P9-CFI-386

Prose of the

Romantic Period

RIVERSIDE EDITIONS

RIVERSIDE EDITIONS

UNDER THE GENERAL EDITORSHIP OF

Gordon N. Ray

Prose of the
Romantic Period

SELECTED WITH AN INTRODUCTION AND NOTES BY

Carl R. Woodring
COLUMBIA UNIVERSITY

HOUGHTON MIFFLIN COMPANY
BOSTON · The Riverside Press Cambridge

COPYRIGHT ©, 1961, BY CARL R. WOODRING

ALL RIGHTS RESERVED

PRINTED IN THE U.S.A.

PREFACE

As IN THE companion volume, *Prose of the Victorian Period*, edited by William E. Buckler, space has been conserved conscientiously in this anthology for the prose of the authors collected. Guidance is therefore afforded economically in an Introduction, a bibliographical note, a brief headnote to each selection, footnotes as needful, and chronological tables for each author who is separately presented and for the critical and the political and social divisions of the book. The notes, except where indicated (by initials) as the author's, have been supplied by the editor. To effect a compromise between students who need factual glosses and readers who wish to savor the authors' styles uninterrupted, glosses have been generally delayed to the end of each imaginative essay. Factual and ideological pieces have been interrupted more freely, but no glosses are supplied for names, words, or phrases that can be found in a good collegiate dictionary. In the chronological tables and elsewhere, unless otherwise noted, works are assigned the date of publication rather than of writing.

The source of each text, identified in the headnotes, is followed typographically except for ligatures, quotation marks (where general Regency practice is standardized), corrections silently made on the authority of manuscripts or editions by the author, and a half-dozen changes in punctuation that would otherwise awkwardly delay comprehension. Original inconsistencies in spelling and mechanics — not then regarded as errors — have been retained.

I am grateful to the Dove Cottage Trustees for permission to reprint selections from the *Journals of Dorothy Wordsworth* edited by Helen Darbishire (World's Classics 568) and published by the Oxford University Press; to Ernest Benn Ltd. for passages of *A Philosophical View of Reform* from the Julian Edition of Shelley's *Complete Works;* to Random House, Inc. for selections from *The Complete Writings of William Blake*. The Keats letters are reprinted by permission of the publishers from *The Letters of John Keats*, edited by Hyder Edward Rollins, Cambridge, Mass.: Harvard University Press, Copyright 1958, by The President and Fellows of Harvard College. The letters of Lamb are printed with generous permission from the Folger Shakespeare Library (to Manning, 15 February 1801), the Huntington Library, San Marino, California (to Barton and three letters to Manning), the University of Texas Library (to Wordsworth), and Harvard University (to Hazlitt and Procter). An anthologist is most indebted of all to earlier editors. For other aid I should like to thank the library staffs of the Universities of Wisconsin and Michigan, the Newberry, Yale, and especially the Houghton Library at Harvard. My wife has been colleagued in this as in all enterprises.

C.R.W.

CONTENTS

LORD BYRON (1788–1824)

PERCY BYSSHE SHELLEY (1792–1822)

JOHN KEATS (1795–1821)

CRITICAL AND IMAGINATIVE

INTRODUCTION

by Carl R. Woodring

AN EXPLOSION of novelty, individuality, and emotional emphasis followed hard upon the French Revolution in the poetry and graphic arts of England. It is sometimes said that the explosion echoed only faintly in English prose. Certainly much that was written between the publication of the *Lyrical Ballads* in 1798 and passage of the Reform Bill in 1832 is free from novelty, individuality, emotion, imagination, and other qualities usually thought of as Romantic. But the distinction to be made is that between the explanatory and the imaginative prose of those years. Even if the limiting dates are extended from the fall of the Bastille in 1789 to the ascension of Victoria in 1837, the Romantic age in England made few alterations in expository style. Instead, it reduced the area in which prose purely expository was chosen for full communication. Burke, Wordsworth, and in his extemporary way Coleridge may be said to have modified expository and argumentative prose toward gusto and singularity. Most other writers of the time either converted exposition into something to be judged for its imaginative coloring or followed the precepts for clarity earlier set down by the Royal Society, John Locke, and Dean Swift.

Romantic literature as a whole continued from the preceding century the work of discussing and embodying fundamental principles, where Victorian literature would turn rather to the application of principles, for identifying and solving current troubles. The Romantic age asserted that change and growth are the laws of life, that particularity is the first requirement for knowledge; the age of Victoria then applied those assertions for the solution of moral and social problems arising at a given stage of growth. First Wordsworth's letter to the Bishop of Llandaff, his tract on the Convention of Cintra, and *The Prelude;* then Carlyle's "Chartism" and Dickens' *Oliver Twist.* It is perhaps surprising that Romantic literature continued the embodiment of ideological principles. Still more surprisingly, prose after 1798 continued the humanistic bias that had begun with the Renaissance. Wordsworth's celandines and Constable's clouds do not make readily evident the emphasis on man which is characteristic of nearly all the prose written for publication in the Romantic era. Lamb, writing to Robert Lloyd in February 1801, epitomized the prose: "A mob of men is better than a flock of sheep. . . ."

Writers properly called Romantic, from Wordsworth to Keats, reacted passionately against the rationalistic, analytical, mechanistic, deterministic, hedonistic, and prudentially utilitarian doctrines of the Enlightenment. Yet most of the ideological lieutenants of the time —

Priestley, Godwin, Malthus, Paley, Ricardo, Owen — accepted the precepts of rationalism as completely as did Bentham, whom J. S. Mill named as the ideological commander opposite to Coleridge. Bentham bound the two centuries of Enlightenment and of Progress with his declaration that every man is to count as one and no man as more than one. Other social and political thinkers agreed with his further declaration that every pleasure counts as one, and pushpin is as good as poetry. The law of physical necessity, derived ultimately from Newton's laws of matter and motion, held most of the expository writers in its usually rigid grip. Thus it is possible to begin the present anthology with some of the most influential pages of the period and yet to represent simultaneously the ideas, style, and methods countered by the major Romantics with full revolt.

In such studies of political theory as Alfred Cobban's *Edmund Burke and the Revolt against the Eighteenth Century,* Burke is treated along with Wordsworth, Coleridge, and Southey as a Romantic. The passion of Burke's rhetoric accords with his organic theory of society. De Quincey called him "the supreme writer of his century." But Burke stands apart from the other political and social writers of his day in the possession of a vitalistic style and faith — if not also in sheer vitality. To take those who might at first seem to be exceptions, the sprightly Sydney Smith is no less a child of the Enlightenment than the aridly sentimental Godwin. Blunt, beef-eating, egotistic, irrational Cobbett, with his apoplectic blows against such clusters of conformity as "the old shuffle-breeches band of the *Quarterly Review,*" is closer than Godwin, Priestley, or Owen to Burke and Hazlitt; yet his vigor, however racy, is external.

We do not find much change of style when we move to the literary quarterlies. Book reviews of the era normally resemble the social disquisitions in both style and organization. In fact, some issues of the *Edinburgh Review* might be taken as the joint transactions of the foremost provincial societies of natural science and political economy. Reviews of belletristic works differed from other reviews only in quoting from the book in hand at unconscionable length (for example, several odes or an entire essay), whether the reviewer was a thirsty hack or the First Secretary to the Admiralty, John Wilson Croker. Somewhat as Byron and Hunt exaggerated the lethal powers of Croker's assault in the *Quarterly Review* on Keat's *Endymion,* so literary historians have exaggerated the reactionary opposition of "blind mouths" to the Romantic originalities halted and sometimes slaughtered on their editorial desks. Reviews were stoutly partisan, and the old term of "tomahawk reviewing" does not suggest more blood than the scalping reviewers hoped to produce. Nor does Keats's complaint to his brother George, in February 1819, misrepresent the power of the *Edinburgh* and *Quarterly* to ruin the sale of a book: "These Reviews

too are getting more and more powerful and especially the Quarterly —
They are like a superstition which the more it prostrates the Crowd
and the longer it continues the more powerful it becomes just in proportion to their increasing weakness —." Nevertheless, several careful
studies have shown that Jeffrey and other Edinburgh reviewers admired many Romantic innovations and after 1815 had moderate praise
for "romantic realism."[1]

When we turn from the reviews to more durable critical writings, we
encounter work that is unmistakably Romantic in doctrine, although not
invariably Romantic in style and method. Much, and perhaps enough,
has been written of late about this criticism.[2] The briefest of summaries
must suffice here. Never given to artistic codes, Great Britain simply
ignored Blake's capsule dogmas, his ability to put the world in an
oyster and serve it on a half-shell. Where most Romantic critics are
expansive, Blake is terse. Besides, as he informed his patron Thomas
Butts in April 1803, he wished to "See Visions, Dream Dreams &
prophecy & speak Parables unobserv'd & at liberty from the Doubts of
other Mortals." No other English Romantic could proclaim the supremacy of the imagination from a position equally strong. Yet the
idealism of Shelley's soaring *Defence* speaks in a form intrinsically
more Romantic than Blake's aphorisms. In Arthur Clutton-Brock's
distinction, the historian of critical documents moves with Shelley's
Defence from a dry style of Justice into the more exuberant style of
Love.

Literary history has traditionally pointed to the *Lyrical Ballads* and
to Wordsworth's Preface of 1800 as together representing the key-
note of a Rousseauistic revolution in England, away from logic and
sophistication, toward feeling and simplicity. Recent decades have
paid more attention to Coleridge, with his insistence upon the active
creativity of the superior or "genial" human mind and his organic
theories of art. Coleridge marks the irreversible change for the Romantics, from the view of the artist as mirror to the view of the artist
as lamp. In England it was Coleridge who made the otherwise
Germanic substitution of Bardolatry for Bibliolatry. Giving a symbolic
rather than literal interpretation of the Jewish and Christian Bible, he
introduced simultaneously the notion that any flaw in a play by
Shakespeare must have been interpolated by some other writer.

Aside from the poets, Coleridge, Wordsworth, and Shelley, the
Romantics were best at practical criticism. Attempting to suggest the

[1] Thomas Crawford, *The Edinburgh Review and Romantic Poetry*, Auck-
land University College Bulletin No. 47, 1955, p. 35. See also John Wain's
Introduction to *Contemporary Reviews of Romantic Poetry*, London, 1953.
[2] For the best, see M. H. Abrams, *The Mirror and the Lamp*, New York,
1953; Walter Jackson Bate, ed., *Criticism: the Major Texts*, New York, 1952;
René Wellek, *A History of Modern Criticism, 1750–1950:* [Volume II] *The
Romantic Age*, New Haven, 1955.

essential qualities of the work before him, the Romantic critic brought his own distinctive style into some degree of harmony with the style of that work, and yet never wholly relinquished the right of the critic to find fault by objective or conventional standards. Edward Gibbon's description of the Longinian method best describes Hazlitt's practice in criticizing a work: "He tells me his own feelings upon it; and tells them with such energy, that he communicates them." Hazlitt, Lamb, and Coleridge are phrase-makers: as critics they frequently fail to hit the nail squarely on the head, but they miss the thumb, and they usually give delight by their near misses.

Perhaps the most famous and least understood aspect of English Romantic criticism, especially in regard to Shakespeare, is its exaggeration. All students have heard, for example, of the exaggerated complaint of Lamb and Hazlitt that the profundity of Shakespeare's tragedies can be either hinted at or grossly travestied on the stage, but never adequately represented there. Fewer students know what this complaint conceals: Lamb's and Hazlitt's intense concern, along with Hunt's, over staging and styles of acting. They protested at the immensity of the licensed theaters (see, in the present volume, Hunt's description in 1809 of the reopened Covent Garden); but Lamb exaggerated for all of them when he exclaimed in "My First Play": "O when shall I be such an expectant again!" What he said of his childhood he could certainly not say of later life: "I knew not players." Romantic attention to the characters of a play, at the cost of attention to other elements, is a critical fault. Yet it also is misinterpreted when it is blamed on too much closet drama and not enough theater. Interest in character is advisable in a director and unavoidable for an actor. Romantic study of character on stage, like Hazlitt's attention to the poetry of Shakespeare's plays, belongs not only to the reader's closet but also to the theater.

To report faithfully on the theater a man must spend time in the city. We are apt to associate the Romantics more readily with the country. "Enough of Science and of Art," said Wordsworth, and recommended instead one impulse from a vernal wood. With notable frequency, the Romantic critics also said, Go to Nature. Yet a common method of their prose, both in their impressionistic, appreciative reports on books and in their familiar essays, is the quotation of favorite authors. Exclude from an essay by Hazlitt or Lamb the imbedded quotations from Shakespeare and Milton, and you leave only scraps. Romantic prose quotes — and vividly misquotes — more than any other English prose before or since. The major imaginative writers of the era loved the stage and they loved books. By Nature they meant life, including living books and other living works of art.

The flower of Romantic prose is the personal essay. In *Plato and Platonism* Walter Pater traced through European history three literary forms: first the metrical ("imaginative, sanguine, often turbid or obscure"), then the formal treatise (dry, dogmatic), and finally the essay, "that characteristic literary type of our own time, a time so rich and various in special apprehensions of truth, so tentative and dubious in its sense of their *ensemble,* and issues." Thinking, let us say, of Montaigne, of Bacon's longer essays, of Mill's shorter works, of Arnold, and of Malthus and his answerers, Pater continued: "Strictly appropriate form of our modern philosophic literature, the essay came into use at what was really the invention of the relative, or 'modern' spirit, in the Renaissance of the sixteenth century." From Nathaniel Bailey's Dictionary, Pater uncovered a suggestive use of the word *essay* by miners: "A little trench or hole, which they dig to search for ore." Linked in origin to the letter, as in the epistles of St. Paul, the essay became more personal, at one leap, with Montaigne. Among the Romantics, Leigh Hunt best illustrates the English tradition in descent through the neat, cryptic, shaped essays of the seventeenth century — as in the Theophrastian "characters" of Overbury, Earle, and Joseph Hall — and through the genial, middle-class, moralistic, informal talk of the periodical essay, so brief in form, so long of life, wholesomely born in the *Spectator* and *Tatler* of Addison and Steele.[3] It was the essay from this tradition that Lamb and Hazlitt personalized.

The twentieth century has been hard on the familiar essay. A sense of haste swept away the genteel tradition of urbanity. Increase in specialization scorned the tentative informality of the amateur. The periodical essay lost its reserved seat to the factual article and the statistic-laden survey. Even in the literary "little magazine," critical writing displaced belles-lettres. Pragmatism of the moment drove out casual reflection. A good short essay moves leisurely; a factual-sounding, best-selling novel of 500,000 words must gallop and pound. Although each personal essay enshrined an idea, it usually enveloped and concealed it. The personal essayist exposed his inner charm and capitalized on an eccentricity not extreme enough to provide full escape from normality. Analytical psychology has changed the approach to character and personality, as most novels illustrate. In the result paradoxically, reading has retrogressed from the essay to the letter. Some of us prefer to catch Lamb, or any other artist, in the undress of his correspondence. In the intricacy and sleight-of-hand of the familiar essay, the writer's innermost drives may elude us; as psychoanalysts, licensed or unlicensed, we are the masters of private letters and diaries. Some have turned in relief from the artist in Keats's poems to the hero in his letters. And yet, of course, what wonderfully vital letters they are!

If the spirit of the personal essay is different from the spirit of our age, we ought to encounter it for that educational and humane reason,

[3] See Melvin R. Watson, *Magazine Serials and the Essay Tradition, 1746–1820,* Baton Rouge, 1956.

as well as for the joy it can bring. If Landor's "Imaginary Conversations" are largely excepted, each familiar or personal essay by the Romantics appeared first in a periodical, and the national fear of revolution and French license can be felt in the editorial fears that intimidated and thus bowdlerized Romantic passions, even when the editor was Leigh Hunt or John Scott of the *London Magazine*. Yet the "inner world of value" evident in Romantic poems, the commitment to subjectivity, the outbreaks of imagination, the personalized solemnity, the organic or emotional unity that displaced external form, these animate the Romantic personal essay in kinship with *The Prelude* and the "Ode to a Nightingale."

Two of these traits, solemnity and the commitment to subjective egoism, seem important enough to treat as central for a discussion of scope and style in the imaginative prose of De Quincey, Hazlitt, Landor, and Lamb.

Romantic egoism may have caused, but it is not identical with, the exploitation of personality in Romantic art. Although the personal essay pretends to reveal "I-myself-I," the Romantic mode of subjectivity should not be mistaken for unrestrained egoism in either poetry or prose. This common mode of the Romantic era, with its emphases on originality, concrete particulars, and emotion, works best when the reader identifies himself with the authorial "I" without any aftertaste of escape from self or of intimate factual disclosure by the author. Both poets and essayists modified their germ of material, what French writers call the *donnée* or "given," in order to provide an ideal moment of emotion for the self of the reader. Wordsworth modified the experience of a group, his starting-point or given for "I wandered lonely as a cloud," in order to unify the tone (he cast off Dorothy's fine image of daffodils pillowing their tired heads) and to achieve the desired subjectivity of solitude. The particular experience around which he shaped "The Solitary Reaper," intensely personal and subjective, was not his but Thomas Wilkinson's. Both in poems and in his letters and journals, Byron exploited subjectivity as a mode admired by the age. He kept flexible the exchanges between self-revelation and the dramatizing of masks — or rather of *personae* created out of experience combined with the artistic needs of his writing. Unlike Wordsworth, Byron had little need to look beyond his own experience for material to intensify.

Oddly enough, the Imaginary Conversations of Landor have been read as far less personal than most of them were intended to be and are. More conventionally, the personality exploited by De Quincey has been taken as his own, not only by relaxed readers but also by biographers straining to find the core of actuality in De Quincey's "imaginative sense of fact." Neither De Quincey's convoluted style nor his whorled structure is purely ornamental embroidery; but both use momentary clarity and the appearance of logic in a very baroque way:

both use experience merely as an "objective correlative" for aesthetically perfected dreams. Like Byron, De Quincey strove to maintain the air of the confessional. Unlike Byron, he prepared himself for confession by donning ceremonial robes. Always, however, the ceremonial was a form of mindplay. His practice followed his definition of rhetoric as "the art of aggrandizing and bringing out into strong relief, by means of various and striking thoughts, some aspect of truth which of itself is supported by no spontaneous feelings, and therefore rests upon artificial aids." Aggrandizing is an objective game played within the mind. As De Quincey describes it, to "hang upon one's own thoughts as an object of conscious interest, to play with them, to watch and pursue them through a maze of inversions, evolutions, and harlequin changes" is to produce his kind of rhetoric. Art, not the ego, wins in such a game.

Hazlitt's method has escaped censure but has also escaped appreciation. His pieces, more than Lamb's and De Quincey's and most of Landor's, belong to the public world of discourse. Go to Hazlitt for ideas. Keeping his eye on the object and keeping the object close enough for emotional comprehension of it, Hazlitt gets us to observe the object and the idea; then suddenly he introduces a personal disclosure, an experience identified in Hazlitt's memory as his own, a self-revelation so unexpectedly apt that it seems an inevitable part of the discourse. More than De Quincey, more even than Byron, Hazlitt had a compulsion to confess, as the *Liber Amoris* somewhat neurotically demonstrates; he thus found it congenial to exploit in his essays both his theory of the necessarily local intensity of our sympathies and the Romantic mode of subjective egoism.

Lamb's case is subtler. By annotating the resemblances between Elia's experiences and Lamb's, and speculating on further resemblances between Lamb's life and his essays (asking, for example, when Lamb sat in the stocks), scholars have furthered the view that Lamb sought to express his self-seen self as faithfully or as vehemently as he could. No doubt Lamb found within himself the sentimental nostalgia of "Dream Children." But his mercurial letters make it evident that no such sentiment ever remained stationary enough within him to have sat for its portrait in "Dream Children." Lamb once suggested that Elia be pronounced with a long *i*. As Geoffrey Tillotson has observed, and doubtlessly Lamb before him, Elia is an anagram of "a lie." There was an actual clerk named Elia (pronounced as Ellia); there was an actual clerk and writer named Lamb — with friends, some eminently creative, some usably curious; and there is the fictional Elia who wrote "the essays under that name" by looking around and under the edges of Lamb's personality.

The mode of subjectivity contains less of intentional deceit, less of calculated artificiality, than is contained in most ascents of Romantic prose toward the sublime. Yet, except in elevated pieces by the prose-wizard De Quincey, the Romantic essay seldom seeks the sublime or the solemn. Kenneth Allott has said that the Victorians inherited through Romanticism three characteristics — "unevenness, seriousness of tone, concreteness and particularity."[4] Concreteness the Romantics energetically sought; unevenness they certainly attained. To go a little further, there is nearly always in Romantic works a seriousness of purpose; but less often, in the prose, is there seriousness of tone. If we set aside the wit of their friends the Smiths — Sydney, Horace, and James — and set aside also, but more at our peril, Romantic irony such as Byron's (what Friedrich Schlegel called transcendental buffoonery), much amusement remains. Wordsworth's prose is sober enough, and most of Shelley's. Elsewhere, wit plays within the seriousness, or humor encircles the tears with smiles and occasional laughter. There is no need to deny that several English Romantics have what Aldous Huxley has found in Goya, "something darker and queerer" than anything in eighteenth-century caricature. The present point concerns the sense of comic intention that we get from most of the dark Romantics as well as from the sunny ones.

Of De Quincey's several styles, one is merely facetious, as on the Malay's visit to Dove Cottage and on crotchets of the later Wordsworth. Another is rather heavily satirical. He calls out "Oh, Reader!" seriously enough in passages variously exalted, exhortatory, or ecstatic. Nevertheless, in De Quincey as in Swinburne, outrage and laughter lie often close abed. A smile is certainly near, a sense of the droll, in the ratiocinative style involved in his arguments on economic theory, in his frequent numbering of paragraphs and points of an argument, and in his depiction of recent murders in full detail, both psychological and physical.

With an even greater range of subjects than De Quincey, but with a much narrower range in style, Hazlitt turns the periodical parallelism of the Augustans into a notched rhythm of risibility:

> Mr. Campbell always seems to me to be thinking how his poetry will look when it comes to be hot-pressed on superfine wove paper, to have a disproportionate eye to points and commas, and dread of errors of the press. He is so afraid of doing wrong, of making the smallest mistake, that he does little or nothing. Lest he should wander irretrievably from the right path, he stands still. He writes according to established etiquette. He offers the Muses no violence.

Or again, more quietly: "The impressions of Mr. Moore's poetry are detached, desultory, and physical." Hazlitt's paradoxical pleasures of hating remain pleasures for the author partly because they are paradoxes; they remain pleasurable for the reader (to use one critical phrase inherited by Wordsworth and Hazlitt and another invented by Cole-

[4] *Victorian Prose 1830–1880,* ed. Kenneth and Miriam Allott, London, 1956, p. xxxiv.

ridge) only as long as the aesthetic similitude in dissimilitude receives from the reader a willing suspension of disbelief. The reader, reacting to Hazlitt as Coleridge did, may be "not displeased to hear of his being knocked down by John Lamb," but his pleasure as a reader would be lessened if he heard that Hazlitt knocked down either one of the Lambs, or even Gifford. When he was asked to shake hands and forgive, according to Tom Moore, Hazlitt answered: "Well, I don't mind if I do. I am a metaphysician and nothing but an *idea* hurts me." And just as much as De Quincey, Lamb, or the Elizabethans, Hazlitt stayed drunk on words — a basically joyous form of intoxication.

Landor is seldom accused of false sublimity, or of true sublimity either; but he is even less frequently given the praise he deserves for wit, comedy, and humor. When his dialogues of Greeks and Romans are regarded as historical, classical re-creations, it is seen that he never rises to the power of archaistic Lamb or jabbing Hazlitt. When, however, these and other Imaginary Conversations are regarded partly as battles in Landor's nineteenth-century wars, his great range of character and idea becomes more noticeable. Wide range, high level of competence, clarity and temperate progression, good humor, frequently keen wit — these are the characteristics to be first observed in Landor's imaginative prose. The casual but apt humor of "La Fontaine and De La Rochefoucault" comes convincingly from the wise characters involved; the wry comedy of "William Wallace and King Edward I" lies in the universal blindness of tyrants to the Romantic values of personal and national liberty. Landor saves less space for argument or humor in the more dramatic "Leofric and Godiva." But the demolition of Seneca's philosophy, in the quiet air of "Epictetus and Seneca," represents a larger group of dialogues than the better-known emotional crises like "Leofric and Godiva" and "Tiberius and Vipsania." Besides his humorous and sometimes comic representations of persons and problems of his own time, Landor made imaginative use of ironic wit, as in his exposure of the confessional (and of privilege) when the learned Bossuet must deal with the volatile child whom Louis XIV has taken as mistress and made Duchess de Fontanges:

Bossuet. To love God, we must hate ourselves. We must detest our bodies, if we would save our souls.
Fontanges. That is hard: how can I do it? I see nothing so detestable in mine. Do you? To love is easier. I love God whenever I think of him, he has been so very good to me; but I cannot hate myself, if I would. As God hath not hated me, why should I? Beside, it was he who made the King to love me; for I heard you say in a sermon that the hearts of kings are in his rule and governance. . . . I am glad to be a duchess. Manon and Lisette have never tied my garter so as to hurt me since, nor has the mischievous old La Grange said anything cross or bold: on the contrary, she told me what a fine color and what a plumpness it gave me. Would not you rather be a

duchess than a waiting-maid or a nun, if the King gave you your
choice?

The comedy resides in Bossuet's words as well as the girl's. In the
Conversations as a whole, wit sometimes alternates, and sometimes
combines, with geniality.

In any just selection, Lamb must be represented in part by the
sentimental warmth of "Dream Children" and the genial hedonism
of "Roast Pig," essays that have made the first issue of the first edition
of *Elia* treasured among collectors next after the First Folio of Shakespeare. But such essays should be read in the light of his vigor and
habitual downrightness, as in his jolting, often joyously profane letters
to friends. He is called whimsical because he enjoyed writing "matter-
of-lie" hoaxes, but he also wrote unwelcome fact and blunt truth.
With Lamb, the problem is to see the seriousness and toughness of
intellect in the humor. He is sober, daring, and typical of himself, in
the essay "Grace before Meat," when he calls rather for "a grace before
Milton — a grace before Shakespeare." When Southey attacked Lamb's
friends and his imperfect sympathy with the true Anglican religion,
Lamb answered publicly, with courage and with comic irony, in defense of a friend he did not at that moment have, William Hazlitt:

> At this instant, he may be preparing for me some compliment, above
> my deserts, as he has sprinkled many such among his admirable books,
> for which I rest his debtor; or, for any thing I know, or can guess to
> the contrary, he may be about to read a lecture on my weaknesses.
> He is welcome to them (as he was to my humble hearth), if they can
> divert a spleen, or ventilate a fit of sullenness. I wish he would not
> quarrel with the world at the rate he does; but the reconciliation must
> be effected by himself, and I despair of living to see that day. But,
> protesting against much that he has written, and some things which
> he chooses to do; judging him by his conversation which I enjoyed so
> long, and relished so deeply; or by his books, in those places where no
> clouding passion intervenes — I should belie my own conscience, if
> I said less, than that I think W. H. to be, in his natural and healthy
> state, one of the wisest and finest spirits breathing. So far from being
> ashamed of that intimacy, which was betwixt us, it is my boast that
> I was able for so many years to have preserved it entire; and I think
> I shall go to my grave without finding, or expecting to find, such an-
> other companion.

A passage like this one should be carried in memory by the reader when
he accompanies Lamb in sentimentally humorous attachment to the
eccentricities and archaic rhythms of Robert Burton and Sir Thomas
Browne.

These paragraphs on the personal essay and related imaginative
prose have urged that the customary one-sidedness in views of Roman-

tic ideas, temper, and style be modified by a look at the opposite side, with egoism and solemnity as two examples of supposed characteristics that deserve close attention. Such an approach must itself be contradicted. The proper attitude for enjoying most Romantic prose is not cautious balance but the attitude recommended by the prose itself: exuberance, an enthusiasm for or against.

BIBLIOGRAPHICAL NOTE

1

Bibliographical Guides

For dependable and convenient guides to editions, scholarship, and criticism, students of Romantic prose can go to *The English Romantic Poets: A Review of Research,* ed. Thomas M. Raysor, revised edition, New York, 1956, and *The English Romantic Poets and Essayists: A Review of Research and Criticism,* ed. Carolyn W. Houtchens and Lawrence H. Houtchens, New York, 1957. Fuller lists can be found in *The Cambridge Bibliography of English Literature,* Volume III, with its *Supplement* (Volume V), and in the annual bibliography of "The Romantic Movement," which appeared from 1937 through 1949 in *ELH: A Journal of English Literary History* and from 1950 in *Philological Quarterly.* These sources point to other useful bibliographies, such as the detailed annual listings for Byron, Hunt, Keats, and Shelley, since 1952, in the *Keats-Shelley Journal.*

2

Standard Works

(a) Standard editions, (b) standard biographies, and (c) a significant critical work are given below for each author treated separately in this anthology. For surveys that include all the authors, see C. H. Herford, *The Age of Wordsworth,* London, 1897, and Oliver Elton, *A Survey of English Literature, 1780–1830,* 2 vols., London, 1912. (The Herford work was twice revised, and both have been often reprinted.)

WORDSWORTH

(a) *Prose Works,* ed. A. B. Grosart. 3 vols. London, 1876.
(b) Mary Moorman. *William Wordsworth: A Biography* . . . *1770–1803.* Oxford, 1957. [See also (c), Harper.]
(c) George M. Harper. *William Wordsworth: His Life, Works, and Influence.* 2 vols. New York, 1916; revised (1 vol.) 1929.

COLERIDGE

(a) *Complete Works,* ed. W. G. T. Shedd. 7 vols. New York, 1853. (Incomplete, but reprinting valuable annotations by Coleridge's children, Sara and Derwent, and his nephew — who married

Sara — Henry Nelson Coleridge. Work has begun on a collected edition with Kathleen Coburn as general editor.)

(b) E. K. Chambers. *Samuel Taylor Coleridge: A Biographical Study.* Oxford, 1938; corrected 1950.

(c) John H. Muirhead. *Coleridge as Philosopher.* London and New York, 1930.

LANDOR

(a) Collected edition, ed. C. G. Crump, London, 1891, including: *Imaginary Conversations,* 6 vols., and *The Longer Prose Works,* 2 vols.

(b) R. H. Super. *Walter Savage Landor: A Biography.* New York, 1954.

(c) Malcolm Elwin. *Landor: A Replevin.* London, 1958. (Revised from *Savage Landor,* 1941.)

LAMB

(a) *Works,* ed. E. V. Lucas. 7 vols. London, 1903–05. Vols. VI–VII, containing letters, have been superseded by: *Letters,* ed. E. V. Lucas. 3 vols. London, 1935.

(b) E. V. Lucas. *The Life of Charles Lamb.* 2 vols. London, 1905; 5th ed. (1 vol.) 1921.

(c) A. C. Ward. *The Frolic and the Gentle: A Centenary Study of Charles Lamb.* London, 1934.

HAZLITT

(a) *Collected Works,* ed. P. P. Howe. 21 vols. London, 1930–34.

(b) P. P. Howe. *The Life of William Hazlitt.* London, 1922; revised 1928, 1947.

(c) Elisabeth Schneider. *The Aesthetics of William Hazlitt.* Philadelphia, 1933; reprinted 1952. (A more general study by Herschel Baker is due in 1962.)

HUNT

(a) Seven of Hunt's many volumes were reprinted, 1870–72. The most representative selection of his essays appears in *Leigh Hunt as Poet and Essayist,* ed. Charles Kent, London, 1889. The fullest and most usefully annotated is a series edited by Lawrence and Carolyn Houtchens: *Dramatic Criticism,* 1949; *Literary Criticism,* 1956; *Political and Occasional Essays* (to come).

(b) Edmund Blunden. *Leigh Hunt: A Biography.* London, 1950.

(c) Louis Landré. *Leigh Hunt: contribution à l'histoire du Romantisme anglais.* 2 vols. Paris, 1935.

DE QUINCEY

(a) *Collected Writings,* ed. David Masson. 14 vols. London, 1896–97.
(b) Horace Ainsworth Eaton. *Thomas De Quincey: A Biography.* London and New York, 1936.
(c) Edward Sackville-West. *Thomas De Quincey: His Life and Work.* New Haven, 1936. (London title: *A Flame in Sunlight.*)

BYRON

(a) *Works: Letters and Journals,* ed. R. E. Prothero. 7 vols. London, 1898–1901. (Incomplete; the most important additional source is *Byron: A Self-Portrait,* ed. Peter Quennell, 2 vols., London, 1950.)
(b) Leslie A. Marchand. *Byron: A Biography.* 3 vols. New York, 1957.
(c) Ernest J. Lovell, Jr. *Byron: The Record of a Quest.* Austin, 1949.

SHELLEY

(a) *Complete Works,* ed. Roger Ingpen and W. E. Peck. 10 vols. London and New York, 1926–30.
(b) Newman Ivey White. *Shelley.* 2 vols. New York. 1940; revised, London, 1947.
(c) Desmond King-Hele. *Shelley: The Man and the Poet.* London and New York, 1960.

KEATS

(a) *Complete Works,* ed. H. B. Forman. 5 vols. Glasgow, 1900–1901. But superseded by *Letters,* ed. Hyder E. Rollins. 2 vols. Cambridge, Mass., 1958.
(b) Dorothy Hewlett. *A Life of John Keats.* 2nd edition. London, 1949, corrected 1950. (Revised from *Adonais,* 1937.)
(c) Lionel Trilling. "The Poet as Hero: Keats in His Letters," in *The Opposing Self.* New York, 1955.

Political and Social

POLITICAL AND SOCIAL

CHRONOLOGY

1789   Onset of the French Revolution.

1790   Edmund Burke, *Reflections on the Revolution in France.*

1791   David Hartley (1705–57), *Observations on Man* (1749), new edition enlarged by H. A. Pistorius.

1791–92   Thomas Paine, *Rights of Man;* James Mackintosh, *Vindiciae Gallicae;* Mary Wollstonecraft, *A Vindication of the Rights of Woman.*

1793   January–February, war declared between Great Britain and France. William Godwin, *An Enquiry concerning Political Justice.*
Dugald Stewart (1753–1828), *Outlines of Moral Philosophy,* Edinburgh.

1794   Pitt's government suspended right of Habeas Corpus and tried liberal "patriots" for treason.
William Paley, *A View of the Evidences of Christianity.*

1794–96   Erasmus Darwin (1731–1802) *Zoonomia, or the Laws of Organic Life.*

1797–98   *Anti-Jacobin* conducted by Canning, Frere, Gifford, and Ellis; succeeded by monthly *Anti-Jacobin Review and Magazine.*

1798   T. R. Malthus, *An Essay on the Principle of Population.*

1802   March 25, treaty of peace at Amiens. Napoleon's power became absolute.

1803   Napoleon began Continental blockade against British shipping; war reopened. Robert Emmet, United Irishman, executed.

1803–35   *Cobbett's Weekly Political Register.*

1805   October 21, Nelson died in victory at Trafalgar.

1807   March 25, coalition government abolished the African slave trade.

1808   Convention of Cintra interrupted military successes against the French in Spain and Portugal. Duke of York, second son of George III, involved by scandalous sale of Army promotions.

1810   July 9, Cobbett sentenced to two years in Newgate prison for "seditious libel" on military flogging.

1811   Tory government retained by Prince Regent (who reigned as George IV, 1820–30).

1812   Sir Humphry Davy (1778–1829), *Elements of Chemical Philosophy.* June, war with the United States (through 1814).

1813   Poet Laureateship refused by Scott; accepted by Robert Southey.

1813–16   Robert Owen, *A New View of Society.*

1814   George Stephenson (1781–1848) constructed first steam locomotive.

1815   March, Corn Laws raised the price of bread. June 18, Napoleon defeated at Waterloo. Bourbon kings restored.

1816–19   Agricultural and laborers' distresses and riots.

1817–24   *Black Dwarf,* Radical weekly edited by T. J. Wooler.

1817–26   *Republican,* Radical weekly edited by Richard Carlile (from prison at Dorchester, 1819–25).

1819   Press and public assembly restricted by Six Acts. Cavalry dispersed crowd at "Peterloo," in Manchester, August 16.

1820   February 24, Cato Street Conspiracy to assassinate the Cabinet; Arthur Thistlewood and accomplices executed May 1.
        December 17, *John Bull,* edited by Theodore Hook, founded to refute Radicals.

1821   After trial for adultery (1820), Queen Caroline was refused admission to coronation of George IV, July 29. She died August 7.

1824   January, *Westminster Review* founded as Benthamite quarterly.
        June, laws against combinations of labor (trade unions) repealed.

1828   Test and Corporation Acts against Dissenters repealed.

1829   Laws restricting Roman Catholics repealed.

1832   June 7, Reform Act gave political power to the middle classes.

Jeremy Bentham

Principles of Morals and Legislation

⟦ Although his style has seldom been praised, and much of his great influence on legal and political reform came through zealous disciples, Jeremy Bentham (1748–1832) communicated directly to many readers the Utilitarian ethic of the least amount of pain and the greatest amount of pleasure for the greatest number of people. This ethic, partially developed by Claude Helvétius, Joseph Priestley, and other rationalists, is presented by Bentham with relentless clarity in *An Introduction to the Principles of Morals and Legislation*, begun about 1776 and first published in 1789. Chapter IV is here taken from the corrected edition of 1823. ⟧

Value of a Lot of Pleasure or Pain, How to Be Measured

I

Pleasures then, and the avoidance of pains, are the *ends* which the legislator has in view: it behoves him therefore to understand their *value*. Pleasures and pains are the *instruments* he has to work with: it behoves him therefore to understand their force, which is again, in other words, their value.

II

To a person considered *by himself*, the value of a pleasure or pain considered *by itself*, will be greater or less, according to the four following circumstances:[1]

1. Its *intensity*.
2. Its *duration*.

---

[1] These circumstances have since been denominated *elements* or *dimensions* of *value* in a pleasure or a pain.

Not long after the publication of the first edition, the following memoriter verses were framed, in the view of lodging more effectually, in the memory, these points, on which the whole fabric of morals and legislation may be seen to rest.

> Intense, long, certain, speedy, fruitful, pure —
> Such marks in *pleasures* and in *pains* endure.
> Such pleasures seek, if *private* be thy end:
> If it be *public*, wide let them *extend*.
> Such *pains* avoid, whichever be thy view:
> If pains *must* come, let them *extend* to few.

[Bentham's note.]

4

3. Its *certainty* or *uncertainty.*
4. Its *propinquity* or *remoteness.*

III

These are the circumstances which are to be considered in estimating a pleasure or a pain considered each of them by itself. But when the value of any pleasure or pain is considered for the purpose of estimating the tendency of any *act* by which it is produced, there are two other circumstances to be taken into the account; these are,

5. Its *fecundity*, or the chance it has of being followed by sensations of the *same* kind: that is, pleasures, if it be a pleasure: pains, if it be a pain.

6. Its *purity*, or the chance it has of *not* being followed by sensations of the *opposite* kind: that is, pains, if it be a pleasure: pleasures, if it be a pain.

These two last, however, are in strictness scarcely to be deemed properties of the pleasure or the pain itself; they are not, therefore, in strictness to be taken into the account of the value of that pleasure or that pain. They are in strictness to be deemed properties only of the act, or other event, by which such pleasure or pain has been produced; and accordingly are only to be taken into the account of the tendency of such act or such event.

IV

To a *number* of persons, with reference to each of whom the value of a pleasure or a pain is considered, it will be greater or less, according to seven circumstances: to wit, the six preceding ones; *viz.*

1. Its *intensity.*
2. Its *duration.*
3. Its *certainty* or *uncertainty.*
4. Its *propinquity* or *remoteness.*
5. Its *fecundity.*
6. Its *purity.*

And one other; to wit:

7. Its *extent;* that is, the number of persons to whom it *extends;* or (in other words) who are affected by it.

V

To take an exact account then of the general tendency of any act, by which the interests of a community are affected, proceed as follows. Begin with any one person of those whose interests seem most immediately to be affected by it: and take an account,

1. Of the value of each distinguishable *pleasure* which appears to be produced by it in the *first* instance.

2. Of the value of each *pain* which appears to be produced by it in the *first* instance.

3. Of the value of each pleasure which appears to be produced by it *after* the first. This constitutes the *fecundity* of the first *pleasure* and the *impurity* of the first *pain*.

4. Of the value of each *pain* which appears to be produced by it after the first. This constitutes the *fecundity* of the first *pain,* and the *impurity* of the first pleasure.

5. Sum up all the values of all the *pleasures* on the one side, and those of all the pains on the other. The balance, if it be on the side of pleasure, will give the *good* tendency of the act upon the whole, with respect to the interests of that *individual* person; if on the side of pain, the *bad* tendency of it upon the whole.

6. Take an account of the *number* of persons whose interests appear to be concerned; and repeat the above process with respect to each. *Sum up* the numbers expressive of the degrees of *good* tendency, which the act has, with respect to each individual, in regard to whom the tendency of it is *good* upon the whole: do this again with respect to each individual, in regard to whom the tendency of it is *good* upon the whole: do this again with respect to each individual, in regard to whom the tendency of it is *bad* upon the whole. Take the *balance;* which, if on the side of *pleasure,* will give the general *good tendency* of the act, with respect to the total number or community of individuals concerned; if on the side of pain, the general *evil tendency,* with respect to the same community.

VI

It is not to be expected that this process should be strictly pursued previously to every moral judgment, or to every legislative or judicial operation. It may, however, be always kept in view: and as near as the process actually pursued on these occasions approaches to it, so near will such process approach to the character of an exact one.

VII

The same process is alike applicable to pleasure and pain, in whatever shape they appear: and by whatever denomination they are distinguished: to pleasure, whether it be called *good* (which is properly the cause or instrument of pleasure) or *profit* (which is distant pleasure, or the cause or instrument of distant pleasure,) or *convenience,* or *advantage, benefit, emolument, happiness,* and so forth: to pain, whether it be called *evil,* (which corresponds to *good*) or *mischief,* or *inconvenience,* or *disadvantage,* or *loss,* or *unhappiness,* and so forth.

VIII

Nor is this a novel and unwarranted, any more than it is a useless theory. In all this there is nothing but what the practice of mankind, wheresoever they have a clear view of their own interest, is perfectly conformable to. An article of property, an estate in land, for instance, is valuable, on what account? On account of the pleasures of all kinds which it enables a man to produce, and what comes to the same thing the pains of all kinds which it enables him to avert. But the value of such an article of property is universally understood to rise or fall according to the length or shortness of the time which a man has in it: the certainty or uncertainty of its coming into possession: and the nearness or remoteness of the time at which, if at all, it is to come into possession. As to the *intensity* of the pleasures which a man may derive from it, this is never thought of, because it depends upon the use which each particular person may come to make of it; which cannot be estimated till the particular pleasures he may come to derive from it, or the particular pains he may come to exclude by means of it, are brought to view. For the same reason, neither does he think of the *fecundity* or *purity* of those pleasures.

Thus much for pleasure and pain, happiness and unhappiness, in *general*. We come now to consider the several particular kinds of pain and pleasure.

❪❫

Edmund Burke

Reflections on the Revolution in France

❪ When the Revolution erupted in Paris, Edmund Burke (1729–97), Irish orator and statesman, was coming to the end of a distinguished career in the Whig cause of liberty. Neither his love of order and tradition nor his hatred of abstract theory had been fully clear to fellow Whigs until November 1790, when he published *Reflections on the Revolution in France and on the Proceedings in Certain Societies in London Relative to That Event*. For an example of the theories to which he objected, see the passages from Priestley's reply. Although Louis XVI had acquiesced in the new constitution of the National Assembly, he and the Queen, Marie Antoinette, had been brought from Versailles to Paris and put under close surveillance. Burke's prophecy of increasing bloodshed and an ultimate dictatorship in France, despite the many prompt answers to the *Reflections*, convinced most members of Parliament and others concerned in politics. The two passages

below are taken from the eighth of eleven London editions that appeared
before the end of 1791. Burke had revised the work slightly since the first
edition, and was to make further small changes in 1793.]▶

[*Rights of Men*]

Far am I from denying in theory, full as far is my heart from
withholding in practice (if I were of power to give or to withhold)
the *real* rights of men. In denying their false claims of right, I do not
mean to injure those which are real, and are such as their pretended
rights would totally destroy. If civil society be made for the advantage
of man, all the advantages for which it is made become his right. It
is an institution of beneficence; and law itself is only beneficence acting
by a rule. Men have a right to live by that rule; they have a right
to justice, as between their fellows, whether their fellows are in public
function or in ordinary occupation. They have a right to the fruits of
their industry; and to the means of making their industry fruitful. They
have a right to the acquisitions of their parents; to the nourishment and
improvement of their offspring; to instruction in life, and to consolation in death. Whatever each man can separately do, without tres-
passing upon others, he has a right to do for himself; and he has a
right to a fair portion of all which society, with all its combinations of
skill and force, can do in his favour. In this partnership all men have
equal rights; but not to equal things. He that has but five shillings in
the partnership, has as good a right to it, as he that has five hundred
pound has to his larger proportion. But he has not a right to an equal
dividend in the product of the joint stock; and as to the share of power,
authority, and direction which each individual ought to have in the
management of the state, that I must deny to be amongst the direct
original rights of man in civil society; for I have in my contemplation
the civil social man, and no other. It is a thing to be settled by convention.

If civil society be the offspring of convention, that convention must
be its law. That convention must limit and modify all the descriptions
of constitution which are formed under it. Every sort of legislative,
judicial, or executory power are its creatures. They can have no being
in any other state of things; and how can any man claim, under the
conventions of civil society, rights which do not so much as suppose
its existence? Rights which are absolutely repugnant to it? One of the
first motives to civil society, and which becomes one of its fundamental
rules, is, *that no man should be judge in his own cause.* By this each
person has at once divested himself of the first fundamental right of
uncovenanted man, that is, to judge for himself, and to assert his
own cause. He abdicates all right to be his own governor. He inclusively, in a great measure, abandons the right of self-defence, the

first law of nature. Men cannot enjoy the rights of an uncivil and of a civil state together. That he may obtain justice he gives up his right of determining what it is in points the most essential to him. That he may secure some liberty, he makes a surrender in trust of the whole of it.

Government is not made in virtue of natural rights, which may and do exist in total independence of it; and exist in much greater clearness, and in a much greater degree of abstract perfection: but their abstract perfection is their practical defect. By having a right to every thing they want every thing. Government is a contrivance of human wisdom to provide for human *wants*. Men have a right that these wants should be provided for by this wisdom. Among these wants is to be reckoned the want, out of civil society, of a sufficient restraint upon their passions. Society requires not only that the passions of individuals should be subjected, but that even in the mass and body as well as in the individuals, the inclinations of men should frequently be thwarted, their will controlled, and their passions brought into subjection. This can only be done *by a power out of themselves;* and not, in the exercise of its function, subject to that will and to those passions which it is its office to bridle and subdue. In this sense the restraints on men, as well as their liberties, are to be reckoned among their rights. But as the liberties and the restrictions vary with times and circumstances, and admit of infinite modifications, they cannot be settled upon any abstract rule; and nothing is so foolish as to discuss them upon that principle.

The moment you abate any thing from the full rights of men, each to govern himself, and suffer any artificial positive limitation upon those rights, from that moment the whole organization of government becomes a consideration of convenience. This it is which makes the constitution of a state, and the due distribution of its powers, a matter of the most delicate and complicated skill. It requires a deep knowledge of human nature and human necessities, and of the things which facilitate or obstruct the various ends which are to be pursued by the mechanism of civil institutions. The state is to have recruits to its strength, and remedies to its distempers. What is the use of discussing a man's abstract right to food or to medicine? The question is upon the method of procuring and administering them. In that deliberation I shall always advise to call in the aid of the farmer and the physician, rather than the professor of metaphysics.

[*Marie Antoinette*]

I hear, and I rejoice to hear, that the great lady, the other object of the triumph, has borne that day, (one is interested that beings made for suffering should suffer well) and that she bears all the succeeding days, that she bears the imprisonment of her husband, and her own captivity, and the exile of her friends, and the insulting adulation of addresses, and the whole weight of her accumulated wrongs, with a serene patience, in a manner suited to her rank and race, and becoming the offspring of a sovereign distinguished for her piety and her courage; that like her she has lofty sentiments; that she feels with the dignity of a Roman matron; that in the last extremity she will save herself from the last disgrace; and that if she must fall, she will fall by no ignoble hand.

It is now sixteen or seventeen years since I saw the queen of France, then the dauphiness, at Versailles; and surely never lighted on this orb, which she hardly seemed to touch, a more delightful vision. I saw her just above the horizon, decorating and cheering the elevated sphere she just began to move in, — glittering like the morning-star, full of life, and splendor, and joy. Oh! what a revolution! and what an heart must I have, to contemplate without emotion that elevation and that fall! Little did I dream when she added titles of veneration to those of enthusiastic, distant, respectful love, that she should ever be obliged to carry the sharp antidote against disgrace concealed in that bosom; little did I dream that I should have lived to see such disasters fallen upon her in a nation of gallant men, in a nation of men of honour and of cavaliers. I thought ten thousand swords must have leaped from their scabbards to avenge even a look that threatened her with in-sult. —— But the age of chivalry is gone. — That of sophisters, œconomists, and calculators, has succeeded; and the glory of Europe is extinguished for ever. Never, never more, shall we behold that generous loyalty to rank and sex, that proud submission, that dignified obedience, that subordination of the heart, which kept alive, even in servitude itself, the spirit of an exalted freedom. The unbought grace of life, the cheap defence of nations, the nurse of manly sentiment and heroic enterprize, is gone! It is gone, that sensibility of principle, that chastity of honour, which felt a stain like a wound, which inspired courage whilst it mitigated ferocity, which ennobled whatever it touched, and under which vice itself lost half its evil, by losing all its grossness.

This mixed system of opinion and sentiment had its origin in the antient chivalry; and the principle, though varied in its appearance by the varying state of human affairs, subsisted and influenced through a long succession of generations, even to the time we live in. If it should ever be totally extinguished, the loss I fear will be great. It is this which has given its character to modern Europe. It is this which has distinguished it under all its forms of government, and distinguished it to its advantage, from the states of Asia, and possibly from those states which flourished in the most brilliant periods of the antique world. It was this, which, without confounding ranks, had produced a noble equality, and handed it down through all the gradations of social life. It was this opinion which mitigated kings into companions, and raised private men to be fellows with kings. Without force, or opposition, it subdued the fierceness of pride and power; it obliged sovereigns to submit to the soft collar of social esteem, compelled stern authority to submit to elegance, and gave a dominating vanquisher of laws, to be subdued by manners.

But now all is to be changed. All the pleasing illusions, which made power gentle, and obedience liberal, which harmonized the different shades of life, and which, by a bland assimilation, incorporated into politics the sentiments which beautify and soften private society, are to be dissolved by this new conquering empire of light and reason. All the decent drapery of life is to be rudely torn off. All the superadded ideas, furnished from the wardrobe of a moral imagination, which the heart owns, and the understanding ratifies, as necessary to cover the defects of our naked shivering nature, and to raise it to dignity in our own estimation, are to be exploded as a ridiculous, absurd, and antiquated fashion.

(|)

Thomas Paine

Rights of Man

❲ Thomas Paine (1737–1809) led a turbulent career as a radical pamphleteer in England, America, and France. Both as a man and as a writer, he won little praise but many converts. Among leaders of thought and literature, his *Rights of Man* was taken far less seriously than *Vindiciae Gallicae*, the reply to Burke by James Mackintosh. For every reader of Mackintosh's legalistic rebuttal, however, there were hundreds who knew Paine's vivid metaphors and bluntly democratic ideas. His *Rights of Man: Being an Answer to Mr. Burke's Attack on the French Revolution*, 1791, was followed by a second part in 1792, "Combining Principle and Practice." The two passages below, the first denying that Englishmen of 1688 could have made a political contract binding on their descendants a century later and the second deriding Burke's concern for Marie Antoinette, are taken from the second London edition of 1791. ❳

There never did, there never will, and there never can exist a parliament, or any description of men, or any generation of men, in any country, possessed of the right or the power of binding and controuling posterity to the "*end of time*," or of commanding for ever how the world shall be governed, or who shall govern it; and therefore, all such clauses, acts or declarations, by which the makers of them attempt to do what they have neither the right nor the power to do, nor the power to execute, are in themselves null and void. — Every age and generation must be as free to act for itself, *in all cases*, as the ages and generations which preceeded it. The vanity and presumption of governing beyond the grave, is the most ridiculous and insolent of all tyrannies. Man has no property in man; neither has any generation a property in the generations which are to follow. The parliament or the people of 1688, or of any other period, had no more right to dispose of the people of the present day, or to bind or controul them *in any shape whatever*, than the parliament or the people of the present day have to dispose of, bind or controul those who are to live a hundred or a thousand years hence. Every generation is, and must be, competent to all the purposes which its occasions require. It is the living, and not the dead, that are to be accommodated. When man ceases to be, his power and his wants cease with him; and having no longer any participation in the concerns of this world, he has no longer any authority in directing who shall be its governors, or how its government shall be organized, or how administered.

*   *   *   *   *

From his violence and his grief, his silence on some points, and his excess on others, it is difficult not to believe that Mr. Burke is sorry, extremely sorry, that arbitrary power, the power of the Pope, and the Bastille, are pulled down.

Not one glance of compassion, not one commiserating reflection, that I can find throughout his book, has he bestowed on those who lingered out the most wretched of lives, a life without hope, in the most miserable of prisons. It is painful to behold a man employing his talents to corrupt himself. Nature has been kinder to Mr. Burke than he is to her. He is not affected by the reality of distress touching his heart, but by the showy resemblance of it striking his imagination. He pities the plumage, but forgets the dying bird. Accustomed to kiss the aristocratical hand that hath purloined him from himself, he degenerates into a composition of art, and the genuine soul of nature forsakes him. His hero or his heroine must be a tragedy-victim expiring in show, and not the real prisoner of misery, sliding into death in the silence of a dungeon.

(I)

Joseph Priestley

Letters to Edmund Burke

❨ Joseph Priestley (1733–1804) is remembered primarily for his discoveries in chemistry, yet his *Letters to the Right Honourable Edmund Burke,* 1791, fairly represents the activity for which he was best known to his contemporaries. Despite his leadership in political and religious dissent, Priestley — rather than Burke — summarizes the political ideas most commonly held in the period of European revolution from dynastic loyalty to fervent nationalism. Priestley published three slightly varying editions of the *Letters* in Birmingham during 1791. The passages below come from Letter III, Of the Nature of Government, and the Rights of Men and of Kings. ❩

You treat with ridicule the ideas of the *rights of men,* and suppose that mankind, when once they have entered into a state of society, necessarily abandon all their proper *natural rights,* and thenceforth have only such as they derive from society. "As to the share of power," you say, p. 87, "authority and direction, which each individual ought to have in the management of the state, that I must deny to be among the direct original rights of man in civil society; for I have in my contemplation the civil, social man, and no other. It is a thing to be settled by convention."

But what does this *convention* respect, beside the secure enjoyment of such *advantages,* or *rights,* as have been usually termed *natural,* as life, liberty, and property, which men had *from nature,* without societies or artificial combinations of men? Men cannot, surely, be said to *give up* their natural rights by entering into a compact for the better securing of them. And if they make a wise compact, they will never wholly exclude themselves from all share in the administration of their government, or some controul over it. For without *this* their stipulated rights would be very insecure.

However, should any people be so unwise as to leave the whole administration of their government, without any express right of controul, in the hands of their magistrates; if those magistrates do not give the people what they deem to be an equivalent for what they gave up for the accommodation of others, they are certainly at liberty to consider the original compact as broken. They then revert to a state of nature, and may enter into a new state of society, and adopt a new form of government, in which they may make better terms for themselves.

* * * * *

Has not the chief magistrate in every country, as well as the chief officer in every town, a certain *duty* to perform, with certain emoluments, and *privileges*, allowed him in consideration of the proper discharge of that duty? And if the town officer, though having chief authority in his district, yet in consequence of being *appointed* and *paid* for his services by the town, is never considered in any other light than that of the *servant of the town;* is not the chief magistrate in any country, let him be called *sovereign, king,* or what you please (for that is only a name) the *servant of the people?* What real difference can there be in the two cases? They each discharge a certain duty, and have a certain stipulated reward for it. The office being *hereditary,* makes no real difference. In our laws, and those of other nations, there are precedents enow of men's whole estates being confiscated for crimes; and this of course excludes the heir.

If, as you expressly acknowledge, the only rational end of the power of a king is the *general advantage,* that is, the *good of the people,* must not the people be of course the judges, whether they derive advantage from him and his government or not, that is, whether they be well or ill *served* by him? Though, there is no express, there is, you must acknowledge, a virtual, *compact between the king and the people.* This, indeed, is particularly mentioned in the Act which implies the abdication of king James, though you say, p. 38, it is *too guarded and too circumstantial;* and what can this compact be, but a stipulation for protection, &c. on the part of the king, and allegiance on the part of the people? If, therefore instead of *protection,* they find *oppression,* certainly allegiance is no longer due. Hence, according to common sense, and the principles of the Revolution,[1] the right of a subject to resist a tyrant, and dethrone him; and what is this, but, in other words, shocking as they may sound to your ears, dismissing, or *cashiering a bad servant,* as a person who had abused his trust.

So fascinating is the situation in which our kings are placed, that it is of great importance to remind them of the true relation they bear to *the people,* or, as they are fond of calling them, *their people.* They are too apt to imagine that their rights are independent of the will of the people, and consequently that they are not accountable to them for any use they may make of their power; and their numerous dependents, and especially the clergy, are too apt to administer this pleasing intoxicating poison. This was the ruin of the Stuarts, and it is a danger that threatens every prince, and every country, from the same quarter. Your whole book, Sir, is little else than a vehicle for the same poison, inculcating, but inconsistently enough, a *respect for princes,* independent of their being originally the choice of the people,

[1] The "Glorious Revolution" of 1688, when Parliament forced the last Stuart king, James II, to abdicate. In honor of this event, Priestley's friend Dr. Richard Price preached the sermon (on the right of cashiering governors) that called forth Burke's *Reflections.*

as if they had some natural and indefeasible right to reign over us, they being born to command, and we to obey; and then, whether the origin of this power be *divine*, or have any other source independent of the people, it makes no difference to us. . . .

(I)

William Godwin

An Enquiry concerning Political Justice

❮ William Godwin (1756–1836), remembered as the husband of Mary Wollstonecraft and father-in-law of Shelley, issued his *Enquiry* in two volumes at the beginning of 1793, just before the declarations of war between Great Britain and the French Revolutionists. As the Government under Pitt had introduced measures for the suppression of subversive political opinion, Godwin issued a challenge in his Preface: "It is to be tried whether a project is formed for suppressing the activity of mind, and putting an end to the disquisitions of science." Editions of 1796 and 1798 considerably toned down, however, the original text here printed. Drawing especially on the principles of necessity, utility, and universal benevolence as found in Claude Helvétius, *De l'esprit*, 1758, and Baron d'Holbach, *Le Système de la nature*, 1770, Godwin argued for equality, "perfectibility" or the infinite improvement of man, and the need to abolish all institutions and vows. In the Preface to his novel *St. Leon*, 1799, he proclaimed a need for "the culture of the heart," but the picture of him as relentlessly rational was already fixed. There is an excellent edition of the *Enquiry* by F. E. L. Priestley, 3 vols., Toronto, 1946. ❯

from Book I, Chapter V

[*Institutions*]

First then, legislation is in almost every country grossly the favourer of the rich against the poor. Such is the character of the game laws, by which the industrious rustic is forbidden to destroy the animal that preys upon the hopes of his future subsistence, or to supply himself with the food that unsought thrusts itself in his path. Such was the spirit of the late revenue laws of France, which in several of their provisions fell exclusively upon the humble and industrious, and exempted from their operation those who were best able to support it. Thus in England the land tax at this moment produces half a million less than it did a century ago, while the taxes on consumption have experienced an addition of thirteen millions per annum during the same period. This is an attempt, whether effectual or no, to throw the burthen from the rich upon the poor, and as such is an exhibition of the spirit of legislation. Upon the same principle robbery and other offences, which the wealthier part of the community have no temptation to commit, are treated as capital crimes, and attended with the most rigorous, often the most inhuman punishments. The rich are encouraged to associate for the execution of the most partial and oppressive positive laws. Monopolies and patents are lavishly dispensed to such as are able to purchase them. While the most vigilant policy is employed to prevent combinations of the poor to fix the price of labour, and they are deprived of the benefit of that prudence and judgment which would select the scene of their industry.[1]

from BOOK II, CHAPTER II

[Justice]

In a loose and general view I and my neighbour are both of us men; and of consequence entitled to equal attention. But in reality it is probable that one of us is a being of more worth and importance than the other. A man is of more worth than a beast; because, being possessed of higher faculties, he is capable of a more refined and genuine happiness. In the same manner the illustrious archbishop of Cambray was of more worth than his chambermaid, and there are few of us that would hesitate to pronounce, if his palace were in flames, and the life of only one of them could be preserved, which of the two ought to be preferred.

But there is another ground of preference, beside the private consideration of one of them being farther removed from the state of a mere animal. We are not connected with one or two percipient beings, but with a society, a nation, and in some sense with the whole family of mankind. Of consequence that life ought to be preferred which will be most conducive to the general good. In saving the life of Fenelon, suppose at the moment when he was conceiving the project of his immortal Telemachus, I should be promoting the benefit of thousands, who have been cured by the perusal of it of some error, vice and consequent unhappiness. Nay, my benefit would extend farther than this, for every individual thus cured has become a better member of society, and has contributed in his turn to the happiness, the information and improvement of others.

Supposing I had been myself the chambermaid, I ought to have chosen to die, rather than that Fenelon should have died. The life of Fenelon was really preferable to that of the chambermaid. But understanding is the faculty that perceives the truth of this and similar propositions; and justice is the principle that regulates my conduct

[1] This passage was omitted in 1796 and thereafter.

accordingly. It would have been just in the chambermaid to have preferred the archbishop to herself. To have done otherwise would have been a breach of justice.

Supposing the chambermaid had been my wife, my mother or my benefactor. This would not alter the truth of the proposition. The life of Fenelon would still be more valuable than that of the chamber-maid; and justice, pure, unadulterated justice, would still have preferred that which was most valuable. Justice would have taught me to save the life of Fenelon at the expence of the other. What magic is there in the pronoun "my," to overturn the decisions of everlasting truth? My wife or my mother may be a fool or a prostitute, malicious, lying or dishonest. If they be, of what consequence is it that they are mine?[2]

*   *   *   *   *

Society is nothing more than an aggregation of individuals. Its claims and its duties must be the aggregate of their claims and duties, the one no more precarious and arbitrary than the other. What has the society a right to require from me? The question is already answered: every thing that it is my duty to do. Any thing more? Certainly not. Can they change eternal truth, or subvert the nature of men and their actions? Can they make it my duty to commit intemperance, to maltreat or assassinate my neighbour? — Again. What is it that the society is bound to do for its members? Every thing that can contribute to their welfare. But the nature of their welfare is defined by the nature of mind. That will most contribute to it, which enlarges the understanding, supplies incitements to virtue, fills us with a generous consciousness of our independence, and carefully removes whatever can impede our exertions.

Should it be affirmed, "that it is not in the power of any political system to secure to us these advantages," the conclusion I am drawing will still be incontrovertible. It is bound to contribute every thing it is able to these purposes, and no man was yet found hardy enough to affirm that it could do nothing. Suppose its influence in the utmost degree limited, there must be one method approaching nearer than any other to the desired object, and that method ought to be universally adopted. There is one thing that political institutions can assuredly do, they can avoid positively counteracting the true interests of their subjects. But all capricious rules and arbitrary distinctions do positively counteract them. There is scarcely any modification of society but has in it some degree of moral tendency. So far as it produces neither mischief nor benefit, it is good for nothing. So far as it tends to the improvement of the community, it ought to be universally adopted.

2 In 1796 Godwin chivalrously changed the chambermaid, wife, and mother to valet, brother, and father, but retained the contrast with Fénelon, archbishop of Cambrai and author of *Les Aventures de Télémaque,* 1699.

from Book III, Chapter II
[*Social Contract*]

Lastly, if government be founded in the consent of the people, it can have no power over any individual by whom that consent is refused. If a tacit consent be not sufficient, still less can I be deemed to have consented to a measure upon which I put an express negative. This immediately follows from the observations of Rousseau. If the people, or the individuals of whom the people is constituted, cannot delegate their authority to a representative; neither can any individual delegate his authority to a majority, in an assembly of which he is himself a member. The rules by which my actions shall be directed are matters of a consideration entirely personal; and no man can transfer to another the keeping of his conscience and the judging of his duties. But this brings us back to the point from which we set out. No consent of ours can divest us of our moral capacity. This is a species of property which we can neither barter nor resign; and of consequence it is impossible for any government to derive its authority from an original contract.

from Book IV, Chapter V
[*Necessity*]

None of these principles seems to be of greater importance than that which affirms that all actions are necessary.

Most of the reasonings upon which we have hitherto been employed, though perhaps constantly built upon this doctrine as a postulate, will yet by their intrinsic evidence, however inconsistently with his opinion upon this primary topic, be admitted by the advocate of free will. But it ought not to be the present design of political enquirers to treat the questions that may present themselves superficially. It will be found upon maturer reflection that this doctrine of moral necessity includes in it consequences of the highest moment, and leads to a bold and comprehensive view of man in society, which cannot possibly be entertained by him who has embraced the opposite opinion. Severe method would have required that this proposition should have been established in the first instance, as an indispensable foundation of moral reasoning of every sort. But there are well disposed persons, who notwithstanding the evidence with which it is attended, have been alarmed at its consequences; and it was perhaps proper, in compliance with their mistake, to shew that the moral reasonings of this work did not stand in need of this support, in any other sense than moral reasonings do upon every other subject.

To the right understanding of any arguments that may be adduced under this head, it is requisite that we should have a clear idea of the

meaning of the term necessity. He who affirms that all actions are
necessary, means, that, if we form a just and complete view of all the
circumstances in which a living or intelligent being is placed, we shall
find that he could not in any moment of his existence have acted otherwise than he has acted. According to this assertion there is in the
transactions of mind nothing loose, precarious and uncertain. Upon
this question the advocate of liberty in the philosophical sense must
join issue. He must, if he mean any thing, deny this certainty of
conjunction between moral antecedents and consequents. Where all is
constant and invariable, and the events that arise uniformly flow from
the circumstances in which they originate, there can be no liberty.

from BOOK VIII, CHAPTER II
[Benefits of Equality]

Accumulated property treads the powers of thought in the dust,
extinguishes the sparks of genius, and reduces the great mass of mankind to be immersed in sordid cares; beside depriving the rich, as we
have already said, of the most salubrious and effectual motives to
activity. If superfluity were banished, the necessity for the greater
part of the manual industry of mankind would be superseded; and
the rest, being amicably shared among all the active and vigorous
members of the community, would be burthensome to none. Every
man would have a frugal, yet wholesome diet; every man would go
forth to that moderate exercise of his corporal functions that would
give hilarity to the spirits; none would be made torpid with fatigue,
but all would have leisure to cultivate the kindly and philanthropical
affections of the soul, and to let loose his faculties in the search of
intellectual improvements. What a contrast does this scene present
us with the present state of human society, where the peasant and
the labourer work, till their understandings are benumbed with toil,
their sinews contracted and made callous by being for ever on the
stretch, and their bodies invaded with infirmities and surrendered
to an untimely grave? What is the fruit of this disproportioned and
unceasing toil? At evening they return to a family, famished with
hunger, exposed half naked to the inclemencies of the sky, hardly
sheltered, and denied the slenderest instruction, unless in a few
instances, where it is dispensed by the hands of ostentatious charity,
and the first lesson communicated is unprincipled servility. All this
while their rich neighbour — but we visited him before.

How rapid and sublime would be the advances of intellect, if all
men were admitted into the field of knowledge? At present ninety-
nine persons in an hundred are no more excited to any regular exertions of general and curious thought, than the brutes themselves.
What would be the state of public mind in a nation, where all were

wise, all had laid aside the shackles of prejudice and implicit faith, all adopted with fearless confidence the suggestions of truth, and the lethargy of the soul was dismissed for ever? It is to be presumed that the inequality of mind would in a certain degree be permanent; but it is reasonable to believe that the geniuses of such an age would far surpass the grandest exertions of intellect that are at present known. Genius would not be depressed with false wants and niggardly patronage. It would not exert itself with a sense of neglect and oppression rankling in its bosom. It would be freed from those apprehensions that perpetually recal us to the thought of personal emolument, and of consequence would expatiate freely among sentiments of generosity and public good.

(I)

Thomas Robert Malthus

An Essay on the Principle of Population

❡ An Essay on the Principle of Population, as It Affects the Future Improvement of Society: With Remarks on the Speculations of Mr. Godwin, M. Condorcet, and Other Writers appeared anonymously in 1798. Its author, T. R. Malthus (1766–1834), a clergyman, converted his urbane essay into a scientific treatise and issued it in his own name in 1803. As he acknowledges, his basic postulates were not original, but he aroused a passionate debate, which has been studied fully by Kenneth Smith, The Malthusian Controversy, London, 1951, and W. P. Albrecht, William Hazlitt and the Malthusian Controversy, Albuquerque, 1950. His early answerers, arguing that reform of social arrangements is to be recommended as long as wretchedness is unequal among groups of the population, included Hazlitt, Godwin, Southey (aided by Coleridge), Cobbett, and Shelley. For a light-hearted defense of Malthus, see the essay below by James Smith, "Modern Criticism in England." De Quincey, in several periodical pieces on economics, weighed the truth on both sides. Although there is no reason to believe that Malthus lacked compassion for the poor, or took delight in declaring their misery inevitable, it should be noted that his cutting irony cancels out each deferential reference to the arguments of Godwin. It will be noted also that his punctuation in 1798, even more than Burke's, corresponds with the pauses of oratorical delivery. ❳

from CHAPTER I
[Outline of the Argument]

The advocate for the present order of things, is apt to treat the sect of speculative philosophers, either as a set of artful and designing knaves, who preach up ardent benevolence, and draw captivating pictures of a happier state of society, only the better to enable them to destroy the present establishments, and to forward their own deep-laid schemes of ambition: or, as wild and mad-headed enthusiasts, whose silly speculations, and absurd paradoxes, are not worthy the attention of any reasonable man.

The advocate for the perfectibility of man, and of society, retorts on the defender of establishments a more than equal contempt. He brands him as the slave of the most miserable, and narrow prejudices; or, as the defender of the abuses of civil society, only because he profits by them. He paints him either as a character who prostitutes his understanding to his interest; or as one whose powers of mind are not of a size to grasp any thing great and noble; who cannot see above five yards before him; and who must therefore be utterly unable to take in the views of the enlightened benefactor of mankind.

In this unamicable contest, the cause of truth cannot but suffer. The really good arguments on each side of the question are not allowed to have their proper weight. Each pursues his own theory, little solicitous to correct, or improve it, by an attention to what is advanced by his opponents.

The friend of the present order of things condemns all political speculations in the gross. He will not even condescend to examine the grounds from which the perfectibility of society is inferred. Much less will he give himself the trouble in a fair and candid manner to attempt an exposition of their fallacy.

The speculative philosopher equally offends against the cause of truth. With eyes fixed on a happier state of society, the blessings of which he paints in the most captivating colours, he allows himself to indulge in the most bitter invectives against every present establishment, without applying his talents to consider the best and safest means of removing abuses, and without seeming to be aware of the tremendous obstacles that threaten, even in theory, to oppose the progress of man towards perfection.

It is an acknowledged truth in philosophy, that a just theory will always be confirmed by experiment. Yet so much friction, and so many minute circumstances occur in practice, which it is next to impossible for the most enlarged and penetrating mind to foresee, that on few subjects can any theory be pronounced just, that has not stood the test of experience. But an untried theory cannot fairly be advanced as probable, much less as just, till all the arguments against it have been maturely weighed, and clearly and consistently refuted.

I have read some of the speculations on the perfectibility of man and of society, with great pleasure. I have been warmed and delighted with the enchanting picture which they hold forth. I ardently wish for such happy improvements. But I see great, and, to my understanding, unconquerable difficulties in the way to them. These difficulties it is my present purpose to state; declaring, at the same time, that so far from exulting in them, as a cause of triumph over the friends of innovation, nothing would give me greater pleasure than to see them completely removed.

The most important argument that I shall adduce is certainly not new. The principles on which it depends have been explained in part by Hume, and more at large by Dr. Adam Smith.[1] It has been advanced and applied to the present subject, though not with its proper weight, or in the most forcible point of view, by Mr. Wallace: and it may probably have been stated by many writers that I have never met with.[2] I should certainly therefore not think of advancing it again, though I mean to place it in a point of view in some degree different from any that I have hitherto seen, if it had ever been fairly and satisfactorily answered.

The cause of this neglect on the part of the advocates for the perfectibility of mankind, is not easily accounted for. I cannot doubt the talents of such men as Godwin and Condorcet. I am unwilling to doubt their candour. To my understanding, and probably to that of most others, the difficulty appears insurmountable. Yet these men of acknowledged ability and penetration, scarcely deign to notice it, and hold on their course in such speculations, with unabated ardour, and undiminished confidence. I have certainly no right to say that they purposely shut their eyes to such arguments. I ought rather to doubt the validity of them, when neglected by such men, however forcibly their truth may strike my own mind. Yet in this respect it must be acknowledged that we are all of us too prone to err. If I saw a glass of wine repeatedly presented to a man, and he took no notice of it, I should be apt to think that he was blind or uncivil. A juster philosophy might teach me rather to think that my eyes deceived me, and that the offer was not really what I conceived it to be.

In entering upon the argument I must premise that I put out of the question, at present, all mere conjectures; that is, all suppositions, the probable realization of which cannot be inferred upon any just philosophical grounds. A writer may tell me that he thinks man will ultimately become an ostrich. I cannot properly contradict him. But before he can expect to bring any reasonable person over to his opinion, he ought to shew, that the necks of mankind have been gradually elongating; that the lips have grown harder, and more prominent; that the legs and feet are daily altering their shape; and that the hair is beginning to change into stubs of feathers. And till the probability of so wonderful a conversion can be shewn, it is surely lost time and lost eloquence to expatiate on the happiness of

[1] David Hume (1711–76), "Of the Populousness of Ancient Nations," 1752; Adam Smith (1723–90), *An Inquiry into . . . the Wealth of Nations,* 1776.
[2] Robert Wallace (1697–1771), *A Dissertation on the Numbers of Mankind,* 1753; *Various Prospects of Mankind, Nature, and Providence,* 1761.

man in such a state; to describe his powers, both of running and flying; to paint him in a condition where all narrow luxuries would be contemned; where he would be employed only in collecting the necessaries of life; and where, consequently, each man's share of labour would be light, and his portion of leisure ample.

I think I may fairly make two postulata.

First, That food is necessary to the existence of man.

Secondly, That the passion between the sexes is necessary, and will remain nearly in its present state.

These two laws ever since we have had any knowledge of mankind, appear to have been fixed laws of our nature; and, as we have not hitherto seen any alteration in them, we have no right to conclude that they will ever cease to be what they now are, without an immediate act of power in that Being who first arranged the system of the universe; and for the advantage of his creatures, still executes, according to fixed laws, all its various operations.

I do not know that any writer has supposed that on this earth man will ultimately be able to live without food. But Mr. Godwin has conjectured that the passion between the sexes may in time be extinguished. As, however, he calls this part of his work, a deviation into the land of conjecture, I will not dwell longer upon it at present, than to say, that the best arguments for the perfectibility of man, are drawn from a contemplation of the great progress that he has already made from the savage state, and the difficulty of saying where he is to stop. But towards the extinction of the passion between the sexes, no progress whatever has hitherto been made. It appears to exist in as much force at present as it did two thousand, or four thousand years ago. There are individual exceptions now as there always have been. But, as these exceptions do not appear to increase in number, it would surely be a very unphilosophical mode of arguing, to infer merely from the existence of an exception, that the exception would, in time, become the rule, and the rule the exception.

Assuming then, my postulata as granted, I say, that the power of population is indefinitely greater than the power in the earth to produce subsistence for man.

Population, when unchecked, increases in a geometrical ratio. Subsistence increases only in an arithmetical ratio. A slight acquaintance with numbers will shew the immensity of the first power in comparison of the second.

By that law of our nature which makes food necessary to the life of man, the effects of these two unequal powers must be kept equal.

This implies a strong and constantly operating check on population from the difficulty of subsistence. This difficulty must fall some where; and must necessarily be severely felt by a large portion of mankind.

Through the animal and vegetable kingdoms, nature has scattered the seeds of life abroad with the most profuse and liberal hand. She has been comparatively sparing in the room, and the nourishment necessary to rear them. The germs of existence contained in this spot of earth, with ample food, and ample room to expand in, would fill millions of worlds in the course of a few thousand years. Necessity, that imperious all pervading law of nature, restrains them within the prescribed bounds. The race of plants, and the race of animals shrink under this great restrictive law. And the race of man cannot, by any efforts of reason, escape from it. Among plants and animals its effects are waste of seed, sickness, and premature death. Among mankind, misery and vice. The former, misery, is an absolutely necessary consequence of it. Vice is a highly probable consequence, and we therefore see it abundantly prevail; but it ought not, perhaps, to be called an absolutely necessary consequence. The ordeal of virtue is to resist all temptation to evil.

This natural inequality of the two powers of population, and of production in the earth, and that great law of our nature which must constantly keep their effects equal, form the great difficulty that to me appears insurmountable in the way to the perfectibility of society. All other arguments are of slight and subordinate consideration in comparison of this. I see no way by which man can escape from the weight of this law which pervades all animated nature. No fancied equality, no agrarian regulations in their utmost extent, could remove the pressure of it even for a single century. And it appears, therefore, to be decisive against the possible existence of a society, all the members of which, should live in ease, happiness, and comparative leisure; and feel no anxiety about providing the means of subsistence for themselves and families.

Consequently, if the premises are just, the argument is conclusive against the perfectibility of the mass of mankind.

from CHAPTER X

[*Critique of Godwin*]

In reading Mr. Godwin's ingenious and able work on political justice, it is impossible not to be struck with the spirit and energy of his style, the force and precision of some of his reasonings, the ardent tone of his thoughts, and particularly with that impressive earnestness of manner which gives an air of truth to the whole. At the same time, it must be confessed, that he has not proceeded in his enquiries with the caution that sound philosophy seems to require. His conclusions are often unwarranted by his premises. He fails sometimes in removing the objections which he himself brings forward. He relies too much on general and abstract propositions which will not admit of application. And his conjectures certainly far outstrip the modesty of nature.

The system of equality which Mr. Godwin proposes, is, without doubt, by far the most beautiful and engaging of any that has yet appeared. An amelioration of society to be produced merely by reason and conviction, wears much more the promise of permanence, than any change effected and maintained by force. The unlimited exercise of private judgment, is a doctrine inexpressibly grand and captivating, and has a vast superiority over those systems where every individual is in a manner the slave of the public. The substitution of benevolence as the master-spring, and moving principle of society, instead of self-love, is a consummation devoutly to be wished. In short, it is impossible to contemplate the whole of this fair structure, without emotions of delight and admiration, accompanied with ardent longing for the period of its accomplishment. But, alas! that moment can never arrive. The whole is little better than a dream, a beautiful phantom of the imagination. These "gorgeous palaces" of happiness and immortality, these "solemn temples" of truth and virtue will dissolve, "like the baseless fabric of a vision,"[3] when we awaken to real life, and contemplate the true and genuine situation of man on earth.

Mr. Godwin, at the conclusion of the third chapter of his eighth book, speaking of population, says, "There is a principle in human society, by which population is perpetually kept down to the level of the means of subsistence. Thus among the wandering tribes of America and Asia, we never find through the lapse of ages that population has so increased as to render necessary the cultivation of the earth." This principle, which Mr. Godwin thus mentions as some mysterious and occult cause, and which he does not attempt to investigate, will be found to be the grinding law of necessity; misery, and the fear of misery.

The great error under which Mr. Godwin labours throughout his whole work, is, the attributing almost all the vices and misery that are seen in civil society to human institutions. Political regulations, and the established administration of property, are with him the fruitful sources of all evil, the hotbeds of all the crimes that degrade mankind. Were this really a true state of the case, it would not seem a hopeless task to remove evil completely from the world; and reason seems to be the proper and adequate instrument for effecting so great a purpose. But the truth is, that though human institutions appear to be the obvious and obtrusive causes of much mischief to mankind; yet, in reality, they are light and superficial, they are mere feathers that float on the surface, in comparison with those deeper seated causes of impurity that corrupt the springs, and render turbid the whole stream of human life.

[3] Cf. *The Tempest* IV.i.151–153.

William Paley
Natural Theology

❨ Two of the works of William Paley (1743–1805), *The Principles of Moral and Political Philosophy* in 1785 and *A View of the Evidences of Christianity* in 1794, became textbooks at Cambridge University almost from the day of publication. As Ben R. Schneider points out in *Wordsworth's Cambridge Education* (Cambridge 1957), Paley's foremost ideals were utility and expediency. His last book, *Natural Theology; or, Evidences of the Existence and Attributes of the Deity Collected from the Appearances of Nature*, 1802, resembles the works of Bentham except in its argument that the ethic of utility receives its ultimate sanction from God, the designer of the universe. The following selections are taken from the Twelfth Edition of 1809. ❩

from CHAPTER I
State of the Argument

In crossing a heath, suppose I pitched my foot against a *stone*, and were asked how the stone came to be there; I might possibly answer, that, for any thing I knew to the contrary, it had lain there for ever: nor would it perhaps be very easy to show the absurdity of this answer. But suppose I had found a *watch* upon the ground, and it should be inquired how the watch happened to be in that place; I should hardly think of the answer which I had before given, that, for any thing I knew, the watch might have always been there. Yet why should not this answer serve for the watch as well as for the stone? why is it not as admissible in the second case, as in the first? For this reason, and for no other, viz. that, when we come to inspect the watch, we perceive (what we could not discover in the stone) that its several parts are framed and put together for a purpose, *e.g.* that they are so formed and adjusted as to produce motion, and that motion so regulated as to point out the hour of the day; that, if the different parts had been differently shaped from what they are, of a different size from what they are, or placed after any other manner, or in any other order, than that in which they are placed, either no motion at all would have been carried on in the machine, or none which would have answered the use that is now served by it. To reckon up a few of the plainest of these parts, and of their offices, all tending to one result: — We see a cylindrical box containing a coiled elastic spring, which, by its endeavour to relax itself, turns round the box. We next observe a flexible chain (artificially wrought for the sake of flexure), communicating the action of the spring from the box to the fusee. We then find a series of wheels, the teeth of which catch in, and apply to, each other, conducting the motion from the fusee to the balance, and from the balance to the pointer; and at the same time, by the size and shape of those wheels, so regulating that motion, as to terminate in causing an index, by an equable and measured progression, to pass over a given space in a given time. We take notice that the wheels are made of brass in order to keep them from rust; the springs of steel, no other metal being so elastic; that over the face of the watch there is placed a glass, a material employed in no other part of the work, but in the room of which, if there had been any other than a transparent substance, the hour could not be seen without opening the case. This mechanism being observed (it requires indeed an examination of the instrument, and perhaps some previous knowledge of the subject, to perceive and understand it; but being once, as we have said, observed and understood), the inference, we think, is inevitable, that the watch must have had a maker: that there must have existed, at some time, and at some place or other, an artificer or artificers who formed it for the purpose which we find it actually to answer; who comprehended its construction, and designed its use. . . .

from Chapter III

Application of the Argument

. . . Every indication of contrivance, every manifestation of design, which existed in the watch, exists in the works of nature; with the difference, on the side of nature, of being greater and more, and that in a degree which exceeds all computation. I mean that the contrivances of nature surpass the contrivances of art, in the complexity, subtility, and curiosity of the mechanism; and still more, if possible, do they go beyond them in number and variety; yet, in a multitude of cases, are not less evidently mechanical, not less evidently accommodated to their end, or suited to their office, than are the most perfect productions of human ingenuity.

I know no better method of introducing so large a subject, than that of comparing a single thing with a single thing; an eye, for example, with a telescope. As far as the examination of the instrument goes, there is precisely the same proof that the eye was made for vision, as there is that the telescope was made for assisting it. They are made upon the same principles; both being adjusted to the laws by which the transmission and refraction of rays of light are regulated. I speak not of the origin of the laws themselves; but such laws being fixed, the construction, in both cases, is adapted to them. For instance; these laws require, in order to produce the same effect, that the rays of light, in passing from water into the eye, should be refracted by a more convex surface, than when it passes out of air into the eye. Accordingly we find that the eye of a fish, in that part of it called the crystalline lens, is much rounder than the eye of terrestrial animals. What plainer manifestation of design can there be than this difference? What could a mathematical-instrument-maker have done more, to show his knowledge of his principle, his application of that knowledge, his suiting of his means to his end; I will not say to display the compass or excellence of his skill and art, for in these all comparison is indecorous, but to testify counsel, choice, consideration, purpose?

To some it may appear a difference sufficient to destroy all similitude between the eye and the telescope, that the one is a perceiving organ, the other an unperceiving instrument. The fact is, that they are both instruments. And, as to the mechanism, at least as to mechanism being employed, and even as to the kind of it, this circumstance varies not the analogy at all. . . .

(I)

James Smith

Modern Criticism in England

No. II

⟪ The "Smith of Smiths" in the Romantic period was Sydney Smith (1771–1845), clergyman, Edinburgh Reviewer, and wit. But Horace (1779–1849) and James (1775–1839) Smith achieved fame in 1812 with *Rejected Addresses*, a collection of parodies of living authors in the form of addresses submitted for the re-opening of Drury Lane Theatre. The comic defense of Malthus, here taken from Horace Smith's edition of his brother's *Comic Miscellanies in Prose and Verse*, 1840, appeared originally in the *Monthly Mirror* for December 1809, as Letter 23 from Endymion the Exile to his friend Ambrose. ⟫

When a man writes a book here, there is generally as much clamour excited against him, as if he had roasted a child. He is looked upon as such a Julius Cæsar in the republic of letters, that every *Brute* who can wield a quill, thinks it meritorious to have a thrust at him.

That this should be the case, on the appearance of a work of imagination, the experience of our own behaviour would prevent us from being surprised: we are extremely loath to allow others to be wittier than ourselves: it is a mark of prodigious wisdom to be dissatisfied, and the cut and dry jokes upon these occasions are in such ready preservation, that it requires no ordinary good-nature to abstain from the use of them. For instance, the blank-verse lines of a sacred poem are mere segments cut out of the Bible, and placed in parallel order, like the steps of a ladder, by means whereof the bard hopes to work miracles, like Peter in the "Tale of a Tub," and to endow himself with poetical inspiration. Pastorals are mere narcotics. Amaryllis reclines her head in slumber under a beech-tree, and her reader reposes his on a mahogany table. If the writer, according to the old customs, presumes to invoke the muse, he is reminded by the reviewer that he has done nothing more than leaving his card at her door, and that the intimacy is not likely to extend further; and if, like the poet Gray, he rushes, *sans ceremonie*, into the thick of the battle, he is informed that Aganippe is not always a cold bath, to invigorate by a single plunge, but that it occasionally emasculates the swimmer, like the streamlet recorded in Ovid. All this, my dear Ambrose, is indubitably funny, and generally gives pleasure to the reader, in proportion as it gives pain to the poet, resembling (to borrow a simile from Fielding) "one of those punches in the stomach exchanged in a boxing-match, which, though they give such exquisite delight to the spectator, are the source of little or no pleasure to the receiver." But when a man publishes a mathematical truth, telling the world that the three angles of a triangle, taken together, are equal to two right angles; or when he broaches an arithmetical truism, such, for instance, as that four multiplied by four produces a greater quantity than when merely added to the same number, it might be supposed that calumny and declamation would be silent, and that ridicule, if awakened at all, would be employed, not in denying the truth of those assertions, but in laughing at the credulity of a writer who should think it necessary to compose two octavo volumes in proving such self-evident propositions. A late fellow of Jesus College, Cambridge,[1] has found out that a newly-married couple, possessed of a small farm, may, in the course of five or six years, be blessed with five or six children; and that if the farm be only adequate to the support of the wedded pair, their offspring must either starve or wander forth in quest of subsistence elsewhere. He then supposes the golden age, so confidently predicted by English philosophers, to have arrived, and the hitherto trackless wilderness to be parcelled out in farms of the above description, in which case the command of seeking a subsistence elsewhere will be liable to this inconvenience, that there will be no subsistence elsewhere to be found. Thus circumstanced, the five or six little unfortunates will share the fate of Ugolino's bantlings.[2] It cannot be denied, that it had been better not to have been born, than to die from want of food. The inference of the philosopher is this: — the source of all evil is the folly, not to say crim-

[1] Malthus.
[2] *I.e.,* starvation, as described by Dante, *Inferno* xxxiii.

inality, of marrying without a fair chance of supporting a family.

I have thus compressed into a few lines the contents of two octavo volumes: and one would suppose that the position they aim at establishing, namely, the certain increase of expense incurred by an increasing family, and the certain limitation of means to meet that expense, are positions too palpable to be contradicted. "My muse," says a lively dramatic writer, of the reign of Queen Anne, "produces me a play every year, and my wife a child; but I find the latter much more disposed to live than the former."[3] I should deem this a secret well worth knowing; and yet, O the ingratitude of man! were I to detail half the outcry that has been raised against this unfortunate late fellow of Jesus College, I should pester you with letters, rivalling in length those of the voluminous Richardson. He has been attacked in weekly publications by apostates, bearded and beardless; he is assailed by the cloudy anarchist,[4] whose novels are dull philosophy, and whose philosophy is dull novelty: he is pounced upon by ravens, and condemned by revelations: grave divines who have theories, and grave matrons who have daughters to establish, join in anathemas against the profane intruder, who has thus dared to lift the sacred veil that covers the altar of Hymen! "What!" cry they, speaking all at once, "shall an ugly fellow, of one of the ugliest colleges in Cambridge, with feelings as sluggish as his own Cam, presume to control the impulses of nature? shall our daughters, whose complexions, natural or acquired, vie with the lily and the rose, be checked in their endeavours to engraft upon the marigold, and thrown back to wither, an encumbrance on their native stalk? Shall our dear boys, whom we are training up to wed an adjoining freehold, and for whom the pious founder of our new national theatre has provided a tier of private boxes, to snatch them from the contagion above and below, be taught presumptuously to look before they leap? Shall domestic happiness, which our own dear Mr. Cowper has called, the "only bliss which has survived the fall,"[5] be cut up by the roots, and the garden of Eden converted into a wilderness, by a sceptic who presumes to judge and decide, where orthodox piety believes and trembles?" "Alas! ladies and gentlemen," replies the alarmed and modest author, "I pretend not to judge and decide — to decide and judge are doughty attributes, and I leave them to my opponents. I am not the manufacturer of the system, I aim only at being its expounder. When they who so loudly talk of the duty of entering into the married state, prove to me that their own marriages were contracted from that motive, and that a new treaty or an old heiress was not the *primum mobile* that introduced them to Hymen, I will bow my head in silence. At present, I have merely to repeat in my appendix

[3] Cf. *An Apology for the Life of Mr. Colley Cibber, Written by Himself*, 1740, ch. viii.

[4] Godwin.

[5] William Cowper (1731–1800), *The Task* III.41–42.

what I have asserted in the body of my work: 'Eating and drinking are necessaries, but marriage is a luxury; a refined and a laudable one I allow, but still a luxury, and as such, not to be encouraged without a reasonable chance of ability to support it.' " The mildness of the reply is vain — the outcry is renewed, and, by a consequence as old as the days of Socrates, his motives are arraigned because his arguments are unanswerable.

Such, Ambrose, is the philosopher, and such are his antagonists. Every bob-wigged citizen, who, as president at a public meeting, strings a bead-roll of silly and disaffected propositions, is thanked for his able and impartial conduct in the chair; but when a grave mathematician expends his nightly oil in enlightening the public, and shows that abstinence from marriage is a more desirable check to population than vice or misery, he is called a prodigal, a misanthrope, a deist, and fifty hard names beside. The British public is like a sick child. It is not enough that the medicine you proffer be conducive to its health, it must also be agreeable to its palate, otherwise you stand a very excellent chance of having the contents of the chalice thrown back into your own face. For my part, had I twenty times the talents of the late fellow of Jesus, I feel too little regard for my species to employ them unsolicited in their behalf. No; my motto is, "Qui vult decipi, decipiatur."[6] Before I would turn oculist to such a race of moles, I would let them grope their own way through mud and mire, like the merchant Abudah in the mountains of Tasgi.[7]

(|)

Robert Southey

Letters from England

❡ In 1797, after six months on the Iberian Peninsula, the prolific Southey (1774–1843) published under his own name *Letters Written During a Short Residence in Spain and Portugal*. Partly because of harsh reviews given to his books of poetry during the next ten years, and partly for the fun of assuming a foreign mask, he issued his *Letters from England*, late in the summer of 1807, as an anonymous translation in three volumes from the Spanish of "Don Manuel Alvarez Espriella," who was supposed to have

[6] Let him be deceived who wishes to be deceived.
[7] Abudah: in James Ridley, *Tales of the Genii*, 1764.
    Jonathan Swift, *A Tale of a Tub*, 1704; Samuel Richardson (1689–1761), author of the long epistolary novels, *Pamela*, *Clarissa*, etc.
    Aganippe: a spring sacred to the Muses.

visited England in 1802–03. Although the book lacks the penetrating satire
of the best works in its tradition (descending from Montesquieu's *Lettres
persanes*, 1721), Southey's biographer, Jack Simmons, has justly called it
"a most lively and readable sketch, giving a brilliant impression of life in
early nineteenth-century England." Simmons published an annotated edition in 1951. The first half of Letter 39 is given below from the Second
Edition of 1808. (The dots of ellipsis in the first paragraph are Southey's.)
There was a further edition in 1814, and others in New York, Boston,
Paris, and Leipzig.])

A place more destitute of all interesting objects than Manchester it
is not easy to conceive. In size and population it is the second city of
the kingdom, containing above fourscore thousand inhabitants. Imagine this multitude crowded together in narrow streets, the houses all
built of brick and blackened with smoke; frequent buildings among
them as large as convents, without their antiquity, without their beauty,
without their holiness; where you hear from within, as you pass along,
the everlasting din of machinery; and where when the bell rings it is
to call wretches to their work instead of their prayers, ... Imagine
this, and you have the materials for a picture of Manchester. The most
remarkable thing which I have seen here is the skin of a snake, fourteen
English feet in length, which was killed in the neighbourhood, and is
preserved in the library of the collegiate church.

We left it willingly on Monday morning, and embarked upon the
canal in a stage boat bound for Chester, a city which we had been
advised by no means to pass by unseen. This was a new mode of
travelling, and a delightful one it proved. The shape of the machine
resembles the common representations of Noah's ark, except that the
roof is flatter, so made for the convenience of passengers. Within this
floating house are two apartments, seats in which are hired at different
prices, the parlour and the kitchen. Two horses, harnessed one before
the other, tow it along at the rate of a league an hour; the very pace
which it is pleasant to keep up with when walking on the bank. The
canal is just wide enough for two boats to pass; sometimes we sprung
ashore, sometimes stood or sate upon the roof, — till to our surprise
we were called down to dinner, and found that as good a meal had been
prepared in the back part of the boat while we were going on, as would
have been supplied at an inn. We joined in a wish that the same kind
of travelling were extended every where: no time was lost; kitchen and
cellar travelled with us; the motion was imperceptible, we could neither
be overturned nor run away with, if we sunk there was not depth of
water to drown us; we could read as conveniently as in a house, or
sleep as quietly as in a bed.

England is now intersected in every direction by canals. This is the
province in which they were first tried by the present duke of Bridgewater, whose fortune has been amply increased by the success of his
experiment. His engineer Brindley was a singular character, a man of

real genius for this particular employment, who thought of nothing but locks and levels, perforating hills, and floating barges upon aqueduct bridges over unmanageable streams. When he had a plan to form he usually went to bed, and lay there working it out in his head till the design was completed. It is recorded of him, that being asked in the course of an examination before the House of Commons for what he supposed rivers were created, he answered after a pause, — To feed navigable canals.

Excellent as these canals are, rail-roads are found to accomplish the same purpose at less expense. In these the wheels of the carriage move in grooves upon iron bars laid all along the road; where there is a descent no draught is required, and the laden waggons as they run down draw the empty ones up. These roads are always used in the neighbourhood of coal-mines and founderies. It has been recommended by speculative men that they should be universally introduced, and a hope held out that at some future time this will be done, and all carriages drawn along by the action of steam-engines erected at proper distances. If this be at present one of the dreams of philosophy, it is a philosophy by which trade and manufactures would be benefited and money saved; and the dream therefore may probably one day be accomplished.

The canal not extending to Chester, we were dismissed from the boat about half way between the two cities, near the town of Warrington, which was just distant enough to form a pleasing object through the intervening trees. A stage to which we were consigned, was ready to receive us; and we exchanged, not very willingly, the silent and imperceptible motion of a water-journey, to be jolted over rough roads in a crowded and noisy coach. The country was little interesting and became less so as we advanced. I saw two bodies swinging from a gibbet by the road side: they had robbed and murdered a post-boy, and, according to the barbarous and indecent custom of England, were hanged up upon the spot till their bones should fall asunder.

We found Chester to be as remarkable a place as our travelling friend at Manchester had represented it. The streets are cut out of a soft red rock, and passengers walk, not upon flag-stones at the side, as in most other cities, nor in the middle of the street, — but through the houses, upon a boarded parade, through what would elsewhere be the front room of the first floor. Wherever a lane or street strikes off, there is a flight of steps into the carriage road. The best shops are upon this covered way, though there are others underneath it on a level with the street. The cathedral is a mean edifice of soft, red, crumbly stone, apparently quarried upon the spot; it would have been folly to have erected any thing better with such wretched materials. I saw nothing in it more notable than the epitaph upon an infant son of the bishop, of whom it was thought proper to record upon marble, that he was born in the palace and baptized in the cathedral.

The old walls are yet standing; there is a walk on the top of them, whence we overlooked the surrounding country, the mountains of Wales not far distant, and the river Dee, which passes by the city and forms an estuary about two leagues below it. The new jail is considered as a perfect model of prison architecture, a branch of the art as much studied by the English of the present day, as ever cathedral-building was by their pious ancestors. The main objects attended to are, that the prisoners be kept apart from each other, and that the cells should be always open to inspection, and well ventilated so as to prevent infectious disorders, which were commonly occurring in old prisons. The structure of this particular prison is singularly curious, the cells being so constructed that the jailor from his dwelling-house can look into every one, — a counterpart to the whispering dungeons in Sicily, which would have delighted Dionysius. I thought of Asmodeus and Don Cleofas.[1] The apartment from whence we were shown the interior of the prison was well, and even elegantly furnished; there were geraniums flowering upon stands, — a piano-forte, and music-books lying open —, and when we looked from the window we saw criminals with irons upon their legs, in solitary dungeons: — one of them, who was intently reading some devotional book, was, we were told, certainly to be executed at the next assizes. Custom soon cauterizes human sympathy; or the situation of the keeper who sits surrounded with comforts, and has these things always in view, would be well nigh as deplorable as that of the wretches under his care. . . .

(I)

Robert Owen

A New View of Society

¶ Robert Owen (1771–1858), industrialist and reformer, is often called the father of English socialism. To replace unregulated competition with economic cooperation and association in communities, Owen hoped to reform the characters of individuals by changing their environment. In behalf of his socialistic program, he opposed the institutions of private property, church, and marriage. Hazlitt gave him a prominent place in the essay "Of People with One Idea." Although the first essay of *A New View of Society* was written as early as 1812, and all four of its essays were widely circulated a year or so later, they were first published as a unit in the "Second Edition" of 1816. The address prefixed to the third essay, in 1814, is given below from the "Fourth Edition" of 1818. ⟩

[1] Characters in *Le Diable boiteux*, 1707, by Alain-René Le Sage.

An Address

To the Superintendants of Manufactories, and to those Individuals generally, who, by giving Employment to an aggregated Population, may easily adopt the Means to form the Sentiments and Manners of such a Population.

Like you, I am a manufacturer for pecuniary profit. But having for many years acted on principles the reverse in many respects of those in which you have been instructed, and having found my procedure beneficial to others and to myself, even in a pecuniary point of view, I am anxious to explain such valuable principles, that you and those under your influence may equally partake of their advantages.

In two Essays, already published, I have developed some of these principles, and in the following pages you will find still more of them explained, with some detail of their application to practice, under the particular local circumstances in which I undertook the direction of the New Lanark Mills and Establishment.

By those details you will find, that from the commencement of my management I viewed the population, with the mechanism and every other part of the establishment, as a system composed of many parts, and which it was my duty and interest so to combine, as that every hand, as well as every spring, lever, and wheel, should effectually co-operate to produce the greatest pecuniary gain to the proprietors.

Many of you have long experienced in your manufacturing operations the advantages of substantial, well-contrived, and well-executed machinery.

Experience has also shown you the difference of the results between mechanism which is neat, clean, well arranged, and always in a high state of repair; and that which is allowed to be dirty, in disorder, without the means of preventing unnecessary friction, and which therefore becomes, and works, much out of repair.

In the first case, the whole economy and management are good; every operation proceeds with ease, order, and success. In the last, the reverse must follow, and a scene be presented of counteraction, confusion, and dissatisfaction among all the agents and instruments interested or occupied in the general process, which cannot fail to create great loss.

If then due care as to the state of your inanimate machines can produce such beneficial results, what may not be expected if you devote equal attention to your vital machines, which are far more wonderfully constructed?

When you shall acquire a right knowledge of these, of their curious mechanism, of their self-adjusting powers; when the proper main spring shall be applied to their varied movements, you will become conscious of their real value, and you will be readily induced to turn your thoughts more frequently from your inanimate to your living machines; you will discover that the latter may be easily trained and directed to procure a large increase of pecuniary gain, while you may also derive from them high and substantial gratification.

Will you then continue to expend large sums of money to procure the best devised mechanism of wood, brass, or iron; to retain it in perfect repair; to provide the best substance for the prevention of unnecessary friction, and to save it from falling into premature decay? Will you also devote years of intense application to understand the connexion of the various parts of these lifeless machines, to improve their effective powers, and to calculate with mathematical precision all their minute and combined movements? And when in these transactions you estimate time by minutes, and the money expended for the chance of increased gain by fractions, will you not afford some of your attention to consider whether a portion of your time and capital would not be more advantageously applied to improve your living machines?

From experience which cannot deceive me, I venture to assure you, that your time and money so applied, if directed by a true knowledge of the subject, would return you not five, ten, or fifteen per cent. for your capital so expended, but often fifty and in many cases a hundred per cent.

I have expended much time and capital upon improvements of the living machinery; and it will soon appear that the time and money so expended in the manufactory at New Lanark, even while such improvements are in progress only, and but half their beneficial effects attained, are now producing a return exceeding fifty per cent., and will shortly create profits equal to cent. per cent. on the original capital expended in them.

Indeed, after experience of the beneficial effects, from due care and attention to the mechanical implements, it became easy to a reflecting mind to conclude at once, that at least equal advantages would arise from the application of similar care and attention to the living instruments. And when it was perceived that inanimate mechanism was greatly improved by being made firm and substantial; that it was the essence of economy to keep it neat, clean, regularly supplied with the best substance to prevent unnecessary friction, and, by proper provision for the purpose, to preserve it in good repair; it was natural to conclude that the more delicate, complex, living mechanism would be equally improved by being trained to strength and activity; and that it would also prove true economy to keep it neat and clean; to treat it with kindness, that its mental movements might not experience too much irritating friction; to endeavour by every means to make it more perfect; to supply it regularly with a sufficient quantity of wholesome food and other necessaries of life, that the body might be preserved in good working condition, and prevented from being out of repair, or falling prematurely to decay.

These anticipations are proved by experience to be just.

Since the general introduction of inanimate mechanism into British manufactories, man, with few exceptions, has been treated as a secondary and inferior machine; and far more attention has been given to perfect the raw materials of wood and metals than those of body and mind. Give but due reflection to the subject, and you will find that man, even as an instrument for the creation of wealth, may be still greatly improved.

But, my friends, a far more interesting and gratifying consideration remains. Adopt the means which ere long shall be rendered obvious to every understanding, and you may not only partially improve those living instruments, but learn how to impart to them such excellence as shall make them infinitely surpass those of the present and all former times.

Here then is an object which truly deserves your attention; and instead of devoting all your faculties to invent improved inanimate mechanism, let your thoughts be, at least in part, directed to discover how to combine the more excellent materials of body and mind, which, by a well-devised experiment, will be found capable of progressive improvement.

Thus seeing with the clearness of noon-day light, thus convinced with the certainty of conviction itself, let us not perpetuate the really unnecessary evils, which our present practices inflict on this large proportion of our fellow subjects. Should your pecuniary interests somewhat suffer by adopting the line of conduct now urged, many of you are so wealthy, that the expense of founding and continuing at your respective establishments the institutions necessary to improve your animate machines, would not be felt. But when you may have ocular demonstration that, instead of any pecuniary loss, a well-directed attention to form the character and increase the comforts of those who are so entirely at your mercy will essentially add to your gains, prosperity, and happiness; no reasons, except those founded on ignorance of your self-interest, can in future prevent you from bestowing your chief care on the living machines which you employ; and by so doing you will prevent an accumulation of human misery, of which it is now difficult to form an adequate conception.

That you may be convinced of this most valuable truth, which due reflection will show you is founded on the evidence of unerring facts, is the sincere wish of

THE AUTHOR.

William Cobbett

Rural Rides

❪ Under slightly varying titles, William Cobbett (1763–1835) conducted his *Political Register* from 1803 until the week of his death. His *Rural Rides,* first published serially in the *Register* between 1821 and 1834, report observations made during his rides on horseback through the country, mostly in periods of agricultural distress. He made a selection in book form in 1830, which was enlarged, annotated, and altered in mechanical details by his son, James Paul Cobbett, in 1853 (the edition here followed, with corrections). The fullest of several subsequent editions was made in 1930 by G. D. H. and Margaret Cole, who there and in other studies contributed to our understanding of Cobbett's relation to his times. Instead of the Corn Laws to keep food prices high, Cobbett recommended Parliamentary Reform, which he expected to reduce governmental sinecures, waste and corruption, the standing army, and the National Debt, and therefore to reduce taxes for the farmer, who could then pay higher wages for labor. Cobbett is one of the most violently prejudiced writers ever to achieve lasting fame, but his vigor is unequaled by writers better educated, more careful of opinion, and more correct in syntax. ❫

Bollitree,
Wednesday, 14 *Nov.* [1821]

Rode to the Forest of Dean, up a very steep hill. The lanes here are between high banks, and, on the sides of the hills, the road is a rock, the water having, long ago, washed all the earth away. Pretty works are, I find, carried on here, as is the case in all the other *public forests!* Are these things *always* to be carried on in this way? Here is a domain of thirty thousand acres of the finest timber-land in the world, and with coal-mines endless! Is this *worth nothing?* Cannot each acre yield ten trees a year? Are not these trees worth a pound a piece? Is not the estate worth three or four hundred thousand pounds a year? And does it yield *anything to the public,* to whom it belongs? But, it is useless to waste one's breath in this way. We must have a *reform of the Parliament:* without it the whole thing will fall to pieces. — The only good purpose that these forests answer is that of furnishing a place of being to labourers' families on their skirts; and here their cottages are very neat, and the people look hearty and well, just as they do round the forests in Hampshire. Every cottage has a pig, or two. These graze in the forest, and, in the fall, eat acorns and beech-nuts and the seed of the ash; for, these last, as well as the others, are very full of oil, and a pig that is put to his shifts will pick the seed very nicely out

from the husks. Some of these foresters keep cows, and all of them
have bits of ground, cribbed, of course, at different times, from the
forest: and, to what better use can the ground be put? I saw several
wheat stubbles from 40 rods to 10 rods. I asked one man how much
wheat he had from about 10 rods. He said more than two bushels.
Here is bread for three weeks, or more, perhaps; and a winter's straw
for the pig besides. Are these things nothing? The dead limbs and old
roots of the forest give *fuel;* and how happy are these people, compared
with the poor creatures about Great Bedwin and Cricklade, where
they have neither land nor shelter, and where I saw the girls carrying
home bean and wheat stubble for fuel! Those countries, always but
badly furnished with fuel, the desolating and damnable system of
paper-money, by sweeping away small homesteads, and laying ten
farms into one, has literally *stripped* of all shelter for the labourer. A
farmer, in such cases, has a whole domain in his hands, and this, not
only to the manifest injury of the public at large, but in *open violation
of positive law.* The poor forger is hanged; but, where is the prosecutor
of the monopolizing farmer, though the *law* is as clear in the one case
as in the other? But, it required this infernal system to render every
wholesome regulation nugatory; and to reduce to such abject misery
a people famed in all ages for the goodness of their food and their
dress. There is one farmer, in the North of Hampshire, who has nearly
eight thousand acres of land in his hands; who grows fourteen hundred
acres of wheat and two thousand acres of barley! He occupies what
was formerly 40 farms! Is it any wonder that *paupers increase?* And is
there not here cause enough for the increase of *poor,* without resorting
to the doctrine of the barbarous and impious MALTHUS and his assistants, the *feelosofers* of the Edinburgh Review, those eulogists and
understrappers of the Whig-Oligarchy? "This farmer has done nothing
unlawful," some one will say. I say he has; for there is a law to forbid
him thus to monopolize land. But, no matter; the laws, the management
of the affairs of a nation, *ought to be such as to prevent the existence of
the temptation to such monopoly.* And, even now, the evil ought to be
remedied, and could be remedied, in the space of half a dozen years.
The disappearance of the paper-money would do the thing in time;
but this might be assisted by legislative measures. — In returning from
the forest we were overtaken by my son, whom I had begged to come
from London to see this beautiful country. On the road-side we saw
two lazy-looking fellows, in long great coats and bundles in their hands,
going into a cottage. "What do you deal in?" said I, to one of them,
who had not yet entered the house. "In the *medical way,"* said he.
And, I find, that vagabonds of this description are seen all over the
country with *tea-licences* in their pockets. They vend *tea, drugs,* and
religious tracts. The first to bring the body into a debilitated state; the
second to finish the corporeal part of the business; and the third to
prepare the spirit for its separation from the clay! Never was a system

so well calculated as the present to degrade, debase, and enslave a people! Law, and, as if that were not sufficient, enormous subscriptions are made; every thing that can be done is done to favour these perambulatory impostors in their depredations on the ignorant. While every thing that can be done is done, to prevent them from reading, or from hearing of, any thing that has a tendency to give them rational notions, or to better their lot. However, all is not buried in ignorance. Down the deep and beautiful valley between Penyard Hill and the Hills on the side of the Forest of Dean, there runs a stream of water. On that stream of water there is a *paper-mill*. In that paper-mill there is a set of workmen. That set of workmen do, I am told, *take the Register*, and have taken it for years! It was to these good and sensible men, it is supposed, that the *ringing of the bells* of Weston church, upon my arrival, was to be ascribed; for, nobody that I visited had any knowledge of the cause. What a subject for lamentation with corrupt hypocrites! That even on this secluded spot there should be a leaven of common sense! No: *all* is not enveloped in brute ignorance yet, in spite of every artifice that hellish Corruption has been able to employ; in spite of all her menaces and all her brutalities and cruelties.

Odiham, Hampshire,
Friday, 27 *Sept.* [1822]

From Lea we set off this morning about six o'clock to get free-quarter again at a worthy old friend's at this nice little plain market-town. Our direct road was right over the heath through Tilford to Farnham; but we veered a little to the left after we came to Tilford, at which place on the Green we stopped to look at an *oak tree*, which, when I was a little boy, was but a very little tree, comparatively, and which is now, take it altogether, by far the finest tree that I ever saw in my life. The stem or shaft is short; that is to say, it is short before you come to the first limbs; but it is full *thirty feet round*, at about eight or ten feet from the ground. Out of the stem there come not less than fifteen or sixteen limbs, many of which are from five to ten feet round, and each of which would, in fact, be considered a decent stick of timber. I am not judge enough of timber to say any thing about the quantity in the whole tree, but my son stepped the ground, and as nearly as we could judge, the diameter of the extent of the branches was upwards of ninety feet, which would make a circumference of about three hundred feet. The tree is in full growth at this moment. There is a little hole in one of the limbs; but with that exception, there appears not the smallest sign of decay. The tree has made great shoots in all parts of it this last summer and spring; and there are no appearances of *white* upon the trunk, such as are regarded as the symptoms of full growth. There are many sorts of oak in England; two very distinct; one with a pale leaf, and one with a dark leaf: this is of the pale leaf. The tree stands upon Tilford-green, the soil of which is a light loam with a hard sand-stone a good way beneath, and, probably, clay beneath that. The spot where the tree stands is about a hundred and twenty feet from the edge of a little river, and the ground on which it stands may be about ten feet higher than the bed of that river.

In quitting Tilford we came on to the land belonging to Waverly Abbey, and then, instead of going on to the town of Farnham, veered away to the left towards Wrecklesham, in order to cross the Farnham and Alton turnpike-road, and to come on by the side of Crondall to Odiham. We went a little out of the way to go to a place called the *Bourne,* which lies in the heath at about a mile from Farnham. It is a winding narrow valley, down which, during the wet season of the year, there runs a stream, beginning at the *Holt Forest,* and emptying itself into the *Wey* just below Moor-Park, which was the seat of Sir William Temple when Swift was residing with him. We went to this Bourne in order that I might show my son the spot where I received the rudiments of my education. There is a little hop-garden in which I used to work when from eight to ten years old; from which I have scores of times run to follow the hounds, leaving the hoe to do the best that it could to destroy the weeds; but the most interesting thing was a *sand-hill,* which goes from a part of the heath down to the rivulet. As a due mixture of pleasure with toil, I, with two brothers, used occasionally to *desport* ourselves, as the lawyers call it, at this sand-hill. Our diversion was this: we used to go to the top of the hill, which was steeper than the roof of a house; one used to draw his arms out of the sleeves of his smock-frock, and lay himself down with his arms by his sides; and then the others, one at head and the other at feet, sent him rolling down the hill like a barrel or a log of wood. By the time he got to the bottom, his hair, eyes, ears, nose, and mouth, were all full of this loose sand; then the others took their turn, and at every roll, there was a monstrous spell of laughter. I had often told my sons of this while they were very little, and I now took one of them to see the spot. But, that was not all. This was the spot where I was receiving my *education;* and this was the sort of education; and I am perfectly satisfied that if I had not received such an education, or something very much like it; that, if I had been brought up a milksop, with a nursery-maid everlastingly at my heels, I should have been at this day as great a fool, as inefficient a mortal, as any of those frivolous idiots that are turned out from Winchester and Westminster School, or from any of those dens of dunces called Colleges and Universities. It is impossible to say how much I owe to that sand-hill; and I went to return it my thanks for the ability which it probably gave me to be one of the greatest terrors, to one of the greatest and most powerful bodies of knaves and fools, that ever were permitted to afflict this or any other country.

From the Bourne we proceeded on to Wrecklesham, at the end of

which, we crossed what is called the river Wey. Here we found a
parcel of labourers at parish-work. Amongst them was an old play-
mate of mine. The account they gave of their situation was very dis-
mal. The harvest was over early. The hop-picking is now over; and
now they are employed *by the Parish;* that is to say, not absolutely
digging holes one day and filling them up the next; but at the expense
of half-ruined farmers and tradesmen and landlords, to break stones
into very small pieces to make nice smooth roads lest the jolting, in
going along them, should create bile in the stomachs of the overfed
tax-eaters. I call upon mankind to witness this scene; and to say,
whether ever the like of this was heard of before. It is a state of things,
where all is out of order; where self-preservation, that great law of
nature, seems to be set at defiance; for here are farmers *unable* to pay
men for working for them, and yet compelled to pay them for working
in doing that which is really of no use to any human being. There lie
the hop-poles unstripped. You see a hundred things in the neighbouring fields that want doing. The fences are not nearly what they ought
to be. The very meadows, to our right and our left in crossing this
little valley, would occupy these men advantageously until the setting
in of the frost; and here are they, not, as I said before, actually digging
holes one day and filling them up the next; but, to all intents and purposes, as uselessly employed. Is this Mr. Canning's *"Sun of Prosperity?"*
Is this the way to increase or preserve a nation's wealth? Is this a sign
of wise legislation and of good government? Does this thing "work
well," Mr. Canning? Does it prove, that we want no change? True, you
were born under a Kingly Government; and so was I as well as you;
but I was not born under *Six-Acts;* nor was I born under a state of
things like this. I was not born under it, and I do not wish to live
under it; and, with God's help, I will change it if I can.[1]

We left these poor fellows, after having given them, not "religious
Tracts," which would, if they could, make the labourer content with
half starvation, but, something to get them some bread and cheese
and beer, being firmly convinced, that it is the body that wants filling
and not the mind. However, in speaking of their low wages, I told
them, that the farmers and hop-planters were as much objects of compassion as themselves, which they acknowledged.

We immediately, after this, crossed the road, and went on towards
Crondall upon a soil that soon became stiff loam and flint at top with
a bed of chalk beneath. . . .

Spittal, near Lincoln, 19th April, 1830.

Here we are, at the end of a pretty decent trip since we left Boston.
The next place, on our way to Hull, was Horncastle, where I preached

[1] Cobbett mocks phrases of complacency used by George Canning (1770–
1827), who had become Foreign Secretary in Lord Liverpool's cabinet after
Castlereagh's suicide on August 12.

politics, in the playhouse, to a most respectable body of farmers, who
had come in the wet to meet me. Mr. John Peniston, who had invited
me to stop there, behaved in a very obliging manner, and made all
things very pleasant.

The country *from* Boston continued, as I said before, flat for about
half the way to Horncastle, and we then began to see the high land.
From Horncastle I set off two hours before the carriage, and going
through a very pretty village called Ashby, got to another at the foot
of a hill, which, they say, forms part of the *Wolds;* that is, a ridge of
hills. This second village is called Scamblesby. The vale in which it
lies is very fine land. A hazel mould, rich and light too. I saw a man
here ploughing for barley, after turnips, with *one horse:* the horse
did not seem to work hard, and the man was *singing:* I need not say
that he was young; and I dare say he had the good sense to keep his
legs under another man's table, and to stretch his body on another man's
bed.

This is a very fine *corn country:* chalk at bottom: stony near the surface, in some places: here and there a chalk-pit in the hills: the shape
of the ground somewhat like that of the broadest valleys in Wiltshire;
but the fields not without fences as they are there: fields from fifteen
to forty acres: the hills not downs, as in Wiltshire; but cultivated all
over. The houses white and thatched, as they are in all chalk-countries.
The valley at Scamblesby has a little rivulet running down it, just as in
all the chalk countries. The land continues nearly the same to Louth,
which lies in a deep dell, with beautiful pastures on the surrounding
hills, like those that I once admired at Shaftesbury, in Dorsetshire, and
like that near St. Austle, in Cornwall, which I described in 1808. . . .

It is time for me now, withdrawing myself from these objects, visible
to the eye, to speak of the state of *the people,* and of the manner in
which their affairs are affected by the workings of the system. With
regard to the labourers, they are, every where, miserable. The wages
for those who are employed on the land are, through all the counties
that I have come, twelve shillings a week for married men, and less for
single ones; but a large part of them are not even at this season employed on the land. The farmers, for want of means of profitable employment, suffer the men to fall upon the parish; and they are employed
in digging and breaking stone for the roads; so that the roads are nice
and smooth for the sheep and cattle to walk on in their way to the all-
devouring jaws of the Jews and other tax-eaters in London and its
vicinity. None of the best meat, except by mere accident, is consumed
here. To-day (the 20th of April), we have seen hundreds upon hundreds of sheep, as fat as hogs, go by this inn door, their toes, like
those of the foot-marks at the entrance of the lion's den, all pointing
towards the Wen; and the landlord gave us for dinner a little skinny,
hard leg of old ewe mutton! Where the man got it, I cannot imagine.
Thus it is: every good thing is literally driven or carried away out of

the country. In walking out yesterday, I saw three poor fellows digging stone for the roads, who told me that they never had any thing
but bread to eat, and water to wash it down. One of them was a wid-
ower, with three children; and his pay was eighteen-pence a-day; that
is to say, about three pounds of bread a day each, for six days in the
week; nothing for Sunday, and nothing for lodging, washing, clothing,
candle-light, or fuel! Just such was the state of things in France at the
eve of the revolution! Precisely such; and precisely the same were the
causes. Whether the effect will be the same, I do not take upon myself positively to determine. Just on the other side of the hedge, while
I was talking to these men, I saw about two hundred fat sheep in a
rich pasture. I did not tell them what I might have told them; but I
explained to them why the farmers were unable to give them a sufficiency of wages. They listened with great attention; and said that
they did believe that the farmers were in great distress themselves. . . .

One of the great signs of the poverty of people in the middle rank of
life, is the falling off of the audiences at the playhouses. There is a
playhouse in almost every country town, where the players used to act
occasionally; and in large towns almost always. In some places they
have of late abandoned acting altogether. In others they have acted,
very frequently, to not more than *ten or twelve persons*. At Norwich,
the playhouse had been shut up for a long time. I heard of one manager who has become a porter to a warehouse, and his company dispersed. In most places, the insides of the buildings seem to be tumbling
to pieces; and the curtains and scenes that they let down, seem to be
abandoned to the damp and the cobwebs. *My* appearance on the
boards seemed to give new life to the drama. I was, until the birth of
my third son, a constant haunter of the playhouse, in which I took
great delight; but when *he* came into the world, I said, "Now, Nancy,
it is time for us to leave off going to the play." It is really melancholy
to look at things now, and to think of things then. I feel great sorrow
on account of these poor players; for, though they are made the tools
of the Government and the corporations and the parsons, it is not their
fault, and they have uniformly, whenever I have come in contact
with them, been very civil to me. I am not sorry that they are left out
of the list of vagrants in the new act; but, in this case, as in so many
others, the men have to be grateful to the *women;* for who believes
that this merciful omission would have taken place, if so many of the
peers had not contracted matrimonial alliances with players; if so
many playeresses had not become peeresses. We may thank God for
disposing the hearts of our law-makers to be guilty of the same sins
and foibles as ourselves; for when a lord had been sentenced to the
pillory, the use of that ancient mode of punishing offences was abolished: when a lord (CASTLEREAGH), who was also a minister of state,
had cut his own throat, the degrading punishment of burial in cross-
roads was abolished; and now, when so many peers and great men

have taken to wife play-actresses, which the law termed *vagrants,* that term, as applied to the children of Melpomene and Thalia, is abolished! Laud we the Gods, that our rulers cannot, after all, divest themselves of flesh and blood! For the Lord have mercy upon us, if their great souls were once to soar above that tenement! . . .

Another respect in which our situation so exactly resembles that of France on the eve of the Revolution, is, the *fleeing from the country* in every direction. When I was in Norfolk, there were four hundred persons, generally young men, labourers, carpenters, wheelwrights, millwrights, smiths, and bricklayers; most of them with some money, and some farmers and others with good round sums. These people were going to Quebec, in timber-ships, and from Quebec, by land, into the United States. They had been told that they would not be suffered to land in the United States from on board of ship. The roguish villains had deceived them: but no matter; they will get into the United States; and going through Canada will do them good, for it will teach them to detest every thing belonging to it. From Boston, two great barge loads had just gone off by canal, to Liverpool, most of them farmers; all carrying some money, and some as much as two thousand pounds each. From the North and West Riding of Yorkshire, numerous wagons have gone carrying people to the canals, leading to Liverpool; and a gentleman, whom I saw at Peterboro', told me that he saw some of them; and that the men all appeared to be respectable farmers. At Hull, the scene would delight the eyes of the wise Burdett; for here the emigration is going on in the "Old Roman Plan." Ten large ships have gone this spring, laden with these fugitives from the fangs of taxation; some bound direct to the ports of the United States; others, like those at Yarmouth, for Quebec. Those that have most money, go direct to the United States. The single men, who are taken for a mere trifle in the Canada ships, go that way, have nothing but their carcasses to carry over the rocks and swamps, and through the myriads of place-men and pensioners in that miserable region; there are about fifteen more ships going from this one port this spring. The ships are fitted up with berths as transports for the carrying of troops. I went on board one morning, and saw the people putting their things on board and stowing them away. Seeing a nice young woman, with a little baby in her arms, I told her that she was going to a country where she would be sure that her children would never want victuals; where she might make her own malt, soap, and candles, without being half put to death for it, and where the blaspheming Jews would not have a mortgage on the life's labour of her children.

There is at Hull one farmer going who is seventy years of age; but who takes out five sons and fifteen hundred pounds! Brave and sensible old man! and good and affectionate father! He is performing a truly parental and sacred duty; and he will die with the blessing of his sons on his head, for having rescued them from this scene of slavery, misery, cruelty, and crime. Come, then, Wilmot Horton, with your sensible associates, Burdett and Poulett Thomson; come into Lincolnshire, Norfolk, and Yorkshire; come and bring Parson Malthus along with you; regale your sight with this delightful "stream of emigration"; congratulate the "greatest captain of the age," and your brethren of the Collective: congratulate the "noblest assembly of free men," on these the happy effects of their measures. Oh! no, Wilmot! Oh! no, generous and sensible Burdett, it is not the aged, the infirm, the halt, the blind, and the idiots, that go: it is the youth, the strength, the wealth, and the spirit, that will no longer brook hunger and thirst, in order that the maws of tax-eaters and Jews may be crammed. You want the Irish to go, and so they will *at our expense,* and all the bad of them, to be kept at our expense on the rocks and swamps of Nova Scotia and Canada. You have no money to send them away with: the tax-eaters want it all; and, thanks to the "improvements of the age," the steam-boats will continue to bring them in shoals in pursuit of the orts of the food, that their task-masters have taken away from them.[2]

After evening lecture, at Horncastle, a very decent farmer came to me and asked me about America, telling me that he was resolved to go, for that, if he staid much longer, he should not have a shilling to go with. I promised to send him a letter from Louth to a friend at New York, who might be useful to him there, and give him good advice. I forgot it at Louth; but I will do it before I go to bed. . . .

[2] Robert Wilmot (who took the name Horton in 1823), Sir Francis Burdett (1770–1844), and Charles Poulett Thomson (later Baron Sydenham and Governor-General of Canada) were all liberal politicians turning conservative. They had recently, in the phrases mocked by Cobbett, supported the Malthusian theory of emigration as one relief for poverty.

William Wordsworth

WILLIAM WORDSWORTH

1770   Born April 7 at Cockermouth in the Lake District.

1787   Entered St. John's College, Cambridge.

1790   During the Long Vacation, walked through France and Switzerland; crossed Alps into Italy.

1791   Received B.A. degree.

1791–92   In Paris, Orleans, and Blois, met supporters of the Revolution.

1792   December 15, daughter born to him and Annette Vallon, a Royalist.

1793   *An Evening Walk* (begun 1787). *Descriptive Sketches* (begun 1791). Wrote and intended to publish "A Letter to the Bishop of Llandaff" as "by a Republican."

1795–97   At Racedown, Somerset, with sister Dorothy.

1797   July 16, moved to Alfoxden, near Bristol and near Coleridge.

1798   September 16, sailed for Germany. October, *Lyrical Ballads*.

1799   May–December, at Sockburn-on-Tees with Hutchinson family. December 21, settled with Dorothy in Dove Cottage, Grasmere (until 1808).

1801   About January 25, second edition of *Lyrical Ballads,* with Preface (dated 1800).

1802   August, visited Annette and daughter at Calais. October 4, married Mary Hutchinson.

1809   May, tract on the Convention of Cintra (parts had appeared in the *Courier*).

1810   "A Description of the Scenery of the Lakes" (as Introduction to Thomas Wilkinson's *Select Views*).

1813   After various other residences in the Lake District, moved to Rydal Mount. Appointed Distributor of Stamps for Westmorland.

1814   July, *The Excursion.*

1815   March, *Poems,* with Essay Supplementary to Preface. May, *The White Doe of Rylstone* (written 1808).

1816   March (?), *A Letter to a Friend of Robert Burns.*

1818   April, *Two Addresses to the Freeholders of Westmorland.*

1819   April, *Peter Bell* (written 1798).

1822   March or April, *Ecclesiastical Sketches.*

1843   April, appointed Poet Laureate, on the death of Southey.

1850   Died April 23. *The Prelude* published posthumously. Dorothy, mentally ill from 1835, died January 25, 1855, aged 83.

Critical Prefaces

❡ Wordsworth believed, somewhat mistakenly, that the *Lyrical Ballads* of 1798 had been received by critics with unusual harshness. For the second edition, after conversations with Coleridge, he produced what is probably the most celebrated and most widely known of English literary manifestoes. This essay of 1800 has been minutely examined by W. J. B. Owen in *Wordsworth's Preface to Lyrical Ballads,* Copenhagen, 1957 (*Anglistica* IX). The language and doctrines of eighteenth-century associational psychology, descended from John Locke through David Hartley, are everywhere evident, especially in the several references to "sensations" and the "known habits of association." Similarly, the Appendix of 1802 assumes the primitivistic theories of "Nature's simple plan" that had become increasingly common in the later decades of the eighteenth century. In 1815, partly to explain why he classified some of his own works as "Poems of the Fancy" and some as "Poems of the Imagination," Wordsworth drew up in a new Preface what Coleridge called a "masterly sketch" of the practical and applied distinction between imagination and fancy. In addition to this second Preface, he published also in 1815 an "Essay, Supplementary to the Preface," in which he presented at some length his views on eighteenth-century English poetry and argued that "poetry is most just to its own divine origin when it administers the comforts and breathes the spirit of religion." The Preface to *Lyrical Ballads* and its Appendix here follow the version of 1802. The ten paragraphs beginning "If it be affirmed that rhyme" first appeared in 1802; at various later dates Wordsworth omitted several passages and made his language more impersonal. The Preface to *Poems,* 1815, is here reprinted, except for the omission of two paragraphs at the beginning and three at the end, from the first edition. ❫

Preface to Lyrical Ballads

The first Volume of these Poems has already been submitted to general perusal. It was published, as an experiment, which, I hoped, might be of some use to ascertain, how far, by fitting to metrical arrangement a selection of the real language of men in a state of vivid sensation, that sort of pleasure and that quantity of pleasure may be imparted, which a Poet may rationally endeavour to impart.

I had formed no very inaccurate estimate of the probable effect of those Poems: I flattered myself that they who should be pleased with them would read them with more than common pleasure: and, on the other hand, I was well aware, that by those who should dislike them they would be read with more than common dislike. The result has differed from my expectation in this only, that I have pleased a greater number, than I ventured to hope I should please.

For the sake of variety, and from a consciousness of my own weakness, I was induced to request the assistance of a Friend, who furnished me with the Poems of the ANCIENT MARINER, the FOSTER-MOTHER'S TALE, the NIGHTINGALE, and the Poem entitled LOVE. I should not, however, have requested this assistance, had I not believed that the Poems of my Friend would in a great measure have the same tendency as my own, and that, though there would be found a difference, there would be found no discordance in the colours of our style; as our opinions on the subject of poetry do almost entirely coincide.

Several of my Friends are anxious for the success of these Poems from a belief, that, if the views with which they were composed were indeed realized, a class of Poetry would be produced, well adapted to interest mankind permanently, and not unimportant in the multiplicity, and in the quality of its moral relations: and on this account they have advised me to prefix a systematic defence of the theory, upon which the poems were written. But I was unwilling to undertake the task, because I knew that on this occasion the Reader would look coldly upon my arguments, since I might be suspected of having been principally influenced by the selfish and foolish hope of *reasoning* him into an approbation of these particular Poems: and I was still more unwilling to undertake the task, because, adequately to display my opinions, and fully to enforce my arguments, would require a space wholly disproportionate to the nature of a preface. For to treat the subject with the clearness and coherence, of which I believe it susceptible, it would be necessary to give a full account of the present state of the public taste in this country, and to determine how far this taste is healthy or depraved; which, again, could not be determined, without pointing out, in what manner language and the human mind act and re-act on each other, and without retracing the revolutions, not of literature alone, but likewise of society itself. I have therefore altogether declined to enter regularly upon this defence; yet I am sensible, that there would be some impropriety in abruptly obtruding upon the Public, without a few words of introduction, Poems so materially different from those, upon which general approbation is at present bestowed.

It is supposed, that by the act of writing in verse an Author makes a formal engagement that he will gratify certain known habits of association; that he not only thus apprizes the Reader that certain classes of ideas and expressions will be found in his book, but that others will be carefully excluded. This exponent or symbol held forth by metrical language must in different æras of literature have excited very different expectations: for example, in the age of Catullus, Terence, and Lucretius and that of Statius or Claudian; and in our own country, in the age of Shakespeare and Beaumont and Fletcher, and that of Donne and Cowley, or Dryden, or Pope.[1] I will not take upon me to determine the exact import of the promise which by the act of writing in

[1] By the late Latin poets Statius and Claudianus, and the English from Donne to Pope, Wordsworth identifies ages of polished, artificial poetry as distinguished from ages of exuberant creativity.

verse an Author, in the present day, makes to his Reader; but I am certain, it will appear to many persons that I have not fulfilled the terms of an engagement thus voluntarily contracted. They who have been accustomed to the gaudiness and inane phraseology of many modern writers, if they persist in reading this book to its conclusion, will, no doubt, frequently have to struggle with feelings of strangeness and aukwardness: they will look round for poetry, and will be induced to inquire by what species of courtesy these attempts can be permitted to assume that title. I hope therefore the Reader will not censure me, if I attempt to state what I have proposed to myself to perform; and also, (as far as the limits of a preface will permit) to explain some of the chief reasons which have determined me in the choice of my purpose: that at least he may be spared any unpleasant feeling of disappointment, and that I myself may be protected from the most dishonorable accusation which can be brought against an Author, namely, that of an indolence which prevents him from endeavouring to ascertain what is his duty, or, when his duty is ascertained, prevents him from performing it.

The principal object, then, which I proposed to myself in these Poems was to chuse incidents and situations from common life, and to relate or describe them, throughout, as far as was possible, in a selection of language really used by men; and, at the same time, to throw over them a certain colouring of imagination, whereby ordinary things should be presented to the mind in an unusual way; and, further, and above all, to make these incidents and situations interesting by tracing in them, truly though not ostentatiously, the primary laws of our nature: chiefly, as far as regards the manner in which we associate ideas in a state of excitement. Low and rustic life was generally chosen, because in that condition, the essential passions of the heart find a better soil in which they can attain their maturity, are less under restraint, and speak a plainer and more emphatic language; because in that condition of life our elementary feelings co-exist in a state of greater simplicity, and, consequently, may be more accurately contemplated, and more forcibly communicated; because the manners of rural life germinate from those elementary feelings; and, from the necessary character of rural occupations, are more easily comprehended; and are more durable; and lastly, because in that condition the passions of men are incorporated with the beautiful and permanent forms of nature. The language, too, of these men is adopted (purified indeed from what appear to be its real defects, from all lasting and rational causes of dislike or disgust) because such men hourly communicate with the best objects from which the best part of language is originally derived; and because, from their rank in society and the sameness and narrow circle of their intercourse, being less under the influence of social vanity they convey their feelings and notions in simple and unelaborated expressions. Accordingly, such a language, arising out of repeated experience and regular feelings, is a more permanent, and a far more philosophical language, than that which is frequently substituted for it by Poets, who think that they are conferring honour upon themselves and their art, in proportion as they separate themselves from the sympathies of men, and indulge in arbitrary and capricious habits of expression, in order to furnish food for fickle tastes, and fickle appetites, of their own creation.[2]

I cannot, however, be insensible of the present outcry against the triviality and meanness both of thought and language, which some of my contemporaries have occasionally introduced into their metrical compositions; and I acknowledge, that this defect, where it exists, is more dishonorable to the Writer's own character than false refinement or arbitrary innovation, though I should contend at the same time that it is far less pernicious in the sum of its consequences. From such verses the Poems in these volumes will be found distinguished at least by one mark of difference, that each of them has a worthy *purpose*. Not that I mean to say, that I always began to write with a distinct purpose formally conceived; but I believe that my habits of meditation have so formed my feelings, as that my descriptions of such objects as strongly excite those feelings, will be found to carry along with them a *purpose*. If in this opinion I am mistaken, I can have little right to the name of a Poet. For all good poetry is the spontaneous overflow of powerful feelings: but though this be true, Poems to which any value can be attached, were never produced on any variety of subjects but by a man, who being possessed of more than usual organic sensibility, had also thought long and deeply. For our continued influxes of feeling are modified and directed by our thoughts, which are indeed the representatives of all our past feelings; and, as by contemplating the relation of these general representatives to each other we discover what is really important to men, so, by the repetition and continuance of this act, our feelings will be connected with important subjects, till at length, if we be originally possessed of much sensibility, such habits of mind will be produced, that, by obeying blindly and mechanically the impulses of those habits, we shall describe objects, and utter sentiments, of such a nature and in such connection with each other, that the understanding of the being to whom we address ourselves, if he be in a healthful state of association, must necessarily be in some degree enlightened, and his affections ameliorated.

I have said that each of these poems has a purpose. I have also informed my Reader what this purpose will be found principally to be: namely to illustrate the manner in which our feelings and ideas are associated in a state of excitement. But, speaking in language somewhat more appropriate, it is to follow the fluxes and refluxes of the

[2] It is worth while here to observe that the affecting parts of Chaucer are almost always expressed in language pure and universally intelligible even to this day. [W. W.]

mind when agitated by the great and simple affections of our nature. This object I have endeavoured in these short essays to attain by various means; by tracing the maternal passion through many of its more subtle windings, as in the poems of the IDIOT BOY and the MAD MOTHER; by accompanying the last struggles of a human being, at the approach of death, cleaving in solitude to life and society, as in the Poem of the FORSAKEN INDIAN; by shewing, as in the Stanzas entitled WE ARE SEVEN, the perplexity and obscurity which in childhood attend our notion of death, or rather our utter inability to admit that notion; or by displaying the strength of fraternal, or to speak more philosophically, of moral attachment when early associated with the great and beautiful objects of nature, as in THE BROTHERS; or, as in the Incident of SIMON LEE, by placing my Reader in the way of receiving from ordinary moral sensations another and more salutary impression than we are accustomed to receive from them. It has also been part of my general purpose to attempt to sketch characters under the influence of less impassioned feelings, as in the TWO APRIL MORNINGS, THE FOUNTAIN, THE OLD MAN TRAVELLING, THE TWO THIEVES, &c. characters of which the elements are simple, belonging rather to nature than to manners, such as exist now, and will probably always exist, and which from their constitution may be distinctly and profitably contemplated. I will not abuse the indulgence of my Reader by dwelling longer upon this subject; but it is proper that I should mention one other circumstance which distinguishes these Poems from the popular Poetry of the day; it is this, that the feeling therein developed gives importance to the action and situation, and not the action and situation to the feeling. My meaning will be rendered perfectly intelligible by referring my Reader to the Poems entitled POOR SUSAN and the CHILDLESS FATHER, particularly to the last Stanza of the latter Poem.

I will not suffer a sense of false modesty to prevent me from asserting, that I point my Reader's attention to this mark of distinction, far less for the sake of these particular Poems than from the general importance of the subject. The subject is indeed important! For the human mind is capable of being excited without the application of gross and violent stimulants; and he must have a very faint perception of its beauty and dignity who does not know this, and who does not further know, that one being is elevated above another, in proportion as he possesses this capability. It has therefore appeared to me, that to endeavour to produce or enlarge this capability is one of the best services in which, at any period, a Writer can be engaged; but this service, excellent at all times, is especially so at the present day. For a multitude of causes, unknown to former times, are now acting with a combined force to blunt the discriminating powers of the mind, and unfitting it for all voluntary exertion to reduce it to a state of almost savage torpor. The most effective of these causes are the great national events which are daily taking place, and the encreasing accumulation of men in cities, where the uniformity of their occupations produces a craving for extraordinary incident, which the rapid communication of intelligence hourly gratifies. To this tendency of life and manners the literature and theatrical exhibitions of the country have conformed themselves. The invaluable works of our elder writers, I had almost said the works of Shakespear and Milton, are driven into neglect by frantic novels, sickly and stupid German Tragedies, and deluges of idle and extravagant stories in verse. — When I think upon this degrading thirst after outrageous stimulation, I am almost ashamed to have spoken of the feeble effort with which I have endeavoured to counteract it; and, reflecting upon the magnitude of the general evil, I should be oppressed with no dishonorable melancholy, had I not a deep impression of certain inherent and indestructible qualities of the human mind, and likewise of certain powers in the great and permanent objects that act upon it which are equally inherent and indestructible; and did I not further add to this impression a belief, that the time is approaching when the evil will be systematically opposed, by men of greater powers, and with far more distinguished success.

Having dwelt thus long on the subjects and aim of these Poems, I shall request the Reader's permission to apprize him of a few circumstances relating to their *style*, in order, among other reasons, that I may not be censured for not having performed what I never attempted. The Reader will find that personifications of abstract ideas rarely occur in these volumes; and, I hope, are utterly rejected as an ordinary device to elevate the style, and raise it above prose. I have proposed to myself to imitate, and, as far as is possible, to adopt the very language of men; and assuredly such personifications do not make any natural or regular part of that language. They are, indeed, a figure of speech occasionally prompted by passion, and I have made use of them as such; but I have endeavoured utterly to reject them as a mechanical device of style, or as a family language which Writers in metre seem to lay claim to by prescription. I have wished to keep my Reader in the company of flesh and blood, persuaded that by so doing I shall interest him. I am, however, well aware that others who pursue a different track may interest him likewise; I do not interfere with their claim, I only wish to prefer a different claim of my own. There will also be found in these volumes little of what is usually called poetic diction; I have taken as much pains to avoid it as others ordinarily take to produce it; this I have done for the reason already alleged, to bring my language near to the language of men, and further, because the pleasure which I have proposed to myself to impart is of a kind very different from that which is supposed by many persons to be the proper object of poetry. I do not know how without being culpably particular I can give my Reader a more exact notion of the style in which I wished these poems to be written than by informing him that I have at all times endeavoured to look steadily at my subject, consequently, I hope that there is in these Poems little falsehood of description, and that my ideas are expressed in language fitted to their respective importance. Something I must have gained by this practice, as it is friendly to one property of all good poetry, namely, good sense; but it has necessarily cut me off from a large portion of phrases and figures of speech which from father to son have long been regarded as the common inheritance of Poets. I have also thought it expedient to restrict myself still further, having abstained from the use of many expressions, in themselves proper and beautiful, but which have been foolishly repeated by bad Poets, till such feelings of disgust are connected with them as it is scarcely possible by any art of association to overpower.

If in a Poem there should be found a series of lines, or even a single line, in which the language, though naturally arranged and according to the strict laws of metre, does not differ from that of prose, there is a numerous class of critics, who, when they stumble upon these prosaisms as they call them, imagine that they have made a notable discovery, and exult over the Poet as over a man ignorant of his own profession. Now these men would establish a canon of criticism which the Reader will conclude he must utterly reject, if he wishes to be pleased with these volumes. And it would be a most easy task to prove to him, that not only the language of a large portion of every good poem, even of the most elevated character, must necessarily, except with reference to the metre, in no respect differ from that of good prose, but likewise that some of the most interesting parts of the best poems will be found to be strictly the language of prose, when prose is well written. The truth of this assertion might be demonstrated by innumerable passages from almost all the poetical writings, even of Milton himself. I have not space for much quotation; but, to illustrate the subject in a general manner, I will here adduce a short composition of Gray, who was at the head of those who by their reasonings have attempted to widen the space of separation betwixt Prose and Metrical composition, and was more than any other man curiously elaborate in the structure of his own poetic diction.

> In vain to me the smiling mornings shine,
> And reddening Phœbus lifts his golden fire:
> The birds in vain their amorous descant join,
> Or chearful fields resume their green attire:
> These ears alas! for other notes repine;
> *A different object do these eyes require;*
> *My lonely anguish melts no heart but mine;*
> *And in my breast the imperfect joys expire;*
> Yet Morning smiles the busy race to cheer,
> And new-born pleasure brings to happier men;
> The fields to all their wonted tribute bear;
> To warm their little loves the birds complain.
> *I fruitless mourn to him that cannot hear*
> *And weep the more because I weep in vain.*

It will easily be perceived that the only part of this Sonnet which is of any value is the lines printed in Italics: it is equally obvious, that, except in the rhyme, and in the use of the single word "fruitless" for fruitlessly, which is so far a defect, the language of these lines does in no respect differ from that of prose.

By the foregoing quotation I have shewn that the language of Prose may yet be well adapted to Poetry; and I have previously asserted that a large portion of the language of every good poem can in no respect differ from that of good Prose. I will go further. I do not doubt that it may be safely affirmed, that there neither is, nor can be, any essential difference between the language of prose and metrical composition. We are fond of tracing the resemblance between Poetry and Painting, and, accordingly, we call them Sisters: but where shall we find bonds of connection sufficiently strict to typify the affinity betwixt metrical and prose composition? They both speak by and to the same organs; the bodies in which both of them are clothed may be said to be of the same substance, their affections are kindred and almost identical, not necessarily differing even in degree; Poetry[3] sheds no tears "such as Angels weep," but natural and human tears; she can boast of no celestial Ichor that distinguishes her vital juices from those of prose; the same human blood circulates through the veins of them both.

If it be affirmed that rhyme and metrical arrangement of themselves constitute a distinction which overturns what I have been saying on the strict affinity of metrical language with that of prose, and paves the way for other artificial distinctions which the mind voluntarily admits, I answer that the language of such Poetry as I am recommending is, as far as is possible, a selection of the language really spoken by men; that this selection, wherever it is made with true taste and feeling, will of itself form a distinction far greater than would at first be imagined, and will entirely separate the composition from the vulgarity and meanness of ordinary life; and, if metre be superadded thereto, I believe that a dissimilitude will be produced altogether sufficient for the gratification of a rational mind. What other distinction would we have? Whence is it to come? And where is it to exist? Not, surely, where the Poet speaks through the mouths of his characters: it cannot be necessary here, either for elevation of style, or any of its supposed ornaments: for, if the Poet's subject be judiciously chosen, it will naturally, and upon fit occasion, lead him to passions the lan-

---

[3] I here use the word "Poetry" (though against my own judgment) as opposed to the word Prose, and synonymous with metrical composition. But much confusion has been introduced into criticism by this contradistinction of Poetry and Prose, instead of the more philosophical one of Poetry and Matter of Fact, or Science. The only strict antithesis to Prose is Metre; nor is this, in truth, a *strict* antithesis; because lines and passages of metre so naturally occur in writing prose, that it would be scarcely possible to avoid them, even were it desirable. [W. W.]

guage of which, if selected truly and judiciously, must necessarily be dignified and variegated, and alive with metaphors and figures. I forbear to speak of an incongruity which would shock the intelligent Reader, should the Poet interweave any foreign splendour of his own with that which the passion naturally suggests: it is sufficient to say that such addition is unnecessary. And, surely, it is more probable that those passages, which with propriety abound with metaphors and figures, will have their due effect, if, upon other occasions where the passions are of a milder character, the style also be subdued and temperate.

But, as the pleasure which I hope to give by the Poems I now present to the Reader must depend entirely on just notions upon this subject, and, as it is in itself of the highest importance to our taste and moral feelings, I cannot content myself with these detached remarks. And if, in what I am about to say, it shall appear to some that my labour is unnecessary, and that I am like a man fighting a battle without enemies, I would remind such persons, that, whatever may be the language outwardly holden by men, a practical faith in the opinions which I am wishing to establish is almost unknown. If my conclusions are admitted, and carried as far as they must be carried if admitted at all, our judgments concerning the works of the greatest Poets both ancient and modern will be far different from what they are at present, both when we praise, and when we censure: and our moral feelings influencing, and influenced by these judgments will, I believe, be corrected and purified.

Taking up the subject, then, upon general grounds, I ask what is meant by the word Poet? What is a Poet? To whom does he address himself? And what language is to be expected from him? He is a man speaking to men: a man, it is true, endued with more lively sensibility, more enthusiasm and tenderness, who has a greater knowledge of human nature, and a more comprehensive soul, than are supposed to be common among mankind; a man pleased with his own passions and volitions, and who rejoices more than other men in the spirit of life that is in him; delighting to contemplate similar volitions and passions as manifested in the goings-on of the Universe, and habitually impelled to create them where he does not find them. To these qualities he has added a disposition to be affected more than other men by absent things as if they were present; an ability of conjuring up in himself passions, which are indeed far from being the same as those produced by real events, yet (especially in those parts of the general sympathy which are pleasing and delightful) do more nearly resemble the passions produced by real events, than any thing which, from the motions of their own minds merely, other men are accustomed to feel in themselves; whence, and from practice, he has acquired a greater readiness and power in expressing what he thinks and feels, and especially those thoughts and feelings which, by his own choice, or from the structure of his own mind, arise in him without immediate external excitement.

But, whatever portion of this faculty we may suppose even the greatest Poet to possess, there cannot be a doubt but that the language which it will suggest to him, must, in liveliness and truth, fall far short of that which is uttered by men in real life, under the actual pressure of those passions, certain shadows of which the Poet thus produces, or feels to be produced, in himself. However exalted a notion we would wish to cherish of the character of a Poet, it is obvious, that, while he describes and imitates passions, his situation is altogether slavish and mechanical, compared with the freedom and power of real and substantial action and suffering. So that it will be the wish of the Poet to bring his feelings near to those of the persons whose feelings he describes, nay, for short spaces of time perhaps, to let himself slip into an entire delusion, and even confound and identify his own feelings with theirs; modifying only the language which is thus suggested to him, by a consideration that he describes for a particular purpose, that of giving pleasure. Here, then, he will apply the principle on which I have so much insisted, namely, that of selection; on this he will depend for removing what would otherwise be painful or disgusting in the passion; he will feel that there is no necessity to trick out or to elevate nature: and, the more industriously he applies this principle, the deeper will be his faith that no words, which his fancy or imagination can suggest, will be to be compared with those which are the emanations of reality and truth.

But it may be said by those who do not object to the general spirit of these remarks, that, as it is impossible for the Poet to produce upon all occasions language as exquisitely fitted for the passion as that which the real passion itself suggests, it is proper that he should consider himself as in the situation of a translator, who deems himself justified when he substitutes excellences of another kind for those which are unattainable by him; and endeavours occasionally to surpass his original, in order to make some amends for the general inferiority to which he feels that he must submit. But this would be to encourage idleness and unmanly despair. Further, it is the language of men who speak of what they do not understand; who talk of Poetry as of a matter of amusement and idle pleasure; who will converse with us as gravely about a *taste* for Poetry, as they express it, as if it were a thing as indifferent as a taste for Rope-dancing, or Frontiniac or Sherry. Aristotle, I have been told, hath said, that Poetry is the most philosophic of all writing: it is so: its object is truth, not individual and local, but general, and operative; not standing upon external testimony, but carried alive into the heart by passion; truth which is its own testimony, which gives strength and divinity to the tribunal to which it appeals, and receives them from the same tribunal. Poetry is the image of man and nature. The obstacles which stand in the way of the fidelity of the

Biographer and Historian, and of their consequent utility, are incalculably greater than those which are to be encountered by the Poet who has an adequate notion of the dignity of his art. The Poet writes under one restriction only, namely, that of the necessity of giving immediate pleasure to a human Being possessed of that information which may be expected from him, not as a lawyer, a physician, a mariner, an astronomer or a natural philosopher, but as a Man. Except this one restriction, there is no object standing between the Poet and the image of things; between this, and the Biographer and Historian there are a thousand.

Nor let this necessity of producing immediate pleasure be considered as a degradation of the Poet's art. It is far otherwise. It is an acknowledgment of the beauty of the universe, an acknowledgment the more sincere because it is not formal, but indirect; it is a task light and easy to him who looks at the world in the spirit of love: further, it is a homage paid to the native and naked dignity of man, to the grand elementary principle of pleasure, by which he knows, and feels, and lives, and moves. We have no sympathy but what is propagated by pleasure: I would not be misunderstood; but wherever we sympathize with pain it will be found that the sympathy is produced and carried on by subtle combinations with pleasure. We have no knowledge, that is, no general principles drawn from the contemplation of particular facts, but what has been built up by pleasure, and exists in us by pleasure alone. The Man of Science, the Chemist and Mathematician, whatever difficulties and disgusts they may have had to struggle with, know and feel this. However painful may be the objects with which the Anatomist's knowledge is connected, he feels that his knowledge is pleasure; and where he has no pleasure he has no knowledge. What then does the Poet? He considers man and the objects that surround him as acting and re-acting upon each other, so as to produce an infinite complexity of pain and pleasure; he considers man in his own nature and in his ordinary life as contemplating this with a certain quantity of immediate knowledge, with certain convictions, intuitions, and deductions which by habit become of the nature of intuitions; he considers him as looking upon this complex scene of ideas and sensations, and finding every where objects that immediately excite in him sympathies which, from the necessities of his nature, are accompanied by an overbalance of enjoyment.

To this knowledge which all men carry about with them, and to these sympathies in which without any other discipline than that of our daily life we are fitted to take delight, the Poet principally directs his attention. He considers man and nature as essentially adapted to each other, and the mind of man as naturally the mirror of the fairest and most interesting qualities of nature. And thus the Poet, prompted by this feeling of pleasure which accompanies him through the whole course of his studies, converses with general nature with affections akin to those, which, through labour and length of time, the Man of Science has raised up in himself, by conversing with those particular parts of nature which are the objects of his studies. The knowledge both of the Poet and the Man of Science is pleasure; but the knowledge of the one cleaves to us as a necessary part of our existence, our natural and unalienable inheritance; the other is a personal and individual acquisition, slow to come to us, and by no habitual and direct sympathy connecting us with our fellow-beings. The Man of Science seeks truth as a remote and unknown benefactor; he cherishes and loves it in his solitude: the Poet, singing a song in which all human beings join with him, rejoices in the presence of truth as our visible friend and hourly companion. Poetry is the breath and finer spirit of all knowledge; it is the impassioned expression which is in the countenance of all Science. Emphatically may it be said of the Poet, as Shakespeare hath said of man, "that he looks before and after." He is the rock of defence of human nature; an upholder and preserver, carrying every where with him relationship and love. In spite of difference of soil and climate, of language and manners, of laws and customs, in spite of things silently gone out of mind and things violently destroyed, the Poet binds together by passion and knowledge the vast empire of human society, as it is spread over the whole earth, and over all time. The objects of the Poet's thoughts are every where; though the eyes and senses of man are, it is true, his favorite guides, yet he will follow wheresoever he can find an atmosphere of sensation in which to move his wings. Poetry is the first and last of all knowledge—it is as immortal as the heart of man. If the labours of men of Science should ever create any material revolution, direct or indirect, in our condition, and in the impressions which we habitually receive, the Poet will sleep then no more than at present, but he will be ready to follow the steps of the man of Science, not only in those general indirect effects, but he will be at his side, carrying sensation into the midst of the objects of the Science itself. The remotest discoveries of the Chemist, the Botanist, or Mineralogist, will be as proper objects of the Poet's art as any upon which it can be employed, if the time should ever come when these things shall be familiar to us, and the relations under which they are contemplated by the followers of these respective Sciences shall be manifestly and palpably material to us as enjoying and suffering beings. If the time should ever come when what is now called Science, thus familiarized to men, shall be ready to put on, as it were, a form of flesh and blood, the Poet will lend his divine spirit to aid the transfiguration, and will welcome the Being thus produced, as a dear and genuine inmate of the household of man. — It is not, then, to be supposed that any one, who holds that sublime notion of Poetry which I have attempted to convey, will break in upon the sanctity and truth of his pictures by transitory and accidental ornaments, and endeavour to excite admiration of himself by arts, the necessity of which must manifestly depend upon the assumed meanness of his subject.

What I have thus far said applies to Poetry in general; but especially to those parts of composition where the Poet speaks through the mouths of his characters; and upon this point it appears to have such weight that I will conclude, there are few persons, of good sense, who would not allow that the dramatic parts of composition are defective, in proportion as they deviate from the real language of nature, and are coloured by a diction of the Poet's own, either peculiar to him as an individual Poet, or belonging simply to Poets in general, to a body of men who, from the circumstance of their compositions being in metre, it is expected will employ a particular language.

It is not, then, in the dramatic parts of composition that we look for this distinction of language; but still it may be proper and necessary where the Poet speaks to us in his own person and character. To this I answer by referring my Reader to the description which I have before given of a Poet. Among the qualities which I have enumerated as principally conducting to form a Poet, is implied nothing differing in kind from other men, but only in degree. The sum of what I have there said is, that the Poet is chiefly distinguished from other men by a greater promptness to think and feel without immediate external excitement, and a greater power in expressing such thoughts and feelings as are produced in him in that manner. But these passions and thoughts and feelings are the general passions and thoughts and feelings of men. And with what are they connected? Undoubtedly with our moral sentiments and animal sensations, and with the causes which excite these; with the operations of the elements and the appearances of the visible universe; with storm and sun-shine, with the revolutions of the seasons, with cold and heat, with loss of friends and kindred, with injuries and resentments, gratitude and hope, with fear and sorrow. These, and the like, are the sensations and objects which the Poet describes, as they are the sensations of other men, and the objects which interest them. The Poet thinks and feels in the spirit of the passions of men. How, then, can his language differ in any material degree from that of all other men who feel vividly and see clearly? It might be *proved* that it is impossible. But supposing that this were not the case, the Poet might then be allowed to use a peculiar language, when expressing his feelings for his own gratification, or that of men like himself. But Poets do not write for Poets alone, but for men. Unless therefore we are advocates for that admiration which depends upon ignorance, and that pleasure which arises from hearing what we do not understand, the Poet must descend from this supposed height, and, in order to excite rational sympathy, he must express himself as other men express themselves. To this it may be added, that while he is only selecting from the real language of men, or, which amounts to the same thing, composing accurately in the spirit of such selection, he is treading upon safe ground, and we know what we are to expect from him. Our feelings are the same with respect to metre; for, as it may be proper to remind the Reader, the distinction of metre is regular and uniform, and not like that which is produced by what is usually called poetic diction, arbitrary, and subject to infinite caprices upon which no calculation whatever can be made. In the one case, the Reader is utterly at the mercy of the Poet respecting what imagery or diction he may choose to connect with the passion, whereas, in the other, the metre obeys certain laws, to which the Poet and Reader both willingly submit because they are certain, and because no interference is made by them with the passion but such as the concurring testimony of ages has shewn to heighten and improve the pleasure which co-exists with it.

It will now be proper to answer an obvious question, namely, why, professing these opinions, have I written in verse? To this, in addition to such answer as is included in what I have already said, I reply in the first place, because, however I may have restricted myself, there is still left open to me what confessedly constitutes the most valuable object of all writing whether in prose or verse, the great and universal passions of men, the most general and interesting of their occupations, and the entire world of nature, from which I am at liberty to supply myself with endless combinations of forms and imagery. Now, supposing for a moment that whatever is interesting in these objects may be as vividly described in prose, why am I to be condemned, if to such description I have endeavoured to superadd the charm which, by the consent of all nations, is acknowledged to exist in metrical language? To this, by such as are unconvinced by what I have already said, it may be answered, that a very small part of the pleasure given by Poetry depends upon the metre, and that it is injudicious to write in metre, unless it be accompanied with the other artificial distinctions of style with which metre is usually accompanied, and that by such deviation more will be lost from the shock which will be thereby given to the Reader's associations, than will be counterbalanced by any pleasure which he can derive from the general power of numbers. In answer to those who still contend for the necessity of accompanying metre with certain appropriate colours of style in order to the accomplishment of its appropriate end, and who also, in my opinion, greatly under-rate the power of metre in itself, it might perhaps, as far as relates to these Poems, have been almost sufficient to observe, that poems are extant, written upon more humble subjects, and in a more naked and simple style than I have aimed at, which poems have continued to give pleasure from generation to generation. Now, if nakedness and simplicity be a defect, the fact here mentioned affords a strong presumption that poems somewhat less naked and simple are capable of affording pleasure at the present day; and, what I wished *chiefly* to attempt, at present, was to justify myself for having written under the impression of this belief.

But I might point out various causes why, when the style is manly, and the subject of some importance, words metrically arranged will long continue to impart such a pleasure to mankind as he who is sensible of the extent of that pleasure will be desirous to impart. The end of Poetry is to produce excitement in co-existence with an overbalance of pleasure. Now, by the supposition, excitement is an unusual and irregular state of the mind; ideas and feelings do not in that state succeed each other in accustomed order. But, if the words by which this excitement is produced are in themselves powerful, or the images and feelings have an undue proportion of pain connected with them, there is some danger that the excitement may be carried beyond its proper bounds. Now the co-presence of something regular, something to which the mind has been accustomed in various moods and in a less excited state, cannot but have great efficacy in tempering and restraining the passion by an intertexture of ordinary feeling, and of feeling not strictly and necessarily connected with the passion. This is unquestionably true, and hence, though the opinion will at first appear paradoxical, from the tendency of metre to divest language in a certain degree of its reality, and thus to throw a sort of half consciousness of unsubstantial existence over the whole composition, there can be little doubt but that more pathetic situations and sentiments, that is, those which have a greater proportion of pain connected with them, may be endured in metrical composition, especially in rhyme, than in prose. The metre of the old Ballads is very artless; yet they contain many passages which would illustrate this opinion, and, I hope, if the following Poems be attentively perused, similar instances will be found in them. This opinion may be further illustrated by appealing to the Reader's own experience of the reluctance with which he comes to the re-perusal of the distressful parts of Clarissa Harlowe, or the Gamester.[4] While Shakespeare's writings, in the most pathetic scenes, never act upon us as pathetic beyond the bounds of pleasure — an effect which, in a much greater degree than might at first be imagined, is to be ascribed to small, but continual and regular impulses of pleasurable surprise from the metrical arrangement. — On the other hand (what it must be allowed will much more frequently happen) if the Poet's words should be incommensurate with the passion, and inadequate to raise the Reader to a height of desirable excitement, then, (unless the Poet's choice of his metre has been grossly injudicious) in the feelings of pleasure which the Reader has been accustomed to connect with metre in general, and in the feeling, whether chearful or melancholy, which he has been accustomed to connect with that particular movement of metre, there will be found something which will greatly contribute to impart passion to the words, and to effect the complex end which the Poet proposes to himself.

[4] Samuel Richardson, *Clarissa*, 1747–48; Edward Moore, *The Gamester*, 1753, a domestic drama.

If I had undertaken a systematic defence of the theory upon which these poems are written, it would have been my duty to develope the various causes upon which the pleasure received from metrical language depends. Among the chief of these causes is to be reckoned a principle which must be well known to those who have made any of the Arts the object of accurate reflection; I mean the pleasure which the mind derives from the perception of similitude in dissimilitude. This principle is the great spring of the activity of our minds, and their chief feeder. From this principle the direction of the sexual appetite, and all the passions connected with it take their origin: It is the life of our ordinary conversation; and upon the accuracy with which similitude in dissimilitude, and dissimilitude in similitude are perceived, depend our taste and our moral feelings. It would not have been a useless employment to have applied this principle to the consideration of metre, and to have shewn that metre is hence enabled to afford much pleasure, and to have pointed out in what manner that pleasure is produced. But my limits will not permit me to enter upon this subject, and I must content myself with a general summary.

I have said that Poetry is the spontaneous overflow of powerful feelings: it takes its origin from emotion recollected in tranquillity: the emotion is contemplated till by a species of reaction the tranquillity gradually disappears, and an emotion, kindred to that which was before the subject of contemplation, is gradually produced, and does itself actually exist in the mind. In this mood successful composition generally begins, and in a mood similar to this it is carried on; but the emotion, of whatever kind and in whatever degree, from various causes is qualified by various pleasures, so that in describing any passions whatsoever, which are voluntarily described, the mind will upon the whole be in a state of enjoyment. Now, if Nature be thus cautious in preserving in a state of enjoyment a being thus employed, the Poet ought to profit by the lesson thus held forth to him, and ought especially to take care, that whatever passions he communicates to his Reader, those passions, if his Reader's mind be sound and vigorous, should always be accompanied with an overbalance of pleasure. Now the music of harmonious metrical language, the sense of difficulty overcome, and the blind association of pleasure which has been previously received from works of rhyme or metre of the same or similar construction, an indistinct perception perpetually renewed of language closely resembling that of real life, and yet, in the circumstance of metre, differing from it so widely, all these imperceptibly make up a complex feeling of delight, which is of the most important use in tempering the painful feeling which will always be found intermingled with powerful descriptions of the deeper passions. This effect is always produced in pathetic and impassioned poetry; while, in lighter compositions, the ease and gracefulness with which the Poet manages his numbers are themselves confessedly a principal source of the gratification of the Reader. I might perhaps include all which it is *necessary* to say upon this subject by affirming, what few persons will deny, that, of two descriptions, either of passions, manners, or characters, each of them equally well executed, the one in prose and the other in verse, the verse will be read a hundred times where the prose is read once. We see that Pope by the power of verse alone, has contrived to render the plainest common sense interesting, and even frequently to invest it with the appearance of passion. In consequence of these convictions I related in metre the Tale of Goody Blake and Harry Gill, which is one of the rudest of this collection. I wished to draw attention to the truth that the power of the human imagination is sufficient to produce such changes even in our physical nature as might almost appear miraculous. The truth is an important one; the fact (for it is a *fact*) is a valuable illustration of it. And I have the satisfaction of knowing that it has been communicated to many hundreds of people who would never have heard of it, had it not been narrated as a Ballad, and in a more impressive metre than is usual in Ballads.

Having thus explained a few of the reasons why I have written in verse, and why I have chosen subjects from common life, and endeavoured to bring my language near to the real language of men, if I have been too minute in pleading my own cause, I have at the same time been treating a subject of general interest; and it is for this reason that I request the Reader's permission to add a few words with reference solely to these particular poems, and to some defects which will probably be found in them. I am sensible that my associations must have sometimes been particular instead of general, and that, consequently, giving to things a false importance, sometimes from diseased impulses I may have written upon unworthy subjects; but I am less apprehensive on this account, than that my language may frequently have suffered from those arbitrary connections of feelings and ideas with particular words and phrases, from which no man can altogether protect himself. Hence I have no doubt, that, in some instances, feelings even of the ludicrous may be given to my Readers by expressions which appeared to me tender and pathetic. Such faulty expressions, were I convinced they were faulty at present, and that they must necessarily continue to be so, I would willingly take all reasonable pains to correct. But it is dangerous to make these alterations on the simple authority of a few individuals, or even of certain classes of men; for where the understanding of an Author is not convinced, or his feelings altered, this cannot be done without great injury to himself: for his own feelings are his stay and support, and, if he sets them aside in one instance, he may be induced to repeat this act till his mind loses all confidence in itself, and becomes utterly debilitated. To this it may be added, that the Reader ought never to forget that he is himself exposed to the same errors as the Poet, and perhaps in a much greater degree: for there can be no presumption in saying, that it is not probable he will be so well acquainted with the various stages of meaning through which words have passed, or with the fickleness or stability of the relations of particular ideas to each other; and above all, since he is so much less interested in the subject, he may decide lightly and carelessly.

Long as I have detained my Reader, I hope he will permit me to caution him against a mode of false criticism which has been applied to Poetry in which the language closely resembles that of life and nature. Such verses have been triumphed over in parodies of which Dr. Johnson's Stanza is a fair specimen.

> "I put my hat upon my head,
> And walk'd into the Strand,
> And there I met another man
> Whose hat was in his hand."

Immediately under these lines I will place one of the most justly admired stanzas of the *"Babes in the Wood."*

> "These pretty Babes with hand in hand
> Went wandering up and down;
> But never more they saw the Man
> Approaching from the Town."[5]

In both these stanzas the words, and the order of the words, in no respect differ from the most unimpassioned conversation. There are words in both, for example, "the Strand," and "the Town," connected with none but the most familiar ideas; yet the one stanza we admit as admirable, and the other as a fair example of the superlatively contemptible. Whence arises this difference? Not from the metre, not from the language, not from the order of the words; but the *matter* expressed in Dr. Johnson's stanza is contemptible. The proper method of treating trivial and simple verses to which Dr. Johnson's stanza would be a fair parallelism is not to say, this is a bad kind of poetry, or this is not poetry; but this wants sense; it is neither interesting in itself, nor can *lead* to any thing interesting; the images neither originate in that same state of feeling which arises out of thought, nor can excite thought or feeling in the Reader. This is the only sensible manner of dealing with such verses: Why trouble yourself about the species till you have previously decided upon the genus? Why take pains to prove that an Ape is not a Newton when it is self-evident that he is not a man?

I have one request to make of my Reader, which is, that in judging these Poems he would decide by his own feelings genuinely, and not

---

[5] Wordsworth does not take the title and text of this ballad from his favorite source, Thomas Percy, *Reliques of Ancient English Poetry*, 1765, but from a broadside version of about 1800. — See F. W. Bateson, *Wordsworth: A Re-interpretation*, London, 1954, p. 135.

by reflection upon what will probably be the judgment of others. How common is it to hear a person say, "I myself do not object to this style of composition or this or that expression, but to such and such classes of people it will appear mean or ludicrous." This mode of criticism, so destructive of all sound unadulterated judgment, is almost universal: I have therefore to request, that the Reader would abide independently by his own feelings, and that if he finds himself affected he would not suffer such conjectures to interfere with his pleasure.

If an Author by any single composition has impressed us with respect for his talents, it is useful to consider this as affording a presumption, that, on other occasions where we have been displeased, he nevertheless may not have written ill or absurdly; and, further, to give him so much credit for this one composition as may induce us to review what has displeased us with more care than we should otherwise have bestowed upon it. This is not only an act of justice, but in our decisions upon poetry especially, may conduce in a high degree to the improvement of our own taste: for an *accurate* taste in poetry, and in all the other arts, as Sir Joshua Reynolds has observed, is an *acquired* talent, which can only be produced by thought and a long continued intercourse with the best models of composition. This is mentioned, not with so ridiculous a purpose as to prevent the most inexperienced Reader from judging for himself, (I have already said that I wish him to judge for himself;) but merely to temper the rashness of decision, and to suggest, that, if Poetry be a subject on which much time has not been bestowed, the judgment may be erroneous; and that in many cases it necessarily will be so.

I know that nothing would have so effectually contributed to further the end which I have in view as to have shewn of what kind the pleasure is, and how that pleasure is produced, which is confessedly produced by metrical composition essentially different from that which I have here endeavoured to recommend: for the Reader will say that he has been pleased by such composition; and what can I do more for him? The power of any art is limited; and he will suspect, that, if I propose to furnish him with new friends, it is only upon condition of his abandoning his old friends. Besides, as I have said, the Reader is himself conscious of the pleasure which he has received from such composition, composition to which he has peculiarly attached the endearing name of Poetry; and all men feel an habitual gratitude, and something of an honorable bigotry for the objects which have long continued to please them: we not only wish to be pleased, but to be pleased in that particular way in which we have been accustomed to be pleased. There is a host of arguments in these feelings; and I should be the less able to combat them successfully, as I am willing to allow, that, in order entirely to enjoy the Poetry which I am recommending, it would be necessary to give up much of what is ordinarily enjoyed. But, would my limits have permitted me to point out how this pleasure

is produced, I might have removed many obstacles, and assisted my
Reader in perceiving that the powers of language are not so limited as
he may suppose; and that it is possible that poetry may give other
enjoyments, of a purer, more lasting, and more exquisite nature. This
part of my subject I have not altogether neglected; but it has been
less my present aim to prove, that the interest excited by some other
kinds of poetry is less vivid, and less worthy of the nobler powers of
the mind, than to offer reasons for presuming, that, if the object which
I have proposed to myself were adequately attained, a species of poetry
would be produced, which is genuine poetry; in its nature well adapted
to interest mankind permanently, and likewise important in the multiplicity and quality of its moral relations.

From what has been said, and from a perusal of the Poems, the
Reader will be able clearly to perceive the object which I have proposed to myself: he will determine how far I have attained this object;
and, what is a much more important question, whether it be worth at-
taining; and upon the decision of these two questions will rest my
claim to the approbation of the public.

(|)

Appendix, 1802

See Preface, page xliii. — "by what is usually called Poetic Diction."
[Wordsworth refers to page 54 above.]

As perhaps I have no right to expect from a Reader of an introduction to a volume of Poems that attentive perusal without which it is
impossible, imperfectly as I have been compelled to express my meaning, that what I have said in the Preface should throughout be fully
understood, I am the more anxious to give an exact notion of the sense
in which I use the phrase *poetic diction;* and for this purpose I will
here add a few words concerning the origin of the phraseology which
I have condemned under that name. — The earliest Poets of all nations generally wrote from passion excited by real events; they wrote
naturally, and as men: feeling powerfully as they did, their language
was daring and figurative. In succeeding times, Poets, and men ambitious of the fame of Poets, perceiving the influence of such language,
and desirous of producing the same effect, without having the same
animating passion, set themselves to a mechanical adoption of those
figures of speech, and made use of them, sometimes with propriety,
but much more frequently applied them to feelings and ideas with
which they had no natural connection whatsoever. A language was
thus insensibly produced, differing materially from the real language
of men in *any situation.* The Reader or Hearer of this distorted lan-

guage found himself in a perturbed and unusual state of mind: when affected by the genuine language of passion he had been in a perturbed and unusual state of mind also: in both cases he was willing that his common judgment and understanding should be laid asleep, and he had no instinctive and infallible perception of the true to make him reject the false; the one served as a passport for the other. The agitation and confusion of mind were in both cases delightful, and no wonder if he confounded the one with the other, and believed them both to be produced by the same, or similar causes. Besides, the Poet spake to him in the character of a man to be looked up to, a man of genius and authority. Thus, and from a variety of other causes, this distorted language was received with admiration; and Poets, it is probable, who had before contented themselves for the most part with misapplying only expressions which at first had been dictated by real passion, carried the abuse still further, and introduced phrases composed apparently in the spirit of the original figurative language of passion, yet altogether of their own invention, and distinguished by various degrees of wanton deviation from good sense and nature.

It is indeed true that the language of the earliest Poets was felt to differ materially from ordinary language, because it was the language of extraordinary occasions; but it was really spoken by men, language which the Poet himself had uttered when he had been affected by the events which he described, or which he had heard uttered by those around him. To this language it is probable that metre of some sort or other was early superadded. This separated the genuine language of Poetry still further from common life, so that whoever read or heard the poems of these earliest Poets felt himself moved in a way in which he had not been accustomed to be moved in real life, and by causes manifestly different from those which acted upon him in real life. This was the great temptation to all the corruptions which have followed: under the protection of this feeling succeeding Poets constructed a phraseology which had one thing, it is true, in common with the genuine language of poetry, namely, that it was not heard in ordinary conversation; that it was unusual. But the first Poets, as I have said, spake a language which though unusual, was still the language of men. This circumstance, however, was disregarded by their successors; they found that they could please by easier means: they became proud of a language which they themselves had invented, and which was uttered only by themselves; and, with the spirit of a fraternity, they arrogated it to themselves as their own. In process of time metre became a symbol or promise of this unusual language, and whoever took upon him to write in metre, according as he possessed more or less of true poetic genius, introduced less or more of this adulterated phraseology into his compositions, and the true and the false became so inseparably interwoven that the taste of men was gradually perverted; and this language was received as a natural language; and, at length, by the influence of books upon men, did to a certain degree really become so. Abuses of this kind were imported from one nation to another, and with the progress of refinement this diction became daily more and more corrupt, thrusting out of sight the plain humanities of nature by a motley masquerade of tricks, quaintnesses, hieroglyphics, and enigmas.

It would be highly interesting to point out the causes of the pleasure given by this extravagant and absurd language; but this is not the place; it depends upon a great variety of causes, but upon none perhaps more than its influence in impressing a notion of the peculiarity and exaltation of the Poet's character, and in flattering the Reader's self-love by bringing him nearer to a sympathy with that character; an effect which is accomplished by unsettling ordinary habits of thinking, and thus assisting the Reader to approach to that perturbed and dizzy state of mind in which if he does not find himself, he imagines that he is *balked* of a peculiar enjoyment which poetry can, and ought to bestow.

The sonnet which I have quoted from Gray, in the Preface, except the lines printed in Italics, consists of little else but this diction, though not of the worst kind; and indeed, if I may be permitted to say so, it is far too common in the best writers, both antient and modern. Perhaps I can in no way, by positive example, more easily give my Reader a notion of what I mean by the phrase *poetic diction* than by referring him to a comparison between the metrical paraphrases which we have of passages in the old and new Testament, and those passages as they exist in our common Translation. See Pope's "Messiah" throughout, Prior's "Did sweeter sounds adorn my flowing tongue," &c. &c. "Though I speak with the tongues of men and of angels," &c. &c. See 1st Corinthians, Chapter 13th. By way of immediate example, take the following of Dr. Johnson.

> "Turn on the prudent Ant thy heedless eyes,
> Observe her labours, Sluggard, and be wise;
> No stern command, no monitory voice,
> Prescribes her duties, or directs her choice;
> Yet timely provident she hastes away,
> To snatch the blessings of a plenteous day;
> When fruitful Summer loads the teeming plain,
> She crops the harvest and she stores the grain.
> How long shall sloth usurp thy useless hours,
> Unnerve thy vigour, and enchain thy powers?
> While artful shades thy downy couch enclose,
> And soft solicitation courts repose,
> Amidst the drowsy charms of dull delight,
> Year chases year with unremitted flight,
> Till want now following, fraudulent and slow,
> Shall spring to seize thee, like an ambushed foe."[6]

[6] Poems cited: Samuel Johnson (1709–84), *The Ant;* Alexander Pope (1688–1744), *Messiah;* Matthew Prior (1664–1721), *Charity.*

From this hubbub of words pass to the original, "Go to the Ant, thou
Sluggard, consider her ways, and be wise: which having no guide,
overseer, or ruler, provideth her meat in the summer, and gathereth
her food in the harvest. How long wilt thou sleep, O Sluggard? when
wilt thou arise out of thy sleep? Yet a little sleep, a little slumber, a
little folding of the hands to sleep. So shall thy poverty come as one
that travaileth, and thy want as an armed man." Proverbs, chap. 6th.

One more quotation and I have done. It is from Cowper's verses
supposed to be written by Alexander Selkirk.

> "Religion! what treasure untold
> Resides in that heavenly word!
> More precious than silver and gold,
> Or all that this earth can afford.
> But the sound of the church-going bell
> These valleys and rocks never heard
> Ne'er sigh'd at the sound of a knell,
> Or smil'd when a sabbath appear'd.
>
> Ye winds, that have made me your sport,
> Convey to this desolate shore
> Some cordial endearing report
> Of a land I must visit no more.
> My Friends, do they now and then send
> A wish or a thought after me?
> O tell me I yet have a friend
> Though a friend I am never to see."[7]

I have quoted this passage as an instance of three different styles of
composition. The first four lines are poorly expressed; some Critics
would call the language prosaic; the fact is, it would be bad prose, so
bad, that it is scarcely worse in metre. The epithet "church-going" applied to a bell, and that by so chaste a writer as Cowper, is an instance
of the strange abuses which Poets have introduced into their language
till they and their Readers take them as matters of course, if they do
not single them out expressly as objects of admiration. The two lines
"Ne'er sigh'd at the sound," &c. are, in my opinion, an instance of the
language of passion wrested from its proper use, and, from the mere
circumstance of the composition being in metre, applied upon an occasion that does not justify such violent expressions, and I should condemn the passage, though perhaps few Readers will agree with me, as
vicious poetic diction. The last stanza is throughout admirably expressed: it would be equally good whether in prose or verse, except
that the Reader has an exquisite pleasure in seeing such natural language so naturally connected with metre. The beauty of this stanza
tempts me here to add a sentiment which ought to be the pervading
spirit of a system, detached parts of which have been imperfectly ex-

[7] The Selkirk of William Cowper's poem, 1782, was the model for Defoe's
Robinson Crusoe.

plained in the Preface, namely, that in proportion as ideas and feelings are valuable, whether the composition be in prose or in verse, they require and exact one and the same language.

(I)

Preface to Poems, 1815

The powers requisite for the production of poetry are, first, those of observation and description, i.e. the ability to observe with accuracy things as they are in themselves, and with fidelity to describe them, unmodified by any passion or feeling existing in the mind of the Describer: whether the things depicted be actually present to the senses, or have a place only in the memory. This power, though indispensable to a Poet, is one which he employs only in submission to necessity, and never for a continuance of time; as its exercise supposes all the higher qualities of the mind to be passive, and in a state of subjection to external objects, much in the same way as the Translator or Engraver ought to be to his Original. 2ndly, Sensibility, — which, the more exquisite it is, the wider will be the range of a Poet's perceptions; and the more will he be incited to observe objects, both as they exist in themselves and as re-acted upon by his own mind. (The distinction between poetic and human sensibility has been marked in the character of the Poet delineated in the original preface, before-mentioned). 3rdly, Reflection, — which makes the Poet acquainted with the value of actions, images, thoughts, and feelings; and assists the sensibility in perceiving their connection with each other. 4thly, Imagination and Fancy, — to modify, to create, and to associate. 5thly, Invention, — by which characters are composed out of materials supplied by observation; whether of the Poet's own heart and mind, or of external life and nature; and such incidents and situations produced as are most impressive to the imagination, and most fitted to do justice to the characters, sentiments, and passions, which the Poet undertakes to illustrate. And, lastly, Judgment, — to decide how and where, and in what degree, each of these faculties ought to be exerted; so that the less shall not be sacrificed to the greater; nor the greater, slighting the less, arrogate, to its own injury, more than its due. By judgment, also, is determined what are the laws and appropriate graces of every species of composition.

The materials of Poetry, by these powers collected and produced, are cast, by means of various moulds, into divers forms. The moulds may be enumerated, and the forms specified, in the following order. 1st, the Narrative, — including the Epopœia, the Historic Poem, the Tale, the Romance, the Mock-heroic, and, if the spirit of Homer will tolerate such neighbourhood, that dear production of our days, the metrical Novel. Of this Class, the distinguishing mark, is, that the Narrator, however liberally his speaking agents be introduced, is himself the source from which every thing primarily flows. Epic Poets, in order that their mode of composition may accord with the elevation of their subject, represent themselves as *singing* from the inspiration of the Muse, Arma virumque *cano;*[1] but this is a fiction, in modern times, of slight value: the Iliad or the Paradise Lost would gain little in our estimation by being chaunted. The other poets who belong to this class are commonly content to *tell* their tale; — so that of the whole it may be affirmed that they neither require nor reject the accompaniment of music.

2ndly, The Dramatic, — consisting of Tragedy, Historic Drama, Comedy, and Masque; in which the poet does not appear at all in his own person, and where the whole action is carried on by speech and dialogue of the agents; music being admitted only incidentally and rarely. The Opera may be placed here, in as much as it proceeds by dialogue; though depending, to the degree that it does, upon music, it has a strong claim to be ranked with the Lyrical. The characteristic and impassioned Epistle, of which Ovid and Pope have given examples, considered as a species of monodrama, may, without impropriety, be placed in this class.

3rdly, The Lyrical, — containing the Hymn, the Ode, the Elegy, the Song, and the Ballad; in all which, for the production of their *full* effect, an accompaniment of music is indispensable.

4thly, The Idyllium, — descriptive chiefly either of the processes and appearances of external nature, as the "Seasons" of Thomson; or of characters, manners, and sentiments, as are Shenstone's School-mistress, The Cotter's Saturday Night of Burns, The Twa Dogs of the same Author; or of these in conjunction with the appearances of Nature, as most of the pieces of Theocritus, the Allegro and Penseroso of Milton, Beattie's Minstrel, Goldsmith's "Deserted Village." The Epitaph, the Inscription, the Sonnet, most of the epistles of poets writing in their own persons, and all loco-descriptive poetry, belong to this class.

5thly, Didactic, — the principal object of which is direct instruction; as the Poem of Lucretius, the Georgics of Virgil, "the Fleece" of Dyer, Mason's "English Garden," &c.

And, lastly, philosophical satire, like that of Horace and Juvenal; personal and occasional Satire rarely comprehending sufficient of the general in the individual to be dignified with the name of Poetry.

Out of the three last classes has been constructed a composite species, of which Young's Night Thoughts and Cowper's Task are excellent examples.

It is deducible from the above, that poems, apparently miscellaneous, may with propriety be arranged either with reference to the powers of mind *predominant* in the production of them; or to the mould in

[1] "Of arms and the man I sing" — the opening of Virgil's *Aeneid.*

which they are cast; or, lastly, to the subjects to which they relate. From each of these considerations, the following Poems have
been divided into classes; which, that the work may more obviously correspond with the course of human life, for the sake of exhibiting in it the three requisites of a legitimate whole, a beginning,
a middle, and an end, have been also arranged, as far as it was possible, according to an order of time, commencing with Childhood, and
terminating with Old Age, Death, and Immortality. My guiding wish
was, that the small pieces of which these volumes consist, thus discriminated, might be regarded under a two-fold view; as composing
an entire work within themselves, and as adjuncts to the philosophical
Poem, "The Recluse."[2] This arrangement has long presented itself
habitually to my own mind. Nevertheless, I should have preferred to
scatter the contents of these volumes at random, if I had been persuaded that, by the plan adopted, any thing material would be taken
from the natural effect of the pieces, individually, on the mind of the
unreflecting Reader. I trust there is a sufficient variety in each class to
prevent this; while, for him who reads with reflection, the arrangement
will serve as a commentary unostentatiously directing his attention to
my purposes, both particular and general. But, as I wish to guard
against the possibility of misleading by this classification, it is proper
first to remind the Reader, that certain poems are placed according to
the powers of mind, in the Author's conception, predominant in the
production of them; *predominant*, which implies the exertion of other
faculties in less degree. Where there is more imagination than fancy
in a poem it is placed under the head of imagination, and vice versâ.
Both the above Classes might without impropriety have been enlarged
from that consisting of "Poems founded on the Affections;" as might
this latter from those, and from the class "Proceeding from Sentiment
and Reflection." The most striking characteristics of each piece, mutual illustration, variety, and proportion, have governed me throughout.

It may be proper in this place to state, that the Extracts in the 2nd
Class entitled "Juvenile Pieces," are in many places altered from the
printed copy, chiefly by omission and compression. The slight alterations of another kind were for the most part made not long after the
publication of the Poems from which the Extracts are taken. These
Extracts seem to have a title to be placed here as they were the productions of youth, and represent implicitly some of the features of a
youthful mind, at a time when images of nature supplied to it the place
of thought, sentiment, and almost of action; or, as it will be found
expressed, of a state of mind when

> "the sounding cataract
> Haunted me like a passion: the tall rock,
> The mountain, and the deep and gloomy wood,
> Their colours and their forms were then to me

[2] *The Excursion* and *The Prelude* are parts of this unfinished poem.

> An appetite, a feeling and a love,
> That had no need of a remoter charm,
> By thought supplied, or any interest
> Unborrowed from the eye" — [3]

I will own that I was much at a loss what to select of these descriptions; and perhaps it would have been better either to have reprinted the whole, or suppressed what I have given.

None of the other Classes, except those of Fancy and Imagination, require any particular notice. But a remark of general application may be made. All Poets, except the dramatic, have been in the practice of feigning that their works were composed to the music of the harp or lyre: with what degree of affectation this has been done in modern times, I leave to the judicious to determine. For my own part, I have not been disposed to violate probability so far, or to make such a large demand upon the Reader's charity. Some of these pieces are essentially lyrical; and, therefore, cannot have their due force without a supposed musical accompaniment; but, in much the greatest part, as a substitute for the classic lyre or romantic harp, I require nothing more than an animated or impassioned recitation, adapted to the subject. Poems, however humble in their kind, if they be good in that kind, cannot read themselves: the law of long syllable and short must not be so inflexible — the letter of metre must not be so impassive to the spirit of versification — as to deprive the Reader of a voluntary power to modulate, in subordination to the sense, the music of the poem; — in the same manner as his mind is left at liberty, and even summoned, to act upon its thoughts and images. But, though the accompaniment of a musical instrument be frequently dispensed with, the true Poet does not therefore abandon his privilege distinct from that of the mere Proseman;

> "He murmurs near the running brooks
> A music sweeter than their own."[4]

I come now to the consideration of the words Fancy and Imagination, as employed in the classification of the following Poems. "A man," says an intelligent Author, has "imagination," in proportion as he can distinctly copy in idea the impressions of sense: it is the faculty which *images* within the mind the phenomena of sensation. A man has fancy in proportion as he can call up, connect, or associate, at pleasure, those internal images (φαντάζειν is to cause to appear) so as to complete ideal representations of absent objects. Imagination is the power of depicting, and fancy of evoking and combining. The imagination is formed by patient observation; the fancy by a voluntary activity in shifting the scenery of the mind. The more accurate the

---

[3] *Tintern Abbey* 76–83. This paragraph, omitted in later editions, refers to selections from *An Evening Walk* and *Descriptive Sketches,* both published in 1793.

[4] Wordsworth, *A Poet's Epitaph* 39–40.

imagination, the more safely may a painter, or a poet, undertake a delineation, or a description, without the presence of the objects to be characterized. The more versatile the fancy, the more original and striking will be the decorations produced. — *British Synonyms discriminated, by W. Taylor.*[5]

Is not this as if a man should undertake to supply an account of a building, and be so intent upon what he had discovered of the foundation as to conclude his task without once looking up at the superstructure? Here, as in other instances throughout the volume, the judicious Author's mind is enthralled by Etymology; he takes up the original word as his guide, his conductor, his escort, and too often does not perceive how soon he becomes its prisoner, without liberty to tread in any path but that to which it confines him. It is not easy to find out how imagination, thus explained, differs from distinct remembrance of images; or fancy from quick and vivid recollection of them: each is nothing more than a mode of memory. If the two words bear the above meaning, and no other, what term is left to designate that Faculty of which the Poet is "all compact;" he whose eye glances from earth to heaven, whose spiritual attributes body-forth what his pen is prompt in turning to shape; or what is left to characterise fancy, as insinuating herself into the heart of objects with creative activity? —— Imagination, in the sense of the word as giving title to a Class of the following Poems, has no reference to images that are merely a faithful copy, existing in the mind, of absent external objects; but is a word of higher import, denoting operations of the mind upon those objects, and processes of creation or of composition, governed by certain fixed laws. I proceed to illustrate my meaning by instances. A parrot *hangs* from the wires of his cage by his beak or by his claws; or a monkey from the bough of a tree by his paws or his tail. Each creature does so literally and actually. In the first Eclogue of Virgil, the Shepherd, thinking of the time when he is to take leave of his Farm, thus addresses his Goats;

> "Non ego vos posthac viridi projectus in antro
> Dumosa *pendere* procul de rupe ordebo."[6]

> —————— "half way up
> *Hangs* one who gathers samphire,"[7]

is the well-known expression of Shakespear, delineating an ordinary image upon the Cliffs of Dover. In these two instances is a slight exertion of the faculty which I denominate imagination, in the use of one word: neither the goats nor the samphire-gatherer do literally

[5] William Taylor of Norwich (1765–1836), *English Synonymes Discriminated,* 1813.

[6] "Never henceforth, stretched out in a green hollow, shall I see you far off, hanging on the rocky, thorn-covered cliff." For *ordebo* read *videbo.*

[7] *King Lear* IV.vi.14–15.

hang, as does the parrot or the monkey; but, presenting to the senses
something of such an appearance, the mind in its activity, for its own
gratification, contemplates them as hanging.

> "As when far off at Sea a Fleet descried
> *Hangs* in the clouds, by equinoxial winds
> Close sailing from Bengala or the Isles
> Of Ternate or Tydore, whence Merchants bring
> Their spicy drugs; they on the trading flood
> Through the wide Ethiopian to the Cape
> Ply, stemming nightly toward the Pole: so seem'd
> Far off the flying Fiend."[8]

Here is the full strength of the imagination involved in the word,
hangs, and exerted upon the whole image: First, the Fleet, an aggregate of many Ships, is represented as one mighty Person, whose
track, we know and feel, is upon the waters; but, taking advantage
of its appearance to the senses, the Poet dares to represent it as *hanging in the clouds,* both for the gratification of the mind in contemplating the image itself, and in reference to the motion and appearance of
the sublime object to which it is compared.

From images of sight we will pass to those of sound:

> "Over his own sweet voice the Stock-dove *broods;*"

of the same bird,

> "His voice was *buried* among trees,
> Yet to be come at by the breeze;"

> "O, Cuckoo! shall I call thee *Bird,*
> Or but a wandering *Voice?*"[9]

The Stock-dove is said to *coo,* a sound well imitating the note of the
bird; but, by the intervention of the metaphor *broods,* the affections are
called in by the imagination to assist in marking the manner in which
the Bird reiterates and prolongs her soft note, as if herself delighting
to listen to it, and participating of a still and quiet satisfaction, like
that which may be supposed inseparable from the continuous process
of incubation. "His voice was buried among trees," a metaphor expressing the love of *seclusion* by which this Bird is marked; and
characterising its note as not partaking of the shrill and the piercing,
and therefore more easily deadened by the intervening shade; yet a
note so peculiar, and withal so pleasing, that the breeze, gifted with
that love of the sound which the Poet feels, penetrates the shade in
which it is entombed, and conveys it to the ear of the listener.

> Shall I call thee Bird
> Or but a wandering Voice?

[8] *Paradise Lost* II.636–643.
[9] *Resolution and Independence* 5; *O Nightingale* 13–14; *To the Cuckoo*
3–4.

This concise interrogation characterises the seeming ubiquity of the voice of the Cuckoo, and dispossesses the creature almost of a corporeal existence; the imagination being tempted to this exertion of her power by a consciousness in the memory that the Cuckoo is almost perpetually heard throughout the season of Spring, but seldom becomes an object of sight.

Thus far of images independent of each other, and immediately endowed by the mind with properties that do not inhere in them, upon an incitement from properties and qualities the existence of which is inherent and obvious. These processes of imagination are carried on either by conferring additional properties upon an object, or abstracting from it some of those which it actually possesses, and thus enabling it to react upon the mind which hath performed the process, like a new existence.

I pass from the Imagination acting upon an individual image to a consideration of the same faculty employed upon images in a conjunction by which they modify each other. The Reader has already had a fine instance before him in the passage quoted from Virgil, where the apparently perilous situation of the Goat, hanging upon the shaggy precipice, is contrasted with that of the Shepherd, contemplating it from the seclusion of the Cavern in which he lies stretched at ease and in security. Take these images separately, and how unaffecting the picture compared with that produced by their being thus connected with, and opposed to, each other!

> "As a huge Stone is sometimes seen to lie
> Couched on the bald top of an eminence,
> Wonder to all who do the same espy
> By what means it could thither come, and whence;
> So that it seems a thing endued with sense,
> Like a Sea-beast crawled forth, which on a shelf
> Of rock or sand reposeth, there to sun himself.
>
> Such seemed this Man; not all alive or dead,
> Nor all asleep, in his extreme old age.
> Motionless as a cloud the old Man stood,
> That heareth not the loud winds when they call,
> And moveth altogether if it move at all."[10]

In these images, the conferring, the abstracting, and the modifying powers of the Imagination, immediately and mediately acting, are all brought into conjunction. The Stone is endowed with something of the power of life to approximate it to the Sea-beast; and the Sea-beast stripped of some of its vital qualities to assimilate it to the stone; which intermediate image is thus treated for the purpose of bringing the original image, that of the stone, to a nearer resemblance to the figure and condition of the aged Man; who is divested of so much of the indications of life and motion as to bring him to the point where

[10] *Resolution and Independence* 57–65, 75–77.

the two objects unite and coalesce in just comparison. After what has been said, the image of the Cloud need not be commented upon.

Thus far of an endowing or modifying power: but the Imagination also shapes and *creates;* and how? By innumerable processes; and in none does it more delight than in that of consolidating numbers into unity, and dissolving and separating unity into number, — alternations proceeding from, and governed by, a sublime consciousness of the soul in her own mighty and almost divine powers. Recur to the passage already cited from Milton. When the compact Fleet, as one Person, has been introduced "Sailing from Bengala," "They," i. e. the "Merchants," representing the Fleet resolved into a Multitude of Ships, 'ply' their voyage towards the extremities of earth: "So" (referring to the word "As" in the commencement) "seemed the flying Fiend;" the image of his Person acting to recombine the multitude of Ships into one body, — the point from which the comparison set out. "So seemed," and to whom seemed? To the heavenly Muse who dictates the poem, to the eye of the Poet's mind, and to that of the Reader, present at one moment in the wide Ethiopian, and the next in the solitudes, then first broken in upon, of the infernal regions!

Modo me Thebis, modo ponit Athenis.[11]

Hear again this mighty Poet, — speaking of the Messiah going forth to expel from Heaven the rebellious Angels,

> Attended by ten thousand, thousand Saints
> He onward came: far off his coming shone, — [12]

the retinue of Saints, and the Person of the Messiah himself, lost almost and merged in the splendour of that indefinite abstraction, "His coming!"

As I do not mean here to treat this subject further than to throw some light upon the present Volumes, and especially upon one division of them, I shall spare myself and the Reader the trouble of considering the Imagination as it deals with thoughts and sentiments, as it regulates the composition of characters, and determines the course of actions: I will not consider it (more than I have already done by implication) as that power which, in the language of one of my most esteemed Friends, "draws all things to one, which makes things animate or inanimate, beings with their attributes, subjects with their accessaries, take one colour and serve to one effect."[13] The grand store-house of enthusiastic and meditative Imagination, of poetical, as contradistinguished from human and dramatic Imagination, is the prophetic and lyrical parts of the holy Scriptures, and the works of

[11] "He sets me now in Thebes, now in Athens" — Horace, *Epistles* II.i.213, in praise of a poet who moves, enchants, and "transports."
[12] *Paradise Lost* VI.767–768.
[13] Charles Lamb upon the genius of Hogarth. [W. W.]

Milton, to which I cannot forbear to add those of Spenser. I select these writers in preference to those of ancient Greece and Rome because the anthropomorphitism of the Pagan religion subjected the minds of the greatest poets in those countries too much to the bondage of definite form; from which the Hebrews were preserved by their abhorrence of idolatry. This abhorrence was almost as strong in our great epic Poet, both from circumstances of his life, and from the constitution of his mind. However imbued the surface might be with classical literature, he was a Hebrew in soul; and all things tended in him towards the sublime. Spenser, of a gentler nature, maintained his freedom by aid of his allegorical spirit, at one time inciting him to create persons out of abstractions; and at another, by a superior effort of genius, to give the universality and permanence of abstractions to his human beings, by means of attributes and emblems that belong to the highest moral truths and the purest sensations, — of which his character of Una is a glorious example. Of the human and dramatic Imagination the works of Shakespear are an inexhaustible source.

> "I tax not you, ye Elements, with unkindness,
> I never gave you Kingdoms, called you Daughters."[14]

And if, bearing in mind the many Poets distinguished by this prime quality, whose names I omit to mention; yet justified by a recollection of the insults which the Ignorant, the Incapable, and the Presumptuous have heaped upon these and my other writings, I may be permitted to anticipate the judgment of posterity upon myself; I shall declare (censurable, I grant, if the notoriety of the fact above stated does not justify me) that I have given, in these unfavourable times, evidence of exertions of this faculty upon its worthiest objects, the external universe, the moral and religious sentiments of Man, his natural affections, and his acquired passions; which have the same ennobling tendency as the productions of men, in this kind, worthy to be holden in undying remembrance.

I dismiss this subject with observing — that, in the series of Poems placed under the head of Imagination, I have begun with one of the earliest processes of Nature in the development of this faculty. Guided by one of my own primary consciousnesses, I have represented a commutation and transfer of internal feelings, co-operating with external accidents to plant, for immortality, images of sound and sight, in the celestial soil of the Imagination. The Boy, there introduced, is listening, with something of a feverish and restless anxiety, for the recurrence of the riotous sounds which he had previously excited; and, at the moment when the intenseness of his mind is beginning to remit, he is surprised into a perception of the solemn and tranquillizing images which the Poem describes. — The Poems next in succession exhibit the faculty exerting itself upon various objects of the external

14 *King Lear* III.ii.16–17.

universe; then follow others, where it is employed upon feelings, characters, and actions; and the Class is concluded with imaginative pictures of moral, political, and religious sentiments.

To the mode in which Fancy has already been characterized as the Power of evoking and combining, or, as my friend Mr. Coleridge has styled it, "the aggregative and associative Power," my objection is only that the definition is too general. To aggregate and to associate, to evoke and to combine, belong as well to the Imagination as to the Fancy; but either the materials evoked and combined are different; or they are brought together under a different law, and for a different purpose. Fancy does not require that the materials which she makes use of should be susceptible of change in their constitution, from her touch; and, where they admit of modification, it is enough for her purpose if it be slight, limited, and evanescent. Directly the reverse of these, are the desires and demands of the Imagination. She recoils from every thing but the plastic, the pliant, and the indefinite. She leaves it to Fancy to describe Queen Mab as coming,

> "In shape no bigger than an agate stone
> On the fore-finger of an Alderman."[15]

Having to speak of stature, she does not tell you that her gigantic Angel was as tall as Pompey's Pillar; much less that he was twelve cubits, or twelve hundred cubits high; or that his dimensions equalled those of Teneriffe or Atlas; — because these, and if they were a million times as high, it would be the same, are bounded: The expression is, "His stature reached the sky!" the illimitable firmament! — When the Imagination frames a comparison, if it does not strike on the first presentation, a sense of the truth of the likeness, from the moment that it is perceived, grows — and continues to grow — upon the mind; the resemblance depending less upon outline of form and feature than upon expression and effect, less upon casual and outstanding, than upon inherent and internal, properties: — moreover, the images invariably modify each other. — The law under which the processes of Fancy are carried on is as capricious as the accidents of things, and the effects are surprizing, playful, ludicrous, amusing, tender, or pathetic, as the objects happen to be appositely produced or fortunately combined. Fancy depends upon the rapidity and profusion with which she scatters her thoughts and images, trusting that their number, and the felicity with which they are linked together, will make amends for the want of individual value: or she prides herself upon the curious subtilty and the successful elaboration with which she can detect their lurking affinities. If she can win you over to her purpose, and impart to you her feelings, she cares not how unstable or transitory may be her influence, knowing that it will not be out of her power to resume it upon an apt occasion. But the Imagination is

[15] *Romeo and Juliet* I.iv.55–56.

conscious of an indestructible dominion; — the Soul may fall away from it, not being able to sustain its grandeur, but, if once felt and acknowledged, by no act of any other faculty of the mind can it be relaxed, impaired, or diminished. — Fancy is given to quicken and to beguile the temporal part of our Nature, Imagination to incite and to support the eternal. — Yet is it not the less true that Fancy, as she is an active, is also, under her own laws and in her own spirit, a creative faculty. In what manner Fancy ambitiously aims at a rivalship with the Imagination, and Imagination stoops to work with the materials of Fancy, might be illustrated from the compositions of all eloquent writers, whether in prose or verse; and chiefly from those of our own Country. Scarcely a page of the impassioned parts of Bishop Taylor's Works can be opened that shall not afford examples.[16] — Referring the Reader to those inestimable Volumes, I will content myself with placing a conceit (ascribed to Lord Chesterfield) in contrast with a passage from the Paradise Lost;

> "The dews of the evening most carefully shun,
> They are the tears of the sky for the loss of the Sun."[17]

After the transgression of Adam, Milton, with other appearances of sympathizing Nature, thus marks the immediate consequence,

> "Sky lowered, and muttering thunder, some sad drops
> Wept at completion of the mortal sin."[18]

The associating link is the same in each instance; — dew or rain, not distinguishable from the liquid substance of tears, are employed as indications of sorrow. A flash of surprize is the effect in the former case, a flash of surprize and nothing more; for the nature of things does not sustain the combination. In the latter, the effects of the act, of which there is this immediate consequence and visible sign, are so momentous that the mind acknowledges the justice and reasonableness of the sympathy in Nature so manifested; and the sky weeps drops of water as if with human eyes, as "Earth had, before, trembled from her entrails, and Nature given a second groan."

Awe-stricken as I am by contemplating the operations of the mind of this truly divine Poet, I scarcely dare venture to add that "An address to an Infant," which the Reader will find under the Class of Fancy in the present Volumes, exhibits something of this communion and interchange of instruments and functions between the two powers; and is, accordingly, placed last in the class, as a preparation for that of Imagination which follows. . . .

[16] Jeremy Taylor (1613–67), theologian and stylist.
[17] Philip Stanhope, 4th Earl of Chesterfield (1694–1773), *Advice to a Lady in Autumn.*
[18] *Paradise Lost* IX.1002–3.

Convention of Cintra

❪ In July 1808 a British army was sent to aid any guerrillas in the Iberian Peninsula, either Spanish or Portuguese, who were rising against Britain's enemy, Napoleon Bonaparte. After news and rumors of victory, the English expected to hear that the French had surrenderd Lisbon, but instead they learned on September 16 that the British generals, in the negotiations known as the Convention of Cintra, had agreed to terms without consulting the Portuguese Government. Wordsworth's tract denounces the Convention on grounds of basic public morality and of nationalism. For the older belief in the sacredness of thrones and dynasties, the newly explosive ideal of nationalism substituted belief in the sacredness of independence for a unified people belonging to a particular soil and speaking a common language. Wordsworth rejects the diplomatic values of utility and expediency. The brief passage below comes from the first edition of the long tract (216 pages) *Concerning the Relations of Great Britain, Spain, and Portugal, to Each Other, and to the Common Enemy, at This Crisis; and Specifically as Affected by the Convention of Cintra: The whole brought to the test of those Principles, by which alone the Independence and Freedom of Nations can be Preserved or Recovered.* Portions had appeared in the *Courier* newspaper; after long delays, while De Quincey supervised corrections for the press, the tract was issued in May 1809. ❫

. . . What an outrage! — We enter the Portugueze territory as allies; and, without their consent — or even consulting them, we proceed to form the basis of an agreement, relating — not to the safety or interests of our own army — but to Portugueze territory, Portugueze persons, liberties, and rights, — and engage, out of our own will and power, to include the Portugueze army, they or their Government willing or not, within the obligation of this agreement. I place these things in contrast, viz. the acknowledgement of Bonaparte as emperor and king, and the utter neglect of the Portugueze Sovereign and Portugueze authorities, to shew in what spirit and temper these agreements were entered upon. I will not here insist upon what was our duty, on this occasion, to the Portugueze — as dictated by those sublime precepts of justice which it has been proved that they and the Spaniards had risen to defend, — and without feeling the force and sanctity of which, they neither could have risen, nor can oppose to their enemy resistance which has any hope in it; but I will ask, of any man who is not dead to the common feelings of his social nature — and besotted in understanding, if this be not a cruel mockery, and which must have been felt, unless it were repelled with hatred and scorn, as a heart-breaking insult. Moreover, this conduct acknowledges, by implication, that principle which by his actions the enemy has for a

long time covertly maintained, and now openly and insolently avows
in his words — that power is the measure of right; — and it is in a
steady adherence to this abominable doctrine that his strength mainly
lies. I do maintain then that, as far as the conduct of our Generals
in framing these instruments tends to reconcile men to this course of
action, and to sanction this principle, they are virtually his Allies:
their weapons may be against him, but he will laugh at their weapons,
— for he knows, though they themselves do not, that their souls are
for him. Look at the preamble to the Armistice! In what is omitted and
what is inserted, the French Ruler could not have fashioned it more
for his own purpose if he had traced it with his own hand. We have
then trampled upon a fundamental principle of justice, and countenanced a prime maxim of iniquity; thus adding, in an unexampled
degree, the foolishness of impolicy to the heinousness of guilt. A
conduct thus grossly unjust and impolitic, without having the hatred
which it inspires neutralised by the contempt, is made contemptible
by utterly wanting that colour of right which authority and power,
put forth in defence of our Allies — in asserting their just claims and
avenging their injuries, might have given. But we, instead of triumphantly displaying our power towards our enemies, have ostentatiously exercised it upon our friends; reversing here, as every where, the
practice of sense and reason; — conciliatory even to abject submission
where we ought to have been haughty and commanding, — and
repulsive and tyrannical where we ought to have been gracious and
kind. Even a common law of good breeding would have served us
here, had we known how to apply it. We ought to have endeavoured
to raise the Portugueze in their own estimation by concealing our
power in comparison with theirs; dealing with them in the spirit of
those mild and humane delusions, which spread such a genial grace
over the intercourse, and add so much to the influence of love in the
concerns of private life. It is a common saying, presume that a man
is dishonest, and that is the readiest way to make him so: in like
manner it may be said, presume that a nation is weak, and that is the
surest course to bring it to weakness, — if it be not rouzed to prove
its strength by applying it to the humiliation of your pride. The
Portugueze had been weak; and, in connection with their allies the
Spaniards, they were prepared to become strong. It was, therefore,
doubly incumbent upon us to foster and encourage them — to look
favourably upon their efforts — generously to give them credit upon
their promises — to hope with them and for them; and, thus anticipating and foreseeing, we should, by a natural operation of love,
have contributed to create the merits which were anticipated and
foreseen. I apply these rules, taken from the intercourse between
individuals, to the conduct of large bodies of men, or of nations towards
each other, because these are nothing but aggregates of individuals;
and because the maxims of all just law, and the measures of all sane

practice, are only an enlarged or modified application of those dispositions of love and those principles of reason, by which the welfare of
individuals, in their connection with each other, is promoted. There
was also here a still more urgent call for these courteous and humane
principles as guides of conduct; because, in exact proportion to the
physical weakness of Governments, and to the distraction and confusion which cannot but prevail, when a people is struggling for
independence and liberty, are the well-intentioned and the wise among
them remitted for their support to those benign elementary feelings
of society, for the preservation and cherishing of which, among other
important objects, government was from the beginning ordained.

Therefore, by the strongest obligations, we were bound to be
studious of a delicate and respectful bearing towards those ill-fated
nations, our allies: and consequently, if the government of the Portugueze, though weak in power, possessed their affections, and was
strong in right, it was incumbent upon us to turn our first thoughts
to that government — to look for it if it were hidden — to call it
forth, — and, by our power combined with that of the people, to
assert its rights. Or, if the government were dissolved and had no
existence, it was our duty, in such an emergency, to have resorted to
the nation, expressing its will through the most respectable and conspicuous authority, through that which seemed to have the best right
to stand forth as its representative. In whatever circumstances Portugal
had been placed, the paramount right of the Portugueze nation, or
government, to appear not merely as a party but a principal, ought to
have been established as a primary position, without the admission of
which, all proposals to treat would be peremptorily rejected. But the
Portugueze *had* a government; they had a lawful prince in Brazil; and
a regency, appointed by him, at home; and generals, at the head of
considerable bodies of troops, appointed also by the regency or the
prince. Well then might one of those generals enter a formal protest
against the treaty, on account of its being "totally void of that deference
due to the prince regent, or the government that represents him; as
being hostile to the sovereign authority and independence of that
government; and as being against the honour, safety, and independence
of the nation." I have already reminded the reader, of the benign
and happy influences which might have attended upon a different
conduct; how much good we might have added to that already in
existence; how far we might have assisted in strengthening, among our
allies, those powers, and in developing those virtues, which were
producing themselves by a natural process, and to which these breath-
ings of insult must have been a deadly check and interruption. Nor
would the evil be merely negative; for the interference of professed
friends, acting in this manner, must have superinduced dispositions
and passions, which were alien to the condition of the Portugueze; —
scattered weeds which could not have been found upon the soil, if

our ignorant hands had not sown them. . . .

Again: independence and liberty were the blessings for which the people of the Peninsula were contending — immediate independence, which was not to be gained but by modes of exertion from which liberty must ensue. Now, liberty — healthy, matured, time-honoured liberty — this is the growth and peculiar boast of Britain; and nature herself, by encircling with the ocean the country which we inhabit, has proclaimed that this mighty nation is for ever to be her own ruler, and that the land is set apart for the home of immortal independence. Judging then from these first fruits of British Friendship, what bewildering and depressing and hollow thoughts must the Spaniards and Portugueze have entertained concerning the real value of these blessings, if the people who have possessed them longest, and who ought to understand them best, could send forth an army capable of enacting the oppression and baseness of the Convention of Cintra; if the government of that people could sanction this treaty; and if, lastly, this distinguished and favoured people themselves could suffer it to be held forth to the eyes of men as expressing the sense of their hearts — as an image of their understandings.

But it did not speak their sense — it was not endured — it was not submitted to in their hearts. Bitter was the sorrow of the people of Great Britain when the tidings first came to their ears, when they first fixed their eyes upon this covenant — overwhelming was their astonishment, tormenting their shame; their indignation was tumultuous; and the burthen of the past would have been insupportable, if it had not involved in its very nature a sustaining hope for the future. Among many alleviations, there was one, which, (not wisely, but overcome by circumstances) all were willing to admit; — that the event was so strange and uncouth, exhibiting such discordant characteristics of innocent fatuity and enormous guilt, that it could not without violence be thought of as indicative of a general constitution of things, either in the country or the government; but that it was a kind of *lusus naturæ* in the moral world — a solitary straggler out of the circumference of nature's law — a monster which could not propagate, and had no birthright in futurity. Accordingly, the first expectation was that the government would deem itself under the necessity of disannulling the Convention; a necessity which, though in itself a great evil, appeared small in the eyes of judicious men, compared with the consequences of admitting that such a contract could be binding. For they, who had signed and ratified it, had not only glaringly exceeded all power which could be supposed to be vested in them as holding a military office; but, in the exercise of political functions, they had framed ordinances which neither the government, nor the nation, nor any power on earth, could confer upon them a right to frame: therefore the contract was self-destroying from the beginning. It is a wretched oversight, or a wilful abuse of terms still more wretched, to speak of the good faith of a nation as being pledged to an act which was not a shattering of the edifice of justice, but a subversion of its foundations. One man cannot sign away the faculty of reason in another; much less can one or two individuals do this for a whole people. Therefore the contract was void, both from its injustice and its absurdity; and the party, with whom it was made, must have known it to be so. It could not then but be expected by many that the government would reject it. Moreover, extraordinary outrages against reason and virtue demand that extraordinary sacrifices of atonement should be made upon their altars; and some were encouraged to think that a government might upon this impulse rise above itself, and turn an exceeding disgrace into true glory, by a public profession of shame and repentance for having appointed such unworthy instruments; that, this being acknowledged, it would clear itself from all imputation of having any further connection with what had been done, and would provide that the nation should as speedily as possible, be purified from all suspicion of looking upon it with other feelings than those of abhorrence. The people knew what had been their own wishes when the army was sent in aid of their allies; and they clung to the faith, that their wishes and the aims of the Government must have been in unison; and that the guilt would soon be judicially fastened upon those who stood forth as principals, and who (it was hoped) would be found to have fulfilled only their own will and pleasure, — to have had no explicit commission or implied encouragement for what they had done, — no accessaries in their crime. The punishment of these persons was anticipated, not to satisfy any cravings of vindictive justice (for these, if they could have existed in such a case, had been thoroughly appeased already: for what punishment could be greater than to have brought upon themselves the sentence passed upon them by the voice of their countrymen?); but for this reason — that a judicial condemnation of the men, who were openly the proximate cause, and who were forgetfully considered as the single and sole originating source, would make our detestation of the effect more signally manifest.

These thoughts, if not welcomed without scruple and relied upon without fear, were at least encouraged; till it was recollected that the persons at the head of government had ordered that the event should be communicated to the inhabitants of the metropolis with signs of national rejoicing. No wonder if, when these rejoicings were called to mind, it was impossible to entertain the faith which would have been most consolatory. The evil appeared no longer as the forlorn monster which I have described. It put on another shape and was endued with a more formidable life — with power to generate and transmit after its kind. A new and alarming import was added to the event by this open testimony of gladness and approbation; which intimated — which declared — that the spirit, which swayed the individuals

who were the ostensible and immediate authors of the Convention,
was not confined to them; but that it was widely prevalent: else it could
not have been found in the very council-seat; there, where if wisdom
and virtue have not some influence, what is to become of the nation
in these times of peril? rather say, into what an abyss is it already
fallen! . . .

Samuel Taylor Coleridge

SAMUEL TAYLOR COLERIDGE

CHRONOLOGY

1772 Born October 21 at Ottery St. Mary, Devonshire.

1782 September, entered Christ's Hospital, London, where he became a Grecian (the highest rank); left in August 1789.

1791–93 Scholarship student at Jesus College, Cambridge.

1793 December 2, enlisted in the Light Dragoons.

1794 April 10, released from Dragoons. Brief periods at Cambridge; with Southey at Oxford and Bristol, planned Pantisocracy; by December, in London with Lamb.

1795 Political and theological lectures at Bristol. October 4, married Sarah Fricker.

1796 March 1–May 13, the *Watchman*. April 16, *Poems on Various Subjects*.

1797–1803 Contributed to the London *Morning Post*.

1798 With Wordsworth, published *Lyrical Ballads,* to offset the cost of study in Germany (to July 1799).

1804–05 In Malta. Returned by way of Rome (1806).

1808 January–June, lectured on poetry, Royal Institution, London.

1809–10 June 1–March 15, the *Friend*.

1811–12 Lectured in London on Shakespeare and Milton; wrote for the *Courier* newspaper.

1813 January 23–February, *Remorse* successfully performed 20 nights at Drury Lane. October 21, at Bristol for lectures (to April 1814).

1814 "On the Principles of Genial Criticism," in *Felix Farley's Bristol Journal*, August–September.

1816 April 15, after long addiction to opium, put himself in the care of James Gillman of Highgate. December, *The Statesman's Manual*.

1817 March, *A Lay Sermon on Distresses and Discontents*. July, *Biographia Literaria* and *Sibylline Leaves*. November, *Zapolya*.

1818 January, "Preliminary Treatise on Method," for the Encyclopaedia Metropolitana. April, wrote and published circulars against the excesses of child labor. November, *The Friend* (expanded to three volumes).

1818–19 Lectured in London on literature, history, and philosophy.

1825 May, *Aids to Reflection*.

1830 *On the Constitution of the Church and State* (2nd edition by July).

1834 Died July 25.

Biographia Literaria

❦ As the result of a plan for an autobiographical introduction to a new edition of his poems, Coleridge produced in 1817 two volumes of what he calls in the work itself an "immethodical miscellany." In several chapters, Coleridge answers Wordsworth's Preface of 1800 to *Lyrical Ballads.* Considered more broadly — as critics like Meyer Abrams, Earl Wasserman, and Morse Peckham have emphasized — the *Biographia* attempts to replace philosophically the crumbling beliefs in an externally ordered universe. Previous critical theory had recommended imitation of an orderly world (holding the mirror up to Nature); Coleridge and others in his time recommended the expression of that which intuition found within (directing one's lamp through the window of the soul). John Shawcross prepared a useful edition of the *Biographia Literaria* in 1907 for the Oxford University Press, and George Watson another for Everyman's Library in 1956. Coleridge's text of 1817 is here followed. ❧

from CHAPTER IV

During the last year of my residence at Cambridge, I became acquainted with Mr. Wordsworth's first publication entitled "Descriptive Sketches;" and seldom, if ever, was the emergence of an original poetic genius above the literary horizon more evidently announced. In the form, style, and manner of the whole poem, and in the structure of the particular lines and periods, there is an harshness and acerbity connected and combined with words and images all a-glow, which might recall those products of the vegetable world, where gorgeous blossoms rise out of the hard and thorny rind and shell, within which the rich fruit was elaborating. The language was not only peculiar and strong, but at times knotty and contorted, as by its own impatient strength; while the novelty and struggling crowd of images acting in conjunction with the difficulties of the style, demanded always a greater closeness of attention, than poetry, (at all events, than descriptive poetry) has a right to claim. It not seldom therefore justified the complaint of obscurity. In the following extract I have sometimes fancied, that I saw an emblem of the poem itself, and of the author's genius as it was then displayed.

> " 'Tis storm; and hid in mist from hour to hour,
> All day the floods a deepening murmur pour;
> The sky is veiled, and every cheerful sight:
> Dark is the region as with coming night;
> And yet what frequent bursts of overpowering light!
> Triumphant on the bosom of the storm,
> Glances the fire-clad eagle's wheeling form;

> Eastward, in long perspective glittering, shine
> The wood-crowned cliffs that o'er the lake recline;
> Wide o'er the Alps a hundred streams unfold,
> At once to pillars turn'd that flame with gold;
> Behind his sail the peasant strives to shun
> The West, that burns like one dilated sun,
> Where in a mighty crucible expire
> The mountains, glowing hot, like coals of fire."[1]

The poetic PSYCHE, in its process to full developement, undergoes as many changes as its Greek name-sake, the[2] butterfly. And it is remarkable how soon genius clears and purifies itself from the faults and errors of its earliest products; faults which, in its earliest compositions, are the more obtrusive and confluent, because as heterogeneous elements, which had only a temporary use, they constitute the very *ferment*, by which themselves are carried off. Or we may compare them to some diseases, which must work on the humours, and be thrown out on the surface, in order to secure the patient from their future recurrence. I was in my twenty-fourth year, when I had the happiness of knowing Mr. Wordsworth personally, and while memory lasts, I shall hardly forget the sudden effect produced on my mind, by his recitation of a manuscript poem, which still remains unpublished,[3] but of which the stanza, and tone of style, were the same as those of the "Female Vagrant" as originally printed in the first volume of the "Lyrical Ballads." There was here, no mark of strained thought, or forced diction, no crowd or turbulence of imagery, and, as the poet hath himself well described in his lines "on re-visiting the Wye,"[4] manly reflection, and human associations had given both variety, and an additional interest to natural objects, which in the passion and appetite of the first love they had seemed to him neither to need or permit. The occasional obscurities, which had risen from an imperfect controul over the resources of his native language, had almost wholly disappeared, together with that worse defect of arbitrary and illogical phrases, at once hackneyed, and fantastic, which hold so distinguished a place in the *technique* of ordinary poetry, and will, more or less, alloy the earlier poems of the truest genius, unless the attention has

[1] *Descriptive Sketches* 332 ff. (text of 1815, not 1793).
[2] The fact, that in Greek Psyche is the common name for the soul, and the butterfly, is thus alluded to in the following stanza from an unpublished poem of the author:
> "The butterfly the ancient Grecians made
> The soul's fair emblem, and its only name —
> But of the soul, escaped the slavish trade
> Of mortal life! For in this earthly frame
> Our's is the reptile's lot, much toil, much blame,
> Manifold motions making little speed,
> And to deform and kill the things, whereon we feed." [S.T.C.]
[3] *Guilt and Sorrow*, published 1842.
[4] Usually, but less accurately, called *Tintern Abbey*.

been specifically directed to their worthlessness and incongruity.[5] I did not perceive any thing particular in the mere style of the poem alluded to during its recitation, except indeed such difference as was not separable from the thought and manner; and the Spencerian stanza, which always, more or less, recalls to the reader's mind Spencer's own style, would doubtless have authorized in my then opinion a more frequent descent to the phrases of ordinary life, than could without an ill effect have been hazarded in the heroic couplet. It was not however the freedom from false taste, whether as to common defects, or to those more properly his own, which made so unusual an impression on my feelings immediately, and subsequently on my judgement. It was the union of deep feeling with profound thought; the fine balance of truth in observing with the imaginative faculty in modifying the objects observed; and above all the original gift of spreading the tone, the *atmosphere*, and with it the depth and height of the ideal world around forms, incidents, and situations, of which, for the common view, custom had bedimmed all the lustre, had dried up the sparkle and the dew drops. "To find no contradiction in the union of old and new; to contemplate the ANCIENT of days and all his works with feelings as fresh, as if all had then sprang forth at the first creative fiat; characterizes the mind that feels the riddle of the world, and may help to unravel it. To carry on the feelings of childhood into the powers of manhood; to combine the child's sense of wonder and novelty with the appearances, which every day for perhaps forty years had rendered familiar;

"With sun and moon and stars throughout the year,
And man and woman;"[6]

this is the character and privilege of genius, and one of the marks which distinguish genius from talents. And therefore is it the prime merit of genius and its most unequivocal mode of manifestation, so

[5] Mr. Wordsworth, even in his two earliest "the Evening Walk and the Descriptive Sketches," is more free from this latter defect than most of the young poets his contemporaries. It may however be exemplified, together with the harsh and obscure construction, in which he more often offended, in the following lines: —

" 'Mid stormy vapours ever driving by,
Where ospreys, cormorants, and herons cry;
Where hardly given the hopeless waste to cheer,
Denied the bread of life the foodful ear,
Dwindles the pear on autumn's latest spray,
And *apple sickens* pale in summer's ray;
*Ev'n here content has fixed her smiling reign
With independence, child of high disdain.*"

I hope, I need not say, that I have quoted these lines for no other purpose than to make my meaning fully understood. It is to be regretted that Mr. Wordsworth has not republished these two poems entire. [S.T.C., quoting *Descriptive Sketches* 317–324.]

[6] Cf. Milton, "Cyriack, this three years' day" 5–6.

to represent familiar objects as to awaken in the minds of others a kindred feeling concerning them and that freshness of sensation which is the constant accompaniment of mental, no less than of bodily, convalescence. Who has not a thousand times seen snow fall on water? Who has not watched it with a new feeling, from the time that he has read Burns' comparison of sensual pleasure

> "To snow that falls upon a river
> A moment white — then gone for ever!"[7]

In poems, equally as in philosophic disquisitions, genius produces the strongest impressions of novelty, while it rescues the most admitted truths from the impotence caused by the very circumstance of their universal admission. Truths of all others the most awful and mysterious, yet being at the same time of universal interest, are too often considered as *so* true, that they lose all the life and efficiency of truth, and lie bed-ridden in the dormitory of the soul, side by side, with the most despised and exploded errors." THE FRIEND,[8] page 76, No. 5.

This excellence, which in all Mr. Wordsworth's writings is more or less predominant, and which constitutes the character of his mind, I no sooner felt, than I sought to understand. Repeated meditations led me first to suspect, (and a more intimate analysis of the human faculties, their appropriate marks, functions, and effects matured my conjecture into full conviction) that fancy and imagination were two distinct and widely different faculties, instead of being, according to the general belief, either two names with one meaning, or at furthest, the lower and higher degree of one and the same power. It is not, I own, easy to conceive a more opposite[9] translation of the Greek *Phantasia*, than the Latin Imaginatio; but it is equally true that in all societies there exists an instinct of growth, a certain collective, unconscious good sense working progressively to desynonymize[10] those

---

[7] Cf. *Tam O'Shanter* 61–62.

[8] As "the Friend" was printed on stampt sheets, and sent only by the post to a very limited number of subscribers, the author has felt less objection to quote from it, though a work of his own. To the public at large indeed it is the same as a volume in manuscript. [S.T.C.]

[9] A misprint, George Watson suggests, for "apposite."

[10] This is effected either by giving to the one word a general, and to the other an exclusive use; as "to put on the back" and "to indorse;" or by an actual distinction of meanings as "naturalist," and "physician;" or by difference of relation as "I" and "Me;" (each of which the rustics of our different provinces still use in all the cases singular of the first personal pronoun). Even the mere difference, or corruption, in the *pronunciation* of the same word, if it have become general, will produce a new word with a distinct signification; thus "property" and "propriety;" the latter of which, even to the time of Charles II. was the *written* word for all the senses of both. Thus too "mister" and "master" both hasty pronunciations of the same word "magister," "mistress," and "miss," "if," and "give," &c. &c. There is a sort of *minim immortal* among the animalcula infusoria which has

words originally of the same meaning, which the conflux of dialects had supplied to the more homogeneous languages, as the Greek and German: and which the same cause, joined with accidents of translation from original works of different countries, occasion in mixt languages like our own. The first and most important point to be proved is, that two conceptions perfectly distinct are confused under one and the same word, and (this done) to appropriate that word exclusively to one meaning, and the synonyme (should there be one) to the other. But if (as will be often the case in the arts and sciences) no synonyme exists, we must either invent or borrow a word. In the present instance the appropriation had already begun, and been legitimated in the derivative adjective: Milton had a highly *imaginative*, Cowley a very *fanciful* mind. If therefore I should succeed in establishing the actual existences of two faculties generally different, the nomenclature would be at once determined. To the faculty by which I had characterized Milton, we should confine the term *imagination;* while the other would be contra-distinguished as *fancy.* Now were it once fully ascertained, that this division is no less grounded in nature, than that of delirium from mania, or Otway's

> "Lutes, lobsters, seas of milk, and ships of amber,"

from Shakespear's

> "What! have his daughters brought him to this pass?"[11]

or from the preceding apostrophe to the elements; the theory of the fine arts, and of poetry in particular, could not, I thought, but derive some additional and important light. It would in its immediate effects furnish a torch of guidance to the philosophical critic; and ultimately to the poet himself. In energetic minds, truth soon changes by domestication into power; and from directing in the discrimination and appraisal of the product, becomes influencive in the production. To admire on principle, is the only way to imitate without loss of originality.

It has been already hinted, that metaphysics and psychology have

---

not naturally either birth, or death, absolute beginning, or absolute end: for at a certain period a small point appears on its back, which deepens and lengthens till the creature divides into two, and the same process recommences in each of the halves now become integral. This may be a fanciful, but it is by no means a bad emblem of the formation of words, and may facilitate the conception, how immense a nomenclature may be organized from a few simple sounds by rational beings in a social state. For each new application, or excitement of the same sound, will call forth a different sensation, which cannot but affect the pronunciation. The after recollection of the sound, without the same vivid sensation, will modify it still further; till at length all trace of the original likeness is worn away. [S.T.C.]

[11] Cf. *Venice Preserved* V.ii.151 (for "lobsters" read "laurels"); *King Lear* III.iv.65.

long been my hobby-horse. But to have a hobby-horse, and to be
vain of it, are so commonly found together, that they pass almost for
the same. I trust therefore, that there will be more good humour than
contempt, in the smile with which the reader chastises my self-
complacency, if I confess myself uncertain, whether the satisfaction
from the perception of a truth new to myself may not have been
rendered more poignant by the conceit, that it would be equally so to
the public. There was a time, certainly, in which I took some little
credit to myself, in the belief that I had been the first of my countrymen, who had pointed out the diverse meaning of which the two
terms were capable, and analyzed the faculties to which they should
be appropriated. Mr. W. Taylor's recent volume of synonimes I have
not yet seen;[12] but his specification of the terms in question has been
clearly shown to be both insufficient and erroneous by Mr. Wordsworth
in the preface added to the late collection of his "Lyrical Ballads and

[12] I ought to have added, with the exception of a single sheet which I
accidentally met with at the printers. Even from this scanty specimen, I
found it impossible to doubt the talent, or not to admire the ingenuity of
the author. That his distinctions were for the greater part unsatisfactory to
my mind, proves nothing against their accuracy; but it may possibly be
serviceable to him in case of a second edition, if I take this opportunity
of suggesting the query; whether he may not have been occasionally misled,
by having assumed, as to me he appeared to have done, the non-existence
of *any* absolute synonimes in our language? Now I cannot but think, that
there are many which remain for our posterity to distinguish and appropriate, and which I regard as so much reversionary wealth in our mother-
tongue. When two distinct meanings are confounded under one or more
words, (and such must be the case, as sure as our knowledge is progressive
and of course imperfect) erroneous consequences will be drawn, and what
is true in one sense of the word, will be affirmed as true in toto. Men of research startled by the consequences, seek in the things themselves (whether
in or out of the mind) for a knowledge of the fact, and having discovered
the difference, remove the equivocation either by the substitution of a new
word, or by the appropriation of one of the two or more words, that had
before been used promiscuously. When this distinction has been so natural-
ized and of such general currency, that the language itself does as it were
think for us (like the sliding rule which is the mechanic's safe substitute for
arithmetical knowledge) we then say, that it is evident to *common sense.*
Common sense, therefore, differs in different ages. What was born and
christened in the schools passes by degrees into the world at large, and
becomes the property of the market and the tea-table. At least I can discover no other meaning of the term, *common sense*, if it is to convey any
specific difference from sense and judgement in genere, and where it is not
used scholastically for the *universal reason.* Thus in the reign of Charles II.
the philosophic world was called to arms by the moral sophisms of Hobbs,
and the ablest writers exerted themselves in the detection of an error, which
a school-boy would now be able to confute by the mere recollection, that
compulsion and *obligation* conveyed two ideas perfectly disparate, and that
what appertained to the one, had been falsely transferred to the other by
a mere confusion of terms. [S.T.C. He refers to Thomas Hobbes, *On Liberty and Necessity,* 1654.]

other poems." The explanation which Mr. Wordsworth has himself given, will be found to differ from mine, chiefly perhaps, as our objects are different. It could scarcely indeed happen otherwise, from the advantage I have enjoyed of frequent conversation with him on a subject to which a poem of his own first directed my attention, and my conclusions concerning which, he had made more lucid to myself by many happy instances drawn from the operation of natural objects on the mind. But it was Mr. Wordsworth's purpose to consider the influences of fancy and imagination as they are manifested in poetry, and from the different effects to conclude their diversity in kind; while it is my object to investigate the seminal principle, and then from the kind to deduce the degree. My friend has drawn a masterly sketch of the branches with their *poetic* fruitage. I wish to add the trunk, and even the roots as far as they lift themselves above ground, and are visible to the naked eye of our common consciousness.

Yet even in this attempt I am aware, that I shall be obliged to draw more largely on the reader's attention, than so immethodical a miscellany can authorize; when in such a work (*the Ecclesiastical Polity*) of such a mind as Hooker's, the judicious author, though no less admirable for the perspicuity than for the port and dignity of his language; and though he wrote for men of learning in a learned age; saw nevertheless occasion to anticipate and guard against "complaints of obscurity," as often as he was to trace his subject "to the highest well-spring and fountain."[13] Which, (continues he) "because men are not accustomed to, the pains we take are more needful a great deal, than acceptable; and the matters we handle, seem by reason of newness (till the mind grow better acquainted with them) dark and intricate." I would gladly therefore spare both myself and others this labor, if I knew how without it to present an intelligible statement of my poetic creed; not as my *opinions,* which weigh for nothing, but as deductions from established premises conveyed in such a form, as is calculated either to effect a fundamental conviction, or to receive a fundamental confutation. If I may dare once more adopt the words of Hooker, "they, unto whom we shall seem tedious, are in no wise injured by us, because it is in their own hands to spare that labour, which they are not willing to endure." Those at least, let me be permitted to add, who have taken so much pains to render me ridiculous for a perversion of taste, and have supported the charge by attributing strange notions to me on no other authority than their own conjectures, owe it to themselves as well as to me not to refuse their attention to my own statement of the theory, which I *do* acknowledge; or shrink from the trouble of examining the grounds on which I rest it, or the arguments which I offer in its justification.

[13] Richard Hooker (c.1554–1600), *Of the Laws of Ecclesiastical Polity* I.i.2.

from CHAPTER XIII

The IMAGINATION then I consider either as primary, or secondary. The primary IMAGINATION I hold to be the living Power and prime Agent of all human Perception, and as a repetition in the finite mind of the eternal act of creation in the infinite I AM. The secondary I consider as an echo of the former, co-existing with the conscious will, yet still as identical with the primary in the *kind* of its agency, and differing only in *degree*, and in the *mode* of its operation. It dissolves, diffuses, dissipates, in order to re-create; or where this process is rendered impossible, yet still at all events it struggles to idealize and to unify. It is essentially *vital*, even as all objects (*as* objects) are essentially fixed and dead.

FANCY, on the contrary, has no other counters to play with, but fixities and definites. The Fancy is indeed no other than a mode of Memory emancipated from the order of time and space; and blended with, and modified by that empirical phenomenon of the will, which we express by the word CHOICE. But equally with the ordinary memory it must receive all its materials ready made from the law of association.

CHAPTER XIV

Occasion of the Lyrical Ballads, and the objects originally proposed — Preface to the second edition — The ensuing controversy, its causes and acrimony — Philosophic definitions of a poem and poetry with scholia.

During the first year that Mr. Wordsworth and I were neighbours, our conversations turned frequently on the two cardinal points of poetry, the power of exciting the sympathy of the reader by a faithful adherence to the truth of nature, and the power of giving the interest of novelty by the modifying colours of imagination. The sudden charm, which accidents of light and shade, which moon-light or sun-set diffused over a known and familiar landscape, appeared to represent the practicability of combining both. These are the poetry of nature. The thought suggested itself (to which of us I do not recollect) that a series of poems might be composed of two sorts. In the one, the incidents and agents were to be, in part at least, supernatural; and the excellence aimed at was to consist in the interesting of the affections by the dramatic truth of such emotions, as would naturally accompany such situations supposing them real. And real in *this* sense they have been to every human being who, from whatever source of delusion, has at any time believed himself under supernatural agency. For the second class, subjects were to be chosen from ordinary life; the characters and incidents were to be such, as will be found in every village and its vicinity, where there is a meditative and feeling mind to seek after them, or to notice them, when they present themselves.

In this idea originated the plan of the "Lyrical Ballads;" in which it was agreed, that my endeavours should be directed to persons and characters supernatural, or at least romantic; yet so as to transfer from our inward nature a human interest and a semblance of truth sufficient to procure for these shadows of imagination that willing suspension of disbelief for the moment, which constitutes poetic faith. Mr. Wordsworth, on the other hand, was to propose to himself as his object, to give the charm of novelty to things of every day, and to excite a feeling analogous to the supernatural, by awakening the mind's attention from the lethargy of custom, and directing it to the loveliness and the wonders of the world before us; an inexhaustible treasure, but for which in consequence of the film of familiarity and selfish solicitude we have eyes, yet see not, ears that hear not, and hearts that neither feel nor understand.

With this view I wrote the "Ancient Mariner," and was preparing among other poems, the "Dark Ladie," and the "Christabel," in which I should have more nearly realized my ideal, than I had done in my first attempt. But Mr. Wordsworth's industry had proved so much more successful, and the number of his poems so much greater, that my compositions, instead of forming a balance, appeared rather an interpolation of heterogeneous matter. Mr. Wordsworth added two or three poems written in his own character, in the impassioned, lofty, and sustained diction, which is characteristic of his genius. In this form the "Lyrical Ballads" were published; and were presented by him, as an *experiment*, whether subjects, which from their nature rejected the usual ornaments and extra-colloquial style of poems in general, might not be so managed in the language of ordinary life as to produce the pleasureable interest, which it is the peculiar business of poetry to impart. To the second edition he added a preface of considerable length; in which notwithstanding some passages of apparently a contrary import, he was understood to contend for the extension of this style to poetry of all kinds, and to reject as vicious and indefensible all phrases and forms of style that were not included in what he (unfortunately, I think, adopting an equivocal expression) called the language of *real* life. From this preface, prefixed to poems in which it was impossible to deny the presence of original genius, however mistaken its direction might be deemed, arose the whole long continued controversy. For from the conjunction of perceived power with supposed heresy I explain the inveteracy and in some instances, I grieve to say, the acrimonious passions, with which the controversy has been conducted by the assailants.

Had Mr. Wordsworth's poems been the silly, the childish things, which they were for a long time described as being; had they been really distinguished from the compositions of other poets merely by meanness of language and inanity of thought; had they indeed contained nothing more than what is found in the parodies and pretended imitations of them; they must have sunk at once, a dead weight, into the slough of oblivion, and have dragged the preface along with them. But year after year increased the number of Mr. Wordsworth's admirers. They were found too not in the lower classes of the reading public, but chiefly among young men of strong sensibility and meditative minds; and their admiration (inflamed perhaps in some degree by opposition) was distinguished by its intensity, I might almost say, by its *religious* fervour. These facts, and the intellectual energy of the author, which was more or less consciously felt, where it was outwardly and even boisterously denied, meeting with sentiments of aversion to his opinions, and of alarm at their consequences, produced an eddy of criticism, which would of itself have borne up the poems by the violence, with which it whirled them round and round. With many parts of this preface in the sense attributed to them and which the words undoubtedly seem to authorise, I never concurred; but on the contrary objected to them as erroneous in principle, and as contradictory (in appearance at least) both to other parts of the same preface, and to the author's own practice in the greater number of the poems themselves. Mr. Wordsworth in his recent collection has, I find, degraded this prefatory disquisition to the end of his second volume, to be read or not at the reader's choice. But he has not, as far as I can discover, announced any change in his poetic creed. At all events, considering it as the source of a controversy, in which I have been honored more, than I deserve, by the frequent conjunction of my name with his, I think it expedient to declare once for all, in what points I coincide with his opinions, and in what points I altogether differ. But in order to render myself intelligible I must previously, in as few words as possible, explain my ideas, first, of a POEM; and secondly, of POETRY itself, in *kind,* and in *essence.*

The office of philosophical *disquisition* consists in just *distinction;* while it is the priviledge of the philosopher to preserve himself constantly aware, that distinction is not division. In order to obtain adequate notions of any truth, we must intellectually separate its distinguishable parts; and this is the technical *process* of philosophy. But having so done, we must then restore them in our conceptions to the unity, in which they actually co-exist; and this is the *result* of philosophy. A poem contains the same elements as a prose composition; the difference therefore must consist in a different combination of them, in consequence of a different object proposed. According to the difference of the object will be the difference of the combination. It is possible, that the object may be merely to facilitate the recollection of any given facts or observations by artificial arrangement; and the composition will be a poem, merely because it is distinguished from prose by metre, or by rhyme, or by both conjointly. In this, the lowest sense, a man might attribute the name of a poem to the well known enumeration of the days in the several months;

> "Thirty days hath September,
> April, June, and November, &c."

and others of the same class and purpose. And as a particular pleasure is found in anticipating the recurrence of sounds and quantities, all compositions that have this charm superadded, whatever be their contents, *may* be entitled poems.

So much for the superficial *form*. A difference of object and contents supplies an additional ground of distinction. The immediate purpose may be the communication of truths; either of truth absolute and demonstrable, as in works of science; or of facts experienced and recorded, as in history. Pleasure, and that of the highest and most permanent kind, may *result* from the *attainment* of the end; but it is not itself the immediate end. In other works the communication of pleasure may be the immediate purpose; and though truth, either moral or intellectual, ought to be the *ultimate* end, yet this will distinguish the character of the author, not the class to which the work belongs. Blest indeed is that state of society, in which the immediate purpose would be baffled by the perversion of the proper ultimate end; in which no charm of diction or imagery could exempt the Bathyllus even of an Anacreon, or the Alexis of Virgil, from disgust and aversion![1]

But the communication of pleasure may be the immediate object of a work not metrically composed; and that object may have been in a high degree attained, as in novels and romances. Would then the mere superaddition of metre, with or without rhyme, entitle *these* to the name of poems? The answer is, that nothing can permanently please, which does not contain in itself the reason why it is so, and not otherwise. If metre be superadded, all other parts must be made consonant with it. They must be such, as to justify the perpetual and distinct attention to each part, which an exact correspondent recurrence of accent and sound are calculated to excite. The final definition then, so deduced, may be thus worded. A poem is that species of composition, which is opposed to works of science, by proposing for its *immediate* object pleasure, not truth; and from all other species (having *this* object in common with it) it is discriminated by proposing to itself such delight from the *whole*, as is compatible with a distinct gratification from each component *part*.

Controversy is not seldom excited in consequence of the disputants attaching each a different meaning to the same word; and in few

[1] Bathyllus and Alexis: beautiful youths celebrated in Anacreon's Ode 29 and Virgil's Eclogue 2.

instances has this been more striking, than in disputes concerning the present subject. If a man chooses to call every composition a poem, which is rhyme, or measure, or both, I must leave his opinion uncontroverted. The distinction is at least competent to characterize the writer's intention. If it were subjoined, that the whole is likewise entertaining or affecting, as a tale, or as a series of interesting reflections, I of course admit this as another fit ingredient of a poem, and an additional merit. But if the definition sought for be that of a *legitimate* poem, I answer, it must be one, the parts of which mutually support and explain each other; all in their proportion harmonizing with, and supporting the purpose and known influences of metrical arrangement. The philosophic critics of all ages coincide with the ultimate judgement of all countries, in equally denying the praises of a just poem, on the one hand, to a series of striking lines or distichs, each of which absorbing the whole attention of the reader to itself disjoins it from its context, and makes it a separate whole, instead of an harmonizing part; and on the other hand, to an unsustained composition, from which the reader collects rapidly the general result unattracted by the component parts. The reader should be carried forward, not merely or chiefly by the mechanical impulse of curiosity, or by a restless desire to arrive at the final solution; but by the pleasureable activity of mind excited by the attractions of the journey itself. Like the motion of a serpent, which the Egyptians made the emblem of intellectual power; or like the path of sound through the air; at every step he pauses and half recedes, and from the retrogressive movement collects the force which again carries him onward. Precipitandus est *liber* spiritus, says Petronius Arbiter most happily.[2] The epithet, *liber*, here balances the preceding verb; and it is not easy to conceive more meaning condensed in fewer words.

But if this should be admitted as a satisfactory character of a poem, we have still to seek for a definition of poetry. The writings of PLATO, and Bishop TAYLOR, and the Theoria Sacra of BURNET, furnish undeniable proofs that poetry of the highest kind may exist without metre, and even without the contradistinguishing objects of a poem.[3] The first chapter of Isaiah (indeed a very large proportion of the whole book) is poetry in the most emphatic sense; yet it would be not less irrational than strange to assert, that pleasure, and not truth, was the immediate object of the prophet. In short, whatever *specific* import we attach to the word, poetry, there will be found involved in it, as a necessary consequence, that a poem of any length neither can be, or ought to be, all poetry. Yet if an harmonious whole is to be produced, the remaining parts must be preserved *in keeping* with the poetry; and this can be no otherwise effected than by such a studied selection and

[2] "The free spirit must be impelled forward" — *Satyricon* 118.
[3] Jeremy Taylor (1613–67); Thomas Burnet, *Telluris theoria sacra*, 1681–89, translated as *The Sacred Theory of the Earth*, 1684–89.

artificial arrangement, as will partake of *one*, though not a *peculiar*, property of poetry. And this again can be no other than the property of exciting a more continuous and equal attention, than the language of prose aims at, whether colloquial or written.

My own conclusions on the nature of poetry, in the strictest use of the word, have been in part anticipated in the preceding disquisition on the fancy and imagination. What is poetry? is so nearly the same question with, what is a poet? that the answer to the one is involved in the solution of the other. For it is a distinction resulting from the poetic genius itself, which sustains and modifies the images, thoughts, and emotions of the poet's own mind. The poet, described in *ideal* perfection, brings the whole soul of man into activity, with the subordination of its faculties to each other, according to their relative worth and dignity. He diffuses a tone, and spirit of unity, that blends, and (as it were) *fuses*, each into each, by that synthetic and magical power, to which we have exclusively appropriated the name of imagination. This power, first put in action by the will and understanding, and retained under their irremissive, though gentle and unnoticed, controul (*laxis effertur habenis*)[4] reveals itself in the balance or reconciliation of opposite or discordant qualities: of sameness, with difference; of the general, with the concrete; the idea, with the image; the individual, with the representative; the sense of novelty and freshness, with old and familiar objects; a more than usual state of emotion, with more than usual order; judgement ever awake and steady self-possession, with enthusiasm and feeling profound or vehement; and while it blends and harmonizes the natural and the artificial, still subordinates art to nature; the manner to the matter; and our admiration of the poet to our sympathy with the poetry. "Doubtless," as Sir John Davies observes of the soul (and his words may with slight alteration be applied, and even more appropriately to the poetic IMAGINATION.)

> "Doubtless this could not be, but that she turns
> Bodies to spirit by sublimation strange,
> As fire converts to fire the things it burns,
> As we our food into our nature change.
>
> From their gross matter she abstracts their forms,
> And draws a kind of quintessence from things;
> Which to her proper nature she transforms
> To bear them light, on her celestial wings.
>
> Thus does she, when from individual states
> She doth abstract the universal kinds;
> Which then re-clothed in divers names and fates
> Steal access through our senses to our minds."[5]

[4] "borne forward on loose reins" — cf. Virgil, *Georgics* II.364.
[5] Altered from Davies, *Nosce Teipsum* (1599) IV.

Finally, GOOD SENSE is the BODY of poetic genius, FANCY its DRAPERY, MOTION its LIFE, and IMAGINATION the SOUL that is every where, and in each; and forms all into one graceful and intelligent whole.

CHAPTER XV

The specific symptoms of poetic power elucidated in a critical analysis of Shakspeare's Venus and Adonis, and Lucrece.[1]

In the application of these principles to purposes of practical criticism as employed in the appraisal of works more or less imperfect, I have endeavoured to discover what the qualities in a poem are, which may be deemed promises and specific symptoms of poetic power, as distinguished from general talent determined to poetic composition by accidental motives, by an act of the will, rather than by the inspiration of a genial and productive nature. In this investigation, I could not, I thought, do better, than keep before me the earliest work of the greatest genius, that perhaps human nature has yet produced, our *myriad-minded*[2] Shakespear. I mean the "Venus and Adonis," and the "Lucrece;" works which give at once strong promises of the strength, and yet obvious proofs of the immaturity, of his genius. From these I abstracted the following marks, as characteristics of original poetic genius in general.

1. In the "Venus and Adonis," the first and most obvious excellence is the perfect sweetness of the versification; its adaptation to the subject; and the power displayed in varying the march of the words without passing into a loftier and more majestic rhythm, than was demanded by the thoughts, or permitted by the propriety of preserving a sense of melody predominant. The delight in richness and sweetness of sound, even to a faulty excess, if it be evidently original, and not the result of an easily imitable mechanism, I regard as a highly favorable promise in the compositions of a young man. "The man that hath not music in his soul"[3] can indeed never be a genuine poet. Imagery (even taken from nature, much more when transplanted from books, as travels, voyages, and works of natural history) affecting incidents; just thoughts; interesting personal or domestic feelings; and with these

---

[1] Chapter XV is based on a lecture Coleridge gave at Scot's Corporation Hall, London, on November 28, 1811.

[2] Ἀνὴρ μυριόνους, a phrase which I have borrowed from a Greek monk, who applies it to a Patriarch of Constantinople. I might have said, that I have *reclaimed*, rather than borrowed it: for it seems to belong to Shakespear, de jure singulari, et ex privilegio naturae. [S.T.C. Naucratius on Theodorus Studites, discussed by Kathleen Coburn in *The Notebooks of Samuel Taylor Coleridge*, London, 1957, I, 1070n.]

[3] Cf. *Merchant of Venice* V.i.83.

the art of their combination or intertexture in the form of a poem; may all by incessant effort be acquired as a trade, by a man of talents and much reading, who, as I once before observed, has mistaken an intense desire of poetic reputation for a natural poetic genius; the love of the arbitrary end for a possession of the peculiar means. But the sense of musical delight, with the power of producing it, is a gift of imagination; and this together with the power of reducing multitude into unity of effect, and modifying a series of thoughts by some one predominant thought or feeling, may be cultivated and improved, but can never be learnt. It is in these that "Poeta nascitur non fit."[4]

2. A second promise of genius is the choice of subjects very remote from the private interests and circumstances of the writer himself. At least I have found, that where the subject is taken immediately from the author's personal sensations and experiences, the excellence of a particular poem is but an equivocal mark, and often a fallacious pledge, of genuine poetic power. We may perhaps remember the tale of the statuary, who had acquired considerable reputation for the legs of his goddesses, though the rest of the statue accorded but indifferently with ideal beauty; till his wife elated by her husband's praises, modestly acknowledged, that she herself had been his constant model. In the Venus and Adonis, this proof of poetic power exists even to excess. It is throughout as if a superior spirit more intuitive, more intimately conscious, even than the characters themselves, not only of every outward look and act, but of the flux and reflux of the mind in all its subtlest thoughts and feelings, were placing the whole before our view; himself meanwhile unparticipating in the passions, and actuated only by that pleasurable excitement, which had resulted from the energetic fervor of his own spirit in so vividly exhibiting, what it had so accurately and profoundly contemplated. I think, I should have conjectured from these poems, that even then the great instinct, which impelled the poet to the drama, was secretly working in him, prompting him by a series and never broken chain of imagery, always vivid and because unbroken, often minute; by the highest effort of the picturesque in words, of which words are capable, higher perhaps than was ever realized by any other poet, even Dante not excepted; to provide a substitute for that visual language, that constant intervention and running comment by tone, look and gesture, which in his dramatic works he was entitled to expect from the players. His "Venus and Adonis" seem at once the characters themselves, and the whole representation of those characters by the most consummate actors. You seem to be *told* nothing, but to see and hear every thing. Hence it is, that from the perpetual activity of attention required on the part of the reader; from the rapid flow, the quick change, and the playful nature of the thoughts and images; and above all from the alienation, and, if I may hazard such an expression, the utter *aloofness* of the

[4] A poet is born, not made.

poet's own feelings, from those of which he is at once the painter and the analyst; that though the very subject cannot but detract from the pleasure of a delicate mind, yet never was poem less dangerous on a moral account. Instead of doing as Ariosto, and as, still more offensively, Wieland has done, instead of degrading and deforming passion into appetite, the trials of love into the struggles of concupiscence; Shakspeare has here represented the animal impulse itself, so as to preclude all sympathy with it, by dissipating the reader's notice among the thousand outward images, and now beautiful, now fanciful circumstances, which form its dresses and its scenery; or by diverting our attention from the main subject by those frequent witty or profound reflections, which the poet's ever active mind has deduced from, or connected with, the imagery and the incidents. The reader is forced into too much action to sympathize with the merely passive of our nature. As little can a mind thus roused and awakened be brooded on by mean and indistinct emotion, as the low, lazy mist can creep upon the surface of a lake, while a strong gale is driving it onward in waves and billows.

3. It has been before observed, that images however beautiful, though faithfully copied from nature, and as accurately represented in words, do not of themselves characterize the poet. They become proofs of original genius only as far as they are modified by a predominant passion; or by associated thoughts or images awakened by that passion; or when they have the effect of reducing multitude to unity, or succession to an instant; or lastly, when a human and intellectual life is transferred to them from the poet's own spirit,

"Which shoots its being through earth, sea, and air."[5]

In the two following lines for instance, there is nothing objectionable, nothing which would preclude them from forming, in their proper place, part of a descriptive poem:

"Behold yon row of pines, that shorn and bow'd
Bend from the sea-blast, seen at twilight eve."

But with the small alteration of rhythm, the same words would be equally in their place in a book of topography, or in a descriptive tour. The same image will rise into a semblance of poetry if thus conveyed:

"Yon row of bleak and visionary pines,
By twilight-glimpse discerned, mark! how they flee
From the fierce sea-blast, all their tresses wild
Streaming before them."

I have given this as an illustration, by no means as an instance, of that particular excellence which I had in view, and in which Shakspeare

[5] Cf. Coleridge, *France: An Ode* 100.

even in his earliest, as in his latest works, surpasses all other poets.
It is by this, that he still gives a dignity and a passion to the objects
which he presents. Unaided by any previous excitement, they burst
upon us at once in life and in power.

> "Full many a glorious morning have I seen
> *Flatter* the mountain tops with sovereign eye."
>   Shakspeare's Sonnet 33rd.

> "Not mine own fears, nor the prophetic soul
> Of the wide world dreaming on things to come —
>
> ❖ ❖ ❖ ❖ ❖ ❖ ❖ ❖ ❖ ❖ ❖ ❖ ❖ ❖ ❖ ❖ ❖
> ❖ ❖ ❖ ❖ ❖ ❖ ❖ ❖ ❖ ❖ ❖ ❖ ❖ ❖ ❖ ❖
>
> The mortal moon hath her eclipse endur'd,
> And the sad augurs mock their own presage;
> Incertainties now crown themselves assur'd,
> And Peace proclaims olives of endless age.
> Now with the drops of this most balmy time
> My Love looks fresh: and DEATH to me subscribes!
> Since spite of him, I'll live in this poor rhyme,
> While he insults o'er dull and speechless tribes.
> And thou in this shalt find thy monument,
> When tyrant's crests, and tombs of brass are spent.
>   Sonnet 107.

As of higher worth, so doubtless still more characteristic of poetic
genius does the imagery become, when it moulds and colors itself to
the circumstances, passion, or character, present and foremost in the
mind. For unrivalled instances of this excellence, the reader's own
memory will refer him to the LEAR, OTHELLO, in short to which not
of the *"great, ever living, dead man's"* dramatic works? Inopem me
copia fecit.[6] How true it is to nature, he has himself finely expressed
in the instance of love in Sonnet 98. . . .[7]

4. The last character I shall mention, which would prove indeed but
little, except as taken conjointly with the former; yet without which the
former could scarce exist in a high degree, and (even if this were
possible) would give promises only of transitory flashes and a meteoric
power; is DEPTH, and ENERGY of THOUGHT. No man was ever yet a
great poet, without being at the same time a profound philosopher.
For poetry is the blossom and the fragrancy of all human knowledge,
human thoughts, human passions, emotions, language. In Shakspeare's
poems, the creative power, and the intellectual energy wrestle as in a
war embrace. Each in its excess of strength seems to threaten the extinction of the other. At length, in the DRAMA they were reconciled,

[6] "The plenty makes me poor" — Ovid, *Metamorphosis* III.466.

[7] Sonnet 98 ("From you have I been absent in the spring"), *Venus and
Adonis* 811–816, and a version of Aristophanes, *Frogs* 96–97, are here
omitted.

and fought each with its shield before the breast of the other. Or like two rapid streams, that at their first meeting within narrow and rocky banks mutually strive to repel each other, and intermix reluctantly and in tumult; but soon finding a wider channel and more yielding shores blend, and dilate, and flow on in one current and with one voice. The Venus and Adonis did not perhaps allow the display of the deeper passions. But the story of Lucretia seems to favor, and even demand their intensest workings. And yet we find in *Shakspeare*'s management of the tale neither pathos, nor any other *dramatic* quality. There is the same minute and faithful imagery as in the former poem, in the same vivid colours, inspirited by the same impetuous vigour of thought, and diverging and contracting with the same activity of the assimilative and of the modifying faculties; and with a yet larger display, a yet wider range of knowledge and reflection; and lastly, with the same perfect dominion, often *domination*, over the whole world of language. What then shall we say? even this; that Shakspeare, no mere child of nature; no automaton of genius; no passive vehicle of inspiration possessed by the spirit, not possessing it; first studied patiently, meditated deeply, understood minutely, till knowledge become habitual and intuitive wedded itself to his habitual feelings, and at length gave birth to that stupendous power, by which he stands alone, with no equal or second in his own class; to that power, which seated him on one of the two glory-smitten summits of the poetic mountain, with Milton as his compeer not rival. While the former darts himself forth, and passes into all the forms of human character and passion, the one Proteus of the fire and the flood; the other attracts all forms and things to himself, into the unity of his own IDEAL. All things and modes of action shape themselves anew in the being of MILTON; while SHAKSPEARE becomes all things, yet for ever remaining himself. O what great men hast thou not produced, England! my country! truly indeed —

> Must *we* be free or die, who speak the tongue,
> Which SHAKSPEARE spake; the faith and morals hold,
> Which MILTON held. In every thing we are sprung
> Of earth's first blood, have titles manifold!
>
> WORDSWORTH.[8]

from CHAPTER XVII

Examination of the tenets peculiar to Mr. Wordsworth — Rustic life (above all, low and rustic life) especially unfavorable to the formation of a human diction — The best parts of language

[8] Cf. Sonnet, "It is not to be thought of that the Flood" 11–14.

the product of philosophers, not clowns or shepherds — Poetry
essentially ideal and generic — The language of Milton as
much the language of real life, yea, incomparably more so than
that of the cottager.

As far then as Mr. Wordsworth in his preface contended, and most
ably contended, for a reformation in our poetic diction, as far as he
has evinced the truth of passion, and the *dramatic* propriety of those
figures and metaphors in the original poets, which stript of their
justifying reasons, and converted into mere artifices of connection or
ornament, constitute the characteristic falsity in the poetic style of the
moderns; and as far as he has, with equal acuteness and clearness,
pointed out the process in which this change was effected, and the
resemblances between that state into which the reader's mind is
thrown by the pleasureable confusion of thought from an unaccustomed
train of words and images; and that state which is induced by the
natural language of empassioned feeling; he undertook a useful task,
and deserves all praise, both for the attempt and for the execution.
The provocations to this remonstrance in behalf of truth and nature
were still of perpetual recurrence before and after the publication of
this preface. I cannot likewise but add, that the comparison of such
poems of merit, as have been given to the public within the last ten
or twelve years, with the majority of those produced previously to the
appearance of that preface, leave no doubt on my mind, that Mr.
Wordsworth is fully justified in believing his efforts to have been by
no means ineffectual. Not only in the verses of those who have professed their admiration of his genius, but even of those who have
distinguished themselves by hostility to his theory, and depreciation of
his writings, are the impressions of his principles plainly visible. It is
possible, that with these principles others may have been blended,
which are not equally evident; and some which are unsteady and
subvertible from the narrowness or imperfection of their basis. But
it is more than possible, that these errors of defect or exaggeration, by
kindling and feeding the controversy, may have conduced not only to
the wider propagation of the accompanying truths, but that by their
frequent presentation to the mind in an excited state, they may have
won for them a more permanent and practical result. A man will
borrow a part from his opponent the more easily, if he feels himself
justified in continuing to reject a part. While there remain important
points in which he can still feel himself in the right, in which he still
finds firm footing for continued resistance, he will gradually adopt
those opinions, which were the least remote from his own convictions,
as not less congruous with his own theory, than with that which he
reprobates. In like manner with a kind of instinctive prudence, he will
abandon by little and little his weakest posts, till at length he seems to
forget that they had ever belonged to him, or affects to consider them

at most as accidental and "petty annexments,"[1] the removal of which leaves the citadel unhurt and unendangered.

My own differences from certain supposed parts of Mr. Wordsworth's theory ground themselves on the assumption, that his words had been rightly interpreted, as purporting that the proper diction for poetry in general consists altogether in a language taken, with due exceptions, from the mouths of men in real life, a language which actually constitutes the natural conversation of men under the influence of natural feelings. My objection is, first, that in *any* sense this rule is applicable only to *certain* classes of poetry; secondly, that even to these classes it is not applicable, except in such a sense, as hath never by any one (as far as I know or have read) been denied or doubted; and lastly, that as far as, and in that degree in which it is *practicable*, yet as a *rule* it is useless, if not injurious, and therefore either need not, or ought not to be practised. The poet informs his reader, that he had generally chosen *low and rustic* life; but not *as* low and rustic, or in order to repeat that pleasure of doubtful moral effect, which persons of elevated rank and of superior refinement oftentimes derive from a happy *imitation* of the rude unpolished manners and discourse of their inferiors. For the pleasure so derived may be traced to three exciting causes. The first is the naturalness, in *fact*, of the things represented. The second is the apparent naturalness of the *representation*, as raised and qualified by an imperceptible infusion of the author's own knowledge and talent, which infusion does, indeed, constitute it an *imitation* as distinguished from a mere *copy*. The third cause may be found in the reader's conscious feeling of his superiority awakened by the contrast presented to him; even as for the same purpose the kings and great barons of yore retained, sometimes *actual* clowns and fools, but more frequently shrewd and witty fellows in that *character*. These, however, were not Mr. Wordsworth's objects. *He* chose low and rustic life, "because in that condition the essential passions of the heart find a better soil, in which they can attain their maturity, are less under restraint, and speak a plainer and more emphatic language; because in that condition of life our elementary feelings coexist in a state of greater simplicity, and consequently may be more accurately contemplated, and more forcibly communicated; because the manners of rural life germinate from those elementary feelings; and from the necessary character of rural occupations are more easily comprehended, and are more durable; and lastly, because in that condition the passions of men are incorporated with the beautiful and permanent forms of nature."

Now it is clear to me, that in the most interesting of the poems, in which the author is more or less dramatic, as the "Brothers," "Michael," "Ruth," the "Mad Mother," &c. the persons introduced are by no means taken *from low or rustic life* in the common acceptation of those words;

[1] Cf. *Hamlet* III.iii.21.

and it is not less clear, that the sentiments and language, as far as they can be conceived to have been really transferred from the minds and conversation of such persons, are attributable to causes and circumstances not necessarily connected with "their occupations and abode." The thoughts, feelings, language, and manners of the shepherd-farmers in the vales of Cumberland and Westmoreland, as far as they are actually adopted in those poems, may be accounted for from causes, which will and do produce the same results in *every* state of life, whether in town or country. As the two principal I rank that INDE-PENDANCE, which raises a man above servitude, or daily toil for the profit of others, yet not above the necessity of industry and a frugal simplicity of domestic life; and the accompanying unambitious, but solid and religious EDUCATION, which has rendered few books familiar, but the bible, and the liturgy or hymn book. To this latter cause, indeed, which is so far *accidental,* that it is the blessing of particular countries and a particular age, not the product of particular places or employments, the poet owes the shew of probability, that his personages might really feel, think, and talk with any tolerable resemblance to his representation. It is an excellent remark of Dr. Henry More's (Enthusiasmus triumphatus, Sec. xxxv) that "a man of confined education, but of good parts, by constant reading of the bible will naturally form a more winning and commanding rhetoric than those that are learned; the intermixture of tongues and of artificial phrases debasing *their* style."

It is, moreover, to be considered that to the formation of healthy feelings, and a reflecting mind, *negations* involve impediments not less formidable, than sophistication and vicious intermixture. I am convinced, that for the human soul to prosper in rustic life, a certain vantage-ground is pre-requisite. It is not every man, that is likely to be improved by a country life or by country labours. Education, or original sensibility, or both, must pre-exist, if the changes, forms, and incidents of nature are to prove a sufficient stimulant. And where these are not sufficient, the mind contracts and hardens by want of stimulants; and the man becomes selfish, sensual, gross, and hard-hearted. Let the management of the POOR LAWS in Liverpool, Manchester, or Bristol be compared with the ordinary dispensation of the poor rates in agricultural villages, where the *farmers* are the overseers and guardians of the poor. If my own experience have not been particularly unfortunate, as well as that of the many respectable country clergymen with whom I have conversed on the subject, the result would engender more than scepticism concerning the desirable influences of low and rustic life in and for itself. Whatever may be concluded on the other side, from the stronger local attachments and enterprizing spirit of the Swiss, and other mountaineers, applies to a particular mode of pastoral life, under forms of property, that permit and beget manners truly republican, not to rustic life in general, or to the absence of artificial cultivation. On the contrary the mountaineers, whose manners have been so often eulogized, are in general better educated and greater readers than men of equal rank elsewhere. But where this is not the case, as among the peasantry of North Wales, the ancient mountains, with all their terrors and all their glories, are pictures to the blind, and music to the deaf.

I should not have entered so much into detail upon this passage, but here seems to be the point, to which all the lines of difference converge as to their source and centre. (I mean, as far as, and in whatever respect, my poetic creed *does* differ from the doctrines promulged in this preface.) I adopt with full faith the principle of Aristotle, that poetry as poetry is essentially[2] *ideal,* that it avoids and excludes all *accident;* that its apparent individualities of rank, character, or occupation must be *representative* of a class; and that the *persons* of poetry must be clothed with *generic* attributes, with the *common* attributes of the class; not with such as one gifted individual might *possibly* possess, but such as from his situation it is most probable before-hand, that he *would* possess. If my premises are right, and my deductions legitimate, it follows that there can be no *poetic* medium between the swains of Theocritus and those of an imaginary golden age.

The characters of the vicar and the shepherd-mariner in the poem of the "BROTHERS," those of the shepherd of Green-head Gill in the

---

[2] Say not that I am recommending abstractions, for these class-characteristics which constitute the instructiveness of a character, are so modified and particularized in each person of the Shaksperian Drama, that life itself does not excite more distinctly that sense of individuality which belongs to real existence. Paradoxical as it may sound, one of the essential properties of Geometry is not less essential to dramatic excellence; and Aristotle has accordingly required of the poet an involution of the universal in the individual. The chief differences are, that in Geometry it is the universal truth, which is uppermost in the consciousness; in poetry the individual form, in which the truth is clothed. With the ancients, and not less with the elder dramatists of England and France, both comedy and tragedy were considered as kinds of poetry. They neither sought in comedy to make us laugh merely; much less to make us laugh by wry faces, accidents of jargon, *slang* phrases for the day, or the clothing of common-place morals in metaphors drawn from the shops or mechanic occupations of their characters. Nor did they condescend in tragedy to wheedle away the applause of the spectators, by representing before them fac-similies of their own mean selves in all their existing meanness, or to work on their sluggish sympathies by a pathos not a whit more respectable than the maudlin tears of drunkenness. Their tragic scenes were meant to *affect* us indeed; but yet within the bounds of pleasure, and in union with the activity both of our understanding and imagination. They wished to transport the mind to a sense of its possible greatness, and to implant the germs of that greatness, during the temporary oblivion of the worthless "thing we are," and of the peculiar state in which each man *happens* to be, suspending our individual recollections and lulling them to sleep amid the music of nobler thoughts. *Friend,* Pages 251, 252. [S.T.C. See Aristotle, *Poetics* IX.1–4.]

"Michael," have all the verisimilitude and representative quality, that the purposes of poetry can require. They are persons of a known and abiding class, and their manners and sentiments the natural product of circumstances common to the class. . . .

On the other hand, in the poems which are pitched at a lower note, as the "Harry Gill," "Idiot Boy," &c. the *feelings* are those of human nature in general; though the poet has judiciously laid the *scene* in the country, in order to place *himself* in the vicinity of interesting images, without the necessity of ascribing a sentimental perception of their beauty to the persons of his drama. In the "Idiot Boy," indeed, the mother's character is not so much a real and native product of a "situation where the essential passions of the heart find a better soil, in which they can attain their maturity and speak a plainer and more emphatic language," as it is an impersonation of an instinct abandoned by judgement. Hence the two following charges seem to me not wholly groundless: at least, they are the only plausible objections, which I have heard to that fine poem. The one is, that the author has not, in the poem itself, taken sufficient care to preclude from the reader's fancy the disgusting images of *ordinary, morbid idiocy,* which yet it was by no means his intention to represent. He has even by the "burr, burr, burr," uncounteracted by any preceding description of the boy's beauty, assisted in recalling them. The other is, that the idiocy of the *boy* is so evenly balanced by the folly of the *mother,* as to present to the general reader rather a laughable burlesque on the blindness of anile dotage, than an analytic display of maternal affection in its ordinary workings.

In the "Thorn," the poet himself acknowledges in a note the necessity of an introductory poem, in which he should have pourtrayed the character of the person from whom the words of the poem are supposed to proceed: a superstitious man moderately imaginative, of slow faculties and deep feelings, "a captain of a small trading vessel, for example, who being past the middle age of life, had retired upon an annuity, or small independent income, to some village or country town of which he was not a native, or in which he had not been accustomed to live. Such men having nothing to do become credulous and talkative from indolence." But in a poem, still more in a lyric poem (and the nurse in Shakspeare's Romeo and Juliet alone prevents me from extending the remark even to dramatic *poetry,* if indeed the Nurse itself can be deemed altogether a case in point) it is not possible to imitate truly a dull and garrulous discourser, without repeating the effects of dulness and garrulity. However this may be, I dare assert, that the parts (and these form the far larger portion of the whole) which might as well or still better have proceeded from the poet's own imagination, and have been spoken in his own character, are those which have given, and which will continue to give universal delight; and that the passages exclusively appropriate to the supposed narrator, such as the last couplet of the third stanza,[3] . . . are felt by many unprejudiced and unsophisticated hearts, as sudden and unpleasant sinkings from the height to which the poet had previously lifted them, and to which he again re-elevates both himself and his reader.

If then I am compelled to doubt the theory, by which the choice of *characters* was to be directed, not only *a priori*, from grounds of reason, but both from the few instances in which the poet himself *need* be supposed to have been governed by it, and from the comparative inferiority of those instances; still more must I hesitate in my assent to the sentence which immediately follows the former citation; and which I can neither admit as particular fact, or as general rule. "The language too of these men is adopted (purified indeed from what appears to be its real defects, from all lasting and rational causes of dislike or disgust) because such men hourly communicate with the best objects from which the best part of language is originally derived; and because, from their rank in society, and the sameness and narrow circle of their intercourse, being less under the action of social vanity, they convey their feelings and notions in simple and unelaborated expressions." To this I reply; that a rustic's language, purified from all provincialism and grossness, and so far re-constructed as to be made consistent with the rules of grammar (which are in essence no other than the laws of universal logic, applied to Psychological materials) will not differ from the language of any other man of common-sense, however learned or refined he may be, except as far as the notions, which the rustic has to convey, are fewer and more indiscriminate. This will become still clearer, if we add the consideration (equally important though less obvious) that the rustic, from the more imperfect development of his faculties, and from the lower state of their cultivation, aims almost solely to convey *insulated facts*, either those of his scanty experience or his traditional belief; while the educated man chiefly seeks to discover and express those *connections* of things, or those relative *bearings* of fact to fact, from which some more or less general law is deducible. For *facts* are valuable to a wise man, chiefly as they lead to the discovery of the indwelling *law*, which is the true *being* of things, the sole solution of their modes of existence, and in the knowledge of which consists our dignity and our power.

As little can I agree with the assertion, that from the objects with which the rustic hourly communicates, the best part of language is formed. For first, if to communicate with an object implies such an acquaintance with it, as renders it capable of being discriminately reflected on; the distinct knowledge of an uneducated rustic would

---

[3] "I've measured it from side to side;
 'Tis three feet long, and two feet wide."
[In the clauses omitted, Coleridge gives as examples other stanzas, which he quotes at length in footnotes.]

furnish a very scanty vocabulary. The few things, and modes of action, requisite for his bodily conveniences, would alone be individualized; while all the rest of nature would be expressed by a small number of confused, general terms. Secondly, I deny that the words and combinations of words derived from the objects, with which the rustic is familiar, whether with distinct or confused knowledge, can be justly said to form the *best* part of language. It is more than probable, that many classes of the brute creation possess discriminating sounds, by which they can convey to each other notices of such objects as concern their food, shelter, or safety. Yet we hesitate to call the aggregate of such sounds a language, otherwise than metaphorically. The best part of human language, properly so called, is derived from reflection on the acts of the mind itself. It is formed by a voluntary appropriation of fixed symbols to internal acts, to processes and results of imagination, the greater part of which have no place in the consciousness of uneducated man; though in civilized society, by imitation and passive remembrance of what they hear from their religious instructors and other superiors, the most uneducated share in the harvest which they neither sowed or reaped. If the history of the phrases in hourly currency among our peasants were traced, a person not previously aware of the fact would be surprized at finding so large a number, which three or four centuries ago were the exclusive property of the universities and the schools; and at the commencement of the Reformation had been transferred from the school to the pulpit, and thus gradually passed into common life. The extreme difficulty, and often the impossibility, of finding words for the simplest moral and intellectual processes in the languages of uncivilized tribes has proved perhaps the weightiest obstacle to the progress of our most zealous and adroit missionaries. Yet these tribes are surrounded by the same nature, as our peasants are; but in still more impressive forms; and they are, moreover, obliged to *particularize* many more of them. When therefore Mr. Wordsworth adds, "accordingly such a language" (meaning, as before, the language of rustic life purified from provincialism) "arising out of repeated experience and regular feelings is a more permanent, and a far more philosophical language, than that which is frequently substituted for it by poets, who think they are conferring honor upon themselves and their art in proportion as they indulge in arbitrary and capricious habits of expression;" it may be answered, that the language, which he has in view, can be attributed to rustics with no greater right, than the style of Hooker or Bacon to Tom Brown or Sir Roger L'Estrange.[4] Doubtless, if what is peculiar to each were omitted in each, the result must needs be the same. Further, that the poet, who uses an illogical diction, or a style fitted to excite only the low and changeable pleasure of wonder by means of ground-

[4] Brown (1663–1704) and L'Estrange (1616–1704), scurrilous writers of topical satire.

less novelty, substitutes a language of *folly* and *vanity*, not for that of the *rustic*, but for that of *good sense* and *natural feeling*.

Here let me be permitted to remind the reader, that the positions, which I controvert, are contained in the sentences — "*a selection of the* REAL *language of men;*" — "*the language of these men* (i. e. men in low and rustic life) *I propose to myself to imitate, and as far as possible, to adopt the very language of men.*" "*Between the language of prose and that of metrical composition, there neither is, nor can be any essential difference.*" It is against these exclusively, that my opposition is directed.

I object, in the very first instance, to an equivocation in the use of the word "real." Every man's language varies, according to the extent of his knowledge, the activity of his faculties, and the depth or quickness of his feelings. Every man's language has, first, its *individualities;* secondly, the common properties of the *class* to which he belongs; and thirdly, words and phrases of *universal* use. The language of Hooker, Bacon, Bishop Taylor, and Burke, differ from the common language of the learned class only by the superior number and novelty of the thoughts and relations which they had to convey. The language of Algernon Sidney differs not at all from that, which every well educated gentleman would wish to write, and (with due allowances for the undeliberateness, and less connected train, of thinking natural and proper to conversation) such as he would wish to talk.[5] Neither one or the other differ half as much from the general language of cultivated society, as the language of Mr. Wordsworth's homeliest composition differs from that of a common peasant. For "real" therefore, we must substitute *ordinary*, or *lingua communis*. And this, we have proved, is no more to be found in the phraseology of low and rustic life, than in that of any other class. Omit the peculiarities of each, and the result of course must be common to all. And assuredly the omissions and changes to be made in the language of rustics, before it could be transferred to any species of poem, except the drama or other professed imitation, are at least as numerous and weighty, as would be required in adapting to the same purpose the ordinary language of tradesmen and manufacturers. Not to mention, that the language so highly extolled by Mr. Wordsworth varies in every county, nay in every village, according to the accidental character of the clergyman, the existence or non-existence of schools; or even, perhaps, as the exciseman, publican, or barber happen to be, or not to be, zealous politicians, and readers of the weekly newspaper *pro bono publico*. Anterior to cultivation the lingua communis of every country, as Dante has well observed, exists every where in parts, and no where as a whole.[6]

Neither is the case rendered at all more tenable by the addition of the words, "*in a state of excitement.*" For the nature of a man's words,

[5] Sidney or Sydney (1622–83), *Discourses concerning Government,* 1698.
[6] *De vulgari eloquentia* I.xvi.

when he is strongly affected by joy, grief, or anger, must necessarily depend on the number and quality of the general truths, conceptions and images, and of the words expressing them, with which his mind had been previously stored. For the property of passion is not to *create;* but to set in increased activity. At least, whatever new connections of thoughts or images, or (which is equally, if not more than equally, the appropriate effect of strong excitement) whatever generalizations of truth or experience, the heat of passion may produce; yet the terms of their conveyance must have pre-existed in his former conversations, and are only collected and crowded together by the unusual stimulation. It is indeed very possible to adopt in a poem the unmeaning repetitions, habitual phrases, and other blank counters, which an unfurnished or confused understanding interposes at short intervals, in order to keep hold of his subject which is still slipping from him, and to give him time for recollection; or in mere aid of vacancy, as in the scanty companies of a country stage the same player pops backwards and forwards, in order to prevent the appearance of empty spaces, in the procession of Macbeth, or Henry VIIIth. But what assistance to the poet, or ornament to the poem, these can supply, I am at a loss to conjecture. Nothing assuredly can differ either in origin or in mode more widely from the *apparent* tautologies of intense and turbulent feeling, in which the passion is greater and of longer endurance, than to be exhausted or satisfied by a single representation of the image or incident exciting it. Such repetitions I admit to be a beauty of the highest kind; as illustrated by Mr. Wordsworth himself from the song of Deborah. *"At her feet he bowed, he fell, he lay down; at her feet he bowed, he fell; where he bowed, there he fell down dead."*[7]

from CHAPTER XXII

*   *   *   *   *

I cannot here enter into a detailed examination of Mr. Wordsworth's works; but I will attempt to give the main results of my own judgement, after an acquaintance of many years, and repeated perusals. And though, to appreciate the defects of a great mind it is necessary to understand previously its characteristic excellences, yet I have already expressed myself with sufficient fulness, to preclude most of the ill effects that might arise from my pursuing a contrary arrangement. I will therefore commence with what I deem the prominent *defects* of his poems hitherto published.

The first *characteristic, though only occasional* defect, which I appear to myself to find in these poems is the INCONSTANCY of the *style.* Under this name I refer to the sudden and unprepared transitions from lines or sentences of peculiar felicity (at all events striking and original) to a style, not only unimpassioned but undistinguished.

[7] Judges 5:27, quoted in a note to *The Thorn.*

He sinks too often and too abruptly to that style, which I should place in the second division of language, dividing it into the three species; *first,* that which is peculiar to poetry; *second,* that which is only proper in prose; and *third,* the neutral or common to both. . . .

The second defect I could generalize with tolerable accuracy, if the reader will pardon an uncouth and new coined word. There is, I should say, not seldom a *matter-of-factness* in certain poems. This may be divided into, *first,* a laborious minuteness and fidelity in the representation of objects, and their positions, as they appeared to the poet himself; *secondly,* the insertion of accidental circumstances, in order to the full explanation of his living characters, their dispositions and actions; which circumstances might be necessary to establish the probability of a statement in real life, where nothing is taken for granted by the hearer, but appear superfluous in poetry, where the reader is willing to believe for his own sake. To this *accidentality,* I object, as contravening the essence of poetry, which Aristotle pronounces to be σπουδαιότατον καὶ φιλοσοφικώτατον γενὸς,[1] the most intense, weighty and philosophical product of human art; adding, as the *reason,* that it is the most catholic and abstract. . . .

Third; an undue predilection for the *dramatic* form in certain poems, from which one or other of two evils result. Either the thoughts and diction are different from that of the poet, and then there arises an incongruity of style; or they are the same and indistinguishable, and then it presents a species of ventriloquism, where two are represented as talking, while in truth one man only speaks.

The fourth class of defects is closely connected with the former; but yet are such as arise likewise from an intensity of feeling disproportionate to *such* knowledge and value of the objects described, as can be fairly anticipated of men in general, even of the most cultivated classes; and with which therefore few only, and those few particularly circumstanced, can be supposed to sympathize: In this class, I comprize occasional prolixity, repetition, and an eddying instead of progression of thought. . . .

Fifth and last; thoughts and images too great for the subject. This is an approximation to what might be called *mental* bombast, as distinguished from verbal: for, as in the latter there is a disproportion of the expressions to the thoughts so in this there is a disproportion of thought to the circumstance and occasion. This, by the bye, is a fault of which none but a man of genius is capable. It is the awkwardness and strength of Hercules with the distaff of Omphale.[2]

It is a well known fact, that bright colours in motion both make and leave the strongest impressions on the eye. Nothing is more

[1] a kind more earnest and more philosophical (than history) — cf. Aristotle, *Poetics* IX.3.

[2] Omphale, queen of Lydia, took Hercules' lion-skin and club and set him to woman's work.

likely too, than that a vivid image or visual spectrum, thus originated, may become the link of association in recalling the feelings and images that had accompanied the original impression. But if we describe this in such lines, as

> "They flash upon that inward eye,
> Which is the bliss of solitude!"

in what words shall we describe the joy of retrospection, when the images and virtuous actions of a whole well-spent life, pass before that conscience which is indeed the *inward* eye: which is indeed *"the bliss of solitude?"* Assuredly we seem to sink most abruptly, not to say burlesquely, and almost as in a *medly* from this couplet to —

> "And then my heart with pleasure fills,
> And dances with the *daffodils*."[3] . . .

To these defects which, as appears by the extracts, are only occasional, I may oppose with far less fear of encountering the dissent of any candid and intelligent reader, the following (for the most part correspondent) excellencies. First, an austere purity of language both grammatically and logically; in short a perfect appropriateness of the words to the meaning. Of how high value I deem this, and how particularly estimable I hold the example at the present day, has been already stated: and in part too the reasons on which I ground both the moral and intellectual importance of habituating ourselves to a strict accuracy of expression. It is noticeable, how limited an acquaintance with the master-pieces of art will suffice to form a correct and even a sensitive taste, where none but master-pieces have been seen and admired: while on the other hand, the most correct notions, and the widest acquaintance with the works of excellence of all ages and countries, will not perfectly secure us against the contagious familiarity with the far more numerous offspring of tastelessness or of a perverted taste. If this be the case, as it notoriously is, with the arts of music and painting, much more difficult will it be, to avoid the infection of multiplied and daily examples in the practice of an art, which uses words, and words only, as its instruments. In poetry, in which every line, every phrase, may pass the ordeal of deliberation and deliberate choice, it is possible, and barely possible, to attain that ultimatum which I have ventured to propose as the infallible test of a blameless style; namely; its *untranslatableness* in words of the same language without injury to the meaning. Be it observed, however, that I include in the *meaning* of a word not only its correspondent object, but likewise all the associations which it recalls. For language is framed to convey not the object alone, but likewise the character, mood and intentions of the person who is representing it. . . .

The second characteristic excellence of Mr. W's work is: a cor-

[3] "I wandered lonely as a cloud" 21–24.

respondent weight and sanity of the Thoughts and Sentiments, — won, not from books; but — from the poet's own meditative observation. They are *fresh* and have the dew upon them. His muse, at least when in her strength of wing, and when she hovers aloft in her proper element,

> Makes audible a linked lay of truth,
> Of truth profound a sweet continuous lay,
> Not learnt, but native, her own natural notes!
>
> S. T. C.[4]

Even throughout his smaller poems there is scarcely one, which is not rendered valuable by some just and original reflection. . . .

Both in respect of this and of the former excellence, Mr. Wordsworth strikingly resembles Samuel Daniel, one of the golden writers of our golden Elizabethian age, now most causelessly neglected: Samuel Daniel, whose diction bears no mark of time, no distinction of age, which has been, and as long as our language shall last, will be so far the language of the to-day and for ever, as that it is more intelligible to us, than the transitory fashions of our own particular age. A similar praise is due to his sentiments. No frequency of perusal can deprive them of their freshness. For though they are brought into the full day-light of every reader's comprehension; yet are they drawn up from depths which few in any age are priviledged to visit, into which few in any age have courage or inclination to descend. If Mr. Wordsworth is not equally with Daniel alike intelligible to all readers of average understanding in all passages of his works, the comparative difficulty does not arise from the greater impurity of the ore, but from the nature and uses of the metal. A poem is not necessarily obscure, because it does not aim to be popular. It is enough, if a work be perspicuous to those for whom it is written, and,

> "Fit audience find, though few."[5] . . .

Third (and wherein he soars far above Daniel) the sinewy strength and originality of single lines and paragraphs: the frequent curiosa felicitas of his diction, of which I need not here give specimens, having anticipated them in a preceding page. This beauty, and as eminently characteristic of Wordsworth's poetry, his rudest assailants have felt themselves compelled to acknowledge and admire.

Fourth; the perfect truth of nature in his images and descriptions as taken immediately from nature, and proving a long and genial intimacy with the very spirit which gives the physiognomic expression to all the works of nature. Like a green field reflected in a calm and perfectly transparent lake, the image is distinguished from the reality

---

[4] *To William Wordsworth* 58–60.
[5] *Paradise Lost* VII.31.

only by its greater softness and lustre. Like the moisture or the polish on a pebble, genius neither distorts nor false-colours its objects; but on the contrary brings out many a vein and many a tint, which escape the eye of common observation, thus raising to the rank of gems, what had been often kicked away by the hurrying foot of the traveller on the dusty high road of custom. . . .

Fifth: a meditative pathos, a union of deep and subtle thought with sensibility; a sympathy with man as man; the sympathy indeed of a contemplator, rather than a fellow-sufferer or co-mate, (*spectator, haud particeps*)[6] but of a contemplator, from whose view no difference of rank conceals the sameness of the nature; no injuries of wind or weather, of toil, or even of ignorance, wholly disguise the human face divine. The superscription and the image of the Creator still remain legible to *him* under the dark lines, with which guilt or calamity had cancelled or cross-barred it. Here the man and the poet lose and find themselves in each other, the one as glorified, the latter as substantiated. In this mild and philosophic pathos, Wordsworth appears to me without a compeer. Such he *is:* so he *writes.* . . .

Last, and pre-eminently I challenge for this poet the gift of IMAGINATION in the highest and strictest sense of the word. In the play of *Fancy*, Wordsworth, to my feelings, is not always graceful, and sometimes *recondite.* The *likeness* is occasionally too strange, or demands too peculiar a point of view, or is such as appears the creature of predetermined research, rather than spontaneous presentation. Indeed his fancy seldom displays itself, as mere and unmodified fancy. But in imaginative power, he stands nearest of all modern writers to Shakespear and Milton; and yet in a kind perfectly unborrowed and his own. To employ his own words, which are at once an instance and an illustration, he does indeed to all thoughts and to all objects—

"—————————— add the gleam,
The light that never was on sea or land,
The consecration, and the poet's dream."[7]

. . . What Mr. Wordsworth *will* produce, it is not for me to prophesy: but I could pronounce with the liveliest convictions what he is capable of producing. It is the FIRST GENUINE PHILOSOPHIC POEM. . . .

[6] an observer, not a sharer.
[7] *Elegiac Stanzas Suggested by a Picture of Peele Castle* 14–16.

[Characteristics of
Shakespeare's Dramas]

❨ This description of seven characteristics of Shakespeare's plays comes from the *Literary Remains* of 1836–39. H. N. Coleridge, the editor, filled out his uncle's extant notes from reports of the lectures given by Coleridge under the auspices of the London Philosophical Society early in 1818. The fragmentary notes have been transcribed and published in two editions of Coleridge's *Shakespearean Criticism* by T. M. Raysor. ❩

The stage in Shakspeare's time was a naked room with a blanket for a curtain; but he made it a field for monarchs. That law of unity, which has its foundations, not in the factitious necessity of custom, but in nature itself, the unity of feeling, is every where and at all times observed by Shakspeare in his plays. Read Romeo and Juliet; — all is youth and spring; — youth with its follies, its virtues, its pre-cipitancies; — spring with its odours, its flowers, and its transiency; it is one and the same feeling that commences, goes through, and ends the play. The old men, the Capulets and the Montagues, are not common old men; they have an eagerness, a heartiness, a ve-hemence, the effect of spring; with Romeo, his change of passion, his sudden marriage, and his rash death, are all the effects of youth; — whilst in Juliet love has all that is tender and melancholy in the nightingale, all that is voluptuous in the rose, with whatever is sweet in the freshness of spring; but it ends with a long deep sigh like the last breeze of the Italian evening. This unity of feeling and character pervades every drama of Shakspeare.

It seems to me that his plays are distinguished from those of all other dramatic poets by the following characteristics:

1. Expectation in preference to surprise. It is like the true reading of the passage; — "God said, Let there be light, and there was *light;*" — not there *was* light.[1] As the feeling with which we startle at a shooting star, compared with that of watching the sunrise at the pre-established moment, such and so low is surprise compared with expectation.

2. Signal adherence to the great law of nature, that all opposites tend to attract and temper each other. Passion in Shakspeare generally displays libertinism, but involves morality; and if there are exceptions to this, they are, independently of their intrinsic value, all of them

[1] Genesis 1:3.

122

indicative of individual character, and, like the farewell admonitions of a parent, have an end beyond the parental relation. Thus the Countess's beautiful precepts to Bertram,[2] by elevating her character, raise that of Helena her favorite, and soften down the point in her which Shakspeare does not mean us not to see, but to see and to forgive, and at length to justify. And so it is in Polonius, who is the personified memory of wisdom no longer actually possessed. This admirable character is always misrepresented on the stage. Shakspeare never intended to exhibit him as a buffoon; for although it was natural that Hamlet, — a young man of fire and genius, detesting formality, and disliking Polonius on political grounds, as imagining that he had assisted his uncle in his usurpation, — should express himself satirically, — yet this must not be taken as exactly the poet's conception of him. In Polonius a certain induration of character had arisen from long habits of business; but take his advice to Laertes, and Ophelia's reverence for his memory, and we shall see that he was meant to be represented as a statesman somewhat past his faculties, — his recollections of life all full of wisdom, and showing a knowledge of human nature, whilst what immediately takes place before him, and escapes from him, is indicative of weakness.

But as in Homer all the deities are in armour, even Venus; so in Shakspeare all the characters are strong. Hence real folly and dullness are made by him the vehicles of wisdom. There is no difficulty for one being a fool to imitate a fool; but to be, remain, and speak like a wise man and a great wit, and yet so as to give a vivid representation of a veritable fool, — *hic labor, hoc opus est.*[3] A drunken constable is not uncommon, nor hard to draw; but see and examine what goes to make up a Dogberry.

3. Keeping at all times in the high road of life. Shakspeare has no innocent adulteries, no interesting incests, no virtuous vice; — he never renders that amiable which religion and reason alike teach us to detest, or clothes impurity in the garb of virtue, like Beaumont and Fletcher, the Kotzebues of the day.[4] Shakspeare's fathers are roused by ingratitude, his husbands stung by unfaithfulness; in him, in short, the affections are wounded in those points in which all may, nay, must, feel. Let the morality of Shakspeare be contrasted with that of the writers of his own, or the succeeding, age, or of those of the present day, who boast their superiority in this respect. No one can dispute that the result of such a comparison is altogether in favour of Shakspeare; — even the letters of women of high rank in his age were often coarser than his writings. If he occasionally disgusts a keen sense of delicacy, he never injures the mind; he neither excites, nor flatters, passion, in order to degrade the subject of it; he does not use the

[2] *All's Well that Ends Well* I.i.70–79.
[3] "This is the task, this the toil." — *Aeneid* VI.129.
[4] Kotzebue (1761–1819), German author of sentimental plays.

faulty thing for a faulty purpose, nor carries on warfare against virtue, by causing wickedness to appear as no wickedness, through the medium of a morbid sympathy with the unfortunate. In Shakspeare vice never walks as in twilight; nothing is purposely out of its place; — he inverts not the order of nature and propriety, — does not make every magistrate a drunkard or glutton, nor every poor man meek, humane, and temperate; he has no benevolent butchers, nor any sentimental rat-catchers.

4. Independence of the dramatic interest on the plot. The interest in the plot is always in fact on account of the characters, not *vice versa*, as in almost all other writers; the plot is a mere canvass and no more. Hence arises the true justification of the same stratagem being used in regard to Benedict and Beatrice, — the vanity in each being alike. Take away from the Much Ado About Nothing all that which is not indispensable to the plot, either as having little to do with it, or, at best, like Dogberry and his comrades, forced into the service, when any other less ingeniously absurd watchmen and night-constables would have answered the mere necessities of the action; — take away Benedict, Beatrice, Dogberry, and the reaction of the former on the character of Hero, — and what will remain? In other writers the main agent of the plot is always the prominent character; in Shakspeare it is so, or is not so, as the character is in itself calculated, or not calculated, to form the plot. Don John is the main-spring of the plot of this play; but he is merely shown and then withdrawn.

5. Independence of the interest on the story as the ground-work of the plot. Hence Shakspeare never took the trouble of inventing stories. It was enough for him to select from those that had been already invented or recorded such as had one or other, or both, of two recommendations, namely, suitableness to his particular purpose, and their being parts of popular tradition, — names of which we had often heard, and of their fortunes, and as to which all we wanted was, to see the man himself. So it is just the man himself, the Lear, the Shylock, the Richard, that Shakspeare makes us for the first time acquainted with. Omit the first scene in Lear, and yet every thing will remain; so the first and second scenes in the Merchant of Venice. Indeed it is universally true.

6. Interfusion of the lyrical — that which in its very essence is poetical — not only with the dramatic, as in the plays of Metastasio,[5] where at the end of the scene comes the *aria* as the *exit* speech of the character, — but also in and through the dramatic. Songs in Shakspeare are introduced as songs only, just as songs are in real life, beautifully as some of them are characteristic of the person who has sung or called for them, as Desdemona's "Willow," and Ophelia's wild snatches, and the sweet carollings in As You Like It. But the whole

[5] Italian author, 1698–1782, of dramas set to music.

of the Midsummer Night's Dream is one continued specimen of the dramatized lyrical. And observe how exquisitely the dramatic of Hotspur; —

> Marry, and I'm glad on't with all my heart;
> I had rather be a kitten and cry — mew, &c.

melts away into the lyric of Mortimer; —

> I understand thy looks: that pretty Welsh
> Which thou pourest down from these swelling heavens,
> I am too perfect in, &c.
>
> Henry IV. part i. act iii. sc. i.

7. The characters of the *dramatis personæ*, like those in real life, are to be inferred by the reader; — they are not told to him. And it is well worth remarking that Shakspeare's characters, like those in real life, are very commonly misunderstood, and almost always understood by different persons in different ways. The causes are the same in either case. If you take only what the friends of the character say, you may be deceived, and still more so, if that which his enemies say; nay, even the character himself sees himself through the medium of his character, and not exactly as he is. Take all together, not omitting a shrewd hint from the clown or the fool, and perhaps your impression will be right; and you may know whether you have in fact discovered the poet's own idea, by all the speeches receiving light from it, and attesting its reality by reflecting it.

Lastly, in Shakspeare the heterogeneous is united, as it is in nature. You must not suppose a pressure or passion always acting on or in the character; — passion in Shakspeare is that by which the individual is distinguished from others, not that which makes a different kind of him. Shakspeare followed the main march of the human affections. He entered into no analysis of the passions or faiths of men, but assured himself that such and such passions and faiths were grounded in our common nature, and not in the mere accidents of ignorance or disease. This is an important consideration, and constitutes our Shakspeare the morning star, the guide and the pioneer, of true philosophy.

[*Romeo and Juliet*]

❦ Coleridge's lectures on Shakespeare provide special problems. Although he was the fountainhead of a century of English Shakespearean criticism, he was occasionally indebted to the German critic A. W. Schlegel, and to others, for terminology and for particular interpretations. As a more serious complication, the lectures have come down to us only through reports and transcriptions by listeners. The best of the transcriptions, covering part of the series delivered in London from November 18, 1811, to January 27, 1812, were made by John Payne Collier and published by him in 1856 as *Seven Lectures on Shakespeare and Milton.* In general, other reports confirm Collier's. Yet Collier, an accomplished forger, almost certainly inserted passages to support his own arguments at the time of publication. Coleridge's seventh lecture, however, on *Romeo and Juliet,* has probably been tampered with very little, if at all, and Collier's text is here followed.]▶

In a former lecture I endeavoured to point out the union of the Poet and the Philosopher, or rather the warm embrace between them, in the "Venus and Adonis" and "Lucrece" of Shakespeare. From thence I passed on to "Love's Labours Lost," as the link between his character as a Poet, and his art as a Dramatist; and I showed that, although in that work the former was still predominant, yet that the germs of his subsequent dramatic power were easily discernible.

I will now, as I promised in my last, proceed to "Romeo and Juliet," not because it is the earliest, or among the earliest of Shakespeare's works of that kind, but because in it are to be found specimens, in degree, of all the excellences which he afterwards displayed in his more perfect dramas, but differing from them in being less forcibly evidenced, and less happily combined: all the parts are more or less present, but they are not united with the same harmony.

There are, however, in "Romeo and Juliet" passages where the poet's whole excellence is evinced, so that nothing superior to them can be met with in the productions of his after years. The main distinction between this play and others is, as I said, that the parts are less happily combined, or to borrow a phrase from the painter, the whole work is less in keeping. Grand portions are produced: we have limbs of giant growth; but the production, as a whole, in which each part gives delight for itself, and the whole, consisting of these delightful parts, communicates the highest intellectual pleasure and satisfaction, is the result of the application of judgment and taste. These are not to be attained but by painful study, and to the sacrifice of the stronger pleasures derived from the dazzling light which a man of genius throws over every circumstance, and where we are chiefly struck by vivid and distinct images. Taste is an attainment after a poet has been disciplined by experience, and has added to genius that talent by which he knows what part of his genius he can make acceptable, and intelligible to the portion of mankind for which he writes.

In my mind it would be a hopeless symptom, as regards genius, if I found a young man with anything like perfect taste. In the earlier works of Shakespeare we have a profusion of double epithets, and sometimes even the coarsest terms are employed, if they convey a more vivid image; but by degrees the associations are connected with the image they are designed to impress, and the poet descends from the ideal into the real world so far as to conjoin both — to give a sphere of active operations to the ideal, and to elevate and refine the real.

In "Romeo and Juliet" the principal characters may be divided into two classes: in one class passion — the passion of love — is drawn and drawn truly, as well as beautifully; but the persons are not individualised farther than as the actor appears on the stage. It is a very just description and development of love, without giving, if I may so express myself, the philosophical history of it — without shewing how the man became acted upon by that particular passion, but leading it through all the incidents of the drama, and rendering it predominant.

Tybalt is, in himself, a common-place personage. And here allow me to remark upon a great distinction between Shakespeare, and all who have written in imitation of him. I know no character in his plays, (unless indeed Pistol be an exception) which can be called the mere portrait of an individual: while the reader feels all the satisfaction arising from individuality, yet that very individual is a sort of class character, and this circumstance renders Shakespeare the poet of all ages.

Tybalt is a man abandoned to his passions — with all the pride of family, only because he thought it belonged to him as a member of that family, and valuing himself highly, simply because he does not care for death. This indifference to death is perhaps more common than any other feeling: men are apt to flatter themselves extravagantly, merely because they possess a quality which it is a disgrace not to have, but which a wise man never puts forward, but when it is necessary.

Jeremy Taylor in one part of his voluminous works, speaking of a great man, says that he was naturally a coward, as indeed most men are, knowing the value of life, but the power of his reason enabled him, when required, to conduct himself with uniform courage and hardihood. The good bishop, perhaps, had in his mind a story, told by one of the ancients, of a Philosopher and a Coxcomb, on board the same ship during a storm: the Coxcomb reviled the Philosopher for betraying marks of fear: "Why are you so frightened? I am not afraid of being drowned: I do not care a farthing for my life." — "You are perfectly right," said the Philosopher, "for your life is not worth a farthing."

Shakespeare never takes pains to make his characters win your esteem, but leaves it to the general command of the passions, and to poetic justice. It is most beautiful to observe, in "Romeo and Juliet," that the characters principally engaged in the incidents are preserved innocent from all that could lower them in our opinion, while the rest of the personages, deserving little interest in themselves, derive it from being instrumental in those situations in which the more important personages develope their thoughts and passions.

Look at Capulet — a worthy, noble-minded old man of high rank, with all the impatience that is likely to accompany it. It is delightful to see all the sensibilities of our nature so exquisitely called forth; as if the poet had the hundred arms of the polypus, and had thrown them out in all directions to catch the predominant feeling. We may see in Capulet the manner in which anger seizes hold of everything that comes in its way, in order to express itself, as in the lines where he reproves Tybalt for his fierceness of behaviour, which led him to wish to insult a Montague, and disturb the merriment. —

> "Go to, go to;
> You are a saucy boy. Is't so, indeed?
> This trick may chance to scath you; — I know what.
> You must contrary me! marry, 'tis time. —
> Well said, my hearts! — You are a princox: go:
> Be quiet or — More light, more light! — For shame!
> I'll make you quiet. — What! cheerly, my hearts!"
>
> *Act I., Scene 5.*

The line

> "This trick may chance to scath you; — I know what,"

was an allusion to the legacy Tybalt might expect; and then, seeing the lights burn dimly, Capulet turns his anger against the servants. Thus we see that no one passion is so predominant, but that it includes all the parts of the character, and the reader never has a mere abstract of a passion, as of wrath or ambition, but the whole man is presented to him — the one predominant passion acting, if I may so say, as the leader of the band to the rest.

It could not be expected that the poet should introduce such a character as Hamlet into every play; but even in those personages, which are subordinate to a hero so eminently philosophical, the passion is at least rendered instructive, and induces the reader to look with a keener eye, and a finer judgment into human nature.

Shakespeare has this advantage over all other dramatists — that he has availed himself of his psychological genius to develope all the minutiæ of the human heart: shewing us the thing that, to common observers, he seems solely intent upon, he makes visible what we should not otherwise have seen: just as, after looking at distant objects through a telescope, when we behold them subsequently with the naked eye, we see them with greater distinctness, and in more detail, than we should otherwise have done.

Mercutio is one of our poet's truly Shakespearian characters; for throughout his plays, but especially in those of the highest order, it is plain that the personages were drawn rather from meditation than from observation, or to speak correctly, more from observation, the child of meditation. It is comparatively easy for a man to go about the world, as if with a pocket-book in his hand, carefully noting down what he sees and hears: by practice he acquires considerable facility in representing what he has observed, himself frequently unconscious of its worth, or its bearings. This is entirely different from the observation of a mind, which, having formed a theory and a system upon its own nature, remarks all things that are examples of its truth, confirming it in that truth, and, above all, enabling it to convey the truths of philosophy, as mere effects derived from, what we may call, the outward watchings of life.

Hence it is that Shakespeare's favourite characters are full of such lively intellect. Mercutio is a man possessing all the elements of a poet: the whole world was, as it were, subject to his law of association. Whenever he wishes to impress anything, all things become his servants for the purpose: all things tell the same tale, and sound in unison. This faculty, moreover, is combined with the manners and feelings of a perfect gentleman, himself utterly unconscious of his powers. By his loss it was contrived that the whole catastrophe of the tragedy should be brought about: it endears him to Romeo, and gives to the death of Mercutio an importance which it could not otherwise have acquired.

I say this in answer to an observation, I think by Dryden, (to which indeed Dr. Johnson has fully replied) that Shakespeare having carried the part of Mercutio as far as he could, till his genius was exhausted, had killed him in the third Act, to get him out of the way. What shallow nonsense! As I have remarked, upon the death of Mercutio the whole catastrophe depends; it is produced by it. The scene in which it occurs serves to show how indifference to any subject but one, and aversion to activity on the part of Romeo, may be overcome and roused to the most resolute and determined conduct. Had not Mercutio been rendered so amiable and so interesting, we could not have felt so strongly the necessity for Romeo's interference, connecting it immediately, and passionately, with the future fortunes of the lover and his mistress.

But what am I to say of the Nurse? We have been told that her character is the mere fruit of observation — that it is like Swift's "Polite Conversation," certainly the most stupendous work of human memory, and of unceasingly active attention to what passes around us, upon record. The Nurse in "Romeo and Juliet" has sometimes been compared to a portrait by Gerard Dow, in which every hair was so exquisitely painted, that it would bear the test of the microscope. Now, I appeal confidently to my hearers whether the closest observation of the manners of one or two old nurses would have enabled Shakespeare to draw this character of admirable generalisation? Surely not. Let any man conjure up in his mind all the qualities and peculiarities that can possibly belong to a nurse, and he will find them in Shakespeare's picture of the old woman: nothing is omitted. This effect is not produced by mere observation. The great prerogative of genius (and Shakespeare felt and availed himself of it) is now to swell itself to the dignity of a god, and now to subdue and keep dormant some part of that lofty nature, and to descend even to the lowest character — to become everything, in fact, but the vicious.

Thus, in the Nurse you have all the garrulity of old-age, and all its fondness; for the affection of old-age is one of the greatest consolations of humanity. I have often thought what a melancholy world this would be without children, and what an inhuman world without the aged.

You have also in the Nurse the arrogance of ignorance, with the pride of meanness at being connected with a great family. You have the grossness, too, which that situation never removes, though it sometimes suspends it; and, arising from that grossness, the little low vices attendant upon it, which, indeed, in such minds are scarcely vices. — Romeo at one time was the most delightful and excellent young man, and the Nurse all willingness to assist him; but her disposition soon turns in favour of Paris, for whom she professes precisely the same admiration. How wonderfully are these low peculiarities contrasted with a young and pure mind, educated under different circumstances!

Another point ought to be mentioned as characteristic of the ignorance of the Nurse: — it is, that in all her recollections, she assists herself by the remembrance of visual circumstances. The great difference, in this respect, between the cultivated and the uncultivated mind is this — that the cultivated mind will be found to recal the past by certain regular trains of cause and effect; whereas, with the uncultivated mind, the past is recalled wholly by coincident images, or facts which happened at the same time. This position is fully exemplified in the following passages put into the mouth of the Nurse: —

> "Even or odd, of all days in the year,
> Come Lammas eve at night shall she be fourteen.
> Susan and she — God rest all Christian souls! —
> Were of an age. — Well, Susan is with God;
> She was too good for me. But, as I said,
> On Lammas eve at night shall she be fourteen;
> That shall she, marry: I remember it well.
> 'Tis since the earthquake now eleven years;
> And she was wean'd, — I never shall forget it, —
> Of all the days of the year, upon that day;
> For I had then laid wormwood to my dug,
> Sitting in the sun under the dove-house wall:
> My lord and you were then at Mantua. —
> Nay, I do bear a brain: — but, as I said,
> When it did taste the wormwood on the nipple
> Of my dug, and felt it bitter, pretty fool,

> To see it tetchy, and fall out with the dug!
> Shake, quoth the dove-house: 'twas no need, I trow,
> To bid me trudge.
> And since that time it is eleven years;
> For then she could stand alone."
>
> *Act I., Scene 3.*

She afterwards goes on with similar visual impressions, so true to the character. — More is here brought into one portrait than could have been ascertained by one man's mere observation, and without the introduction of a single incongruous point.

I honour, I love, the works of Fielding as much, or perhaps more, than those of any other writer of fiction of that kind: take Fielding in his characters of postillions, landlords, and landladies, waiters, or indeed, of any-body who had come before his eye, and nothing can be more true, more happy, or more humorous; but in all his chief personages, Tom Jones for instance, where Fielding was not directed by observation, where he could not assist himself by the close copying of what he saw, where it is necessary that something should take place, some words be spoken, or some object described, which he could not have witnessed, (his soliloquies for example, or the interview between the hero and Sophia Western before the reconciliation) and I will venture to say, loving and honouring the man and his productions as I do, that nothing can be more forced and unnatural: the language is without vivacity or spirit, the whole matter is incongruous, and totally destitute of psychological truth.

On the other hand, look at Shakespeare: where can any character be produced that does not speak the language of nature? where does he not put into the mouths of his *dramatis personæ*, be they high or low, Kings or Constables, precisely what they must have said? Where, from observation, could he learn the language proper to Sovereigns, Queens, Noblemen or Generals? yet he invariably uses it. — Where, from observation, could he have learned such lines as these, which are put into the mouth of Othello, when he is talking to Iago of Brabantio?

> "Let him do his spite:
> My services, which I have done the signiory,
> Shall out-tongue his complaints. 'Tis yet to know,
> Which, when I know that boasting is an honour,
> I shall promulgate, I fetch my life and being
> From men of royal siege; and my demerits
> May speak, unbonneted, to as proud a fortune
> As this that I have reach'd: for know, Iago,
> But that I love the gentle Desdemona,
> I would not my unhoused free condition
> Put into circumscription and confine
> For the sea's worth."
>
> *Act I., Scene 2.*

I ask where was Shakespeare to observe such language as this? If he did observe it, it was with the inward eye of meditation upon his own nature: for the time, he became Othello, and spoke as Othello, in such circumstances, must have spoken.

Another remark I may make upon "Romeo and Juliet" is, that in this tragedy the poet is not, as I have hinted, entirely blended with the dramatist, — at least, not in the degree to be afterwards noticed in "Lear," "Hamlet," "Othello," or "Macbeth." Capulet and Montague not unfrequently talk a language only belonging to the poet, and not so characteristic of, and peculiar to, the passions of persons in the situations in which they are placed — a mistake, or rather an indistinctness, which many of our later dramatists have carried through the whole of their productions.

When I read the song of Deborah, I never think that she is a poet, although I think the song itself a sublime poem: it is as simple a dithyrambic production as exists in any language; but it is the proper and characteristic effusion of a woman highly elevated by triumph, by the natural hatred of oppressors, and resulting from a bitter sense of wrong: it is a song of exultation on deliverance from these evils, a deliverance accomplished by herself. When she exclaims, "The inhabitants of the villages ceased, they ceased in Israel, until that I, Deborah, arose, that I arose a mother in Israel," it is poetry in the highest sense: we have no reason, however, to suppose that if she had not been agitated by passion, and animated by victory, she would have been able so to express herself; or that if she had been placed in different circumstances, she would have used such language of truth and passion. We are to remember that Shakespeare, not placed under circumstances of excitement, and only wrought upon by his own vivid and vigorous imagination, writes a language that invariably, and intuitively, becomes the condition and position of each character.

On the other hand, there is a language not descriptive of passion, nor uttered under the influence of it, which is at the same time poetic, and shows a high and active fancy, as when Capulet says to Paris, —

> "Such comfort as do lusty young men feel,
> When well-apparell'd April on the heel
> Of limping winter treads, even such delight
> Among fresh female buds, shall you this night
> Inherit at my house."
>
> *Act I., Scene 2.*

Here the poet may be said to speak, rather than the dramatist; and it would be easy to adduce other passages from this play, where Shakespeare, for a moment forgetting the character, utters his own words in his own person.

In my mind, what have often been censured as Shakespeare's conceits are completely justifiable, as belonging to the state, age, or feeling of the individual. Sometimes, when they cannot be vindicated on these grounds, they may well be excused by the taste of his own and of the preceding age; as for instance, in Romeo's speech,

> "Here's much to do with hate, but more with love: —
> Why then, O brawling love! O loving hate!
> O anything, of nothing first created!
> O heavy lightness! serious vanity!
> Misshapen chaos of well-seeming forms!
> Feather of lead, bright smoke, cold fire, sick health!
> Still-waking sleep, that is not what it is!"
>
> *Act I., Scene* 1.

I dare not pronounce such passages as these to be absolutely unnatural, not merely because I consider the author a much better judge than I can be, but because I can understand and allow for an effort of the mind, when it would describe what it cannot satisfy itself with the description of, to reconcile opposites and qualify contradictions, leaving a middle state of mind more strictly appropriate to the imagination than any other, when it is, as it were, hovering between images. As soon as it is fixed on one image, it becomes understanding; but while it is unfixed and wavering between them, attaching itself permanently to none, it is imagination. Such is the fine description of Death in Milton: —

> "The other shape,
> If shape it might be call'd, that shape had none
> Distinguishable in member, joint, or limb,
> Or substance might be call'd, that shadow seem'd,
> For each seem'd either: black it stood as night;
> Fierce as ten furies, terrible as hell,
> And shook a dreadful dart: what seem'd his head
> The likeness of a kingly crown had on."
>
> *Paradise Lost,* Book II.

The grandest efforts of poetry are where the imagination is called forth, not to produce a distinct form, but a strong working of the mind, still offering what is still repelled, and again creating what is again rejected; the result being what the poet wishes to impress, namely, the substitution of a sublime feeling of the unimaginable for a mere image. I have sometimes thought that the passage just read might be quoted as exhibiting the narrow limit of painting, as compared with the boundless power of poetry: painting cannot go beyond a certain point; poetry rejects all control, all confinement. Yet we know that sundry painters have attempted pictures of the meeting between Satan and Death at the gates of Hell; and how was Death represented? Not as Milton has described him, but by the most defined thing that can be imagined — a skeleton, the dryest and hardest image that it is possible to discover; which, instead of keeping the mind in a state of activity, reduces it to the merest passivity, — an image, compared with which a square, a triangle, or any other mathematical figure, is a luxuriant fancy.

It is a general but mistaken notion that, because some forms of writing, and some combinations of thought, are not usual, they are not natural; but we are to recollect that the dramatist represents his characters in every situation of life and in every state of mind, and there is no form of language that may not be introduced with effect by a great and judicious poet, and yet be most strictly according to nature. Take punning, for instance, which may be the lowest, but at all events is the most harmless, kind of wit, because it never excites envy. A pun may be a necessary consequence of association: one man, attempting to prove something that was resisted by another, might, when agitated by strong feeling, employ a term used by his adversary with a directly contrary meaning to that for which that adversary had resorted to it: it might come into his mind as one way, and sometimes the best, of replying to that adversary. This form of speech is generally produced by a mixture of anger and contempt, and punning is a natural mode of expressing them.

It is my intention to pass over none of the important so-called conceits of Shakespeare, not a few of which are introduced into his later productions with great propriety and effect. We are not to forget, that at the time he lived there was an attempt at, and an affectation of, quaintness and adornment, which emanated from the Court, and against which satire was directed by Shakespeare in the character of Osrick in Hamlet. Among the schoolmen of that age, and earlier, nothing was more common than the use of conceits: it began with the revival of letters, and the bias thus given was very generally felt and acknowledged.

I have in my possession a dictionary of phrases, in which the epithets applied to love, hate, jealousy, and such abstract terms, are arranged; and they consist almost entirely of words taken from Seneca and his imitators, or from the schoolmen, showing perpetual antithesis, and describing the passions by the conjunction and combination of things absolutely irreconcileable. In treating the matter thus, I am aware that I am only palliating the practice in Shakespeare: he ought to have had nothing to do with merely temporary peculiarities: he wrote not for his own only, but for all ages, and so far I admit the use of some of his conceits to be a defect. They detract sometimes from his universality as to time, person, and situation.

If we were able to discover, and to point out the peculiar faults, as well as the peculiar beauties of Shakespeare, it would materially assist us in deciding what authority ought to be attached to certain portions of what are generally called his works. If we met with a play, or certain scenes of a play, in which we could trace neither his defects nor his excellences, we should have the strongest reason for believing that he had had no hand in it. In the case of scenes so circumstanced we might come to the conclusion that they were taken from the older plays, which, in some instances, he reformed or altered, or that they were inserted afterwards by some under-hand, in order to please the mob. If a drama by Shakespeare turned out to be too heavy for popular audiences, the clown might be called in to lighten the representation; and if it appeared that what was added was not in Shakespeare's manner, the conclusion would be inevitable, that it was not from Shakespeare's pen.

It remains for me to speak of the hero and heroine, of Romeo and Juliet themselves; and I shall do so with unaffected diffidence, not merely on account of the delicacy, but of the great importance of the subject. I feel that it is impossible to defend Shakespeare from the most cruel of all charges, — that he is an immoral writer — without entering fully into his mode of pourtraying female characters, and of displaying the passion of love. It seems to me, that he has done both with greater perfection than any other writer of the known world, perhaps with the single exception of Milton in his delineation of Eve.

When I have heard it said, or seen it stated, that Shakespeare wrote for man, but the gentle Fletcher for woman, it has always given me something like acute pain, because to me it seems to do the greatest injustice to Shakespeare: when, too, I remember how much character is formed by what we read, I cannot look upon it as a light question, to be passed over as a mere amusement, like a game of cards or chess. I never have been able to tame down my mind to think poetry a sport, or an occupation for idle hours.

Perhaps there is no more sure criterion of refinement in moral character, of the purity of intellectual intention, and of the deep conviction and perfect sense of what our own nature really is in all its combinations, than the different definitions different men would give of love. I will not detain you by stating the various known definitions, some of which it may be better not to repeat: I will rather give you one of my own, which, I apprehend, is equally free from the extravagance of pretended Platonism (which, like other things which supermoralise, is sure to demoralise) and from its grosser opposite.

Considering myself and my fellow-men as a sort of link between heaven and earth, being composed of body and soul, with power to reason and to will, and with that perpetual aspiration which tells us that this is ours for a while, but it is not ourselves; considering man, I say, in this two-fold character, yet united in one person, I conceive that there can be no correct definition of love which does not correspond with our being, and with that subordination of one part to another which constitutes our perfection. I would say therefore that —

"Love is a desire of the whole being to be united to some thing, or some being, felt necessary to its completeness, by the most perfect means that nature permits, and reason dictates."

It is inevitable to every noble mind, whether man or woman, to feel itself, of itself, imperfect and insufficient, not as an animal only, but as a moral being. How wonderfully, then, has Providence contrived for us, by making that which is necessary to us a step in our exaltation to a higher and nobler state! The Creator has ordained that one should possess qualities which the other has not, and the union of both is the most complete ideal of human character. In everything the blending of the similar with the dissimilar is the secret of all pure delight. Who shall dare to stand alone, and vaunt himself, in himself, sufficient? In poetry it is the blending of passion with order that constitutes perfection: this is still more the case in morals, and more than all in the exclusive attachment of the sexes.

True it is, that the world and its business may be carried on without marriage; but it is so evident that Providence intended man (the only animal of all climates, and whose reason is pre-eminent over instinct) to be the master of the world, that marriage, or the knitting together of society by the tenderest, yet firmest ties, seem ordained to render him capable of maintaining his superiority over the brute creation. Man alone has been privileged to clothe himself, and to do all things so as to make him, as it were, a secondary creator of himself, and of his own happiness or misery: in this, as in all, the image of the Deity is impressed upon him.

Providence, then, has not left us to prudence only; for the power of calculation, which prudence implies, cannot have existed, but in a state which pre-supposes marriage. If God has done this, shall we suppose that he has given us no moral sense, no yearning, which is something more than animal, to secure that, without which man might form a herd, but could not be a society? The very idea seems to breathe absurdity.

From this union arise the paternal, filial, brotherly and sisterly relations of life; and every state is but a family magnified. All the operations of mind, in short, all that distinguishes us from brutes, originate in the more perfect state of domestic life. — One infallible criterion in forming an opinion of a man is the reverence in which he holds women. Plato has said, that in this way we rise from sensuality to affection, from affection to love, and from love to the pure intellectual delight by which we become worthy to conceive that infinite in ourselves, without which it is impossible for man to believe in a God. In a word, the grandest and most delightful of all promises has been expressed to us by this practical state — our marriage with the Redeemer of mankind.

I might safely appeal to every man who hears me, who in youth has been accustomed to abandon himself to his animal passions, whether when he first really fell in love, the earliest symptom was not a complete change in his manners, a contempt and a hatred of himself for having excused his conduct by asserting, that he acted according to the dictates of nature, that his vices were the inevitable consequences of youth, and that his passions at that period of life could not be conquered? The surest friend of chastity is love: it leads us, not to sink the mind in the body, but to draw up the body to the mind — the immortal part of our nature. See how contrasted in this respect are some portions of the works of writers, whom I need not name, with other portions of the same works: the ebullitions of comic humour have at times, by a lamentable confusion, been made the means of debasing our nature, while at other times, even in the same volume, we are happy to notice the utmost purity, such as the purity of love, which above all other qualities renders us most pure and lovely.

Love is not, like hunger, a mere selfish appetite: it is an associative quality. The hungry savage is nothing but an animal, thinking only of the satisfaction of his stomach: what is the first effect of love, but to associate the feeling with every object in nature? the trees whisper, the roses exhale their perfumes, the nightingales sing, nay the very skies smile in unison with the feeling of true and pure love. It gives to every object in nature a power of the heart, without which it would indeed be spiritless.

Shakespeare has described this passion in various states and stages, beginning, as was most natural, with love in the young. Does he open his play by making Romeo and Juliet in love at first sight — at the first glimpse, as any ordinary thinker would do? Certainly not: he knew what he was about, and how he was to accomplish what he was about: he was to develope the whole passion, and he commences with the first elements — that sense of imperfection, that yearning to combine itself with something lovely. Romeo became enamoured of the idea he had formed in his own mind, and then, as it were, christened the first real being of the contrary sex as endowed with the perfections he desired. He appears to be in love with Rosaline; but, in truth, he is in love only with his own idea. He felt that necessity of being beloved which no noble mind can be without. Then our poet, our poet who so well knew human nature, introduces Romeo to Juliet, and makes it not only a violent, but a permanent love — a point for which Shakespeare has been ridiculed by the ignorant and unthinking. Romeo is first represented in a state most susceptible of love, and then, seeing Juliet, he took and retained the infection.

This brings me to observe upon a characteristic of Shakespeare, which belongs to a man of profound thought and high genius. It has been too much the custom, when anything that happened in his dramas could not easily be explained by the few words the poet has employed, to pass it idly over, and to say that it is beyond our reach, and beyond the power of philosophy — a sort of terra incognita for discoverers — a great ocean to be hereafter explored. Others have treated such passages as hints and glimpses of something now non-existent, as the sacred fragments of an ancient and ruined temple, all the portions of which are beautiful, although their particular relation to each other is unknown. Shakespeare knew the human mind, and its most minute and intimate workings, and he never introduces a word, or a thought, in vain or out of place: if we do not understand him, it is our own fault or the fault of copyists and typographers; but study, and the possession of some small stock of the knowledge by which he worked, will enable us often to detect and explain his meaning. He never wrote at random, or hit upon points of character and conduct by chance; and the smallest fragment of his mind not unfrequently gives a clue to a most perfect, regular, and consistent whole.

As I may not have another opportunity, the introduction of Friar Laurence into this tragedy enables me to remark upon the different manner in which Shakespeare has treated the priestly character, as compared with other writers. In Beaumont and Fletcher priests are represented as a vulgar mockery; and, as in others of their dramatic personages, the errors of a few are mistaken for the demeanour of the many: but in Shakespeare they always carry with them our love and respect. He made no injurious abstracts: he took no copies from the worst parts of our nature; and, like the rest, his characters of priests are truly drawn from the general body.

It may strike some as singular, that throughout all his productions he has never introduced the passion of avarice. The truth is, that it belongs only to particular parts of our nature, and is prevalent only in particular states of society; hence it could not, and cannot, be permanent. The Miser of Moliere and Plautus is now looked upon as a species of madman, and avarice as a species of madness. Elwes, of whom everybody has heard, was an individual influenced by an insane condition of mind; but, as a passion, avarice has disappeared. How admirably, then, did Shakespeare foresee, that if he drew such a character it could not be permanent! he drew characters which would always be natural, and therefore permanent, inasmuch as they were not dependent upon accidental circumstances.

There is not one of the plays of Shakespeare that is built upon anything but the best and surest foundation; the characters must be permanent — permanent while men continue men, — because they stand upon what is absolutely necessary to our existence. This cannot be said even of some of the most famous authors of antiquity. Take the capital tragedies of Orestes, or of the husband of Jocasta: great as was the genius of the writers, these dramas have an obvious fault, and the fault lies at the very root of the action. In Œdipus a man is represented oppressed by fate for a crime of which he was not morally guilty; and while we read we are obliged to say to ourselves, that in those days they considered actions without reference to the real guilt of the persons.

There is no character in Shakespeare in which envy is pourtrayed, with one solitary exception — Cassius, in "Julius Cæsar;" yet even there the vice is not hateful, inasmuch as it is counterbalanced by a number of excellent qualities and virtues. The poet leads the reader to suppose that it is rather something constitutional, something derived from his parents, something that he cannot avoid, and not something that he has himself acquired; thus throwing the blame from the will of man to some inevitable circumstance, and leading us to suppose that it is hardly to be looked upon as one of those passions that actually debase the mind.

Whenever love is described as of a serious nature, and much more when it is to lead to a tragical result, it depends upon a law of the mind, which, I believe, I shall hereafter be able to make intelligible, and which would not only justify Shakespeare, but show an analogy to all his other characters.[1]

The Friend

([In 1809–10, almost without help from others, Coleridge conducted the *Friend,* an ill-conceived, heavily philosophical "essay periodical." In the prolific year 1817 he projected and carried forward with some success an expansion of these essays into three volumes. Later in the year, for the *Encyclopaedia Metropolitana,* he wrote a *Treatise on Method,* which was revised by other editors, published in six editions by 1854, and reprinted in 1934 with introduction and notes by Alice D. Snyder. With the manuscript of the *Treatise* before him, in the summer of 1818, Coleridge wrote eight essays on method for *The Friend* (Section II, essays iv–xi). The first of these, given below in the text of 1818, will interest many readers as Shakespearean criticism rather than as methodology.])

from SECTION II

On the Grounds of Morals and Religion, and the Discipline of the Mind Requisite for a True Understanding of the Same

ESSAY IV

Ὅ δὲ δίκαιον ἐσι ποιεῖν, ἄκουε πῶς χρὴ ἔχειν ἐμὲ καὶ σὲ πρὸς ἀλλήλους. Εἰ μὲν ὅλως φιλοσοφίας καταπεφρόνηκας, ἐᾶν καίρειν· ἐι δὲ παρ' ἑτέρου ἀκήκοας ἤ αὐτὸς βελτίονα εὕρηκας τῶν παρ' ἐμοὶ,

[1] Pistol: braggart companion of Falstaff; John Elwes (1714–89), a miser; Jocasta: mother and wife of Oedipus.

ἐκεῖνα τίμα· ἐι δ' ἄρα τὰ παρ' ἡμῶν σοὶ ἀρέσκει, τιμητέον καὶ ἐμὲ μάλισα.   ΠΛΑΤΩΝ· ΔΙΩΝ : επις· δευτερα.

(*Translation.*) — Hear then what are the terms on which you and I ought to stand toward each other. If you hold philosophy altogether in contempt, bid it farewell. Or if you have heard from any other person, or have yourself found out a better than mine, then give honor to that, which ever it be. But if the doctrine taught in these our works please you, then it is but just that you should honor me too in the same proportion.

Plato's 2d Letter to Dion.

What is that which first strikes us, and strikes us at once, in a man of education? And which, among educated men, so instantly distinguishes the man of superior mind, that (as was observed with eminent propriety of the late Edmund Burke) "we cannot stand under the same arch-way during a shower of rain, *without finding him out?*" Not the weight or novelty of his remarks; not any unusual interest of facts communicated by him; for we may suppose both the one and the other precluded by the shortness of our intercourse, and the triviality of the subjects. The difference will be impressed and felt, though the conversation should be confined to the state of the weather or the pavement. Still less will it arise from any peculiarity in his words and phrases. For if he be, as we now assume, a *well*-educated man as well as a man of superior powers, he will not fail to follow the golden rule of Julius Cæsar, *Insolens verbum, tanquam scopulum, evitare.*[1] Unless where new things necessitate new terms, he will avoid an unusual word as a rock. It must have been among the earliest lessons of his youth, that the breach of this precept, at all times hazardous, becomes ridiculous in the topics of ordinary conversation. There remains but one other point of distinction possible; and this must be, and in fact is, the true cause of the impression made on us. It is the unpremeditated and evidently habitual *arrangement* of his words, grounded on the habit of foreseeing, in each integral part, or (more plainly) in every sentence, the whole that he then intends to communicate. However irregular and desultory his talk, there is *method* in the fragments.

Listen, on the other hand, to an ignorant man, though perhaps shrewd and able in his particular calling; whether he be describing or relating. We immediately perceive, that his memory alone is called into action; and that the objects and events recur in the narration in the same order, and with the same accompaniments, however accidental or impertinent, as they had first occurred to the narrator. The necessity of taking breath, the efforts of recollection, and the abrupt rectification of its failures, produce all his pauses; and with exception of the "*and then,*" the "*and there,*" and the still less significant, "*and so,*" they constitute likewise all his connections.

[1] Avoid the unusual word as you would a rock. — Adapted from a surviving fragment of Caesar's *De Analogia.*

Our discussion, however, is confined to Method as employed in the formation of the understanding, and in the constructions 'of science and literature. It would indeed be superfluous to attempt a proof of its importance in the business and economy of active or domestic life. From the cotter's hearth or the workshop of the artisan, to the palace or the arsenal, the first merit, that which admits neither substitute nor equivalent, is, that *every thing is in its place*. Where this charm is wanting, every other merit either loses its name, or becomes an additional ground of accusation and regret. Of one, by whom it is eminently possessed, we say proverbially, he is like clock-work. The resemblance extends beyond the point of regularity, and yet falls short of the truth. Both do, indeed, at once divide and announce the silent and otherwise indistinguishable lapse of time. But the man of methodical industry and honorable pursuits, does more: he realizes its ideal divisions, and gives a character and individuality to its moments. If the idle are described as killing time, he may be justly said to call it into life and moral being, while he makes it the distinct object not only of the consciousness, but of the conscience. He organizes the hours, and gives them a soul: and that, the very essence of which is to fleet away, and evermore *to have been*, he takes up into his own permanence, and communicates to it the imperishableness of a spiritual nature. Of the good and faithful servant, whose energies, thus directed, are thus methodized, it is less truly affirmed, that He lives in time, than that Time lives in him. His days, months, and years, as the stops and punctual marks in the records of duties performed, will survive the wreck of worlds, and remain extant when time itself shall be no more.

But as the importance of Method in the duties of social life is incomparably greater, so are its practical elements proportionably obvious, and such as relate to the will far more than to the understanding. Henceforward, therefore, we contemplate its bearings on the latter.

The difference between the products of a well-disciplined and those of an uncultivated understanding, in relation to what we will now venture to call the *Science of Method,* is often and admirably exhibited by our great Dramatist. We scarcely need refer our readers to the Clown's evidence, in the first scene of the second act of "Measure for Measure," or the Nurse in "Romeo and Juliet." But not to leave the position, without an instance to illustrate it, we will take the "easy-yielding" Mrs. Quickley's relation of the circumstances of Sir John Falstaff's debt to her.

FALSTAFF. What is the gross sum that I owe thee?

Mrs. QUICKLEY. Marry, if thou wert an honest man, thyself and the money too. Thou didst swear to me upon a parcel-gilt goblet, sitting in my dolphin chamber, at the round table, by a sea-coal fire, on Wednesday in Whitsun week, when the prince broke thy head for likening his father to a singing-man in Windsor — thou didst swear to me then, as I was washing thy wound, to marry me and make me my

lady thy wife. Canst thou deny it? Did not goodwife Keech, the
butcher's wife, come in then and call me gossip Quickley? — coming
in to borrow a mess of vinegar: telling us she had a good dish of prawns
— whereby thou didst desire to eat some — whereby I told thee they
were ill for a green wound, &c. &c. &c.

                                          Henry IV. 1st. pt. act ii. sc. 1.[2]

And this, be it observed, is so far from being carried beyond the
bounds of a fair imitation, that "the poor soul's" thoughts and sentences
are more closely interlinked than the truth of nature would have required, but that the connections and sequence, which the habit of
Method can alone give, have in this instance a substitute in the fusion
of passion. For the absence of Method, which characterizes the uneducated, is occasioned by an habitual submission of the understanding
to mere events and images as such, and independent of any power in
the mind to classify or appropriate them. The general accompaniments
of time and place are the only relations which persons of this class
appear to regard in their statements. As this constitutes *their* leading
feature, the contrary excellence, as distinguishing the well-educated
man, must be referred to the contrary habit. METHOD, therefore, becomes natural to the mind which has been accustomed to contemplate
not *things* only, or for their own sake alone, but likewise and chiefly
the *relations* of things, either their relations to each other, or to the
observer, or to the state and apprehension of the hearers. To enumer-
ate and analyze these relations, with the conditions under which alone
they are discoverable, is to teach the science of Method.

The enviable results of this science, when knowledge has been
ripened into those habits which at once secure and evince its possession, can scarcely be exhibited more forcibly as well as more pleasingly,
than by contrasting with the former extract from Shakspeare the narration given by Hamlet to Horatio of the occurrences during his proposed transportation to England, and the events that interrupted his
voyage.

> HAM. Sir, in my heart there was a kind of fighting
> That would not let me sleep: methought I lay
> Worse than the mutines in the bilboes. Rashly,
> And prais'd be rashness for it — *Let us know,*
> *Our indiscretion sometimes serves us well,*
> *When our deep plots do fail: and that should teach us,*
> *There's a divinity that shapes our ends,*
> *Rough-hew them how we will.*
> HOR. That is most certain.
> HAM. Up from my cabin,
> My sea-gown scarf'd about me, in the dark
> Grop'd I to find out them; had my desire;
> Finger'd their pocket; and, in fine, withdrew

---

[2] Actually *2 Henry IV* II.i.91ff.

To my own room again: making so bold,
My fears forgetting manners, to unseal
Their grand commission; where *I* found, Horatio,
A royal knavery — an exact command,
Larded with many several sorts of reasons,
Importing Denmark's health, and England's too,
With, ho! such bugs and goblins in *my* life,
That on the supervize, no leisure bated,
No, not to stay the grinding of the axe,
My head should be struck off!
    Hor. Is't possible?
    Ham. Here's the commission. — Read it at more leisure.
Act v. sc. 2.

Here the events, with the circumstances of time and place, are all
stated with equal compression and rapidity, not one introduced which
could have been omitted without injury to the intelligibility of the
whole process. If any tendency is discoverable, as far as the mere
facts are in question, it is the tendency to omission: and, accordingly,
the reader will observe, that the attention of the narrator is called back
to one material circumstance, which he was hurrying by, by a direct
question from the friend to whom the story is communicated, "How
WAS THIS SEALED?" But by a trait which is indeed peculiarly characteristic of Hamlet's mind, ever disposed to generalize, and meditative
to excess (but which, with due abatement and reduction, is distinctive
of every powerful and methodizing intellect), all the digressions and
enlargements consist of reflections, truths, and principles of general
and permanent interest, either directly expressed or disguised in playful satire.

    ————— I sat me down;
Devis'd a new commission; wrote it fair.
I once did hold it, as our statists do,
A baseness to write fair, and laboured much
How to forget that learning; but, sir, now
It did me yeoman's service. Wilt thou know
The effect of what I wrote?
    Hor. Aye, good my lord.
    Ham. An earnest conjuration from the king,
As England was his faithful tributary;
As love between them, like the palm, might flourish;
As peace should still her wheaten garland wear,
And many such like As's of great charge —
That on the view and knowing of these contents
He should the bearers put to sudden death,
No shriving time allowed.
    Hor. How was this sealed?
    Ham. Why, even in that was heaven ordinant.
I had my father's signet in my purse,
Which was the model of that Danish seal:

Folded the writ up in the form of the other;
Subscribed it; gave't the impression; placed it safely,
The changeling never known. Now, the next day
Was our sea-fight; and what to this was sequent,
Thou knowest already.
HOR. So Guildenstern and Rosencrantz go to't?
HAM. Why, man, they did make love to this employment.
They are not near my conscience: their defeat
Doth by their own insinuation grow.
'Tis dangerous when the baser nature comes
Between the pass and fell incensed points
Of mighty opposites.

[V.ii.31–62]

It would, perhaps, be sufficient to remark of the preceding passage, in connection with the humorous specimen of narration,

"Fermenting o'er with frothy circumstance,"

in Henry IV.; that if overlooking the different value of the *matter* in each, we considered the *form* alone, we should find both *immethodical;* Hamlet from the excess, Mrs. Quickley from the want, of reflection and generalization; and that Method, therefore, must result from the due mean or balance between our passive impressions and the mind's own re-action on the same. (Whether this re-action do not suppose or imply a primary act positively *originating* in the mind itself, and prior to the object in order of nature, though co-instantaneous in its manifestation, will be hereafter discussed.) But we had a further purpose in thus contrasting these extracts from our "myriad-minded Bard," (μυριονοῦς ἄνηρ.) We wished to bring forward, each for itself, these two elements of Method, or (to adopt an arithmetical term) its two main *factors*.

Instances of the want of generalization are of no rare occurrence in real life: and the narrations of Shakspeare's Hostess and the Tapster, differ from those of the ignorant and unthinking in general, by their superior humor, the poet's own gift and infusion, not by their want of Method, which is not greater than we often meet with in that class, of which they are the dramatic representatives. Instances of the opposite fault, arising from the excess of generalization and reflection in minds of the opposite class, will, like the minds themselves, occur less frequently in the course of our own personal experience. Yet they will not have been wanting to our readers, nor will they have passed unobserved, though the great poet himself (ὁ τὴν ἑαυτοῦ ψυχὴν ὥσει ὕλην τίνα ἀσώματον μορφαῖς ποικιλαῖς μορφώσας)[3] has more conveniently supplied the illustrations. To complete, therefore, the purpose aforementioned, that of presenting each of the two components as

[3] *Translation.* — He that moulded his own soul, as some incorporeal material, into various forms. THEMISTIUS. [S.T.C.]

separately as possible, we chose an instance in which, by the surplus
of its own activity, Hamlet's mind disturbs the arrangement, of which
that very activity had been the cause and impulse.

Thus exuberance of mind, on the one hand, interferes with the
forms of Method; but sterility of mind, on the other, wanting the spring
and impulse to mental action, is wholly destructive of Method itself.
For in attending too exclusively to the relations which the past or
passing events and objects bear to general truth, and the moods of his
own Thought, the most intelligent man is sometimes in danger of overlooking that other relation, in which they are likewise to be placed to
the apprehension and sympathies of his hearers. His discourse appears
like soliloquy intermixed with dialogue. But the uneducated and unreflecting talker overlooks *all* mental relations, both logical and psychological; and consequently precludes all Method, that is not purely
accidental. Hence the nearer the things and incidents in time and
place, the more distant, disjointed, and impertinent to each other, and
to any common purpose, will they appear in his narration: and this
from the want of a *staple*, or *starting-post*, in the narrator himself;
from the absence of *the leading Thought*, which, borrowing a phrase
from the nomenclature of legislation, we may not inaptly call the
INITIATIVE. On the contrary, where the habit of Method is present
and effective, things the most remote and diverse in time, place, and
outward circumstance, are brought into mental contiguity and succession, the more striking as the less expected. But while we would impress the necessity of this habit, the illustrations adduced give proof
that in undue preponderance, and when the prerogative of the mind is
stretched into despotism, the discourse may degenerate into the grotesque or the fantastical.

With what a profound insight into the constitution of the human
soul is this exhibited to us in the character of the Prince of Denmark,
where flying from the sense of reality, and seeking a reprieve from the
pressure of its duties, in that ideal activity, the overbalance of which,
with the consequent indisposition to action, is his disease, he compels
the reluctant good sense of the high yet healthful-minded Horatio, to
follow him in his wayward meditation amid the graves? *"To what base
uses we may return, Horatio! Why may not imagination trace the noble
dust of Alexander, till he find it stopping a bung-hole?* HOR. *It were
to consider too curiously to consider so.* HAM. *No, faith, not a jot; but
to follow him thither with modesty enough and likelihood to lead it.
As thus: Alexander died, Alexander was buried, Alexander returneth
to dust — the dust is earth; of earth we make loam: and why of that
loam, whereto he was converted, might they not stop a beer-barrel?*

> *Imperial Cæsar, dead and turn'd to clay,*
> *Might stop a hole to keep the wind away!"*

[V.i.223–237]

But let it not escape our recollection, that when the objects thus connected are proportionate to the connecting energy, relatively to the real, or at least to the desirable sympathies of mankind; it is from the same character that we derive the genial method in the famous soliloquy, *"To be? or not to be?"*[4] which, admired as it is, and has been, has yet received only the first-fruits of the admiration due to it.

We have seen that from the confluence of innumerable impressions in each moment of time the mere passive memory must needs tend to confusion — a rule, the seeming exceptions to which (the thunder-bursts in Lear, for instance) are really confirmations of its truth. For, in many instances, the predominance of some mighty Passion takes the place of the guiding Thought, and the result presents the method of Nature, rather than the habit of the Individual. For Thought, Imagination (and we may add, Passion), are, in their very essence, the first, connective, the latter co-adunative: and it has been shown, that if the excess lead to Method misapplied, and to connections of the moment, the absence, or marked deficiency, either precludes Method altogether, both form and substance: or (as the following extract will exemplify) retains the outward form only.

> *My liege and madam! to expostulate*
> *What majesty should be, what duty is,*
> *Why day is day, night night, and time is time,*
> *Were nothing but to waste night, day and time.*
> *Therefore — since brevity is the soul of wit,*
> *And tediousness the limbs and outward flourishes,*
> *I will be brief. Your noble son is mad:*
> *Mad call I it — for to define true madness,*
> *What is't, but to be nothing else but mad!*
> *But let that go.*
>   QUEEN. *More matter with less art.*
>   POL.
> *Madam! I swear, I use no art at all.*
> *That he is mad, tis true: tis true, tis pity:*
> *And pity tis, tis true (a foolish figure!*
> *But farewell it, for I will use no art.)*
> *Mad let us grant him then: and now remains,*
> *That we find out the cause of this effect,*
> *Or rather say the cause of this defect:*
> *For this effect defective comes by cause.*
> *Thus it remains, and the remainder thus*
> *Perpend!*
>   *Hamlet,* act ii. scene 2.

Does not the irresistible sense of the ludicrous in this flourish of the soul-surviving body of old Polonius's intellect, not less than in the endless confirmations and most undeniable matters of fact, of Tapster

[4] III.i.56ff.

Pompey or "the hostess of the tavern" prove to our feelings, even before the word is found which presents the truth to our understandings, that confusion and formality are but the opposite poles of the same null-point?

It is Shakspeare's peculiar excellence, that throughout the whole of his splendid picture gallery (the reader will excuse the confest inadequacy of this metaphor), we find individuality every where, mere portrait no where. In all his various characters, we still feel ourselves communing with the same human nature, which is every where present as the vegetable sap in the branches, sprays, leaves, buds, blossoms, and fruits, their shapes, tastes, and odours. Speaking of the effect, i. e. his works themselves, we may define the excellence of *their* method as consisting in that just proportion, that union and interpenetration of the universal and the particular, which must ever pervade all works of decided genius and true science. For Method implies a *progressive transition*, and it is the meaning of the word in the original language. The Greek Μεθοδος is literally *a way*, or *path of Transit*. Thus we extol the Elements of Euclid, or Socrates' discourse with the slave in the Menon, as *methodical*, a term which no one who holds himself bound to think or speak correctly, would apply to the alphabetical order or arrangement of a common dictionary.[5] But as, without continuous transition, there can be no Method, so without a pre-conception there can be no transition with continuity. The term, Method, cannot therefore, otherwise than by abuse, be applied to a mere dead arrangement, containing in itself no principle of progression.

The Statesman's Manual

(The full title of the first edition of 1816, from which the two selections below are taken, tells little about the contents of the book, but much about its tone and its awkward structure: *The Statesman's Manual; or, The Bible the Best Guide to Political Skill and Foresight: A Lay Sermon, addressed to the Higher Classes of Society, with an Appendix, containing Comments and Essays connected with the Study of the Inspired Writings.* In the first passage from the essay, with specific reference to the current economic and religious disturbances in England and Ireland, Coleridge attacks the arrogance of the rationalistic Enlightenment. In the second, from the Appendix, he borrows, but modifies toward idealism, a distinction made by Immanuel

[5] In Plato's *Meno* (or *Menon*), Socrates leads a slave through the steps of a geometric proof.

Kant between mechanistic understanding and what Coleridge describes as transcendent reason.]❭

. . . The Bible differs from all the books of Greek philosophy, and in a two-fold manner. It doth not affirm a Divine Nature only, but a God: and not a God only, but the living God. Hence in the Scriptures alone is the *Jus divinum*, or direct Relation of the State and its Magistracy to the Supreme Being, taught as a vital and indispensable part of all moral and of all political wisdom, even as the Jewish alone was a true theocracy.

But I refer to the demand. Were it my object to touch on the present state of public affairs in this kingdom, or on the prospective measures in agitation respecting our sister island, I would direct your most serious meditations to the latter period of the reign of Solomon, and to the revolutions in the reign of Rehoboam, his successor. But I should tread on glowing embers. I will turn to a subject on which all men of reflection are at length in agreement — the causes of the revolution and fearful chastisement of France. We have learned to trace them back to the rising importance of the commercial and manufacturing class, and its incompatibility with the old feudal privileges and prescriptions; to the spirit of sensuality and ostentation, which from the court had spread through all the towns and cities of the empire; to the predominance of a presumptuous and irreligious philosophy; to the extreme over-rating of the knowledge and power given by the improvements of the arts and sciences, especially those of astronomy, mechanics, and a wonder-working chemistry; to an assumption of prophetic power, and the general conceit that states and governments might be and ought to be constructed as machines, every movement of which might be foreseen and taken into previous calculation; to the consequent multitude of plans and constitutions, of planners and constitution-makers, and the remorseless arrogance with which the authors and proselytes of every new proposal were ready to realize it, be the cost what it might in the established rights, or even in the lives, of men; in short, to restlessness, presumption, sensual indulgence, and the idolatrous reliance on false philosophy in the whole domestic, social, and political life of the stirring and effective part of the community: these all acting, at once and together, on a mass of materials supplied by the unfeeling extravagance and oppressions of the government, which "shewed no mercy, and very heavily laid its yoke."

Turn then to the chapter from which the last words were cited, and read the following seven verses; and I am deceived if you will not be compelled to admit, that the Prophet Isaiah revealed the true philosophy of the French revolution more than two thousand years before it became a sad irrevocable truth of history. "And thou saidst, I shall be a lady for ever: so that thou didst not lay these things to thy heart, neither didst remember the latter end of it. Therefore, hear now this, thou that art given to pleasures, that dwellest carelessly, that sayest in thine heart, I am, and none else besides me! . . ."[1]

from Appendix, Note C

Of the *discursive* understanding, which forms for itself general notions and terms of classification for the purpose of comparing and arranging phænomena, the Characteristic is Clearness without Depth. It contemplates the unity of things in their *limits* only, and is consequently a knowledge of superficies without substance. So much so indeed, that it entangles itself in contradictions in the very effort of comprehending the *idea* of substance. The completing power which unites clearness with depth, the plenitude of the sense with the comprehensibility of the understanding, is the IMAGINATION, impregnated with which the understanding itself becomes intuitive, and a living power. The REASON, (not the abstract reason, not the reason as the mere *organ* of science, or as the faculty of scientific principles and schemes a priori; but reason) as the integral *spirit* of the regenerated man, reason substantiated and vital, "one only, yet manifold, overseeing all, and going through all understanding; the breath of the power of God, and a pure influence from the glory of the Almighty; which remaining in itself regenerateth all other powers, and in all ages entering into holy souls maketh them friends of God and prophets;" (Wisdom of Solomon, c. vii.) the REASON without being either the SENSE, the UNDERSTANDING or the IMAGINATION contains all three within itself, even as the mind contains its thoughts, and is present in and through them all; or as the expression pervades the different features of an intelligent countenance. Each individual must bear witness of it to his own mind, even as he describes life and light: and with the silence of light it describes itself, and dwells in *us* only as far as we dwell in *it*. It cannot in strict language be called a faculty, much less a personal property, of any human mind! He, with whom it is present, can as little appropriate it, whether, totally or by partition, as he can claim ownership in the breathing air or make an inclosure in the cope of heaven.

[1] Cf. Isaiah 47:6–8.

On the Constitution
of the Church and State

❨ In 1830 Coleridge cast *On the Constitution of the Church and State* in the form of a letter, explaining to a friend why the Catholic Emancipation Act of 1829 was right in intention but wrong in its failure to exclude Catholic priests explicitly from the group he calls the "clerisy." He had contemplated writing the work in 1825, and had begun it in 1827 as an attempt to give the Prime Minister, Lord Liverpool, a philosophical basis for action on questions concerning the Church. Aging and discouraged, Coleridge could not foresee — as John Colmer has observed in *Coleridge: Critic of Society*, Oxford, 1959 — that his last book "would leave a permanent mark on the thought of the nineteenth century." The edition of 1839, from which Chapter V is here taken, was "edited from the author's copies with notes by Henry Nelson Coleridge." Some of the extensive clarification in method is probably the work of the nephew. ❩

CHAPTER V

Of the Church of England, or National Clergy, according to the Constitution; its characteristic ends, purposes and functions; and of the persons comprehended under the Clergy, or the functionaries of the National Church.

After these introductory preparations, I can have no difficulty in setting forth the right idea of a national Church as, in the language of Queen Elizabeth, the third great venerable estate of the realm; the first being the estate of the land-owners or possessors of fixed property, consisting of the two classes of the Barons and the Franklins; and the second comprising the merchants, the manufacturers, free artizans, and the distributive class. To comprehend, therefore, the true character of this third estate, in which the reserved Nationalty was vested, we must first ascertain the end or national purpose, for which such reservation was made.

Now, as in the first estate the permanency of the nation was provided for; and in the second estate its progressiveness and personal freedom; while in the king the cohesion by interdependence, and the unity of the country, were established; there remains for the third estate only that interest which is the ground, the necessary antecedent condition, of both the former. These depend on a continuing and progressive civilization. But civilization is itself but a mixed good, if not far more a corrupting influence, the hectic of disease, not the bloom of health, and a nation so distinguished more fitly to be called a varnished than a polished people, where this civilization is not grounded in cultivation, in the harmonious developement of those qualities and faculties that characterize our humanity. We must be men in order to be citizens.

The Nationalty, therefore, was reserved for the support and maintenance of a permanent class or order with the following duties. A certain smaller number were to remain at the fountain heads of the humanities, in cultivating and enlarging the knowledge already possessed, and in watching over the interests of physical and moral science; being, likewise, the instructors of such as constituted, or were to constitute, the remaining more numerous classes of the order. The members of this latter and far more numerous body were to be distributed throughout the country, so as not to leave even the smallest integral part or division without a resident guide, guardian, and instructor; the objects and final intention of the whole order being these — to preserve the stores and to guard the treasures of past civilization, and thus to bind the present with the past; to perfect and add to the same, and thus to connect the present with the future; but especially to diffuse through the whole community and to every native entitled to its laws and rights that quantity and quality of knowledge which was indispensable both for the understanding of those rights, and for the performance of the duties correspondent: finally, to secure for the nation, if not a superiority over the neighbouring states, yet an equality at least, in that character of general civilization, which equally with, or rather more than, fleets, armies, and revenue, forms the ground of its defensive and offensive power. The object of the two former estates of the realm, which conjointly form the State, was to reconcile the interests of permanence with that of progression — law with liberty. The object of the national Church, the third remaining estate of the realm, was to secure and improve that civilization, without which the nation could be neither permanent nor progressive.

That, in all ages, individuals who have directed their meditations and their studies to the nobler characters of our nature, to the cultivation of those powers and instincts which constitute the man, at least separate him from the animal, and distinguish the nobler from the animal part of his own being, will be led by the supernatural in themselves to the contemplation of a power which is likewise superhuman; that science, and especially moral science, will lead to religion, and remain blended with it, — this, I say, will in all ages be the course of things. That in the earlier ages, and in the dawn of civility, there will be a twilight in which science and religion give light, but a light refracted through the dense and the dark, a superstition; — this is what we learn from history, and what philosophy would have taught us to expect. But I affirm that in the spiritual purpose of the word, and as understood in reference to a future state, and to the abiding essential interest of the individual as a person, and not as the citizen, neighbour, or subject, religion may be an indispensable ally, but is not the essential constitutive end, of that national institute, which is unfortunately, at least improperly, styled the Church; a name which in its best sense is exclusively appropriate to the Church of Christ. If this latter be *ecclesia*, the communion of such as are called out of the world, that is, in reference to the especial ends and purposes of that communion; this other might more expressively have been entitled *enclesia*, or an order of men chosen in and of the realm, and constituting an estate of that realm. And in fact, such was the original and proper sense of the more appropriately named clergy. It comprehended the learned of all names, and the clerk was the synonyme of the man of learning. Nor can any fact more strikingly illustrate the conviction entertained by our ancestors respecting the intimate connexion of this clergy with the peace and weal of the nation, than the privilege formerly recognized by our laws, in the well-known phrase, "benefit of clergy."

Deeply do I feel, for clearly do I see, the importance of my theme. And had I equal confidence in my ability to awaken the same interest in the minds of others, I should dismiss as affronting to my readers all apprehension of being charged with prolixity, while I am labouring to compress in two or three brief chapters the principal sides and aspects of a subject so large and multilateral as to require a volume for its full exposition; — with what success will be seen in what follows, commencing with the Churchmen, or (a far apter and less objectionable designation,) the national Clerisy.

The Clerisy of the nation, or national Church, in its primary acceptation and original intention, comprehended the learned of all denominations, the sages and professors of the law and jurisprudence, of medicine and physiology, of music, of military and civil architecture, of the physical sciences, with the mathematical as the common organ of the preceding; in short, all the so called liberal arts and sciences, the possession and application of which constitute the civilization of a country, as well as the theological. The last was, indeed, placed at the head of all; and of good right did it claim the precedence. But why? Because under the name of theology or divinity were contained the interpretation of languages, the conservation and tradition of past events, the momentous epochs and revolutions of the race and nation, the continuation of the records, logic, ethics, and the determination of ethical science, in application to the rights and duties of men in all their various relations, social and civil; and lastly, the ground-knowledge, the *prima scientia* as it was named, — philosophy, or the doctrine and discipline of ideas.[1]

[1] That is, of knowledges immediate, yet real, and herein distinguished in kind from logical and mathematical truths, which express not realities, but

Theology formed only a part of the objects, the theologians formed only a portion of the clerks or clergy, of the national Church. The theological order had precedency indeed, and deservedly; but not because its members were priests, whose office was to conciliate the invisible powers, and to superintend the interests that survive the grave; nor as being exclusively, or even principally, sacerdotal or templar, which, when it did occur, is to be considered as an accident of the age, a mis-growth of ignorance and oppression, a falsification of the constitutive principle, not a constituent part of the same. No, the theologians took the lead, because the science of theology was the root and the trunk of the knowledges that civilized man, because it gave unity and the circulating sap of life to all other sciences, by virtue of which alone they could be contemplated as forming, collectively, the living tree of knowledge. It had the precedency because, under the name theology, were comprised all the main aids, instruments, and materials of national education, the *nisus formativus*[2] of the body politic, the shaping and informing spirit, which, educing or eliciting the latent man in all the natives of the soil, trains them up to be citizens of the country, free subjects of the realm. And lastly, because to divinity belong those fundamental truths, which are the common ground-work of our civil and our religious duties, not less indispensable to a right view of our temporal concerns, than to a rational faith respecting our immortal well-being. Not without celestial observations can even terrestrial charts be accurately constructed. And of especial importance is it to the objects here contemplated, that only by the vital warmth diffused by these truths throughout the many, and by the guiding light from the philosophy, which is the basis of divinity, possessed by the few, can either the community or its rulers fully comprehend, or rightly appreciate, the permanent distinction and the occasional contrast between cultivation and civiliza-

---

only the necessary forms of conceiving and perceiving, and are therefore named the formal or abstract sciences. Ideas, on the other hand, or the truths of philosophy, properly so called, correspond to substantial beings, to objects the actual subsistence of which is implied in their idea, though only by the idea revealable. To adopt the language of the great philosophic Apostle, they are *spiritual realities that can only spiritually be discerned*, and the inherent aptitude and moral preconfiguration to which constitutes what we mean by ideas, and by the presence of ideal truth and of ideal power, in the human being. They, in fact, constitute his humanity. For try to conceive a man without the ideas of God, eternity, freedom, will, absolute truth, of the good, the true, the beautiful, the infinite. An animal endowed with a memory of appearances and of facts might remain. But the man will have vanished, and you have instead a creature, *more subtle than any beast of the field*, but likewise *cursed above every beast of the field; upon the belly must it go and dust must it eat all the days of its life.* But I recal myself from a train of thoughts little likely to find favour in this age of sense and selfishness. [S.T.C.]

[2] formative thrust.

tion; or be made to understand this most valuable of the lessons taught by history, and exemplified alike in her oldest and her most recent records — that a nation can never be a too cultivated, but may easily become an over-civilized, race.

Walter Savage Landor

WALTER SAVAGE LANDOR

CHRONOLOGY

1775   Born January 30 at Warwick, as heir to large estates.

1783   Entered Rugby School.

1791   Removed from Rugby because of rebellious conduct.

1793   Entered Trinity College, Oxford.

1794   Rusticated from Oxford for firing a gun at the window opposite his.

1798   July (?), *Gebir: A Poem, in Seven Books.*

1803   *Gebirus,* a Latin version of *Gebir.*

1808   August–October, led his own small troop in the defense of Spain.

1811   May 24, after earlier affairs, married Julia Thuillier, aged 17.

1814   *Letters by Calvus.* Ruined by extravagance and lawsuits; left England.

1818–35   In Italy, mostly in and near Florence.

1824   March, *Imaginary Conversations,* Volumes I, II. (III in 1828; IV, V in 1829; others in 1846, 1848, 1853, and posthumously.)

1834•   October, *Citation and Examination of William Shakespeare.*

1835–58   Moved about in England, before returning to Italy.

1836   March, *Pericles and Aspasia.*

1837   November (?), *The Pentameron and Pentalogia.*

1847   November, *Hellenics.* (Enlarged, 1859.)

1852–53   Caricatured in Dickens' *Bleak House* as the violent, litigious Boythorn.

1853   November, *The Last Fruit off an Old Tree.*

1858   December, *Dry Sticks, Fagoted.*

1863   *Heroic Idyls.*

1864   Died September 17 at Florence.

Imaginary Conversations

❡ Although Landor was learned in Greek and Latin literature, history, and languages, he used the form of essay particularly associated with his name not so much to re-create with historical accuracy the celebrities and situations of the past as to illustrate and discuss the moral, social, and literary questions alive in his own day. He designed pieces like "Tiberius and Vipsania" and "Leofric and Godiva" to be imaginatively compressed and classically restrained drama. Neither the first two volumes of *Imaginary Conversations*, 1824, nor their enlargement in 1826 contained any of the conversations here reprinted. In Volume III, 1828, first appeared "Tiberius and Vipsania," "Epictetus and Seneca," and the conversation then entitled "Landor, English Visitor, and Florentine Visitor." Only the third of these was greatly modified later. "Leofric and Godiva" was first published in Volume V, 1829, and "Archdeacon Hare and Walter Landor" in *The Last Fruit off an Old Tree*, 1853. The present text follows *The Works and Life of Walter Savage Landor*, 1874–76, edited in eight volumes by John Forster, who had access to Landor's corrected copies. ❫

Tiberius and Vipsania[1]

Tiberius. Vipsania, my Vipsania, whither art thou walking?
Vipsania. Whom do I see? my Tiberius?
Tiberius. Ah! no, no, no! but thou seest the father of thy little Drusus. Press him to thy heart the more closely for this meeting, and give him . .
Vipsania. Tiberius! the altars, the gods, the destinies, are between us . . I will take it from this hand; thus, thus shall he receive it.

[1] Vipsania, the daughter of Agrippa, was divorced from Tiberius by Augustus and Livia, in order that he might marry Julia, and hold the empire by inheritance. He retained such an affection for her, and showed it so intensely when he once met her afterward, that every precaution was taken lest they should meet again.
There can be no doubt that the Claudii were deranged in intellect. Those of them who succeeded to the empire were by nature no worse than several of their race in the times of the republic. Appius Claudius, Appius Cœcus, Publius, Appia, and after these the enemy of Cicero, exhibited as ungovernable a temper as the imperial ones, some breaking forth into tyranny and lust, others into contempt of, and imprecations against, their country. Tiberius was meditative, morose, suspicious. In the pupil of Seneca were dispositions the opposite to these, with many talents, and some good qualities. They could not disappear on a sudden without one of those shocks under which had been engulfed almost every member of the family.
[W.S.L.]

157

Tiberius. Raise up thy face, my beloved! I must not shed tears. Augustus! Livia! ye shall not extort them from me. Vipsania! I may kiss thy head . . for I have saved it. Thou sayest nothing. I have wronged thee; ay?

Vipsania. Ambition does not see the earth she treads on: the rock and the herbage are of one substance to her. Let me excuse you to my heart, O Tiberius. It has many wants; this is the first and greatest.

Tiberius. My ambition, I swear by the immortal gods, placed not the bar of severance between us. A stronger hand, the hand that composes Rome and sways the world . . .

Vipsania. . . . Overawed Tiberius. I know it; Augustus willed and commanded it.

Tiberius. And overawed Tiberius! Power bent, Death terrified, a Nero! What is our race, that any should look down on us and spurn us! Augustus, my benefactor, I have wronged thee! Livia, my mother, this one cruel deed was thine! To reign forsooth is a lovely thing! O womanly appetite! Who would have been before me, though the palace of Cæsar cracked and split with emperors, while I, sitting in idleness on a cliff of Rhodes, eyed the sun as he swang his golden censer athwart the heaven, or his image as it overstrode the sea.[2] I have it before me; and though it seems falling on me, I can smile at it; just as I did from my little favourite skiff, painted round with the marriage of Thetis, when the sailors drew their long shaggy hair across their eyes, many a stadium away from it, to mitigate its effulgence.

These too were happy days: days of happiness like these I could recall and look back upon with unaching brow.

O land of Greece! Tiberius blesses thee, bidding thee rejoice and flourish.

Why can not one hour, Vipsania, beauteous and light as we have led, return?

Vipsania. Tiberius! is it to me that you were speaking? I would not interrupt you; but I thought I heard my name as you walked away and looked up toward the East. So silent!

Tiberius. Who dared to call thee? Thou wert mine before the gods . . do they deny it? Was it my fault . .

Vipsania. Since we are separated, and for ever, O Tiberius, let us think no more on the cause of it. Let neither of us believe that the other was to blame: so shall separation be less painful.

[2] The Colossus was thrown down by an earthquake during the war between Antiochus and Ptolemy, who sent the Rhodians three thousand talents for the restoration of it. Again in the time of Vespasian, "Coæ Veneris, item *Colossi* refectorem congiario magnâque mercede donavit." *Suetonius in Vesp.* The first residence of Tiberius in Rhodes was when he returned from his Armenian expedition, the last was after his divorce from Vipsania and his marriage with Julia. [W.S.L.]

Tiberius. O mother! and did I not tell thee what she was? patient in injury, proud in innocence, serene in grief!

Vipsania. Did you say that too? but I think it was so: I had felt little. One vast wave has washed away the impression of smaller from my memory. Could Livia, could your mother, could she who was so kind to me . . .

Tiberius. The wife of Cæsar did it. But hear me now, hear me: be calm as I am. No weaknesses are such as those of a mother who loves her only son immoderately; and none are so easily worked upon from without. Who knows what impulses she received? She is very, very kind; but she regards me only; and that which at her bidding is to encompass and adorn me. All the weak look after power, protectress of weakness. Thou art a woman, O Vipsania! is there nothing in thee to excuse my mother? So good she ever was to me! so loving!

Vipsania. I quite forgive her: be tranquil, O Tiberius!

Tiberius. Never can I know peace . . never can I pardon . . any-one. Threaten me with thy exile, thy separation, thy seclusion! remind me that another climate might endanger thy health! . . There death met me and turned me round. Threaten me to take our son from us! our one boy! our helpless little one! him whom we made cry because we kissed him both together. Rememberest thou? or dost thou not hear? turning thus away from me!

Vipsania. I hear; I hear. O cease, my sweet Tiberius! Stamp not upon that stone: my heart lies under it.

Tiberius. Ay, there again death, and more than death, stood before me. O she maddened me, my mother did, she maddened me . . she threw me to where I am at one breath. The gods can not replace me where I was, nor atone to me, nor console me, nor restore my senses. To whom can I fly? to whom can I open my heart? to whom speak plainly?[3] There was upon the earth a man I could converse with, and fear nothing: there was a woman too I could love, and fear nothing. What a soldier, what a Roman, was thy father, O my young bride! How could those who never saw him have discoursed so rightly upon virtue!

Vipsania. These words cool my breast like pressing his urn against it. He was brave: shall Tiberius want courage?

Tiberius. My enemies scorn me. I am a garland dropped from a triumphal car, and taken up and looked on for the place I occupied: and tossed away and laughed at. Senators! laugh, laugh! Your merits may be yet rewarded . . be of good cheer! Counsel me, in your wisdom, what services I can render you, conscript fathers!

[3] The regret of Tiberius at the death of Agrippa may be imagined to arise from a cause of which at this moment he was unconscious. If Agrippa had lived, Julia, who was his wife, could not have been Tiberius's, nor would he and Vipsania have been separated. [W.S.L.]

Vipsania. This seems mockery: Tiberius did not smile so, once.

Tiberius. They had not then congratulated me.

Vipsania. On what?

Tiberius. And it was not because she was beautiful, as they thought her, and virtuous as I know she is, but because the flowers on the altar were to be tied together by my heart-string. On this they congratulated me. Their day will come. Their sons and daughters are what I would wish them to be: worthy to succeed them.

Vipsania. Where is that quietude, that resignation, that sanctity, that heart of true tenderness?

Tiberius. Where is my love? my love?

Vipsania. Cry not thus aloud, Tiberius! there is an echo in the place. Soldiers and slaves may burst in upon us.

Tiberius. And see my tears? There is no echo, Vipsania! why alarm and shake me so? We are too high here for the echoes: the city is below us. Methinks it trembles and totters: would it did! from the marble quays of the Tiber to this rock. There is a strange buzz and murmur in my brain; but I should listen so intensely, I should hear the rattle of its roofs, and shout with joy.

Vipsania. Calm, O my life! calm this horrible transport.

Tiberius. Spake I so loud? Did I indeed then send my voice after a lost sound, to bring it back; and thou fanciedest it an echo? Wilt not thou laugh with me, as thou wert wont to do, at such an error? What was I saying to thee, my tender love, when I commanded . . I know not whom . . to stand back, on pain of death? Why starest thou on me in such agony? Have I hurt thy fingers, child? I loose them; now let me look! Thou turnest thine eyes away from me. Oh! oh! I hear my crime! Immortal gods! I cursed then audibly, and before the sun, my mother!

Epictetus and Seneca

Seneca. Epictetus! I desired your master Epaphroditus to send you hither, having been much pleased with his report of your conduct, and much surprised at the ingenuity of your writings.[1]

Epictetus. Then I am afraid, my friend . . .

Seneca. My friend! are these the expressions . . Well, let it pass. Philosophers must bear bravely. The people expect it.

Epictetus. Are philosophers then only philosophers for the people?

---

[1] Like Epictetus, who was freed from slavery by Epaphroditus, Seneca was a Stoic, a follower of the severe Greek philosophers Crates, Zeno, and Cleanthes. But Seneca had been Nero's tutor, and he lived in great wealth at the emperor's increasingly corrupt court from 54 A.D. until his voluntary withdrawal in 62 A.D.

and, instead of instructing them, must they play tricks before them? Give me rather the gravity of dancing dogs. Their motions are for the rabble; their reverential eyes and pendent paws are under the pressure of awe at a master; but they are dogs, and not below their destinies.

Seneca. Epictetus! I will give you three talents to let me take that sentiment for my own.

Epictetus. I would give thee twenty, if I had them, to make it thine.

Seneca. You mean, by lending to it the graces of my language.

Epictetus. I mean, by lending it to thy conduct. And now let me console and comfort thee, under the calamity I brought on thee by calling thee *my friend.* If thou art not my friend, why send for me? Enemy I can have none: being a slave, Fortune has now done with me.

Seneca. Continue then your former observations. What were you saying?

Epictetus. That which thou interruptedst.

Seneca. What was it?

Epictetus. I should have remarked that, if thou foundest ingenuity in my writings, thou must have discovered in them some deviation from the plain homely truths of Zeno and Cleanthes.

Seneca. We all swerve a little from them.

Epictetus. In practice too?

Seneca. Yes, even in practice, I am afraid.

Epictetus. Often?

Seneca. Too often.

Epictetus. Strange! I have been attentive, and yet have remarked but one difference among you great personages at Rome.

Seneca. What difference fell under your observation?

Epictetus. Crates and Zeno and Cleanthes taught us, that our desires were to be subdued by philosophy alone. In this city, their acute and inventive scholars take us aside, and show us that there is not only one way, but two.

Seneca. Two ways?

Epictetus. They whisper in our ear, "These two ways are philosophy and enjoyment: the wiser man will take the readier, or, not finding it, the alternative." Thou reddenest.

Seneca. Monstrous degeneracy.

Epictetus. What magnificent rings! I did not notice them until thou liftedst up thy hands to heaven, in detestation of such effeminacy and impudence.

Seneca. The rings are not amiss: my rank rivets them upon my fingers: I am forced to wear them. Our emperor gave me one, Epaphroditus another, Tigellinus the third. I cannot lay them aside a single day, for fear of offending the gods, and those whom they love the most worthily.

Epictetus. Although they make thee stretch out thy fingers, like the arms and legs of one of us slaves upon a cross.

Seneca. O horrible! Find some other resemblance.

Epictetus. The extremities of a fig-leaf.

Seneca. Ignoble!

Epictetus. The claws of a toad, trodden on or stoned.

Seneca. You have great need, Epictetus, of an instructor in eloquence and rhetoric: you want topics and tropes and figures.

Epictetus. I have no room for them. They make such a buzz in the house, a man's own wife can not understand what he says to her.

Seneca. Let us reason a little upon style. I would set you right, and remove from before you the prejudices of a somewhat rustic education. We may adorn the simplicity of the wisest.

Epictetus. Thou canst not adorn simplicity. What is naked or defective is susceptible of decoration: what is decorated is simplicity no longer. Thou mayest give another thing in exchange for it; but if thou wert master of it, thou wouldst preserve it inviolate. It is no wonder that we mortals, little able as we are to see truth, should be less able to express it.

Seneca. You have formed at present no idea of style.

Epictetus. I never think about it. First I consider whether what I am about to say is true; then whether I can say it with brevity, in such a manner as that others shall see it as clearly as I do in the light of truth; for if they survey it as an ingenuity, my desire is ungratified, my duty unfulfilled. I go not with those who dance round the image of Truth, less out of honour to her than to display their agility and address.

Seneca. We must attract the attention of readers by novelty and force and grandeur of expression.

Epictetus. We must. Nothing is so grand as truth, nothing so forcible, nothing so novel.

Seneca. Sonorous sentences are wanted, to awaken the lethargy of indolence.

Epictetus. Awaken it to what? Here lies the question; and a weighty one it is. If thou awakenest men where they can see nothing and do no work, it is better to let them rest: but will not they, thinkest thou, look up at a rainbow, unless they are called to it by a clap of thunder?

Seneca. Your early youth, Epictetus, has been I will not say neglected, but cultivated with rude instruments and unskilful hands.

Epictetus. I thank God for it. Those rude instruments have left the turf lying yet toward the sun; and those unskilful hands have plucked out the docks.

Seneca. We hope and believe that we have attained a vein of eloquence, brighter and more varied than has been hitherto laid open to the world.

Epictetus. Than any in the Greek?

Seneca. We trust so.

Epictetus. Than your Cicero's?

Seneca. If the declaration may be made without an offence to modesty. Surely you can not estimate or value the eloquence of that noble pleader.

Epictetus. Imperfectly; not being born in Italy; and the noble pleader is a much less man with me than the noble philosopher. I regret that having farms and villas, he would not keep his distance from the pumping up of foul words, against thieves, cut-throats, and other rogues: and that he lied, sweated, and thumped his head and thighs, in behalf of those who were no better.

Seneca. Senators must have clients, and must protect them.

Epictetus. Innocent or guilty?

Seneca. Doubtless.

Epictetus. If it becomes a philosopher to regret at all, and if I regret what is, and might not be, I may regret more what both is and must be. However it is an amiable thing, and no small merit in the wealthy, even to trifle and play at their leisure hours with philosophy. It can not be expected that such a personage should espouse her, or should recommend her as an inseparable mate to his heir.

Seneca. I would.

Epictetus. Yes, Seneca, but thou hast no son to make the match for; and thy recommendation, I suspect, would be given him before he could consummate the marriage. Every man wishes his sons to be philosophers while they are young; but takes especial care, as they grow older, to teach them its insufficiency and unfitness for their intercourse with mankind. The paternal voice says, "You must not be particular: you are about to have a profession to live by: follow those who have thriven the best in it." Now among these, whatever be the profession, canst thou point out to me one single philosopher?

Seneca. Not just now. Nor, upon reflection, do I think it feasible.

Epictetus. Thou indeed mayest live much to thy ease and satisfaction with philosophy, having (they say) two thousand talents.

Seneca. And a trifle to spare . . pressed upon me by that godlike youth, my pupil Nero.

Epictetus. Seneca! where God hath placed a mine, he hath placed the materials of an earthquake.

Seneca. A true philosopher is beyond the reach of Fortune.

Epictetus. The false one thinks himself so. Fortune cares little about philosophers; but she remembers where she hath set a rich man, and she laughs to see the Destinies at his door.

Leofric and Godiva

Godiva. There is a dearth in the land, my sweet Leofric! Remember how many weeks of drought we have had, even in the deep pas-

tures of Leicestershire; and how many Sundays we have heard the
same prayers for rain, and supplications that it would please the Lord
in his mercy to turn aside his anger from the poor pining cattle. You,
my dear husband, have imprisoned more than one malefactor for
leaving his dead ox in the public way; and other hinds have fled before
you out of the traces, in which they and their sons and their daughters,
and haply their old fathers and mothers, were dragging the abandoned
wain homeward. Although we were accompanied by many brave
spearmen and skilful archers, it was perilous to pass the creatures
which the farm-yard dogs, driven from the hearth by the poverty of
their masters, were tearing and devouring; while others, bitten and
lamed, filled the air either with long and deep howls or sharp and quick
barkings, as they struggled with hunger and feebleness or were exasperated by heat and pain. Nor could the thyme from the heath, nor
the bruised branches of the fir-tree, extinguish or abate the foul odour.

Leofric. And now, Godiva my darling, thou art afraid we should
be eaten up before we enter the gates of Coventry; or perchance that
in the gardens there are no roses to greet thee, no sweet herbs for thy
mat and pillow.

Godiva. Leofric, I have no such fears. This is the month of roses:
I find them everywhere since my blessed marriage: they, and all other
sweet herbs, I know not why, seem to greet me wherever I look at
them, as though they knew and expected me. Surely they can not
feel that I am fond of them.

Leofric. O light laughing simpleton! But what wouldst thou? I
came not hither to pray; and yet if praying would satisfy thee, or
remove the drought, I would ride up straightway to Saint Michael's
and pray until morning.

Godiva. I would do the same, O Leofric! but God hath turned
away his ear from holier lips than mine. Would my own dear husband
hear me, if I implored him for what is easier to accomplish? what he
can do like God.

Leofric. How! what is it?

Godiva. I would not, in the first hurry of your wrath, appeal to
you, my loving lord, in behalf of these unhappy men who have offended you.

Leofric. Unhappy! is that all?

Godiva. Unhappy they must surely be, to have offended you so
grievously. What a soft air breathes over us! how quiet and serene
and still an evening! how calm are the heavens and the earth! shall
none enjoy them? not even we, my Leofric! The sun is ready to set:
let it never set, O Leofric, on your anger. These are not my words;
they are better than mine; should they lose their virtue from my un-
worthiness in uttering them!

Leofric. Godiva, wouldst thou plead to me for rebels?

Godiva. They have then drawn the sword against you! Indeed I
knew it not.

Leofric. They have omitted to send me my dues, established by my ancestors, well knowing of our nuptials, and of the charges and festivities they require, and that in a season of such scarcity my own lands are insufficient.

Godiva. If they were starving as they said they were . . .

Leofric. Must I starve too? Is it not enough to lose my vassals?

Godiva. Enough! O God! too much! too much! may you never lose them! Give them life, peace, comfort, contentment. There are those among them who kissed me in my infancy, and who blessed me at the baptismal font. Leofric, Leofric! the first old man I meet I shall think is one of those; and I shall think on the blessing he gave, and (ah me!) on the blessing I bring back to him. My heart will bleed, will burst . . and he will weep at it! he will weep, poor soul! for the wife of a cruel lord who denounces vengeance on him, who carries death into his family.

Leofric. We must hold solemn festivals.

Godiva. We must indeed.

Leofric. Well then.

Godiva. Is the clamorousness that succeeds the death of God's dumb creatures, are crowded halls, are slaughtered cattle, festivals? are maddening songs and giddy dances, and hireling praises from party-coloured coats? Can the voice of a minstrel tell us better things of ourselves than our own internal one might tell us; or can his breath make our breath softer in sleep? O my beloved! let everything be a joyance to us: it will, if we will. Sad is the day, and worse must follow, when we hear the blackbird in the garden and do not throb with joy. But, Leofric, the high festival is strown by the servant of God upon the heart of man. It is gladness, it is thanksgiving; it is the orphan, the starveling, pressed to the bosom, and bidden as its first commandment to remember its benefactor. We will hold this festival; the guests are ready: we may keep it up for weeks, and months, and years together, and always be the happier and the richer for it. The beverage of this feast, O Leofric, is sweeter than bee or flower or vine can give us: it flows from heaven; and in heaven will it abundantly be poured out again, to him who pours it out here unsparingly.

Leofric. Thou art wild.

Godiva. I have indeed lost myself. Some Power, some good kind Power, melts me (body and soul and voice) into tenderness and love. O my husband, we must obey it. Look upon me! look upon me! lift your sweet eyes from the ground! I will not cease to supplicate; I dare not.

Leofric. We may think upon it.

Godiva. Never say that! What! think upon goodness when you can be good? Let not the infants cry for sustenance! The mother of our blessed Lord will hear them; us never, never afterward.

Leofric. Here comes the bishop: we are but one mile from the walls. Why dismountest thou? no bishop can expect it. Godiva! my honour and rank among men are humbled by this: Earl Godwin will hear of it: up! up! the bishop hath seen it: he urgeth his horse onward: dost thou not hear him now upon the solid turf behind thee?

Godiva. Never, no, never will I rise, O Leofric, until you remit this most impious tax, this tax on hard labour, on hard life.

Leofric. Turn round: look how the fat nag canters, as to the tune of a sinner's psalm, slow and hard-breathing. What reason or right can the people have to complain, while their bishop's steed is so sleek and well caparisoned? Inclination to change, desire to abolish old usages . . . Up! up! for shame! They shall smart for it, idlers! Sir bishop, I must blush for my young bride.

Godiva. My husband, my husband! will you pardon the city?

Leofric. Sir bishop! I could not think you would have seen her in this plight. Will I pardon? yea, Godiva, by the holy rood, will I pardon the city, when thou ridest naked at noontide through the streets.

Godiva. O my dear cruel Leofric, where is the heart you gave me! It was not so! can mine have hardened it!

Bishop. Earl, thou abashest thy spouse; she turneth pale and weepeth. Lady Godiva, peace be with thee.

Godiva. Thanks, holy man! peace will be with me when peace is with your city. Did you hear my lord's cruel word?

Bishop. I did, lady.

Godiva. Will you remember it, and pray against it?

Bishop. Wilt *thou* forget it, daughter?

Godiva. I am not offended.

Bishop. Angel of peace and purity!

Godiva. But treasure it up in your heart: deem it an incense, good only when it is consumed and spent, ascending with prayer and sacrifice. And now what was it?

Bishop. Christ save us! that he will pardon the city when thou ridest naked through the streets at noon.

Godiva. Did he not swear an oath?

Bishop. He sware by the holy rood.

Godiva. My Redeemer! thou hast heard it! save the city!

Leofric. We are now upon the beginning of the pavement: these are the suburbs: let us think of feasting: we may pray afterward: to-morrow we shall rest.

Godiva. No judgments then to-morrow, Leofric?

Leofric. None: we will carouse.

Godiva. The saints of heaven have given me strength and confidence: my prayers are heard: the heart of my beloved is now softened.

Leofric (aside). Ay, ay . . they shall smart though.

Godiva. Say, dearest Leofric, is there indeed no other hope, no other mediation?

Leofric. I have sworn: beside, thou hast made me redden and turn my face away from thee, and all the knaves have seen it: this adds to the city's crime.

Godiva. I have blushed too, Leofric, and was not rash nor obdurate.

Leofric. But thou, my sweetest, art given to blushing; there is no conquering it in thee. I wish thou hadst not alighted so hastily and roughly: it hath shaken down a sheaf of thy hair: take heed thou sit not upon it, lest it anguish thee. Well done! it mingleth now sweetly with the cloth of gold upon the saddle, running here and there, as if it had life and faculties and business, and were working thereupon some newer and cunninger device. O my beauteous Eve! there is a Paradise about thee! the world is refreshed as thou movest and breathest on it. I can not see or think of evil where thou art. I could throw my arms even here about thee. No signs for me! no shaking of sunbeams! no reproof or frown or wonderment . . . I *will* say it . . . now then for worse . . . I could close with my kisses thy half-open lips, ay, and those lovely and loving eyes, before the people.

Godiva. To-morrow you shall kiss me, and they shall bless you for it. I shall be very pale, for to-night I must fast and pray.

Leofric. I do not hear thee; the voices of the folk are so loud under this archway.

Godiva (to herself). God help them! good kind souls! I hope they will not crowd about me so to-morrow. O Leofric! could my name be forgotten! and yours alone remembered! But perhaps my innocence may save me from reproach! and how many as innocent are in fear and famine! No eye will open on me but fresh from tears. What a young mother for so large a family! Shall my youth harm me! Under God's hand it gives me courage. Ah, when will the morning come! ah, when will the noon be over![1]

---

[1] The story of Godiva, at one of whose festivals or fairs I was present in my boyhood, has always much interested me; and I wrote a poem on it, sitting, I remember, by the *square pool* at Rugby. When I showed it to the friend in whom I had most confidence, he began to scoff at the subject; and on his reaching the last line, his laughter was loud and immoderate. This conversation has brought both laughter and stanza back to me, and the earnestness with which I entreated and implored my friend *not to tell the lads;* so heart-strickenly and desperately was I ashamed. The verses are these, if anyone else should wish another laugh at me.

> In every hour, in every mood,
> O lady, it is sweet and good
>   To bathe the soul in prayer,
> And, at the close of such a day,
> When we have ceased to bless and pray,
>   To dream on thy long hair.

May the peppermint be still growing on the bank in that place! W. S. L. [Landor began this note in 1829 with praise for Leigh Hunt: "This Conversation was suggested by the *Indicator,* an excellent book, stored with sound criticisms, and what are better still, with manly, just, and generous reflexions."]

FROM *Florentine, English Visitor, and Landor*

* * * * *

English Visitor. One objection to your *Imaginary Conversations* is, that you represent some living characters as speaking with greater powers of mind than they possess, vile as they are in conduct.

Landor. It can not be expected, by those who know of what materials the cabinets of Europe are composed, that any person in them should reason so conclusively, and with such illustrations, as some who are introduced. This, if it is a blemish in a book, is one which the book would be worse without. The practice of Shakespeare and Sophocles is a better apology for me than I could offer of my own. If men were to be represented as they show themselves, encrusted with all the dirtiness they contract in public life, in all the debility of ignorance, in all the distortion of prejudice, in all the reptile trickery of partisanship, who would care about the greater part of what are called the greatest? Principles and ideas are my objects: they must be reflected from high and low, but they must also be exhibited where people can see them best, and are most inclined to look at them.

English Visitor. You, by proper attention, or even by abstinence from attack, might have gone out among the commissioners to America.

Landor. I go out nowhere: here I live, here I die perhaps. A sea-voyage of very few days, although I suffer no sickness, makes me weary of life itself. What a situation is that in which, next to the sight of port, a tempest is the thing most desirable! I would not be embarked two months, to possess the kingdom of Montezuma united with that of Aurungzebe.

English Visitor. You appear to have no ambition, at least of this kind: you live upon a fifth of your income, willingly or unwillingly, and live handsomely and hospitably: what do you want then?

Landor. That which I told you before . . to become a *king's friend.* Peace, freedom, independence for nations, these shall buy me: and, if nothing but the humiliation of their betters can win the hearts of rulers, I would almost kiss their hands to obtain them. Had avarice or ambition guided me, remember I started with a larger hereditary estate than those of Pitt, Fox, Canning, and twenty more such, amounted to; and not scraped together in this, or the last, or the preceding century, in ages of stockjobbing and peculation, of cabinet-adventure and counterfeit nobility. My education, and that which education works upon or produces, was not below theirs: yet certain I am that, if I had applied to be made a tide-waiter on the Thames, the minister would have refused me. In the county where my chief estate lies, a waste and unprofitable one, but the third I believe in extent of any there, it was represented to me that the people were the most lawless in Great Britain; and the two most enlightened among the magistrates wished and exhorted me to become one. It would have been a great hinderance to my studies; yet a sense of public good, and a desire to promote it by any sacrifice, induced me to propose the thing to the duke of Beaufort, the lord-lieutenant. He could have heard nothing more of me, good or evil, than that I was a studious man, and that, although I belonged to no society, club, or party, and never sat in my life at a public dinner, I should oppose his family in elections. The information, however probable, was wrong. I had votes in four counties, and could influence fifty or sixty, and perhaps many more; yet I never did or will influence one in any case, nor ever give one while Representation is either cheat or coaxer. The noble duke declined my proposal.

These bells recall my attention from what is personal and from what is worthless.

Florentine. How they clatter and jingle! The ringers are pulling every bell-rope in the whole city as fast and as furiously as they can.

Landor. The sound of one only, the largest in the place, tolling slowly at equal intervals, makes a different impression on the hearer. We are impatient of these, which are rung in the same manner to announce a festival: instead of impatience at the others, we wait in suspense for every stroke, and the pulse of the heart replies to it. No people but the English can endure a long continuation of gravity and sadness: none pay the same respect to the dead.

English Visitor. Here not only the poorer, but householders and fathers of families, are thrown together into a covered cart; and when enow of them are collected, they are carried off by night, and cast naked into the ditch in the burial-ground. No sheet about them, no shroud externally, no coffin, no bier, no emblem of mortality; none of sorrow, none of affection, none of hope. Corpses are gathered like rotten gourds and cracked cucumbers, and thrown aside where none could find if any looked for them. Among people in easy circumstances, wife, children, relatives, friends, all leave the house when one of the family is dying: the priest alone remains with him: the last sacrament solves and sunders every human tie. The eyes, after wandering over the altered scenes of domestic love, over the silent wastes of friendship, are reconciled to whatever is most lugubrious in death, and are closed at last by mercenaries and strangers. . . .

Landor. The greatest power on earth, or that ever existed on earth, is the power of the British public; its foundation morals, its fabric wisdom, its circumvallation wealth. Yet this mighty power, which could overawe the universe, and (what is better) could fix its destinies, was, in less embarrassing circumstances, almost inert. Far am I from the inclination of lighting up a fire to invite around it the idle, the malevolent, the seditious: I would however subscribe my name, to ensure the maintenance of those persons who shall have lost their country for having punished with death its oppressor, or for having attempted it and failed. Let it first be demonstrated that he hath annulled the constitutional laws, or retracted his admissal or violated his promise of them, or that he holds men not born his subjects, nor reduced to that condition by legitimate war, in servitude and thraldom, or hath assisted or countenanced another in such offences. No scorn, no contumely, no cruelty, no single, no multiplied, injustice, no destruction, is enough, excepting the destruction of that upon which all society is constituted, under which all security rests, and all hope lies at anchor, faith. Public wrongs may and ought to be punished by private vindication, where the tongue of Law is paralysed by the bane of Despotism; and the action which in civil life is the worst, becomes, where civism lies beneath power, the most illustrious that magnanimity can achieve. The calmest and wisest men that ever lived were unanimous in this sentence; such men were Algernon Sydney and Milton: it is sanctioned by the laws of Solon, and sustained by the authority of Cicero and Aristoteles. The latter, mild and moderate as he was, goes a great way farther than I have ventured. . . .

It has been my fortune to love, in general, those men most who have thought most differently from me, on subjects wherein others pardon no discordance. In my opinion, I have no more right to be angry with a man whose reason has followed up a process different from what mine has, and is satisfied with the result, than with one who has gone to Venice while I am at Florence, and who writes to me that he likes the place, and that, although he said once he should settle elsewhere, he shall reside in that city. My political opinions are my only ones, beyond square demonstration, that I am certain will never change. If my muscles have hardened in them and are fit for no other, I have not on this account the right or inclination to consider a friend untrue or insincere, who declares that he sees more of practical good in a quarter opposite to that where we agreed to fix the speculative; and that he abandons the dim astounding majesty of mountain scenery, for the refreshing greenness and easy paths of the plain. I have walked always where I must breathe hard, and where such breathing was my luxury: I now sit somewhat stiller and have fewer aspirations, but I inhale the same atmosphere yet. . . .[1]

FROM *Archdeacon Hare and Walter Landor*

Walter Landor. Johnson had somewhat of the medlar in his nature; one side hard and austere, the other side unsound. We call him

[1] Beaufort: Landor applied to him for a magistracy, for the estate of Llanthony in Monmouthshire, in 1812. Montezuma II: Aztec emperor of Mexico, 1503–20; Aurungzebe: emperor of Hindustan, 1658–1707.

affected for his turgidity: this was not affected; it was the most natural part of him. He hated both affectation and tameness.

Archdeacon Hare. Two things intolerable, whether in prose or poetry. Wordsworth is guiltless at least of affectation.

Walter Landor. True; but he often is as tame as an abbess's cat, which in kittenhood has undergone the same operation as the Holy Father's choristers.

Archdeacon Hare. Sometimes indeed he might be more succinct. A belt is good for the breath, and without it we fail in the long run. And yet a man will always be more lookt at whose dress flutters in the air than he whose dress sits tight upon him: but he will soon be left on the roadside. Wherever there is a word beyond what is requisite to express the meaning, that word must be peculiarly beautiful in itself or strikingly harmonious; either of which qualities may be of some service in fixing the attention and enforcing the sentiment. But the proper word in the proper place seldom leaves anything to be desiderated on the score of harmony. The beauty of health and strength is more attractive and impressive than any beauty conferred by ornament. I know the delight you feel, not only in Milton's immortal verse, but (although less) in Wordsworth's.

Walter Landor. A Mozart to a Handel! But who is not charmed by the melody of Mozart? Critics have their favourites; and, like the same rank of people at elections, they chair one candidate and pelt another.

Archdeacon Hare. A smaller object may be so placed before a greater as to intercept the view of it in its just proportions. This is the favourite manœuvre in the Review-field. Fierce malignity is growing out of date. Nothing but fairness is spoken of; regret at the exposure of faults, real or imaginary, has taken place of derision, sarcasm, and arrogant condemnation. Nothing was wanting to Byron's consistency when he had exprest his contempt of Shakespeare.

Walter Landor. Giffords, who sniffed at the unsavory skirts of Juvenal, and took delight in paddling among the bubbles of azote, no longer ply the trade of critics to the same advantage. Generosity, in truth or semblance, is expected and required. Chattertons may die in poverty and despair; but Keatses are exposed no longer to a lingering death under that poison which paralyzes the heart, contempt.

Archdeacon Hare. In youth the appetite for fame is strongest. It is cruel and inhuman to withhold the sustenance which is necessary to the growth, if not the existence, of genius; sympathy, encouragement, commendation. Praise is not fame; but the praise of the intelligent is its precursor. *Vaticide* is no crime in the statute-book; but a crime, and a heavy crime, it is: and the rescue of a poet from a murderous enemy, although there is no oaken crown decreed for it, is among the higher virtues.

Walter Landor. Many will pass by; many will take the other side; many will cherish the less deserving; but some one, considerate and compassionate, will raise up the neglected: and, where a strong hand does it, several less strong will presently be ready to help. Alas! not always. There is nothing in the ruins of Rome which throws so chilling a shadow over the heart as the monument of Keats.

Our field of poetry at the present time is both wider and better cultivated than it has ever been. But if the tyrant of old who walked into the growing corn, to inculcate a lesson of *order* by striking off the heads of the higher poppies, were to enter ours, he would lay aside his stick, so nearly on a level is the crop. Every year there is more good poetry written now, in this our country, than was written between the *Metamorphoses* and the *Divina Commedia*.[1] We walk no longer in the cast-off clothes of the ancients, often ill sewn at first, and now ill fitting. We have pulpier flesh, stouter limbs, we take longer walks, explore wider fields, and surmount more craggy and more lofty eminences. From these let us take a leisurely look at Fancy and Imagination. Your friend Wordsworth was induced to divide his minor Poems under the separate heads of these two; probably at the suggestion of Coleridge, who persuaded him, as he himself told me, to adopt the name of *Lyrical Ballads*. He was sorry, he said, that he took the advice. And well he might be; for *lyre* and *ballad* belong not to the same age or the same people. It would have puzzled Coleridge to have drawn a strait boundary-line between the domains of Fancy and those of Imagination, on a careful survey of these pieces; or perhaps to have given a satisfactory definition of their qualities.

Archdeacon Hare. Do you believe you yourself can?

Walter Landor. I doubt it. The face is not the same, but the resemblance is sisterly; and, even by the oldest friends and intimates of the family, one is often taken for the other, so nearly are they alike. Fancy is Imagination in her youth and adolescence. Fancy is always excursive; Imagination, not seldom, is sedate. It is the business of Imagination, in her maturity, to create and animate such Beings as are worthy of her plastic hand; certainly not by invisible wires to put marionettes in motion, nor to pin butterflies on blotting-paper. Vigorous thought, elevated sentiment, just expression, developement of character, power to bring man out from the secret haunts of his soul, and to place him in strong outline against the sky, belong to Imagination. Fancy is thought to dwell among the Faeries and their congeners; and they frequently lead the weak and ductile poet far astray. He is fond of playing at *little-go* among them; and, when he grows bolder, he acts among the Witches and other such creatures; but his hankering after the Faeries still continues. Their tiny rings, in which the intelligent see only the growth of fungusses, are no arena for action and passion. It was not in these circles that Homer and Æschylus and Dante strove.

Archdeacon Hare. But Shakespeare sometimes entered them, who,

[1] *I.e.,* between Ovid (43 B.C.–A.D. 18) and Dante (1265–1321).

with infinitely greater power, moulded his composite and consistent Man, breathing into him an immortality never to be forfeited.

Walter Landor. Shakespeare's full strength and activity were exerted on Macbeth and Othello: he trifled with Ariel and Titania; he played with Caliban: but no other would have thought of playing with him, any more than of playing with Cerberus. Shakespeare and Milton and Chaucer have more imagination than any of those to whom the quality is peculiarly attributed. It is not inconsistent with vigour and gravity. There may be a large and effuse light without

"the motes that people the sunbeams."[2]

Imagination follows the steps of Homer throughout the Troad, from the ships on the strand to Priam and Helen on the city-wall: Imagination played with the baby Astyanax at the departure of Hector from Andromache, and was present at the noblest scene of the Iliad, where, to repeat a verse of Cowper's on Achilles, more beautiful than Homer's own,

"his hand he placed
On the old man's hand, *and pusht it gently away.*"

No less potently does Imagination urge Æschylus on, from the range of beacons to the bath of Agamemnon; nor expand less potently the vulture's wing over the lacerated bosom on the rocks of Caucasus. With the earliest flowers of the freshly created earth Imagination strewed the nuptial couch of Eve. Not Ariel, nor Caliban, nor Witches who ruled the elements, but Eve, and Satan, and Prometheus, are the most wonderous and the most glorious of her works.[3] Imagination takes the weaker hand of Virgil out of Dante's who grasps it, and guides the Florentine exile thro the triple world.

Archdeacon Hare. Whatever be your enthusiasm for the great old masters, you must often feel, if less of so strong an impulse, yet a cordial self-congratulation in having bestowed so many eulogies on poetical contemporaries, and on others whose genius is apart from poetry.

Walter Landor. Indeed I do. Every meed of Justice is delivered out of her own full scale. The poets, and others who may rank with them, indeed all the great men, have borne toward me somewhat more than civility. The few rudenesses I have ever heard of, are from such as neither I nor you ever meet in society, and such as warm their fingers and stomachs round less ornamental hearths.

When they to whom we have been unknown, or indifferent, begin to speak a little well of us, we are sure to find some honest old friend

---

[2] Milton, *Il Penseroso* 8.

[3] *I.e.,* not the supernatural beings in *The Tempest* and *Macbeth,* but the beings psychologically human in Milton's *Paradise Lost* and Aeschylus' *Prometheus Bound.*

ready to trim the balance. I have had occasion to smile at this.

Archdeacon Hare. We sometimes stumble upon sly invidiousness and smouldering malignity, quite unexpectedly, and in places which we should have believed were above the influence of such malaria. When Prosperity pays to Wisdom her visit in state, would we not, rather than halloo the yard-dog against her, clear the way for her, and adorn the door with garlands? How fond are people in general of clinging to a great man's foibles! they can climb no higher. It is not the solid, it is the carious, that grubs feed upon.

Walter Landor. The practice of barring out the master is still continued in the world's great schoolroom. Our sturdy boys do not fear a flogging; they fear only a book or a lecture.

Archdeacon Hare. Authors are like cattle going to a fair; those of the same field can never move on without butting one another.

Walter Landor. It has been my fortune and felicity, from my earliest days, to have avoided all competitions. My tutor at Oxford could never persuade me to write a piece of Latin poetry for the Prize, earnest as he was that his pupil should be a winner at the forthcoming *Encænia.* Poetry was always my amusement, prose my study and business. I have publisht five volumes of *Imaginary Conversations:* cut the worst of them thro the middle, and there will remain in this decimal fraction quite enough to satisfy my appetite for fame. I shall dine late; but the diningroom will be well lighted, the guests few and select.

In this age of discovery it may haply be discovered, who first among our Cisalpine nations led Greek to converse like Greek, Roman like Roman, in poetry or prose. Gentlemen of fashion have patronized them occasionally, have taken them under the arm, have recommended their own tailor, their own perfumer, and have lighted a cigar for them from their own at the door of the *Traveler's* or *Athenæum:* there they parted.

Archdeacon Hare. Before we go into the house again, let me revert to what you seem to have forgotten, the hasty and inaccurate remarks on *Gebir.*

Walter Landor. It is hardly worth our while. Evidently they were written by a very young person, who with a little encouragement, and induced to place his confidence in somewhat safer investment than himself, may presently do better things.

Archdeacon Hare. Southey too, I remember, calls the poem in some parts obscure.

Walter Landor. It must be, if Southey found it so. I never thought of asking him where lies the obscurity: I would have attempted to correct whatever he disapproved.

Archdeacon Hare. He himself, the clearest of writers, professes that he imitated your versification: and the style of his *Colloquies* is in some degree modified by yours.

Walter Landor. Little cause had he for preferring any other to his own. . . .[4]

Pericles and Aspasia

❪ *Pericles and Aspasia* appeared in two volumes in 1836. In its final form, achieved in 1846, it consists of 237 letters imagined as exchanges between the Greek statesman Pericles and his wife and between each of them and various friends. There is significant action, and much charm, but little narrative development. ❫

LXXIX. *Aspasia to Cleone*

Anaxagoras is the true, firm, constant friend of Pericles; the golden lamp that shines perpetually on the image I adore. Yet sometimes he speaks severely. On one of these occasions, Pericles took him by the hand, saying,

"O Anaxagoras! sincere and ardent lover of Truth! why do not you love her in such a manner as never to let her see you out of humour?"

"Because," said Anaxagoras, "you divide my affections with her, much to my shame."

Pericles was called away on business; I then said:

"O Anaxagoras! is not Pericles a truly great man?"

He answered, "If Pericles were a truly great man, he would not wish to appear different from what he is; he would know himself, and make others know him; he seems to guard against both. Much is wanting to constitute his greatness. He possesses, it is true, more comprehensiveness and concentration than any living; perhaps more than any since Solon; but he thinks that power over others is better than power over himself; as if a mob were worth a man, and an acclamation were worth a Pericles."

"But," said I, "he has absolute command over himself; and it is chiefly by exerting it that he has obtained an ascendancy over the minds of others."

[4] Robert Southey, *Sir Thomas More; or, Colloquies on the Progress and Prospects of Society,* 1829.

William Gifford (1756–1826) translated, imitated, and defended the satires of Juvenal.

Traveler's and Athenaeum: adjacent clubs in London. *Vaticide:* murder of a poet.

"Has he rendered them wiser and more virtuous?" said he.

"You know best," replied I, "having lived much longer among them."

"Perhaps," said Anaxagoras, "I may wrong him; perhaps he has saved them from worse disasters."

"You think him then ambitious?" said I, with some sadness.

"Ambitious!" cried he; "how so! He might have been a philosopher, and he is content to be a ruler."

I was ill at ease.

"Come," said I, "Anaxagoras, come into the garden with me. It is rather too warm indeed out of doors, but we have many evergreens, high and shady, and those who, like you and me, never drink wine, have little to dread from the heat."

Whether the ilexes and bays and oleanders struck his imagination, and presented the simile, I can not tell, but he thus continued in illustration of his discourse.

"There are no indeciduous plants, Aspasia! the greater part lose their leaves in winter, the rest in summer. It is thus with men. The generality yield and are stripped under the first chilly blasts that shake them. They who have weathered these, drop leaf after leaf in the sunshine. The virtues by which they arose to popularity, take another garb, another aspect, another form, and totally disappear. Be not uneasy; the heart of Pericles will never dry up, so many streams run into it."

He retired to his studies; I spoke but little that evening, and slept late.

The Pentameron

❆ As the subtitle of the first edition in 1837 indicated, *The Pentameron* consists of imaginary interviews, or lengthy conversations, between Giovanni Boccaccio (1313–75) and Francesco Petrarca (1304–74), at Boccaccio's villa near Certaldo. The title might be translated as "five sessions" — half as many as in Boccaccio's *Decameron*. The air of pomp and ceremony present in much of Landor's work is subdued, though perceptible, in the dreams recounted by the two speakers in the Fifth Day's Interview. The dream attributed to Petrarch was written at Heidelberg in July 1836; Landor then intended to find a place for it in *Pericles and Aspasia*. ❊

FROM *First Day's Interview*

Boccaccio. We admire by tradition; we censure by caprice; and there is nothing in which we are more ingenious and inventive. A wrong step in politics sprains a foot in poetry; eloquence is never so unwelcome as when it issues from a familiar voice; and praise hath no echo but from a certain distance. Our critics, who know little about them, would gaze with wonder at anything similar, in our days, to Pindar and Sophocles, and would cast it aside, as quite impracticable. They are in the right: for sonnet and canzonet charm greater numbers. There are others, or may be hereafter, to whom far other things will afford far higher gratification.

Petrarca. But our business at present is with prose and Cicero; and our question now is, what is Ciceronian. He changed his style according to his matter and his hearers. His speeches to the people vary from his speeches to the senate. Toward the one he was impetuous and exacting; toward the other he was usually but earnest and anxious, and sometimes but submissive and imploring, yet equally unwilling, on both occasions, to conceal the labour he had taken to captivate their attention and obtain success. At the tribunal of Cæsar the dictator he laid aside his costly armour, contracted the folds of his capacious robe, and became calm, insinuating, and adulative, showing his spirit not utterly extinguished, his dignity not utterly fallen, his consular year not utterly abolished from his memory, but Rome, and even himself, lowered in the presence of his judge.

Boccaccio. And after all this, can you bear to think what I am?

Petrarca. Complacently and joyfully; venturing, nevertheless, to offer you a friend's advice.

Enter into the mind and heart of your own creatures: think of them long, entirely, solely: never of style, never of self, never of critics, cracked or sound. Like the miles of an open country, and of an ignorant population, when they are correctly measured they become smaller. In the loftiest rooms and richest entablatures are suspended the most spider-webs; and the quarry out of which palaces are erected is the nursery of nettle and bramble.

Boccaccio. It is better to keep always in view such writers as Cicero, than to run after those idlers who throw stones that can never reach us.

Petrarca. If you copied him to perfection, and on no occasion lost sight of him, you would be an indifferent, not to say a bad writer.

Boccaccio. I begin to think you are in the right. Well then, retrenching some of my licentious tales, I must endeavour to fill up the vacancy with some serious and some pathetic.

Petrarca. I am heartily glad to hear of this decision; for, admirable as you are in the jocose, you descend from your natural position when you come to the convivial and the festive. You were placed among the Affections, to move and master them, and gifted with the rod that sweetens the fount of tears. My nature leads me also to the pathetic; in which, however, an imbecile writer may obtain celebrity. Even the hard-hearted are fond of such reading, when they are fond of any; and nothing is easier in the world than to find and accumulate its suf-

ferings. Yet this very profusion and luxuriance of misery is the reason
why few have excelled in describing it. The eye wanders over the
mass without noticing the peculiarities. To mark them distinctly is the
work of genius; a work so rarely performed, that, if time and space
may be compared, specimens of it stand at wider distances than the
trophies of Sesostris. Here we return again to the *Inferno* of Dante,
who overcame the difficulty. In this vast desert are its greater and its
less oasis; Ugolino and Francesca di Rimini. The peopled region is
peopled chiefly with monsters and moschitoes: the rest for the most
part is sand and suffocation.

Boccaccio. Ah! had Dante remained through life the pure solitary
lover of Bice, his soul had been gentler, tranquiller, and more generous. He scarcely hath described half the curses he went through, nor
the roads he took on the journey: theology, politics, and that barbican
of the *Inferno*, marriage, surrounded with its

> Selva selvaggia ed aspra e forte.[1]

Admirable is indeed the description of Ugolino, to whoever can endure the sight of an old soldier gnawing at the scalp of an old archbishop.

Petrarca. The thirty lines from

> Ed io sentj,   [xxxiii.46]

are unequalled by any other continuous thirty in the whole dominions
of poetry.

Boccaccio. Give me rather the six on Francesca: for if in the
former I find the simple, vigorous, clear narration, I find also what I
would not wish, the features of Ugolino reflected full in Dante. The
two characters are similar in themselves; hard, cruel, inflexible, malig-
nant, but, whenever moved, moved powerfully. In Francesca, with the
faculty of divine spirits, he leaves his own nature (not indeed the
exact representative of theirs) and converts all his strength into
tenderness. The great poet, like the original man of the Platonists, is
double, possessing the further advantage of being able to drop one
half at his option, and to resume it. Some of the tenderest on paper
have no sympathies beyond: and some of the austerest in their intercourse with their fellow-creatures, have deluged the world with tears.
It is not from the rose that the bee gathers her honey, but often from
the most acrid and the most bitter leaves and petals.

> Quando legemmo il disiato viso
> Esser baciato di cotanto amante,
> Questi, chi mai da me non sia diviso!
> La bocca mi baciò tutto tremante . . .

[1] "Wild, rough, and stubborn forest" — *Inferno* I.5.
Sesostris: Ramses II (1292–1225 B.C.), who defeated the Hittites and built
imperial temples in Egypt. Bice: Dante's Beatrice.

> *Galeotto* fù il libro, e chi lo scrisse . . .
> Quel giorno più non vi legemmo avante.[2]

In the midst of her punishment, Francesca, when she comes to the tenderest part of her story, tells it with complacency and delight; and, instead of naming Paolo, which indeed she never has done from the beginning, she now designates him as

> Questi chi mai da me non sia diviso!

Are we not impelled to join in her prayer, wishing them happier in their union?

Petrarca. If there be no sin in it.

Boccaccio. Ay, and even if there be . . . God help us!

What a sweet aspiration in each cesura of the verse! three love-sighs fixed and incorporate! Then, when she hath said

> La bocca mi baciò, tutto tremante,

she stops: she would avert the eyes of Dante from her: he looks for the sequel: she thinks he looks severely: she says,

"*Galeotto* is the name of the book,"

fancying by this timorous little flight she has drawn him far enough from the nest of her young loves. No, the eagle beak of Dante and his piercing eyes are yet over her.

"*Galeotto* is the name of the book."

"What matters that?"

"And of the writer."

"Or that either?"

At last she disarms him: but how?

"*That* day we read no more."

Such a depth of intuitive judgment, such a delicacy of perception, exists not in any other work of human genius; and from an author who, on almost all occasions, in this part of the work, betrays a deplorable want of it.

Petrarca. Perfection of poetry! The greater is my wonder at discovering nothing else of the same order or cast in this whole section of the poem. He who fainted at the recital of Francesca,

> And he who fell as a dead body falls,   [V.142]

would exterminate all the inhabitants of every town in Italy! What execrations against Florence, Pistoia, Siena, Pisa, Genoa! what hatred against the whole human race! what exultation and merriment at eternal and immitigable sufferings! Seeing this, I can not but consider

---

[2] "When we read how the desiring smile was kissed by such a lover, he, who shall never be divided from me, kissed my mouth all trembling. Galeotto is the name of the book, and of him who wrote it. That day we read no more." — V.133–138. For *viso* read *riso;* for *sia* read *fia.*

the *Inferno* as the most immoral and impious book that ever was written. Yet, hopeless that our country shall ever see again such poetry, and certain that without it our future poets would be more feebly urged forward to excellence, I would have dissuaded Dante from cancelling it, if this had been his intention. Much however as I admire his vigour and severity of style in the description of Ugolino, I acknowledge with you that I do not discover so much imagination, so much creative power, as in the Francesca. I find indeed a minute detail of probable events: but this is not all I want in a poet: it is not even all I want most in a scene of horror. Tribunals of justice, dens of murderers, wards of hospitals, schools of anatomy, will afford us nearly the same sensations, if we hear them from an accurate observer, a clear reporter, a skilful surgeon, or an attentive nurse. . . .

FROM *Fifth Day's Interview*

Boccaccio. I prayed; and my breast, after some few tears, grew calmer. Yet sleep did not ensue until the break of morning, when the dropping of soft rain on the leaves of the fig-tree at the window, and the chirping of a little bird, to tell another there was shelter under them, brought me repose and slumber. Scarcely had I closed my eyes, if indeed time can be reckoned any more in sleep than in heaven, when my Fiametta seemed to have led me into the meadow. You will see it below you: turn away that branch: gently! gently! do not break it; for the little bird sat there.

Petrarca. I think, Giovanni, I can divine the place. Although this fig-tree, growing out of the wall between the cellar and us, is fantastic enough in its branches, yet that other which I see yonder, bent down and forced to crawl along the grass by the prepotency of the young shapely walnut-tree, is much more so. It forms a seat, about a cubit above the ground, level and long enough for several.

Boccaccio. Ha! you fancy it must be a favourite spot with me, because of the two strong forked stakes wherewith it is propped and supported!

Petrarca. Poets know the haunts of poets at first sight; and he who loved Laura . . . O Laura! did I say he who *loved* thee? . . . hath whisperings where those feet would wander which have been restless after Fiametta.

Boccaccio. It is true, my imagination has often conducted her thither; but here in this chamber she appeared to me more visibly in a dream.

"Thy prayers have been heard, O Giovanni," said she.

I sprang to embrace her.

"Do not spill the water! Ah! you have spilt a part of it."

I then observed in her hand a crystal vase. A few drops were
sparkling on the sides and running down the rim: a few were trickling
from the base and from the hand that held it.

"I must go down to the brook," said she, "and fill it again as it
was filled before."

What a moment of agony was this to me! Could I be certain how
long might be her absence? She went: I was following: she made a
sign for me to turn back: I disobeyed her only an instant: yet my
sense of disobedience, increasing my feebleness and confusion, made
me lose sight of her. In the next moment she was again at my side,
with the cup quite full. I stood motionless: I feared my breath might
shake the water over. I looked her in the face for her commands . .
and to see it . . to see it so calm, so beneficent, so beautiful. I was forgetting what I had prayed for, when she lowered her head, tasted of
the cup, and gave it me. I drank; and suddenly sprang forth before
me, many groves and palaces and gardens, and their statues and their
avenues, and their labyrinths of alaternus and bay, and alcoves of
citron, and watchful loopholes in the retirements of impenetrable
pomegranate. Farther off, just below where the fountain slipt away
from its marble hall and guardian gods, arose, from their beds of moss
and drosera and darkest grass, the sisterhood of oleanders, fond of
tantalising with their bosomed flowers and their moist and pouting
blossoms the little shy rivulet, and of covering its face with all the
colours of the dawn. My dream expanded and moved forward. I
trod again the dust of Posilipo, soft as the feathers in the wings of
Sleep. I emerged on Baia; I crossed her innumerable arches; I loitered
in the breezy sunshine of her mole; I trusted the faithful seclusion of
her caverns, the keepers of so many secrets; and I reposed on the
buoyancy of her tepid sea. Then Naples, and her theatres and her
churches, and grottoes and dells and forts and promontories, rushed
forward in confusion, now among soft whispers, now among sweetest
sounds, and subsided, and sank, and disappeared. Yet a memory
seemed to come fresh from every one: each had time enough for its
tale, for its pleasure, for its reflection, for its pang. As I mounted with
silent steps the narrow staircase of the old palace, how distinctly did I
feel against the palm of my hand the coldness of that smooth stone-
work, and the greater of the cramps of iron in it!

"Ah me! is this forgetting?" cried I anxiously to Fiametta.

"We must recall these scenes before us," she replied: "such is the
punishment of them. Let us hope and believe that the apparition, and
the compunction which must follow it, will be accepted as the full
penalty, and that both will pass away almost together."

I feared to lose anything attendant on her presence: I feared to
approach her forehead with my lips: I feared to touch the lily on its
long wavy leaf in her hair, which filled my whole heart with fragrance.
Venerating, adoring, I bowed my head at last to kiss her snow-white

robe, and trembled at my presumption. And yet the effulgence of her countenance vivified while it chastened me. I loved her . . . I must not say *more* than ever . . . *better* than ever; it was Fiametta who had inhabited the skies. As my hand opened toward her,

"Beware!" said she, faintly smiling; "beware, Giovanni! Take only the crystal; take it, and drink again."

"Must all be then forgotten?" said I sorrowfully.

"Remember your prayer and mine, Giovanni? Shall both have been granted . . . O how much worse than in vain?"

I drank instantly; I drank largely. How cool my bosom grew; how could it grow so cool before her! But it was not to remain in its quiescency; its trials were not yet over. I will not, Francesco! no, I may not commemorate the incidents she related to me, nor which of us said, "I blush for having loved *first;*" nor which of us replied, "Say *least,* say *least,* and blush again."

The charm of the words (for I felt not the encumbrance of the body nor the acuteness of the spirit) seemed to possess me wholly. Although the water gave me strength and comfort, and somewhat of celestial pleasure, many tears fell around the border of the vase as she held it up before me, exhorting me to take courage, and inviting me with more than exhortation to accomplish my deliverance. She came nearer, more tenderly, more earnestly; she held the dewy globe with both hands, leaning forward, and sighed and shook her head, drooping at my pusillanimity. It was only when a ringlet had touched the rim, and perhaps the water (for a sun-beam on the surface could never have given it such a golden hue) that I took courage, clasped it, and exhausted it. Sweet as was the water, sweet as was the serenity it gave me . . . alas! that also which it moved away from me was sweet!

"This time you can trust me alone," said she, and parted my hair, and kissed my brow. Again she went toward the brook: again my agitation, my weakness, my doubt, came over me: nor could I see her while she raised the water, nor knew I whence she drew it. When she returned, she was close to me at once: she smiled: her smile pierced me to the bones: it seemed an angel's. She sprinkled the pure water on me; she looked most fondly; she took my hand; she suffered me to press hers to my bosom; but, whether by design I cannot tell, she let fall a few drops of the chilly element between.

"And now, O my beloved!" said she, "we have consigned to the bosom of God our earthly joys and sorrows. The joys can not return, let not the sorrows. These alone would trouble my repose among the blessed."

"Trouble thy repose! Fiametta! Give me the chalice!" cried I . . . "not a drop will I leave in it, not a drop."

"Take it!" said that soft voice. "O now most dear Giovanni! I know thou hast strength enough; and there is but little . . . at the bottom lies our first kiss."

"Mine! didst thou say, beloved one? and is that left thee still?"

"*Mine,*" said she, pensively; and as she abased her head, the broad leaf of the lily hid her brow and her eyes; the light of heaven shone through the flower.

"O Fiametta! Fiametta!" cried I in agony, "God is the God of mercy, God is the God of love . . . can I, can I ever?" I struck the chalice against my head, unmindful that I held it; the water covered my face and my feet. I started up, not yet awake, and I heard the name of Fiametta in the curtains.

Petrarca. Love, O Giovanni, and life itself, are but dreams at best. I do think

> Never so gloriously was Sleep attended
> As with the pageant of that heavenly maid.

But to dwell on such subjects is sinful. The recollection of them, with all their vanities, brings tears into my eyes.

Boccaccio. And into mine too . . they were so very charming.

Petrarca. Alas, alas! the time always comes when we must regret the enjoyments of our youth.

Boccaccio. If we have let them pass us.

Petrarca. I mean our indulgence in them.

Boccaccio. Francesco! I think you must remember Raffaellino degli Alfani.

Petrarca. Was it Raffaellino who lived near San Michele in Orto?

Boccaccio. The same. He was an innocent soul, and fond of fish. But whenever his friend Sabbatelli sent him a trout from Pratolino, he always kept it until next day or the day after, just long enough to render it unpalatable. He then turned it over in the platter, smelt at it closer, although the news of its condition came undeniably from a distance, touched it with his forefinger, solicited a testimony from the gills which the eyes had contradicted, sighed over it, and sent it for a present to somebody else. Were I a lover of trout as Raffaellino was, I think I should have taken an opportunity of enjoying it while the pink and crimson were glittering on it.

Petrarca. Trout, yes.

Boccaccio. And all other fish I could encompass.

Petrarca. O thou grave mocker! I did not suspect such slyness in thee: proof enough I had almost forgotten thee.

Boccaccio. Listen! listen! I fancied I caught a footstep in the passage. Come nearer; bend your head lower, that I may whisper a word in your ear. Never let Assunta hear you sigh. She is mischievous: she may have been standing at the door: not that I believe she would be guilty of any such impropriety: but who knows what girls are capable of! She has no malice, only in laughing; and a sigh sets her windmill at work, van over van, incessantly.

Petrarca. I should soon check her. I have no notion . . .

Boccaccio. After all, she is a good girl . . a trifle of the wilful. She must have it that many things are hurtful to me . . reading in particular . . it makes people so odd. Tina is a small matter of the madcap . . in her own particular way . . but exceedingly discreet, I do assure you, if they will only leave her alone.

I find I was mistaken, there was nobody.

Petrarca. A cat perhaps.

Boccaccio. No such thing. I order him over to Certaldo while the birds are laying and sitting: and he knows by experience, favourite as he is, that it is of no use to come back before he is sent for. Since the first impetuosities of youth, he has rarely been refractory or disobliging. We have lived together now these five years, unless I miscalculate; and he seems to have learnt something of my manners, wherein violence and enterprise by no means predominate. I have watched him looking at a large green lizard; and, their eyes being opposite and near, he has doubted whether it might be pleasing to me if he began the attack; and their tails on a sudden have touched one another at the decision.

Petrarca. Seldom have adverse parties felt the same desire of peace at the same moment, and none ever carried it more simultaneously and promptly into execution.

Boccaccio. He enjoys his *otium cum dignitate* at Certaldo: there he is my castellan, and his chase is unlimited in those domains. After the doom of relegation is expired, he comes hither at midsummer. And then if you could see his joy! His eyes are as deep as a well, and as clear as a fountain: he jerks his tail into the air like a royal sceptre, and waves it like the wand of a magician. You would fancy that, as Horace with his head, he was about to smite the stars with it. There is ne'er such another cat in the parish; and he knows it, a rogue! We have rare repasts together in the bean-and-bacon time, although in regard to the bean he sides with the philosopher of Samos; but after due examination. In cleanliness he is a very nun; albeit in that quality which lies between cleanliness and godliness, there is a smack of Fra Biagio about him.[1] What is that book in your hand?

Petrarca. My breviary.

Boccaccio. Well, give me mine too . . there, on the little table in the corner, under the glass of primroses. We can do nothing better.

Petrarca. What prayer were you looking for? let me find it.

Boccaccio. I don't know how it is: I am scarcely at present in a frame of mind for it. We are of one faith: the prayers of the one will do for the other: and I am sure, if you omitted my name, you would say them all over afresh. I wish you could recollect in any book as dreamy a thing to entertain me as I have been just repeating. We have had enough of Dante: I believe few of his beauties have escaped

[1] Biagio: St. Blasius, martyred with iron combs about A.D. 316. Samos: birthplace of Pythagoras, an abstemious ascetic.

us: and small faults, which we readily pass by, are fitter for small folks, as grubs are the proper bait for gudgeons.

Petrarca. I have had as many dreams as most men. We are all made up of them, as the webs of the spider are particles of her own vitality. But how infinitely less do we profit by them! I will relate to you, before we separate, one among the multitude of mine, as coming the nearest to the poetry of yours, and as having been not totally useless to me. Often have I reflected on it; sometimes with pensiveness, with sadness never.

Boccaccio. Then, Francesco, if you had with you as copious a choice of dreams as clustered on the elm-trees where the Sibyl led Æneas,[2] this, in preference to the whole swarm of them, is the queen dream for me.

Petrarca. When I was younger I was fond of wandering in solitary places, and never was afraid of slumbering in woods and grottoes. Among the chief pleasures of my life, and among the commonest of my occupations, was the bringing before me such heroes and heroines of antiquity, such poets and sages, such of the prosperous and the unfortunate, as most interested me by their courage, their wisdom, their eloquence, or their adventures. Engaging them in the conversation best suited to their characters, I knew perfectly their manners, their steps, their voices: and often did I moisten with my tears the models I had been forming of the less happy.

Boccaccio. Great is the privilege of entering into the studies of the intellectual; great is that of conversing with the guides of nations, the movers of the mass, the regulators of the unruly will, stiff, in its impurity and rust, against the finger of the Almighty Power that formed it; but give me, Francesco, give me rather the creature to sympathize with; apportion me the sufferings to assuage. Ah, gentle soul! thou wilt never send them over to another; they have better hopes from thee.

Petrarca. We both alike feel the sorrows of those around us. He who suppresses or allays them in another, breaks many thorns off his own; and future years will never harden fresh ones.

My occupation was not always in making the politician talk politics, the orator toss his torch among the populace, the philosopher run down from philosophy to cover the retreat or the advances of his sect; but sometimes in devising how such characters must act and discourse, on subjects far remote from the beaten track of their career. In like manner the philologist, and again the dialectician, were not indulged in the review and parade of their trained bands, but, at times, brought forward to show in what manner and in what degree external habits had influenced the conformation of the internal man. It was far from unprofitable to set passing events before past actors, and to record the

[2] *Aeneid* VI.282–284.

decisions of those whose interests and passions are unconcerned in them.

Boccaccio. This is surely no easy matter. The thoughts are in fact your own, however you distribute them.

Petrarca. All can not be my own; if you mean by *thoughts* the opinions and principles I should be the most desirous to inculcate. Some favourite ones perhaps may obtrude too prominently, but otherwise no misbehaviour is permitted them: reprehension and rebuke are always ready, and the offence is punished on the spot.

Boccaccio. Certainly you thus throw open, to its full extent, the range of poetry and invention; which can not but be very limited and sterile, unless where we find displayed much diversity of character as disseminated by nature, much peculiarity of sentiment as arising from position, marked with unerring skill through every shade and gradation; and finally and chiefly, much intertexture and intensity of passion. You thus convey to us more largely and expeditiously the stores of your understanding and imagination, than you ever could by sonnets or canzonets, or sinewless and sapless allegories.

But weightier works are less captivating. If you had published any such as you mention, you must have waited for their acceptance. Not only the fame of Marcellus, but every other,

Crescit occulto velut arbor ævo;[3]

and that which makes the greatest vernal shoot is apt to make the least autumnal. Authors in general who have met celebrity at starting, have already had their reward; always their utmost due, and often much beyond it. We can not hope for both celebrity and fame: supremely fortunate are the few who are allowed the liberty of choice between them. We two prefer the strength that springs from exercise and toil, acquiring it gradually and slowly: we leave to others the earlier blessing of that sleep which follows enjoyment. How many at first sight are enthusiastic in their favour! Of these how large a portion come away empty-handed and discontented! like idlers who visit the seacoast, fill their pockets with pebbles bright from the passing wave, and carry them off with rapture. After a short examination at home, every streak seems faint and dull, and the whole contexture coarse, uneven, and gritty: first one is thrown away, then another; and before the week's end the store is gone, of things so shining and wonderful.

Petrarca. Allegory, which you named with sonnets and canzonets, had few attractions for me, believing it to be the delight in general of idle, frivolous, inexcursive minds, in whose mansions there is neither hall nor portal to receive the loftier of the Passions. A stranger to the Affections, she holds a low station among the handmaidens of Poetry, being fit for little but an apparition in a mask. I had reflected

[3] "Grows like a tree unmarked by time" — Horace, *Odes* I.xii.45.

for some time on this subject, when, wearied with the length of my walk over the mountains, and finding a soft old molehill, covered with grey grass, by the way-side, I laid my head upon it, and slept. I can not tell how long it was before a species of dream or vision came over me.

Two beautiful youths appeared beside me; each was winged; but the wings were hanging down, and seemed ill adapted to flight. One of them, whose voice was the softest I ever heard, looking at me frequently, said to the other,

"He is under my guardianship for the present: do not awaken him with that feather."

Methought, hearing the whisper, I saw something like the feather on an arrow; and then the arrow itself; the whole of it, even to the point; although he carried it in such a manner that it was difficult at first to discover more than a palm's length of it: the rest of the shaft, and the whole of the barb, was behind his ankles.

"This feather never awakens any one," replied he, rather petulantly; "but it brings more of confident security, and more of cherished dreams, than you without me are capable of imparting."

"Be it so!" answered the gentler . . "none is less inclined to quarrel or dispute than I am. Many whom you have wounded grievously, call upon me for succour. But so little am I disposed to thwart you, it is seldom I venture to do more for them than to whisper a few words of comfort in passing. How many reproaches on these occasions have been cast upon me for indifference and infidelity! Nearly as many, and nearly in the same terms, as upon you!"

"Odd enough that we, O Sleep! should be thought so alike!" said Love, contemptuously. "Yonder is he who bears a nearer resemblance to you: the dullest have observed it." I fancied I turned my eyes to where he was pointing, and saw at a distance the figure he designated. Meanwhile the contention went on uninterruptedly. Sleep was slow in asserting his power or his benefits. Love recapitulated them; but only that he might assert his own above them. Suddenly he called on me to decide, and to choose my patron. Under the influence, first of the one, then of the other, I sprang from repose to rapture, I alighted from rapture on repose . . and knew not which was sweetest. Love was very angry with me, and declared he would cross me throughout the whole of my existence. Whatever I might on other occasions have thought of his veracity, I now felt too surely the conviction that he would keep his word. At last, before the close of the altercation, the third Genius had advanced, and stood near us. I can not tell how I knew him, but I knew him to be the Genius of Death. Breathless as I was at beholding him, I soon became familiar with his features. First they seemed only calm; presently they grew contemplative; and lastly beautiful: those of the Graces themselves are less regular, less harmonious, less composed. Love glanced at him unsteadily, with a countenance in which there was somewhat of anxiety, somewhat of disdain; and cried, "Go away! go away! nothing that thou touchest, lives!"

"Say rather, child!" replied the advancing form, and advancing grew loftier and statelier, "Say rather that nothing of beautiful or of glorious lives its own true life until my wing hath passed over it."

Love pouted, and rumpled and bent down with his forefinger the stiff short feathers on his arrow-head; but replied not. Although he frowned worse than ever, and at me, I dreaded him less and less, and scarcely looked toward him. The milder and calmer Genius, the third, in proportion as I took courage to contemplate him, regarded me with more and more complacency. He held neither flower nor arrow, as the others did; but, throwing back the clusters of dark curls that over-shadowed his countenance, he presented to me his hand, openly and benignly. I shrank on looking at him so near, and yet I sighed to love him. He smiled, not without an expression of pity, at perceiving my diffidence, my timidity: for I remembered how soft was the hand of Sleep, how warm and entrancing was Love's. By degrees, I became ashamed of my ingratitude; and turning my face away, I held out my arms, and felt my neck within his. Composure strewed and allayed all the throbbings of my bosom; the coolness of freshest morning breathed around; the heavens seemed to open above me; while the beautiful cheek of my deliverer rested on my head. I would now have looked for those others; but knowing my intention by my gesture, he said consolatorily,

"Sleep is on his way to the Earth, where many are calling him; but it is not to these he hastens; for every call only makes him fly farther off. Sedately and gravely as he looks, he is nearly as capricious and volatile as the more arrogant and ferocious one."

"And Love!" said I, "whither is he departed? If not too late, I would propitiate and appease him."

"He who can not follow me, he who can not overtake and pass me," said the Genius, "is unworthy of the name, the most glorious in earth or heaven. Look up! Love is yonder, and ready to receive thee."

I looked: the earth was under me: I saw only the clear blue sky, and something brighter above it.

Charles Lamb

CHARLES LAMB

CHRONOLOGY

1775 Born February 10 in London.

1782 October 9, entered Christ's Hospital, London, where he established friendship with Coleridge.

1789 November 23, as a Deputy Grecian, completed course at Christ's Hospital.

1791–92 Worked for five months in South Sea House.

1792 April 5, entered employment as clerk in East India House.

1795–96 Confined for six weeks in a mad house.

1796 Accepted lifelong responsibility for sister Mary, aged 32, who on September 21 stabbed their mother in one of many periods of insanity.

1796–98 Contributed poems to volumes by Coleridge and Charles Lloyd; wrote, as afterward, for newspapers and periodicals.

1798 Summer, *A Tale of Rosamund Gray*.

1802 January (?), *John Woodvil: A Tragedy*.

1806 December 10, *Mr. H.*, a farce, hissed at Drury Lane.

1807 January, *Tales from Shakespear*, with Mary.

1808 Summer, *Specimens of English Dramatic Poets*.

1811–21 Contributed to Hunt's *Reflector, Examiner*, and *Indicator*.

1818 June, *Works*, a miscellaneous collection in two volumes.

1819 Proposed marriage to Fanny Kelly, who declined.

1820–25 Contributed essays, including those signed "Elia," to *London Magazine*.

1823 January, *Elia*, a selection from essays first published 1819–22.

1825 March 29, retired with a pension from East India House.

1830 July, *Album Verses*.

1833 January, *The Last Essays of Elia*. With Mary and adopted daughter, Emma Isola, moved in May from Enfield to Edmonton. In July, Emma married Lamb's publisher, Edward Moxon.

1834 Died December 27. Mary died in 1847, aged 82.

Preface.
By a Friend of the Late Elia

❲ Under the title of "A Character of the Late Elia," an earlier version of this "Preface" appeared in the *London Magazine* for January 1823, to mark the recent publication of *Elia* as a book. With the omission of several paragraphs, it took its present form at the head of *The Last Essays of Elia*, 1833. The essay claims for Elia the kind of amiable, humorous eccentricity ascribed to Yorick in Laurence Sterne's *Tristram Shandy*. For examples of the character as a literary type, turn to the essays of Leigh Hunt. ❳

This poor gentleman, who for some months past had been in a declining way, hath at length paid his final tribute to nature.

To say truth, it is time he were gone. The humour of the thing, if there was ever much in it, was pretty well exhausted; and a two years' and a half existence has been a tolerable duration for a phantom.

I am now at liberty to confess, that much which I have heard objected to my late friend's writings was well-founded. Crude they are, I grant you — a sort of unlicked, incondite things — villainously pranked in an affected array of antique modes and phrases. They had not been *his*, if they had been other than such; and better it is, that a writer should be natural in a self-pleasing quaintness, than to affect a naturalness (so called) that should be strange to him. Egotistical they have been pronounced by some who did not know, that what he tells us, as of himself, was often true only (historically) of another; as in a former Essay (to save many instances) — where under the *first person* (his favourite figure) he shadows forth the forlorn estate of a country-boy placed at a London school, far from his friends and connections — in direct opposition to his own early history. If it be egotism to imply and twine with his own identity the griefs and affections of another — making himself many, or reducing many unto himself — then is the skilful novelist, who all along brings in his hero, or heroine, speaking of themselves, the greatest egotist of all; who yet has never, therefore, been accused of that narrowness. And how shall the intenser dramatist escape being faulty, who doubtless, under cover of passion uttered by another, oftentimes gives blameless vent to his most inward feelings, and expresses his own story modestly?

My late friend was in many respects a singular character. Those who did not like him, hated him; and some, who once liked him, afterwards became his bitterest haters. The truth is, he gave himself too

191

little concern what he uttered, and in whose presence. He observed neither time' nor place, and would e'en out with what came uppermost. With the severe religionist he would pass for a free-thinker; while the other faction set him down for a bigot, or persuaded themselves that he belied his sentiments. Few understood him; and I am not certain that at all times he quite understood himself. He too much affected that dangerous figure — irony. He sowed doubtful speeches, and reaped plain, unequivocal hatred. — He would interrupt the gravest discussion with some light jest; and yet, perhaps, not quite irrelevant in ears that could understand it. Your long and much talkers hated him. The informal habit of his mind, joined to an inveterate impediment of speech, forbade him to be an orator; and he seemed determined that no one else should play that part when he was present. He was *petit* and ordinary in his person and appearance. I have seen him sometimes in what is called good company, but where he has been a stranger, sit silent, and be suspected for an odd fellow; till some unlucky occasion provoking it, he would stutter out some senseless pun (not altogether senseless perhaps, if rightly taken), which has stamped his character for the evening. It was hit or miss with him; but nine times out of ten, he contrived by this device to send away a whole company his enemies. His conceptions rose kindlier than his utterance, and his happiest *impromptus* had the appearance of effort. He has been accused of trying to be witty, when in truth he was but struggling to give his poor thoughts articulation. He chose his companions for some individuality of character which they manifested. — Hence, not many persons of science, and few professed *literati*, were of his councils. They were, for the most part, persons of an uncertain fortune; and, as to such people commonly nothing is more obnoxious than a gentleman of settled (though moderate) income, he passed with most of them for a great miser. To my knowledge this was a mistake. His *intimados*, to confess a truth, were in the world's eye a ragged regiment. He found them floating on the surface of society; and the colour, or something else, in the weed pleased him. The burrs stuck to him — but they were good and loving burrs for all that. He never greatly cared for the society of what are called good people. If any of these were scandalised (and offences were sure to arise), he could not help it. When he has been remonstrated with for not making more concessions to the feelings of good people, he would retort by asking, what one point did these good people ever concede to him? He was temperate in his meals and diversions, but always kept a little on this side of abstemiousness. Only in the use of the Indian weed he might be thought a little excessive. He took it, he would say, as a solvent of speech. Marry — as the friendly vapour ascended, how his prattle would curl up sometimes with it! the ligaments, which tongue-tied him, were loosened, and the stammerer proceeded a statist!

I do not know whether I ought to bemoan or rejoice that my old friend is departed. His jests were beginning to grow obsolete, and his stories to be found out. He felt the approaches of age; and while he pretended to cling to life, you saw how slender were the ties left to bind him. Discoursing with him latterly on this subject, he expressed himself with a pettishness, which I thought unworthy of him. In our walks about his suburban retreat (as he called it) at Shacklewell, some children belonging to a school of industry had met us, and bowed and curtseyed, as he thought, in an especial manner to *him*. "They take me for a visiting governor," he muttered earnestly. He had a horror, which he carried to a foible, of looking like anything important and parochial. He thought that he approached nearer to that stamp daily. He had a general aversion from being treated like a grave or respectable character, and kept a wary eye upon the advances of age that should so entitle him. He herded always, while it was possible, with people younger than himself. He did not conform to the march of time, but was dragged along in the procession. His manners lagged behind his years. He was too much of the boy-man. The *toga virilis* never sate gracefully on his shoulders. The impressions of infancy had burnt into him, and he resented the impertinence of manhood. These were weaknesses; but such as they were, they are a key to explicate some of his writings.

Christ's Hospital
Five and Thirty Years Ago

❬ Lamb wrote "Recollections" of his schooldays for the *Gentleman's Magazine* of June 1813, reprinted in his *Works* of 1818. Actually that first essay contained more general information and fewer recollections than "Christ's Hospital Five and Thirty Years Ago," which was reprinted in *Elia* from the *London Magazine* of November 1820. This later essay is more representative of Lamb stylistically and structurally. Especially in the opening paragraphs, he imagines himself in Coleridge's circumstances at the school rather than his own. The text here is taken from *Elia*, 1823. ❭

In Mr. Lamb's "Works," published a year or two since, I find a magnificent eulogy on my old school,[1] such as it was, or now appears to him to have been, between the years 1782 and 1789. It happens, very oddly, that my own standing at Christ's was nearly corresponding

[1] Recollections of Christ's Hospital. [C.L.]

with his; and, with all gratitude to him for his enthusiasm for the
cloisters, I think he has contrived to bring together whatever can be
said in praise of them, dropping all the other side of the argument most
ingeniously.

I remember L. at school; and can well recollect that he had some
peculiar advantages, which I and others of his schoolfellows had not.
His friends lived in town, and were near at hand; and he had the
privilege of going to see them, almost as often as he wished, through
some invidious distinction, which was denied to us. The present
worthy sub-treasurer to the Inner Temple can explain how that happened. He had his tea and hot rolls in a morning, while we were
battening upon our quarter of a penny loaf — our *crug* — moistened
with attenuated small beer, in wooden piggins, smacking of the
pitched leathern jack it was poured from. Our Monday's milk porritch,
blue and tasteless, and the pease soup of Saturday, coarse and choking,
were enriched for him with a slice of "extraordinary bread and
butter," from the hot-loaf of the Temple. The Wednesday's mess of
millet, somewhat less repugnant — (we had three banyan to four
meat days in the week) — was endeared to his palate with a lump of
double-refined, and a smack of ginger (to make it go down the more
glibly) or the fragrant cinnamon. In lieu of our *half-pickled* Sundays,
or *quite fresh* boiled beef on Thursdays (strong as *caro equina*), with
detestable marigolds floating in the pail to poison the broth — our
scanty mutton crags on Fridays — and rather more savoury, but
grudging, portions of the same flesh, rotten-roasted or rare, on the
Tuesdays (the only dish which excited our appetites, and disappointed
our stomachs, in almost equal proportion) — he had his hot plate
of roast veal, or the more tempting griskin (exotics unknown to our
palates), cooked in the paternal kitchen (a great thing), and brought
him daily by his maid or aunt! I remember the good old relative (in
whom love forbade pride) squatting down upon some odd stone in a
by-nook of the cloisters, disclosing the viands (of higher regale than
those cates which the ravens ministered to the Tishbite); and the contending passions of L. at the unfolding. There was love for the
bringer; shame for the thing brought, and the manner of its bringing;
sympathy for those who were too many to share in it; and, at top of
all, hunger (eldest, strongest of the passions!) predominant, breaking
down the stony fences of shame, and awkwardness, and a troubling
over-consciousness.[2]

I was a poor friendless boy. My parents, and those who should care
for me, were far away. Those few acquaintances of theirs, which they
could reckon upon being kind to me in the great city, after a little
forced notice, which they had the grace to take of me on my first

[2] Tishbite: Elijah, in *Paradise Regained* II.266–270 from 1 Kings 17:6;
piggins: pails; banyan: vegetable (in Christ's Hospital slang); double-
refined: sugar; *caro equina:* horsemeat; crags: necks.

arrival in town, soon grew tired of my holiday visits. They seemed
to them to recur too often, though I thought them few enough; and,
one after another, they all failed me, and I felt myself alone among six
hundred playmates.

O the cruelty of separating a poor lad from his early homestead!
The yearnings which I used to have towards it in those unfledged
years! How, in my dreams, would my native town (far in the west)
come back, with its church, and trees, and faces! How I would wake
weeping, and in the anguish of my heart exclaim upon sweet Calne
in Wiltshire!

To this late hour of my life, I trace impressions left by the recollection of those friendless holidays. The long warm days of summer never
return but they bring with them a gloom from the haunting memory
of those *whole-day-leaves,* when, by some strange arrangement, we
were turned out, for the live-long day, upon our own hands, whether
we had friends to go to, or none. I remember those bathing-excursions
to the New-River, which L. recalls with such relish, better, I think,
than he can — for he was a home-seeking lad, and did not much care
for such water-pastimes: — How merrily we would sally forth into
the fields; and strip under the first warmth of the sun; and wanton like
young dace in the streams; getting us appetites for noon, which those
of us that were pennyless (our scanty morning crust long since exhausted) had not the means of allaying — while the cattle, and the
birds, and the fishes, were at feed about us, and we had nothing to
satisfy our cravings — the very beauty of the day, and the exercise of
the pastime, and the sense of liberty, setting a keener edge upon them!
— How faint and languid, finally, we would return, towards nightfall,
to our desired morsel, half-rejoicing, half-reluctant, that the hours of
our uneasy liberty had expired!

It was worse in the days of winter, to go prowling about the streets
objectless — shivering at cold windows of print-shops, to extract a
little amusement; or haply, as a last resort, in the hope of a little
novelty, to pay a fifty-times repeated visit (where our individual faces
should be as well known to the warden as those of his own charges) to
the Lions in the Tower — to whose levée, by courtesy immemorial,
we had a prescriptive title to admission.

L.'s governor (so we called the patron who presented us to the
foundation) lived in a manner under his paternal roof. Any complaint which he had to make was sure of being attended to. This was
understood at Christ's, and was an effectual screen to him against the
severity of masters, or worse tyranny of the monitors. The oppressions
of these young brutes are heart-sickening to call to recollection. I
have been called out of my bed, and *waked for the purpose,* in the
coldest winter nights — and this not once, but night after night — in
my shirt, to receive the discipline of a leathern thong, with eleven
other sufferers, because it pleased my callow overseer, when there has

been any talking heard after we were gone to bed, to make the six last
beds in the dormitory, where the youngest children of us slept, answerable for an offience they neither dared to commit, nor had the power
to hinder. — The same execrable tyranny drove the younger part of
us from the fires, when our feet were perishing with snow; and, under
the cruelest penalties, forbad the indulgence of a drink of water, when
we lay in sleepless summer nights, fevered with the season, and the
day's sports.

There was one H——, who, I learned, in after days, was seen
expiating some maturer offence in the hulks. (Do I flatter myself in
fancying that this might be the planter of that name, who suffered
— at Nevis, I think, or St. Kits, — some few years since? My
friend Tobin was the benevolent instrument of bringing him to the
gallows.) This petty Nero actually branded a boy, who had offended
him, with a red hot iron; and nearly starved forty of us, with exacting
contributions, to the one half of our bread, to pamper a young ass,
which, incredible as it may seem, with the connivance of the nurse's
daughter (a young flame of his) he had contrived to smuggle in, and
keep upon the leads of the *ward*, as they called our dormitories. This
game went on for better than a week, till the foolish beast, not able to
fare well but he must cry roast meat — happier than Caligula's minion,
could he have kept his own counsel — but, foolisher, alas! than any of
his species in the fables — waxing fat, and kicking, in the fulness of
bread, one unlucky minute would needs proclaim his good fortune to
the world below; and, laying out his simple throat, blew such a ram's
horn blast, as (toppling down the walls of his own Jericho) set concealment any longer at defiance.[3] The client was dismissed, with certain attentions, to Smithfield; but I never understood that the patron
underwent any censure on the occasion. This was in the stewardship
of L.'s admired Perry.

Under the same *facile* administration, can L. have forgotten the
cool impunity with which the nurses used to carry away openly, in
open platters, for their own tables, one out of two of every hot joint,
which the careful matron had been seeing scrupulously weighed out
for our dinners? These things were daily practised in that magnificent
apartment, which L. (grown connoisseur since, we presume) praises
so highly for the grand paintings "by Verrio, and others," with which
it is "hung round and adorned." But the sight of sleek well-fed blue-
coat boys in pictures was, at that time, I believe, little consolatory to
him, or us, the living ones, who saw the better part of our provisions
carried away before our faces by harpies; and ourselves reduced
(with the Trojan in the hall of Dido)

> To feed our mind with idle portraiture.[4]

[3] According to Seutonius, Caligula proposed to make his favorite horse a
Roman consul. On Jericho, see Joshua 6:5.

[4] *Aeneid* I.464.

L. has recorded the repugnance of the school to *gags*, or the fat of fresh beef boiled; and sets it down to some superstition. But these unctuous morsels are never grateful to young palates (children are universally fat-haters) and in strong, coarse, boiled meats, *unsalted*, are detestable. A *gag-eater* in our time was equivalent to a *goul*, and held in equal detestation. —— suffered under the imputation.

> —————— 'Twas said,
> He ate strange flesh.[5]

He was observed, after dinner, carefully to gather up the remnants left at his table (not many, nor very choice fragments, you may credit me) — and, in an especial manner, these disreputable morsels, which he would convey away, and secretly stow in the settle that stood at his bed-side. None saw when he ate them. It was rumoured that he privately devoured them in the night. He was watched, but no traces of such midnight practices were discoverable. Some reported, that, on leave-days, he had been seen to carry out of the bounds a large blue check handkerchief, full of something. This then must be the accursed thing. Conjecture next was at work to imagine how he could dispose of it. Some said he sold it to the beggars. This belief generally prevailed. He went about moping. None spake to him. No one would play with him. He was excommunicated; put out of the pale of the school. He was too powerful a boy to be beaten, but he underwent every mode of that negative punishment, which is more grievous than many stripes. Still he persevered. At length he was observed by two of his school-fellows, who were determined to get at the secret, and had traced him one leave-day for that purpose, to enter a large worn-out building, such as there exist specimens of in Chancery-lane, which are let out to various scales of pauperism with open door, and a common staircase. After him they silently slunk in, and followed by stealth up four flights, and saw him tap at a poor wicket, which was opened by an aged woman, meanly clad. Suspicion was now ripened into certainty. The informers had secured their victim. They had him in their toils. Accusation was formally preferred, and retribution most signal was looked for. Mr. Hathaway, the then steward (for this happened a little after my time), with that patient sagacity which tempered all his conduct, determined to investigate the matter, before he proceeded to sentence. The result was, that the supposed mendicants, the receivers or purchasers of the mysterious scraps, turned out to be the parents of ——, an honest couple come to decay, — whom this seasonable supply had, in all probability, saved from mendicancy; and that this young stork, at the expense of his own good name, had all this while been only feeding the old birds! — The governors on this occasion, much to their honour, voted a present relief to the family of

[5] Cf. *Antony and Cleopatra* I.iv.67.

———, and presented him with a silver medal. The lesson which the steward read upon RASH JUDGMENT, on the occasion of publicly delivering the medal to ———, I believe, would not be lost upon his auditory. — I had left school then, but I well remember ———. He was a tall, shambling youth, with a cast in his eye, not at all calculated to conciliate hostile prejudices. I have since seen him carrying a baker's basket. I think I heard he did not do quite so well by himself, as he had done by the old folks.

I was a hypochondriac lad; and the sight of a boy in fetters, upon the day of my first putting on the blue clothes, was not exactly fitted to assuage the natural terrors of initiation. I was of tender years, barely turned of seven; and had only read of such things in books, or seen them but in dreams. I was told he had *run away*. This was the punishment for the first offence. — As a novice I was soon after taken to see the dungeons. These were little, square, Bedlam cells, where a boy could just lie at his length upon straw and a blanket — a mattress, I think, was afterwards substituted — with a peep of light, let in askance, from a prison-orifice at top, barely enough to read by. Here the poor boy was locked in by himself all day, without sight of any but the porter who brought him his bread and water — who *might not speak to him;* — or of the beadle, who came twice a week to call him out to receive his periodical chastisement, which was almost welcome, because it separated him for a brief interval from solitude: — and here he was shut up by himself *of nights*, out of the reach of any sound, to suffer whatever horrors the weak nerves, and superstition incident to his time of life, might subject him to.[6] This was the penalty for the second offence. — Wouldst thou like, reader, to see what became of him in the next degree?

The culprit, who had been a third time an offender, and whose expulsion was at this time deemed irreversible, was brought forth, as at some solemn *auto da fe*, arrayed in uncouth and most appalling attire — all trace of his late "watchet weeds" carefully effaced, he was exposed in a jacket, resembling those which London lamplighters formerly delighted in, with a cap of the same. The effect of this divestiture was such as the ingenious devisers of it could have anticipated. With his pale and frighted features, it was as if some of those disfigurements in Dante had seized upon him. In this disguisement he was brought into the hall (*L.'s favourite stateroom*), where awaited him the whole number of his school-fellows, whose joint lessons and sports he was thenceforth to share no more; the awful presence of the

---

[6] One or two instances of lunacy, or attempted suicide, accordingly, at length convinced the governors of the impolicy of this part of the sentence, and the midnight torture to the spirits was dispensed with. — This fancy of dungeons for children was a sprout of Howard's brain; for which (saving the reverence due to Holy Paul) methinks, I could willingly spit upon his statue. [C.L. John Howard (c.1726–90) was a penal reformer.]

steward, to be seen for the last time; of the executioner beadle, clad in his state robe for the occasion; and of two faces more, of direr import, because never but in these extremities visible. These were governors; two of whom, by choice, or charter, were always accustomed to officiate at these *Ultima Supplicia;* not to mitigate (so at least we understood it), but to enforce the uttermost stripe. Old Bamber Gascoigne, and Peter Aubert, I remember, were colleagues on one occasion, when the beadle turning rather pale, a glass of brandy was ordered to prepare him for the mysteries. The scourging was, after the old Roman fashion, long and stately. The lictor accompanied the criminal quite round the hall. We were generally too faint with attending to the previous disgusting circumstances, to make accurate report with our eyes of the degree of corporal suffering inflicted. Report, of course, gave out the back knotty and livid. After scourging, he was made over, in his *San Benito,* to his friends, if he had any (but commonly such poor runagates were friendless), or to his parish officer, who, to enhance the effect of the scene, had his station allotted to him on the outside of the hall gate.[7]

These solemn pageantries were not played off so often as to spoil the general mirth of the community. We had plenty of exercise and recreation *after* school hours; and, for myself, I must confess, that I was never happier, than *in* them. The Upper and the Lower Grammar Schools were held in the same room; and an imaginary line only divided their bounds. Their character was as different as that of the inhabitants on the two sides of the Pyrenees. The Rev. James Boyer was the Upper Master; but the Rev. Matthew Field presided over that portion of the apartment, of which I had the good fortune to be a member. We lived a life as careless as birds. We talked and did just what we pleased, and nobody molested us. We carried an accidence, or a grammar, for form; but, for any trouble it gave us, we might take two years in getting through the verbs deponent, and another two in forgetting all that we had learned about them. There was now and then the formality of saying a lesson, but if you had not learned it, a brush across the shoulders (just enough to disturb a fly) was the sole remonstrance. Field never used the rod; and in truth he wielded the cane with no great good will — holding it "like a dancer."[8] It looked in his hands rather like an emblem than an instrument of authority; and an emblem, too, he was ashamed of. He was a good easy man, that did not care to ruffle his own peace, nor perhaps set any great consideration upon the value of juvenile time. He came among us,

[7] Divested of his "watchet weeds" (blue coat), the culprit in this paragraph undergoes *Ultima Supplicia* (extreme penalties) as formally as if under the Roman Empire or the Spanish Inquisition, and is thus left as in a sanbenito, the penitential garment worn by the heretic at an auto-da-fé.

[8] *Antony and Cleopatra* III.xi.36. In another essay, Mrs. Battle holds her cards "like a dancer."

now and then, but often staid away whole days from us; and when he
came, it made no difference to us — he had his private room to retire
to, the short time he staid, to be out of the sound of our noise. Our
mirth and uproar went on. We had classics of our own, without being
beholden to "insolent Greece or haughty Rome,"[9] that passed current
among us — Peter Wilkins — the Adventures of the Hon. Capt.
Robert Boyle — the Fortunate Blue Coat Boy — and the like. Or we
cultivated a turn for mechanic or scientific operations; making little
sun-dials of paper; or weaving those ingenious parentheses, called
cat-cradles; or making dry peas to dance upon the end of a tin pipe;
or studying the art military over that laudable game "French and English,"[10] and a hundred other such devices to pass away the time —
mixing the useful with the agreeable — as would have made the souls
of Rousseau and John Locke chuckle to have seen us.

Matthew Field belonged to that class of modest divines who affect
to mix in equal proportion the *gentleman,* the *scholar,* and the *Christian;* but, I know not how, the first ingredient is generally found to be
the predominating dose in the composition. He was engaged in gay
parties, or with his courtly bow at some episcopal levée, when he
should have been attending upon us. He had for many years the
classical charge of a hundred children, during the four or five first
years of their education; and his very highest form seldom proceeded
further than two or three of the introductory fables of Phædrus. How
things were suffered to go on thus, I cannot guess. Boyer, who was
the proper person to have remedied these abuses, always affected,
perhaps felt, a delicacy in interfering in a province not strictly his
own. I have not been without my suspicions, that he was not altogether displeased at the contrast we presented to his end of the
school. We were a sort of Helots to his young Spartans. He would
sometimes, with ironic deference, send to borrow a rod of the Under
Master, and then, with Sardonic grin, observe to one of his upper boys,
"how neat and fresh the twigs looked." While his pale students were
battering their brains over Xenophon and Plato, with a silence as deep
as that enjoined by the Samite, we were enjoying ourselves at our
ease in our little Goshen. We saw a little into the secrets of his discipline, and the prospect did but the more reconcile us to our lot. His
thunders rolled innocuous for us; his storms came near, but never
touched us; contrary to Gideon's miracle, while all around were
drenched, our fleece was dry.[11] His boys turned out the better
scholars; we, I suspect, have the advantage in temper. His pupils
cannot speak of him without something of terror allaying their grati-

[9] Ben Jonson, *To the Memory of Shakespeare* 39.
[10] The winner, with his eyes closed, slashed a pencil through more dots
than the loser.
[11] Cowley. [C.L. Abraham Cowley (1618–67), *The Complaint* IV.12,
drawing upon Judges 6:37–38.]

tude; the remembrance of Field comes back with all the soothing images of indolence, and summer slumbers, and work like play, and innocent idleness, and Elysian exemptions, and life itself a "playing holiday."[12]

Though sufficiently removed from the jurisdiction of Boyer, we were near enough (as I have said) to understand a little of his system. We occasionally heard sounds of the *Ululantes,* and caught glances of Tartarus. B. was a rabid pedant. His English style was crampt to barbarism. His Easter anthems (for his duty obliged him to those periodical flights) were grating as scrannel pipes.[13] — He would laugh, ay, and heartily, but then it must be at Flaccus's quibble about *Rex* — or at the *tristis severitas in vultu,* or *inspicere in patinas,* of Terence — thin jests, which at their first broaching could hardly have had *vis* enough to move a Roman muscle.[14] — He had two wigs, both pedantic, but of differing omen. The one serene, smiling, fresh powdered, betokening a mild day. The other, an old discoloured, unkempt, angry caxon, denoting frequent and bloody execution. Woe to the school, when he made his morning appearance in his *passy,* or *passionate wig.* No comet expounded surer. — J. B. had a heavy hand. I have known him double his knotty fist at a poor trembling child (the maternal milk hardly dry upon its lips) with a "Sirrah, do you presume to set your wits at me?" — Nothing was more common than to see him make a head-long entry into the schoolroom, from his inner recess, or library, and, with turbulent eye, singling out a lad, roar out, "Od's my life, Sirrah," (his favourite adjuration) "I have a great mind to whip you," — then, with as sudden a retracting impulse, fling back into his lair — and, after a cooling lapse of some minutes (during which all but the culprit had totally forgotten the context) drive headlong out again, piecing out his imperfect sense, as if it had been some Devil's Litany, with the expletory yell — "*and I* WILL, *too.*" — In his gentler moods, when the *rabidus furor* was assuaged, he had

12 Cf. *1 Henry IV* I.ii.228.

Helots: Spartans exhibited drunken slaves to their sons as a warning. Samite: Pythagoras of Samos required each new pupil to listen in silence for five years. Goshen: free of plagues, from Exodus 8:22.

13 In this and every thing B. was the antipodes of his co-adjutor. While the former was digging his brains for crude anthems, worth a pig-nut, F. would be recreating his gentlemanly fancy in the more flowery walks of the Muses. A little dramatic effusion of his, under the name of Vertumnus and Pomona, is not yet forgotten by the chroniclers of that sort of literature. It was accepted by Garrick, but the town did not give it their sanction. — B. used to say of it, in a way of half-compliment, half-irony, that it was *too classical for representation.* [C.L.]

Ululantes: howling sufferers; *scrannel:* harsh, from *Lycidas* 124.

14 See Horace (Flaccus), *Satires* I.vii.35; Terence, *Andrea* V.ii ("sad rigor in the face" — of a liar) and *The Adelphi* III.iii ("to look into the stewpans" — for a reflection of life).

resort to an ingenious method, peculiar, for what I have heard, to himself, of whipping the boy, and reading the Debates, at the same time; a paragraph, and a lash between; which in those times, when parliamentary oratory was most at a height and flourishing in these realms, was not calculated to impress the patient with a veneration for the diffuser graces of rhetoric.

Once, and but once, the uplifted rod was known to fall ineffectual from his hand — when droll squinting W — having been caught putting the inside of the master's desk to a use for which the architect had clearly not designed it, to justify himself, with great simplicity averred, that *he did not know that the thing had been forewarned.* This exquisite irrecognition of any law antecedent to the *oral* or *declaratory,* struck so irresistibly upon the fancy of all who heard it (the pedagogue himself not excepted) that remission was unavoidable.

L. has given credit to B.'s great merits as an instructor. Coleridge, in his literary life, has pronounced a more intelligible and ample encomium on them. The author of the Country Spectator doubts not to compare him with the ablest teachers of antiquity. Perhaps we cannot dismiss him better than with the pious ejaculation of C. — when he heard that his old master was on his death-bed — "Poor J. B.! — may all his faults be forgiven; and may he be wafted to bliss by little cherub boys, all head and wings, with no *bottoms* to reproach his sublunary infirmities."

Under him were many good and sound scholars bred. — First Grecian of my time was Lancelot Pepys Stevens, kindest of boys and men, since Co-grammar-master (and inseparable companion) with Dr. T——e. What an edifying spectacle did this brace of friends present to those who remembered the anti-socialities of their predecessors! — You never met the one by chance in the street without a wonder, which was quickly dissipated by the almost immediate sub-appearance of the other. Generally arm in arm, these kindly coadjutors lightened for each other the toilsome duties of their profession, and when, in advanced age, one found it convenient to retire, the other was not long in discovering that it suited him to lay down the fasces also. Oh, it is pleasant, as it is rare, to find the same arm linked in yours at forty, which at thirteen helped it to turn over the *Cicero De Amicitia,* or some tale of Antique Friendship, which the young heart even then was burning to anticipate! — Co-Grecian with S. was Th——, who has since executed with ability various diplomatic functions at the Northern courts. Th—— was a tall, dark, saturnine youth, sparing of speech, with raven locks. — Thomas Fanshaw Middleton followed him (now Bishop of Calcutta) a scholar and a gentleman in his teens. He has the reputation of an excellent critic; and is author (besides the Country Spectator) of a Treatise on the Greek Article, against Sharpe. — M. is said to bear his mitre high in India, where the *regni novitas*[15] (I dare say) sufficiently justifies the bearing. A humility quite as primitive as that of Jewel or Hooker might not be exactly fitted to impress the minds of those Anglo-Asiatic diocesans with a reverence for home institutions, and the church which those fathers watered. The manners of M. at school, though firm, were mild, and unassuming. — Next to M. (if not senior to him) was Richards, author of the *Aboriginal Britons*, the most spirited of the Oxford Prize Poems; a pale, studious Grecian. — Then followed poor S——, ill-fated M——! of these the Muse is silent.

> Finding some of Edward's race
> Unhappy, pass their annals by.[16]

Come back into memory, like as thou wert in the day-spring of thy fancies, with hope like a fiery column before thee — the dark pillar not yet turned — Samuel Taylor Coleridge — Logician, Metaphysician, Bard! — How have I seen the casual passer through the Cloisters stand still, intranced with admiration (while he weighed the disproportion between the *speech* and the *garb* of the young Mirandula), to hear thee unfold, in thy deep and sweet intonations, the mysteries of Jamblichus, or Plotinus (for even in those years thou waxedst not pale at such philosophic draughts), or reciting Homer in his Greek, or Pindar — while the walls of the old Grey Friars re-echoed to the accents of the *inspired charity-boy!* — Many were the "wit-combats," (to dally awhile with the words of old Fuller,) between him and C. V. Le G——, "which two I behold like a Spanish great gallion, and an English man of war; Master Coleridge, like the former, was built far higher in learning, solid, but slow in his performances. C. V. L., with the English man of war, lesser in bulk, but lighter in sailing, could turn with all tides, tack about, and take advantage of all winds, by the quickness of his wit and invention."[17]

Nor shalt thou, their compeer, be quickly forgotten, Allen, with the cordial smile, and still more cordial laugh, with which thou wert wont to make the old Cloisters shake, in thy cognition of some poignant jest of theirs; or the anticipation of some more material, and, peradventure, practical one, of thine own. Extinct are those smiles, with that beautiful countenance, with which (for thou wert the *Nireus formosus* of the school), in the days of thy maturer waggery, thou didst disarm the wrath of infuriated town-damsel, who, incensed by provoking pinch, turning tigress-like round, suddenly converted by thy angel-look, exchanged the half-formed terrible "*bl*——," for a

[15] "newness of the reign" (*Aeneid* I.562). Middleton was the first Anglican Bishop of Calcutta.

[16] Matthew Prior, *Carmen Seculare* for 1700, VIII.4–5.

[17] Adapted from Thomas Fuller, *Worthies of England*, 1662, on exchanges of wit between Shakespeare and Jonson.

gentler greeting — *"bless thy handsome face!"*

Next follow two, who ought to be now alive, and the friends of Elia — the junior Le G—— and F——; who impelled, the former by a roving temper, the latter by too quick a sense of neglect — ill capable of enduring the slights poor Sizars are sometimes subject to in our seats of learning — exchanged their Alma Mater for the camp; perishing, one by climate, and one on the plains of Salamanca: — Le G——, sanguine, volatile, sweet-natured; F—— dogged, faithful, anticipative of insult, warm-hearted, with something of the old Roman height about him.

Fine, frank-hearted Fr——, the present master of Hertford, with Marmaduke T——, mildest of Missionaries — and both my good friends still — close the catalogue of Grecians in my time.[18]

The Two Races of Men

❰ The germ of this essay, which was published in the *London Magazine* of December 1820, is evident in a letter to Wordsworth dated April 9, 1816. As in other essays, Lamb fits metaphors mock-heroically to his subject: when Coleridge has failed to return the best of ten volumes in the set of Dodsley's *Old Plays,* Lamb likens himself to Priam, who regarded his nine remaining sons as useless because the Fates at the siege of Troy had "borrowed" his best son, Hector; again, the remaining volume of *The Life of John Buncle,* by Thomas Amory, mourns its lost mate just as Buncle mourned one of his wives, with "eyes closed." Thus Lamb inweaves literary judgments with humorous remarks on human conduct. He relies on metaphor to unify the whole. The text here follows *Elia,* 1823. ❱

[18] Initials in the essay, according to a key by Lamb, accurately represent Joseph Favell, killed at Salamanca in 1812; F. W. Franklin, died 1836; Charles V. Le Grice and his brother Samuel; "Maunde, dismiss'd school"; "Scott, died in Bedlam"; Marmaduke Thompson, to whom Lamb dedicated *Rosamund Gray;* Sir Edward Thornton (1766–1852), diplomat; Dr. Arthur W. Trollope, headmaster 1799–1826. T— and H— are unknown.

"L.'s governor" was a senior lawyer of the Inner Temple, Samuel Salt, whom Lamb's father served as secretary and valet.

Antonio Verrio (c.1639–1707), decorated the Windsor and Hampton Court palaces as well as Christ's Hospital. Robert Paltock's *The Life and Adventures of Peter Wilkins,* 1751, has outlived the other romances mentioned. John Jewel (1522–71), Bishop of Salisbury; Richard Hooker (c.1554–1600), author of *The Laws of Ecclesiastical Polity;* G. Pico della Mirandola (1463–94), precocious philosopher.

Nireus: in *Iliad* II.673, handsomest of the Greeks at Troy.

The human species, according to the best theory I can form of it, is composed of two distinct races, *the men who borrow,* and *the men who lend.* To these two original diversities may be reduced all those impertinent classifications of Gothic and Celtic tribes, white men, black men, red men. All the dwellers upon earth, "Parthians, and Medes, and Elamites,"[1] flock hither, and do naturally fall in with one or other of these primary distinctions. The infinite superiority of the former, which I choose to designate as the *great race,* is discernible in their figure, port, and a certain instinctive sovereignty. The latter are born degraded. "He shall serve his brethren."[2] There is something in the air of one of this cast, lean and suspicious; contrasting with the open, trusting, generous manners of the other.

Observe who have been the greatest borrowers of all ages — Alcibiades — Falstaff — Sir Richard Steele — our late incomparable Brinsley — what a family likeness in all four!

What a careless, even deportment hath your borrower! what rosy gills! what a beautiful reliance on Providence doth he manifest, — taking no more thought than lilies! What contempt for money, — accounting it (yours and mine especially) no better than dross! What a liberal confounding of those pedantic distinctions of *meum* and *tuum!* or rather, what a noble simplification of language (beyond Tooke), resolving these supposed opposites into one clear, intelligible pronoun adjective! — What near approaches doth he make to the primitive *community,* — to the extent of one half of the principle at least! —

He is the true taxer who "calleth all the world up to be taxed;"[3] and the distance is as vast between him and *one of us,* as subsisted betwixt the Augustan Majesty and the poorest obolary Jew that paid it tribute-pittance at Jerusalem! — His exactions, too, have such a cheerful, voluntary air! So far removed from your sour parochial or state-gatherers, — those ink-horn varlets, who carry their want of welcome in their faces! He cometh to you with a smile, and troubleth you with no receipt; confining himself to no set season. Every day is his Candlemas, or his Feast of Holy Michael. He applieth the *lene tormentum*[4] of a pleasant look to your purse, — which to that gentle warmth expands her silken leaves, as naturally as the cloak of the traveller, for which sun and wind contended! He is the true Propontic which never ebbeth![5] The sea which taketh handsomely at each man's hand. In vain the victim, whom he delighteth to honour, struggles with destiny; he is in the net. Lend therefore cheerfully, O

[1] Acts 2:9.
[2] Cf. Genesis 9:25.
[3] Cf. Luke 2:1.
[4] "gentle stimulus" — Horace, *Odes* III.xxi.13. Candlemas and Michaelmas were quarter-days, for paying rent.
[5] Cf. *Othello* III.iii.453–456.

man ordained to lend — that thou lose not in the end, with thy
worldly penny, the reversion promised. Combine not preposterously
in thine own person the penalties of Lazarus and of Dives![6] — but,
when thou seest the proper authority coming, meet it smilingly, as it
were half-way. Come, a handsome sacrifice! See how light *he* makes
of it! Strain not courtesies with a noble enemy.

Reflections like the foregoing were forced upon my mind by the
death of my old friend, Ralph Bigod, Esq., who departed this life on
Wednesday evening; dying, as he had lived, without much trouble.
He boasted himself a descendant from mighty ancestors of that name,
who heretofore held ducal dignities in this realm. In his actions and
sentiments he belied not the stock to which he pretended. Early in
life he found himself invested with ample revenues; which, with that
noble disinterestedness which I have noticed as inherent in men of the
great race, he took almost immediate measures entirely to dissipate
and bring to nothing: for there is something revolting in the idea of
a king holding a private purse; and the thoughts of Bigod were all
regal. Thus furnished, by the very act of disfurnishment; getting rid
of the cumbersome luggage of riches, more apt (as one sings)

> To slacken virtue, and abate her edge,
> Than prompt her to do aught may merit praise,[7]

he set forth, like some Alexander, upon his great enterprise, "borrowing and to borrow!"[8]

In his periegesis, or triumphant progress throughout this island, it
has been calculated that he laid a tythe part of the inhabitants under
contribution. I reject this estimate as greatly exaggerated: — but having had the honour of accompanying my friend, divers times, in his
perambulations about this vast city, I own I was greatly struck at
first with the prodigious number of faces we met, who claimed a sort
of respectful acquaintance with us. He was one day so obliging as
to explain the phenomenon. It seems, these were his tributaries;
feeders of his exchequer; gentlemen, his good friends (as he was
pleased to express himself), to whom he had occasionally been beholden for a loan. Their multitudes did no way disconcert him. He
rather took a pride in numbering them; and, with Comus, seemed
pleased to be "stocked with so fair a herd."[9]

With such sources, it was a wonder how he contrived to keep his
treasury always empty. He did it by force of an aphorism, which he
had often in his mouth, that "money kept longer than three days
stinks." So he made use of it while it was fresh. A good part he drank
away (for he was an excellent toss-pot), some he gave away, the

[6] Cf. Proverbs 19:17; Luke 16:20–31.
[7] *Paradise Regained* II.455–456.
[8] Cf. Revelation 6:2, "conquering and to conquer."
[9] Cf. Milton, *Comus* 152.

rest he threw away, literally tossing and hurling it violently from him — as boys do burrs, or as if it had been infectious, — into ponds, or ditches, or deep holes, — inscrutable cavities of the earth; — or he would bury it (where he would never seek it again) by a river's side under some bank, which (he would facetiously observe) paid no interest — but out away from him it must go peremptorily, as Hagar's offspring into the wilderness, while it was sweet. He never missed it. The streams were perennial which fed his fisc. When new supplies became necessary, the first person that had the felicity to fall in with him, friend or stranger, was sure to contribute to the deficiency. For Bigod had an *undeniable* way with him. He had a cheerful, open exterior, a quick jovial eye, a bald forehead, just touched with grey (*cana fides*).[10] He anticipated no excuse, and found none. And, waiving for a while my theory as to the *great race*, I would put it to the most untheorising reader, who may at times have disposable coin in his pocket, whether it is not more repugnant to the kindliness of his nature to refuse such a one as I am describing, than to say *no* to a poor petitionary rogue (your bastard borrower), who, by his mumping visnomy, tells you, that he expects nothing better; and, therefore, whose preconceived notions and expectations you do in reality so much less shock in the refusal.

When I think of this man; his fiery glow of heart; his swell of feeling; how magnificent, how *ideal* he was; how great at the midnight hour; and when I compare with him the companions with whom I have associated since, I grudge the saving of a few idle ducats, and think that I am fallen into the society of *lenders*, and *little men*.

To one like Elia, whose treasures are rather cased in leather covers than closed in iron coffers, there is a class of alienators more formidable than that which I have touched upon; I mean your *borrowers of books* — those mutilators of collections, spoilers of the symmetry of shelves, and creators of odd volumes. There is Comberbatch, matchless in his depredations!

That foul gap in the bottom shelf facing you, like a great eye-tooth knocked out — (you are now with me in my little back study in Bloomsbury, reader!) —— with the huge Switzer-like tomes on each side (like the Guildhall giants, in their reformed posture, guardant of nothing) once held the tallest of my folios, *Opera Bonaventuræ*, choice and massy divinity, to which its two supporters (school divinity also, but of a lesser calibre, — Bellarmine, and Holy Thomas), showed but as dwarfs, — itself an Ascapart! — *that* Comberbatch abstracted upon the faith of a theory he holds, which is more easy, I confess, for me to suffer by than to refute, namely, that "the title to property in a book (my Bonaventure, for instance), is in exact ratio to the claimant's powers of understanding and appreciating the same." Should he

[10] the "hoary honor" (*Aeneid* I.292) of gray hair.

go on acting upon this theory, which of our shelves is safe?

The slight vacuum in the left-hand case — two shelves from the ceiling — scarcely distinguishable but by the quick eye of a loser —— was whilom the commodious resting-place of Brown on Urn Burial. C. will hardly allege that he knows more about that treatise than I do, who introduced it to him, and was indeed the first (of the moderns) to discover its beauties — but so have I known a foolish lover to praise his mistress in the presence of a rival more qualified to carry her off than himself. — Just below, Dodsley's dramas want their fourth volume, where Vittoria Corombona is! The remainder nine are as distasteful as Priam's refuse sons, when the Fates *borrowed* Hector. Here stood the Anatomy of Melancholy, in sober state. — There loitered the Complete Angler; quiet as in life, by some stream side. — In yonder nook, John Buncle, a widower-volume, with "eyes closed," mourns his ravished mate.

One justice I must do my friend, that if he sometimes, like the sea, sweeps away a treasure, at another time, sea-like, he throws up as rich an equivalent to match it. I have a small under-collection of this nature (my friend's gatherings in his various calls), picked up, he has forgotten at what odd places, and deposited with as little memory as mine. I take in these orphans, the twice-deserted. These proselytes of the gate are welcome as the true Hebrews. There they stand in conjunction; natives, and naturalised. The latter seem as little disposed to inquire out their true lineage as I am. — I charge no warehouse-room for these deodands, nor shall ever put myself to the ungentlemanly trouble of advertising a sale of them to pay expenses.

To lose a volume to C. carries some sense and meaning in it. You are sure that he will make one hearty meal on your viands, if he can give no account of the platter after it. But what moved thee, wayward, spiteful K., to be so importunate to carry off with thee, in spite of tears and adjurations to thee to forbear, the Letters of that princely woman, the thrice noble Margaret Newcastle? — knowing at the time, and knowing that I knew also, thou most assuredly wouldst never turn over one leaf of the illustrious folio: — what but the mere spirit of contradiction, and childish love of getting the better of thy friend? — Then, worst cut of all! to transport it with thee to the Gallican land —

> Unworthy land to harbour such a sweetness,
> A virtue in which all ennobling thoughts dwelt,
> Pure thoughts, kind thoughts, high thoughts, her sex's wonder![11]

—— hadst thou not thy play-books, and books of jests and fancies, about thee, to keep thee merry, even as thou keepest all companies with thy quips and mirthful tales? — Child of the Green-room, it

[11] Unidentified; sometimes attributed to Lamb.

was unkindly done of thee. Thy wife, too, that part-French, better-part Englishwoman! — that *she* could fix upon no other treatise to bear away, in kindly token of remembering us, than the works of Fulke Greville, Lord Brook — of which no Frenchman, nor woman of France, Italy, or England, was ever by nature constituted to comprehend a tittle! *Was there not Zimmerman on Solitude?*

Reader, if haply thou art blessed with a moderate collection, be shy of showing it; or if thy heart overfloweth to lend them, lend thy books; but let it be to such a one as S. T. C. — he will return them (generally anticipating the time appointed) with usury; enriched with annotations, tripling their value. I have had experience. Many are these precious MSS. of his — (in *matter* oftentimes, and almost in *quantity* not unfrequently, vying with the originals) — in no very clerkly hand — legible in my Daniel; in old Burton; in Sir Thomas Browne; and those abstruser cogitations of the Greville, now, alas! wandering in Pagan lands. —— I counsel thee, shut not thy heart, nor thy library, against S. T. C.[12]

[12] Coleridge (who had enlisted in the Dragoons as "Silas Tomkyn Comberbache") borrowed John Webster, *The White Devil, or Vittoria Corombona* (in Dodsley's collection); theological works of St. Bonaventura (1221–74), Roberto Bellarmino (1542–1621), and St. Thomas Aquinas (c.1225–74); Robert Burton, *The Anatomy of Melancholy*, 1621; Izaak Walton, *The Compleat Angler;* Samuel Daniel, *Poetical Works*, 1718; Sir Thomas Browne, *Pseudodoxia Epidemica*, 1658 edition (returned), and *Hydriotaphia, or Urn-Burial* (not returned). James Kenney (1780-1849), actor and playwright, and his wife borrowed J. G. von Zimmermann, *Solitude* (translated about 1791); Margaret Cavendish, Duchess of Newcastle, *CCXI Sociable Letters*, 1664; and works of Fulke Greville, Baron Brooke (1554–1628).

Brinsley: Richard Brinsley Sheridan (1751–1816), dramatist, theater manager, and Whig orator. Tooke: John Horne Tooke (1736–1812), author of *The Diversions of Purley*, 1786–98, a work of philological reform. Bigod: actually John Fenwick, editor of the short-lived *Albion* newspaper. Hagar's offspring: Ishmael, in Genesis 21. Ascapart: giant converted by Bevis of Hampton, in a medieval romance retold by Michael Drayton, *Polyolbion* II.259–384.

lilies: in Matthew 6:28; *community:* in Acts 2:44; obolary: possessing an obolus, or penny; visnomy: physiognomy, face (here of a mumbling beggar); Switzer: tall Swiss Guard.

Mrs. Battle's Opinions on Whist

❲ First published in the *London Magazine* for February 1821, the essay is here taken from *Elia*, 1823. The chief living model for Mrs. Battle was Sarah Burney. She and her husband had begun to play cards with the Lambs about 1803. In 1830 Lamb asked his friend Ayrton to remember Mrs. Burney's "obstinate questioning of the score, after the game was absolutely lost to the devil." ❳

"A clear fire, a clean hearth, and the rigour of the game." This was the celebrated *wish* of old Sarah Battle (now with God) who, next to her devotions, loved a good game at whist. She was none of your lukewarm gamesters, your half and half players, who have no objection to take a hand, if you want one to make up a rubber; who affirm that they have no pleasure in winning; that they like to win one game, and lose another; that they can while away an hour very agreeably at a card-table, but are indifferent whether they play or no; and will desire an adversary, who has slipt a wrong card, to take it up and play another. These insufferable triflers are the curse of a table. One of these flies will spoil a whole pot. Of such it may be said, that they do not play at cards, but only play at playing at them.

Sarah Battle was none of that breed. She detested them, as I do, from her heart and soul; and would not, save upon a striking emergency, willingly seat herself at the same table with them. She loved a thorough-paced partner, a determined enemy. She took, and gave, no concessions. She hated favours. She never made a revoke, nor ever passed it over in her adversary without exacting the utmost forfeiture. She fought a good fight: cut and thrust. She held not her good sword (her cards) "like a dancer." She sate bolt upright; and neither showed you her cards, nor desired to see yours. All people have their blind side — their superstitions; and I have heard her declare, under the rose, that Hearts was her favourite suit.

I never in my life — and I knew Sarah Battle many of the best years of it — saw her take out her snuff-box when it was her turn to play; or snuff a candle in the middle of a game; or ring for a servant, till it was fairly over. She never introduced, or connived at, miscellaneous conversation during its process. As she emphatically observed, cards were cards: and if I ever saw unmingled distaste in her fine last-century countenance, it was at the airs of a young gentleman of a literary turn, who had been with difficulty persuaded to take a hand; and who, in his excess of candour, declared, that he thought there was no harm in unbending the mind now and then, after serious studies, in recreations of that kind! She could not bear to have her noble occupation, to which she wound up her faculties, considered in that light. It was her business, her duty, the thing she came into the world to do, — and she did it. She unbent her mind afterwards — over a book.

Pope was her favourite author: his Rape of the Lock her favourite work. She once did me the favour to play over with me (with the cards) his celebrated game of Ombre in that poem; and to explain to me how far it agreed with, and in what points it would be found to differ from, tradrille. Her illustrations were apposite and poignant; and I had the pleasure of sending the substance of them to Mr. Bowles: but I suppose they came too late to be inserted among his ingenious notes upon that author.

Quadrille, she has often told me, was her first love; but whist had engaged her maturer esteem. The former, she said, was showy and specious, and likely to allure young persons. The uncertainty and quick shifting of partners — a thing which the constancy of whist abhors; — the dazzling supremacy and regal investiture of Spadille — absurd, as she justly observed, in the pure aristocrasy of whist, where his crown and garter give him no proper power above his brother-nobility of the Aces; — the giddy vanity, so taking to the inexperienced, of playing alone; — above all, the overpowering attractions of a *Sans Prendre Vole*,[1] — to the triumph of which there is certainly nothing parallel or approaching, in the contingencies of whist; — all these, she would say, make quadrille a game of captivation to the young and enthusiastic. But whist was the *solider* game: that was her word. It was a long meal; not, like quadrille, a feast of snatches. One or two rubbers might co-extend in duration with an evening. They gave time to form rooted friendships, to cultivate steady enmities. She despised the chance-started, capricious, and ever fluctuating alliances of the other. The skirmishes of quadrille, she would say, reminded her of the petty ephemeral embroilments of the little Italian states, depicted by Machiavel; perpetually changing postures and connexions; bitter foes to-day, sugared darlings to-morrow; kissing and scratching in a breath; — but the wars of whist were comparable to the long, steady, deep-rooted, rational, antipathies of the great French and English nations.

A grave simplicity was what she chiefly admired in her favourite game. There was nothing silly in it, like the nob in cribbage — nothing superfluous. No *flushes* — that most irrational of all pleas that a reasonable being can set up: — that any one should claim four by virtue of holding cards of the same mark and colour, without

---

[1] Taking all the tricks without a partner. Spadille: the ace of spades. Rules for playing quadrille (four-handed ombre) and whist can be found in early editions of Edmond Hoyle's books on games and in modern histories of bridge.

reference to the playing of the game, or the individual worth or pretensions of the cards themselves! She held this to be a solecism; as
pitiful an ambition at cards as alliteration is in authorship. She
despised superficiality, and looked deeper than the colours of things.
— Suits were soldiers, she would say, and must have a uniformity of
array to distinguish them: but what should we say to a foolish squire,
who should claim a merit from dressing up his tenantry in red jackets,
that never were to be marshalled — never to take the field? — She
even wished that whist were more simple than it is; and, in my mind,
would have stript it of some appendages, which, in the state of human
frailty, may be venially, and even commendably allowed of. She saw
no reason for the deciding of the trump by the turn of the card. Why
not one suit always trumps? — Why two colours, when the mark of
the suits would have sufficiently distinguished them without it? —

"But the eye, my dear Madam, is agreeably refreshed with the
variety. Man is not a creature of pure reason — he must have his
senses delightfully appealed to. We see it in Roman Catholic countries, where the music and the paintings draw in many to worship,
whom your quaker spirit of unsensualizing would have kept out. —
You, yourself, have a pretty collection of paintings — but confess to
me, whether, walking in your gallery at Sandham, among those clear
Vandykes, or among the Paul Potters in the ante-room, you ever felt
your bosom glow with an elegant delight, at all comparable to *that*
you have it in your power to experience most evenings over a well-
arranged assortment of the court cards? — the pretty antic habits, like
heralds in a procession — the gay triumph-assuring scarlets — the
contrasting deadly-killing sables — the 'hoary majesty of spades' —
Pam in all his glory! —[2]

"All these might be dispensed with; and, with their naked names
upon the drab pasteboard, the game might go on very well, picture-
less. But the *beauty* of cards would be extinguished for ever. Stripped
of all that is imaginative in them, they must degenerate into mere
gambling. — Imagine a dull deal board, or drum head, to spread them
on, instead of that nice verdant carpet (next to nature's), fittest arena
for those courtly combatants to play their gallant jousts and turneys
in! — Exchange those delicately-turned ivory markers — (work of
Chinese artist, unconscious of their symbol, — or as profanely slighting their true application as the arrantest Ephesian journeyman that
turned out those little shrines for the goddess) — exchange them for
little bits of leather (our ancestors' money) or chalk and a slate!" —

The old lady, with a smile, confessed the soundness of my logic; and
to her approbation of my arguments on her favorite topic that evening,
I have always fancied myself indebted for the legacy of a curious
cribbage board, made of the finest Sienna marble, which her maternal
uncle (old Walter Plumer, whom I have elsewhere celebrated)

[2] *The Rape of the Lock* III.56. Pam: the knave of clubs.

brought with him from Florence: — this, and a trifle of five hundred pounds, came to me at her death.

The former bequest (which I do not least value) I have kept with religious care; though she herself, to confess a truth, was never greatly taken with cribbage. It was an essentially vulgar game, I have heard her say, — disputing with her uncle, who was very partial to it. She could never heartily bring her mouth to pronounce *"go"* — or *"that's a go."* She called it an ungrammatical game. The pegging teased her. I once knew her to forfeit a rubber (a five dollar stake), because she would not take advantage of the turn-up knave, which would have given it her, but which she must have claimed by the disgraceful tenure of declaring *"two for his heels."* There is something extremely genteel in this sort of self-denial. Sarah Battle was a gentlewoman born.

Piquet she held the best game at the cards for two persons, though she would ridicule the pedantry of the terms — such as pique — repique — the capot — they savoured (she thought) of affectation. But games for two, or even three, she never greatly cared for. She loved the quadrate, or square. She would argue thus: — Cards are warfare: the ends are gain, with glory. But cards are war, in disguise of a sport: when single adversaries encounter, the ends proposed are too palpable. By themselves, it is too close a fight; with spectators, it is not much bettered. No looker on can be interested, except for a bet, and then it is a mere affair of money; he cares not for your luck *sympathetically,* or for your play. — Three are still worse; a mere naked war of every man against every man, as in cribbage, without league or alliance; or a rotation of petty and contradictory interests, a succession of heartless leagues, and not much more hearty infractions of them, as in tradrille. — But in square games (*she meant whist*) all that is possible to be attained in card-playing is accomplished. There are the incentives of profit with honour, common to every species — though the *latter* can be but very imperfectly enjoyed in those other games, where the spectator is only feebly a participator. But the parties in whist are spectators and principals too. They are a theatre to themselves, and a looker-on is not wanted. He is rather worse than nothing, and an impertinence. Whist abhors neutrality, or interests beyond its sphere. You glory in some surprising stroke of skill or fortune, not because a cold — or even an interested — by-stander witnesses it, but because your *partner* sympathises in the contingency. You win for two. You triumph for two. Two are exalted. Two again are mortified; which divides their disgrace, as the conjunction doubles (by taking off the invidiousness) your glories. Two losing to two are better reconciled, than one to one in that close butchery. The hostile feeling is weakened by multiplying the channels. War becomes a civil game. — By such reasonings as these the old lady was accustomed to defend her favourite pastime.

No inducement could ever prevail upon her to play at any game, where chance entered into the composition, *for nothing*. Chance, she would argue — and here again, admire the subtlety of her conclusion! — chance is nothing, but where something else depends upon it. It is obvious, that cannot be *glory*. What rational cause of exultation could it give to a man to turn up size ace a hundred times together by himself? or before spectators, where no stake was depending? — Make a lottery of a hundred thousand tickets with but one fortunate number — and what possible principle of our nature, except stupid wonderment, could it gratify to gain that number as many times successively, without a prize? — Therefore she disliked the mixture of chance in backgammon, where it was not played for money. She called it foolish, and those people idiots, who were taken with a lucky hit under such circumstances. Games of pure skill were as little to her fancy. Played for a stake, they were a mere system of over-reaching. Played for glory, they were a mere setting of one man's wit, — his memory, or combination-faculty rather — against another's; like a mock-engagement at a review, bloodless and profitless. — She could not conceive a *game* wanting the spritely infusion of chance, — the handsome excuses of good fortune. Two people playing at chess in a corner of a room, whilst whist was stirring in the centre, would inspire her with insufferable horror and ennui. Those well-cut similitudes of Castles, and Knights, the *imagery* of the board, she would argue, (and I think in this case justly) were entirely misplaced and senseless. Those hard head-contests can in no instance ally with the fancy. They reject form and colour. A pencil and dry slate (she used to say) were the proper arena for such combatants.

To those puny objectors against cards, as nurturing the bad passions, she would retort, that man is a gaming animal. He must be always trying to get the better in something or other: — that this passion can scarcely be more safely expended than upon a game at cards: that cards are a temporary illusion; in truth, a mere drama; for we do but *play* at being mightily concerned, where a few idle shillings are at stake, yet during the illusion, we *are* as mightily concerned as those whose stake is crowns and kingdoms. They are a sort of dream-fighting; much ado; great battling, and little bloodshed; mighty means for disproportioned ends; quite as diverting, and a great deal more innoxious, than many of those more serious *games* of life, which men play, without esteeming them to be such. ——

With great deference to the old lady's judgment on these matters, I think I have experienced some moments in my life, when playing at cards *for nothing* has even been agreeable. When I am in sickness, or not in the best spirits, I sometimes call for the cards, and play a game at piquet *for love* with my cousin Bridget — Bridget Elia.

I grant there is something sneaking in it: but with a tooth-ache, or a sprained ancle, — when you are subdued and humble, — you are glad to put up with an inferior spring of action.

There is such a thing in nature, I am convinced, as *sick whist*. —
I grant it is not the highest style of man — I deprecate the manes
of Sarah Battle — she lives not, alas! to whom I should apologise. —
At such times, those *terms* which my old friend objected to, come
in as something admissible. — I love to get a tierce or a quatorze,
though they mean nothing. I am subdued to an inferior interest.
Those shadows of winning amuse me.

That last game I had with my sweet cousin (I capotted her) —
(dare I tell thee, how foolish I am?) — I wished it might have
lasted for ever, though we gained nothing, and lost nothing, though
it was a mere shade of play: I would be content to go on in that idle
folly for ever. The pipkin should be ever boiling, that was to prepare
the gentle lenitive to my foot, which Bridget was doomed to apply
after the game was over: and, as I do not much relish appliances, there
it should ever bubble. Bridget and I should be ever playing.[3]

Dream Children: A Reverie

⟨ This essay, which first appeared in the *London Magazine* for January
1822, is here reprinted from *Elia*, 1823. It will seem cloyingly sentimental
only if it is taken as raw autobiography. Among those who have admired
its delicately balanced design, A. C. Ward has concentrated on the technique by which Lamb built up a unified whole, in *Dream Children* as
in *Old China*, through a pattern of parenthetical insertions. ⟩

Children love to listen to stories about their elders, when *they* were
children; to stretch their imagination to the conception of a traditionary
great-uncle, or grandame, whom they never saw. It was in this spirit
that my little ones crept about me the other evening to hear about
their great-grandmother Field, who lived in a great house in Norfolk (a
hundred times bigger than that in which they and papa lived) which
had been the scene — so at least it was generally believed in that part
of the country — of the tragic incidents which they had lately become
familiar with from the ballad of the Children in the Wood. Certain

---

[3] William Lisle Bowles (1762–1850) edited Pope's works in 1806; when
Lamb wrote this essay, controversy raged over Byron's charge that Bowles
underestimated Pope. Machiavel: Niccolo Machiavelli, *Istorie Florentine*,
1532, translated in 1595.

Ephesian: in Acts 19:24; Plumer: in Lamb's essay *The South-Sea House*.

"*go*": in cribbage — to Mrs. Battle's disgust — a forfeiture from inability
to play (in other games, to "go better" is to outbid); size ace: six and one,
a good throw of the dice in backgammon; to capot: to win all the tricks.

it is that the whole story of the children and their cruel uncle was to
be seen fairly carved out in wood upon the chimney-piece of the great
hall, the whole story down to the Robin Redbreasts, till a foolish
rich person pulled it down to set up a marble one of modern invention in its stead, with no story upon it. Here Alice put out one of
her dear mother's looks, too tender to be called upbraiding. Then I
went on to say, how religious and how good their great-grandmother
Field was, how beloved and respected by every body, though she was
not indeed the mistress of this great house, but had only the charge of
it (and yet in some respects she might be said to be the mistress of it
too) committed to her by the owner, who preferred living in a newer
and more fashionable mansion which he had purchased somewhere in
the adjoining county; but still she lived in it in a manner as if it had
been her own, and kept up the dignity of the great house in a sort
while she lived, which afterwards came to decay, and was nearly pulled
down, and all its old ornaments stripped and carried away to the
owner's other house, where they were set up, and looked as awkward
as if some one were to carry away the old tombs they had seen lately
at the Abbey, and stick them up in Lady C.'s tawdry gilt drawing-
room. Here John smiled, as much as to say, "that would be foolish
indeed." And then I told how, when she came to die, her funeral was
attended by a concourse of all the poor, and some of the gentry too,
of the neighbourhood for many miles round, to show their respect for
her memory, because she had been such a good and religious woman;
so good indeed that she knew all the Psaltery by heart, ay, and a great
part of the Testament besides. Here little Alice spread her hands. Then
I told what a tall, upright, graceful person their great-grandmother
Field once was; and how in her youth she was esteemed the best
dancer — here Alice's little right foot played an involuntary movement, till, upon my looking grave, it desisted — the best dancer, I was
saying, in the county, till a cruel disease, called a cancer, came, and
bowed her down with pain; but it could never bend her good spirits,
or make them stoop, but they were still upright, because she was so
good and religious. Then I told how she was used to sleep by herself
in a lone chamber of the great lone house; and how she believed that
an apparition of two infants was to be seen at midnight gliding up and
down the great staircase near where she slept, but she said "those innocents would do her no harm;" and how frightened I used to be,
though in those days I had my maid to sleep with me, because I was
never half so good or religious as she — and yet I never saw the infants. Here John expanded all his eye-brows and tried to look coura-
geous. Then I told how good she was to all her grand-children, having
us to the great-house in the holydays, where I in particular used to
spend many hours by myself, in gazing upon the old busts of the
Twelve Cæsars, that had been Emperors of Rome, till the old marble
heads would seem to live again, or I to be turned into marble with

them; how I never could be tired with roaming about that huge
mansion, with its vast empty rooms, with their worn-out hangings,
fluttering tapestry, and carved oaken pannels, with the gilding almost
rubbed out — sometimes in the spacious old-fashioned gardens, which
I had almost to myself, unless when now and then a solitary gardening
man would cross me — and how the nectarines and peaches hung upon
the walls, without my ever offering to pluck them, because they were
forbidden fruit, unless now and then, — and because I had more
pleasure in strolling about among the old melancholy-looking yew
trees, or the firs, and picking up the red berries, and the fir apples,
which were good for nothing but to look at — or in lying about upon
the fresh grass, with all the fine garden smells around me — or basking
in the orangery, till I could almost fancy myself ripening too along
with the oranges and the limes in that grateful warmth — or in watching the dace that darted to and fro in the fish-pond, at the bottom of
the garden, with here and there a great sulky pike hanging midway
down the water in silent state, as if it mocked at their impertinent
friskings, — I had more pleasure in these busy-idle diversions than in
all the sweet flavours of peaches, nectarines, oranges, and such like
common baits of children. Here John slyly deposited back upon the
plate a bunch of grapes, which, not unobserved by Alice, he had
mediated dividing with her, and both seemed willing to relinquish
them for the present as irrelevant. Then in somewhat a more heightened tone, I told how, though their great-grandmother Field loved all
her grand-children, yet in an especial manner she might be said to love
their uncle, John L——, because he was so handsome and spirited a
youth, and a king to the rest of us; and, instead of moping about in
solitary corners, like some of us, he would mount the most mettlesome
horse he could get, when but an imp no bigger than themselves, and
make it carry him half over the county in a morning, and join the
hunters when there were any out — and yet he loved the old great
house and gardens too, but had too much spirit to be always pent
up within their boundaries — and how their uncle grew up to man's
estate as brave as he was handsome, to the admiration of every body,
but of their great-grandmother Field most especially; and how he
used to carry me upon his back when I was a lame-footed boy — for
he was a good bit older than me — many a mile when I could not
walk for pain; — and how in after life he became lame-footed too, and
I did not always (I fear) make allowances enough for him when he
was impatient, and in pain, nor remember sufficiently how considerate
he had been to me when I was lame-footed; and how when he died,
though he had not been dead an hour, it seemed as if he had died a
great while ago, such a distance there is betwixt life and death; and
how I bore his death as I thought pretty well at first, but afterwards it
haunted and haunted me; and though I did not cry or take it to heart
as some do, and as I think he would have done if I had died, yet I

missed him all day long, and knew not till then how much I had loved him. I missed his kindness, and I missed his crossness, and wished him to be alive again, to be quarrelling with him (for we quarreled sometimes), rather than not have him again, and was as uneasy without him, as he their poor uncle must have been when the doctor took off his limb. Here the children fell a crying, and asked if their little mourning which they had on was not for uncle John, and they looked up, and prayed me not to go on about their uncle, but to tell them some stories about their pretty dead mother. Then I told how for seven long years, in hope sometimes, sometimes in despair, yet persisting ever, I courted the fair Alice W——n; and, as much as children could understand, I explained to them what coyness, and difficulty, and denial meant in maidens — when suddenly, turning to Alice, the soul of the first Alice looked out at her eyes with such a reality of re-presentment, that I became in doubt which of them stood there before me, or whose that bright hair was; and while I stood gazing, both the children gradually grew fainter to my view, receding, and still receding till nothing at last but two mournful features were seen in the uttermost distance, which, without speech, strangely impressed upon me the effects of speech; "We are not of Alice, nor of thee, nor are we children at all. The children of Alice call Bartrum father. We are nothing; less than nothing, and dreams. We are only what might have been, and must wait upon the tedious shores of Lethe millions of ages before we have existence, and a name" — and immediately awaking, I found myself quietly seated in my bachelor arm-chair, where I had fallen asleep, with the faithful Bridget unchanged by my side — but John L. (or James Elia) was gone for ever.[1]

A Dissertation upon Roast Pig

(This essay, the most famous in the long history of pseudo-oriental fantasies, is easily the best treatment of an idea already commonplace when Lamb heard it from his friend Thomas Manning: how the eating of raw meat ended by accident. First published in the London Magazine for September 1822, the "dissertation" is here taken from Elia, 1823.)

Mankind, says a Chinese manuscript, which my friend M. was obliging enough to read and explain to me, for the first seventy thousand ages ate their meat raw, clawing or biting it from the living animal,

[1] Lamb's brother John had died on October 26, 1821. On the association of Lethe with rebirth, see Aeneid VI.748–751.

just as they do in Abyssinia to this day. This period is not obscurely
hinted at by their great Confucius in the second chapter of his Mundane Mutations, where he designates a kind of golden age by the
term Cho-fang, literally the Cooks' holiday. The manuscript goes on
to say, that the art of roasting, or rather broiling (which I take to be
the elder brother) was accidentally discovered in the manner following. The swine-herd, Ho-ti, having gone out into the woods one morning, as his manner was, to collect mast for his hogs, left his cottage in
the care of his eldest son Bo-bo, a great lubberly boy, who being fond
of playing with fire, as younkers of his age commonly are, let some
sparks escape into a bundle of straw, which kindling quickly, spread
the conflagration over every part of their poor mansion, till it was
reduced to ashes. Together with the cottage (a sorry antediluvian
make-shift of a building, you may think it), what was of much more
importance, a fine litter of new-farrowed pigs, no less than nine in
number, perished. China pigs have been esteemed a luxury all over
the East from the remotest periods that we read of. Bo-bo was in the
utmost consternation, as you may think, not so much for the sake of
the tenement, which his father and he could easily build up again with
a few dry branches, and the labour of an hour or two, at any time, as
for the loss of the pigs. While he was thinking what he should say
to his father, and wringing his hands over the smoking remnants of
one of those untimely sufferers, an odour assailed his nostrils, unlike
any scent which he had before experienced. What could it proceed
from? — not from the burnt cottage — he had smelt that smell before
— indeed this was by no means the first accident of the kind which
had occurred through the negligence of this unlucky young fire-brand.
Much less did it resemble that of any known herb, weed, or flower. A
premonitory moistening at the same time overflowed his nether lip.
He knew not what to think. He next stooped down to feel the pig, if
there were any signs of life in it. He burnt his fingers, and to cool
them he applied them in his booby fashion to his mouth. Some of the
crums of the scorched skin had come away with his fingers, and for
the first time in his life (in the world's life indeed, for before him no
man had known it) he tasted — *crackling!* Again he felt and fumbled
at the pig. It did not burn him so much now, still he licked his
fingers from a sort of habit. The truth at length broke into his slow
understanding, that it was the pig that smelt so, and the pig that
tasted so delicious; and, surrendering himself up to the new-born
pleasure, he fell to tearing up whole handfuls of the scorched skin
with the flesh next it, and was cramming it down his throat in his
beastly fashion, when his sire entered amid the smoking rafters, armed
with retributory cudgel, and finding how affairs stood, began to rain
blows upon the young rogue's shoulders, as thick as hail-stones, which
Bo-bo heeded not any more than if they had been flies. The tickling
pleasure, which he experienced in his lower regions, had rendered him

quite callous to any inconveniences he might feel in those remote quarters. His father might lay on, but he could not beat him from his pig, till he had fairly made an end of it, when, becoming a little more sensible of his situation, something like the following dialogue ensued.

"You graceless whelp, what have you got there devouring? Is it not enough that you have burnt me down three houses with your dog's tricks, and be hanged to you, but you must be eating fire, and I know not what — what have you got there, I say?"

"O father, the pig, the pig, do come and taste how nice the burnt pig eats."

The ears of Ho-ti tingled with horror. He cursed his son, and he cursed himself that ever he should beget a son that should eat burnt pig.

Bo-bo, whose scent was wonderfully sharpened since morning, soon raked out another pig, and fairly rending it asunder, thrust the lesser half by main force into the fists of Ho-ti, still shouting out "Eat, eat, eat the burnt pig, father, only taste — O Lord," — with such-like barbarous ejaculations, cramming all the while as if he would choke.

Ho-ti trembled every joint while he grasped the abominable thing, wavering whether he should not put his son to death for an unnatural young monster, when the crackling scorching his fingers, as it had done his son's, and applying the same remedy to them, he in his turn tasted some of its flavour, which, make what sour mouths he would for a pretence, proved not altogether displeasing to him. In conclusion (for the manuscript here is a little tedious) both father and son fairly sat down to the mess, and never left off till they had despatched all that remained of the litter.

Bo-bo was strictly enjoined not to let the secret escape, for the neighbours would certainly have stoned them for a couple of abominable wretches, who could think of improving upon the good meat which God had sent them. Nevertheless, strange stories got about. It was observed that Ho-ti's cottage was burnt down now more frequently than ever. Nothing but fires from this time forward. Some would break out in broad day, others in the night-time. As often as the sow farrowed, so sure was the house of Ho-ti to be in a blaze; and Ho-ti himself, which was the more remarkable, instead of chastising his son, seemed to grow more indulgent to him than ever. At length they were watched, the terrible mystery discovered, and father and son summoned to take their trial at Pekin, then an inconsiderable assize town. Evidence was given, the obnoxious food itself produced in court, and verdict about to be pronounced, when the foreman of the jury begged that some of the burnt pig, of which the culprits stood accused, might be handed into the box. He handled it, and they all handled it, and burning their fingers, as Bo-bo and his father had done before them, and nature prompting to each of them the same remedy, against the face of all the facts, and the clearest charge which judge had ever given, — to the surprise of the whole court, townsfolk, strangers, reporters, and all present — without leaving the box, or any manner of consultation whatever, they brought in a simultaneous verdict of Not Guilty.

The judge, who was a shrewd fellow, winked at the manifest iniquity of the decision; and, when the court was dismissed, went privily, and bought up all the pigs that could be had for love or money. In a few days his Lordship's town house was observed to be on fire. The thing took wing, and now there was nothing to be seen but fires in every direction. Fuel and pigs grew enormously dear all over the district. The insurance offices one and all shut up shop. People built slighter and slighter every day, until it was feared that the very science of architecture would in no long time be lost to the world. Thus this custom of firing houses continued, till in process of time, says my manuscript, a sage arose, like our Locke, who made a discovery, that the flesh of swine, or indeed of any other animal, might be cooked (*burnt,* as they called it) without the necessity of consuming a whole house to dress it. Then first began the rude form of a gridiron. Roasting by the string, or spit, came in a century or two later, I forget in whose dynasty. By such slow degrees, concludes the manuscript, do the most useful, and seemingly the most obvious arts, make their way among mankind. ——

Without placing too implicit faith in the account above given, it must be agreed, that if a worthy pretext for so dangerous an experiment as setting houses on fire (especially in these days) could be assigned in favour of any culinary object, that pretext and excuse might be found in ROAST PIG.

Of all the delacacies in the whole *mundus edibilis,* I will maintain it to be the most delicate — *princeps obsoniorum.*[1]

I speak not of your grown porkers — things between pig and pork — those hobbydehoys — but a young and tender suckling — under a moon old — guiltless as yet of the sty — with no original speck of the *amor immunditiæ,*[2] the hereditary failing of the first parent, yet manifest — his voice as yet not broken, but something between a childish treble, and a grumble — the mild forerunner, or *præludium,* of a grunt.

He must be roasted. I am not ignorant that our ancestors ate them seethed, or boiled — but what a sacrifice of the exterior tegument!

There is no flavour comparable, I will contend, to that of the crisp, tawny, well-watched, not over-roasted, *crackling* as it is well called — the very teeth are invited to their share of the pleasure at this banquet in overcoming the coy, brittle resistance — with the adhesive oleaginous — O call it not fat — but an indefinable sweetness growing up to it — the tender blossoming of fat — fat cropped in the

[1] Of "the world of things to eat," the "chief of delicacies."
[2] "love of dirt," the original sin of pigs.

bud — taken in the shoot — in the first innocence — the cream and
quintessence of the child-pig's yet pure food —— the lean, no lean, but
a kind of animal manna — or, rather, fat and lean (if it must be so) so
blended and running into each other, that both together make but
one ambrosian result, or common substance.

Behold him, while he is doing — it seemeth rather a refreshing
warmth, than a scorching heat, that he is so passive to. How equably
he twirleth round the string! — Now he is just done. To see the extreme sensibility of that tender age, he hath wept out his pretty eyes
— radiant jellies — shooting stars —[3]

See him in the dish, his second cradle, how meek he lieth! —
wouldst thou have had this innocent grow up to the grossness and
indocility which too often accompany maturer swinehood? Ten to
one he would have proved a glutton, a sloven, an obstinate, disagreeable animal — wallowing in all manner of filthy conversation — from
these sins he is happily snatched away —

> Ere sin could blight, or sorrow fade,
> Death came with timely care —[4]

his memory is odoriferous — no clown curseth, while his stomach half
rejecteth, the rank bacon — no coalheaver bolteth him in reeking
sausages — he hath a fair sepulchre in the grateful stomach of the
judicious epicure — and for such a tomb might be content to die.

He is the best of Sapors. Pine-apple is great. She is indeed almost
too transcendent — a delight, if not sinful, yet so like to sinning, that
really a tender-conscienced person would do well to pause — too
ravishing for mortal taste, she woundeth and excoriateth the lips that
approach her — like lovers' kisses, she biteth — she is a pleasure bor-
dering on pain from the fierceness and insanity of her relish — but she
stoppeth at the palate — she meddleth not with the appetite — and
the coarsest hunger might barter her consistently for a mutton chop.

Pig — let me speak his praise — is no less provocative of the appetite, than he is satisfactory to the criticalness of the censorious
palate. The strong man may batten on him, and the weakling refuseth
not his mild juices.

Unlike to mankind's mixed characters, a bundle of virtues and
vices, inexplicably intertwisted, and not to be unravelled without
hazard, he is — good throughout. No part of him is better or worse
than another. He helpeth, as far as his little means extend, all
around. He is the least envious of banquets. He is all neighbours' fare.

I am one of those, who freely and ungrudgingly impart a share of
the good things of this life which fall to their lot (few as mine are in

---

[3] An allusion to the superstition that shooting stars leave jelly where they
fall.

[4] Cf. Coleridge, *Epitaph on an Infant* 1–2.

this kind) to a friend. I protest I take as great an interest in my friend's pleasures, his relishes, and proper satisfactions, as in mine own. "Presents," I often say, "endear Absents." Hares, pheasants, partridges, snipes, barn-door chickens (those "tame villatic fowl"),[5] capons, plovers, brawn, barrels of oysters, I dispense as freely as I receive them. I love to taste them, as it were, upon the tongue of my friend. But a stop must be put somewhere. One would not, like Lear, "give every thing."[6] I make my stand upon pig. Methinks it is an ingratitude to the Giver of all good flavours, to extra-domiciliate, or send out of the house, slightingly, (under pretext of friendship, or I know not what) a blessing so particularly adapted, predestined, I may say, to my individual palate — It argues an insensibility.

I remember a touch of conscience in this kind at school. My good old aunt, who never parted from me at the end of a holiday without stuffing a sweetmeat, or some nice thing, into my pocket, had dismissed me one evening with a smoking plum-cake, fresh from the oven. In my way to school (it was over London bridge) a grey-headed old beggar saluted me (I have no doubt at this time of day that he was a counterfeit). I had no pence to console him with, and in the vanity of self-denial, and the very coxcombry of charity, school-boy-like, I made him a present of — the whole cake! I walked on a little, buoyed up, as one is on such occasions, with a sweet soothing of self-satisfaction; but before I had got to the end of the bridge, my better feelings returned, and I burst into tears, thinking how ungrateful I had been to my good aunt, to go and give her good gift away to a stranger, that I had never seen before, and who might be a bad man for aught I knew; and then I thought of the pleasure my aunt would be taking in thinking that I — I myself, and not another — would eat her nice cake — and what should I say to her the next time I saw her — how naughty I was to part with her pretty present — and the odour of that spicy cake came back upon my recollection, and the pleasure and the curiosity I had taken in seeing her make it, and her joy when she sent it to the oven, and how disappointed she would feel that I had never had a bit of it in my mouth at last — and I blamed my impertinent spirit of alms-giving, and out-of-place hypocrisy of goodness, and above all I wished never to see the face again of that insidious, good-for-nothing, old grey impostor.

Our ancestors were nice in their method of sacrificing these tender victims. We read of pigs whipt to death with something of a shock, as we hear of any other obsolete custom. The age of discipline is gone by, or it would be curious to inquire (in a philosophical light merely) what effect this process might have towards intenerating and dulcifying a substance, naturally so mild and dulcet as the flesh of young

---

[5] Milton, *Samson Agonistes* 1695.
[6] *King Lear* II.iv.253.

pigs. It looks like refining a violet. Yet we should be cautious, while
we condemn the inhumanity, how we censure the wisdom of the
practice. It might impart a gusto —

I remember an hypothesis, argued upon by the young students,
when I was at St. Omer's, and maintained with much learning and
pleasantry on both sides, "Whether, supposing that the flavour of a
pig who obtained his death by whipping (*per flagellationem extre-
mam*)[7] superadded a pleasure upon the palate of a man more intense
than any possible suffering we can conceive in the animal, is man
justified in using that method of putting the animal to death?" I
forget the decision.

His sauce should be considered. Decidedly, a few bread crums,
done up with his liver and brains, and a dash of mild sage. But,
banish, dear Mrs. Cook, I beseech you, the whole onion tribe. Barbe-
cue your whole hogs to your palate, steep them in shalots, stuff them
out with plantations of the rank and guilty garlic; you cannot poison
them, or make them stronger than they are — but consider, he is a
weakling — a flower.[8]

Old China

(After its appearance in the *London Magazine* for March 1823, "Old
China" was reprinted in *The Last Essays of Elia*, 1833, the text here followed.)

I have an almost feminine partiality for old china. When I go to see
any great house, I inquire for the china-closet, and next for the picture
gallery. I cannot defend the order of preference, but by saying, that
we have all some taste or other, of too ancient a date to admit of our
remembering distinctly that it was an acquired one. I can call to mind
the first play, and the first exhibition, that I was taken to; but I am
not conscious of a time when china jars and saucers were introduced
into my imagination.

I had no repugnance then — why should I now have? — to those
little, lawless, azure-tinctured grotesques, that under the notion of
men and women, float about, uncircumscribed by any element, in that
world before perspective — a china tea-cup.

[7] by flogging to death.
[8] St. Omer's: a Jesuit college, where Lamb supposes that training in dis-
putation would be subtle and severe.
filthy conversation: lewd behavior, as in 2 Peter 2:7.

I like to see my old friends — whom distance cannot diminish — figuring up in the air (so they appear to our optics), yet on *terra firma* still — for so we must in courtesy interpret that speck of deeper blue, which the decorous artist, to prevent absurdity, has made to spring up beneath their sandals.

I love the men with women's faces, and the women, if possible, with still more womanish expressions.

Here is a young and courtly Mandarin, handing tea to a lady from a salver — two miles off. See how distance seems to set off respect! And here the same lady, or another — for likeness is identity on tea-cups — is stepping into a little fairy boat, moored on the hither side of this calm garden river, with a dainty mincing foot, which in a right angle of incidence (as angles go in our world) must infallibly land her in the midst of a flowery mead — a furlong off on the other side of the same strange stream!

Farther on — if far or near can be predicated of their world — see horses, trees, pagodas, dancing the hays.

Here — a cow and rabbit couchant, and co-extensive — so objects show, seen through the lucid atmosphere of fine Cathay.

I was pointing out to my cousin last evening, over our Hyson, (which we are old fashioned enough to drink unmixed still of an afternoon) some of these *speciosa miracula*[1] upon a set of extraordinary old blue china (a recent purchase) which we were now for the first time using; and could not help remarking, how favourable circumstances had been to us of late years, that we could afford to please the eye sometimes with trifles of this sort — when a passing sentiment seemed to over-shade the brows of my companion. I am quick at detecting these summer clouds in Bridget.

"I wish the good old times would come again," she said, "when we were not quite so rich. I do not mean, that I want to be poor; but there was a middle state;" — so she was pleased to ramble on, — "in which I am sure we were a great deal happier. A purchase is but a purchase, now that you have money enough and to spare. Formerly it used to be a triumph. When we coveted a cheap luxury (and, O! how much ado I had to get you to consent in those times!) we were used to have a debate two or three days before, and to weigh the *for* and *against*, and think what we might spare it out of, and what saving we could hit upon, that should be an equivalent. A thing was worth buying then, when we felt the money that we paid for it.

"Do you remember the brown suit, which you made to hang upon you, till all your friends cried shame upon you, it grew so thread-bare — and all because of that folio Beaumont and Fletcher, which you dragged home late at night from Barker's in Covent-garden? Do you remember how we eyed it for weeks before we

---

[1] "shining marvels" — Horace, *Ars poetica* 144.

could make up our minds to the purchase, and had not come to a
determination till it was near ten o'clock of the Saturday night, when
you set off from Islington, fearing you should be too late — and when
the old bookseller with some grumbling opened his shop, and by the
twinkling taper (for he was setting bedwards) lighted out the relic
from his dusty treasures — and when you lugged it home, wishing it
were twice as cumbersome — and when you presented it to me —
and when we were exploring the perfectness of it (*collating* you called
it) — and while I was repairing some of the loose leaves with paste,
which your impatience would not suffer to be left till day-break — was
there no pleasure in being a poor man? or can those neat black clothes
which you wear now, and are so careful to keep brushed, since we
have become rich and finical, give you half the honest vanity, with
which you flaunted it about in that over-worn suit — your old corbeau — for four or five weeks longer than you should have done,
to pacify your conscience for the mighty sum of fifteen — or sixteen
shillings was it? — a great affair we thought it then — which you had
lavished on the old folio. Now you can afford to buy any book that
pleases you, but I do not see that you ever bring me home any nice
old purchases now.

"When you came home with twenty apologies for laying out a less
number of shillings upon that print after Lionardo, which we christened the 'Lady Blanch;' when you looked at the purchase, and
thought of the money — and thought of the money, and looked again
at the picture — was there no pleasure in being a poor man? Now,
you have nothing to do but to walk into Colnaghi's, and buy a
wilderness of Lionardos. Yet do you?

"Then, do you remember our pleasant walks to Enfield, and Potter's
Bar, and Waltham, when we had a holyday — holydays, and all other
fun, are gone, now we are rich — and the little hand-basket in which
I used to deposit our day's fare of savory cold lamb and salad — and
how you would pry about at noon-tide for some decent house, where
we might go in, and produce our store — only paying for the ale
that you must call for — and speculate upon the looks of the landlady, and whether she was likely to allow us a table-cloth — and wish
for such another honest hostess, as Izaak Walton has described many
a one on the pleasant banks of the Lea, when he went a fishing —
and sometimes they would prove obliging enough, and sometimes
they would look grudgingly upon us — but we had cheerful looks still
for one another, and would eat our plain food savorily, scarcely grudging Piscator his Trout Hall?[2] Now, when we go out a day's pleasuring,
which is seldom moreover, we *ride* part of the way — and go into a
fine inn, and order the best of dinners, never debating the expense —
which, after all, never has half the relish of those chance country

[2] See Walton, *The Compleat Angler*, 1653, I.ii, and 1676, II.iii–iv (a
continuation of Walton's work by Charles Cotton).

snaps, when we were at the mercy of uncertain usage, and a precarious welcome.

"You are too proud to see a play anywhere now but in the pit. Do you remember where it was we used to sit, when we saw the battle of Hexham, and the surrender of Calais, and Bannister and Mrs. Bland in the Children in the Wood — when we squeezed out our shillings a-piece to sit three or four times in a season in the one-shilling gallery — where you felt all the time that you ought not to have brought me — and more strongly I felt obligation to you for having brought me — and the pleasure was the better for a little shame — and when the curtain drew up, what cared we for our place in the house, or what mattered it where we were sitting, when our thoughts were with Rosalind in Arden, or with Viola at the Court of Illyria?[3] You used to say, that the gallery was the best place of all for enjoying a play socially — that the relish of such exhibitions must be in proportion to the infrequency of going — that the company we met there, not being in general readers of plays, were obliged to attend the more, and did attend, to what was going on, on the stage — because a word lost would have been a chasm, which it was impossible for them to fill up. With such reflections we consoled our pride then — and I appeal to you, whether, as a woman, I met generally with less attention and accommodation, than I have done since in more expensive situations in the house? The getting in indeed, and the crowding up those inconvenient staircases, was bad enough, — but there was still a law of civility to woman recognised to quite as great an extent as we ever found in the other passages — and how a little difficulty overcome heightened the snug seat, and the play, afterwards! Now we can only pay our money, and walk in. You cannot see, you say, in the galleries now. I am sure we saw, and heard too, well enough then — but sight, and all, I think, is gone with our poverty.

"There was pleasure in eating strawberries, before they became quite common — in the first dish of peas, while they were yet dear — to have them for a nice supper, a treat. What treat can we have now? If we were to treat ourselves now — that is, to have dainties a little above our means, it would be selfish and wicked. It is the very little more that we allow ourselves beyond what the actual poor can get at, that makes what I call a treat — when two people living together, as we have done, now and then indulge themselves in a cheap luxury, which both like; while each apologises, and is willing to take both halves of the blame to his single share. I see no harm in people making much of themselves in that sense of the word. It may give them a hint how to make much of others. But now — what I

[3] *The Battle of Hexham,* 1789, and *The Surrender of Calais,* 1791: comedies by George Colman, the younger; John Bannister (1760–1836) and Mrs. Maria Bland (1769–1838): actors in *The Children in the Wood,* 1793, by Thomas Morton; Rosalind: in *As You Like It;* Viola: in *Twelfth Night.*

mean by the word — we never do make much of ourselves. None but
the poor can do it. I do not mean the veriest poor of all, but persons
as we were, just above poverty.

"I know what you were going to say, that it is mighty pleasant at the
end of the year to make all meet — and much ado we used to have
every Thirty-first Night of December to account for our exceedings —
many a long face did you make over your puzzled accounts, and in
contriving to make it out how we had spent so much — or that we had
not spent so much — or that it was impossible we should spend so
much next year — and still we found our slender capital decreasing
— but then, betwixt ways, and projects, and compromises of one
sort or another, and talk of curtailing this charge, and doing without
that for the future — and the hope that youth brings, and laughing
spirits (in which you were never poor till now,) we pocketed up our
loss, and in conclusion, with 'lusty brimmers' (as you used to quote it
out of *hearty cheerful Mr. Cotton,* as you called him), we used to
welcome in the 'coming guest.'⁴ Now we have no reckoning at all at
the end of the old year — no flattering promises about the new
year doing better for us."

Bridget is so sparing of her speech on most occasions, that when she
gets into a rhetorical vein, I am careful how I interrupt it. I could not
help, however, smiling at the phantom of wealth which her dear
imagination had conjured up out of a clear income of poor — hundred
pounds a year. "It is true we were happier when we were poorer, but
we were also younger, my cousin. I am afraid we must put up with
the excess, for if we were to shake the superflux into the sea, we should
not much mend ourselves. That we had much to struggle with, as
we grew up together, we have reason to be most thankful. It strengthened, and knit our compact closer. We could never have been what
we have been to each other, if we had always had the sufficiency
which you now complain of. The resisting power — those natural
dilations of the youthful spirit, which circumstances cannot straiten —
with us are long since passed away. Competence to age is supplementary youth; a sorry supplement indeed, but I fear the best that is to
be had. We must ride, where we formerly walked: live better, and lie
softer — and shall be wise to do so — than we had means to do in
those good old days you speak of. Yet could those days return — could
you and I once more walk our thirty miles a-day — could Bannister
and Mrs. Bland again be young, and you and I be young to see them
— could the good old one shilling gallery days return — they are
dreams, my cousin, now — but could you and I at this moment, instead of this quiet argument, by our well-carpeted fire-side, sitting on
this luxurious sofa — be once more struggling up those inconvenient
stair-cases, pushed about, and squeezed, and elbowed by the poorest

⁴ Charles Cotton (1630–87), *The New Year* 49–50.

rabble of poor gallery scramblers — could I once more hear those anxious shrieks of yours — and the delicious *Thank God, we are safe,* which always followed when the topmost stair, conquered, let in the first light of the whole cheerful theatre down beneath us — I know not the fathom line that ever touched a descent so deep as I would be willing to bury more wealth in than Crœsus had, or the great Jew R—— is supposed to have, to purchase it. And now do just look at that merry little Chinese waiter holding an umbrella, big enough for a bed-tester, over the head of that pretty insipid half-Madona-ish chit of a lady in that very blue summer house."[5]

On the Tragedies of Shakspeare

❲ Lamb's first distinctive critical essay, on Hogarth, appeared in Hunt's *Reflector*, No. III. It was followed in No. IV, for October–December 1811, by the essay reprinted in *Works*, 1818, as "On the Tragedies of Shakspeare, Considered with Reference to Their Fitness for Stage Representation." E. M. W. Tillyard, in the introduction to his selections from Lamb's applied criticism (Cambridge, 1923), asks us to recognize in this essay "nobility, high seriousness and a passionate emphasis." The text below, from the version of 1818, omits passages on *Othello* and *Richard III* as further examples of the argument that Shakespeare's tragedies are deformed and reduced by performance in Regency theaters. ❳

Taking a turn the other day in the Abbey, I was struck with the affected attitude of a figure, which I do not remember to have seen before, and which upon examination proved to be a whole-length of the celebrated Mr. Garrick. Though I would not go so far with some good catholics abroad as to shut players altogether out of consecrated ground, yet I own I was not a little scandalized at the introduction of theatrical airs and gestures into a place set apart to remind us of the saddest realities. Going nearer, I found inscribed under this harlequin figure the following lines: —

> To paint fair Nature, by divine command,
> Her magic pencil in his glowing hand,

[5] Lamb's copy of the plays of Beaumont and Fletcher, purchased in 1799 (presumably from the bookseller Barker), is in the British Museum.

Paul Colnaghi (1751–1833), print dealer; Leonardo da Vinci (1452–1519), Italian painter, engineer, sculptor, musician. R—: Nathan Rothschild (1777–1836), financier.

hays, or hay: intricate rustic dance; Cathay: old China (a pun); corbeau: raven (here describing a dark brown suit).

A Shakspeare rose; then, to expand his fame
Wide o'er this breathing world, a Garrick came.
Though sunk in death the forms the Poet drew,
The Actor's genius bade them breathe anew;
Though, like the bard himself, in night they lay,
Immortal Garrick call'd them back to day:
And till Eternity with pow'r sublime
Shall mark the mortal hour of hoary Time,
Shakspeare and Garrick like twin-stars shall shine,
And earth irradiate with a beam divine.

It would be an insult to my readers' understandings to attempt any thing like a criticism on this farrago of false thoughts and nonsense. But the reflection it led me into was a kind of wonder, how, from the days of the actor here celebrated to our own, it should have been the fashion to compliment every° performer in his turn, that has had the luck to please the town in any of the great characters of Shakspeare, with the notion of possessing a *mind congenial with the poet's:* how people should come thus unaccountably to confound the power of originating poetical images and conceptions with the faculty of being able to read or recite the same when put into words;[1] or what connection that absolute mastery over the heart and soul of man, which a great dramatic poet possesses, has with those low tricks upon the eye and ear, which a player by observing a few general effects, which some common passion, as grief, anger, &c. usually has upon the gestures and exterior, can so easily compass. To know the internal workings and movements of a great mind, of an Othello or a Hamlet for instance, the *when* and the *why* and the *how far* they should be moved; to what pitch a passion is becoming; to give the reins and to pull in the curb exactly at the moment when the drawing in or the slackening is most graceful; seems to demand a reach of intellect of a vastly different extent from that which is employed upon the bare imitation of the signs of these passions in the countenance or gesture, which signs are usually observed to be most lively and emphatic in the weaker sort of minds, and which signs can after all but indicate some passion, as I said before, anger, or grief, generally; but of the motives and grounds of the passion, wherein it differs from the same passion in low and vulgar natures, of these the actor can give no more idea by his face or gesture than the eye (without a metaphor) can speak, or the muscles utter intelligible sounds. But such is the instantaneous nature

---

[1] It is observable that we fall into this confusion only in *dramatic* recitations. We never dream that the gentleman who reads Lucretius in public with great applause, is therefore a great poet and philosopher; nor do we find that Tom Davies, the bookseller, who is recorded to have recited the Paradise Lost better than any man in England in his day (though I cannot help thinking there must be some mistake in this tradition) was therefore, by his intimate friends, set upon a level with Milton. [C.L.]

of the impressions which we take in at the eye and ear at a playhouse, compared with the slow apprehension oftentimes of the understanding in reading, that we are apt not only to sink the play-writer in the consideration which we pay to the actor, but even to identify in our minds in a perverse manner, the actor with the character which he represents. It is difficult for a frequent playgoer to disembarrass the idea of Hamlet from the person and voice of Mr. K. We speak of Lady Macbeth, while we are in reality thinking of Mrs. S.[2] Nor is this confusion incidental alone to unlettered persons, who, not possessing the advantage of reading, are necessarily dependent upon the stage-player for all the pleasure which they can receive from the drama, and to whom the very idea of *what an author is* cannot be made comprehensible without some pain and perplexity of mind: the error is one from which persons otherwise not meanly lettered, find it almost impossible to extricate themselves.

Never let me be so ungrateful as to forget the very high degree of satisfaction which I received some years back from seeing for the first time a tragedy of Shakespeare performed, in which those two great performers sustained the principal parts. It seemed to embody and realize conceptions which had hitherto assumed no distinct shape. But dearly do we pay all our life after for this juvenile pleasure, this sense of distinctness. When the novelty is past, we find to our cost that instead of realizing an idea, we have only materialized and brought down a fine vision to the standard of flesh and blood. We have let go a dream, in quest of an unattainable substance.

How cruelly this operates upon the mind, to have its free conceptions thus crampt and pressed down to the measure of a strait-lacing actuality, may be judged from that delightful sensation of freshness, with which we turn to those plays of Shakspeare which have escaped being performed, and to those passages in the acting plays of the same writer which have happily been left out in the performance. How far the very custom of hearing any thing *spouted*, withers and blows upon a fine passage, may be seen in those speeches from Henry the Fifth, &c. which are current in the mouths of school-boys from their being to be found in *Enfield Speakers*, and such kind of books. I confess myself utterly unable to appreciate that celebrated soliloquy in Hamlet, beginning "To be or not to be," or to tell whether it be good, bad, or indifferent, it has been so handled and pawed about by declamatory boys and men, and torn so inhumanly from its living place and principle of continuity in the play, till it is become to me a perfect dead member.

It may seem a paradox, but I cannot help being of opinion that the plays of Shakspeare are less calculated for performance on a stage, than those of almost any other dramatist whatever. Their distinguish-

2 John Philip Kemble (1757–1853) and his sister, Sarah Siddons (1755–1831), shared the renown earlier enjoyed by David Garrick (1717–79).

ing excellence is a reason that they should be so. There is so much in them, which comes not under the province of acting, with which eye, and tone, and gesture, have nothing to do.

The glory of the scenic art is to personate passion, and the turns of passion; and the more coarse and palpable the passion is, the more hold upon the eyes and ears of the spectators the performer obviously possesses. For this reason, scolding scenes, scenes where two persons talk themselves into a fit of fury, and then in a surprising manner talk themselves out of it again, have always been the most popular upon our stage. And the reason is plain, because the spectators are here most palpably appealed to, they are the proper judges in this war of words, they are the legitimate ring that should be formed round such "intellectual prize-fighters." Talking is the direct object of the imitation here. But in all the best dramas, and in Shakspeare above all, how obvious it is, that the form of *speaking*, whether it be in soliloquy or dialogue, is only a medium, and often a highly artificial one, for putting the reader or spectator into possession of that knowledge of the inner structure and workings of mind in a character, which he could otherwise never have arrived at *in that form of composition* by any gift short of intuition. We do here as we do with novels written in the *epistolary form*. How many improprieties, perfect solecisms in letter-writing, do we put up with in Clarissa and other books, for the sake of the delight which that form upon the whole gives us.[3]

But the practice of stage representation reduces every thing to a controversy of elocution. Every character, from the boisterous blasphemings of Bajazet to the shrinking timidity of womanhood, must play the orator. The love-dialogues of Romeo and Juliet, those silver-sweet sounds of lovers' tongues by night; the more intimate and sacred sweetness of nuptial colloquy between an Othello or a Posthumus with their married wives, all those delicacies which are so delightful in the reading, as when we read of those youthful dalliances in Paradise —

————————————— As beseem'd
Fair couple link'd in happy nuptial league,
Alone:[4]

by the inherent fault of stage representation, how are these things sullied and turned from their very nature by being exposed to a large assembly; when such speeches as Imogen addresses to her lord, come drawling out of the mouth of a hired actress, whose courtship, though nominally addressed to the personated Posthumus, is manifestly aimed

[3] Samuel Richardson, *Clarissa*, 1747–48.
[4] *Paradise Lost* IV.338–340.
Bajazet: in Christopher Marlowe's *Tamburlaine*, c.1590; Posthumus: husband of Imogen in *Cymbeline*.

at the spectators, who are to judge of her endearments and her returns of love.

The character of Hamlet is perhaps that by which, since the days of Betterton, a succession of popular performers have had the greatest ambition to distinguish themselves. The length of the part may be one of their reasons. But for the character itself, we find it in a play, and therefore we judge it a fit subject of dramatic representation. The play itself abounds in maxims and reflexions beyond any other, and therefore we consider it as a proper vehicle for conveying moral instruction. But Hamlet himself — what does he suffer meanwhile by being dragged forth as the public schoolmaster, to give lectures to the crowd! Why, nine parts in ten of what Hamlet does, are transactions between himself and his moral sense, they are the effusions of his solitary musings, which he retires to holes and corners and the most sequestered parts of the palace to pour forth; or rather, they are the silent meditations with which his bosom is bursting, reduced to *words* for the sake of the reader, who must else remain ignorant of what is passing there. These profound sorrows, these light-and-noise-abhorring ruminations, which the tongue scarce dares utter to deaf walls and chambers, how can they be represented by a gesticulating actor, who comes and mouths them out before an audience, making four hundred people his confidants at once. I say not that it is the fault of the actor so to do; he must pronounce them *ore rotundo,* he must accompany them with his eye, he must insinuate them into his auditory by some trick of eye, tone, or gesture, or he fails. *He must be thinking all the while of his appearance, because he knows that all the while the spectators are judging of it.* And this is the way to represent the shy, negligent, retiring Hamlet.

It is true that there is no other mode of conveying a vast quantity of thought and feeling to a great portion of the audience, who otherwise would never earn it for themselves by reading, and the intellectual acquisition gained this way may, for aught I know, be inestimable; but I am not arguing that Hamlet should not be acted, but how much Hamlet is made another thing by being acted. I have heard much of the wonders which Garrick performed in this part; but as I never saw him, I must have leave to doubt whether the representation of such a character came within the province of his art. Those who tell me of him, speak of his eye, of the magic of his eye, and of his commanding voice: physical properties, vastly desirable in an actor, and without which he can never insinuate meaning into an auditory, — but what have they to do with Hamlet? what have they to do with intellect? In fact, the things aimed at in theatrical representation, are to arrest the spectator's eye upon the form and the gesture, and so to gain a more favourable hearing to what is spoken: it is not what the character is, but how he looks; not what he says, but how he

speaks it. I see no reason to think that if the play of Hamlet were
written over again by some such writer as Banks or Lillo, retaining
the process of the story, but totally omitting all the poetry of it, all
the divine features of Shakspeare, his stupendous intellect; and only
taking care to give us enough of passionate dialogue, which Banks
or Lillo were never at a loss to furnish; I see not how the effect could
be much different upon an audience, nor how the actor has it in his
power to represent Shakspeare to us differently from his representation of Banks or Lillo. Hamlet would still be a youthful accomplished
prince, and must be gracefully personated; he might be puzzled in
his mind, wavering in his conduct, seemingly-cruel to Ophelia, he
might see a ghost, and start at it, and address it kindly when he found
it to be his father; all this in the poorest and most homely language
of the servilest creeper after nature that ever consulted the palate of
an audience; without troubling Shakspeare for the matter: and I see
not but there would be room for all the power which an actor has, to
display itself. All the passions and changes of passion might remain:
for those are much less difficult to write or act than is thought, it is
a trick easy to be attained, it is but rising or falling a note or two in
the voice, a whisper with a significant foreboding look to announce its
approach, and so contagious the counterfeit appearance of any emotion is, that let the words be what they will, the look and tone shall
carry it off and make it pass for deep skill in the passions.

It is common for people to talk of Shakspeare's plays being *so
natural;* that every body can understand him. They are natural indeed, they are grounded deep in nature, so deep that the depth of
them lies out of the reach of most of us. You shall hear the same
persons say that George Barnwell is very natural, and Othello is
very natural, that they are both very deep; and to them they are the
same kind of thing. At the one they sit and shed tears, because a
good sort of young man is tempted by a naughty woman to commit
a trifling peccadillo, the murder of an uncle or so,[5] that is all, and so
comes to an untimely end, which is *so moving;* and at the other, because a blackamoor in a fit of jealousy kills his innocent white wife:
and the odds are that ninety-nine out of a hundred would willingly
behold the same catastrophe happen to both the heroes, and have
thought the rope more due to Othello than to Barnwell. For of the
texture of Othello's mind, the inward construction marvellously laid
open with all its strengths and weaknesses, its heroic confidences and
its human misgivings, its agonies of hate springing from the depths
of love, they see no more than the spectators at a cheaper rate, who
pay their pennies a-piece to look through the man's telescope in
Leicester-fields, see into the inward plot and topography of the moon.

[5] A note of Lamb's, advising managers on moral grounds not to perform
George Lillo's *The London Merchant; or, The History of George Barnwell,*
1731, is here omitted.

Some dim thing or other they see, they see an actor personating a passion, of grief, or anger, for instance, and they recognize it as a copy of the usual external effects of such passions; or at least as being true to *that symbol of the emotion which passes current at the theatre for it*, for it is often no more than that: but of the grounds of the passion, its correspondence to a great or heroic nature, which is the only worthy object of tragedy, — that common auditors know any thing of this, or can have any such notions dinned into them by the mere strength of an actor's lungs, — that apprehensions foreign to them should be thus infused into them by storm, I can neither believe, nor understand how it can be possible.

We talk of Shakspeare's admirable observation of life, when we should feel, that not from a petty inquisition into those cheap and every-day characters which surrounded him, as they surround us, but from his own mind, which was, to borrow a phrase of Ben Jonson's, the very "sphere of humanity,"[6] he fetched those images of virtue and of knowledge, of which every one of us recognizing a part, think we comprehend in our natures the whole; and oftentimes mistake the powers which he positively creates in us, for nothing more than indigenous faculties of our own minds, which only waited the application of corresponding virtues in him to return a full and clear echo of the same.

To return to Hamlet. — Among the distinguishing features of that wonderful character, one of the most interesting (yet painful) is that soreness of mind which makes him treat the intrusions of Polonius with harshness, and that asperity which he puts on in his interviews with Ophelia. These tokens of an unhinged mind (if they be not mixed in the latter case with a profound artifice of love, to alienate Ophelia by affected discourtesies, so to prepare her mind for the breaking off of that loving intercourse, which can no longer find a place amidst business so serious as that which he has to do) are parts of his character, which to reconcile with our admiration of Hamlet, the most patient consideration of his situation is no more than necessary; they are what we *forgive afterwards*, and explain by the whole of his character, but *at the time* they are harsh and unpleasant. Yet such is the actor's necessity of giving strong blows to the audience, that I have never seen a player in this character, who did not exaggerate and strain to the utmost these ambiguous features, — these temporary deformities in the character. They make him express a vulgar scorn at Polonius which utterly degrades his gentility, and which no explanation can render palateable; they make him shew contempt, and curl up the nose at Ophelia's father, — contempt in its very grossest and most hateful form; but they get applause by it: it is natural, people say; that is, the words are scornful, and the actor expresses

---

[6] Cf. *To the Immortal Memory of Cary and Morison* 52.

scorn, and that they can judge of: but why so much scorn, and of
that sort, they never think of asking.

So to Ophelia. — All the Hamlets that I have ever seen, rant and
rave at her as if she had committed some great crime, and the audience are highly pleased, because the words of the part are satirical,
and they are enforced by the strongest expression of satirical indignation of which the face and voice are capable. But then, whether
Hamlet is likely to have put on such brutal appearances to a lady
whom he loved so dearly, is never thought on. The truth is, that in all
such deep affections as had subsisted between Hamlet and Ophelia,
there is a stock of *supererogatory love,* (if I may venture to use the
expression) which in any great grief of heart, especially where that
which preys upon the mind cannot be communicated, confers a kind
of indulgence upon the grieved party to express itself, even to its
heart's dearest object, in the language of a temporary alienation; but
it is not alienation, it is a distraction purely, and so it always makes
itself to be felt by that object: it is not anger, but grief assuming the
appearance of anger, — love awkwardly counterfeiting hate, as sweet
countenances when they try to frown: but such sternness and fierce
disgust as Hamlet is made to shew, is no counterfeit, but the real
face of absolute aversion, — of irreconcileable alienation. It may be
said he puts on the madman; but then he should only so far put on
this counterfeit lunacy as his own real distraction will give him leave;
that is, incompletely, imperfectly; not in that confirmed, practised
way, like a master of his art, or as Dame Quickly would say, "like one
of those harlotry players."[7]

I mean no disrespect to any actor, but the sort of pleasure which
Shakspeare's plays give in the acting seems to me not at all to differ
from that which the audience receive from those of other writers;
and, *they being in themselves essentially so different from all others,*
I must conclude that there is something in the nature of acting which
levels all distinctions. . . .

The truth is, the Characters of Shakspeare are so much the objects
of meditation rather than of interest or curiosity as to their actions,
that while we are reading any of his great criminal characters, —
Macbeth, Richard, even Iago, — we think not so much of the crimes
which they commit, as of the ambition, the aspiring spirit, the intellectual activity, which prompts them to overleap those moral fences.
Barnwell is a wretched murderer; there is a certain fitness between his
neck and the rope; he is the legitimate heir to the gallows; nobody
who thinks at all can think of any alleviating circumstances in his
case to make him a fit object of mercy. Or to take an instance from the
higher tragedy, what else but a mere assassin is Glenalvon! Do we
think of any thing but of the crime which he commits, and the rack

---

[7] *1 Henry IV* II.iv.437.

which he deserves? That is all which we really think about him. Whereas in corresponding characters in Shakspeare so little do the actions comparatively affect us, that while the impulses, the inner mind in all its perverted greatness, solely seems real and is exclusively attended to, the crime is comparatively nothing. But when we see these things represented, the acts which they do are comparatively every thing, their impulses nothing. The state of sublime emotion into which we are elevated by those images of night and horror which Macbeth is made to utter, that solemn prelude with which he entertains the time till the bell shall strike which is to call him to murder Duncan, — when we no longer read it in a book, when we have given up that vantage-ground of abstraction which reading possesses over seeing, and come to see a man in his bodily shape before our eyes actually preparing to commit a murder, if the acting be true and impressive, as I have witnessed it in Mr. K.'s performance of that part, the painful anxiety about the act, the natural longing to prevent it while it yet seems unperpetrated, the too close pressing semblance of reality, give a pain and an uneasiness which totally destroy all the delight which the words in the book convey, where the deed doing never presses upon us with the painful sense of presence: it rather seems to belong to history, — to something past and inevitable, if it has any thing to do with time at all. The sublime images, the poetry alone, is that which is present to our minds in the reading.

So to see Lear acted, — to see an old man tottering about the stage with a walking-stick, turned out of doors by his daughters in a rainy night, has nothing in it but what is painful and disgusting. We want to take him into shelter and relieve him. That is all the feeling which the acting of Lear ever produced in me. But the Lear of Shakspeare cannot be acted. The contemptible machinery by which they mimic the storm which he goes out in, is not more inadequate to represent the horrors of the real elements, than any actor can be to represent Lear: they might more easily propose to personate the Satan of Milton upon a stage, or one of Michael Angelo's terrible figures. The greatness of Lear is not in corporal dimension, but in intellectual: the explosions of his passion are terrible as a volcano: they are storms turning up and disclosing to the bottom that sea, his mind, with all its vast riches. It is his mind which is laid bare. This case of flesh and blood seems too insignificant to be thought on; even as he himself neglects it. On the stage we see nothing but corporal infirmities and weakness, the impotence of rage; while we read it, we see not Lear, but we are Lear, — we are in his mind, we are sustained by a grandeur which baffles the malice of daughters and storms; in the aberrations of his reason, we discover a mighty irregular power of reasoning, immethodized from the ordinary purposes of life, but exerting its powers, as the wind blows where it listeth, at will upon the corruptions and abuses of mankind. What have looks, or tones, to do with that sub-

lime identification of his age with that of the *heavens themselves,*
when in his reproaches to them for conniving at the injustice of his
children, he reminds them that "they themselves are old."[8] What
gesture shall we appropriate to this? What has the voice or the eye
to do with such things? But the play is beyond all art, as the tamper-
ings with it shew: it is too hard and stony; it must have love-scenes,
and a happy ending. It is not enough that Cordelia is a daughter, she
must shine as a lover too. Tate has put his hook in the nostrils of
this Leviathan, for Garrick and his followers, the showmen of the
scene, to draw the mighty beast about more easily. A happy ending!
— as if the living martyrdom that Lear had gone through, — the
flaying of his feelings alive, did not make a fair dismissal from the
stage of life the only decorous thing for him. If he is to live and be
happy after, if he could sustain this world's burden after, why all this
pudder and preparation, — why torment us with all this unnecessary
sympathy? As if the childish pleasure of getting his gilt robes and
sceptre again could tempt him to act over again his misused station,
— as if at his years, and with his experience, any thing was left but
to die.

Lear is essentially impossible to be represented on a stage. But
how many dramatic personages are there in Shakspeare, which though
more tractable and feasible (if I may so speak) than Lear, yet from
some circumstance, some adjunct to their character, are improper to
be shewn to our bodily eye. Othello for instance. Nothing can be
more soothing, more flattering to the nobler parts of our natures, than
to read of a young Venetian lady of highest extraction, through the
force of love and from a sense of merit in him whom she loved, laying
aside every consideration of kindred, and country, and colour, and
wedding with a *coal-black Moor* . . .

Much has been said, and deservedly, in reprobation of the vile
mixture which Dryden has thrown into the Tempest: doubtless without some such vicious alloy, the impure ears of that age would never
have sate out to hear so much innocence of love as is contained in
the sweet courtship of Ferdinand and Miranda. But is the Tempest
of Shakspeare at all a subject for stage representation? It is one thing
to read of an enchanter, and to believe the wondrous tale while we are
reading it; but to have a conjuror brought before us in his conjuring-
gown, with his spirits about him, which none but himself and some
hundred of favoured spectators before the curtain are supposed to see,
involves such a quantity of the *hateful incredible,* that all our reverence for the author cannot hinder us from perceiving such gross attempts upon the senses to be in the highest degree childish and inefficient. Spirits and fairies cannot be represented, they cannot even
be painted, — they can only be believed. But the elaborate and

[8] II.iv.194.

anxious provision of scenery, which the luxury of the age demands, in these cases works a quite contrary effect to what is intended. That which in comedy, or plays of familiar life, adds so much to the life of the imitation, in plays which appeal to the higher faculties, positively destroys the illusion which it is introduced to aid. A parlour or a drawing-room, — a library opening into a garden, — a garden with an alcove in it, — a street, or the piazza of Covent-garden, does well enough in a scene; we are content to give as much credit to it as it demands; or rather, we think little about it, — it is little more than reading at the top of a page, "Scene, a Garden;" we do not imagine ourselves there, but we readily admit the imitation of familiar objects. But to think by the help of painted trees and caverns, which we know to be painted, to transport our minds to Prospero, and his island and his lonely cell;[9] or by the aid of a fiddle dexterously thrown in, in an interval of speaking, to make us believe that we hear those supernatural noises of which the isle was full: — the Orrery Lecturer at the Haymarket might as well hope, by his musical glasses cleverly stationed out of sight behind his apparatus, to make us believe that we do indeed hear the chrystal spheres ring out that chime, which if it were to inwrap our fancy long, Milton thinks,

> Time would run back and fetch the age of gold,
> And speckled vanity
> Would sicken soon and die,
> And leprous Sin would melt from earthly mould;
> Yea Hell itself would pass away,
> And leave its dolorous mansions to the peering day.[10]

The Garden of Eden, with our first parents in it, is not more impossible to be shewn on a stage, than the Enchanted Isle, with its no less interesting and innocent first settlers.

The subject of Scenery is closely connected with that of the Dresses, which are so anxiously attended to on our stage. I remember the last time I saw Macbeth played, the discrepancy I felt at the changes of garment which he varied, — the shiftings and re-shiftings, like a Romish priest at mass. The luxury of stage-improvements, and the importunity of the public eye, require this. The coronation robe of the Scottish monarch was fairly a counterpart to that which our King wears when he goes to the Parliament-house, — just so full and cumbersome, and set out with ermine and pearls. And if things must be represented, I see not what to find fault with in this. But in reading,

[9] It will be said these things are done in pictures. But pictures and scenes are very different things. Painting is a world of itself, but in scene-painting there is the attempt to deceive; and there is the discordancy, never to be got over, between painted scenes and real people. [C.L.]

[10] *On the Morning of Christ's Nativity* 135–140. Scientific lectures were given at the Theatre Royal, Haymarket.

what robe are we conscious of? Some dim images of royalty — a crown and sceptre, may float before our eyes, but who shall describe the fashion of it? Do we see in our mind's eye what Webb or any other robe-maker could pattern? This is the inevitable consequence of imitating every thing, to make all things natural. Whereas the reading of a tragedy is a fine abstraction. It presents to the fancy just so much of external appearances as to make us feel that we are among flesh and blood, while by far the greater and better part of our imagination is employed upon the thoughts and internal machinery of the character. But in acting, scenery, dress, the most contemptible things, call upon us to judge of their naturalness.

Perhaps it would be no bad similitude, to liken the pleasure which we take in seeing one of these fine plays acted, compared with that quiet delight which we find in the reading of it, to the different feelings with which a reviewer, and a man that is not a reviewer, reads a fine poem. The accursed critical habit, — the being called upon to judge and pronounce, must make it quite a different thing to the former. In seeing these plays acted, we are affected just as judges. When Hamlet compares the two pictures of Gertrude's first and second husband, who wants to see the pictures? But in the acting, a miniature must be lugged out; which we know not to be the picture, but only to shew how finely a miniature may be represented. This shewing of every thing, levels all things: it makes tricks, bows, and curtesies, of importance. Mrs. S. never got more fame by any thing than by the manner in which she dismisses the guests in the banquet-scene in Macbeth: it is as much remembered as any of her thrilling tones or impressive looks. But does such a trifle as this enter into the imaginations of the readers of that wild and wonderful scene? Does not the mind dismiss the feasters as rapidly as it can? Does it care about the gracefulness of the doing it? But by acting, and judging of acting, all these non-essentials are raised into an importance, injurious to the main interest of the play.

I have confined my observations to the tragic parts of Shakspeare. It would be no very difficult task to extend the enquiry to his comedies; and shew why Falstaff, Shallow, Sir Hugh Evans, and the rest, are equally incompatible with stage representation. The length to which this Essay has run, will make it, I am afraid, sufficiently distasteful to the Amateurs of the Theatre, without going any deeper into the subject at present.[11]

---

[11] William Enfield, *The Speaker; or, Miscellaneous Pieces, Selected from the Best English Writers,* 1785. Thomas Betterton, active in London theaters from 1659 to 1710. In 1681 Nahum Tate devised for *King Lear* a happy ending, in which Lear survives and Cordelia marries Edgar. Glenalvon: in John Home's *Douglas,* 1756.

Sanity of True Genius

❨ In a series on "Popular Fallacies" in the *New Monthly Magazine,* May 1826, Lamb attacked the idea expressed in Dryden's line, "Great wits are sure to madness near allied." With minor changes, in *Last Essays,* 1833, Lamb's piece took the form that here follows. ❩

So far from the position holding true, that great wit (or genius, in our modern way of speaking), has a necessary alliance with in-sanity, the greatest wits, on the contrary, will ever be found to be the sanest writers. It is impossible for the mind to conceive of a mad Shakspeare. The greatness of wit, by which the poetic talent is here chiefly to be understood, manifests itself in the admirable bal-ance of all the faculties. Madness is the disproportionate straining or excess of any one of them. "So strong a wit," says Cowley, speaking of a poetical friend,

> "—— did Nature to him frame,
> As all things but his judgment overcame,
> His judgment like the heavenly moon did show,
> Tempering that mighty sea below."[1]

The ground of the mistake is, that men, finding in the raptures of the higher poetry a condition of exaltation, to which they have no parallel in their own experience, besides the spurious resemblance of it in dreams and fevers, impute a state of dreaminess and fever to the poet. But the true poet dreams being awake. He is not possessed by his subject, but has dominion over it. In the groves of Eden he walks familiar as in his native paths. He ascends the empyrean heaven, and is not intoxicated. He treads the burning marl without dismay; he wins his flight without self-loss through realms of chaos "and old night."[2] Or if, abandoning himself to that severer chaos of a "human mind untuned," he is content awhile to be mad with Lear, or to hate mankind (a sort of madness) with Timon, neither is that madness, nor this misanthropy, so unchecked, but that, — never letting the reins of reason wholly go, while most he seems to do so, — he has his bet-ter genius still whispering at his ear, with the good servant Kent suggesting saner counsels, or with the honest steward Flavius recom-mending kindlier resolutions.[3] Where he seems most to recede from

[1] Abraham Cowley, *On the Death of Mr. William Hervey* 97–100.
[2] *Paradise Lost* I.296,543.
[3] Cf. *King Lear* IV.vii.17 (and for Kent, Act III); Flavius in *Timon of Athens* IV.iii.482–545.

humanity, he will be found the truest to it. From beyond the scope of Nature if he summon possible existences, he subjugates them to the law of her consistency. He is beautifully loyal to that sovereign directress, even when he appears most to betray and desert her. His ideal tribes submit to policy; his very monsters are tamed to his hand, even as that wild sea-brood, shepherded by Proteus. He tames, and he clothes them with attributes of flesh and blood, till they wonder at themselves, like Indian Islanders forced to submit to European vesture. Caliban, the Witches, are as true to the laws of their own nature (ours with a difference), as Othello, Hamlet, and Macbeth. Herein the great and the little wits are differenced; that if the latter wander ever so little from nature or actual existence, they lose themselves, and their readers. Their phantoms are lawless; their visions nightmares. They do not create, which implies shaping and consistency. Their imaginations are not active — for to be active is to call something into act and form — but passive, as men in sick dreams. For the super-natural, or something super-added to what we know of nature, they give you the plainly non-natural. And if this were all, and that these mental hallucinations were discoverable only in the treatment of subjects out of nature, or transcending it, the judgment might with some plea be pardoned if it ran riot, and a little wantonized: but even in the describing of real and every day life, that which is before their eyes, one of these lesser wits shall more deviate from nature — show more of that inconsequence, which has a natural alliance with frenzy, — than a great genius in his "maddest fits," as Withers somewhere calls them.[4] We appeal to any one that is acquainted with the common run of Lane's novels, — as they existed some twenty or thirty years back, — those scanty intellectual viands of the whole female reading public, till a happier genius arose, and expelled for ever the innutritious phantoms, — whether he has not found his brain more "betossed," his memory more puzzled, his sense of when and where more confounded, among the improbable events, the incoherent incidents, the inconsistent characters, or no-characters, of some third-rate love intrigue — where the persons shall be a Lord Glendamour and a Miss Rivers, and the scene only alternate between Bath and Bond-street — a more bewildering dreaminess induced upon him, than he has felt wandering over all the fairy grounds of Spenser. In the productions we refer to, nothing but names and places is familiar; the persons are neither of this world nor of any other conceivable one; an endless string of activities without purpose, of purposes destitute of motive: — we meet phantoms in our known walks; *fantasques* only christened. In the poet we have names which announce fiction; and we have absolutely no place at all, for the things and persons of the Fairy Queen prate not of their "whereabout."[5]

4 George Wither (1588–1667), *The Shepherds Hunting* IV.409.
5 *Macbeth* II.i.58.

But in their inner nature, and the law of their speech and actions, we are at home and upon acquainted ground. The one turns life into a dream; the other to the wildest dreams gives the sobrieties of every day occurrences. By what subtle art of tracing the mental processes it is effected, we are not philosophers enough to explain, but in that wonderful episode of the cave of Mammon, in which the Money God appears first in the lowest form of a miser, is then a worker of metals, and becomes the god of all the treasures of the world; and has a daughter, Ambition, before whom all the world kneels for favours — with the Hesperian fruit, the waters of Tantalus, with Pilate washing his hands vainly, but not impertinently, in the same stream — that we should be at one moment in the cave of an old hoarder of treasures, at the next at the forge of the Cyclops, in a palace and yet in hell, all at once, with the shifting mutations of the most rambling dream, and our judgment yet all the time awake, and neither able nor willing to detect the fallacy, — is a proof of that hidden sanity which still guides the poet in his widest seeming-aberrations.[6]

It is not enough to say that the whole episode is a copy of the mind's conceptions in sleep; it is, in some sort — but what a copy! Let the most romantic of us, that has been entertained all night with the spectacle of some wild and magnificent vision, recombine it in the morning, and try it by his waking judgment. That which appeared so shifting, and yet so coherent, while that faculty was passive, when it comes under cool examination, shall appear so reasonless and so unlinked, that we are ashamed to have been so deluded; and to have taken, though but in sleep, a monster for a god. But the transitions in this episode are every whit as violent as in the most extravagant dream, and yet the waking judgment ratifies them.[7]

Stage Illusion

(First given the title "Imperfect Dramatic Illusion" in the *London Magazine* of August 1825, this essay was reprinted in *Last Essays*, 1833 — the text here followed. Lamb's chief contribution to the theory of "willing suspension of disbelief," as Sylvan Barnet has pointed out (in *PMLA*, December 1954), rests on his perception that most comedy appeals to the intellect and should not, by realistic illusion, involve the audience in emotional self-identification with the characters.)

[6] *The Faerie Queene* II.vii.
[7] William Lane (1738–1814) published fashionable romances "expelled" by the Waverley Novels of Sir Walter Scott.
"betossed": from *Romeo and Juliet* V.iii.76.

A play is said to be well or ill acted in proportion to the scenical illusion produced. Whether such illusion can in any case be perfect, is not the question. The nearest approach to it, we are told, is, when the actor appears wholly unconscious of the presence of spectators. In tragedy — in all which is to affect the feelings — this undivided attention to his stage business, seems indispensable. Yet it is, in fact, dispensed with every day by our cleverest tragedians; and while these references to an audience, in the shape of rant or sentiment, are not too frequent or palpable, a sufficient quantity of illusion for the purposes of dramatic interest may be said to be produced in spite of them. But, tragedy apart, it may be inquired whether, in certain characters in comedy, especially those which are a little extravagant, or which involve some notion repugnant to the moral sense, it is not a proof of the highest skill in the comedian when, without absolutely appealing to an audience, he keeps up a tacit understanding with them; and makes them, unconsciously to themselves, a party in the scene. The utmost nicety is required in the mode of doing this; but we speak only of the great artists in the profession.

The most mortifying infirmity in human nature, to feel in ourselves, or to contemplate in another, is, perhaps, cowardice. To see a coward *done to the life* upon a stage would produce anything but mirth. Yet we most of us remember Jack Bannister's cowards. Could any thing be more agreeable, more pleasant? We loved the rogues. How was this effected but by the exquisite art of the actor in a perpetual sub-insinuation to us, the spectators, even in the extremity of the shaking fit, that he was not half such a coward as we took him for? We saw all the common symptoms of the malady upon him; the quivering lip, the cowering knees, the teeth chattering; and could have sworn "that man was frightened." But we forgot all the while — or kept it almost a secret to ourselves — that he never once lost his self-possession; that he let out by a thousand droll looks and gestures — meant at *us*, and not at all supposed to be visible to his fellows in the scene, that his confidence in his own resources had never once deserted him. Was this a genuine picture of a coward? or not rather a likeness, which the clever artist contrived to palm upon us instead of an original; while we secretly connived at the delusion for the purpose of greater pleasure, than a more genuine counterfeiting of the imbecility, helplessness, and utter self-desertion, which we know to be concomitants of cowardice in real life, could have given us?

Why are misers so hateful in the world, and so endurable on the stage, but because the skilful actor, by a sort of sub-reference, rather than direct appeal to us, disarms the character of a great deal of its odiousness, by seeming to engage *our* compassion for the insecure tenure by which he holds his money bags and parchments? By this subtle vent half of the hatefulness of the character — the self-closeness with which in real life it coils itself up from the sympathies of men —

evaporates. The miser becomes sympathetic; *i. e.* is no genuine miser. Here again a diverting likeness is substituted for a very disagreeable reality.

Spleen, irritability — the pitiable infirmities of old men, which produce only pain to behold in the realities, counterfeited upon a stage, divert not altogether for the comic appendages to them, but in part from an inner conviction that they are *being acted* before us; that a likeness only is going on, and not the thing itself. They please by being done under the life, or beside it; not *to the life.* When Gatty acts an old man, is he angry indeed? or only a pleasant counterfeit, just enough of a likeness to recognise, without pressing upon us the uneasy sense of reality?

Comedians, paradoxical as it may seem, may be too natural. It was the case with a late actor. Nothing could be more earnest or true than the manner of Mr. Emery; this told excellently in his Tyke, and characters of a tragic cast. But when he carried the same rigid exclusiveness of attention to the stage business, and wilful blindness and oblivion of everything before the curtain into his comedy, it produced a harsh and dissonant effect. He was out of keeping with the rest of the *Personæ Dramatis.* There was as little link between him and them as betwixt himself and the audience. He was a third estate, dry, repulsive, and unsocial to all. Individually considered, his execution was masterly. But comedy is not this unbending thing; for this reason, that the same degree of credibility is not required of it as to serious scenes. The degrees of credibility demanded to the two things may be illustrated by the different sort of truth which we expect when a man tells us a mournful or a merry story. If we suspect the former of falsehood in any one tittle, we reject it altogether. Our tears refuse to flow at a suspected imposition. But the teller of a mirthful tale has latitude allowed him. We are content with less than absolute truth. 'Tis the same with dramatic illusion. We confess we love in comedy to see an audience naturalised behind the scenes, taken in into the interest of the drama, welcomed as by-standers however. There is something ungracious in a comic actor holding himself aloof from all participation or concern with those who are come to be diverted by him. Macbeth must see the dagger, and no ear but his own be told of it; but an old fool in farce may think he *sees something,* and by conscious words and looks express it, as plainly as he can speak, to pit, box, and gallery. When an impertinent in tragedy, an Osric, for instance, breaks in upon the serious passions of the scene, we approve of the contempt with which he is treated.[1] But when the pleasant impertinent of comedy, in a piece purely meant to give delight, and raise mirth out of whimsical perplexities, worries the studious man with taking up his leisure, or making his house his home,

[1] *Macbeth* I.ii.33; *Hamlet* V.ii.81–190.

the same sort of contempt expressed (however *natural*) would destroy
the balance of delight in the spectators. To make the intrusion comic,
the actor who plays the annoyed man must a little desert nature; he
must, in short, be thinking of the audience, and express only so much
dissatisfaction and peevishness as is consistent with the pleasure of
comedy. In other words, his perplexity must seem half put on. If
he repel the intruder with the sober set face of a man in earnest, and
more especially if he deliver his expostulations in a tone which in the
world must necessarily provoke a duel; his real-life manner will
destroy the whimsical and purely dramatic existence of the other
character (which to render it comic demands an antagonist comicality
on the part of the character opposed to it), and convert what was
meant for mirth, rather than belief, into a downright piece of impertinence indeed, which would raise no diversion in us, but rather stir
pain, to see inflicted in earnest upon any unworthy person. A very
judicious actor (in most of his parts) seems to have fallen into an error
of this sort in his playing with Mr. Wrench in the farce of Free and
Easy.

Many instances would be tedious; these may suffice to show that
comic acting at least does not always demand from the performer
that strict abstraction from all reference to an audience, which is
exacted of it; but that in some cases a sort of compromise may take
place, and all the purposes of dramatic delight be attained by a
judicious understanding, not too openly announced, between the
ladies and gentlemen — on both sides of the curtain.[2]

On the Artificial Comedy
of the Last Century

(Lamb published a series of three articles on "The Old Actors" in the
London Magazine for February, April, and October 1822. Reduced and
rearranged, these articles became the last three essays in *Elia*, 1823. The
argument of the middle essay, that Restoration comedy and its eighteenth-
century sequel comprise an "Artificial Comedy," is inaccurate if applied

---

[2] John Bannister, famous as Bob Acres in R. B. Sheridan's *The Rivals*,
retired in 1815. Henry Gattie (1774–1844), Dr. Caius in *The Merry Wives
of Windsor;* John Emery (1777–1822), Tyke in Thomas Morton's *The
School for Reform,* 1805. The leading roles in Samuel J. Arnold's *Free and
Easy,* 1816, were played by Benjamin Wrench (1788–1843) and George
Bartley (c.1782–1858).

historically to the intentions of the playwrights; but Lamb refers primarily to the artificial and stylized revivals of these plays on the stage. In *The Amiable Humorist* (Chicago, 1960), Stuart M. Tave has explained Lamb's essay in the context of a view common in its time, that the comic can be relief and defense, a "necessary moral sustenance to a melancholic man."]]

The artificial Comedy, or Comedy of manners, is quite extinct on our stage. Congreve and Farquhar show their heads once in seven years only, to be exploded and put down instantly. The times cannot bear them. Is it for a few wild speeches, an occasional license of dialogue? I think not altogether. The business of their dramatic characters will not stand the moral test. We screw every thing up to that. Idle gallantry in a fiction, a dream, the passing pageant of an evening, startles us in the same way as the alarming indications of profligacy in a son or ward in real life should startle a parent or guardian. We have no such middle emotions as dramatic interests left. We see a stage libertine playing his loose pranks of two hours' duration, and of no after consequence, with the severe eyes which inspect real vices with their bearings upon two worlds. We are spectators to a plot or intrigue (not reducible in life to the point of strict morality) and take it all for truth. We substitute a real for a dramatic person, and judge him accordingly. We try him in our courts, from which there is no appeal to the *dramatis personæ*, his peers. We have been spoiled with — not sentimental comedy — but a tyrant far more pernicious to our pleasures which has succeeded to it, the exclusive and all devouring drama of common life; where the moral point is every thing; where, instead of the fictitious half-believed personages of the stage (the phantoms of old comedy) we recognise ourselves, our brothers, aunts, kinsfolk, allies, patrons, enemies, — the same as in life, — with an interest in what is going on so hearty and substantial, that we cannot afford our moral judgment, in its deepest and most vital results, to compromise or slumber for a moment. What is *there* transacting, by no modification is made to affect us in any other manner than the same events or characters would do in our relationships of life. We carry our fire-side concerns to the theatre with us. We do not go thither, like our ancestors, to escape from the pressure of reality, so much as to confirm our experience of it; to make assurance double, and take a bond of fate. We must live our toilsome lives twice over, as it was the mournful privilege of Ulysses to descend twice to the shades. All that neutral ground of character, which stood between vice and virtue; or which in fact was indifferent to neither, where neither properly was called in question; that happy breathing-place from the burthen of a perpetual moral questioning — the sanctuary and quiet Alsatia of hunted casuistry — is broken up and disfranchised, as injurious to the interests of society. The privileges of the place are taken away by law. We dare not dally with images, or names, of wrong. We bark like foolish dogs at shadows. We dread infection from the scenic representation of disorder; and fear a painted pustule. In our anxiety that our morality should not take cold, we wrap it up in a great blanket surtout of precaution against the breeze and sunshine.

I confess for myself that (with no great delinquencies to answer for) I am glad for a season to take an airing beyond the diocese of the strict conscience, — not to live always in the precincts of the law-courts, — but now and then, for a dream-while or so, to imagine a world with no meddling restrictions — to get into recesses, whither the hunter cannot follow me —

> ————————— Secret shades
> Of woody Ida's inmost grove,
> While yet there was no fear of Jove —[1]

I come back to my cage and my restraint the fresher and more healthy for it. I wear my shackles more contentedly for having respired the breath of an imaginary freedom. I do not know how it is with others, but I feel the better always for the perusal of one of Congreve's — nay, why should I not add even of Wycherley's — comedies. I am the gayer at least for it; and I could never connect those sports of a witty fancy in any shape with any result to be drawn from them to imitation in real life. They are a world of themselves almost as much as fairyland. Take one of their characters, male or female (with few exceptions they are alike), and place it in a modern play, and my virtuous indignation shall rise against the profligate wretch as warmly as the Catos of the pit could desire; because in a modern play I am to judge of the right and the wrong. The standard of *police* is the measure of *political justice*. The atmosphere will blight it, it cannot live here. It has got into a moral world, where it has no business, from which it must needs fall headlong; as dizzy, and incapable of making a stand, as a Swedenborgian bad spirit that has wandered unawares into the sphere of one of his Good Men, or Angels. But in its own world do we feel the creature is so very bad? — The Fainalls and the Mirabels, the Dorimants and the Lady Touchwoods, in their own sphere, do not offend my moral sense; in fact they do not appeal to it at all. They seem engaged in their proper element. They break through no laws, or conscientious restraints. They know of none. They have got out of Christendom into the land — what shall I call it? — of cuckoldry — the Utopia of gallantry, where pleasure is duty, and the manners perfect freedom. It is altogether a speculative scene of things, which has no reference whatever to the world that is. No good person can be justly offended as a spectator, because no good person suffers on the stage. Judged morally, every character in these plays — the few exceptions only are *mistakes* — is alike essentially vain and

[1] Milton, *Il Penseroso* 28–30.

worthless. The great art of Congreve is especially shown in this, that he has entirely excluded from his scenes, — some little generosities in the part of Angelica perhaps excepted, — not only any thing like a faultless character, but any pretensions to goodness or good feelings whatsoever. Whether he did this designedly, or instinctively, the effect is as happy, as the design (if design) was bold. I used to wonder at the strange power which his Way of the World in particular possesses of interesting you all along in the pursuits of characters, for whom you absolutely care nothing — for you neither hate nor love his personages — and I think it is owing to this very indifference for any, that you endure the whole. He has spread a privation of moral light, I will call it, rather than by the ugly name of palpable darkness, over his creations; and his shadows flit before you without distinction or preference. Had he introduced a good character, a single gush of moral feeling, a revulsion of the judgment to actual life and actual duties, the impertinent Goshen would have only lighted to the discovery of deformities, which now are none, because we think them none.

Translated into real life, the characters of his, and his friend Wycherley's dramas, are profligates and stumpets, — the business of their brief existence, the undivided pursuit of lawless gallantry. No other spring of action, or possible motive of conduct, is recognised; principles which, universally acted upon, must reduce this frame of things to a chaos. But we do them wrong in so translating them. No such effects are produced in *their* world. When we are among them, we are amongst a chaotic people. We are not to judge them by our usages. No reverend institutions are insulted by their proceedings, — for they have none among them. No peace of families is violated, — for no family ties exist among them. No purity of the marriage bed is stained, — for none is supposed to have a being. No deep affections are disquieted, — no holy wedlock bands are snapped asunder, — for affection's depth and wedded faith are not of the growth of that soil. There is neither right nor wrong, — gratitude or its opposite, — claim or duty, — paternity or sonship. Of what consequence is it to virtue, or how is she at all concerned about it, whether Sir Simon, or Dapperwit, steal away Miss Martha; or who is the father of Lord Froth's, or Sir Paul Pliant's children.

The whole is a passing pageant, where we should sit as unconcerned at the issues, for life or death, as at a battle of the frogs and mice. But, like Don Quixote, we take part against the puppets, and quite as impertinently. We dare not contemplate an Atlantis, a scheme, out of which our coxcombical moral sense is for a little transitory ease excluded. We have not the courage to imagine a state of things for which there is neither reward nor punishment. We cling to the painful necessities of shame and blame. We would indict our very dreams.

Amidst the mortifying circumstances attendant upon growing old,

it is something to have seen the School for Scandal in its glory. This
comedy grew out of Congreve and Wycherley, but gathered some
allays of the sentimental comedy which followed theirs. It is impossible
that it should be now *acted*, though it continues, at long intervals, to
be announced in the bills. Its hero, when Palmer played it at least, was
Joseph Surface. When I remember the gay boldness, the graceful
solemn plausibility, the measured step, the insinuating voice — to express it in a word — the downright *acted* villany of the part, so different from the pressure of conscious actual wickedness, — the hypo-
critical assumption of hypocrisy, — which made Jack so deservedly a
favourite in that character, I must needs conclude the present generation of play-goers more virtuous than myself, or more dense. I freely
confess that he divided the palm with me with his better brother; that,
in fact, I liked him quite as well. Not but there are passages, — like
that, for instance, where Joseph is made to refuse a pittance to a poor
relation, — incongruities which Sheridan was forced upon by the attempt to join the artificial with the sentimental comedy, either of which
must destroy the other — but over these obstructions Jack's manner
floated him so lightly, that a refusal from him no more shocked you, than
the easy compliance of Charles gave you in reality any pleasure; you got
over the paltry question as quickly as you could, to get back into
the regions of pure comedy, where no cold moral reigns. The highly
artificial manner of Palmer in this character counteracted every disagreeable impression which you might have received from the contrast, supposing them real, between the two brothers. You did not
believe in Joseph with the same faith with which you believed in
Charles. The latter was a pleasant reality, the former a no less pleasant
poetical foil to it. The comedy, I have said, is incongruous; a mixture
of Congreve with sentimental incompatibilities: the gaiety upon the
whole is buoyant; but it required the consummate art of Palmer to
reconcile the discordant elements.

A player with Jack's talents, if we had one now, would not dare
to do the part in the same manner. He would instinctively avoid every
turn which might tend to unrealise, and so to make the character
fascinating. He must take his cue from his spectators, who would
expect a bad man and a good man as rigidly opposed to each other as
the death-beds of those geniuses are contrasted in the prints, which
I am sorry to say have disappeared from the windows of my old friend
Carrington Bowles, of St. Paul's Church-yard memory — (an exhibition as venerable as the adjacent cathedral, and almost coeval) of the
bad and good man at the hour of death; where the ghastly apprehensions of the former, — and truly the grim phantom with his reality of
a toasting fork is not to be despised, — so finely contrast with the
meek complacent kissing of the rod, — taking it in like honey and
butter, — with which the latter submits to the scythe of the gentle
bleeder, Time, who wields his lancet with the apprehensive finger of a

popular young ladies' surgeon. What flesh, like loving grass, would not covet to meet half-way the stroke of such a delicate mower? — John Palmer was twice an actor in this exquisite part. He was playing to you all the while that he was playing upon Sir Peter and his lady. You had the first intimation of a sentiment before it was on his lips. His altered voice was meant to you, and you were to suppose that his fictitious co-flutterers on the stage perceived nothing at all of it. What was it to you if that half-reality, the husband, was over-reached by the puppetry — or the thin thing (Lady Teazle's reputation) was persuaded it was dying of a plethory? The fortunes of Othello and Desdemona were not concerned in it. Poor Jack has past from the stage in good time, that he did not live to this our age of seriousness. The pleasant old Teazle *King*, too, is gone in good time. His manner would scarce have past current in our day. We must love or hate — acquit or condemn — censure or pity — exert our detestable coxcombry of moral judgment upon every thing. Joseph Surface, to go down now, must be a downright revolting villain — no compromise — his first appearance must shock and give horror — his specious plausibilities, which the pleasurable faculties of our fathers welcomed with such hearty greetings, knowing that no harm (dramatic harm even) could come, or was meant to come of them, must inspire a cold and killing aversion. Charles (the real canting person of the scene — for the hypocrisy of Joseph has its ulterior legitimate ends, but his brother's professions of a good heart centre in downright self-satisfaction) must be *loved*, and Joseph *hated*. To balance one disagreeable reality with another, Sir Peter Teazle must be no longer the comic idea of a fretful old bachelor bridegroom, whose teasings (while King acted it) were evidently as much played off at you, as they were meant to concern any body on the stage, — he must be a real person, capable in law of sustaining an injury — a person towards whom duties are to be acknowledged — the genuine crim-con antagonist of the villanous seducer Joseph. To realise him more, his sufferings under his unfortunate match must have the downright pungency of life — must (or should) make you not mirthful but uncomfortable, just as the same predicament would move you in a neighbour or old friend. The delicious scenes which give the play its name and zest, must affect you in the same serious manner as if you heard the reputation of a dear female friend attacked in your real presence. Crabtree, and Sir Benjamin — those poor snakes that live but in the sunshine of your mirth — must be ripened by this hot-bed process of realization into asps or amphisbænas;[2] and Mrs. Candour — O! frightful! become a hooded serpent. Oh who that remembers Parsons and Dodd — the wasp and butterfly of the School for Scandal — in those two characters; and charming natural Miss Pope, the perfect gentlewoman as

[2] Cf. *Paradise Lost* X.524.

distinguished from the fine lady of comedy, in this latter part — would forego the true scenic delight — the escape from life — the oblivion of consequences — the holiday barring out the pedant Reflection — those Saturnalia of two or three brief hours, well won from the world — to sit instead at one of our modern plays — to have his coward conscience (that forsooth must not be left for a moment) stimulated with perpetual appeals — dulled rather, and blunted, as a faculty without repose must be — and his moral vanity pampered with images of notional justice, notional beneficence, lives saved without the spectators' risk, and fortunes given away that cost the author nothing?

No piece was, perhaps, ever so completely cast in all its parts as this *manager's comedy*. Miss Farren had succeeded to Mrs. Abingdon in Lady Teazle; and Smith, the original Charles, had retired, when I first saw it. The rest of the characters, with very slight exceptions, remained. I remember it was then the fashion to cry down John Kemble, who took the part of Charles after Smith; but, I thought, very unjustly. Smith, I fancy, was more airy, and took the eye with a certain gaiety of person. He brought with him no sombre recollections of tragedy. He had not to expiate the fault of having pleased before-hand in lofty declamation. He had no sins of Hamlet or of Richard to atone for. His failure in these parts was a passport to success in one of so opposite a tendency. But, as far as I could judge, the weighty sense of Kemble made up for more personal incapacity than he had to answer for. His harshest tones in this part came steeped and dulcified in good humour. He made his defects a grace. His exact declamatory manner, as he managed it, only served to convey the points of his dialogue with more precision. It seemed to head the shafts to carry them deeper. Not one of his sparkling sentences was lost. I remember minutely how he delivered each in succession, and cannot by any effort imagine how any of them could be altered for the better. No man could deliver brilliant dialogue — the dialogue of Congreve or of Wycherley — because none understood it — half so well as John Kemble. His Valentine, in Love for Love, was, to my recollection, faultless. He flagged sometimes in the intervals of tragic passion. He would slumber over the level parts of an heroic character. His Macbeth has been known to nod. But he always seemed to me to be particularly alive to pointed and witty dialogue. The relaxing levities of tragedy have not been touched by any since him — the playful court-bred spirit in which he condescended to the players in Hamlet — the sportive relief which he threw into the darker shades of Richard — disappeared with him. He had his sluggish moods, his torpors — but they were the halting-stones and resting-places of his tragedy — politic savings, and fetches of the breath — husbandry of the lungs, where nature pointed him to be an economist — rather, I think, than errors of the judgment. They were, at worst, less painful than the eternal tormenting unappeasable vigilance, the "lidless dragon eyes,"[3] of present fashionable tragedy.[4]

On the Acting of Munden

❨ The last essay in *Elia*, 1823, on Joseph Shepherd Munden (1758–1832), illustrates in brief space Lamb's rivalry of Hazlitt and Hunt in the description of acting techniques and theatrical effects. ❩

Not many nights ago I had come home from seeing this extraordinary performer in Cockletop; and when I retired to my pillow, his whimsical image still stuck by me, in a manner as to threaten sleep. In vain I tried to divest myself of it, by conjuring up the most opposite associations. I resolved to be serious. I raised up the gravest topics of life; private misery, public calamity. All would not do.

———— There the antic sate
Mocking our state —[1]

his queer visnomy — his bewildering costume — all the strange things which he had raked together — his serpentine rod, swagging about in his pocket — Cleopatra's tear, and the rest of his relics — O'Keefe's wild farce, and *his* wilder commentary — till the passion of laughter, like grief in excess, relieved itself by its own weight, inviting the sleep which in the first instance it had driven away.

But I was not to escape so easily. No sooner did I fall into slumbers, than the same image, only more perplexing, assailed me in the shape

---

[3] Coleridge, *Ode on the Departing Year* 145.

[4] Roles referred to: William Congreve's Fainall in *The Way of the World*, 1700, Lady Touchwood in *The Double Dealer*, 1694, Angelica in *Love for Love*, 1695; George Farquhar's Mirabel in *The Inconstant*, 1702; Sir George Etherege's Dorimant in *The Man of Mode*, 1676; William Wycherley's Martha in *Love in a Wood*, 1671; Richard Brinsley Sheridan's Joseph and Charles Surface and other characters in *The School for Scandal*, 1777. Prominent actors: Thomas King (1730–1805), the original Sir Peter Teazle, and Jane Pope (1742–1818), the original Mrs. Candour, in *The School for Scandal*. John Philip Kemble (1757–1823), leader of a severe but declamatory school of acting, performed most of Shakespeare's heroic roles, including that of Richard III.

Alsatia: a district in London providing sanctuary for debtors until 1697; Cato (234–149 B.C.), a Roman censor, combated luxury; Atlantis: a fabulous island, leading Francis Bacon to entitle his Utopian treatise *The New Atlantis.*

[1] Cf. *Richard II* III.ii.162–163.

of dreams. Not one Munden, but five hundred, were dancing before
me, like the faces which, whether you will or no, come when you have
been taking opium — all the strange combinations, which this strangest
of all strange mortals ever shot his proper countenance into, from the
day he came commissioned to dry up the tears of the town for the loss
of the now almost forgotten Edwin. O for the power of the pencil to
have fixed them when I awoke! A season or two since there was exhibited a Hogarth gallery. I do not see why there should not be a
Munden gallery. In richness and variety the latter would not fall far
short of the former.

There is one face of Farley, one face of Knight, one (but what a
one it is!) of Liston; but Munden has none that you can properly pin
down, and call *his*. When you think he has exhausted his battery of
looks, in unaccountable warfare with your gravity, suddenly he sprouts
out an entirely new set of features, like Hydra. He is not one, but
legion. Not so much a comedian, as a company. If his name could be
multiplied like his countenance, it might fill a play-bill. He, and he
alone, literally *makes faces:* applied to any other person, the phrase is
a mere figure, denoting certain modifications of the human countenance. Out of some invisible wardrobe he dips for faces, as his friend
Suett used for wigs, and fetches them out as easily. I should not be
suprised to see him some day put out the head of a river horse; or come
forth a pewitt, or lapwing, some feathered metamorphosis.

I have seen this gifted actor in Sir Christopher Curry — in Old
Dornton — diffuse a glow of sentiment which has made the pulse of
a crowded theatre beat like that of one man; when he has come in aid
of the pulpit, doing good to the moral heart of a people. I have seen
some faint approaches to this sort of excellence in other players. But
in the grand grotesque of farce, Munden stands out as single and
unaccompanied as Hogarth. Hogarth, strange to tell, had no followers.
The school of Munden began, and must end with himself.

Can any man *wonder*, like him? can any man *see ghosts,* like him?
or *fight with his own shadow* — "SESSA"[2] — as he does in that
strangely-neglected thing, the Cobbler of Preston — where his alternations from the Cobbler to the Magnifico, and from the Magnifico to the
Cobbler, keep the brain of the spectator in as wild a ferment, as if
some Arabian Night were being acted before him. Who like him
can throw, or ever attempted to throw, a preternatural interest over the
commonest daily-life objects? A table, or a joint stool, in his conception, rises into a dignity equivalent to Cassiopeia's chair. It is invested
with constellatory importance. You could not speak of it with more
deference, if it were mounted into the firmament. A beggar in the
hands of Michael Angelo, says Fuseli, rose the Patriarch of Poverty.
So the gusto of Munden antiquates and ennobles what it touches. His

[2] Cf. *King Lear* III.iv.58,104 (E. V. Lucas).

pots and his ladles are as grand and primal as the seething-pots and
hooks seen in old prophetic vision. A tub of butter, contemplated by
him, amounts to a Platonic idea. He understands a leg of mutton in its
quiddity. He stands wondering, amid the common-place materials of
life, like primæval man with the sun and stars about him.[3]

Letters

❨ Of the known letters by Lamb, numbering about 1100, a large portion
gave full imaginative value in days when the recipient paid the postage.
Several of his most famous essays amplify ideas and fantasies tried out in
the letters. He was nearly as witty, if not as discerning, to nonentities as to
men of fame. Some of his letters to Coleridge suggest strain, but those to
Wordsworth do not. He was at his best to Thomas Manning (1772–1840),
bachelor, linguist, semi-official traveler, and tutor in mathematics. Although
it is partly in jest that Manning is called in the letters Trismegistus, Archimedes, and other "geometric" names, Lamb described him in 1801 as a
"man of great Power — an enchanter almost," far "beyond Coleridge or any
man in power of impressing." Contrary to his usual practice, Lamb preserved most of the answering letters from Manning, which were edited by
Gertrude Anderson and published in 1925. Lamb's letters below are taken
from photostats of the manuscripts. Editorial insertions are enclosed in
square brackets ([]). Canceled words and letters are enclosed in shaped
brackets (⟨⟩). ❩

TO WILLIAM WORDSWORTH

[30 January 1801]

Thanks for your Letter and Present.[1] I had already borrowed your
second volume — What most please me are, the Song of Lucy. . . .
Simon's sickly daughter in the Sexton made me *cry*. Next to these
are the description of the continuous Echoes in the story of Joanna's
laugh, where the mountains and all the scenery absolutely seem alive

---

[3] Cockletop, in John O'Keeffe, *Modern Antiques*, 1791; Curry, in George
Colman the younger, *Inkle and Yariko*, 1787; Dornton, in Thomas Holcroft,
The Road to Ruin, 1792; Charles Johnson, *The Cobbler of Preston*, 1716.
    William Hogarth (1697–1764), whose engravings Lamb praised for their
ethical and narrative power. Henry Fuseli (1741–1825), Swiss painter and
author in London, a friend of Blake.
[1] *Lyrical Ballads*, 1800, with new poems in Volume II.

— and that fine Shakesperian character of the Happy Man, in the Brothers,

> that creeps about the fields,
> Following his fancies by the hour, to bring
> Tears down his cheek, or solitary smiles
> Into his face, UNTIL THE SETTING SUN
> WRITE FOOL UPON HIS FOREHEAD.

I will mention one more: the delicate and curious feeling, in the wish for the Cumberland Beggar, that he may have about him the melody of Birds, altho' he hear them not. Here the mind knowingly passes a fiction upon herself, first substituting her own feelings for the Beggar's, and, in the same breath detecting the fallacy, will not part with the wish. — The Poets Epitaph is disfigured, to my taste by the vulgar satire upon parsons and lawyers in the beginning, and the coarse epithet of pin point in the 6ᵗʰ stanza. All the rest is eminently good, and your own. I will just add that it appears to me a fault in the Beggar, that the instructions conveyed in it are too direct and like' a lecture: they dont slide into the mind of the reader, while he is imagining no such matter. An intelligent reader finds a sort of insult in being told, I will teach you how to think upon this subject. This fault, if I am right, is in a ten thousandth worse degree to be found in Sterne and many many novelists & modern poets, who continually put a sign post up to shew where you are to feel. They set out with assuming their readers to be stupid. Very different from Robinson Crusoe, the Vicar of Wakefield, Roderick Random, and other beautiful bare narratives. There is implied an unwritten compact between Author and reader; I will tell you a story, and I suppose you will understand it. Modern Novels "Sᵗ. Leons" and the like are full of such flowers as these "Let not my reader suppose" — "Imagine, IF YOU CAN" — modest! — &c. — I will here have done with praise and blame. I have written so much, only that you may not think I have passed over your book without observation. — I am sorry that Coleridge has christened his Ancient Marinere "a poet's Reverie" — it is as bad as Bottom the Weaver's declaration that he is not a Lion but only the scenical representation of a Lion. What new idea is gained by this Title, but one subversive of all credit, which the Tale should force upon us, of its truth? — For me, I was never so affected with any human Tale. After first reading it, I was totally possessed with it for many days. — I dislike all the miraculous part of it, but the feelings of the man under the operation of such scenery dragged me along like Tom Piper's magic whistle. I totally differ from your idea that the Marinere should have had a character and profession. This is a Beauty in Gulliver's Travels, where the mind is kept in a placid state of little wonderments; but the Ancient Marinere undergoes such Trials, as overwhelm and bury all individuality or memory of what he was. Like the state of a man in a Bad dream, one terrible peculiarity of which is, that all consciousness of personality is gone. — Your other observation is I think as well a little unfounded: the Marinere from being conversant in supernatural events HAS acquired a supernatural and strange cast of *phrase*, eye, appearance &c. which frighten the wedding guest. — You will excuse my remarks, because I am hurt and vexed that you should think it necessary, with a prose apology, to open they [*for* the] eyes of dead men that cannot see . . — To sum up a general opinion of the second vol. — I do not ⟨like any⟩ feel any one poem in it so forcibly as the Ancient Marinere, the Mad mother,[2] and the Lines at Tintern Abbey in the first. — I could, too, have wished that the Critical preface had appeared in a separate treatise. All its dogmas are true and just, and most of them new, *as* criticism. . But they associate a *diminishing* idea with the Poems which follow, as ⟨being⟩ having been written for EXPERIMENTS on the public taste, more than having sprung (as they must have done) from living and daily circumstances. — I am prolix, because I am gratified in the opportunity of writing to you, and I dont well know when to leave off. — I ought before this to have reply'd to your very kind invitation into Cumberland. — With you and your Sister I could gang any where. But I am afraid whether I shall ever be able to afford so desperate a Journey. — Separate from the pleasure of your company, I dont much care if I never see a mountain in my life. . I have passed all my days in London, until I have formed as many and intense local attachments, as any of you Mountaineers can have done with dead nature. . The Lighted shops of the Strand and Fleet Street, the innumerable trades, tradesmen and customers, coaches, waggons, playhouses, all the bustle and wickedness round about Covent Garden, the very women of the Town, the Watchmen, drunken scenes, rattles; — life awake, if you awake, at all hours of the night, the impossibility of being dull in Fleet Street, the crowds, the very dirt & mud, the Sun shining upon houses and pavements, the print shops, the OLD BOOK stalls, parsons cheap'ning books, coffee houses, steams of soup from kitchens, the pantomimes, London itself a pantomime and a masquerade, all these things work themselves into my mind and feed me without a power of satiating me. The wonder of these sights impells me into night-walks about her crowded streets, and I often shed tears in the motley Strand from fullness of joy at so much Life. — All these emotions must be strange to you. So are your rural emotions to me. . But consider, what must I have been doing all my life, not to have lent great portions of my heart with usury to such scenes? —— My attachments are ⟨not⟩ all local, purely local — I have no passion (or have had none since I was in love, and then it was the spurious engendering of poetry & books) to groves and vallies. . The rooms where I was born, the furniture which has been

---

[2] "Her eyes are wild."

before my eyes all my life, a book case which has followed me about
(like a faithful dog, only exceeding him in knowledge) wherever I
have moved — old chairs, old tables, streets, squares, where I have
sunned myself, my old school, — these are my mistresses — have I
not enough, without your mountains? — I do not envy you. I should
pity you, did I not know, that the Mind will make friends of any
thing. Your sun & moon and skys and hills & lakes affect me no more,
or scarcely come to me in more venerable characters, than as a gilded
room with tapestry and tapers, where I might live with handsome
visible objects. — I consider the clouds above me but as a roof
beautifully painted, but unable to satisfy the mind, and at last, like the
pictures of the apartment of a connoisseur, unable to afford him any
longer a pleasure. So fading upon me, from disuse, have been the
Beauties of Nature, as they have been confinedly called; so ever fresh
& green and warm are all the inventions of men and assemblies of men
in this great city. I should certainly have laughed with dear Joanna.

Give my kindest love, *and my sister's*, to Dorothy & yourself And a
kiss from me to little Barbara Lewthwaite.

C Lamb

Thank you for Liking my Play! ![3]

TO THOMAS MANNING

[15 February 1801]

I had need be cautious henceforward what opinion I give of the
Lyrical Bal[l]ads. — All the north of England are in a turmoil. Cumberland and Westmorland have already declared a state of war. — I
lately received from Wordsw[orth]. a copy of the second volume,
accompanied by an acknowledgment of having received from me many
months since a copy of a certain Tragedy,[1] with excuses for not having
made any acknowledgment sooner, it being owing to an "almost insurmountable aversion from Letter writing." — This letter I answered
in due form and time, and enumerated several of the passages which
had most affected me, adding, unfortunately, that no single piece
had moved me so forcibly as the Ancient Marinere, the Mad Mother,

---

[3] *John Woodvil.*
Wordsworth later changed the "pin point" to "ever-dwindling." He had
noted for his readers, among three defects in Coleridge's mariner, that he
"has no distinct character," either in "his profession of Mariner" or as a
human being under supernatural influences. For Barbara and Joanna, see
his poems "The Pet-Lamb" and "To Joanna."

St. Leon: by Godwin, 1799; Bottom: *A Midsummer Night's Dream*
V.i.222–229.

[1] *John Woodvil.*

or the Lines at Tintern Abbey. The Post did not sleep a moment. I
received almost instantaneously a long letter of four sweating pages
from my RELUCTANT LETTERWRITER, the purport of which was, that
he was sorry his 2^d vol. had not given me more pleasure (Devil a hint
did I give that it had *not pleased me*) and "was compelled to wish that
my range of Sensibility was more extended, being obliged to believe
that I should receive large influxes of happiness & happy Thoughts"
(I suppose from the L. B. —) With a deal of stuff about a certain
"Union of Tenderness & Imagination, which in the sense he used Imag.
was not the characteristic of Shakesp. but which Milton possessed in
a degree far exceeding other Poets: which Union, as the highest
species of Poetry, and chiefly deserving that name, He was most
proud to aspire to" — then illustrating the said Union by two quotations from his own 2^d vol. (which I had been so unfortunate as to
miss) — 1st Specimen — A father addresses his Son —

> When thou
> First cam'st into the world, as it befalls
> To newborn Infants, thou didst sleep away
> Two days: *And Blessings from thy father's tongue*
> *Then fell upon thee.*[2]

The lines were thus undermark'd & then followed "This Passage as
combining in an extraordinary degree that union of Imagination &
Tenderness, which I am speaking of, I consider as one of the Best I
ever wrote." —

2^d Specimen. — A Youth after years of absence revisits his native
place, and thinks (as most people do) that there has been strange
alteration in his absence —

> And that the rocks
> And Everlasting Hills themselves were chang'd.[3]

You see both these are good Poetry: but after one has been reading
Shaksp. twenty of the best years of one's life, to have a fellow start
up, and prate about some unknown quality, which Shakspere possess'd
in a degree inferior to Milton and somebody else! ! —— This was not
to be *all* my castigation. — Coleridge, who had not written to me
some months before, starts up from his bed of sickness, to reprove me
for my hardy presumption: four long pages, equally sweaty, and more
tedious, came from him: assuring me, that, when the works of a man
of true Genius, such as W. undoubtedly was, do not please me at first
sight, I should suspect the fault to lie "in me & not in them" — &c.
&c. &c. &c. &c. What am I to do with such people? — I certainly
shall write them a very merry Letter. — . — . —— Writing to *you*,
I may say, that the 2^d vol. has no such pieces as the 3 I enumerated. . It

[2] Cf. *Michael* 339–343.
[3] *The Brothers* 98–99.

is full of original thinking and an observing mind, but it does not often
make you laugh or cry. — It too artfully aims at simplicity of expression. And you sometimes doubt if simplicity be not a cover for Poverty.
The best Piece in it I will send you, being *short* — I have grievously
offended my friends in the North by declaring my undue preference.
But I need not fear you —

> She dwelt among the untrodden ways
> [Here follows the poem.]

This is choice and genuine, and so are many many more. But one
does not like to have 'em ramm'd down one's throat — "Pray take it
— its very good — let me help you — eat faster." — . —

At length George Dyer's 1st vol. is come to a birth. — One volume
of three. — Subscribers being *allowed* by the Prospectus to pay for all
at once (tho its very doubtful if the rest ever come to any thing, this
having been already some years getting out)[4] I paid two Guineas for
you and myself, which entitle us to the whole. — I will send you your
copy, if you are in a *great hurry*. Meantime you owe me a Guinea.
George skipped about like a pea with its arse scorched, at the receipt of
so much cash. — To give you one specimen of the beautiful absurdity
of the Notes, which defys imitation, take one. "Discrimination is not
the *aim* of the present volume. It will be more strictly attended to in
the next." — One of the Sonnets purports to have been written in
Bedlam! This for a man to *own*. — ! — The rest are addrest to Science, Genius, Melancholy, &c. — two to the River Cam. — an ode to
the Nightingale. Another to Howard, beginning, Spirit of meek
Philanthropy. — One is entitled the Madman, "being collected by the
Author from several madhouses" it begins, Yes, yes, tis He. — A long
poetical Satire is inscribed to John Disney D. D. His Wife And Daughter! ! !

Now to my own affairs — I have not taken that Thing to Colman,[5]
but I have proceeded one step in the business. I have enquir'd his address, and am promis'd it in a few days. — Meantime 3 Acts and a
half are finished gallopping, of a Play on a Persian Story, which I
must father in April. — But far, very far, below Antonio[6] in composition. O Jeptha, judge of Israel, what a fool I was. —

C Lamb

---

[4] Dyer (1775–1841), *Poems*, 1801; *Poems and Critical Essays*, 1802.
[5] George Colman (1762–1836), manager of the Haymarket Theater.
[6] Godwin's *Antonio: A Tragedy*, with an epilogue by Lamb, opened (and
closed) on December 13, 1800. Hence Lamb's reference to the unfortunate
vow of Jephthah, in Judges 11:30–34.

TO THOMAS MANNING

[15 February 1802]

Not a sentence, not a syllable, of Trismegistus shall be lost through my neglect. I am his word-banker, his store-keeper of puns & syllogisms. You cannot conceive (and if Trismegistus cannot, no man can) the strange joy, which I felt at the Receipt of a Letter from Paris. It seemed to give me a learned importance, which placed me above all, who had not Parisian Correspondents. Believe, that I shall carefully husband every Scrap, which will save you the trouble of memory, when you come back. You cannot write things so trifling, let them only be about Paris, which I shall not treasure. In particular, I must have parallels of Actors & Actresses. I must be told if any Building in Paris is at all comparable to S^t. Paul's, which contrary to the usual mode of that part of our Nature, called Admiration, I have looked up to with unfading Wonder, every morning at ten oClock, ever since it has lain in my way to business. At noon I casually glance upon it, being hungry; and Hunger has not much taste for the fine arts. Is any night-walk comparable to a walk from S^t. Pauls to Charing Cross, for Lighting, & Paving, Crowds going & coming without respite, the rattle of coaches, & the chearfulness of shops? Have you seen a man Guillotined yet? is it as good as Hanging? are the women *all* painted, & the men *all* monkeys? or are there not a *few* that look like *rational* of *both sexes?* Are you & the first Consul *thick?* All this expence of ink I may fairly put you to, as your Letters will not be solely for my proper pleasure, but are to serve as memoranda & notices, helps for short memory, a kind of Rumfordizing recollection, for yourself on your return. Your Letter was just what a letter should be, crammed, and very funny. Every part of it pleased me, till you came to Paris, & your damned philosophical indolence or indifference stung me. You cannot stir from your rooms till you know the Language! what the devil! are men nothing but word-trumpets? are men all tongue & ear? have these creatures, that you & I profess to know *something about,* no faces, gestures, gabble; no folly, no absurdity, no induction of French education upon the Abstract Idea of Men & Women, no similitude nor dissimilitude to English! Why, thou *damned* Smelfungus! Your account of your Landing and reception & Bullen (I forget how you spell it) it was spelt my way in Harry the 8^{ths} time, — was exactly in that *minute* style which strong impressions INSPIRE (writing to a Frenchman I write as a Frenchman would). It appears to me, as if I should die with joy at the first Landing in a foreign Country. It is the nearest Pleasure, which a grown man can substitute for that unknown one, which he can never know, the pleasure of the first entrance into Life from the womb. — I dare say, in a short time my Habits would come

back like a "stronger man" armed, and drive out that new pleasure;
& I should soon sicken for known objects. Nothing has transpired here
that seems to me of sufficient importance to send dry-shod over the
Water: but I suppose you will want to be told some news. The Best
& the Worst to me is, that I have given up Two Guineas a week at the
Post, & regained my health & spirits, which were upon the wane. I
grew sick, & Stuart unsatisfied. Ludisti satis, tempus abire est.[1] I
must cut closer that's all. In all this time I have done but one thing,
which I reckon tolerable: & that I will transcribe, because it may give
you pleasure, being a Picture of *my* humours. You will find it in my
last Page. It absurdly is a first Number of a Series, thus strangled in
Embryo. MORE NEWS. The Professor's Rib has come out to be a
damn'd disagreeable woman, so much as to drive me & some more old
cronies from his House. If a man will keep Snakes in his House, he
must not wonder if People are shy of coming to see him because of the
Snakes. Mister Fell or as you with your usual faceteness and drollery
call him M[r]. F+ll has stopt short in the middle of his Play, like what
is called being taken short. Some *friend* has told him that it has not
the least merit in it. O! that I had the rectifying of the Litany! I would
put in a Libera *Nos* (*Scriptores* videlicet) ab *amicis!*[2] That's all the
News. *Apropos* (is it *Pedantry*, writing to a Frenchman, to express
myself sometimes by a French word, when an English one would not
do as well? methinks, my thoughts fall naturally into it) *Apropos*, I
think you wrong about *my* Play. *All* the omissions are *right*. And the
supplementary Scene in which Sandford *narrates* the manner in which
his master is affected, is the Best in the Book. It stands, where a Hodge
podge of German puerilities used to stand. I insist upon it, that you
like that Scene. Love me, love that scene. I will now transcribe the
Londoner (N[o]. 1) & wind up all with Affection & Humble Servant at
the end.

THE LONDONER (I write *small*, in regard to your good eyesight.
"In compliance with my own particular humour, no less than with thy
laudable curiosity, Reader, I proceed to give thee some acco[un]t of
my history & habits. I was born under the Nose of S[t]. Dunstan's
Steeple, just where the conflux of the eastern & western inhabitants of
this Two-fold City meet & justle in friendly opposition at Temple Bar.
The same day, which gave me to the world, saw London happy in the
celebration of her great Annual Feast. This I cannot help looking upon
as a lively type or omen of the great good will, which I was destined
to bear toward the City, resembling in kind that Solicitude, which
every Chief Magistrate is supposed to feel for whatever concerns her
interest & well being. Indeed I consider myself in some sort a
speculative Lord Mayor of London: for tho' circumstances unhappily

---

[1] "You have played enough; it is time to go" — from the close of Horace's
Epistles.
[2] "Deliver us (meaning authors) from our *friends.*"

preclude me from ever arriving at the dignity of a gold chain & spital sermon, yet thus much will I say of myself in truth, that Whittington himself with his *Cat* (just emblem of *vigilance* & a *furred gown*) never went beyond me in affection, which I bear to the Citizens. Shut out from serving them in the most honorable mode, I aspire to do them benefit in another scarcely less honorable: & if I cannot by virtue of office commit vice & irregularity to the *material Counter*, I will at least erect a *spiritual one*, where they shall be laid fast by the heels. In plain words, I will do my best endeavors to write them down. To return to Myself (from whence my zeal for the public good is perpetually causing me to digress) I will let thee, Reader, into certain more of my peculiarities. I was born (as you have heard) bred, & have past most part of my time in a *crowd*. This has begot in me an entire affection for that way of life, amounting to an almost insurmountable aversion from solitude & rural scenes. This aversion was never interrupted or suspended, except for a few years in the younger part of my Life, during a period, in which I had fixed my affections upon a charming young woman. Every man, while the *Passion* is upon him, is for a time at least addicted to groves & meadows, & purling streams. During this short period of my existence, I contracted just enough familiarity with rural objects, to understand tolerably well ever after the Poets, when they declaim in such passionate terms in favor of a country Life. For my own part, now the fit is long past, I have no hesitation in declaring, that a mob of happy faces, crowding up at the Pit Door of Drury Lane Theatre just at the hour of 5, give me ten thousand finer pleasures, than I ever received from all the flocks of silly sheep, that have whitened the plains of Arcadia or Epsom Downs. This passion for Crowds is no where feasted so full as in London. The man must have a rare recipe for melancholy, who can be dull in Fleet Street. I am naturally inclined to Hypochondria, but in London it vanishes, like all other ills. Often, when I have felt a weariness or distaste at home, have I rushed out into her crowded *Strand,* and fed my humour till tears have wetted my cheek for inutterable sympathies with the multitudinous moving picture, which she never fails to present at all hours, like the shifting scenes of a skilful Pantomime. The very deformities of London, which give distaste to others, from habit do not displease me. The endless succession of Shops, where Fancy (miscalled Folly) is supplied with perpetual new gauds & toys, excite in me no puritanical aversion. I gladly behold every appetite supplied with its proper food. The obliging Customer, & the obliged Tradesman — things which live by bowing, & things which exist but for homage, do not affect me with disgust; from habit, I perceive nothing but urbanity, where other men, more refined, discover meanness. I love the very Smoke of London, because it has been the medium most familiar to my vision. I see grand principles of honor at work in the dirty ring, which encompasses two Combatants with fists, & prin-

ciples of no less eternal justice in the tumultuous detectors of a pick-
pocket. The salutary astonishment, with which an Execution is surveyed, convinces me more forcibly than an 100 vol^s. of abstract Polity,
that the universal instinct of man in all ages has leaned to order &
good government. Thus, an Art of extracting Morality from the
commonest incidents of a Town Life is attained by the same well-
natured alchemy, with which the *Forresters* of *Arden,* in a beautiful
country, 'Found tongues in trees, books in the running brooks, Sermons
in stones, & Good in ev'ry thing.'^{3} Where has Spleen her food but in
London? — humour, interest, curiosity, suck at her measureless breasts
without a possibility of being satiated. Nursed amid her noise, her
crowds, her beloved smoke, what have I been doing all my life, if I
have not lent out my heart with *usury* to such scenes? Reader, in the
course of my peregrinations about this Great City, it is hard, if I have
not picked up Matter, which may serve to amuse thee, as it has done
me, a summer evening long. Farewell." ——^{4}

What is all this about? said M^{rs}. Shandy — A story of a Cock & a Bull,
said Yorick; & so it is — but Manning will take good-naturedly what
God will send him across the water: only I hope he won't *shut* his
eyes & open his *mouth,* as the Children say, for that is a way to *gape*
& not to *read.* Manning, continue your Laudable Purpose of making
me your Register. I will render back all your Remarks, & *I, not you,*
shall have received Usury by having read them. — In the mean time,
may the Great Spirit, have you in his keeping; & preserve our Englishman from the inoculation of frivolity & sin upon French Earth. —

Allons (or what is it you say instead of *good bye?* —

Mary sends her kind Remembrance, & covets the Remarks equally
with me.^{5}

                                                              C Lamb
Monday 15th February 1802

^{3} Cf. *As You Like It* II.i.16–17.
^{4} The published version closed: ". . . a winter evening long. When next
we meet, I purpose opening my budget — Till when, farewell."
^{5} Manning had asked that his letters from France be kept for his own
use. He had written of the published *John Woodvil:* "I miss the Beautiful
Branches you have lopped off . . . ."
  Lamb had been writing for the *Morning Post,* edited by Daniel Stuart.
"The Londoner," which appeared there February 1, 1802, was slightly re-
vised in *Works,* 1818. It echoes Lamb's letters of early 1801.
  Rumfordizing: Sir Benjamin Thompson, Count von Rumford (1753–
1814), was inventor, reformer, and "efficiency expert"; Smelfungus: dis-
gruntled traveler in Laurence Sterne, *A Sentimental Journey,* 1768; Bullen:
Boulogne (French port) and Anne Boleyn (second wife of Henry VIII).
  Annual Feast, gold chain, furred gown, etc., all appertain to the Lord
Mayor of London; Counter: the Mayor's court and its prison.
  Yorick, etc.: altered from the close of Sterne's *Tristram Shandy.*

TO THOMAS MANNING

24th Sep. 1802
London

My dear Manning,

Since the date of my last letter, I have been a traveller. A strong
desire seized me of visiting remote regions. My first impulse was to
go and see Paris. It was a trivial objection to my aspiring mind, that
I did not understand a word of the language: since, I certainly intend
some time in my life to see ⟨life⟩ Paris, and equally certainly intend
never to learn the language: therefore that could be no objection.
However, I am very glad I did not go, because you had left Paris
(I see) before I could have set out. — I believe, Stoddart promising
to go with me another year prevented that plan. My next scheme
(for to my restless ambitious mind London was become a bed of
thorns) was to visit the far famed Peak in Derbyshire, where the
Devil sits, they say, without breeches. *This* my purer mind rejected
as indelicate. And my final resolve was a Tour to the Lakes. I set
out with Mary to Keswick, without giving Coleridge any notice, for
my time being precious did not admit of it; he received us with all the
hospitality in the world, and gave up his time to shew us all the
wonders of the country. He dwells upon a small hill by the side of
Keswick, in a comfortable house, quite enveloped on all sides by a net
of mountains: great floundering bears & monsters they seem'd, all
couchant & asleep. We got in in the evening, travelling in a Post
Chaise from Pe[n]rith, in the midst of a gorgeous sun shine, which
transmuted all the mountains into colours, purple &c. &c. We thought
we had got into Fairy Land. But that went off (as it never came
again, while we stayed, we had no more fine sun sets) and we entered
Coleridge's comfortable study just in the dusk, when the mountains
were all dark with clouds upon their heads. Such an impression I
never received from objects of sight before, nor do I suppose that I
can ever again. Glorious creatures, fine old fellows, Skiddaw &c. I
never shall forget ye, how ye lay about that night, like an intrench-
ment, gone to bed as it seemed for the night, but promising that ye
were to be seen in the morning. Coleridge had got a blazing fire in his
study; which is a large antique ill-shaped room, with an old fashioned
organ, never play'd upon, big enough for a church, shelves of scattered
folios, an Eolian Harp, & an old sofa, half bed &c. And all looking out
upon the last fading view of Skiddaw & his broad-breasted brethren:
What a night! Here we staid three full weeks, in which time I visited
Wordsworth's cottage, where we stayed a day or two with the Clarksons (good people & most hospitable, at whose house we tarried one

day & night) & saw Lloyd. Wordsworths were gone to Calais. They have since been in London, & past much time with us: he is now gone into Yorkshire to be married, to a girl of small fortune, but he is in expectation of augmenting his own, in consequence of the death of Lord Lonsdale, who kept him out of his own, in conformity with a plan my Lord had taken up in early life of making every body unhappy. So we have seen Keswick, Grasmere, Ambleside, Ulswater (where the Clarksons live) and a place at the other end of Ulswater, I forget the name, to which we travelled on a very sultry day over the middle of Helvellyn. — We have clambered up to the top of Skiddaw, & I have waded up the bed of Lodore. In fine I have satisfied myself, that there is such a thing as that, which tourists call *romantic*, which I very much suspected before: they make such a spluttering about it, and toss their splendid epithets around them, till they give as dim a light, as four oClock next morning the Lamps do after an illumination. Mary was excessively tired, when she got about half way up Skiddaw, but we came to a cold rill (than which nothing can be imagined more cold, running over cold stones) & with the reinforcem^t. of a draught of cold water, she surmounted it most manfully. — O its fine black head & the bleak air a top of it, with a prospect of mountains all about & about, making you giddy, & then Scotland afar off & the border countries so famous in song & ballad — It was a day that will stand out, like a mountain, I am sure, in my life. — But I am returned (I have now been come home near 3 weeks (I was a month out) & you cannot conceive the degradation I felt at first, from being accustomed to wander free as air among mountains, & bathe in rivers without being controuled by any one, to come home & *work:* I felt very *little*. I had been dreaming I was a very great man. But that is going off, & I find I shall conform in time to that state of Life, to which it has pleased God to call me. Besides, after all, Fleet Street & the Strand are better places to live in for good & all than among Skiddaw: still, I turn back to those great places, where I wandered about, participating in their greatness. After all I could not *live* in Skiddaw: I could spend a year, two, three years, among them, but I must have a prospect of seeing Fleet Street at the End of that time: or I should mope & pine away, I know. Still Skiddaw is a fine Creature. My habits are changing, I think; i.e. from drunk to sober: whether I shall be happier or no, remains to be proved. I shall certainly be more happy in a morning, but whether I shall not sacrifice the fat & the marrow & the kidneys, i.e. the Night, the glorious, care-drowning, night, that heals all our wrongs, pours wine into our mortifications, changes the scene from indifferent & flat to bright & brilliant — O Manning, if I should have formed a diabolical resolution, by the time you come to England, of not admitting any spirituous liquors into my house, will you be my guest on such shameworthy terms? Is life, with such limitations, worth trying. — The truth is that my liquors bring a nest

of friendly harpies about my house, who consume me. — This is a
pitiful tale to be read at S^t. Gothard: but it is just now nearest my
heart. — Fenwick is a ruined man. He is hiding himself from his
Creditors, and has sent his wife & children into the Country. Fell, my
other drunken companion (that has been: nam hic cæstus artemque
repono)[1] is turned Editor of a Naval Chronicle. Godwin (with a pitiful artificial Wife) continues a steady friend: tho' the same facility
does not remain of visiting him often. That Bitch has detached
Marshall from his house: Marshall, the man who went to sleep when
the Ancient Mariner was reading, the old steady, unalterable, friend of
the Professor. Holcroft is not yet come to town. I expect to see him
& will deliver your message. How I hate *this part* of a letter. Things
come crowding in to say, & no room for 'em. Some things are too
little to be told, i.e. to have a preference: some are too big & circumstantial. — Thanks for yours, which was most delicious. Would I
had been with you, benighted &c — I fear, my head is turned with
wandering. I shall never be the same acquiesc^t. being. — Farewell.
—— Write again quickly, for I shall not like to hazard a letter, not
knowing where the fates have carried you. Farewell, my dear fellow.[2]

C Lamb.

TO THOMAS MANNING

[27 July 1805 ?]

Dear Archimedes,

Things have gone on badly with thy ungeometrical friend, but they
are on the turn. My old housekeeper has shewed signs of convalescence, and will shortly resume the power of the Keys. So I
shan't be cheated of my tea and liquors. Wind in the west, which
promotes tranquillity. Have leisure now to anticipate seeing thee
again. Have been taking leave of Tobacco in a rhyming address. Had
thought *that vein* had been long since closed up. But the L—d
opened Sara's bag after years of unproduction. Find I can rhime &
reason too. Think of studying mathematics, to restrain the fire of my
genius: which G. D[yer]. recommends. Have frequent bleedings at the
nose: which shews plethoric. May'be shall try the sea myself, that

---

[1] "Now I lay down my gloves and skill"; see Virgil, *Aeneid* V.484.
[2] John Stoddart (1773–1856), brother-in-law of Hazlitt (1808), knighted
in 1826; Thomas Clarkson (1760–1846), Quaker agitator against slavery,
and his wife Catherine; Charles Lloyd (1775–1839), poet, pupil (1796–
97) of Coleridge; Wordsworths: William and Dorothy; Thomas Holcroft
(1745–1809), novelist, dramatist, "radical."

great scene of wonders. Got incredibly sober & regular: shave oftener,
& hum a tune, to signify chearfulness & gallantry.

Suddenly disposed to sleep, having taken a quart of peas with
bacon, and stout. Will not refuse Nature, who has done such things
for me! —

Nurse, dont call me, unless M^r. Manning comes. What, the Gentleman in spectacles? Yes.

Saturd^y —   Dormit
Hot Noon —   C L.[1]

TO WILLIAM HAZLITT

[7 January 1806]

Dear Hazlitt

I have been a long time without writing to you, but I don't know
that it has deprived you of any valuable communications. Nothing
has occurrd to deserve a special dispatch. I have also had upon my
mind to write a long letter to Malta,[1] and whenever that duty came
over me, I thought I must write to you, and how could I make out two
letters? & which should I set about first? and in the same manner that
occurr'd, when I thought of setting about one to you. So it is in
contradictory duties, when one cannot reconcile interest to pleasure,
or virtue to ease, or industry to indolence, which I take to be duties
all pretty equally alike. — You know Lord Nelson is dead. He is also
to be buried. And the whole town is in a fever. Seats erecting, seats
to be let, sold, lent &c. Customers crowding in to every ⟨house⟩ shop
between Whitehall and S^t. Pauls, and the tradesman & the customer
changing parts, the latter being willing to become the obliged person,
and the former assuming new airs of choice & selection. "A favor to
beg of you M^r. Tape. — to let my young Ladies come and see the
funeral procession on Thursday — my girls are come home from school,
and young folks love sights." — M^r. Tape very grave "how many,
Maam?" — "O! there'll be only me, and my three daughters, and perhaps their cousin Betty, and two young men to escort them, unless my
Cousin Elbowroom happens to come to town, then there'll be nine
of us." — "I am afraid it will be impossible to accommodate so many,
if one of the young ladies will come we perhaps shall be able to put
her in the second floor." — Exit Customer with thanks, & returns on
Thursday with fourteen more than the number first begg'd for. Cold

---

[1] "Lamb sleeps." housekeeper: Mary; Sara: in Genesis 21:1–2.
"A Farewell to Tobacco" was first published in Hunt's *Reflector* in 1811.
[1] *I.e.*, to Coleridge.

Edgebone of Beef and Small Beer suffer for it about three oClock. — The Streets are in a perfect fever. The whole town as unsettled as a young Lady the day before being married. S^t. Paul's virgers making their hundred pounds a day in sixpences for letting people see the scaffolding inside, & ⟨at the⟩ hole where he is to be let down; which money they under the Rose share with the Dean and Præcentors at night. — Great aquatic bustle tomorrow. Body to come up from Greenwich with Lord Mayor & City Barges. Fillets of veal predestined to be demolish'd at the Temple in the afternoon. All Chiswick, Pimlico, & Pancras emptying out in the morning into the Temple. Templars don't pay for Militia men tho', so one tax to be set off against another. If you with your refinements were here, you would be as fidgety as a Scotchman's hand between the fingers, you could neither eat, sit, read nor paint, till the corpse were fairly laid. The ⟨old⟩ ghost of the funeral will walk till over Sunday night I'm sure, & the streets be perturb'd. You can't get along for People going about staring to see where it will come by, or asking when it will come by, and Have you got a Seat? — "I for my part am indifferent about it, only it looks foolish not to see it." And "I suppose it will be like all other shows, but the Crowd and the Bustle is agreeable." "I for my part have no relish for spectacles, ⟨my⟩ but my Husband is going to take the young Miss Squeezes out of the country, that are come up out ⟨of the⟩ 100 miles to see it, & he don't like to disappoint them." And then the eldest Miss Squeeze declares she dont know whether she shall like to see it or no, for she is afraid it will be too affecting. She is sure she shall turn her head away from the window as it goes by. O the immortal Man! — but when the time comes it is odds but the pressing & thrusting dont constrain her to turn her eyes into the street against her will, & who can help it? —— ⟨I am⟩ ⟨Tuesday⟩

Just to get the Buzzing out of my head let me remember something vastly different. — The American Farmer. I thank you for sending it to us, and am a little sorry that I cannot say so much in its praise as the usual compliments in these cases require. To shame the Devil, then, at once, it does appear to me a very stupid uninteresting Book. In what kind mood you pick'd it up I can't guess, or how Wordsworth also came to give his testimony for it, but to me it is perfectly disagreeable. Why should a book be pleasant to one, that if it were made into a man (the binding a coat, the leaves a shirt with a frill, the &c. &c. make out the rest of the metamorphosis yourself, I have no time, — Lord Nelson & one thing or other, my head's dizzy) if the said book were a man & not a book, would be odious? A wretched purse-proud American Farmer with no virtue but industry & its ostentatious concomitant charity, no ideas but of clearing land & setting the poor to work (damn him for that if I was a lousy Beggar ⟨in⟩ happy in the Sun) calling Ladies young women & praising them for decent mirth & needle work & possibilities of being notable mothers:

things too tradesman-quaker-like (quakers the worst of tradesmen) to
come into that agreeable book the young man's best companion or the
Apprentices Guide: cold and chill and barren as D^r. Franklin's
Golden rules or Poor John's Thoughts in an American almanac. Thou
that hast read Romeo & Juliet & Midsummers Nights Dream, to feed
on the garbage & husk of dried leaves of le[d]gers & journals & swallow ploughs & harrows! If I didn't like it as you expected, it might be
in part (principally, no doubt, its own stupidity) in part because we
had just read thro' Bruce's Travels with infinite delight where all is
alive & novel, & about Kings & Queens & fabulous Heads of Rivers, &
Abyssinian wars & the Line of Solomon & he's a fine dashing fellow &
intrigues with Empresses & gets into Harams of Black Women, & was
himself descended from Kings of Scotland: not farmers & mechanics
& industry —

The above written in great precipitation, so can't answer for the
style & grammar, just to get rid of a vapour fit which comes often &
clouds us over. Shall be more cool when Lord Nelson is buried, & one
can walk the streets with less justling, & when the crowding & madness
of the people is still. — Believe me, dull or Giddy,[2]

> Yours as ever.   C Lamb   7th Jan^y.

TO WILLIAM WORDSWORTH

20th March 1822

My dear Wordsworth,

A letter from you is very grateful, I have not seen a Kendal post-
mark so long! — we are pretty well save colds & rheumatics, and a
certain deadness to every thing, which I think I may date from poor
John's Loss,[1] and another accident or two at the same time, that has
made me almost bury myself at Dalston, where I yet see more faces
than I could wish. Deaths over-set one and put one out long after the
recent grief. Two or three have died within this last two twelve^ths.
and so many parts of me have been numbed — One sees a picture,
reads an ane[c]dote, ⟨puts up⟩ starts a casual fancy, and thinks to tell
of it to this person in preference to every other — the person is gone
whom it would have peculiarly suited. It wont do for *another*. Every
departure destroys a class of sympathies. There's Capt Burney gone!

[2] J. Hector St. John (pseud. of Michel de Crèvecœur), *Letters from an
American Farmer*, 1782; James Bruce, *Travels to Discover the Source of the
Nile*, 5 vols., 1790; Benjamin Franklin (1706–90), *Poor Richard's Almanack*,
1732–57.
[1] Lamb's brother John died October 26, 1821.

— what fun has whist now; what matters it what you lead, if you can
no longer fancy him looking over you? — One never hears any thing,
but the image of the particular person occurs with whom alone almost
you would care to share the intelligence — Thus one distributes oneself about — & now for so many parts of me I have lost the market.
Common natures do not suffice me. Good people, as they are called,
won't serve. I want individuals. I am made up of queer points and
I want so many answering needles. The going away of friends does
not make the remainder more precious. It takes so much from them
as there was a common link. A. B. & C. make a party. A. dies. B.
not only loses A. but all A's part in C. C loses A's part in B. and so
the Alphabet sickens by su[b]traction of interchan[g]eables — I express myself muddily, capite dolente.[2] I have a dulling cold. — My
theory is to enjoy life, but the practice is against it. I grow ominously
tired of official confinement. Thirty years have I served the Philistines,
and my neck is not subdued to the yoke. You dont know how wearisome it is to breathe the air of four pent walls without relief day after
day all the golden hours of the day between 10 & 4 without ease or
interposition. Tædet me harum quotidianarum formarum,[3] these
pestilential clerk faces always in ones dish. O for a few years between
the grave & the desk! they are the same, save at the latter you are
outside the machine. The foul enchanter ⟨B⟩— letters four do form
his name[4] — Busirane is his name in hell — that has curtailed you of
some domestic comforts, hath laid a heavier hand on me, not in
present infliction, but in the taking away the hope of enfranchise-
ment. I dare not whisper to myself a Pension on this side of absolute
incapacitation & infirmity, till years have sucked me dry. Otium cum
indignitate.[5] I had thought in a green old age (O green thought!)[6]
to have retired to Ponders End — emblematic name how beautiful! in
the Ware road, there to have made up my accounts with Heaven &
the Company, toddling about between it & Cheshunt, anon stretching
on some fine Isaac Walton morning to Hoddesdon or Amwell, careless
as a Beggar, but walking walking ever till I fairly walkd myself off
my legs, dying walking!

The hope is gone. I sit like Philomel all day (but not singing) with
my breast against this thorn of a Desk, with the only hope that some
Pulmonary affliction may relieve me. Vide Lord Palmerston's report

[2] having a headache.

[3] "I am weary of these everyday beauties," Terence, *The Eunuch* II.iii.6.

[4] Coleridge, *Fire, Famine, and Slaughter*, refrain; here Joseph Hume,
M. P. whose reforms had affected both the East India Company and the
revenue of Wordsworth's Distributorship. Busirane: in Spenser, *Faerie
Queene* III.xi.

[5] Ease with indignity.

[6] Cf. "a green thought in a green shade," Andrew Marvell (1621–78),
The Garden 48.

of the Clerks in the war office (Debates, this morning's Times) by
which it appears in 20 years, as many Clerks have been coughd &
catarrhd out of it into their freer graves ——

Thank you for asking about the Pictures. Milton hangs over my
fire side in Cov[ent] Gard[en] (when I am there), the rest have sold
for an old song, wanting the eloquent tongue that should have set
them off! —

You have gratifyd me with liking my meeting with Dodd. For the
Malvolio story — the thing is become in verity a sad task & I eke it
out with any thing. If I could slip out of it I sh^d be happy, but our
chief reputed assistants have forsaken us — The opium eater crossed
us once with a dazzling path, & hath as suddenly left us darkling; &
in short I shall go on from dull to worse, because I cannot resist the
Bookseller's importunity — the old plea you know of authors, but I
believe on my part sincere. — Hartley I do not so often see, but I
never see him in unwelcome hour. I thoro[u]ghly love & honor him.
— I send you a frozen Epistle, but it is winter & dead time of the
year with me. May heaven keep something like spring & summer up
with you, strengthen your eyes & make mine a little lighter to encounter with them, ⟨I⟩ as I hope they shall yet & again, before all are
closed.

                    Yours, with every kind rem^be.
                                                    C L. —

I had almost forgot to say, I think you thoroughly right about
presentation copies. — I should like to see you print a book I should
grudge to purchase for its size! D—n me, but I would have it
though![7]

TO BERNARD BARTON

[15 May 1824]

Dear B B. — I am oppressed with business all day and Company all
night. But I will snatch a quarter of an hour. Your recent acquisitions
of the Picture and the Letter are greatly to be congratulated. I too
have a picture of my father, and the copy of his first Love verses, but
they have been mine long. Blake is a real name, I assure you, and a
most extraordinary man, if he be still living. He is the Robert [for

---

[7] Dalston: rural retreat, now in London; Capt. James Burney (1750–
1821), father of Martin and brother of Fanny (the novelist); Philomel:
nightingale, in Greek mythology; Milton's portrait: left to Lamb by John
and now in the New York Public Library; Dodd and Malvolio: in "On
Some of the Old Actors," *London Magazine*, February 1822; reputed assistants: Hazlitt and De Quincey; Bookseller: publisher; Hartley: Coleridge's
son (1796–1849), a poet, in London after dismissal from a Probationary
Fellowship at Oxford.

William] Blake, whose wild designs accompany a splendid folio edition of the Night Thoughts,[1] which you may have seen, in one of which he pictures the parting of soul & body by a solid mass of human form floating off God knows how from a lumpish mass (facsimile to itself) left behin[d] on the dying bed. He paints in water colours, marvellous strange pictures, visions of his brain which he asserts that he has seen. They have great merit. He has *seen* the old Welch bards on Snowdon — he has seen the Beautifullest, the Strongest, & the Ugliest Man, left alone from the Massacre of the Britons by the Romans, & has painted them from memory (I have seen his paintings) and asserts them to be as good as the figures of Raphael & Angelo, but not better, as they had precisely the same retro-visions & prophetic visions with themself [*for* himself]. The painters in Oil (which he will have it that neither of them practised) he affirms to have been the ruin of art, and affirms that all the while he was engaged in his water-paintings, Titian was disturbing him, Titian the Ill Genius of Oil Painting. His Pictures, one in particular the Canterbury Pilgrims (far above Stothard's) have great merit, but hard, dry, yet with grace. He has written a Catalogue of them, with a most spirited criticism on Chaucer, but mystical and full of Vision. His poems have been sold hitherto only in Manuscript. I never read them, but a friend at my desire procured the Sweep Song. There is one to a Tiger, which I have heard recited, beginning

> Tiger Tiger burning bright
> Thro' the desarts of the night —

which is glorious. But alas! I have not the Book, for the man is flown, whither I know not, to Hades, or a Mad House — but I must look on him as one of the most extraordinary persons of the age. Montgomery's Book I have not much hopes from.[2] The Society, with the affected name, have been laboring at it for these 20 Years & made few Converts. I think it was injudicious to mix stories avowedly colour'd by fiction with the sad true statements from the parliamentary records &c. but I wish the little Negroes all the good that can come from it. I batter'd my brains (not butter'd them — but it is a bad *a*) for a few verses ⟨from⟩ for them, but I could ⟨do⟩ make nothing of it. You have been luckier. But Blake's are the flower of the set you will I am sure agree, tho' some of Montgom[ys]. at the end are pretty — but the Dream awkwardly paraphrased from B[lake].

With the exception of an Epilogue for a Private Theatrical, I have written nothing now for near 6 months. It is in vain to spur me on. I must wait. I cannot write without a genial impulse & I have none.

[1] by Edward Young, engraved by Blake in 1796–97.
[2] James Montgomery, *The Chimney-Sweeper's Friend and Climbing-Boy's Album*, 1824, published for The Society for Ameliorating the Condition of Infant Chimney-Sweepers, including verses by Barton and Blake's "The Chimney Sweeper," sent by Lamb.

Tis barren all & dearth — No matter, life is something without scribbling. I have got rid of my bad spirits, & hold up pretty well this
rain-damn'd May. So we have lost another Poet. I never much rel-
ished his Lordship's mind, and shall be sorry if the Greeks have cause
to miss him. He was to me offensive, and I never can make out his
great *power,* which his admirers talk of. Why, a line of Wordsworths
is a lever to lift the immortal Spirit! Byrons can only move the Spleen.
He was at best a Satyrist — in any other way he was mean enough. I
dare say I do him injustice, but I cannot love him, nor squeeze a tear
to his memory. He did not like the world, and he has left it, as Alderman Curtis advised the Radicals, "if they dont like their Country,
damn 'em let 'em leave it" — they possessing no rood of Ground in
England, & he 10000 acres. Byron was better than many Curtises —

Farewell & accept this apology for a Letter from one who owes you
so much in that kind. Yours ever Truly[3]

C L

TO BRYAN WALLER PROCTER

[19 January 1829]

My dear Proctor,[1] I am ashamed to have not taken the drift of your
pleasant letter, which I find to have been pure invention. But jokes
are not suspected in Boeotian Enfield. We are plain people, and our
talk is of corn, and cattle, and Waltham markets. Besides I was a little
out of sorts when I received it. The fact is, I am involved in a case
which has fretted me to death, and I have no reliance except on you to
extricate me. I am sure you will give me your best legal advice, having no professional friend besides but Robinson & Talfourd, with
neither of whom at present I am on the best terms. My brothers
widow left a will, made during the life time of my brother, in which
I am named sole Executor, by which she bequeaths forty acres of
arable property, which it seems she held under Covert Baron, unknown to my Brother, to the heirs of the body of Elizabeth Dowden,
her married daughter by a first husband, in fee simple, recoverable
by fine, — invested property, mind, for there is the difficulty — subject to leet and quit rent — in short, worded in the most guarded
terms, to shut out the property from Isaac Dowden the husband. Intelligence has just come of the death of this person in India, where
he made a will, entailing this property (which seem'd entangled

---

[3] Bernard Barton (1784–1849), bank clerk, Quaker, poet.

Thomas Stothard's painting of the Canterbury pilgrims was exhibited in
1807. Sir William Curtis (1752–1829), alderman, had been Lord Mayor of
London in 1795.

[1] Bryan Waller Procter (1787–1874), a solicitor who published poems
under the name of "Barry Cornwall."

enough already) to the heirs of his body, that should not be born of his wife, for it seems by the Law in India Natural children can recover. They have put the cause into Exchecquer Process here, removed by Certiorari from the Native Courts, and the question is whether I should, as Executor, try the cause here, or again re-move it to the Supreme Sessions at Bangalore, which I understand I can, or plead a hearing before the Privy Council here. As it involves all the little property of Elizabeth Dowden, I am anxious to take the fittest steps, and what may be least expensive. For God's sake assist me, for the case is so embarrassed that it deprives me of sleep & appetite. M. Burney thinks there is a Case like it in Chapt. 170 Sect 5 in Fearn's Contingent Remainders. Pray read it over with him dispassionately, and let me have the result. The complexity lies in the questionable power of the husband to alienate in usum enfoeofments whereof he was only collaterally seized &c — . . .[2]

I had another favour to beg, which is the beggarliest of beggings. A few lines of verse for a young friend's Album (six will be enough) — M Burney will tell you who she is I want 'em for. A girl of gold. Six lines — make 'em eight — signed Barry C—— They need not be very good, as I chiefly want 'em as a foil to mine. But I shall be seriously obliged by any refuse scrap. We are in the last ages of the world, when S[t]. Paul prophesied that women should be "headstrong, lovers of their own wills, having Albums." I fled hither to escape the Albumean persecution, & had not been in my new house 24 hours, when the Daughter of the next house came in with a friends Album to beg a contribution, & the following day intimated she had one of her own. Two more have sprung up since. If I take the wings of the morning & fly unto the uttermost parts of the earth, there will Albums be — New Holland has Albums. But the age is to be complied with. M. B will tell you the sort of girl I request the 10 lines for. Somewhat of a pensive cast, what you admire. The lines may come before the Law question, as that cannot be determined before Hilary Term, & I wish your deliberate judgment on that. The other may be flimsy & superficial. And if you have not burnt your return'd letter, pray re-send it me, as a monumental token of my stupidity. Twas a little unthinking of you to touch upon a sore subject. Why, by dabbling in those accursed Annuals, I have become a byword of infamy all over the Kingdom. I have sickend decent women for asking me to write in Albums. There be "dark jests" abroad, Master Cornwall, & some riddles may live to be clear'd up. And tisn't every saddle is put on the right steed. And forgeries & false Gospels are not peculiar to the age following the Apostles. And some tubs don't stand on their right Bottoms. Which is all I wish to say in these ticklish Times — & so your Servant, Ch[s] Lamb —

[2] The legal case is an invention, in retaliation for a successful hoax on Lamb by Procter. Its terminology was presumably supplied by Martin Burney, a barrister.

William Hazlitt

WILLIAM HAZLITT

CHRONOLOGY

1778   Born April 10 at Maidstone, Kent, son of a Unitarian minister.

1783–87   Lived in the United States, in Philadelphia and near Boston.

1793–98   Attended Hackney Theological College (Unitarian) in London.

1799–1806   Studied painting under his brother and in Paris (1802); did portraits of Wordsworth, Coleridge, and Lamb.

1805   *An Essay on the Principles of Human Action* (anonymous).

1807   March–May, in Cobbett's *Register,* and then as a book, *A Reply to the Essay on Population by the Rev. T. R. Malthus* (anonymous).

1808   May 1, married Sarah Stoddart.

1812   For the leading Whig newspaper, the London *Morning Chronicle,* began the career of journalism on which most of his books were based.

1817   January, *The Round Table* (from the *Examiner,* with twelve essays by Hunt). April (?), *Characters of Shakespear's Plays.*

1818   May, *A View of the English Stage* (from *Examiner, Champion, Morning Chronicle,* and *Times*). May 1 (?), *Lectures on the English Poets.*

1819   January 5 (?), *A Letter to William Gifford, Esq.* April, *Lectures on the English Comic Writers.* About December, separated from his wife (divorced in Edinburgh, July 17, 1822).

1820   January, *Lectures Chiefly on the Dramatic Literature of the Age of Elizabeth.* August, love at first sight for Sarah Walker, aged 19 or 20.

1821   (April?)–1822 (June?)   *Table Talk,* 2 volumes.

1823   Early May, *Liber Amoris* (anonymous).

1824   April, married Mrs. Isabella Bridgewater, who left him at the end of a year's honeymoon in France, Switzerland, and Italy.

1825   April (?), *The Spirit of the Age.*

1826   May, *The Plain Speaker.*

1828–30   *The Life of Napoleon Buonaparte.*

1830   Died September 18.

My First Acquaintance with Poets

❪ For a letter in the *Examiner,* January 12, 1817, Hazlitt had recovered some of the memories recorded more fully in this essay, which appeared in the *Liberal,* No. 3, published about April 23, 1823. Later scholarship has confirmed most of Hazlitt's details concerning Coleridge's and Wordsworth's lives, ideas, and tastes in 1798. From about 1810, most of Hazlitt's reviews and other writings on Wordsworth and especially Coleridge show greater disillusion than this essay does with their politics and their persons. ❫

My father was a Dissenting Minister at W——m in Shropshire; and in the year 1798 (the figures that compose that date are to me like the "dreaded name of Demogorgon")[1] Mr. Coleridge came to Shrewsbury, to succeed Mr. Rowe in the spiritual charge of a Unitarian Congregation there. He did not come till late on the Saturday afternoon before he was to preach; and Mr. Rowe, who himself went down to the coach in a state of anxiety and expectation, to look for the arrival of his successor, could find no one at all answering the description but a round-faced man in a short black coat (like a shooting-jacket) which hardly seemed to have been made for him, but who seemed to be talking at a great rate to his fellow-passengers. Mr. Rowe had scarce returned to give an account of his disappointment, when the round-faced man in black entered, and dissipated all doubts on the subject, by beginning to talk. He did not cease while he staid; nor has he since, that I know of. He held the good town of Shrewsbury in delightful suspense for three weeks that he remained there, "fluttering the *proud Salopians* like an eagle in a dove-cote;"[2] and the Welch mountains that skirt the horizon with their tempestuous confusion, agree to have heard no such mystic sounds since the days of

"High-born Hoel's harp or soft Llewellyn's lay!"[3]

As we passed along between W——m and Shrewsbury, and I eyed their blue tops seen through the wintry branches, or the red rustling leaves of the sturdy oak-trees by the roadside, a sound was in my ears as of a Siren's song; I was stunned, startled with it, as from deep sleep; but I had no notion then that I should ever be able to express my admiration to others in motley imagery or quaint allusion, till the light of his genius shone into my soul, like the sun's rays glittering in the puddles of the road. I was at that time dumb, inarticulate, helpless,

[1] *Paradise Lost* II.964–965.
[2] Cf. *Coriolanus* V.vi.114–115. Salopia is the Latin name of Shropshire.
[3] Gray, *The Bard* 28.

like a worm by the way side, crushed, bleeding, lifeless; but now,
bursting from the deadly bands that "bound them,

"With Styx nine times round them,"[4]

my ideas float on winged words, and as they expand their plumes,
catch the golden light of other years. My soul has indeed remained
in its original bondage, dark, obscure, with longings infinite and unsatisfied; my heart, shut up in the prison-house of this rude clay, has
never found, nor will it ever find, a heart to speak to; but that my
understanding also did not remain dumb and brutish, or at length
found a language to express itself, I owe to Coleridge. But this is
not to my purpose.

My father lived ten miles from Shrewsbury, and was in the habit of
exchanging visits with Mr. Rowe, and with Mr. Jenkins of Whit-
church (nine miles farther on) according to the custom of Dissenting
Ministers in each other's neighbourhood. A line of communication is
thus established, by which the flame of civil and religious liberty is
kept alive, and nourishes its smouldering fire unquenchable, like the
fires in the Agamemnon of Æschylus, placed at different stations, that
waited for ten long years to announce with their blazing pyramids the
destruction of Troy. Coleridge had agreed to come over to see my
father, according to the courtesy of the country, as Mr. Rowe's probable successor; but in the mean time I had gone to hear him preach
the Sunday after his arrival. A poet and a philosopher getting up into
a Unitarian pulpit to preach the Gospel, was a romance in these degenerate days, a sort of revival of the primitive spirit of Christianity,
which was not to be resisted.

It was in January, 1798, that I rose one morning before day-light, to
walk ten miles in the mud, and went to hear this celebrated person
preach. Never, the longest day I have to live, shall I have such
another walk as this cold, raw, comfortless one, in the winter of the
year 1798. — *Il y a des impressions que ni le tems ni les circonstances
peuvent effacer. Dusse-je vivre des siècles entiers, le doux tems de ma
jeunesse ne peut renaitre pour moi, ni s'effacer jamais dans ma
mémoire.*[5] When I got there, the organ was playing the 100th psalm,
and, when it was done, Mr. Coleridge rose and gave out his text, "And
he went up into the mountain to pray, HIMSELF, ALONE."[6] As he gave
out this text, his voice "rose like a steam of rich distilled perfumes,"[7]
and when he came to the two last words, which he pronounced loud,

[4] Cf. Pope, *Ode on St. Cecilia's Day* 90–91.
[5] "There are impressions which neither time nor circumstances can efface.
Were I to live whole ages, the sweet days of my youth could not return
to me, nor ever be effaced from my memory." — Rousseau, *Confessions*
II.vii.
[6] Cf. John 6:15.
[7] Milton, *Comus* 556.

deep, and distinct, it seemed to me, who was then young, as if the
sounds had echoed from the bottom of the human heart, and as if that
prayer might have floated in solemn silence through the universe.
The idea of St. John came into mind, "of one crying in the wilderness,
who had his loins girt about, and whose food was locusts and wild
honey."[8] The preacher then launched into his subject, like an eagle
dallying with the wind. The sermon was upon peace and war; upon
church and state — not their alliance, but their separation — on the
spirit of the world and the spirit of Christianity, not as the same, but
as opposed to one another. He talked of those who had "inscribed the
cross of Christ on banners dripping with human gore." He made a
poetical and pastoral excursion, — and to shew the fatal effects of war,
drew a striking contrast between the simple shepherd boy, driving his
team afield, or sitting under the hawthorn, piping to his flock, "as
though he should never be old,"[9] and the same poor country-lad,
crimped, kidnapped, brought into town, made drunk at an alehouse,
turned into a wretched drummer-boy, with his hair sticking on end
with powder and pomatum, a long cue at his back, and tricked out
in the loathsome finery of the profession of blood.

"Such were the notes our once-lov'd poet sung."[10]

And for myself, I could not have been more delighted if I had heard
the music of the spheres. Poetry and Philosophy had met together,
Truth and Genius had embraced, under the eye and with the sanction
of Religion. This was even beyond my hopes. I returned home well
satisfied. The sun that was still labouring pale and wan through the
sky, obscured by thick mists, seemed an emblem of the *good cause;*
and the cold dank drops of dew that hung half melted on the beard
of the thistle, had something genial and refreshing in them; for there
was a spirit of hope and youth in all nature, that turned every thing
into good. The face of nature had not then the brand of Jus Divinum
on it:

"Like to that sanguine flower inscrib'd with woe."[11]

On the Tuesday following, the half-inspired speaker came. I was
called down into the room where he was, and went half-hoping, half-
afraid. He received me very graciously, and I listened for a long time
without uttering a word. I did not suffer in his opinion by my silence.
"For those two hours," he afterwards was pleased to say, "he was conversing with W. H.'s forehead!" His appearance was different from
what I had anticipated from seeing him before. At a distance, and in
the dim light of the chapel, there was to me a strange wildness in his

[8] Cf. Matthew 3:3–4.
[9] Sidney, *Arcadia* I.ii.
[10] Cf. Pope, *Epistle to Earl of Oxford* 1.
[11] Milton, *Lycidas* 106.

aspect, a dusky obscurity, and I thought him pitted with the small-pox. His complexion was at that time clear, and even bright —

"As are the children of yon azure sheen."[12]

His forehead was broad and high, light as if built of ivory, with large projecting eyebrows, and his eyes rolling beneath them like a sea with darkened lustre. "A certain tender bloom his face o'erspread,"[13] a purple tinge as we see it in the pale thoughtful complexions of the Spanish portrait-painters, Murillo and Velasquez. His mouth was gross, voluptuous, open, eloquent; his chin good-humoured and round; but his nose, the rudder of the face, the index of the will, was small, feeble, nothing — like what he has done. It might seem that the genius of his face as from a height surveyed and projected him (with sufficient capacity and huge aspiration) into the world unknown of thought and imagination, with nothing to support or guide his veering purpose, as if Columbus had launched his adventurous course for the New World in a scallop, without oars or compass. So at least I comment on it after the event. Coleridge in his person was rather above the common size, inclining to the corpulent, or like Lord Hamlet, "somewhat fat and pursy."[14] His hair (now, alas! grey) was then black and glossy as the raven's, and fell in smooth masses over his forehead. This long pendulous hair is peculiar to enthusiasts, to those whose minds tend heavenward; and is traditionally inseparable (though of a different colour) from the pictures of Christ. It ought to belong, as a character, to all who preach *Christ crucified*, and Coleridge was at that time one of those!

It was curious to observe the contrast between him and my father, who was a veteran in the cause, and then declining into the vale of years. He had been a poor Irish lad, carefully brought up by his parents, and sent to the University of Glasgow (where he studied under Adam Smith) to prepare him for his future destination. It was his mother's proudest wish to see her son a Dissenting Minister. So if we look back to past generations (as far as eye can reach) we see the same hopes, fears, wishes, followed by the same disappointments, throbbing in the human heart; and so we may see them (if we look forward) rising up for ever, and disappearing, like vapourish bubbles, in the human breast! After being tossed about from congregation to congregation in the heats of the Unitarian controversy, and squabbles about the American war, he had been relegated to an obscure village, where he was to spend the last thirty years of his life, far from the only converse that he loved, the talk about disputed texts of Scripture and the cause of civil and religious liberty. Here he passed his days, repining but resigned, in the study of the Bible, and the perusal of

12 Cf. Thomson, *Castle of Indolence* II.295.
13 *Ibid.*, I.507.
14 Cf. *Hamlet* III.iv.153, V.ii.298.

the Commentators, — huge folios, not easily got through, one of which would outlast a winter! Why did he pore on these from morn to night (with the exception of a walk in the fields or a turn in the garden to gather brocoli-plants or kidney-beans of his own rearing, with no small degree of pride and pleasure)? — Here were "no figures nor no fantasies,"[15] — neither poetry nor philosophy — nothing to dazzle, nothing to excite modern curiosity; but to his lack-lustre eyes there appeared, within the pages of the ponderous, unwieldy, neglected tomes, the sacred name of JEHOVAH in Hebrew capitals: pressed down by the weight of the style, worn to the last fading thinness of the understanding, there were glimpses, glimmering notions of the patri-archal wanderings, with palm-trees hovering in the horizon, and pro-cessions of camels at the distance of three thousand years; there was Moses with the Burning Bush, the number of the Twelve Tribes, types, shadows, glosses on the law and the prophets; there were discussions (dull enough) on the age of Methuselah, a mighty speculation! there were outlines, rude guesses at the shape of Noah's Ark and of the riches of Solomon's Temple; questions as to the date of the creation, predictions of the end of all things; the great lapses of time, the strange mutations of the globe were unfolded with the voluminous leaf, as it turned over; and though the soul might slumber with an hieroglyphic veil of inscrutable mysteries drawn over it, yet it was in a slumber ill-exchanged for all the sharpened realities of sense, wit, fancy, or reason. My father's life was comparatively a dream; but it was a dream of infinity and eternity, of death, the resurrection, and a judgment to come!

No two individuals were ever more unlike than were the host and his guest. A poet was to my father a sort of nondescript: yet what-ever added grace to the Unitarian cause was to him welcome. He could hardly have been more surprised or pleased, if our visitor had worn wings. Indeed, his thoughts had wings; and as the silken sounds rustled round our little wainscoted parlour, my father threw back his spectacles over his forehead, his white hairs mixing with its sanguine hue; and a smile of delight beamed across his rugged cordial face, to think that Truth had found a new ally in Fancy![16] Besides, Cole-ridge seemed to take considerable notice of me, and that of itself was enough. He talked very familiarly, but agreeably, and glanced over a variety of subjects. At dinner-time he grew more animated, and dilated in a very edifying manner on Mary Wolstonecraft and Mackintosh. The last, he said, he considered (on my father's speaking

---

[15] *Julius Caesar* II.i.231.

[16] My father was one of those who mistook his talent after all. He used to be very much dissatisfied that I preferred his Letters to his Sermons. The last were forced and dry; the first came naturally from him. For ease, half-plays on words, and a supine, monkish, indolent pleasantry, I have never seen them equalled. [W.H.]

of his *Vindiciæ Gallicæ* as a capital performance) as a clever scholastic man — a master of the topics, — or as the ready warehouseman of letters, who knew exactly where to lay his hand on what he wanted, though the goods were not his own. He thought him no match for Burke, either in style or matter. Burke was a metaphysician, Mackintosh a mere logician. Burke was an orator (almost a poet) who reasoned in figures, because he had an eye for nature: Mackintosh, on the other hand, was a rhetorician, who had only an eye to commonplaces. On this I ventured to say that I had always entertained a great opinion of Burke, and that (as far as I could find) the speaking of him with contempt might be made the test of a vulgar democratical mind. This was the first observation I ever made to Coleridge, and he said it was a very just and striking one. I remember the leg of Welsh mutton and the turnips on the table that day had the finest flavour imaginable. Coleridge added that Mackintosh and Tom. Wedgwood (of whom, however, he spoke highly) had expressed a very indifferent opinion of his friend Mr. Wordsworth, on which he remarked to them — "He strides on so far before you, that he dwindles in the distance!" Godwin had once boasted to him of having carried on an argument with Mackintosh for three hours with dubious success; Coleridge told him — "If there had been a man of genius in the room, he would have settled the question in five minutes." He asked me if I had ever seen Mary Wolstonecraft, and I said, I had once for a few moments, and that she seemed to me to turn off Godwin's objections to something she advanced with quite a playful, easy air. He replied, that "this was only one instance of the ascendancy which people of imagination exercised over those of mere intellect." He did not rate Godwin very high[17] (this was caprice or prejudice, real or affected) but he had a great idea of Mrs. Wolstonecraft's powers of conversation, none at all of her talent for book-making. We talked a little about Holcroft. He had been asked if he was not much struck *with* him, and he said, he thought himself in more danger of being struck *by* him. I complained that he would not let me get on at all, for he required a definition of every the commonest word, exclaiming, "What do you mean by a *sensation*, Sir? What do you mean by an *idea?*" This, Coleridge said, was barricadoing the road to truth: — it was setting up a turnpike-gate at every step we took. I forget a great number of things, many more than I remember; but the day passed off pleasantly, and the next morning Mr. Coleridge was to return to Shrewsbury. When I came down to breakfast, I found that he had just received a letter from his friend, T. Wedgwood, making him an offer of £150. a-year if he chose to wave his present pursuit, and

---

[17] He complained in particular of the presumption of his attempting to establish the future immortality of man, "without" (as he said) "knowing what Death was or what Life was" — and the tone in which he pronounced these two words seemed to convey a complete image of both. [W.H.]

devote himself entirely to the study of poetry and philosophy. Coleridge seemed to make up his mind to close with this proposal in the act of tying on one of his shoes. It threw an additional damp on his departure. It took the wayward enthusiast quite from us to cast him into Deva's winding vales, or by the shores of old romance. Instead of living at ten miles distance, of being the pastor of a Dissenting congregation at Shrewsbury, he was henceforth to inhabit the Hill of Parnassus, to be a Shepherd on the Delectable Mountains. Alas! I knew not the way thither, and felt very little gratitude for Mr. Wedgwood's bounty. I was presently relieved from this dilemma; for Mr. Coleridge, asking for a pen and ink, and going to a table to write something on a bit of card, advanced towards me with undulating step, and giving me the precious document, said that that was his address, *Mr. Coleridge, Nether-Stowey, Somersetshire;* and that he should be glad to see me there in a few weeks' time, and, if I chose, would come half-way to meet me. I was not less surprised than the shepherd-boy (this simile is to be found in Cassandra) when he sees a thunder-bolt fall close at his feet. I stammered out my acknowledgments and acceptance of this offer (I thought Mr. Wedgwood's annuity a trifle to it) as well as I could; and this mighty business being settled, the poet-preacher took leave, and I accompanied him six miles on the road. It was a fine morning in the middle of winter, and he talked the whole way. The scholar in Chaucer is described as going

—— "Sounding on his way."[18]

So Coleridge went on his. In digressing, in dilating, in passing from subject to subject, he appeared to me to float in air, to slide on ice. He told me in confidence (going along) that he should have preached two sermons before he accepted the situation at Shrewsbury, one on Infant Baptism, the other on the Lord's Supper, shewing that he could not administer either, which would have effectually disqualified him for the object in view. I observed that he continually crossed me on the way by shifting from one side of the foot-path to the other. This struck me as an odd movement; but I did not at that time connect it with any instability of purpose or involuntary change of principle, as I have done since. He seemed unable to keep on in a strait line. He spoke slightingly of Hume (whose Essay on Miracles he said was stolen from an objection started in one of South's Sermons — *Credat Judæus Apella!*).[19] I was not very much pleased at this account of Hume, for I had just been reading, with infinite relish, that completest of all metaphysical *choke-pears,* his *Treatise on Human Nature,* to which the *Essays,* in point of scholastic subtlety and close reasoning, are mere elegant trifling, light summer-reading. Coleridge even denied

[18] Cf. *Canterbury Tales,* Prologue 307.

[19] Cf. Horace, *Satires* I.v.101: "Let the Jew Apella believe it" — for he will believe anything.

the excellence of Hume's general style, which I think betrayed a want
of taste or candour. He however made me amends by the manner in
which he spoke of Berkeley. He dwelt particularly on his *Essay on
Vision* as a masterpiece of analytical reasoning. So it undoubtedly is.
He was exceedingly angry with Dr. Johnson for striking the stone
with his foot, in allusion to this author's Theory of Matter and Spirit,
and saying, "Thus I confute him, Sir."[20] Coleridge drew a parallel
(I don't know how he brought about the connection) between Bishop
Berkeley and Tom Paine. He said the one was an instance of a
subtle, the other of an acute mind, than which no two things could
be more distinct. The one was a shop-boy's quality, the other the
characteristic of a philosopher. He considered Bishop Butler as a true
philosopher, a profound and conscientious thinker, a genuine reader
of nature and of his own mind. He did not speak of his *Analogy,* but
of his *Sermons at the Rolls' Chapel,* of which I had never heard.
Coleridge somehow always contrived to prefer the *unknown* to the
known. In this instance he was right. The *Analogy* is a tissue of
sophistry, of wire-drawn, theological special-pleading; the *Sermons*
(with the Preface to them) are in a fine vein of deep, matured reflection, a candid appeal to our observation of human nature, without
pedantry and without bias. I told Coleridge I had written a few remarks, and was sometimes foolish enough to believe that I had made
a discovery on the same subject (the *Natural Disinterestedness of the
Human Mind*)[21] — and I tried to explain my view of it to Coleridge,
who listened with great willingness, but I did not succeed in making
myself understood. I sat down to the task shortly afterwards for the
twentieth time, got new pens and paper, determined to make clear
work of it, wrote a few meagre sentences in the skeleton-style of a
mathematical demonstration, stopped half-way down the second page;
and, after trying in vain to pump up any words, images, notions, apprehensions, facts, or observations, from that gulph of abstraction in
which I had plunged myself for four or five years preceding, gave up
the attempt as labour in vain, and shed tears of helpless despondency
on the blank unfinished paper. I can write fast enough now. Am I
better than I was then? Oh no! One truth discovered, one pang of
regret at not being able to express it, is better than all the fluency
and flippancy in the world. Would that I could go back to what I
then was! Why can we not revive past times as we can revisit old
places? If I had the quaint Muse of Sir Philip Sidney to assist me, I
would write a *Sonnet to the Road between W—m and Shrewsbury,*
and immortalise every step of it by some fond enigmatical conceit.
I would swear that the very milestones had ears, and that Harmer-hill
stooped with all its pines, to listen to a poet, as he passed! I remember but one other topic of discourse in this walk. He mentioned

[20] Boswell, *Life of Johnson,* episode of 1763.
[21] Subtitle of *An Essay on the Principles of Human Action,* 1805.

Paley, praised the naturalness and clearness of his style, but condemned his sentiments, thought him a mere time-serving casuist, and said that "the fact of his work on Moral and Political Philosophy being made a text-book in our Universities was a disgrace to the national character." We parted at the six-mile stone; and I returned homeward, pensive but much pleased. I had met with unexpected notice from a person, whom I believed to have been prejudiced against me. "Kind and affable to me had been his condescension, and should be honoured ever with suitable regard."[22] He was the first poet I had known, and he certainly answered to that inspired name. I had heard a great deal of his powers of conversation, and was not disappointed. In fact, I never met with any thing at all like them, either before or since. I could easily credit the accounts which were circulated of his holding forth to a large party of ladies and gentlemen, an evening or two before, on the Berkeleian Theory, when he made the whole material universe look like a transparency of fine words; and another story (which I believe he has somewhere told himself) of his being asked to a party at Birmingham, of his smoking tobacco and going to sleep after dinner on a sofa, where the company found him to their no small surprise, which was increased to wonder when he started up of a sudden, and rubbing his eyes, looked about him, and launched into a three-hours' description of the third heaven, of which he had had a dream, very different from Mr. Southey's Vision of Judgment, and also from that other Vision of Judgment, which Mr. Murray, the Secretary of the Bridge-street Junto, has taken into his especial keeping![23]

On my way back, I had a sound in my ears, it was the voice of Fancy: I had a light before me, it was the face of Poetry. The one still lingers there, the other has not quitted my side! Coleridge in truth met me half-way on the ground of philosophy, or I should not have been won over to his imaginative creed. I had an uneasy, pleasurable sensation all the time, till I was to visit him. During those months the chill breath of winter gave me a welcoming; the vernal air was balm and inspiration to me. The golden sun-sets, the silver star of evening, lighted me on my way to new hopes and prospects. *I was to visit Coleridge in the Spring.* This circumstance was never absent from my thoughts, and mingled with all my feelings. I wrote to him at the time proposed, and received an answer postponing my intended visit for a week or two, but very cordially urging me to complete my promise then. This delay did not damp, but rather increase my ardour. In the mean time, I went to Llangollen Vale, by way of initiating myself in the mysteries of natural scenery; and I must say I was enchanted with it. I had been reading Coleridge's description of Eng-

---

[22] Cf. *Paradise Lost* VIII.648–650.
[23] See *Biographia Literaria,* ch. x. The Constitutional Association in Bridge Street, headed by Charles Murray, prosecuted John Hunt for publishing *The Vision of Judgment* by Byron.

land, in his fine *Ode on the Departing Year,* and I applied it, *con amore,* to the objects before me. That valley was to me (in a manner) the cradle of a new existence: in the river that winds through it, my spirit was baptised in the waters of Helicon!

I returned home, and soon after set out on my journey with un-worn heart and untried feet. My way lay through Worcester and Gloucester, and by Upton, where I thought of Tom Jones and the ad-venture of the muff. I remember getting completely wet through one day, and stopping at an inn (I think it was at Tewkesbury) where I sat up all night to read Paul and Virginia. Sweet were the showers in early youth that drenched my body, and sweet the drops of pity that fell upon the books I read! I recollect a remark of Coleridge's upon this very book, that nothing could shew the gross indelicacy of French manners and the entire corruption of their imagination more strongly than the behaviour of the heroine in the last fatal scene, who turns away from a person on board the sinking vessel, that offers to save her life, because he has thrown off his clothes to assist him in swimming. Was this a time to think of such a circumstance? I once hinted to Wordsworth, as we were sailing in his boat on Grasmere lake, that I thought he had borrowed the idea of his *Poems on the Naming of Places* from the local inscriptions of the same kind in Paul and Virginia. He did not own the obligation, and stated some distinc-tion without a difference, in defence of his claim to originality. Any the slightest variation would be sufficient for this purpose in his mind; for whatever *he* added or omitted would inevitably be worth all that any one else had done, and contain the marrow of the sentiment. — I was still two days before the time fixed for my arrival, for I had taken care to set out early enough. I stopped these two days at Bridge-water, and when I was tired of sauntering on the banks of its muddy river, returned to the inn, and read Camilla. So have I loitered my life away, reading books, looking at pictures, going to plays, hearing, thinking, writing on what pleased me best. I have wanted only one thing to make me happy; but wanting that, have wanted every thing!

I arrived, and was well received. The country about Nether Stowey is beautiful, green and hilly, and near the sea-shore. I saw it but the other day, after an interval of twenty years, from a hill near Taunton. How was the map of my life spread out before me, as the map of the country lay at my feet! In the afternoon, Coleridge took me over to All-Foxden, a romantic old family-mansion of the St. Aubins, where Wordsworth lived. It was then in the possession of a friend of the poet's, who gave him the free use of it. Somehow that period (the time just after the French Revolution) was not a time when *nothing was given for nothing.* The mind opened, and a softness might be per-ceived coming over the heart of individuals, beneath "the scales that fence" our self-interest. Wordsworth himself was from home, but his sister kept house, and set before us a frugal repast; and we had free

access to her brother's poems, the *Lyrical Ballads,* which were still in
manuscript, or in the form of *Sybilline Leaves.* I dipped into a few
of these with great satisfaction, and with the faith of a novice. I slept
that night in an old room with blue hangings, and covered with the
round-faced family-portraits of the age of George I. and II. and from
the wooded declivity of the adjoining park that overlooked my window,
at the dawn of day, could

———— "hear the loud stag speak."[24]

In the outset of life (and particularly at this time I felt it so) our
imagination has a body to it. We are in a state between sleeping and
waking, and have indistinct but glorious glimpses of strange shapes,
and there is always something to come better than what we see. As
in our dreams the fulness of the blood gives warmth and reality to
the coinage of the brain, so in youth our ideas are clothed, and fed,
and pampered with our good spirits; we breathe thick with thoughtless happiness, the weight of future years presses on the strong pulses
of the heart, and we repose with undisturbed faith in truth and good.
As we advance, we exhaust our fund of enjoyment and of hope. We
are no longer wrapped in *lamb's-wool,* lulled in Elysium. As we taste
the pleasures of life, their spirit evaporates, the sense palls; and nothing
is left but the phantoms, the lifeless shadows of what *has been!*

That morning, as soon as breakfast was over, we strolled out into the
park, and seating ourselves on the trunk of an old ash-tree that
stretched along the ground, Coleridge read aloud with a sonorous and
musical voice, the ballad of *Betty Foy.* I was not critically or scepti-
cally inclined. I saw touches of truth and nature, and took the rest
for granted. But in the *Thorn,* the *Mad Mother,* and the *Complaint
of a Poor Indian Woman,* I felt that deeper power and pathos which
have been since acknowledged,

"In spite of pride, in erring reason's spite,"[25]

as the characteristics of this author; and the sense of a new style and
a new spirit in poetry came over me. It had to me something of the
effect that arises from the turning up of the fresh soil, or of the first
welcome breath of Spring,

"While yet the trembling year is unconfirmed."[26]

Coleridge and myself walked back to Stowey that evening, and his
voice sounded high

"Of Providence, foreknowledge, will, and fate,
Fix'd fate, free-will, foreknowledge absolute,"[27]

[24] Ben Jonson, *To Sir Robert Wroth* 22.
[25] Pope, *Essay on Man* I.293.
[26] Cf. Thomson, *Seasons,* Spring 18.
[27] *Paradise Lost* II.559–560.

as we passed through echoing grove, by fairy stream or waterfall, gleaming in the summer moonlight! He lamented that Wordsworth was not prone enough to belief in the traditional superstitions of the place, and that there was a something corporeal, a *matter-of-fact-ness*, a clinging to the palpable, or often to the petty, in his poetry, in consequence. His genius was not a spirit that descended to him through the air; it sprung out of the ground like a flower, or unfolded itself from a green spray, on which the gold-finch sang. He said, however (if I remember right) that this objection must be confined to his descriptive pieces, that his philosophic poetry had a grand and comprehensive spirit in it, so that his soul seemed to inhabit the universe like a palace, and to discover truth by intuition, rather than by deduction. The next day Wordsworth arrived from Bristol at Coleridge's cottage. I think I see him now. He answered in some degree to his friend's description of him, but was more gaunt and Don Quixote-like. He was quaintly dressed (according to the *costume* of that unconstrained period) in a brown fustian jacket and striped pantaloons. There was something of a roll, a lounge in his gait, not unlike his own Peter Bell. There was a severe, worn pressure of thought about his temples, a fire in his eye (as if he saw something in objects more than the outward appearance) an intense high narrow forehead, a Roman nose, cheeks furrowed by strong purpose and feeling, and a convulsive inclination to laughter about the mouth, a good deal at variance with the solemn, stately expression of the rest of his face. Chantry's bust wants the marking traits; but he was teazed into making it regular and heavy: Haydon's head of him, introduced into the *Entrance of Christ into Jerusalem,* is the most like his drooping weight of thought and expression. He sat down and talked very naturally and freely, with a mixture of clear gushing accents in his voice, a deep guttural intonation, and a strong tincture of the northern *burr,* like the crust on wine. He instantly began to make havoc of the half of a Cheshire cheese on the table, and said triumphantly that "his marriage with experience had not been so unproductive as Mr. Southey's in teaching him a knowledge of the good things of this life." He had been to see the *Castle Spectre* by Monk Lewis, while at Bristol, and described it very well. He said "it fitted the taste of the audience like a glove." This *ad captandum* merit was however by no means a recommendation of it, according to the severe principles of the new school, which reject rather than court popular effect. Wordsworth, looking out of the low, latticed window, said, "How beautifully the sun sets on that yellow bank!" I thought within myself, "With what eyes these poets see nature!" and ever after, when I saw the sun-set stream upon the objects facing it, conceived I had made a discovery, or thanked Mr. Wordsworth for having made one for me! We went over to All-Foxden again the day following, and Wordsworth read us the story of Peter Bell in the open air; and the comment made upon it by his face and voice was very different from that of some later critics! Whatever might be thought of the poem, "his face was as a book where men might read strange matters,"[28] and he announced the fate of his hero in prophetic tones. There is a *chaunt* in the recitation both of Coleridge and Wordsworth, which acts as a spell upon the hearer, and disarms the judgment. Perhaps they have deceived themselves by making habitual use of this ambiguous accompaniment. Coleridge's manner is more full, animated, and varied; Wordsworth's more equable, sustained, and internal. The one might be termed more *dramatic*, the other more *lyrical*. Coleridge has told me that he himself liked to compose in walking over uneven ground, or breaking through the straggling branches of a copsewood; whereas Wordsworth always wrote (if he could) walking up and down a strait gravel-walk, or in some spot where the continuity of his verse met with no collateral interruption. Returning that same evening, I got into a metaphysical argument with Wordsworth, while Coleridge was explaining the different notes of the nightingale to his sister, in which we neither of us succeeded in making ourselves perfectly clear and intelligible. Thus I passed three weeks at Nether Stowey and in the neighbourhood, generally devoting the afternoons to a delightful chat in an arbour made of bark by the poet's friend Tom Poole, sitting under two fine elm-trees, and listening to the bees humming round us, while we quaffed our *flip*. It was agreed, among other things, that we should make a jaunt down the Bristol-Channel, as far as Linton. We set off together on foot, Coleridge, John Chester, and I. This Chester was a native of Nether Stowey, one of those who were attracted to Coleridge's discourse as flies are to honey, or bees in swarming-time to the sound of a brass pan. He "followed in the chace, like a dog who hunts, not like one that made up the cry."[29] He had a brown cloth coat, boots, and corduroy breeches, was low in stature, bow-legged, had a drag in his walk like a drover, which he assisted by a hazel switch, and kept on a sort of trot by the side of Coleridge, like a running footman by a state coach, that he might not lose a syllable or sound, that fell from Coleridge's lips. He told me his private opinion, that Coleridge was a wonderful man. He scarcely opened his lips, much less offered an opinion the whole way: yet of the three, had I to chuse during that journey, I would be John Chester. He afterwards followed Coleridge into Germany, where the Kantean philosophers were puzzled how to bring him under any of their categories. When he sat down at table with his idol, John's felicity was complete; Sir Walter Scott's, or Mr. Blackwood's, when they sat down at the same table with the King, was not more so. We passed Dunster on our right, a small town between the brow of a hill and the sea. I remember eying it wistfully as it lay below us:

[28] Cf. *Macbeth* I.v.62–63.
[29] Cf. *Othello* II.iii.370.

contrasted with the woody scene around, it looked as clear, as pure, as *embrowned* and ideal as any landscape I have seen since, of Gaspar Poussin's or Domenichino's. We had a long day's march — (our feet kept time to the echoes of Coleridge's tongue) — through Minehead and by the Blue Anchor, and on to Linton, which we did not reach till near midnight, and where we had some difficulty in making a lodgment. We however knocked the people of the house up at last, and we were repaid for our apprehensions and fatigue by some excellent rashers of fried bacon and eggs. The view in coming along had been splendid. We walked for miles and miles on dark brown heaths overlooking the channel, with the Welsh hills beyond, and at times descended into little sheltered valleys close by the sea-side, with a smuggler's face scowling by us, and then had to ascend conical hills with a path winding up through a coppice to a barren top, like a monk's shaven crown, from one of which I pointed out to Coleridge's notice the bare masts of a vessel on the very edge of the horizon and within the red-orbed disk of the setting sun, like his own spectre-ship in the *Ancient Mariner*. At Linton the character of the sea-coast becomes more marked and rugged. There is a place called the *Valley of Rocks* (I suspect this was only the poetical name for it) bedded among precipices overhanging the sea, with rocky caverns beneath, into which the waves dash, and where the sea-gull for ever wheels its screaming flight. On the tops of these are huge stones thrown trans-verse, as if an earthquake had tossed them there, and behind these is a fretwork of perpendicular rocks, something like the *Giant's Cause-way*. A thunder-storm came on while we were at the inn, and Cole-ridge was running out bareheaded to enjoy the commotion of the elements in the *Valley of Rocks*, but as if in spite, the clouds only muttered a few angry sounds, and let fall a few refreshing drops. Coleridge told me that he and Wordsworth were to have made this place the scene of a prose-tale, which was to have been in the man-ner of, but far superior to, the *Death of Abel*, but they had relin-quished the design. In the morning of the second day, we break-fasted luxuriously in an old-fashioned parlour, on tea, toast, eggs, and honey, in the very sight of the bee-hives from which it had been taken, and a garden full of thyme and wild flowers that had produced it. On this occasion Coleridge spoke of Virgil's Georgics, but not well. I do not think he had much feeling for the classical or elegant. It was in this room that we found a little worn-out copy of the *Seasons*, lying in a window-seat, on which Coleridge exclaimed, *"That* is true fame!" He said Thomson was a great poet, rather than a good one; his style was as meretricious as his thoughts were natural. He spoke of Cowper as the best modern poet. He said the *Lyrical Ballads* were an experi-ment about to be tried by him and Wordsworth, to see how far the public taste would endure poetry written in a more natural and simple style than had hitherto been attempted; totally discarding the artifices of poetical diction, and making use only of such words as had probably been common in the most ordinary language since the days of Henry II. Some comparison was introduced between Shakespear and Milton. He said "he hardly knew which to prefer. Shakespear seemed to him a mere stripling in the art; he was as tall and as strong, with infinitely more activity than Milton, but he never appeared to have come to man's estate; or if he had, he would not have been a man, but a monster." He spoke with contempt of Gray, and with intolerance of Pope. He did not like the versification of the latter. He observed that "the ears of these couplet-writers might be charged with having short memories, that could not retain the harmony of whole passages." He thought little of Junius as a writer; he had a dislike of Dr. Johnson; and a much higher opinion of Burke as an orator and politician, than of Fox or Pitt. He however thought him very inferior in richness of style and imagery to some of our elder prose-writers, particularly Jeremy Taylor. He liked Richardson, but not Fielding; nor could I get him to enter into the merits of *Caleb Williams*.[30] In short, he was profound and discriminating with respect to those authors whom he liked, and where he gave his judgment fair play; capricious, perverse, and prejudiced in his antipathies and distastes. We loitered on the "ribbed sea-sands,"[31] in such talk as this, a whole morning, and I recollect met with a curious sea-weed, of which John Chester told us the country name! A fisherman gave Coleridge an account of a boy that had been drowned the day before, and that they had tried to save him at the risk of their own lives. He said "he did not know how it was that they ventured, but, Sir, we have a *nature* towards one another." This expression, Coleridge remarked to me, was a fine illustration of that theory of disinterestedness which I (in common with Butler) had adopted. I broached to him an argument of mine to prove that *likeness* was not mere association of ideas. I said that the mark in the sand put one in mind of a man's foot, not because it was part of a former impression of a man's foot (for it was quite new) but because it was like the shape of a man's foot. He assented to the justness of this distinction (which I have explained at length elsewhere, for the benefit of the curious) and John Chester listened; not from any interest in the subject, but because he was astonished that I should be able to suggest any thing to Coleridge that he did not already know. We returned on the third morning, and Coleridge remarked the silent cottage-smoke curling up the valleys where, a few evenings before, we had seen the lights gleaming through the dark.

[30] He had no idea of pictures, of Claude or Raphael, and at this time I had as little as he. He sometimes gives a striking account at present of the Cartoons at Pisa, by Buffamalco and others; of one in particular, where Death is seen in the air brandishing his scythe, and the great and mighty of the earth shudder at his approach, while the beggars and the wretched kneel to him as their deliverer. He would of course understand so broad and fine a moral as this at any time. [W.H.]

[31] *Ancient Mariner* 227.

In a day or two after we arrived at Stowey, we set out, I on my return home, and he for Germany. It was a Sunday morning, and he was to preach that day for Dr. Toulmin of Taunton. I asked him if he had prepared any thing for the occasion? He said he had not even thought of the text, but should as soon as we parted. I did not go to hear him, — this was a fault, — but we met in the evening at Bridgewater. The next day we had a long day's walk to Bristol, and sat down, I recollect, by a well-side on the road, to cool ourselves and satisfy our thirst, when Coleridge repeated to me some descriptive lines from his tragedy of Remorse; which I must say became his mouth and that occasion better than they, some years after, did Mr. Elliston's and the Drury-lane boards, —

> "Oh memory! shield me from the world's poor strife,
> And give those scenes thine everlasting life."

I saw no more of him for a year or two, during which period he had been wandering in the Hartz Forest in Germany; and his return was cometary, meteorous, unlike his setting out. It was not till some time after that I knew his friends Lamb and Southey. The last always appears to me (as I first saw him) with a common-place book under his arm, and the first with a *bon-mot* in his mouth. It was at Godwin's that I met him with Holcroft and Coleridge, where they were disputing fiercely which was the best — *Man as he was, or man as he is to be.* "Give me," says Lamb, "man as he is *not* to be."[32] This saying was the beginning of a friendship between us, which I believe still continues. — Enough of this for the present.

> "But there is matter for another rhyme,
> And I to this may add a second tale."[33]

W. H.

[32] Cf. William Godwin, *Caleb Williams, or Things as They Are*, 1794; Robert Bage, *Hermsprong, or Man as He Is Not*, 1796.

[33] Cf. Wordsworth, *Hart-Leap Well* 95–96.

W—m: Wem; Deva: the river Dee; Delectable Mountains: in Bunyan's *Pilgrim's Progress;* the muff: in Fielding's *Tom Jones* X.v.; Betty Foy: in Wordsworth's *Idiot Boy.*

Thomas and Josiah Wedgwood, sons of the famous potter, philanthropists; Thomas Holcroft (1745–1809), dramatist, novelist, radical; Robert South (1643–1716), theologian admired by Coleridge; Joseph Butler, *Analogy of Religion*, 1736; Bernardin de St. Pierre, *Paul et Virginie*, a simple story translated in 1795; Fanny Burney D'Arblay, *Camilla*, 1796, domestic novel.

Death of Abel: Coleridge was comparing "The Wanderings of Cain," which he continued without Wordsworth, with Salomon Gessner's *Tod Abels*, 1758. Francis Chantrey's bust of Wordsworth, executed in 1820, was exhibited in the Royal Academy. Robert Elliston acted Alvar in Coleridge's *Remorse*, 1813, but the lines quoted are not in that play.

choke-pears: harsh, hard to swallow; *ad captandum:* to catch the rabble; scallop: probably an error for *shallop*, a sloop or dinghy.

On Going a Journey

❲ The first volume of Hazlitt's *Table Talk; or, Original Essays* was published in 1821; the second in 1822. Several of his most popular essays belong to these volumes. For the second edition, 1824, the words *of Men and Manners* were added to the title. Hazlitt made a selection from these and other volumes for a Paris edition of 1825. "On Going a Journey" is here taken from the volume of 1822; it had appeared in January in the *New Monthly Magazine,* and was reprinted by Hazlitt in the later editions of *Table Talk.* He wrote crisp essays also "On Living to One's-Self" and "On the Pleasures of Hating." Lamb, by contrast, wrote on "Imperfect Sympathies." ❳

One of the pleasantest things in the world is going a journey; but I like to go by myself. I can enjoy society in a room; but out of doors, nature is company enough for me. I am then never less alone than when alone.

> "The fields his study, nature was his book."[1]

I cannot see the wit of walking and talking at the same time. When I am in the country, I wish to vegetate like the country. I am not for criticising hedge-rows and black cattle. I go out of town in order to forget the town and all that is in it. There are those who for this purpose go to watering-places, and carry the metropolis with them. I like more elbow-room, and fewer incumbrances. I like solitude, when I give myself up to it, for the sake of solitude; nor do I ask for

> ——— "a friend in my retreat,
> Whom I may whisper solitude is sweet."[2]

The soul of a journey is liberty, perfect liberty, to think, feel, do just as one pleases. We go a journey chiefly to be free of all impediments and of all inconveniences; to leave ourselves behind, much more to get rid of others. It is because I want a little breathing-space to muse on indifferent matters, where Contemplation

> "May plume her feathers and let grow her wings,
> That in the various bustle of resort
> Were all too ruffled, and sometimes impair'd,"[3]

that I absent myself from the town for awhile, without feeling at a

[1] Robert Bloomfield (1766–1823), *The Farmer's Boy,* Spring 32.
[2] Cowper, *Retirement* 741–742.
[3] Cf. Milton, *Comus* 378–380.

loss the moment I am left by myself. Instead of a friend in a post-chaise or in a Tilbury, to exchange good things with, and vary the same stale topics over again, for once let me have a truce with impertinence. Give me the clear blue sky over my head, and the green turf beneath my feet, a winding road before me, and a three hours' march to dinner — and then to thinking! It is hard if I cannot start some game on these lone heaths. I laugh, I run, I leap, I sing for joy. From the point of yonder rolling cloud, I plunge into my past being, and revel there, as the sun-burnt Indian plunges headlong into the wave that wafts him to his native shore. Then long-forgotten things, like "sunken wrack and sumless treasuries,"[4] burst upon my eager sight, and I begin to feel, think, and be myself again. Instead of an awkward silence, broken by attempts at wit or dull commonplaces, mine is that undisturbed silence of the heart which alone is perfect eloquence. No one likes puns, alliterations, antitheses, argument, and analysis better than I do; but I sometimes had rather be without them. "Leave, oh, leave me to my repose!" I have just now other business in hand, which would seem idle to you, but is with me "very stuff of the conscience."[5] Is not this wild rose sweet without a comment? Does not this daisy leap to my heart set in its coat of emerald? Yet if I were to explain to you the circumstance that has so endeared it to me, you would only smile. Had I not better then keep it to myself, and let it serve me to brood over, from here to yonder craggy point, and from thence onward to the far-distant horizon? I should be but bad company all that way, and therefore prefer being alone. I have heard it said that you may, when the moody fit comes on, walk or ride on by yourself, and indulge your reveries. But this looks like a breach of manners, a neglect of others, and you are thinking all the time that you ought to rejoin your party. "Out upon such half-faced fellowship,"[6] say I. I like to be either entirely to myself, or entirely at the disposal of others; to talk or be silent, to walk or sit still, to be sociable or solitary. I was pleased with an observation of Mr. Cobbett's, that "he thought it a bad French custom to drink our wine with our meals, and that an Englishman ought to do only one thing at a time." So I cannot talk and think, or indulge in melancholy musing and lively conversation by fits and starts. "Let me have a companion of my way," says Sterne, "were it but to remark how the shadows lengthen as the sun declines."[7] It is beautifully said: but in my opinion, this continual comparing of notes interferes with the involuntary impression of things upon the mind, and hurts the sentiment. If you only hint what you feel in a kind of dumb show, it is insipid: if you have to explain it, it is making a toil

---

[4] *Henry V* I.ii.165.
[5] Cf. Gray, *Descent of Odin* 50; *Othello* I.ii.2.
[6] *1 Henry IV* I.iii.208.
[7] Cf. *Sermons*, 1760, xviii.

of a pleasure. You cannot read the book of nature without being perpetually put to the trouble of translating it for the benefit of others. I am for the synthetical method on a journey, in preference to the analytical. I am content to lay in a stock of ideas then, and to examine and anatomise them afterwards. I want to see my vague notions float like the down of the thistle before the breeze, and not to have them entangled in the briars and thorns of controversy. For once, I like to have it all my own way; and this is impossible unless you are alone, or in such company as I do not covet. I have no objection to argue a point with any one for twenty miles of measured road, but not for pleasure. If you remark the scent of a bean-field crossing the road, perhaps your fellow-traveller has no smell. If you point to a distant object, perhaps he is short-sighted, and has to take out his glass to look at it. There is a feeling in the air, a tone in the colour of a cloud which hits your fancy, but the effect of which you are unable to account for. There is then no sympathy, but an uneasy craving after it, and a dissatisfaction which pursues you on the way, and in the end probably produces ill humour. Now I never quarrel with myself, and take all my own conclusions for granted till I find it necessary to defend them against objections. It is not merely that you may not be of accord on the objects and circumstances that present themselves before you — these may recal a number of objects, and lead to associations too delicate and refined to be possibly communicated to others. Yet these I love to cherish, and sometimes still fondly clutch them, when I can escape from the throng to do so. To give way to our feelings before company, seems extravagance or affectation; and on the other hand, to have to unravel this mystery of our being at every turn, and to make others take an equal interest in it (otherwise the end is not answered) is a task to which few are competent. We must "give it an understanding, but no tongue."[8] My old friend C——, however, could do both. He could go on in the most delightful explanatory way over hill and dale, a summer's day, and convert a landscape into a didactic poem or a Pindaric ode. "He talked far above singing,"[9] If I could so clothe my ideas in sounding and flowing words, I might perhaps wish to have some one with me to admire the swelling theme; or I could be more content, were it possible for me still to hear his echoing voice in the woods of All-Foxden. They had "that fine madness in them which our first poets had;"[10] and if they could have been caught by some rare instrument, would have breathed such strains as the following.

> —— "Here be woods as green
> As any, air likewise as fresh and sweet
> As when smooth Zephyrus plays on the fleet

[8] *Hamlet* I.ii.250.
[9] Cf. Beaumont and Fletcher, *Philaster* V.v.165–166.
[10] Cf. Drayton, *Elegy to Henry Reynolds* 109–110.

Face of the curled stream, with flow'rs as many
As the young spring gives, and as choice as any;
Here be all new delights, cool streams and wells,
Arbours o'ergrown with woodbine, caves and dells;
Choose where thou wilt, while I sit by and sing,
Or gather rushes to make many a ring
For thy long fingers; tell thee tales of love,
How the pale Phœbe, hunting in a grove,
First saw the boy Endymion, from whose eyes
She took eternal fire that never dies;
How she convey'd him softly in a sleep,
His temples bound with poppy, to the steep
Head of old Latmos, where she stoops each night,
Gilding the mountain with her brother's light,
To kiss her sweetest." ———

FAITHFUL SHEPHERDESS. [I.iii.26–43]

Had I words and images at command like these, I would attempt to
wake the thoughts that lie slumbering on golden ridges in the evening
clouds: but at the sight of nature my fancy, poor as it is, droops and
closes up its leaves, like flowers at sunset. I can make nothing out
on the spot: — I must have time to collect myself. —

In general, a good thing spoils out-of-door prospects: it should be
reserved for Table-talk. L——— is for this reason, I take it, the worst
company in the world out of doors; because he is the best within. I
grant, there is one subject on which it is pleasant to talk on a journey;
and that is, what one shall have for supper when we get to our inn at
night. The open air improves this sort of conversation or friendly
altercation, by setting a keener edge on appetite. Every mile of the
road heightens the flavour of the viands we expect at the end of it.
How fine it is to enter some old town, walled and turreted, just at
the approach of night-fall, or to come to some straggling village, with
the lights streaming through the surrounding gloom; and then after
inquiring for the best entertainment that the place affords, to "take
one's ease at one's inn!"[11] These eventful moments in our lives' history are too precious, too full of solid, heart-felt happiness to be frittered and dribbled away in imperfect sympathy. I would have them
all to myself, and drain them to the last drop: they will do to talk
of or to write about afterwards. What a delicate speculation it is,
after drinking whole goblets of tea,

"The cups that cheer, but not inebriate,"[12]

and letting the fumes ascend into the brain, to sit considering what
we shall have for supper — eggs and a rasher, a rabbit smothered in
onions, or an excellent veal-cutlet! Sancho in such a situation once
fixed upon cow-heel; and his choice, though he could not help it, is

[11] Cf. 1 Henry IV III.iii.93. L — is probably Lamb.
[12] Cowper, The Task IV.39–40.

not to be disparaged. Then, in the intervals of pictured scenery and Shandean contemplation, to catch the preparation and the stir in the kitchen — *Procul, O procul este profani!*[13] These hours are sacred to silence and to musing, to be treasured up in the memory, and to feed the source of smiling thoughts hereafter. I would not waste them in idle talk; or if I must have the integrity of fancy broken in upon, I would rather it were by a stranger than a friend. A stranger takes his hue and character from the time and place; he is a part of the furniture and costume of an inn. If he is a Quaker, or from the West Riding of Yorkshire, so much the better. I do not even try to sympathise with him, and he breaks no squares. I associate nothing with my travelling companion but present objects and passing events. In his ignorance of me and my affairs, I in a manner forget myself. But a friend reminds one of other things, rips up old grievances, and destroys the abstraction of the scene. He comes in ungraciously between us and our imaginary character. Something is dropped in the course of conversation that gives a hint of your profession and pursuits; or from having some one with you that knows the less sublime portions of your history, it seems that other people do. You are no longer a citizen of the world: but your "unhoused free condition is put into circumscription and confine." The *incognito* of an inn is one of its striking privileges — "lord of one's-self, uncumber'd with a name."[14] Oh, it is great to shake off the trammels of the world and of public opinion — to lose our importunate, tormenting, everlasting personal identity in the elements of nature, and become the creature of the moment, clear of all ties — to hold to the universe only by a dish of sweet-breads, and to owe nothing but the score of the evening — and no longer seeking for applause and meeting with contempt, to be known by no other title than *the Gentleman in the parlour!* One may take one's choice of all characters in this romantic state of uncertainty as to one's real pretensions, and become indefinitely respectable and negatively right-worshipful. We baffle prejudice and disappoint conjecture; and from being so to others, begin to be objects of curiosity and wonder even to ourselves. We are no more those hackneyed commonplaces that we appear in the world: an inn restores us to the level of nature, and quits scores with society! I have certainly spent some enviable hours at inns — sometimes when I have been left entirely to myself, and have tried to solve some metaphysical problem, as once at Witham-common, where I found out the proof that likeness is not a case of the association of ideas — at other times, when there have been pictures in the room, as at St. Neot's, (I think it was) where I first met with Gribelin's engravings of the Cartoons, into which I

[13] "Ye unhallowed, stand far off." — *Aeneid* VI.258. Shandean: like Sterne's digressive Walter Shandy. Sancho: in *Don Quixote* II.iii.ch.59.
[14] Cf. *Othello* I.ii.26; Dryden, *To John Driden* 18: "uncumber'd with a wife."

entered at once, and at a little inn on the borders of Wales, where there happened to be hanging some of Westall's drawings, which I compared triumphantly (for a theory that I had, not for the admired artist) with the figure of a girl who had ferried me over the Severn, standing up in the boat between me and the twilight — at other times I might mention luxuriating in books, with a peculiar interest in this way, as I remember sitting up half the night to read Paul and Virginia, which I picked up at an inn at Bridgewater, after being drenched in the rain all day; and at the same place I got through two volumes of Madame D'Arblay's Camilla. It was on the tenth of April, 1798, that I sat down to a volume of the New Eloise, at the inn at Llangollen, over a bottle of sherry and a cold chicken. The letter I chose was that in which St. Preux describes his feelings as he first caught a glimpse from the heights of the Jura of the Pays de Vaud, which I had brought with me as a *bon bouche* to crown the evening with.[15] It was my birth-day, and I had for the first time come from a place in the neighbourhood to visit this delightful spot. The road to Llangollen turns off between Chirk and Wrexham; and on passing a certain point, you come all at once upon the valley, which opens like an amphitheatre, broad, barren hills rising in majestic state on either side, with "green upland swells that echo to the bleat of flocks" below, and the river Dee babbling over its stony bed in the midst of them. The valley at this time "glittered green with sunny showers," and a budding ash-tree dipped its tender branches in the chiding stream. How proud, how glad I was to walk along the high road that overlooks the delicious prospect, repeating the lines which I have just quoted from Mr. Coleridge's poems![16] But besides the prospect which opened beneath my feet, another also opened to my inward sight, a heavenly vision, on which were written, in letters large as Hope could make them, these four words, LIBERTY, GENIUS, LOVE, VIRTUE; which have since faded into the light of common day, or mock my idle gaze.

"The beautiful is vanished, and returns not."[17]

Still I would return some time or other to this enchanted spot; but I would return to it alone. What other self could I find to share that influx of thoughts, of regret, and delight, the fragments of which I could hardly conjure up to myself, so much have they been broken and defaced! I could stand on some tall rock, and overlook the precipice of years that separates me from what I then was. I was at that time going shortly to visit the poet whom I have above named. Where is he now? Now only I myself have changed; the world, which was

---

[15] Rousseau, *Nouvelle Héloïse* IV.xvii. *Bonne bouche:* choice morsel.

[16] Cf. *Ode on the Departing Year* 124–126.

[17] Coleridge, translation of Schiller, *Death of Wallenstein* V.i.68. With "common day" cf. Wordsworth, *Intimations Ode* 77.

then new to me, has become old and incorrigible. Yet will I turn to thee in thought, O sylvan Dee, in joy, in youth and gladness as thou then wert; and thou shalt always be to me the river of Paradise, where I will drink of the waters of life freely!

There is hardly any thing that shows the short-sightedness or capriciousness of the imagination more than travelling does. With change of place we change our ideas; nay, our opinions and feelings. We can by an effort indeed transport ourselves to old and long-forgotten scenes, and then the picture of the mind revives again; but we forget those that we have just left. It seems that we can think but of one place at a time. The canvas of the fancy is but of a certain extent, and if we paint one set of objects upon it, they immediately efface every other. We cannot enlarge our conceptions, we only shift our point of view. The landscape bares its bosom to the enraptured eye, we take our fill of it, and seem as if we could form no other image of beauty or grandeur. We pass on, and think no more of it: the horizon that shuts it from our sight, also blots it from our memory like a dream. In travelling through a wild barren country, I can form no idea of a woody and cultivated one. It appears to me that all the world must be barren, like what I see of it. In the country we forget the town, and in town we despise the country. "Beyond Hyde Park," says Sir Fopling Flutter, "all is a desert."[18] All that part of the map that we do not see before us is a blank. The world in our conceit of it is not much bigger than a nutshell. It is not one prospect expanded into another, county joined to county, kingdom to kingdom, lands to seas, making an image voluminous and vast; — the mind can form no larger idea of space than the eye can take in at a single glance. The rest is a name written in a map, a calculation of arithmetic. For instance, what is the true signification of that immense mass of territory and population, known by the name of China to us? An inch of paste-board on a wooden globe, of no more account than a China orange! Things near us are seen of the size of life: things at a distance are diminished to the size of the understanding. We measure the universe by ourselves, and even comprehend the texture of our own being only piece-meal. In this way, however, we remember an infinity of things and places. The mind is like a mechanical instrument that plays a great variety of tunes, but it must play them in succession. One idea recalls another, but it at the same time excludes all others. In trying to renew old recollections, we cannot as it were unfold the whole web of our existence; we must pick out the single threads. So in coming to a place where we have formerly lived and with which we have intimate associations, every one must have found that the feeling grows more vivid the nearer we approach the spot, from the mere anticipation of the actual impression: we remember

[18] Cf. Harriet in Etherege, *The Man of Mode; or, Sir Fopling Flutter* V.ii.

circumstances, feelings, persons, faces, names, that we had not thought of for years; but for the time all the rest of the world is forgotten! — To return to the question I have quitted above.

I have no objection to go to see ruins, aqueducts, pictures, in company with a friend or a party, but rather the contrary, for the former reason reversed. They are intelligible matters, and will bear talking about. The sentiment here is not tacit, but communicable and overt. Salisbury Plain is barren of criticism, but Stonehenge will bear a discussion antiquarian, picturesque, and philosophical. In setting out on a party of pleasure, the first consideration always is where we shall go to: in taking a solitary ramble, the question is what we shall meet with by the way. "The mind is its own place;" nor are we anxious to arrive at the end of our journey. I can myself do the honours indifferently well to works of art and curiosity. I once took a party to Oxford with no mean *eclat* — shewed them that seat of the Muses at a distance,

"With glistering spires and pinnacles adorn'd" —[19]

descanted on the learned air that breathes from the grassy quadrangles and stone walls of halls and colleges — was at home in the Bodleian; and at Blenheim quite superseded the powdered Ciceroni that attended us, and that pointed in vain with his wand to common-place beauties in matchless pictures. — As another exception to the above reasoning, I should not feel confident in venturing on a journey in a foreign country without a companion. I should want at intervals to hear the sound of my own language. There is an involuntary antipathy in the mind of an Englishman to foreign manners and notions that requires the assistance of social sympathy to carry it off. As the distance from home increases, this relief, which was at first a luxury, becomes a passion and an appetite. A person would almost feel stifled to find himself in the deserts of Arabia without friends and countrymen: there must be allowed to be something in the view of Athens or old Rome that claims the utterance of speech; and I own that the Pyramids are too mighty for any single contemplation. In such situations, so opposite to all one's ordinary train of ideas, one seems a species by one's-self, a limb torn off from society, unless one can meet with instant fellowship and support. — Yet I did not feel this want or craving very pressing once, when I first set my foot on the laughing shores of France. Calais was peopled with novelty and delight. The confused, busy murmur of the place was like oil and wine poured into my ears; nor did the mariners' hymn, which was sung from the top of an old crazy vessel in the harbour, as the sun went down, send an alien sound into my soul. I only breathed the air of general humanity. I walked over "the vine-covered hills and gay regions of France,"[20] erect and satisfied;

[19] *Paradise Lost* I.254, III.550.
[20] Cf. William Roscoe, *Song for 14 August 1791* 1.

for the image of man was not cast down and chained to the foot of arbitrary thrones: I was at no loss for language, for that of all the great schools of painting was open to me. The whole is vanished like a shade. Pictures, heroes, glory, freedom, all are fled: nothing remains but the Bourbons and the French people! — There is undoubtedly a sensation in travelling into foreign parts that is to be had nowhere else: but it is more pleasing at the time than lasting. It is too remote from our habitual associations to be a common topic of discourse or reference, and, like a dream or another state of existence, does not piece into our daily modes of life. It is an animated but a momentary hallucination. It demands an effort to exchange our actual for our ideal identity; and to feel the pulse of our old transports revive very keenly, we must "jump" all our present comforts and connexions. Our romantic and itinerant character is not to be domesticated. Dr. Johnson remarked how little foreign travel added to the facilities of conversation in those who had been abroad. In fact, the time we have spent there is both delightful and in one sense instructive; but it appears to be cut out of our substantial, downright existence, and never to join kindly on to it. We are not the same, but another, and perhaps more enviable individual, all the time we are out of our own country. We are lost to ourselves, as well as our friends. So the poet somewhat quaintly sings,

"Out of my country and myself I go."

Those who wish to forget painful thoughts, do well to absent themselves for a while from the ties and objects that recal them: but we can be said only to fulfill our destiny in the place that gave us birth. I should on this account like well enough to spend the whole of my life in travelling abroad, if I could any where borrow another life to spend afterwards at home! —[21]

[21] Bodleian: great library of Oxford University; Blenheim: ducal palace, near Oxford, rewarding Marlborough's victory at Blenheim, 1704 (Hazlitt took the Lambs there in August 1810). Simon Gribelin (1661–1733) made engravings from Raphael's cartoons for the Sistine Chapel, seven of which were in England. Richard Westall (1765–1836), painter of historical subjects.

On Genius and Common Sense

❲ Essays IV and V of *Table Talk* bore the titles "On Genius and Common Sense" and "The Same Subject Continued." The first paragraph of Essay IV serves here as an introduction to Essay V, which is given in full from the first edition of 1821. ❳

I

We hear it maintained by people of more gravity than understanding, that genius and taste are strictly reducible to rules, and that there is a rule for every thing. So far is it from being true that the finest breath of fancy is a definable thing, that the plainest common sense is only what Mr. Locke would have called a *mixed mode*, subject to a particular sort of acquired and undefinable tact.[1] It is asked, "If you do not know the rule by which a thing is done, how can you be sure of doing it a second time?" And the answer is, "If you do not know the muscles by the help of which you walk, how is it you do not fall down at every step you take?" In art, in taste, in life, in speech, you decide from feeling, and not from reason; that is, from the impression of a number of things on the mind, which impression is true and well-founded, though you may not be able to analyse or account for it in the several particulars. In a gesture you use, in a look you see, in a tone you hear, you judge of the expression, propriety, and meaning from habit, not from reason or rules; that is to say, from innumerable instances of like gestures, looks, and tones, in innumerable other circumstances, variously modified, which are too many and too refined to be all distinctly recollected, but which do not therefore operate the less powerfully upon the mind and eye of taste. Shall we say that these impressions (the immediate stamp of nature) do not operate in a given manner till they are classified and reduced to rules, or is not the rule itself grounded upon the truth and certainty of that natural operation? How then can the distinction of the understanding as to the manner in which they operate be necessary to their producing their due and uniform effect upon the mind? If certain effects did not regularly arise out of certain causes in mind as well as matter, there could be no rule given for them: nature does not follow the rule, but suggests it. Reason is the interpreter and critic of nature and genius, not their lawgiver and judge. He must be a poor creature indeed whose practical convictions do not in almost all cases outrun his de-

[1] *Essay concerning Human Understanding* II.xii.4.

liberate understanding, or who does not feel and know much more than he can give a reason for. — Hence the distinction between eloquence and wisdom, between ingenuity and common sense. A man may be dextrous and able in explaining the grounds of his opinions, and yet may be a mere sophist, because he only sees one half of a subject. Another may feel the whole weight of a question, nothing relating to it may be lost upon him, and yet he may be able to give no account of the manner in which it affects him, or to drag his reasons from their silent lurking-places. This last will be a wise man, though neither a logician nor rhetorician. Goldsmith was a fool to Dr. Johnson in argument; that is, in assigning the specific grounds of his opinions: Dr. Johnson was a fool to Goldsmith in the fine tact, the airy, intuitive faculty with which he skimmed the surfaces of things, and unconsciously formed his opinions. Common sense is the just result of the sum-total of such unconscious impressions in the ordinary occurrences of life, as they are treasured up in the memory, and called out by the occasion. Genius and taste depend much upon the same principle exercised on loftier ground and in more unusual combinations. . . .

II

Genius or originality is, for the most part, *some strong quality in the mind, answering to and bringing out some new and striking quality in nature.*

Imagination is, more properly, the power of carrying on a given feeling into other situations, which must be done best according to the hold which the feeling itself has taken of the mind.[2] In new and unknown combinations, the impression must act by sympathy, and not by rule; but there can be no sympathy, where there is no passion, no original interest. The personal interest may in some cases oppress and circumscribe the imaginative faculty, as in the instance of Rousseau: but in general the strength and consistency of the imagination will be in proportion to the strength and depth of feeling; and it is rarely that a man even of lofty genius will be able to do more than carry on his own feelings and character, or some prominent and ruling passion, into fictitious and uncommon situations. Milton has by allusion embodied a great part of his political and personal history in the chief characters and incidents of Paradise Lost. He has, no doubt, wonderfully adapted and heightened them, but the elements are the same; you trace the bias and opinions of the man in the creations of the poet. Shakespear (almost alone) seems to have been a man of genius, raised above the definition of genius. "Born universal heir to all hu-

---

[2] I do not here speak of the figurative or fanciful exercise of the imagination, which consists in finding out some striking object or image to illustrate another. [W.H.]

manity," he was "as one, in suffering all who suffered nothing;" with a perfect sympathy with all things, yet alike indifferent to all: who did not tamper with nature or warp her to his own purposes; who "knew all qualities with a learned spirit," instead of judging of them by his own predilections; and was rather "a pipe for the Muse's finger to play what stop she pleased,"[3] than anxious to set up any character or pretensions of his own. His genius consisted in the faculty of transforming himself at will into whatever he chose: his originality was the power of seeing every object from the exact point of view in which others would see it. He was the Proteus of human intellect. Genius in ordinary is a more obstinate and less versatile thing. It is sufficiently exclusive and self-willed, quaint and peculiar. It does some one thing by virtue of doing nothing else: it excels in some one pursuit by being blind to all excellence but its own. It is just the reverse of the cameleon; for it does not borrow, but lend its colours to all about it: or like the glow-worm, discloses a little circle of gorgeous light in the twilight of obscurity, in the night of intellect, that surrounds it. So did Rembrandt. If ever there was a man of genius, he was one, in the proper sense of the term. He lived in and revealed to others a world of his own, and might be said to have invented a new view of nature. He did not discover things *out of* nature, in fiction or fairy land, or make a voyage to the moon "to descry new lands, rivers, or mountains in her spotty globe,"[4] but saw things *in* nature that every one had missed before him, and gave others eyes to see them with. This is the test and triumph of originality, not to shew us what has never been, and what we may therefore very easily never have dreamt of, but to point out to us what is before our eyes and under our feet, though we have had no suspicion of its existence, for want of sufficient strength of intuition, of determined grasp of mind to seize and retain it. Rembrandt's conquests were not over the *ideal,* but the real. He did not contrive a new story or character, but we nearly owe to him a fifth part of painting, the knowledge of *chiaroscuro* — a distinct power and element in art and nature. He had a steadiness, a firm keeping of mind and eye, that first stood the shock of "fierce extremes" in light and shade, or reconciled the greatest obscurity and the greatest brilliancy into perfect harmony; and he therefore was the first to hazard this appearance upon canvas, and give full effect to what he saw and delighted in. He was led to adopt this style of broad and startling contrast from its congeniality to his own feelings: his mind grappled with that which afforded the best exercise to its master-powers: he was bold in act, because he was urged on by a strong native impulse. Originality is then nothing but nature and feeling working in the mind. A man does not affect to be original: he is so, because he cannot help it, and often without knowing it. This

---

[3] Cf. *Hamlet* III.ii.71,75–76; *Othello* III.iii.259.
[4] *Paradise Lost* I.290–291.

extraordinary artist indeed might be said to have had a particular organ for colour. His eye seemed to come in contact with it as a feeling, to lay hold of it as a substance, rather than to contemplate it as a visual object. The texture of his landscapes is "of the earth, earthy" — his clouds are humid, heavy, slow; his shadows are "darkness that may be felt," a "palpable obscure;" his lights are lumps of liquid splendour![5] There is something more in this than can be accounted for from design or accident: Rembrandt was not a man made up of two or three rules and directions for acquiring genius.

I am afraid I shall hardly write so satisfactory a character of Mr. Wordsworth, though he, too, like Rembrandt, has a faculty of making something out of nothing, that is, out of himself, by the medium through which he sees and with which he clothes the barrenest subject. Mr. Wordsworth is the last man to "look abroad into universality," if that alone constituted genius: he looks at home into himself, and is "content with riches fineless."[6] He would in the other case be "poor as winter," if he had nothing but general capacity to trust to. He is the greatest, that is, the most original poet of the present day, only because he is the greatest egotist. He is "self-involved, not dark." He sits in the centre of his own being, and there "enjoys bright day."[7] He does not waste a thought on others. Whatever does not relate exclusively and wholly to himself, is foreign to his views. He contemplates a whole-length figure of himself, he looks along the unbroken line of his personal identity. He thrusts aside all other objects, all other interests with scorn and impatience, that he may repose on his own being, that he may dig out the treasures of thought contained in it, that he may unfold the precious stores of a mind, for ever brooding over itself. His genius is the effect of his individual character. He stamps that character, that deep individual interest, on whatever he meets. The object is nothing but as it furnishes food for internal meditation, for old associations. If there had been no other being in the universe, Mr. Wordsworth's poetry would have been just what it is. If there had been neither love nor friendship, neither ambition nor pleasure nor business in the world, the author of the Lyrical Ballads need not have been greatly changed from what he is — might still have "kept the noiseless tenour of his way,"[8] retired in the sanctuary of his own heart, hallowing the Sabbath of his own thoughts. With the passions, the pursuits, and imaginations of other men he does not profess to sympathise, but "finds tongues in the trees, books in the running brooks, sermons in stones, and good in every thing."[9] With a

[5] 1 Corinthians 15:47; Exodus 10:21; *Paradise Lost* II.406.

[6] Bacon, *Advancement of Learning*, Bk. I.

[7] Cf. *Othello* III.iii.173; James Thomson, *Castle of Indolence* I.508; Milton, *Comus* 382.

[8] Cf. Gray, *Elegy* 76.

[9] *As You Like It* II.i.16–17.

mind averse from outward objects, but ever intent upon its own workings, he hangs a weight of thought and feeling upon every trifling circumstance connected with his past history. The note of the cuckoo sounds in his ear like the voice of other years; the daisy spreads its leaves in the rays of boyish delight, that stream from his thoughtful eyes; the rainbow lifts its proud arch in heaven but to mark his progress from infancy to manhood; an old thorn is buried, bowed down under the mass of associations he has wound about it; and to him, as he himself beautifully says,

> —— "The meanest flow'r that blows can give
> Thoughts that do often lie too deep for tears."[10]

It is this power of habitual sentiment, or of transferring the interest of our conscious existence to whatever gently solicits attention, and is a link in the chain of association, without rousing our passions or hurting our pride, that is the striking feature in Mr. Wordsworth's mind and poetry. Others have felt and shown this power before, as Withers, Burns, &c. but none have felt it so intensely and absolutely as to lend to it the voice of inspiration, as to make it the foundation of a new style and school in poetry. His strength, as it so often happens, arises from the excess of his weakness. But he has opened a new avenue to the human heart, has explored another secret haunt and nook of nature, "sacred to verse, and sure of everlasting fame." Compared with his lines, Lord Byron's stanzas are but exaggerated common-place, and Walter Scott's poetry (not his prose) old wives' fables.[11] There is no one in whom I have been more disappointed than in the writer here spoken of, nor with whom I am more disposed on certain points to quarrel: but the love of truth and justice which obliges me to do this, will not suffer me to blench his merits. Do what he can, he cannot help being an original-minded man. His poetry is not servile. While the cuckoo returns in the spring, while the daisy looks bright in the sun, while the rainbow lifts its head above the storm —

> "Yet I'll remember thee, Glencairn,
> And all that thou hast done for me!"[12]

Sir Joshua Reynolds, in endeavouring to show that there is no such thing as proper originality, a spirit emanating from the mind of the artist and shining through his works, has traced Raphael through a number of figures which he has borrowed from Masaccio and others.[13] This is a bad calculation. If Raphael had only borrowed those figures from others, would he, even in Sir Joshua's sense, have been entitled

---

10 *Intimations Ode* 203–204.

11 Mr. Wordsworth himself should not say this, and yet I am not sure he would not. [W.H.]

12 Cf. Burns, *Lament for Glencairn* 79–80.

13 See Reynolds, Discourse XII.

to the praise of originality? Plagiarism, I presume, in so far as it is plagiarism, is not originality. Salvator is considered by many as a great genius. He was what they call an irregular genius. My notion of genius is not exactly the same as theirs. It has also been made a question whether there is not more genius in Rembrandt's *Three Trees* than in all Claude Lorraine's landscapes? I do not know how that may be: but it was enough for Claude to have been a perfect land-scape-painter.

Capacity is not the same thing as genius. Capacity may be described to relate to the quantity of knowledge, however acquired; genius to its quality and the mode of acquiring it. Capacity is a power over given ideas or combinations of ideas; genius is the power over those which are not given, and for which no obvious or precise rule can be laid down. Or capacity is power of any sort: genius is power of a different sort from what has yet been shown. A retentive memory, a clear understanding is capacity, but it is not genius. The admirable Crichton was a person of prodigious capacity; but there is no proof (that I know) that he had an atom of genius. His verses that remain are dull and sterile. He could learn all that was known of any subject: he could do any thing if others could show him the way to do it. This was very wonderful: but that is all you can say of it. It requires a good capacity to play well at chess: but, after all, it is a game of skill, and not of genius. Know what you will of it, the understanding still moves in certain tracks in which others have trod before it, quicker or slower, with more or less comprehension and presence of mind. The greatest skill strikes out nothing for itself, from its own peculiar re-sources; the nature of the game is a thing determinate and fixed: there is no royal or poetical road to check-mate your adversary. There is no place for genius but in the indefinite and unknown. The discovery of the binomial theorem was an effort of genius; but there was none shown in Jedediah Buxton's being able to multiply 9 figures by 9 in his head. If he could have multiplied 90 figures by 90 instead of 9, it would have been equally useless toil and trouble.[14] He is a man of capacity who possesses considerable intellectual riches: he is a man

---

[14] The only good thing I ever heard come of this man's singular faculty of memory was the following. A gentleman was mentioning his having been sent up to London from the place where he lived to see Garrick act. When he went back into the country, he was asked what he thought of the player and the play. "Oh!" he said, "he did not know: he had only seen a little man strut about the stage, and repeat 7956 words." We all laughed at this, but a person in one corner of the room, holding one hand to his fore-head, and seeming mightily delighted, called out, "Ay, indeed! And pray, was he found to be correct?" This was the supererogation of literal matter-of-fact curiosity. Jedediah Buxton's counting the number of words was idle enough; but here was a fellow who wanted some one to count them over again to see if he was correct.

"The force of *dulness* could no farther go!" [W.H. Cf. Dryden's *Lines under the Portrait of Milton:* "The force of Nature could no farther go."]

of genius who finds out a vein of new ore. Originality is the seeing nature differently from others, and yet as it is in itself. It is not singularity or affectation, but the discovery of new and valuable truth. All the world do not see the whole meaning of any object they have been looking at. Habit blinds them to some things: short-sightedness to others. Every mind is not a gauge and measure of truth. Nature has her surface and her dark recesses. She is deep, obscure, and infinite. It is only minds on whom she makes her fullest impressions that can penetrate her shrine or unveil her *Holy of Holies*. It is only those whom she has filled with her spirit that have the boldness or the power to reveal her mysteries to others. But nature has a thousand aspects, and one man can only draw out one of them. Whoever does this, is a man of genius. One displays her force, another her refinement, one her power of harmony, another her suddenness of contrast, one her beauty of form, another her splendour of colour. Each does that for which he is best fitted by his particular genius, that is to say, by some quality of mind into which the quality of the object sinks deepest, where it finds the most cordial welcome, is perceived to its utmost extent, and where again it forces its way out from the fulness with which it has taken possession of the mind of the student. The imagination gives out what it has first absorbed by congeniality of temperament, what it has attracted and moulded into itself by elective affinity, as the loadstone draws and impregnates iron. A little originality is more esteemed and sought for than the greatest acquired talent, because it throws a new light upon things, and is peculiar to the individual. The other is common; and may be had for the asking, to any amount.

The value of any work is to be judged of by the quantity of originality contained in it. A very little of this will go a great way. If Goldsmith had never written any thing but the two or three first chapters of the Vicar of Wakefield, or the character of a Village-Schoolmaster, they would have stamped him a man of genius. The Editors of Encyclopedias are not usually reckoned the first literary characters of the age. The works, of which they have the management, contain a great deal of knowledge, like chests or warehouses, but the goods are not their own. We should as soon think of admiring the shelves of a library; but the shelves of a library are useful and respectable. I was once applied to, in a delicate emergency, to write an article on a difficult subject for an Encyclopedia, and was advised to take time and give it a systematic and scientific form, to avail myself of all the knowledge that was to be obtained on the subject, and arrange it with clearness and method. I made answer that as to the first, I had taken time to do all that I ever pretended to do, as I had thought incessantly on different matters for twenty years of my life;[15] that I had no particular knowledge of the subject in question, and no head for arrange-

[15] Sir Joshua Reynolds being asked how long it had taken him to do a certain picture, made answer, "All his life." [W.H.]

ment; and that the utmost I could do in such a case would be, when a systematic and scientific article was prepared, to write marginal notes upon it, to insert a remark or illustration of my own (not to be found in former Encyclopedias) or to suggest a better definition than had been offered in the text. There are two sorts of writing. The first is compilation; and consists in collecting and stating all that is already known of any question in the best possible manner, for the benefit of the uninformed reader. An author of this class is a very learned amanuensis of other people's thoughts. The second sort proceeds on an entirely different principle. Instead of bringing down the account of knowledge to the point at which it has already arrived, it professes to start from that point on the strength of the writer's individual reflections; and supposing the reader in possession of what is already known, supplies deficiencies, fills up certain blanks, and quits the beaten road in search of new tracts of observation or sources of feeling. It is in vain to object to this last style that it is disjointed, disproportioned, and irregular. It is merely a set of additions and corrections to other men's works, or to the common stock of human knowledge, printed separately. You might as well expect a continued chain of reasoning in the notes to a book. It skips all the trite, intermediate, level common-places of the subject, and only stops at the difficult passages of the human mind, or touches on some striking point that has been overlooked in previous editions. A view of a subject, to be connected and regular, cannot be all new. A writer will always be liable to be charged either with paradox or common-place, either with dulness or affectation. But we have no right to demand from any one more than he pretends to. There is indeed a medium in all things, but to unite opposite excellencies, is a task ordinarily too hard for mortality. He who succeeds in what he aims at, or who takes the lead in any one mode or path of excellence, may think himself very well off. It would not be fair to complain of the style of an Encyclopedia as dull, as wanting volatile salt; nor of the style of an Essay because it is too light and sparkling, because it is not a *caput mortuum.* So it is rather an odd objection to a work that it is made up entirely of "brilliant passages" — at least it is a fault that can be found with few works, and the book might be pardoned for its singularity. The censure might indeed seem like adroit flattery, if it were not passed on an author whom any objection is sufficient to render unpopular and ridiculous. I grant it is best to unite solidity with show, general information with particular ingenuity. This is the pattern of a perfect style: but I myself do not pretend to be a perfect writer. In fine, we do not banish light French wines from our tables, or refuse to taste sparkling Champagne when we can get it, because it has not the body of Old Port. Besides, I do not know that dulness is strength, or that an observation is slight, because it is striking. Mediocrity, insipidity, want of character is the great fault. *Mediocribus esse poetis non Dii, non*

homines, non concessère columnæ.[16] Neither is this privilege allowed
to prose-writers in our time, any more than to poets formerly.

It is not then acuteness of organs or extent of capacity that constitutes rare genius or produces the most exquisite models of art, but
an intense sympathy with some one beauty or distinguishing characteristic in nature. Irritability alone, or the interest taken in certain things,
may supply the place of genius in weak and otherwise ordinary minds.
As there are certain instruments fitted to perform certain kinds of
labour, there are certain minds so framed as to produce certain *chef-
d'œuvres* in art and literature, which is surely the best use they can
be put to. If a man had all sorts of instruments in his shop and wanted
one, he would rather have that one than be supplied with a double set
of all the others. If he had them all twice over, he could only do what
he can do as it is, whereas without that one he perhaps cannot finish
any one work he has in hand. So if a man can do one thing better
than any body else, the value of this one thing is what he must stand
or fall by, and his being able to do a hundred other things merely
as well as any body else, would not alter the sentence or add to his
respectability; on the contrary, his being able to do so many other
things well would probably interfere with and incumber him in the
execution of the only thing that others cannot do as well as he, and
so far be a draw-back and a disadvantage. More people in fact fail
from a multiplicity of talents and pretensions than from an absolute
poverty of resources. I have given instances of this elsewhere. Perhaps Shakespear's tragedies would in some respects have been better,
if he had never written comedies at all; and in that case, his comedies
might well have been spared, though they must have cost us some
regret. Racine, it is said, might have rivalled Moliere in comedy; but
he gave up the cultivation of his comic talents to devote himself wholly
to the tragic Muse. If, as the French tell us, he in consequence attained to the perfection of tragic composition, this was better than
writing comedies as well as Moliere and tragedies as well as Crebillon.
Yet I count those persons fools who think it a pity Hogarth did not
succeed better in serious subjects. The division of labour is an excellent principle in taste as well as in mechanics. Without this, I find
from Adam Smith, we could not have a pin made to the degree of
perfection it is.[17] We do not, on any rational scheme of criticism, inquire into the variety of a man's excellences, or the number of his
works, or his facility of production. Venice Preserved is sufficient for
Otway's fame. I hate all those nonsensical stories about Lope de Vega
and his writing a play in a morning before breakfast. He had time
enough to do it after. If a man leaves behind him any work which is
a model in its kind, we have no right to ask whether he could do any

[16] "Mediocrity in poetry is authorized by neither gods nor men." —
Horace, *Ars Poetica* 372–373.
[17] *Wealth of Nations*, Bk. I, ch. i.

thing else, or how he did it, or how long he was about it. All that talent which is not necessary to the actual quantity of excellence existing in the world, loses its object, is so much waste talent or *talent to let.* I heard a sensible man say he should like to do some one thing better than all the rest of the world, and in every thing else to be like all the rest of the world. Why should a man do more than his part? The rest is vanity and vexation of spirit. We look with jealous and grudging eyes at all those qualifications which are not essential; first, because they are superfluous, and next, because we suspect they will be prejudicial. Why does Mr. Kean play all those harlequin tricks of singing, dancing, fencing, &c.? They say, "It is for his benefit." It is not for his reputation. Garrick indeed shone equally in comedy and tragedy. But he was first, not second-rate in both. There is not a greater impertinence than to ask, if a man is clever out of his profession. I have heard of people trying to cross-examine Mrs. Siddons. I would as soon try to entrap one of the Elgin Marbles into an argument. Good nature and common sense are required from all people: but one proud distinction is enough for any one individual to possess or to aspire to![18]

On Familiar Style

(Essay VIII in the second volume of *Table Talk*, 1822, "On Familiar Style" was not reprinted by Hazlitt.)

It is not easy to write a familiar style. Many people mistake a familiar for a vulgar style, and suppose that to write without affectation is to write at random. On the contrary, there is nothing that requires more precision, and, if I may so say, purity of expression, than the style I am speaking of. It utterly rejects not only all unmeaning pomp, but all low, cant phrases, and loose, unconnected, *slipshod* allusions. It is not to take the first word that offers, but the best word in common use; it is not to throw words together in any combinations we please, but to follow and avail ourselves of the true idiom of the language. To write a genuine familiar or truly English

---

[18] Hazlitt puns on "benefit," a performance from which all proceeds went (in this case) to Edmund Kean (1787–1833).

James Crichton (c.1560–82), Scottish linguist and adventurer; Thomas Otway, *Venice Preserv'd*, 1682.

caput mortuum: "dead head," lifeless sediment.

style, is to write as any one would speak in common conversation, who had a thorough command and choice of words, or who could discourse with ease, force, and perspicuity, setting aside all pedantic and oratorical flourishes. Or to give another illustration, to write naturally is the same thing in regard to common conversation, as to read naturally is in regard to common speech. It does not follow that it is an easy thing to give the true accent and inflection to the words you utter, because you do not attempt to rise above the level of ordinary life and colloquial speaking. You do not assume indeed the solemnity of the pulpit, or the tone of stage-declamation: neither are you at liberty to gabble on at a venture, without emphasis or discretion, or to resort to vulgar dialect or clownish pronunciation. You must steer a middle course. You are tied down to a given and appropriate articulation, which is determined by the habitual associations between sense and sound, and which you can only hit by entering into the author's meaning, as you must find the proper words and style to express yourself by fixing your thoughts on the subject you have to write about. Any one may mouth out a passage with a theatrical cadence, or get upon stilts to tell his thoughts: but to write or speak with propriety and simplicity is a more difficult task. Thus it is easy to affect a pompous style, to use a word twice as big as the thing you want to express: it is not so easy to pitch upon the very word that exactly fits it. Out of eight or ten words equally common, equally intelligible, with nearly equal pretensions, it is a matter of some nicety and discrimination to pick out the very one, the preferableness of which is scarcely perceptible, but decisive. The reason why I object to Dr. Johnson's style is, that there is no discrimination, no selection, no variety in it. He uses none but "tall, opaque words," taken from the "first row of the rubric:"[1] — words with the greatest number of syllables, or Latin phrases with merely English terminations. If a fine style depended on this sort of arbitrary pretension, it would be fair to judge of an author's elegance by the measurement of his words, and the substitution of foreign circumlocutions (with no precise associations) for the mother-tongue.[2] How simple is it to be dignified without ease, to be pompous without meaning! Surely, it is but a mechanical rule for avoiding what is low to be always pedantic and affected. It is clear you cannot use a vulgar English word, if you never use a common English word at all. A fine tact is shewn in adhering to those which are perfectly common, and yet never falling into any expressions which are debased by disgusting circumstances, or which owe their signification and point to technical or professional allusions. A truly

[1] Cf. Sterne, *Tristram Shandy* III.xx; *Hamlet* II.ii.438 (variant).
[2] I have heard of such a thing as an author, who makes it a rule never to admit a monosyllable into his vapid verse. Yet the charm and sweetness of Marlow's lines depended often on their being made up almost entirely of monosyllables. [W.H. Christopher Marlowe (1564–93), the dramatist.]

natural or familiar style can never be quaint or vulgar, for this reason, that it is of universal force and applicability, and that quaintness and vulgarity arise out of the immediate connection of certain words with coarse and disagreeable, or with confined ideas. The last form what we understand by *cant* or *slang* phrases. — To give an example of what is not very clear in the general statement. I should say that the phrase *To cut with a knife*, or *To cut a piece of wood*, is perfectly free from vulgarity, because it is perfectly common: but to *cut an acquaintance* is not quite unexceptionable, because it is not perfectly common or intelligible, and has hardly yet escaped out of the limits of slang phraseology. I should hardly therefore use the word in this sense without putting it in italics as a license of expression, to be received *cum grano salis*. All provincial or bye-phrases come under the same mark of reprobation — all such as the writer transfers to the page from his fire-side or a particular *coterie*, or that he invents for his own sole use and convenience. I conceive that words are like money, not the worse for being common, but that it is the stamp of custom alone that gives them circulation or value. I am fastidious in this respect, and would almost as soon coin the currency of the realm as counterfeit the King's English. I never invented or gave a new and unauthorised meaning to any word but one single one (the term *impersonal* applied to feelings) and that was in an abstruse metaphysical discussion to express a very difficult distinction.[3] I have been (I know) loudly accused of revelling in vulgarisms and broken English. I cannot speak to that point: but so far I plead guilty to the determined use of acknowledged idioms and common elliptical expressions. I am not sure that the critics in question know the one from the other, that is, can distinguish any medium between formal pedantry and the most barbarous solecism. As an author, I endeavour to employ plain words and popular modes of construction, as were I a chapman and dealer, I should common weights and measures.

The proper force of words lies not in the words themselves, but in their application. A word may be a fine-sounding word, of an unusual length, and very imposing from its learning and novelty, and yet in the connection in which it is introduced, may be quite pointless and irrelevant. It is not pomp or pretension, but the adaptation of the expression to the idea that clenches a writer's meaning: — as it is not the size or glossiness of the materials, but their being fitted each to its place, that gives strength to the arch; or as the pegs and nails are as necessary to the support of the building as the larger timbers, and more so than the mere shewy, unsubstantial ornaments. I hate any thing that occupies more space than it is worth. I hate to see a load of band-boxes go along the street, and I hate to see a parcel of big words without any thing in them. A person who does not

[3] In *An Essay on the Principles of Human Action:* "a perfectly disinterested, or if I may so say *impersonal* feeling".

deliberately dispose of all his thoughts alike in cumbrous draperies and
flimsy disguises, may strike out twenty varieties of familiar every-day
language, each coming somewhat nearer to the feeling he wants to
convey, and at last not hit upon that particular and only one, which
may be said to be identical with the exact impression in his mind.
This would seem to shew that Mr. Cobbett is hardly right in saying
that the first word that occurs is always the best.[4] It may be a very
good one; and yet a better may present itself on reflection or from
time to time. It should be suggested naturally, however, and spontaneously, from a fresh and lively conception of the subject. We
seldom succeed by trying at improvement, or by merely substituting
one word for another that we are not satisfied with, as we cannot
recollect the name of a place or person by merely plaguing ourselves
about it. We wander farther from the point by persisting in a wrong
scent; but it starts up accidentally in the memory when we least expected it, by touching some link in the chain of previous association.

There are those who hoard up and make a cautious display of
nothing but rich and rare phraseology; — ancient medals, obscure
coins, and Spanish pieces of eight. They are very curious to inspect;
but I myself would neither offer nor take them in the course of exchange. A sprinkling of archaisms is not amiss; but a tissue of obsolete expressions is more fit *for keep than wear.* I do not say I would
not use any phrase that had been brought into fashion before the
middle or the end of the last century; but I should be shy of using
any that had not been employed by any approved author during the
whole of that time. Words, like clothes, get old-fashioned, or mean
and ridiculous, when they have been for some time laid aside. Mr.
Lamb is the only imitator of old English style I can read with pleasure;
and he is so thoroughly imbued with the spirit of his authors, that the
idea of imitation is almost done away. There is an inward unction,
a marrowy vein both in the thought and feeling, an intuition, deep
and lively, of his subject, that carries off any quaintness or awkwardness arising from an antiquated style and dress. The matter is completely his own, though the manner is assumed. Perhaps his ideas
are altogether so marked and individual, as to require their point and
pungency to be neutralised by the affectation of a singular but traditional form of conveyance. Tricked out in the prevailing costume, they
would probably seem more startling and out of the way. The old
English authors, Burton, Fuller, Coryate, Sir Thomas Brown, are a
kind of mediators between us and the more eccentric and whimsical
modern, reconciling us to his peculiarities. I do not however know how
far this is the case or not, till he condescends to write like one of
us. I must confess that what I like best of his papers under the signature of Elia (still I do not presume, amidst such excellence, to de-

---

[4] In *A Grammar of the English Language,* 1818, Letter xxiii.

cide what is most excellent) is the account of *Mrs. Battle's Opinions on Whist,* which is also the most free from obsolete allusions and turns of expression —

"A well of native English undefiled."[5]

To those acquainted with his admired prototypes, these Essays of the ingenious and highly gifted author have the same sort of charm and relish, that Erasmus's Colloquies or a fine piece of modern Latin have to the classical scholar. Certainly, I do not know any borrowed pencil that has more power or felicity of execution than the one of which I have here been speaking.

It is as easy to write a gaudy style without ideas, as it is to spread a pallet of shewy colours, or to smear in a flaunting transparency. "What do you read?" — "Words, words, words." — "What is the matter?" — *"Nothing,"* it might be answered.[6] The florid style is the reverse of the familiar. The last is employed as an unvarnished medium to convey ideas; the first is resorted to as a spangled veil to conceal the want of them. When there is nothing to be set down but words, it costs little to have them fine. Look through the dictionary, and cull out a *florilegium,* rival the *tulippomania. Rouge* high enough, and never mind the natural complexion. The vulgar, who are not in the secret, will admire the look of preternatural health and vigour; and the fashionable, who regard only appearances, will be delighted with the imposition. Keep to your sounding generalities, your tinkling phrases, and all will be well. Swell out an unmeaning truism to a perfect tympany of style. A thought, a distinction is the rock on which all this brittle cargo of verbiage splits at once. Such writers have merely *verbal* imaginations, that retain nothing but words. Or their puny thoughts have dragon-wings, all green and gold. They soar far above the vulgar failing of the *Sermo humi obrepens* —[7] their most ordinary speech is never short of an hyperbole, splendid, imposing, vague, incomprehensible, magniloquent, a cento of sounding commonplaces. If some of us, whose "ambition is more lowly," pry a little too narrowly into nooks and corners to pick up a number of "unconsidered trifles,"[8] they never once direct their eyes or lift their hands to seize on any but the most gorgeous, tarnished, thread-bare patchwork set of phrases, the left-off finery of poetic extravagance, transmitted down through successive generations of barren pretenders. If they criticise actors and actresses, a huddled phantasmagoria of feathers, spangles, floods of light, and oceans of sound float before their morbid sense, which they paint in the style of Ancient Pistol. Not a glimpse can you get of the merits or defects of the performers:

[5] Cf. *The Faerie Queene* IV.ii.32.
[6] Cf. *Hamlet* II.ii.193–195.
[7] "Speech creeping on the ground" — cf. Horace, *Epistles* II.i.250–251.
[8] Cf. *Julius Caesar* II.i.22; *The Winter's Tale* IV.iii.26.

they are hidden in a profusion of barbarous epithets and wilful rhodomontade. Our hypercritics are not thinking of these little fantoccini
beings —

"That strut and fret their hour upon the stage" —[9]

but of tall phantoms of words, abstractions, *genera* and *species,* sweeping clauses, periods that unite the Poles, forced alliterations, astounding antitheses —

"And on their pens *Fustian* sits plumed."[10]

If they describe kings and queens, it is an Eastern pageant. The
Coronation at either House is nothing to it. We get at four repeated
images — a curtain, a throne, a sceptre, and a foot-stool. These are
with them the wardrobe of a lofty imagination; and they turn their
servile strains to servile uses. Do we read a description of pictures?
It is not a reflection of tones and hues which "nature's own sweet
and cunning hand laid on,"[11] but piles of precious stones, rubies,
pearls, emeralds, Golconda's mines, and all the blazonry of art. Such
persons are in fact besotted with words, and their brains are turned
with the glittering, but empty and sterile phantoms of things. Personifications, capital letters, seas of sunbeams, visions of glory, shining
inscriptions, the figures of a transparency, Britannia with her shield, or
Hope leaning on an anchor, make up their stock in trade. They may
be considered as *hieroglyphical* writers. Images stand out in their
minds isolated and important merely in themselves, without any
ground-work of feeling — there is no context in their imaginations.
Words affect them in the same way, by the mere sound, that is, by
their possible, not by their actual application to the subject in hand.
They are fascinated by first appearances, and have no sense of consequences. Nothing more is meant by them than meets the ear: they
understand or feel nothing more than meets their eye. The web and
texture of the universe, and of the heart of man, is a mystery to them:
they have no faculty that strikes a chord in unison with it. They cannot get beyond the daubings of fancy, the varnish of sentiment. Objects are not linked to feelings, words to things, but images revolve
in splendid mockery, words represent themselves in their strange
rhapsodies. The categories of such a mind are pride and ignorance
— pride in outside show, to which they sacrifice every thing, and
ignorance of the true worth and hidden structure both of words and
things. With a sovereign contempt for what is familiar and natural,
they are the slaves of vulgar affectation — of a routine of high-flown
phrases. Scorning to imitate realities, they are unable to invent any
thing, to strike out one original idea. They are not copyists of nature,

[9] Cf. *Macbeth* V.v.25.
[10] Cf. *Paradise Lost* IV.988–989: "and on his crest Sat Horror plumed."
[11] *Twelfth Night* I.v.258.

it is true: but they are the poorest of all plagiarists, the plagiarists of words. All is far-fetched, dear-bought, artificial, oriental in subject and allusion: all is mechanical, conventional, vapid, formal, pedantic in style and execution. They startle and confound the understanding of the reader, by the remoteness and obscurity of their illustrations: they soothe the ear by the monotony of the same everlasting round of circuitous metaphors. They are the *mock-school* in poetry and prose. They flounder about between fustian in expression, and bathos in sentiment. They tantalise the fancy, but never reach the head nor touch the heart. Their Temple of Fame is like a shadowy structure raised by Dulness to Vanity, or like Cowper's description of the Empress of Russia's palace of ice, "as worthless as in shew 'twas glittering" —

"It smiled, and it was cold!"[12]

On Gusto

‖ After its appearance in the *Examiner* for May 26, 1816, as No. 40 in the Round Table series, Hazlitt admitted "On *Gusto*" as No. 29 in the more select company of *The Round Table* in two volumes, 1817, whence it is here reprinted. ‖

Gusto in art is power or passion defining any object. — It is not so difficult to explain this term in what relates to expression (of which it may be said to be the highest degree) as in what relates to things without expression, to the natural appearances of objects, as mere colour or form. In one sense, however, there is hardly any object entirely devoid of expression, without some character of power belonging to it, some precise association with pleasure or pain: and it is in giving this truth of character from the truth of feeling, whether in the highest or the lowest degree, but always in the highest degree of which the subject is capable, that gusto consists.

There is a gusto in the colouring of Titian. Not only do his heads seem to think — his bodies seem to feel. This is what the Italians mean by the *morbidezza* of his flesh-colour. It seems sensitive and

[12] Cf. Cowper, *The Task* V.173–176.

Thomas Coryate, traveler, author of *Coryats Crudities*, 1611; Pistol: braggart companion of Falstaff.

florilegium: catalogue of flowers; *tulippomania:* rage for growing tulips.

alive all over; not merely to have the look and texture of flesh, but the feeling in itself. For example, the limbs of his female figures have a luxurious softness and delicacy, which appears conscious of the pleasure of the beholder. As the objects themselves in nature would produce an impression on the sense, distinct from every other object, and having something divine in it, which the heart owns and the imagination consecrates, the objects in the picture preserve the same impression, absolute, unimpaired, stamped with all the truth of passion, the pride of the eye, and the charm of beauty. Rubens makes his flesh-colour like flowers; Albano's is like ivory; Titian's is like flesh, and like nothing else. It is as different from that of other painters, as the skin is from a piece of white or red drapery thrown over it. The blood circulates here and there, the blue veins just appear, the rest is distinguished throughout only by that sort of tingling sensation to the eye, which the body feels within itself. This is gusto. — Vandyke's flesh-colour, though it has great truth and purity, wants gusto. It has not the internal character, the living principle in it. It is a smooth surface, not a warm, moving mass. It is painted without passion, with indifference. The hand only has been concerned. The impression slides off from the eye, and does not, like the tones of Titian's pencil, leave a sting behind it in the mind of the spectator. The eye does not acquire a taste or appetite for what it sees. In a word, gusto in painting is where the impression made on one sense excites by affinity those of another.

Michael Angelo's forms are full of gusto. They every where obtrude the sense of power upon the eye. His limbs convey an idea of muscular strength, of moral grandeur, and even of intellectual dignity: they are firm, commanding, broad, and massy, capable of executing with ease the determined purposes of the will. His faces have no other expression than his figures, conscious power and capacity. They appear only to think what they shall do, and to know that they can do it. This is what is meant by saying that his style is hard and masculine. It is the reverse of Correggio's, which is effeminate. That is, the gusto of Michael Angelo consists in expressing energy of will without proportionable sensibility, Correggio's in expressing exquisite sensibility without energy of will. In Correggio's faces as well as figures we see neither bones nor muscles, but then what a soul is there, full of sweetness and of grace — pure, playful, soft, angelical! There is sentiment enough in a hand painted by Correggio to set up a school of history painters. Whenever we look at the hands of Correggio's women or of Raphael's, we always wish to touch them.

Again, Titian's landscapes have a prodigious gusto, both in the colouring and forms. We shall never forget one that we saw many years ago in the Orleans Gallery of Acteon hunting. It had a brown, mellow, autumnal look. The sky was of the colour of stone. The winds seemed to sing through the rustling branches of the trees, and already you might hear the twanging of bows resound through the tangled mazes of the wood. Mr West, we understand, has this landscape. He will know if this description of it is just. The landscape back-ground of the St Peter Martyr is another well known instance of the power of this great painter to give a romantic interest and an appropriate character to the objects of his pencil, where every circumstance adds to the effect of the scene, — the bold trunks of the tall forest trees, the trailing ground plants, with that cold convent spire rising in the distance, amidst the blue sapphire mountains and the golden sky.

Rubens has a great deal of gusto in his Fauns and Satyrs, and in all that expresses motion, but in nothing else. Rembrandt has it in every thing; every thing in his pictures has a tangible character. If he puts a diamond in the ear of a Burgomaster's wife, it is of the first water; and his furs and stuffs are proof against a Russian winter. Raphael's gusto was only in expression; he had no idea of the character of any thing but the human form. The dryness and poverty of his style in other respects is a phenomenon in the art. His trees are like sprigs of grass stuck in a book of botanical specimens. Was it that Raphael never had time to go beyond the walls of Rome? That he was always in the streets, at church, or in the bath? He was not one of the Society of Arcadians.[1]

Claude's landscapes, perfect as they are, want gusto. This is not easy to explain. They are perfect abstractions of the visible images of things; they speak the visible language of nature truly. They resemble a mirror or a microscope. To the eye only they are more perfect than any other landscapes that ever were or will be painted; they give more of nature, as cognizable by one sense alone; but they lay an equal stress on all visible impressions; they do not interpret one sense by another; they do not distinguish the character of different objects as we are taught, and can only be taught, to distinguish them by their effect on the different senses. That is, his eye wanted imagination: it did not strongly sympathize with his other faculties. He saw the atmosphere, but he did not feel it. He painted the trunk of a tree or a rock in the foreground as smooth — with as complete an abstraction of the gross, tangible impression, as any other part of the picture; his trees are perfectly beautiful, but quite immoveable; they have a look of enchantment. In short, his landscapes are unequalled imitations of nature, released from its subjection to the elements, — as if all objects

---

[1] Raphael not only could not paint a landscape; he could not paint people in a landscape. He could not have painted the heads or the figures, or even the dresses of the St Peter Martyr. His figures have always an *in-door* look, that is, a set, determined, voluntary, dramatic character, arising from their own passions, or a watchfulness of those of others, and want that wild uncertainty of expression, which is connected with the accidents of nature and the changes of the elements. He has nothing *romantic* about him. [W.H.]

were become a delightful fairy vision, and the eye had rarefied and refined away the other senses.

The gusto in the Greek statues is of a very singular kind. The sense of perfect form nearly occupies the whole mind, and hardly suffers it to dwell on any other feeling. It seems enough for them *to be,* without acting or suffering. Their forms are ideal, spiritual. Their beauty is power. By their beauty they are raised above the frailties of pain or passion; by their beauty they are deified.

The infinite quantity of dramatic invention in Shakspeare takes from his gusto. The power he delights to shew is not intense, but discursive. He never insists on any thing as much as he might, except a quibble. Milton has great gusto. He repeats his blow twice; grapples with and exhausts his subject. His imagination has a double relish of its objects, an inveterate attachment to the things he describes, and to the words describing them.

> ———————— "Or where Chineses drive
> With sails and wind their *cany* waggons *light.*"
> ❖ ❖ ❖ ❖ ❖ ❖ ❖ ❖ ❖ ❖ ❖
> "Wild above rule or art, *enormous* bliss."[2]

There is a gusto in Pope's compliments, in Dryden's satires, and Prior's tales; and among prose-writers, Boccacio and Rabelais had the most of it. We will only mention one other work which appears to us to be full of gusto, and that is the *Beggar's Opera.*[3] If it is not, we are altogether mistaken in our notions on this delicate subject.

W. H.

On Poetry in General

❡ In January and February of 1818 Hazlitt gave a series of lectures on English poets at the Surrey Institution in London. His first lecture, "On Poetry in General," formed the first chapter when the series was published in May. To correct the common misconception that Hazlitt views poetry as passionate self-expression rather than as a passionate grasp of objective reality, W. J. Bate points out in *Criticism: The Major Texts* (New York,

---

[2] Cf. *Paradise Lost* III.438–439, V.297.
[3] by John Gay, 1728.

Francesco Albani (or Albano, 1578–1660), studied with Guido Reni under the Carracci. Orleans Gallery: an exhibition of Italian masters in 1798–99. Benjamin West, president of the Royal Academy, 1792–1820. Hazlitt saw Titian's *St. Peter Martyr* (since destroyed by fire) at the Louvre in 1802.

1952), that Hazlitt supports "the conception of art as intense naturalistic expression — that is, the sympathetic and objective expression of the particular and concrete." The text here is taken from *Lectures on the English Poets,* 1818, which differs slightly in phrasing from the Second Edition of 1819.]⟩

The best general notion which I can give of poetry is, that it is the natural impression of any object or circumstance, by its vividness exciting an involuntary movement of imagination and passion, and producing, by sympathy, a certain modulation of the voice, or sounds, expressing it.

In treating of poetry, I shall speak first of the subject-matter of it, next of the forms of expression to which it gives birth, and afterwards of its connection with harmony of sound.

Poetry is the language of the imagination and the passions. It relates to whatever gives immediate pleasure or pain to the human mind. It comes home to the bosoms and businesses of men; for nothing but what so comes home to them in the most general and intelligible shape, can be a subject for poetry. Poetry is the universal language which the heart holds with nature and itself. He who has a contempt for poetry, cannot have much respect for himself, or for any thing else. It is not a mere frivolous accomplishment, (as some persons have been led to imagine) the trifling amusement of a few idle readers or leisure hours — it has been the study and delight of mankind in all ages. Many people suppose that poetry is something to be found only in books, contained in lines of ten syllables, with like endings: but wherever there is a sense of beauty, or power, or harmony, as in the motion of a wave of the sea, in the growth of a flower that "spreads its sweet leaves to the air, and dedicates its beauty to the sun,"[1] — *there* is poetry, in its birth. If history is a grave study, poetry may be said to be a graver: its materials lie deeper, and are spread wider. History treats, for the most part, of the cumbrous and unwieldy masses of things, the empty cases in which the affairs of the world are packed, under the heads of intrigue or war, in different states, and from century to century: but there is no thought or feeling that can have entered into the mind of man, which he would be eager to communicate to others, or which they would listen to with delight, that is not a fit subject for poetry. It is not a branch of authorship: it is "the stuff of which our life is made." The rest is "mere oblivion," a dead letter: for all that is worth remembering in life, is the poetry of it. Fear is poetry, hope is poetry, love is poetry, hatred is poetry, contempt, jealousy, remorse, admiration, wonder, pity, despair, or madness, are all poetry. Poetry is that fine particle within us, that expands, rarefies, refines, raises our whole being: without it "man's life is poor as beast's." Man is a poetical animal: and those of us who

[1] Cf. *Romeo and Juliet* I.i.159–160.

do not study the principles of poetry, act upon them all our lives, like Moliere's *Bourgeois Gentilhomme*, who had always spoken prose without knowing it.[2] The child is a poet in fact, when he first plays at hide-and-seek, or repeats the story of Jack the Giant-killer; the shepherd-boy is a poet, when he first crowns his mistress with a garland of flowers; the countryman, when he stops to look at the rainbow; the city-apprentice, when he gazes after the Lord-Mayor's show; the miser, when he hugs his gold; the courtier, who builds his hopes upon a smile; the savage, who paints his idol with blood; the slave, who worships a tyrant, or the tyrant, who fancies himself a god; — the vain, the ambitious, the proud, the choleric man, the hero and the coward, the beggar and the king, the rich and the poor, the young and the old, all live in a world of their own making; and the poet does no more than describe what all the others think and act. If his art is folly and madness, it is folly and madness at second hand. "There is warrant for it." Poets alone have not "such seething brains, such shaping fantasies, that apprehend more than cooler reason" can.

"The lunatic, the lover, and the poet
Are of imagination all compact.
One sees more devils than vast hell can hold;
The madman. While the lover, all as frantic,
Sees Helen's beauty in a brow of Egypt.
The poet's eye in a fine frenzy rolling,
Doth glance from heav'n to earth, from earth to heav'n;
And as imagination bodies forth
The forms of things unknown, the poet's pen
Turns them to shape, and gives to airy nothing
A local habitation and a name.
Such tricks hath strong imagination."[3]

If poetry is a dream, the business of life is much the same. If it is a fiction, made up of what we wish things to be, and fancy that they are, because we wish them so, there is no other nor better reality. Ariosto has described the loves of Angelica and Medoro: but was not Medoro, who carved the name of his mistress on the barks of trees, as much enamoured of her charms as he? Homer has celebrated the anger of Achilles: but was not the hero as mad as the poet? Plato banished the poets from his Commonwealth, lest their descriptions of the natural man should spoil his mathematical man, who was to be without passions and affections, who was neither to laugh nor weep, to feel sorrow nor anger, to be cast down nor elated by any thing. This was a chimera, however, which never existed but in the brain of the inventor; and Homer's poetical world has outlived Plato's philosophical Republic.

[2] Cf. *The Tempest* IV.i.156–157; *As You Like It* II.vii.165; *King Lear* II.iv.270; *Le Bourgeois Gentilhomme* (1670) II.vi.
[3] Cf. *Macbeth* II.iii.151; *A Midsummer Night's Dream* V.i.4–18.

Poetry then is an imitation of nature, but the imagination and the passions are a part of man's nature. We shape things according to our wishes and fancies, without poetry; but poetry is the most perfect language that can be found for those creations of the mind "which ecstacy is very cunning in."[4] Neither a mere description of natural objects, nor a mere delineation of natural feelings, however distinct or forcible, constitutes the ultimate end and aim of poetry, without the heightenings of the imagination. The light of poetry is not only a direct but also a reflected light, that while it shews us the object, throws a sparkling radiance on all around it: the flame of the passions, communicated to the imagination, reveals to us, as with a flash of lightning, the inmost recesses of thought, and penetrates our whole being. Poetry represents forms chiefly as they suggest other forms; feelings, as they suggest forms or other feelings. Poetry puts a spirit of life and motion into the universe. It describes the flowing, not the fixed. It does not define the limits of sense, or analyze the distinctions of the understanding, but signifies the excess of the imagination beyond the actual or ordinary impression of any object or feeling. The poetical impression of any object is that uneasy, exquisite sense of beauty or power that cannot be contained within itself; that is impatient of all limit; that (as flame bends to flame) strives to link itself to some other image of kindred beauty or grandeur; to enshrine itself, as it were, in the highest forms of fancy, and to relieve the aching sense of pleasure by expressing it in the boldest manner, and by the most striking examples of the same quality in other instances. Poetry, according to Lord Bacon, for this reason, "has something divine in it, because it raises the mind and hurries it into sublimity, by conforming the shows of things to the desires of the soul, instead of subjecting the soul to external things, as reason and history do."[5] It is strictly the language of the imagination; and the imagination is that faculty which represents objects, not as they are in themselves, but as they are moulded by other thoughts and feelings, into an infinite variety of shapes and combinations of power. This language is not the less true to nature, because it is false in point of fact; but so much the more true and natural, if it conveys the impression which the object under the influence of passion makes on the mind. Let an object, for instance, be presented to the senses in a state of agitation or fear — and the imagination will distort or magnify the object, and convert it into the likeness of whatever is most proper to encourage the fear. "Our eyes are made the fools" of our other faculties. This is the universal law of the imagination,

"That if it would but apprehend some joy,
It comprehends some bringer of that joy:

[4] *Hamlet* III.iv.138–139.
[5] Cf. *The Advancement of Learning* II.xiii.2.

> Or in the night imagining some fear,
> How easy is each bush suppos'd a bear!"

When Iachimo says of Imogen,

> "— The flame o' th' taper
> Bows toward her, and would under-peep her lids
> To see the enclosed lights" —[6]

this passionate interpretation of the motion of the flame to accord with the speaker's own feelings, is true poetry. The lover, equally with the poet, speaks of the auburn tresses of his mistress as locks of shining gold, because the least tinge of yellow in the hair has, from novelty and a sense of personal beauty, a more lustrous effect to the imagination than the purest gold. We compare a man of gigantic stature to a tower: not that he is any thing like so large, but because the excess of his size beyond what we are accustomed to expect, or the usual size of things of the same class, produces by contrast a greater feeling of magnitude and ponderous strength than another object of ten times the same dimensions. The intensity of the feeling makes up for the disproportion of the objects. Things are equal in imagination, which have the power of affecting the mind with an equal degree of terror, admiration, delight, or love. When Lear calls upon the heavens to avenge his cause, "for they are old like him," there is nothing extravagant or impious in this sublime identification of his age with theirs; for there is no other image which could do justice to the agonising sense of his wrongs and his despair!

Poetry is the high-wrought enthusiasm of fancy and feeling. As in describing natural objects, it impregnates sensible impressions with the forms of fancy, so it describes the feelings of pleasure or pain, by blending them with the strongest movements of passion, and the most striking forms of nature.

Tragic poetry, which is the most impassioned species of it, strives to carry on the feeling to the utmost point of sublimity or pathos, by all the force of comparison or contrast; loses the sense of present suffering in the imaginary exaggeration of it; exhausts the terror or pity by an unlimited indulgence of it; grapples with impossibilities in its desperate impatience of restraint; throws us back upon the past, forward into the future; brings every moment of our being or object of nature in startling review before us; and in the rapid whirl of events, lifts us from the depths of woe to the highest contemplations on human life. When Lear says of Edgar, "Nothing but his unkind daughters could have brought him to this;" what a bewildered amazement, what a wrench of the imagination, that cannot be brought to conceive of any

---

[6] Cf. *Macbeth* II.i.44; *A Midsummer Night's Dream* V.i.19–22; *Cymbeline* II.ii.19–21.

other cause of misery than that which has bowed it down, and absorbs all other sorrow in its own! His sorrow, like a flood, supplies the sources of all other sorrow. Again, when he exclaims in the mad scene, "The little dogs and all, Tray, Blanche, and Sweetheart, see, they bark at me!" it is imagination lending occasion to passion to make every creature in league against him, conjuring up ingratitude and insult in their least looked-for and most galling shapes, searching every thread and fibre of his heart, and finding out the last remaining image of respect or attachment in the bottom of his breast, only to torture and kill it! In like manner, the "So I am" of Cordelia, gushes from her heart like a torrent of tears, relieving it of a weight of love and of supposed ingratitude, which had pressed upon it for years.[7] What a fine return of the passion upon itself is that in Othello — with what a parting agony of mingled regret and despair he clings to the last traces of departed happiness — when he exclaims,

> —— "Oh now, for ever
> Farewel the tranquil mind. Farewel content;
> Farewel the plumed troops and the big war,
> That make ambition virtue! Oh farewel!
> Farewel the neighing steed, and the shrill trump,
> The spirit-stirring drum, th' ear-piercing fife,
> The royal banner, and all quality,
> Pride, pomp, and circumstance of glorious war:
> And O you mortal engines, whose rude throats
> Th' immortal Jove's dread clamours counterfeit,
> Farewel! Othello's occupation's gone!"

How his passion lashes itself up and swells and rages like a tide in its sounding course, when in answer to the doubts expressed of his returning love, he says,

> "Never, Iago. Like to the Pontic sea,
> Whose icy current and compulsive course
> Ne'er feels retiring ebb, but keeps due on
> To the Propontic and the Hellespont:
> Even so my bloody thoughts, with violent pace,
> Shall ne'er look back, ne'er ebb to humble love,
> Till that a capable and wide revenge
> Swallow them up." —

The climax of his expostulation afterwards with Desdemona is at that line,

> "But there where I had garner'd up my heart,
> To be discarded thence!" —[8]

This is like that fine stroke of pathos in the Paradise Lost, where Milton makes Adam say to Eve,

[7] Cf. *King Lear* II.iv.192–195; III.iv.69–70; III.vi.65–66; IV.vii.70.
[8] *Othello* III.iii.347–357, 453–460; IV.ii.57–58.

> "Should God create another Eve, and I
> Another rib afford, yet loss of thee
> Would never from my heart!" —9

One mode in which the dramatic exhibition of passion excites our sympathy without raising our disgust is, that in proportion as it sharpens the edge of calamity and disappointment, it strengthens the desire of good. It enhances our consciousness of the blessing, by making us sensible of the magnitude of the loss. The storm of passion lays bare and shews us the rich depths of the human soul: the whole of our existence, the sum total of our passions and pursuits, of that which we desire and that which we dread, is brought before us by contrast; the action and re-action are equal; the keenness of immediate suffering only gives us a more intense aspiration after, and a more intimate participation with the antagonist world of good; makes us drink deeper of the cup of human life; tugs at the heart-strings; loosens the pressure about them; and calls the springs of thought and feeling into play with tenfold force.

Impassioned poetry is an emanation of the moral and intellectual part of our nature, as well as of the sensitive — of the desire to know, the will to act, and the power to feel; and ought to appeal to these different parts of our constitution, in order to be perfect. The domestic or prose tragedy, which is thought to be the most natural, is in this sense the least so, because it appeals almost exclusively to one of these faculties, our sensibility. The tragedies of Moore and Lillo, for this reason, however affecting at the time, oppress and lie like a dead weight upon the mind, a load of misery which it is unable to throw off: the tragedy of Shakspeare, which is true poetry, stirs our inmost affections; abstracts evil from itself by combining it with all the forms of imagination, and with the deepest workings of the heart, and rouses the whole man within us.

The pleasure, however, derived from tragic poetry, is not any thing peculiar to it as poetry, as a fictitious and fanciful thing. It is not an anomaly of the imagination. It has its source and ground-work in the common love of strong excitement. As Mr. Burke observes, people flock to see a tragedy; but if there were a public execution in the next street, the theatre would very soon be empty.10 It is not then the difference between fiction and reality that solves the difficulty. Children are satisfied with the stories of ghosts and witches in plain prose: nor do the hawkers of full, true, and particular accounts of murders and executions about the streets, find it necessary to have them turned into penny ballads, before they can dispose of these interesting and authentic documents. The grave politician drives a thriving trade of

9 *Paradise Lost* IX.911–913.
10 *A Philosophical Enquiry into the Origin of Our Ideas of the Sublime and Beautiful* (1757) I.xv.

abuse and calumnies poured out against those whom he makes his enemies for no other end than that he may live by them. The popular preacher makes less frequent mention of heaven than of hell. Oaths and nicknames are only a more vulgar sort of poetry or rhetoric. We are as fond of indulging our violent passions as of reading a description of those of others. We are as prone to make a torment of our fears, as to luxuriate in our hopes of good. If it be asked, Why we do so? the best answer will be, because we cannot help it. The sense of power is as strong a principle in the mind as the love of pleasure. The objects of terror and pity exercise the same despotic control over it as those of love or beauty. It is as natural to hate as to love, to despise as to admire, to express our hatred or contempt, as our love or admiration.

> "Masterless passion sways us to the mood
> Of what it likes or loathes."[11]

Not that we like what we loathe; but we like to indulge our hatred and scorn of it; to dwell upon it, to exasperate our idea of it by every refinement of ingenuity and extravagance of illustration; to make it a bugbear to ourselves, to point it out to others in all the splendour of deformity, to embody it to the senses, to stigmatise it in words, to grapple with it in thought, in action, to sharpen our intellect, to arm our will against it, to know the worst we have to contend with, and to contend with it to the utmost. Poetry is only the highest eloquence of passion, the most vivid form of expression that can be given to our conception of any thing, whether pleasurable or painful, mean or dignified, delightful or distressing. It is the perfect coincidence of the image and the words with the feeling we have, and of which we cannot get rid in any other way, that gives an instant "satisfaction to the thought." This is equally the origin of wit and fancy, of comedy and tragedy, of the sublime and pathetic. When Pope says of the Lord Mayor's shew, —

> "Now night descending, the proud scene is o'er,
> But lives in Settle's numbers one day more!"

— when Collins makes Danger, "with limbs of giant mould,"

> — — "Throw him on the steep
> Of some loose hanging rock asleep:"

when Lear calls out in extreme anguish,

> "Ingratitude, thou marble-hearted fiend,
> How much more hideous shew'st in a child
> Than the sea-monster!"[12]

— the passion of contempt in the one case, of sublimity in the other,

---

[11] Cf. *The Merchant of Venice* IV.i.51–52.
[12] Cf. *Othello* III.iii.97; *The Dunciad* I:89–90; William Collins, *Ode to Fear* 10, 14–15; *King Lear* I.iv.281–283.

and of indignation in the last, is perfectly satisfied. We see the thing ourselves, and show it to others as we feel it to exist, and as, in spite of ourselves, we are compelled to think of it. The imagination, by embodying them and turning them to shape, gives a kind of relief to the indistinct and importunate cravings of the will. — We do not wish the thing to be so; but we wish it to appear what it is. For knowledge is conscious power; and the mind is no longer, in this case, the dupe, though it may be the victim of vice or folly.

Poetry is in all its shapes the language of the imagination and the passions, of fancy and will. Nothing, therefore, can be more absurd than the outcry which has been sometimes raised by frigid and pedantic critics, for reducing the language of poetry to the standard of common sense and reason: for the end and use of poetry, "both at the first and now, was and is to hold the mirror up to nature,"[13] seen through the medium of passion and imagination, not divested of that medium by means of literal truth or abstract reason. The painter of history might as well be required to represent the face of a person who has just trod upon a serpent with the still-life expression of a common portrait, as the poet to describe the most striking and vivid impressions which things can be supposed to make upon the mind, in the language of common conversation. Let who will strip nature of the colours and the shapes of fancy, the poet is not bound to do so: the impressions of common sense and strong imagination, that is, of passion and indifference, cannot be the same, and they must have a separate language to do justice to either. Objects must strike differently upon the mind, independently of what they are in themselves, as long as we have a different interest in them, as we see them in a different point of view, nearer or at a greater distance (morally or physically speaking) from novelty, from old acquaintance, from our ignorance of them, from our fear of their consequences, from contrast, from unexpected likeness. We can no more take away the faculty of the imagination, than we can see all objects without light or shade. Some things must dazzle us by their preternatural light; others must hold us in suspense, and tempt our curiosity to explore their obscurity. Those who would dispel these various illusions, to give us their drab-coloured creation in their stead, are not very wise. Let the naturalist, if he will, catch the glow-worm, carry it home with him in a box, and find it next morning nothing but a little grey worm; let the poet or the lover of poetry visit it at evening, when beneath the scented hawthorn and the crescent moon it has built itself a palace of emerald light. This is also one part of nature, one appearance which the glow-worm presents, and that not the least interesting; so poetry is one part of the history of the human mind, though it is neither science nor philosophy. It cannot be concealed, however, that the progress of

[13] *Hamlet* III.ii.25–26.

knowledge and refinement has a tendency to circumscribe the limits
of the imagination, and to clip the wings of poetry. The province of
the imagination is principally visionary, the unknown and undefined:
the understanding restores things to their natural boundaries, and
strips them of their fanciful pretensions. Hence the history of religious and poetical enthusiasm is much the same; and both have
received a sensible shock from the progress of experimental philosophy.
It is the undefined and uncommon that gives birth and scope to the
imagination: we can only fancy what we do not know. As in looking
into the mazes of a tangled wood we fill them with what shapes we
please, with ravenous beasts, with caverns vast, and drear enchant-
ments, so in our ignorance of the world about us, we make gods or
devils of the first object we see, and set no bounds to the wilful
suggestions of our hopes and fears. . . .

Poetry in its matter and form is natural imagery or feeling, combined
with passion and fancy. In its mode of conveyance, it is the ordinary
use of language, combined with musical expression. There is a question of long standing, in what the essence of poetry consists, or what it
is that determines why one set of ideas should be expressed in prose,
another in verse. Milton has told us his idea of poetry in a single
line —

> "Thoughts that voluntary move
> Harmonious numbers."[14]

As there are certain sounds that excite certain motions, and the
song and dance go together, so there are, no doubt, certain thoughts
that lead to certain tones of voice, or modulations of sound, and change
"the words of Mercury into the songs of Apollo."[15] . . . On the contrary,
there is nothing either musical or natural in the ordinary construction
of language. It is a thing altogether arbitrary and conventional.
Neither in the sounds themselves, which are the voluntary signs of
certain ideas, nor in their grammatical arrangements in common
speech, is there any principle of natural imitation, or correspondence
to the individual ideas, or to the tone of feeling with which they are
conveyed to others. The jerks, the breaks, the inequalities, and harsh-
nesses of prose, are fatal to the flow of a poetical imagination, as a
jolting road or a stumbling horse disturbs the reverie of an absent man.
But poetry makes these odds all even. It is the music of language,
answering to the music of the mind, untying as it were "the secret soul
of harmony."[16] Wherever any object takes such a hold of the mind
as to make us dwell upon it, and brood over it, melting the heart in
tenderness, or kindling it to a sentiment of enthusiasm; — wherever
a movement of imagination or passion is impressed on the mind, by

[14] *Paradise Lost* III.37–38.
[15] Cf. *Love's Labor's Lost* V.ii.940.
[16] Cf. Milton, *L'Allegro* 144.

which it seeks to prolong and repeat the emotion, to bring all other objects into accord with it, and to give the same movement of harmony, sustained and continuous, or gradually varied according to the occasion, to the sounds that express it — this is poetry. The musical in sound is the sustained and continuous; the musical in thought is the sustained and continuous also. There is a close connection between music and deep-rooted passion. Mad people sing. As often as articulation passes naturally into intonation, there poetry begins. Where one idea gives a tone and colour to others, where one feeling melts others into it, there can be no reason why the same principle should not be extended to the sounds by which the voice utters these emotions of the soul, and blends syllables and lines into each other. It is to supply the inherent defect of harmony in the customary mechanism of language, to make the sound an echo to the sense, when the sense becomes a sort of echo to itself — to mingle the tide of verse, "the golden cadences of poetry," with the tide of feeling, flowing and murmuring as it flows — in short, to take the language of the imagination from off the ground, and enable it to spread its wings where it may indulge its own impulses —

> "Sailing with supreme dominion
> Through the azure deep of air —"[17]

without being stopped, or fretted, or diverted with the abruptnesses and petty obstacles, and discordant flats and sharps of prose, that poetry was invented. It is, to common language, what springs are to a carriage, or wings to feet. In ordinary speech we arrive at a certain harmony by the modulations of voice: in poetry the same thing is done systematically by a regular collocation of syllables. It has been well observed, that every one who declaims warmly, or grows intent upon a subject, rises into a sort of blank verse or measured prose. The merchant, as described in Chaucer, went on his way "sounding always the increase of his winning."[18] Every prose-writer has more or less of rhythmical adaptation, except poets, who, when deprived of the regular mechanism of verse, seem to have no principle of modulation left in their writings. . . .[19]

[17] Cf. *Love's Labor's Lost* IV.ii.126; Gray, *The Progress of Poesy* 116–117.
[18] *Canterbury Tales*, Prologue 275.
[19] Medoro: in *Orlando Furioso*, 1516, translated by Sir John Harington, 1591. Edward Moore (1712–57), *The Gamester*, 1753; George Lillo (1693–1739), *The London Merchant*, 1731.

On Modern Comedy

❡ Hazlitt conceived and published this essay for the *Morning Chronicle* of London, September 25, 1813. After modifying it slightly for Hunt as the weekly Theatrical Examiner of August 20, 1815, he included it in the first volume of *The Round Table*, 1817. Among other changes, he restored the fourth paragraph from the version in the *Morning Chronicle*. The text of 1817 is here followed. ❱

The question which has often been asked, *Why there are so few good modern Comedies?* appears in a great measure to answer itself. It is because so many excellent Comedies have been written, that there are none written at present. Comedy naturally wears itself out — destroys the very food on which it lives; and by constantly and successfully exposing the follies and weaknesses of mankind to ridicule, in the end leaves itself nothing worth laughing at. It holds the mirror up to nature; and men, seeing their most striking peculiarities and defects pass in gay review before them, learn either to avoid or conceal them. It is not the criticism which the public taste exercises upon the stage, but the criticism which the stage exercises upon public manners, that is fatal to comedy, by rendering the subject-matter of it tame, correct, and spiritless. We are drilled into a sort of stupid decorum, and forced to wear the same dull uniform of outward appearance; and yet it is asked, why the Comic Muse does not point, as she was wont, at the peculiarities of our gait and gesture, and exhibit the picturesque contrast of our dress and costume, in all that graceful variety in which she delights. The genuine source of comic writing,

"Where it must live, or have no life at all,"[1]

is undoubtedly to be found in the distinguishing peculiarities of men and mannners. Now, this distinction can subsist, so as to be strong, pointed, and general, only while the manners of different classes are formed immediately by their particular circumstances, and the characters of individuals by their natural temperament and situation, without being everlastingly modified and neutralized by intercourse with the world — by knowledge and education. In a certain stage of society, men may be said to vegetate like trees, and to become rooted to the soil in which they grow. They have no idea of any thing beyond themselves and their immediate sphere of action; they are, as it were,

[1] Cf. *Othello* II.iv.258.

circumscribed, and defined by their particular circumstances; they are what their situation makes them, and nothing more. Each is absorbed in his own profession or pursuit, and each in his turn contracts that habitual peculiarity of manners and opinions, which makes him the subject of ridicule to others, and the sport of the Comic Muse. Thus the physician is nothing but a physician, the lawyer is a mere lawyer, the scholar degenerates into a pedant, the country squire is a different species of being from the fine gentleman, the citizen and the courtier inhabit a different world, and even the affectation of certain characters, in aping the follies or vices of their betters, only serves to shew the immeasurable distance which custom or fortune has placed between them. Hence the early comic writers, taking advantage of this mixed and solid mass of ignorance, folly, pride, and prejudice, made those deep and lasting incisions into it, — have given those sharp and nice touches, that bold relief to their characters, — have opposed them in every variety of contrast and collision, of conscious self-satisfaction and mutual antipathy, with a power which can only find full scope in the same rich and inexhaustible materials. But in proportion as comic genius succeeds in taking off the mask from ignorance and conceit, as it teaches us to—

"See ourselves as others see us," —[2]

in proportion as we are brought out on the stage together, and our prejudices clash one against the other, our sharp angular points wear off; we are no longer rigid in absurdity, passionate in folly, and we prevent the ridicule directed at our habitual foibles, by laughing at them ourselves.

If it be said, that there is the same fund of absurdity and prejudice in the world as ever — that there are the same unaccountable perversities lurking at the bottom of every breast, — I should answer, be it so: but at least we keep our follies to ourselves as much as possible — we palliate, shuffle, and equivocate with them — they sneak into bye-corners, and do not, like *Chaucer's Canterbury Pilgrims,* march along the high road, and form a procession — they do not entrench themselves strongly behind custom and precedent — they are not embodied in professions and ranks in life — they are not organized into a system — they do not openly resort to a standard, but are a sort of straggling nondescripts, that, like *Wart,* "Present no mark to the foeman."[3] As to the gross and palpable absurdities of modern manners, they are too shallow and barefaced, and those who affect, are too little *serious* in them, to make them worth the detection of the Comic Muse. They proceed from an idle, impudent affectation of folly in general, in the dashing *bravura* style, not from an infatuation with any of its characteristic modes. In short, the proper object of ridicule is *egotism;* and a

---

[2] Cf. Robert Burns (1759–96), *To a Louse* 44.
[3] Cf. *2 Henry IV* III.ii.286 (of Shadow, not Wart).

man cannot be a very great egotist, who every day sees himself represented on the stage. We are deficient in Comedy, because we are without characters in real life — as we have no historical pictures, because we have no faces proper for them.

It is, indeed, the evident tendency of all literature to generalize and *dissipate* character, by giving men the same artificial education, and the same common stock of ideas; so that we see all objects from the same point of view, and through the same reflected medium; — we learn to exist, not in ourselves, but in books; — all men become alike mere readers — spectators, not actors in the scene, and lose all proper personal identity. The templar, the wit, the man of pleasure, and the man of fashion, the courtier and the citizen, the knight and the squire, the lover and the miser — *Lovelace, Lothario, Will. Honeycomb*, and *Sir Roger de Coverley, Sparkish*, and *Lord Foppington, Western* and *Tom Jones, my Father*, and *my Uncle Toby, Millamant* and *Sir Sampson Legend, Don Quixote* and *Sancho, Gil Blas* and *Guzman d'Alfarache, Count Fathom* and *Joseph Surface*,[4] — have all met, and exchanged common-places on the barren plains of the *haute littérature* — toil slowly on to the Temple of Science, seen a long way off upon a level, and end in one dull compound of politics, criticism, chemistry, and metaphysics!

We cannot expect to reconcile opposite things. If, for example, any of us were to put ourselves into the stage-coach from Salisbury to London, it is more than probable we should not meet with the same number of odd accidents, or ludicrous distresses on the road, that befel *Parson Adams*;[5] but why, if we get into a common vehicle, and submit to the conveniences of modern travelling, should we complain of the want of adventures? Modern manners may be compared to a modern stage-coach: our limbs may be a little cramped with the confinement, and we may grow drowsy; but we arrive safe, without any very amusing or very sad accident, at our journey's end.

Again, the alterations which have taken place in conversation and dress in the same period, have been by no means favourable to Comedy. The present prevailing style of conversation is not *personal*, but critical and analytical. It consists almost entirely in the discussion of general topics, in dissertations on philosophy or taste: and Congreve would be able to derive no better hints from the conversations of our toilettes or drawing-rooms, for the exquisite raillery or poignant repartee of his dialogues, than from a deliberation of the Royal Society. In the same manner, the extreme simplicity and graceful uniformity of modern dress, however favourable to the arts, has certainly stript Comedy of one of its richest ornaments and most expressive symbols. The sweeping pall and buskin, and nodding plume, were never more

[4] For less jaundiced discussion of Hazlitt's favorite characters see his *Lectures on the English Comic Writers.*

[5] in Henry Fielding's *Joseph Andrews,* 1742.

serviceable to Tragedy, than the enormous hoops and stiff stays worn by the belles of former days were to the intrigues of Comedy. They assisted wonderfully in heightening the mysteries of the passion, and adding to the intricacy of the plot. Wycherley and Vanbrugh could not have spared the dresses of Vandyke. These strange fancy-dresses, perverse disguises, and counterfeit shapes, gave an agreeable scope to the imagination. "That sevenfold fence"[6] was a sort of foil to the lusciousness of the dialogue, and a barrier against the sly encroachments of *double entendre*. The greedy eye and bold hand of indiscretion were repressed, which gave a greater licence to the tongue. The senses were not to be gratified in an instant. Love was entangled in the folds of the swelling handkerchief, and the desires might wander for ever round the circumference of a quilted petticoat, or find a rich lodging in the flowers of a damask stomacher. There was room for years of patient contrivance, for a thousand thoughts, schemes, conjectures, hopes, fears, and wishes. There seemed no end of difficulties and delays; to overcome so many obstacles was the work of ages. A mistress was an angel concealed behind whalebone, flounces, and brocade. What an undertaking to penetrate through the disguise! What an impulse must it give to the blood, what a keenness to the invention, what a volubility to the tongue! "Mr. Smirk, you are a brisk man," was then the most significant commendation. But now-a-days — A woman can be *but undressed!*[7]

The same account might be extended to Tragedy. Aristotle has long since said, that Tragedy purifies the mind by terror and pity; that is, substitutes an artificial and intellectual interest for real passion. Tragedy, like Comedy, must therefore defeat itself; for its patterns must be drawn from the living models within the breast, from feeling or from observation; and the materials of Tragedy cannot be found among a people, who are the habitual spectators of Tragedy, whose interests and passions are not their own, but ideal, remote, sentimental, and abstracted. It is for this reason chiefly, we conceive, that the highest efforts of the Tragic Muse are in general the earliest; where the strong impulses of nature are not lost in the refinements and glosses of art; where the writers themselves, and those whom they saw about them, had "warm hearts of flesh and blood beating in their bosoms, and were not embowelled of their natural entrails, and stuffed with paltry blurred sheets of paper."[8] Shakspeare, with all his genius, could not have written as he did, if he had lived in the present times. Nature would not have presented itself to him in the same freshness and vigour; he must have seen it through all the refractions of successive dulness, and his powers would have languished in the dense atmos-

---

[6] Cf. *Antony and Cleopatra* IV.xiv.38.

[7] The second half of this paragraph had appeared in Hazlitt's *Reply to Malthus*, 1807. Smirk: in Samuel Foote, *The Minor*, 1760.

[8] Altered from Burke, *Reflections on the Revolution in France.*

phere of logic and criticism. "Men's minds," he somewhere says, "are parcel of their fortunes;"[9] and his age was necessary to him. It was this which enabled him to grapple at once with nature, and which stamped his characters with her image and superscription.

W. H.

He will never write a
more wrong essay !

Hamlet

❨ Hazlitt completed and dated the Preface to *Characters of Shakespear's Plays* on April 15, 1817. In the Second Edition of 1818, here followed for the essay on *Hamlet,* he made and announced a "few alterations and corrections." Like other Romantic critics, Hazlitt emphasized the characters of drama from interest in the actor's problems of interpretation and concern for objective moral judgment. Verbal discrepancies between modern editions of *Hamlet* and those used by Hazlitt are enlarged by his habit of quoting from memory. ❩

This is that Hamlet the Dane, whom we read of in our youth, and whom we may be said almost to remember in our after-years; he who made that famous soliloquy on life, who gave the advice to the players, who thought "this goodly frame, the earth, a steril promontory, and this brave o'er-hanging firmament, the air, this majestical roof fretted with golden fire, a foul and pestilent congregation of vapours;" whom "man delighted not, nor woman neither;" he who talked with the grave-diggers, and moralised on Yorick's skull; the school-fellow of Rosencraus and Guildenstern at Wittenberg; the friend of Horatio; the lover of Ophelia; he that was mad and sent to England; the slow avenger of his father's death; who lived at the court of Horwendillus five hundred years before we were born, but all whose thoughts we seem to know as well as we do our own, because we have read them in Shakespear.

Hamlet is a name; his speeches and sayings but the idle coinage of the poet's brain. What then, are they not real? They are as real as our own thoughts. Their reality is in the reader's mind. It is *we* who are Hamlet. This play has a prophetic truth, which is above that of history. Whoever has become thoughtful and melancholy through his own mishaps or those of others; whoever has borne about with him the clouded brow of reflection, and thought himself "too much i' th' sun;" whoever has seen the golden lamp of day dimmed by envious mists rising in his own breast, and could find in the world before him only

[9] Cf. *Antony and Cleopatra* III.xiii.31–32.

a dull blank with nothing left remarkable in it; whoever has known "the pangs of despised love, the insolence of office, or the spurns which patient merit of the unworthy takes;" he who has felt his mind sink within him, and sadness cling to his heart like a malady, who has had his hopes blighted and his youth staggered by the apparitions of strange things; who cannot be well at ease, while he sees evil hovering near him like a spectre; whose powers of action have been eaten up by thought, he to whom the universe seems infinite, and himself nothing; whose bitterness of soul makes him careless of consequences, and who goes to a play as his best resource to shove off, to a second remove, the evils of life by a mock representation of them — this is the true Hamlet.

We have been so used to this tragedy that we hardly know how to criticise it any more than we should know how to describe our own faces. But we must make such observations as we can. It is the one of Shakespear's plays that we think of the oftenest, because it abounds most in striking reflections on human life, and because the distresses of Hamlet are transferred, by the turn of his mind, to the general account of humanity. Whatever happens to him we apply to ourselves, because he applies it so himself as a means of general reasoning. He is a great moraliser; and what makes him worth attending to is, that he moralises on his own feelings and experience. He is not a commonplace pedant. If *Lear* is distinguished by the greatest depth of passion, HAMLET is the most remarkable for the ingenuity, originality, and unstudied developement of character. Shakespear had more magnanimity than any other poet, and he has shewn more of it in this play than in any other. There is no attempt to force an interest: every thing is left for time and circumstances to unfold. The attention is excited without effort, the incidents succeed each other as matters of course, the characters think and speak and act just as they might do, if left entirely to themselves. There is no set purpose, no straining at a point. The observations are suggested by the passing scene — the gusts of passion come and go like sounds of music borne on the wind. The whole play is an exact transcript of what might be supposed to have taken place at the court of Denmark, at the remote period of time fixed upon, before the modern refinements in morals and manners were heard of. It would have been interesting enough to have been admitted as a by-stander in such a scene, at such a time, to have heard and witnessed something of what was going on. But here we are more than spectators. We have not only "the outward pageants and the signs of grief;" but "we have that within which passes shew." We read the thoughts of the heart, we catch the passions living as they rise. Other dramatic writers give us very fine versions and paraphrases of nature; but Shakespear, together with his own comments, gives us the original text, that we may judge for ourselves. This is a very great advantage.

The character of Hamlet stands quite by itself. It is not a character marked by strength of will or even of passion, but by refinement of thought and sentiment. Hamlet is as little of the hero as a man can well be: but he is a young and princely novice, full of high enthusiasm and quick sensibility — the sport of circumstances, questioning with fortune and refining on his own feelings, and forced from the natural bias of his disposition by the strangeness of his situation. He seems incapable of deliberate action, and is only hurried into extremities on the spur of the occasion, when he has no time to reflect, as in the scene where he kills Polonius, and again, where he alters the letters which Rosencraus and Guildenstern are taking with them to England, purporting his death. At other times, when he is most bound to act, he remains puzzled, undecided, and sceptical, dallies with his purposes, till the occasion is lost, and finds out some pretence to relapse into indolence and thoughtfulness again. For this reason he refuses to kill the King when he is at his prayers, and by a refinement in malice, which is in truth only an excuse for his own want of resolution, defers his revenge to a more fatal opportunity, when he shall be engaged in some act "that has no relish of salvation in it."

> "He kneels and prays,
> And now I'll do't, and so he goes to heaven,
> And so am I reveng'd: *that would be scann'd.*
> He kill'd my father, and for that,
> I, his sole son, send him to heaven.
> Why this is reward, not revenge.
> Up sword and know thou a more horrid time,
> When he is drunk, asleep, or in a rage." [III.iii.74–89]

He is the prince of philosophical speculators; and because he cannot have his revenge perfect, according to the most refined idea his wish can form, he declines it altogether. So he scruples to trust the suggestions of the ghost, contrives the scene of the play to have surer proof of his uncle's guilt, and then rests satisfied with this confirmation of his suspicions, and the success of his experiment, instead of acting upon it. Yet he is sensible of his own weakness, taxes himself with it, and tries to reason himself out of it.

> "How all occasions do inform against me,
> And spur my dull revenge! What is a man,
> If his chief good and market of his time
> Be but to sleep and feed? A beast; no more.
> Sure he that made us with such large discourse,
> Looking before and after, gave us not
> That capability and god-like reason
> To rust in us unus'd. Now whether it be
> Bestial oblivion, or some craven scruple
> Of thinking too precisely on th' event, —

> A thought which quarter'd, hath but one part wisdom,
> And ever three parts coward; — I do not know
> Why yet I live to say, this thing's to do;
> Sith I have cause, and will, and strength, and means
> To do it. Examples gross as earth exhort me:
> Witness this army of such mass and charge,
> Led by a delicate and tender prince,
> Whose spirit with divine ambition puff'd,
> Makes mouths at the invisible event,
> Exposing what is mortal and unsure
> To all that fortune, death, and danger dare,
> Even for an egg-shell. 'Tis not to be great
> Never to stir without great argument;
> But greatly to find quarrel in a straw,
> When honour's at the stake. How stand I then,
> That have a father kill'd, a mother stain'd,
> Excitements of my reason and my blood,
> And let all sleep, while to my shame I see
> The imminent death of twenty thousand men,
> That for a fantasy and trick of fame,
> Go to their graves like beds, fight for a plot
> Whereon the numbers cannot try the cause,
> Which is not tomb enough and continent
> To hide the slain? — O, from this time forth,
> My thoughts be bloody or be nothing worth." [IV.iv.32–66]

Still he does nothing; and this very speculation on his own infirmity only affords him another occasion for indulging it. It is not from any want of attachment to his father or of abhorrence of his murder that Hamlet is thus dilatory, but it is more to his taste to indulge his imagination in reflecting upon the enormity of the crime and refining on his schemes of vengeance, than to put them into immediate practice. His ruling passion is to think, not to act: and any vague pretext that flatters this propensity instantly diverts him from his previous purposes.

The moral perfection of this character has been called in question, we think, by those who did not understand it. It is more interesting than according to rules; amiable, though not faultless. The ethical delineations of "that noble and liberal casuist" (as Shakespear has been well called)[1] do not exhibit the drab-coloured quakerism of morality. His plays are not copied either from the Whole Duty of Man, or from The Academy of Compliments![2] We confess we are a little shocked at the want of refinement in those who are shocked at the want of refinement in Hamlet. The neglect of punctilious exactness in his behaviour either partakes of the "licence of the time," or else belongs to the very excess of intellectual refinement in the character, which makes the com-

[1] Lamb, on Elizabethan dramatists generally, in *Specimens of English Dramatic Poets:* "those noble and liberal casuists."

[2] Popular 17th-century tracts on morals and manners.

mon rules of life, as well as his own purposes, sit loose upon him. He may be said to be amenable only to the tribunal of his own thoughts, and is too much taken up with the airy world of contemplation to lay as much stress as he ought on the practical consequences of things. His habitual principles of action are unhinged and out of joint with the time. His conduct to Ophelia is quite natural in his circumstances. It is that of assumed severity only. It is the effect of disappointed hope, of bitter regrets, of affection suspended, not obliterated, by the distractions of the scene around him! Amidst the natural and preternatural horrors of his situation, he might be excused in delicacy from carrying on a regular courtship. When "his father's spirit was in arms," it was not a time for the son to make love in. He could neither marry Ophelia, nor wound her mind by explaining the cause of his alienation, which he durst hardly trust himself to think of. It would have taken him years to have come to a direct explanation on the point. In the harassed state of his mind, he could not have done much otherwise than he did. His conduct does not contradict what he says when he sees her funeral,

> "I loved Ophelia: forty thousand brothers
> Could not with all their quantity of love
> Make up my sum." [V. i. 292–294]

Nothing can be more affecting or beautiful than the Queen's apostrophe to Ophelia on throwing the flowers into the grave.

> ———— "Sweets to the sweet, farewell.
> I hop'd thou should'st have been my Hamlet's wife:
> I thought thy bride-bed to have deck'd, sweet maid,
> And not have strew'd thy grave." [V.i.266–269]

Shakespear was thoroughly a master of the mixed motives of human character, and he here shews us the Queen, who was so criminal in some respects, not without sensibility and affection in other relations of life. — Ophelia is a character almost too exquisitely touching to be dwelt upon. Oh rose of May, oh flower too soon faded! Her love, her madness, her death, are described with the truest touches of tenderness and pathos. It is a character which nobody but Shakespear could have drawn in the way that he has done, and to the conception of which there is not even the smallest approach, except in some of the old romantic ballads.[3] Her brother, Laertes, is a character we do not

---

[3] In the account of her death, a friend has pointed out an instance of the poet's exact observation of nature: —
> "There is a willow growing o'er a brook,
> That shews its hoary leaves i' th' glassy stream."
> [IV.vii.167–168]
The inside of the leaves of the willow, next the water, is of a whitish colour, and the reflection would therefore be "hoary." [W.H.]

like so well: he is too hot and choleric, and somewhat rhodomontade. Polonius is a perfect character in its kind; nor is there any foundation for the objections which have been made to the consistency of this part. It is said that he acts very foolishly and talks very sensibly. There is no inconsistency in that. Again, that he talks wisely at one time and foolishly at another; that his advice to Laertes is very excellent, and his advice to the King and Queen on the subject of Hamlet's madness very ridiculous. But he gives the one as a father, and is sincere in it; he gives the other as a mere courtier, a busy-body, and is accordingly officious, garrulous, and impertinent. In short, Shakespear has been accused of inconsistency in this and other characters, only because he has kept up the distinction which there is in nature, between the understandings and the moral habits of men, between the absurdity of their ideas and the absurdity of their motives. Polonius is not a fool, but he makes himself so. His folly, whether in his actions or speeches, comes under the head of impropriety of intention.

We do not like to see our author's plays acted, and least of all, HAMLET. There is no play that suffers so much in being transferred to the stage. Hamlet himself seems hardly capable of being acted. Mr. Kemble unavoidably fails in this character from a want of ease and variety. The character of Hamlet is made up of undulating lines; it has the yielding flexibility of "a wave o' th' sea." Mr. Kemble plays it like a man in armour, with a determined inveteracy of purpose, in one undeviating straight line, which is as remote from the natural grace and refined susceptibility of the character, as the sharp angles and abrupt starts which Mr. Kean introduces into the part. Mr. Kean's Hamlet is as much too splenetic and rash as Mr. Kemble's is too deliberate and formal. His manner is too strong and pointed. He throws a severity, approaching to virulence, into the common observations and answers. There is nothing of this in Hamlet. He is, as it were, wrapped up in his reflections, and only *thinks aloud*. There should therefore be no attempt to impress what he says upon others by a studied exaggeration of emphasis or manner; no *talking at* his hearers. There should be as much of the gentleman and scholar as possible infused into the part, and as little of the actor. A pensive air of sadness should sit reluctantly upon his brow, but no appearance of fixed and sullen gloom. He is full of weakness and melancholy, but there is no harshness in his nature. He is the most amiable of misanthropes.

Mr. Kean's Macbeth

⁣❨ Edmund Kean (1787–1833), in defeat of John Philip Kemble (1757–1823), is easily the hero of *A View of the English Stage*, 1818, a selection from the theatrical criticisms Hazlitt wrote between January 1814 and June 1817 for the *Morning Chronicle, Champion, Examiner,* and *Times*. Hazlitt often contrasted Kemble's "grace and dignity" with Kean's "force and nature." "Mr. Kean's Macbeth" is a review, for the *Champion* of November 13, 1814, of a performance at Drury Lane on November 5. It is here reprinted from the edition of 1818. ❩

The genius of SHAKESPEAR was as much shewn in the subtlety and nice discrimination, as in the force and variety of his characters. The distinction is not preserved more completely in those which are the most opposite, than in those which in their general features and obvious appearance most nearly resemble each other. It has been observed, with very little exaggeration, that not one of his speeches could be put into the mouth of any other character than the one to which it is given, and that the transposition, if attempted, might be always detected from some circumstance in the passage itself. *If to invent according to nature,* be the true definition of genius, SHAKESPEAR had more of this quality than any other writer. He might be said to have been a joint-worker with Nature, and to have created an imaginary world of his own, which has all the appearance and the truth of reality. His mind, while it exerted an absolute controul over the stronger workings of the passions, was exquisitely alive to the slightest impulses and most evanescent shades of character and feeling. The broad distinctions and governing principles of human nature are presented not in the abstract, but in their immediate and endless application to different persons and things. The local details, the particular accidents have the fidelity of history, without losing any thing of their general effect.

It is the business of poetry, and indeed of all works of imagination, to exhibit the species through the individual. Otherwise, there can be no opportunity for the exercise of the imagination, without which the descriptions of the painter or the poet are lifeless, unsubstantial, and vapid. If some modern critics are right, with their sweeping generalities and vague abstractions, SHAKESPEAR was quite wrong. In the French dramatists, only the class is represented, never the individual: their kings, their heroes, and their lovers are all the same, and they are all French — that is, they are nothing but the mouth-pieces of certain rhetorical common-place sentiments on the favourite topics of morality and the passions. The characters in SHAKESPEAR do not declaim like pedantic school-boys, but speak and act like men, placed in real circumstances, with "real hearts of flesh and blood beating in their bosoms."[1] No two of his characters are the same, more than they would be so in nature. Those that are the most alike, are distinguished by positive differences, which accompany and modify the leading principle of the character through its most obscure ramifications, embodying the habits, gestures, and almost the looks of the individual. These touches of nature are often so many, and so minute, that the poet cannot be supposed to have been distinctly aware of the operation of the springs by which his imagination was set at work: yet every one of the results is brought out with a truth and clearness, as if his whole study had been directed to that peculiar trait of character, or subordinate train of feeling.

Thus Macbeth, and Richard the Third, King Henry the Sixth, and Richard the Second, — characters that, in their general description, and in common hands, would be merely repetitions of the same idea — are distinguished by traits as precise, though of course less violent, than those which separate Macbeth from Henry the Sixth, or Richard the Third from Richard the Second. SHAKESPEAR has, with wonderful accuracy, and without the smallest appearance of effort, varied the portraits of imbecility and effeminacy in the two deposed monarchs. With still more powerful and masterly strokes, he has marked the different effects of ambition and cruelty, operating on different dispositions and in different circumstances, in his Macbeth and Richard the Third. Both are tyrants and usurpers, both violent and ambitious, both cruel and treacherous. But, Richard is cruel from nature and constitution. Macbeth becomes so from accidental circumstances. He is urged to the commission of guilt by golden opportunity, by the instigations of his wife, and by prophetic warnings. "Fate and metaphysical aid," conspire against his virtue and loyalty.[2] Richard needs no prompter, but wades through a series of crimes to the height of his ambition, from ungovernable passions and the restless love of mischief. He is never gay but in the prospect, or in the success of his villanies: Macbeth is full of horror at the thoughts of the murder of Duncan, and of remorse after its perpetration. Richard has no mixture of humanity in his composition, no tie which binds him to the kind; he owns no fellowship with others, but is himself alone. Macbeth is not without feelings of sympathy, is accessible to pity, is even the dupe of his uxoriousness, and ranks the loss of friends and of his good name among the causes that have made him sick of life. He becomes more callous indeed as he plunges deeper in guilt, "direness is thus made familiar to his slaughterous thoughts," and he anticipates his wife in the boldness

[1] Burke, *Reflections on the Revolution in France.*
[2] *Macbeth* I.v.30.

and bloodiness of his enterprises, who, for want of the same stimulus of action, is "troubled with thick-coming fancies," walks in her sleep, goes mad, and dies.[3] Macbeth endeavours to escape from reflection on his crimes, by repelling their consequences, and banishes remorse for the past, by meditating future mischief. This is not the principle of Richard's cruelty, which resembles the cold malignity of a fiend, rather than the frailty of human nature. Macbeth is goaded on by necessity; to Richard, blood is a pastime. —

There are other essential differences. Richard is a man of the world, a vulgar, plotting, hardened villain, wholly regardless of every thing but his own ends, and the means to accomplish them. Not so Macbeth. The superstitions of the time, the rude state of society, the local scenery and customs, all give a wildness and imaginary grandeur to his character. From the strangeness of the events which surround him, he is full of amazement and fear, and stands in doubt between the world of reality and the world of fancy. He sees sights not shewn to mortal eye, and hears unearthly music. All is tumult and disorder within and without his mind. In thought, he is absent and perplexed, desperate in act: his purposes recoil upon himself, are broken, and disjointed: he is the double thrall of his passions and his evil destiny. He treads upon the brink of fate, and grows dizzy with his situation. Richard is not a character of imagination, but of pure will or passion. There is no conflict of opposite feelings in his breast. The apparitions which he sees are in his sleep, nor does he live like Macbeth, in a waking dream.

Such, at least, is our conception of the two characters, as drawn by SHAKESPEAR. Mr. KEAN does not distinguish them so completely as he might. His Richard comes nearer to the original than his Macbeth. He was deficient in the poetry of the character. He did not look like a man who had encountered the Weird Sisters. There should be nothing tight or compact in Macbeth, no tenseness of fibre, nor pointed decision of manner. He has, indeed, energy and manliness of soul, but "subject to all the skyey influences."[4] He is sure of nothing. All is left at issue. He runs a-tilt with fortune, and is baffled with preternatural riddles. The agitation of his mind resembles the rolling of the sea in a storm; or, he is like a lion in the toils — fierce, impetuous, and ungovernable. In the fifth act in particular, which is in itself as busy and turbulent as possible, there was not that giddy whirl of the imagination — the character did not burnish out on all sides with those flashes of genius, of which Mr. KEAN had given so fine an earnest in the conclusion of his Richard. The scene stood still — the parts might be perfect in themselves, but they were not joined together; they wanted vitality. The pauses in the speeches were too long — the actor seemed to be studying the part, rather than performing it — striving to make every word more emphatic than the last, and "lost too poorly

---

[3] *Ibid.*, V.v.14, V.iii.38.
[4] Cf. *Measure for Measure* III.i.9.

in himself," instead of being carried away with the grandeur of his subject. The text was not given accurately. Macbeth is represented in the play, arming before the castle, which adds to the interest of the scene.

In the delivery of the beautiful soliloquy, "My way of life is fallen into the sear, the yellow leaf," Mr. KEAN was unsuccessful. That fine thoughtful melancholy did not seem to come over his mind, which characterises Mr. KEMBLE's recitation of these lines. The very tone of Mr. KEMBLE's voice has something retrospective in it — it is an echo of the past. Mr. KEAN in his dress was occasionally too much docked and curtailed for the gravity of the character. His movements were too agile and mercurial, and he fought more like a modern fencing-master than a Scottish chieftain of the eleventh century. He fell at last finely, with his face downwards, as if to cover the shame of his defeat. We recollect that Mr. COOKE discovered the great actor both in the death-scene in Macbeth, and in that of Richard. He fell like the ruin of a state, like a king with his regalia about him.[5]

The two finest things that Mr. KEAN has ever done, are his recitation of the passage in Othello, "Then, oh, farewell the tranquil mind," and the scene in Macbeth after the murder. The former was the highest and most perfect effort of his art. To enquire whether his manner in the latter scene was that of a king who commits a murder, or of a man who commits a murder to become a king, would be "to consider too curiously." But, as a lesson of common humanity, it was heart-rending. The hesitation, the bewildered look, the coming to himself when he sees his hands bloody; the manner in which his voice clung to his throat, and choaked his utterance; his agony and tears, the force of nature overcome by passion — beggared description. It was a scene, which no one who saw it can ever efface from his recollection.

Liber Amoris

⟨ The title of Hazlitt's anonymous but scarcely disguised revelations, *Liber Amoris; or, The New Pygmalion*, published in May 1823, may be translated as "The Book of Love, from one who created the illusory ideal by which he was stricken." Part I of the work reports conversations between Hazlitt and Sarah Walker, the girl who infatuated him. Part III, beginning "It is all over, and I know my fate," consists of letters purportedly sent to J. S. K. (the playwright James Sheridan Knowles). Part II relates the middle of the story by altering very slightly letters actually exchanged between Hazlitt

[5] George Frederick Cooke (1756–1811).

and Peter George Patmore. Hazlitt wrote Letter VIII on June 9, 1822, from Renton Inn, forty miles south of Edinburgh. Not until recently has *Liber Amoris* been much praised as a notable work of psychological confession. Concerning Hazlitt's ability to produce some of his best essays during this period of agony, see Stewart C. Wilcox, *Hazlitt in the Workshop*, Baltimore, 1943.]⟩

LETTER VIII

MY DEAR FRIEND,

Your letter raised me for a moment from the depths of despair; but not hearing from you yesterday or to-day (as I hoped) I have had a relapse. You say I want to get rid of her. I hope you are more right in your conjectures about her than in this about me. Oh no! believe it, I love her as I do my own soul; my very heart is wedded to her (be she what she may) and I would not hesitate a moment between her and "an angel from Heaven." I grant all you say about my self-tormenting folly: but has it been without cause? Has she not refused me again and again with a mixture of scorn and resentment, after going the utmost lengths with a man for whom she now disclaims all affection; and what security can I have for her reserve with others, who will not be restrained by feelings of delicacy towards her, and whom she has probably preferred to me for their want of it? *"She can make no more confidences"* — these words ring for ever in my ears, and will be my death-watch. They can have but one meaning, be sure of it — she always expressed herself with the exactest propriety. That was one of the things for which I loved her — shall I live to hate her for it? My poor fond heart, that brooded over her and the remains of her affections as my only hope of comfort upon earth, cannot brook this new degradation. Who is there so low as me? Who is there besides (I ask) after the homage I have paid her and the caresses she has lavished on me, so vile, so abhorrent to love, to whom such an indignity could have happened? When I think of this (and I think of nothing else) it stifles me. I am pent up in burning, fruitless desires, which can find no vent or object. Am I not hated, repulsed, derided by her whom alone I love or ever did love? I cannot stay in any place, and seek in vain for relief from the sense of her contempt and her ingratitude. I can settle to nothing: what is the use of all I have done? Is it not that very circumstance (my thinking beyond my strength, my feeling more than I need about so many things) that has withered me up, and made me a thing for Love to shrink from and wonder at? Who could ever feel that peace from the touch of her dear hand that I have done; and is it not torn from me for ever? My state is this, that I shall never lie down again at night nor rise up in the morning in peace, nor ever behold my little boy's face with pleasure while I live — unless I am restored to her favour. Instead of that delicious feeling I had when she was heavenly-kind to me, and my heart softened and melted in its own tenderness and her sweetness, I am now inclosed in a dungeon of despair. The sky is marble to my thoughts; nature is dead around me, as hope is within me; no object can give me one gleam of satisfaction now, nor the prospect of it in time to come. I wander by the sea-side; and the eternal ocean and lasting despair and her face are before me. Slighted by her, on whom my heart by its last fibre hung, where shall I turn? I wake with her by my side, not as my sweet bedfellow, but as the corpse of my love, without a heart in her bosom, cold, insensible, or struggling from me; and the worm gnaws me, and the sting of unrequited love, and the canker of a hopeless, endless sorrow. I have lost the taste of my food by feverish anxiety; and my favourite beverage, which used to refresh me when I got up, has no moisture in it. Oh! cold, solitary, sepulchral breakfasts, compared with those which I promised myself with her; or which I made when she had been standing an hour by my side, my guardian-angel, my wife, my sister, my sweet friend, my Eve, my all; and had blest me with her seraph-kisses! Ah! what I suffer at present only shews what I have enjoyed. But "the girl is a good girl, if there is goodness in human nature." I thank you for those words; and I will fall down and worship you, if you can prove them true: and I would not do much less for him that proves her a demon. She is one or the other, that's certain; but I fear the worst. Do let me know if any thing has passed: suspense is my greatest punishment. I am going into the country to see if I can work a little in the three weeks I have yet to stay here. Write on the receipt of this, and believe me ever your unspeakably obliged friend.

Leigh Hunt

JAMES HENRY LEIGH HUNT

1784   Born October 19 at Southgate near London, youngest son of a clergyman from Barbados.

1791   November 24, entered Christ's Hospital, London.

1799   November 20, as a Deputy Grecian, completed the course at Christ's Hospital, London.

1801   Spring, *Juvenilia,* poems (fourth edition in 1803).

1805–08   Drama critic for the *News, Times,* and other periodicals; worked as clerk in War Office.

1808   January, *Critical Essays on the Performers of the London Theatres* (dated 1807).

1808 (January)–1821 (October)   Edited the weekly *Examiner.*

1809   July 3, married Marianne Kent.

1810–12   Edited the quarterly *Reflector* (dated October 1810–December 1811).

1813   February 3, sentenced to two years in Horsemonger Lane Gaol for a libel on the Prince Regent.

1816   February (?), *The Story of Rimini.*

1818–21   Edited *The Literary Pocket Book* and the weekly *Indicator* (October 13, 1819–March 21, 1821).

1822–25   In Italy, where he edited the *Liberal,* October 1822–April 1823, with Byron and Shelley.

1828   January 1 (?), *Lord Byron and Some of His Contemporaries.* Edited the weekly *Companion,* January 9–July 23.

1830 (September 4)–1832 (March 31)   Edited the *Tatler: A Daily Journal of Literature and the Stage.*

1832   January, *Sir Ralph Esher,* a novel, and (printed only) *Christianism,* both anonymous. December, *Poetical Works,* a selection.

1834 (April 2)–1835 (December 25)   Edited the weekly *Leigh Hunt's London Journal.*

1840   February 7, *A Legend of Florence* opened at Covent Garden.

1844   March, *Imagination and Fancy.*

1847   June, *Men, Women, and Books,* one of several gatherings from his periodical prose.

1850   June 8, *Autobiography.* December 7, began the weekly *Leigh Hunt's Journal* (to March 29, 1851).

1853   *The Religion of the Heart* (enlarged from *Christianism*).

1859   Died August 28.

Autobiography

¶ In *Lord Byron and Some of His Contemporaries* Hunt combined general reminiscences with severe attacks on Byron, Gifford, and other friends and enemies. In the *Autobiography* of 1850, from which the following pages are taken, he greatly expanded the account of his own life. He also mollified his remarks on Byron and even reduced his strictures against William Gifford (1756–1826). With further modifications, reductions, and editorial interpolations, the *Autobiography* was reissued in 1859 (dated 1860) by Hunt's son Thornton. Byron considered Gifford a satirist worth imitating, but Hunt makes a strong case against him. Hunt's objections to Gifford as well as to Scott were originally political but ultimately literary. ¶

from CHAPTER XII

Literary Warfare

The *Examiner* had been established about three years, when my brother projected a quarterly magazine of literature and politics, entitled the *Reflector,* which I edited. Lamb, Dyer, Barnes, Mitchell, the present Greek Professor Scholefield (all Christ-Hospital men), together with Dr. Aikin and his family wrote in it; and it was rising in sale every quarter, when it stopped at the close of the fourth number for want of funds.[1] Its termination was not owing to want of liberality in the payments. But the radical reformers in those days were not sufficiently rich or numerous to support such a publication.

Some of the liveliest effusions of Lamb first appeared in this magazine; and in order that I might retain no influential class for my good wishers, after having angered the stage, dissatisfied the Church, offended the State, not very well pleased the Whigs, and exasperated the Tories, I must needs commence the maturer part of my versemaking with contributing to its pages the *Feast of the Poets.*

The *Feast of the Poets* was (perhaps, I may say, is) a *jeu-d'esprit* suggested by the *Session of the Poets* of Sir John Suckling. Apollo gives the poets a dinner; and many verse-makers, who have no claim to the title, present themselves, and are rejected.

With this effusion, while thinking of nothing but showing my wit, and reposing under the shadow of my "laurels" (of which I expected

---

[1] George Dyer (1755–1841), innocent poet and friend of Lamb; Thomas Barnes (1785–1841), editor of the London *Times,* 1817–41; John Aikin (1747–1822), of a literary family including Mrs. Anna Barbauld; Thomas Mitchell and James Scholefield, friends of Hunt.

a harvest as abundant as my self-esteem), I made almost every living poet and poetaster my enemy, and particularly exasperated those among the Tories. I speak of the shape in which it first appeared, before time and reflection had moderated its judgment. It drew upon my head all the personal hostility which had hitherto been held in a state of suspense by the vaguer daring of the *Examiner;* and I have reason to believe that its inconsiderate, and I am bound to confess, in some respects, unwarrantable levity, was the origin of the gravest, and far less warrantable attacks which I afterwards sustained from political antagonists, and which caused the most serious mischief to my fortunes. Let the young satirist take warning; and consider how much self-love he is going to wound, by the indulgence of his own.

Not that I have to apologize to the memory of every one whom I attacked. I am sorry to have had occasion to differ with any of my fellow-creatures, knowing the mistakes to which we are all liable, and the circumstances that help to cause them. But I can only regret it, personally, in proportion to the worth or personal regret on the side of the enemy.

The *Quarterly Review,* for instance, had lately been set up, and its editor was Gifford, the author of the *Baviad and Mæviad.* I had been invited, nay, pressed by the publisher, to write in the new review; which surprised me, considering its politics and the great difference of my own. I was not aware of the little faith that was held in the politics of any beginner of the world; and I have no doubt, that the invitation had been made at the instance of ,Gifford himself, of whom, as the dictum of a "man of vigorous learning," and the "first satirist of his time," I had quoted in the *Critical Essays* the gentle observation, that "all the fools in the kingdom seemed to have risen up with one accord, and exclaimed, 'let us write for the theatres!' "

Strange must have been Gifford's feelings, when, in the *Feast of the Poets,* he found his eulogizer falling as trenchantly on the author of the *Baviad and Mæviad* as the *Baviad and Mæviad* had fallen on the dramatists. The Tory editor discerned plainly enough, that if a man's politics were of no consideration with the *Quarterly Review,* provided the politician was his critical admirer, they were very different things with the editor Radical. He found also, that the new satirist had ceased to regard the old one as a "critical authority;" and he might not have unwarrantably concluded, that I had conceived some personal disgust against him as a man; for such, indeed, was the secret of my attack.

The reader is perhaps aware, that George the Fourth, when he was Prince of Wales, had a mistress of the name of Robinson. She was the wife of a man of no great character; had taken to the stage for a livelihood; was very handsome, wrote verses, and is said to have excited a tender emotion in the bosom of Charles Fox. The Prince allured her from the stage, and lived with her for some years. After their separation, and during her decline, which took place before she

was old, she became afflicted with rheumatism; and as she solaced her
pains, and perhaps added to her subsistence, by writing verses, and
as her verses turned upon her affections, and she could not discon-
tinue her old vein of love and sentiment, she fell under the lash of
this masculine and gallant gentleman, Mr. Gifford, who, in his *Baviad
and Mæviad,* amused himself with tripping up her "crutches," particularly as he thought her on her way to her last home. This he
considered the climax of the fun.

"See," exclaimed he, after a hit or two at other women, like a boy
throwing stones in the street, —

> "See Robinson forget her state, and move
> *On crutches tow'rds the grave* to 'Light o' Love.' "

This is the passage which put all the gall into anything which I
said, then or afterwards, of Gifford, till he attacked myself and my
friends. At least, it disposed me to think the worst of whatever he
wrote; and as reflection did not improve nor suffering soften him, he
is the only man I ever attacked, respecting whom I have felt no
regret.

It would be easy for me, at this distance of time, to own that Gifford possessed genius, had such been the case. It would have been
easy for me at any time. But he had not a particle. The scourger of
poetasters was himself a poetaster. When he had done with his whip,
everybody had a right to take it up, and lay it over the scourger's
shoulders; for though he had sense enough to discern glaring faults,
he abounded in commonplaces. His satire itself, which at its best
never went beyond smartness, was full of them. . . .

His satire consists, not in a critical exposure, — in showing why
the objects of his contempt are wrong, — but in simply asserting that
they are so. He turns a commonplace of his own in his verses, quotes
a passage from his author in a note, expresses his amazement at it,
and thus thinks he has proved his case, when he has made out nothing
but an overweening assumption at the expense of what was not worth
noticing. "I was born," says he,

> "To *brand* obtrusive ignorance with scorn,
> On bloated pedantry to *pour my rage,*
> And *hiss preposterous fustian* from the stage."

What commonplace talking is that? And so he goes on: —

> "Lo! Della Crusca, in his closet pent,
> *He toils to give the crude conceptions vent.*
> Abortive thoughts, that *right and wrong confound,*
> Truth *sacrificed* to letters, [why 'letters'?] *sense to sound;*
> *False glare,* incongruous images, *combine;*
> And noise and nonsense clatter through the line."

What is the example of writing here which is shown to the poor
Della Cruscans? What the masterly novelty of style or imagery?
What the right evinced to speak in the language of a teacher? Yet

Gifford never doubted himself on these points. He stood uttering
his didactic nothings as if other literary defaulters were but so many
children, whom it taxed his condescension to instruct. Here is some
more of the same stuff: —

> "Then let your style be brief, your meaning clear,
> Nor, like Lorenzo, tire the labouring ear
> With a wild waste of words; sound without sense,
> And all the florid glare of impotence.
> Still, with your characters your language change, —
> From grave to gay, *as nature dictates,* range:
> Now droop in all the plaintiveness of woe, — (!!)
> Now in glad numbers light and airy flow;
> Now shake the stage with guilt's alarming *tone,* (!!)
> And make the aching bosom *all your own.*"

Was there ever a fonder set of complacent old phrases, such as any
schoolboy might utter? Yet this is the man who undertook to despise
Charles Lamb, and to trample on Keats and Shelley. . . .

I believe, that with reference to high standards of poetry and criticism, superior to mere description, however lively, to the demands of
rhyme for its own sake, to prosaical groundworks of style, metaphors
of common property, conventionalities in general, and the prevalence
of a material over a spiritual treatment, my estimate of Walter Scott's
then publications, making allowance for the manner of it, will still be
found not far from the truth, by those who have profited by a more
advanced age of æsthetical culture.

There is as much difference, for instance, poetically speaking, between Coleridge's brief poem, *Christabel,* and all the narrative poems
of Walter Scott, or as Wordsworth called them, "novels in verse," as
between a precious essence and a coarse imitation of it, got up for
sale. Indeed, Coleridge, not unnaturally, though not with entire
reason (for the story and the characters were the real charm), lamented that an endeavour, unavowed, had been made to catch his
tone, and had succeeded just far enough to recommend to unbounded
popularity what had nothing in common with it.

But though Walter Scott was no novelist at that time except in
verse, the tone of personal assumption towards him in the *Feast of
the Poets* formed a just ground of offence. Not that I had not as much
right to differ with any man on any subject, as he had to differ with
others; but it would have become me, especially at that time of life,
and in speaking of a living person, to express the difference with
modesty. I ought to have taken care also not to fall into one of the
very prejudices I was reproving, and think ill or well of people in
proportion as they differed or agreed with me in politics. Walter
Scott saw the good of mankind in a Tory or restropective point of
view. I saw it from a Whig, a Radical, or prospective one; and
though I still think he was mistaken, and though circumstances have
shown that the world think so too, I ought to have discovered, even

by the writings which I condemned, that he was a man of a kindly
nature; and it would have become me to have given him credit for
the same good motives, which I arrogated exclusively for my own
side of the question. It is true, it might be supposed, that I should
have advocated that side with less ardour, had I been more temperate
in this kind of judgment; but I do not think so. Or if I had, the want
of ardour would probably have been compensated by the presence
of qualities, the absence of which was injurious to its good effect.
At all events, I am now of opinion, that whatever may be the immediate impression, a cause is advocated to the most permanent advantage by persuasive, instead of provoking manners; and certain I
am, that whether this be the case or not, no human being, be he the
best and wisest of his kind, much less a confident young man, can be
so sure of the result of his confidence, as to warrant the substitution
of his will and pleasure in that direction, for the charity which befits
his common modesty and his participation of error.

It is impossible for me, in other respects, to regret the war I had
with the Tories. I rejoice in it as far as I can rejoice at anything
painful to myself and others, and I am paid for the consequences in
what I have lived to see; nay, in the respect and regrets of the best
of my enemies. But I am sorry, that in aiming wounds which I had
no right to give, I cannot deny that I brought on myself others which
they had still less right to inflict; and I make the amends of this
confession, not only in return for what they have expressed themselves,
but in justice to the feelings which honest men of all parties experience as they advance in life, and when they look back calmly upon
their common errors. . . .

Every party has a right side and a wrong. The right side of Whig-
gism, Radicalism, or the love of liberty, is the love of justice; the wish
to see fair-play to all men, and the advancement of knowledge and
competence. The wrong side is the wish to pull down those above
us, instead of the desire of raising those who are below. The right
side of Toryism is the love of order, and the disposition to reverence
and personal attachment; the wrong side is the love of power for
power's sake, and the determination to maintain it in the teeth of
all that is reasonable and humane. A strong spice of superstition, generated by the habit of success, tended to confuse the right and wrong
sides of Toryism, in minds not otherwise unjust or ungenerous. They
seemed to imagine, that heaven and earth would "come together," if
the supposed favourites of Providence were to be considered as
favourites no longer; and hence the unbounded license which they
gave to their resentment, and the strange self-permission of a man
like Walter Scott, not only to lament over the progress of society, as
if the future had been ordained only to carry on the past, but to
countenance the border-like forages of his friends into provinces
which they had no business to invade, and to speculate upon still
greater organizations of them, which circumstances, luckily for his

fame, prevented. I allude to the intended establishment of a journal, which, as it never existed, it is no longer necessary to name.

Readers in these kindlier days of criticism have no conception of the extent to which personal hostility allowed itself to be transported, in the periodicals of those times. Personal habits, appearances, connections, domesticities, nothing was safe from misrepresentations, begun perhaps in the gaiety of a saturnalian license, but gradually carried to an excess which would have been ludicrous, had it not sometimes produced tragical consequences. It threatened a great many more, and scattered, meantime, a great deal of wretchedness among unoffending as well as offending persons, sometimes in proportion to the delicacy which hindered them from exculpating themselves, and which could only have vindicated one portion of a family by sacrificing another. I was so caricatured, it seems, among the rest, upon matters great and small (for I did not see a tenth part of what was said of me), that persons, on subsequently becoming acquainted with me, sometimes expressed their surprise at finding me no other than I was in face, dress, manners, and very walk; to say nothing of the conjugality which they found at my fireside, and the affection which I had the happiness of enjoying among my friends in general. I never retaliated in the same way; first, because I had never been taught to respect it, even by the jests of Aristophanes; secondly, because I observed the sorrow it caused both to right and wrong; thirdly, because it is impossible to know the truth of any story if related of a person, without hearing all the parties concerned; and fourthly, because, while people thought me busy with politics and contention, I was almost always absorbed in my books and verses, and did not, perhaps, sufficiently consider the worldly consequences of the indulgence. . . .

If Sir Walter Scott was a poet of a purely conventional order, warmed with a taste for old books, and if he was a critic more agreeable than subtle, and a bitter and not very large-minded politician, unwilling, and perhaps unable, to turn his eyes from the past to the future, and to look with patience on the prospects of the many, he was a man of singular and admirable genius in the points in which he excelled, great in some respects, and charming almost in all. I beg leave to think that he did not possess that attribute of genius, which is said to partake of the feminine as well as the masculine; if feminine only it be to excel in sweet as well as strong, to be musical and graceful, and be able to paint women themselves; and I will not do such discredit to his memory, in this or in any masculine respect, as to repeat the comparisons of him with Shakspeare, who painted both women and men to admiration, and was a great poet, and a profound universalist, and excelled as much in nature as in manners; for certainly Scott was in all these respects (and rare is the excellence that can be put even to such a disadvantage) but a half, or even a third or fourth kind of Shakspeare, with all the poetry (so to speak) taken out of him, and all the expression and the quotability besides; Sir Walter being, perhaps, the least quotable for sententiousness or wit, or any other memorable brevity, in the whole circle of illustrious writers. But he was an agreeable and kindly biographer, a most entertaining selector from history, an exquisite antiquary, a charming companion, a warm-hearted friend, a good father, husband, and man; and though his novels, as works of art and style, were inferior to Fielding, and I think it was a want of imagination in him, and a self-abasement, to wish to build a great house and be a feudal lord, instead of being content to write about houses and lords, and living among us all to this day in a cottage that still would have been a shrine for princes to visit; yet, assuredly, he was the most wonderful combiner of the novel and romance that ever existed. He was Shakspearian in the abundance and variety of his characters, unsurpassed, if ever equalled, in the substantial flow of his pen; and in spite of admirable Burns and delightful Thomson, and all the historical and philosophical names of Edinburgh during the last and present century, was upon the whole the greatest writer that Scotland has produced.

It can be of no consequence to the memory of such a man what I said or thought of him, whether before his death or after; but for my own sake, since I am forced to speak of such things in a work like the present, I may be allowed to state, that whatever hostility I was forced to maintain with his politics, and so far with himself, I had the pleasure of expressing my regret for the mistakes which I had made about him, long before I experienced their ill effects. I will add, that long after those effects, and when he was lying sick in London on his way to his last home, I called every morning at his door (anonymously; for I doubted whether my name would please him) to furnish a respectful bulletin of his health to a daily paper, in which I suggested its appearance; and I will not conceal, that as I loved the humanities in his wonderful pages, in spite of the politics which accompanied them, so I mourned for his closing days, and shed tears at his death.

To return to the *Feast of the Poets*. I offended all the critics of the old or French school, by objecting to the monotony of Pope's versification, and all the critics of the new or German school, by laughing at Wordsworth, with whose writings I was then unacquainted, except through the medium of his deriders. On reading him for myself, I became such an admirer, that Lord Byron accused me of making him popular upon town. I had not very well pleased Lord Byron himself, by counting him inferior to Wordsworth. Indeed, I offended almost everybody whom I noticed; some by finding any fault at all with them; some, by not praising them on their favourite points; some, by praising others on any point; and some, I am afraid, and those among the most good-natured, by needlessly bringing them on the carpet, and turning their very good-nature into a subject for caricature. . . .

Getting Up on Cold Mornings

❨ This, one of the most often reprinted of Hunt's essays, appeared in *Indicator* No. 15, for January 19, 1820. It is here taken from the shorter version in *The Indicator and The Companion: A Miscellany for the Fields and the Fireside*, 1834. Among other differences, the essay continued in 1820 for two further paragraphs, with advice to women on getting their men to rise from bed, and assurances to "Madam" (the reader) that a look from her would rouse Mr. Indicator at an unaccustomed six o'clock. ❩

An Italian author — Giulio Cordara, a Jesuit — has written a poem upon insects, which he begins by insisting, that those troublesome and abominable little animals were created for our annoyance, and that they were certainly not inhabitants of Paradise. We of the north may dispute this piece of theology; but on the other hand, it is as clear as the snow on the housetops, that Adam was not under the necessity of shaving; and that when Eve walked out of her delicious bower, she did not step upon ice three inches thick.

Some people say it is a very easy thing to get up of a cold morning. You have only, they tell you, to take the resolution; and the thing is done. This may be very true; just as a boy at school has only to take a flogging, and the thing is over. But we have not at all made up our minds upon it; and we find it a very pleasant exercise to discuss the matter, candidly, before we get up. This at least is not idling, though it may be lying. It affords an excellent answer to those, who ask how lying in bed can be indulged in by a reasoning being, — a rational creature. How? Why with the argument calmly at work in one's head, and the clothes over one's shoulder. Oh — it is a fine way of spending a sensible, impartial half-hour.

If these people would be more charitable, they would get on with their argument better. But they are apt to reason so ill, and to assert so dogmatically, that one could wish to have them stand round one's bed of a bitter morning, and *lie* before their faces. They ought to hear both sides of the bed, the inside and out. If they cannot entertain themselves with their own thoughts for half an hour or so, it is not the fault of those who can.

Candid enquiries into one's decumbency, besides the greater or less privileges to be allowed a man in proportion to his ability of keeping early hours, the work given his faculties, &c. will at least concede their due merits to such representations as the following. In the first place, says the injured but calm appealer, I have been warm all night, and find my system in a state perfectly suitable to a warm-blooded animal. To get out of this state into the cold, besides the inharmonious and uncritical abruptness of the transition, is so unnatural to such a creature, that the poets, refining upon the tortures of the damned, make one of their greatest agonies consist in being suddenly transported from heat to cold, — from fire to ice. They are "haled" out of their "beds," says Milton, by "harpy-footed furies,"[1] — fellows who come to call them. On my first movement towards the anticipation of getting up, I find that such parts of the sheets and bolster, as are exposed to the air of the room, are stone-cold. On opening my eyes, the first thing that meets them is my own breath rolling forth, as if in the open air, like smoke out of a chimney. Think of this symptom. Then I turn my eyes sideways and see the window all frozen over. Think of that. Then the servant comes in. "It is very cold this morning, is it not?" — "Very cold, Sir." — "Very cold indeed, isn't it?" — "Very cold indeed, Sir." — "More than usually so, isn't it, even for this weather?" (Here the servant's wit and good-nature are put to a considerable test, and the enquirer lies on thorns for the answer.) "Why, Sir - - - - I think it *is*." (Good creature! There is not a better, or more truth-telling servant going.) "I must rise however — get me some warm water." — Here comes a fine interval between the departure of the servant and the arrival of the hot water; during which, of course, it is of "no use?" to get up. The hot water comes. "Is it quite hot?" — "Yes, Sir." — "Perhaps too hot for shaving: I must wait a little?" — "No, Sir; it will just do." (There is an over-nice propriety sometimes, an officious zeal of virtue, a little troublesome.) "Oh — the shirt — you must air my clean shirt; — linen gets very damp this weather." — "Yes, Sir." Here another delicious five minutes. A knock at the door. "Oh, the shirt — very well. My stockings — I think the stockings had better be aired too." — "Very well, Sir." — Here another interval. At length every thing is ready, except myself. I now, continues our incumbent (a happy word, by the bye, for a country vicar) — I now cannot help thinking a good deal — who can? — upon the unnecessary and villainous custom of shaving: it is a thing so unmanly (here I nestle closer) — so effeminate (here I recoil from an unlucky step into the colder part of the bed.) — No wonder, that the Queen of France took part with the rebels against that degenerate King, her husband, who first affronted her smooth visage with a face like her own.[2] The Emperor Julian never shewed the luxuriancy of his genius to better advantage than in reviving the flowing beard. Look at Cardinal Bembo's picture — at Michael Angelo's — at Titian's — at Shakspeare's — at Fletcher's — at Spenser's — at Chaucer's — at Alfred's — at Plato's — I could name a great man for every tick of my watch. — Look at the Turks, a grave and otiose people. — Think of

[1] *Paradise Lost* II.596.
[2] Louis VII shaved off his beard in submission to ecclesiastical edict.

Haroun Al Raschid and Bed-ridden Hassan. — Think of Wortley
Montague, the worthy son of his mother, above the prejudice of his
time — Look at the Persian gentlemen, whom one is ashamed of
meeting about the suburbs, their dress and appearance are so much
finer than our own — Lastly, think of the razor itself — how totally
opposed to every sensation of bed — how cold, how edgy, how hard!
how utterly different from any thing like the warm and circling
amplitude, which

> Sweetly recommends itself
> Unto our gentle senses.[3]

Add to this, benumbed fingers, which may help you to cut yourself,
a quivering body, a frozen towel, and an ewer full of ice, and he
that says there is nothing to oppose in all this, only shews, that he
has no merit in opposing it.

Thomson the poet, who exclaims in his Seasons —

> Falsely luxurious! Will not man awake?

used to lie in bed till noon, because he said he had no motive in
getting up. He could imagine the good of rising; but then he could
also imagine the good of lying still; and his exclamation, it must be
allowed, was made upon summer-time, not winter. We must proportion the argument to the individual character. A money-getter may
be drawn out of his bed by three or four-pence; but this will not
suffice for a student. A proud man may say, "What shall I think of
myself, if I don't get up?" but the more humble one will be content
to waive this prodigious notion of himself, out of respect to his kindly
bed. The mechanical man shall get up without any ado at all; and
so shall the barometer. An ingenious lier in bed will find hard matter of discussion even on the score of health and longevity. He will
ask us for our proofs and precedents of the ill effects of lying later in
cold weather; and sophisticate much on the advantages of an even
temperature of body; of the natural propensity (pretty universal) to
have one's way; and of the animals that roll themselves up, and sleep
all the winter. As to longevity, he will ask whether the longest is of
necessity the best; and whether Holborn is the handsomest street in
London.[4]

[3] *Macbeth* I.vi.2–3.
[4] Holborn: then a long dirty street.

On Washerwomen

❦ Hunt begins this piece with a defense of the slight and casual as a worthy modification of the stricter tradition from Theophrastus (c.371–c.287 B.C.), whose *Characters* consists of sketches in which the definition of a particular human weakness serves as introduction to a list of actions typical of a person with that weakness. "On Washerwomen" appeared in Hazlitt's and Hunt's Round Table series, first in the *Examiner* of September 15, 1816, and then in the second volume of *The Round Table* in 1817, which bore Hazlitt's name on the title page, with "L.H." at the foot of each essay by Hunt. It may be assumed that Hunt did not first conceive as a single essay the piece as we have it, for a footnote in the *Examiner* says: "Part of this article has appeared in another publication." The text of 1817 is here corrected by that of 1816. ❧

Writers, we think, might oftener indulge themselves in direct picture-making, that is to say, in detached sketches of men and things, which should be to *manners*, what those of Theophrastus are to *character*.

Painters do not always think it necessary to paint epics, or to fill a room with a series of pictures on one subject. They deal sometimes in single figures and groups; and often exhibit a profounder feeling in these little concentrations of their art, than in subjects of a more numerous description. Their *gusto*, perhaps, is less likely to be lost on that very account. They are no longer Sultans in a seraglio, but lovers with a favourite mistress, retired and absorbed. A Madonna of Correggio's, the Bath of Michael Angelo, the Standard of Leonardo da Vinci, Titian's Mistress, and other single subjects or groups of the great masters, are acknowledged to be among their greatest performances, some of them their greatest of all.

It is the same with music. Overtures, which are supposed to make allusion to the whole progress of the story they precede, are not always the best productions of the master; still less are chorusses, and quintetts, and other pieces involving a multiplicity of actors. The overture to Mozart's *Magic Flute* (*Zauberflöte*) is worthy of the title of the piece; it is truly enchanting; but what are so intense, in their way, as the duet of the two lovers, *Ah Perdona,* — or the laughing trio in *Cosi Fan Tutte,* — or that passionate serenade in Don Giovanni, *Deh vieni alla finestra,*[1] which breathes the very soul of refined sensuality! The gallant is before you, with his mandolin and his cap and feather,

---

[1] "Ah, come to the window" — Don Giovanni to Zerlina, II.iii.

taking place of the nightingale for that amorous hour; and you feel
that the sounds must inevitably draw his mistress to the window.
Their intenseness even renders them pathetic; and his heart seems in
earnest, because his senses are.

We do not mean to say, that, in proportion as the work is large and
the subject numerous, the merit may not be the greater if all is good.
Raphael's Sacrament is a greater work than his Adam and Eve; but
his Transfiguration would still have been the finest picture in the
world, had the second group in the foreground been away; nay, the
latter is supposed, and, we think, with justice, to injure its effect. We
only say that there are times, when the numerousness may scatter the
individual gusto; — that the greatest possible feeling may be proved
without it; — and, above all, returning to our more immediate subject,
that writers, like painters, may sometimes have leisure for excellent
detached pieces, when they want it for larger productions. Here, then,
is an opportunity for them. Let them, in their intervals of history, or,
if they want time for it, give us portraits of humanity. People lament
that Sappho did not write more: but, at any rate, her two odes are
worth twenty epics like Tryphiodorus.[2]

But, in portraits of this kind, writing will also have a great advantage; and may avoid what seems to be an inevitable stumbling-block
in paintings of a similar description. Between the matter-of-fact works
of the Dutch artists, and the subtle compositions of Hogarth, there
seems to be a medium reserved only for the pen. The writer only can
tell you all he means, — can let you into his whole mind and intention. The moral insinuations of the painter are, on the one hand,
apt to be lost for want of distinctness, or tempted, on the other, by
their visible nature, to put on too gross a shape. If he leaves his meanings to be imagined, he may unfortunately speak to unimaginate spectators, and generally does; if he wishes to explain himself so as not
to be mistaken, he will paint a set of comments upon his own incidents
and characters, rather than let them tell for themselves. Hogarth himself, for instance, who never does any thing without a sentiment or a
moral, is too apt to perk them both in your face, and to be over-
redundant in his combinations. His persons, in many instances, seem
too much taken away from their proper indifference to effect, and to
be made too much of conscious agents and joint contributors. He "o'er-
informs his tenements."[3] His very goods and chattels are didactic. He
makes a capital remark of a cow's horn, and brings up a piece of cannon in aid of a satire on vanity.[4] It is the writer only who, without

[2] A minor Greek poem on the fall of Troy.
[3] Cf. Dryden, *Absalom and Achitophel* 158.
[4] See the cannon going off in the turbulent portrait of a General Officer:
and the cow's head coming just over that of the citizen who is walking with
his wife. [L.H. In William Hogarth's *Evening* the cow's horns rudely declare the citizen a cuckold.]

hurting the most delicate propriety of the representation, can leave no doubt of all his intentions, — who can insinuate his object in two or three words, to the dullest conception, and, in conversing with the most foreign minds, take away all the awkwardness of interpretation. What painting gains in universality to the eye, it loses by an infinite proportion in power of suggestion to the understanding.

There is something of the sort of sketches we are recommending in Sterne: but Sterne had a general connected object before him, of which the parts apparently detached were still connecting links: and while he also is apt to overdo his subject like Hogarth, is infinitely less various and powerful. The greatest master of detached portrait is Steele: but his pictures too form a sort of link in a chain. Perhaps the completest specimen of what we mean in the English language is Shenstone's *School-Mistress*, by far his best production, and a most natural, quiet, and touching old dame. — But what? Are we leaving out *Chaucer?* Alas, we thought to be doing something a little original, and find it all existing already, and in unrivalled perfection, in his portraits of the Canterbury Pilgrims! We can only dilate, and vary upon his principle.

But we are making a very important preface to what may turn out a very trifling subject; and must request the reader not to be startled at the homely specimen we are about to give him, after all this gravity of recommendation. Not that we would apologise for homeliness, as homeliness. The beauty of this unlimited power of suggestion in writing is, that you may take up the driest and most common-place of all possible subjects, and strike a light out of it to warm your intellect and your heart by. The fastidious habits of polished life generally incline us to reject, as incapable of interesting us, whatever does not present itself in a graceful shape of its own, and a ready-made suit of ornaments. But some of the plainest weeds become beautiful under the microscope. It is the benevolent provision of nature, that in proportion as you feel the necessity of extracting interest from common things, you are enabled to do so; — and the very least that this familiarity with homeliness will do for us is to render our artificial delicacy less liable to annoyance, and to teach us how to grasp the nettles till they obey us.

The reader sees that we are Wordsworthians enough not to confine our tastes to the received elegancies of society; and, in one respect, we go farther than Mr Wordsworth, for, though as fond, perhaps, of the country as he, we can manage to please ourselves in the very thick of cities, and even find there as much reason to do justice to Providence, as he does in the haunts of sportsmen, and anglers, and all-devouring insects.

To think, for instance, of that laborious and inelegant class of the community, — *Washerwomen*, and of all the hot, disagreeable, dabbing, smoaking, splashing, kitcheny, cold-dining, anti-company-receiv-

ing associations, to which they give rise. — What can be more annoy-
ing to any tasteful lady or gentleman, at their first waking in the
morning, than when that dreadful thump at the door comes, announcing the tub-tumbling viragoes, with their brawny arms and
brawling voices? We must confess, for our own parts, that our taste,
in the abstract, is not for washerwomen; we prefer Dryads and Naiads,
and the figures that resemble them; —

> "Fair forms, that glance amid the green of woods,
> Or from the waters give their sidelong shapes
> Half swelling."

Yet, we have lain awake sometimes in a street in town, after this first
confounded rap, and pleased ourselves with reflecting how equally the
pains and enjoyments of this world are dealt out, and what a pleasure
there is in the mere contemplation of any set of one's fellow-creatures
and their humours, when our knowledge has acquired humility enough
to look at them steadily.

The reader knows the knock which we mean. It comes like a lump
of lead, and instantly wakes the maid, whose business it is to get up,
though she pretends not to hear it. Another knock is inevitable, and
it comes, and then another; but still Betty does not stir, or stirs only
to put herself in a still snugger posture, knowing very well that they
must knock again. "How, 'drat that Betty," says one of the washerwomen; "she hears as well as we do, but the deuce a bit will she
move till we give her another;" and at the word another, down goes
the knocker again. "It's very odd," says the master of the house,
mumbling from under the bed-clothes, "that Betty does not get up to
let the people in; I've heard that knocker three times." — "Oh," returns
the mistress, "she's as lazy as she's high," — and off goes the chamber-
bell; — by which time Molly, who begins to lose her sympathy with
her fellow-servant in impatience of what is going on, gives her one
or two conclusive digs in the side; when the other gets up, and rubbing her eyes and mumbling, and hastening and shrugging herself
down stairs, opens the door with — "Lard, Mrs Watson, I hope you
haven't been standing here long?" — "Standing here long! Mrs Betty!
Oh don't tell me; people might stand starving their legs off, before
you'd put a finger out of bed." — "Oh don't say so, Mrs Watson; I'm
sure I always rises at the first knock; and there — you'll find every
thing comfortable below, with a nice hock of ham, which I made John
leave for you." At this the washerwomen leave their mumbling, and
shuffle down stairs, hoping to see Mrs Betty early at breakfast. Here,
after warming themselves at the copper, taking a mutual pinch of
snuff, and getting things ready for the wash, they take a snack at the
promised hock; for people of this profession have always their appetite at hand, and every interval of labour is invariably cheered by
the prospect of *having something* at the end of it. "Well," says Mrs

Watson, finishing the last cut, "some people thinks themselves mighty generous for leaving one what little they can't eat; but, howsomever, it's better than nothing." — "Ah," says Mrs Jones, who is a minor genius, "one must take what one can get now-a-days; but Squire Hervey's for my money." — "Squire Hervey!" rejoins Mrs Watson, "what's that the great what's-his-name as lives yonder?" — "Aye," returns Mrs Jones, "him as has a niece and nevvy, as they say eats him out of house and land;" — and here commences the history of all the last week of the whole neighbourhood round, which continues amidst the dipping of splashing fists, the rumbling of suds, and the creaking of wringings out, till an hour or two are elapsed; and then for another snack and a pinch of snuff, till the resumption of another hour's labour or so brings round the time for first breakfast. Then, having had nothing to signify since five, they sit down at half-past six in the wash-house, to take their own meal before the servants meet at the general one. This is the chief moment of enjoyment. They have just laboured enough to make the tea and bread and butter welcome, are at an interesting point of the conversation, (for there they contrive to leave off on purpose,) and so down they sit, fatigued and happy, with their red elbows and white corrugated fingers, to a tub turned upside down, and a dish of good christian souchong, fit for a body to drink.

We could dwell a good deal upon this point of time, but we have already, we fear, ran out our limits; and shall only admonish the fastidious reader, who thinks he has all the taste and means of enjoyment to himself, how he looks with scorn upon two persons, who are perhaps at this moment the happiest couple of human beings in the street, — who have discharged their duty, have earned their enjoyment, and have health and spirits to relish it to the full. A washerwoman's cup of tea may vie with the first drawn cork at a bonvivant's table, and the complacent opening of her snuff-box with that of the most triumphant politician over a scheme of partition. We say nothing of the continuation of their labours, of the scandal they resume, or the complaints they pour forth, when they first set off again in the indolence of a satisfied appetite, at the quantity of work which the mistress of the house, above all other mistresses, is sure to heap upon them. Scandal and complaint, in these instances, do not hurt the complacency of our reflections; they are in their proper sphere; and are nothing but a part, as it were, of the day's work, and are so much vent to the animal spirits. Even the unpleasant day which the work causes up stairs in some houses, — the visitors which it excludes, and the leg of mutton which it hinders from roasting, are only so much enjoyment kept back and contracted, in order to be made keener the rest of the week. Beauty itself is indebted to it, and draws from that steaming out-house and splashing tub the well-fitting robe that gives out its figure, and the snowy cap that contrasts its curls and its complexion. In short, whenever we hear a washerwoman at her foaming work, or see her plodding towards us with her jolly warm face, her mob cap, her black stockings, clattering pattens, and tub at arm's length resting on her hip-joint, we look upon her as a living lesson to us to make the most both of time and comfort, and as a sort of allegorical union of pain and pleasure, a little too much, perhaps, in the style of Rubens.

L. H.

A "Now": Descriptive of a Hot Day

¶ This essay appeared in *Indicator* No. 38, for June 28, 1820. Like "Getting Up on Cold Mornings," it was shortened by Hunt for the edition of 1834, which is here followed except for the omission of a closing passage quoted by Hunt from Beaumont and Fletcher's play, *The Woman Hater*. Several of Hunt's essays, such as "The Old Lady" and "The Maid-Servant," follow the convention of the Theophrastian "character," or brief essay analyzing a human type. Emulating the pithy style and neat form of the "character" as practiced by seventeenth-century essayists like Sir Thomas Overbury and John Earle, Hunt refines still further on the genre by portraying a single moment as experienced by several social types. In a sequel, "A 'Now': Descriptive of a Cold Day," published in *Leigh Hunt's London Journal* for December 3, 1834, he explained that he had been first struck by the convenience of the word *Now* for descriptive writers like the poet James Thomson. He emphasized the Englishness of it: "No other *Now* can be so present, so instantaneous, so extremely *Now* as our own Now."]▶

Now the rosy- (and lazy-) fingered Aurora, issuing from her saffron house, calls up the moist vapours to surround her, and goes veiled with them as long as she can; till Phœbus, coming forth in his power, looks every thing out of the sky, and holds sharp uninterrupted empire from his throne of beams. Now the mower begins to make his sweeping cuts more slowly, and resorts oftener to the beer. Now the carter sleeps a-top of his load of hay, or plods with double slouch of shoulder, looking out with eyes winking under his shading hat, and with a hitch upward of one side of his mouth. Now the little girl at her grandmother's cottage-door watches the coaches that go by, with her hand held up over her sunny forehead. Now labourers look well resting in their white shirts at the doors of rural alehouses. Now an elm is fine there, with a seat under it; and horses drink out of the trough, stretching their yearning necks with loosened collars; and the traveller calls for his glass of ale, having been without one for more than ten minutes; and his horse stands wincing at the flies, giving sharp shivers of his skin, and moving to and fro his ineffectual docked tail; and now Miss Betty Wilson, the host's daughter, comes streaming forth in a flowered gown and ear-rings, carrying with four of her beautiful fingers the foaming glass, for which, after the traveller has drank it, she receives with an indifferent eye, looking another way, the lawful two-pence. Now grasshoppers "fry," as Dryden says.[1] Now cattle stand in water, and ducks are envied. Now boots and shoes, and trees by the road side, are thick with dust; and dogs, rolling in it, after issuing out of the water, into which they have been thrown to fetch sticks, come scattering horror among the legs of the spectators. Now a fellow who finds he has three miles further to go in a pair of tight shoes, is in a pretty situation. Now rooms with the sun upon them become intolerable; and the apothecary's apprentice, with a bitterness beyond aloes, thinks of the pond he used to bathe in at school. Now men with powdered heads (especially if thick) envy those that are unpowdered, and stop to wipe them up hill, with countenances that seem to expostulate with destiny. Now boys assemble round the village pump with a ladle to it, and delight to make a forbidden splash and get wet through the shoes. Now also they make suckers of leather, and bathe all day long in rivers and ponds, and make mighty fishings for "tittle-bats." Now the bee, as he hums along, seems to be talking heavily of the heat. Now doors and brick-walls are burning to the hand; and a walled lane, with dust and broken bottles in it, near a brick-field, is a thing not to be thought of. Now a green lane, on the contrary, thick-set with hedge-row elms, and having the noise of a brook "rumbling in pebble-stone,"[2] is one of the pleasantest things in the world.

Now, in town, gossips talk more than ever to one another, in rooms, in door-ways, and out of window, always beginning the conversation with saying that the heat is overpowering. Now blinds are let down, and doors thrown open, and flannel waistcoats left off, and cold meat preferred to hot, and wonder expressed why tea continues so refreshing, and people delight to sliver lettuces into bowls, and apprentices water door-ways with tin-canisters that lay several atoms of dust. Now the water-cart, jumbling along the middle of the street, and jolting the showers out of its box of water, really does something. Now fruiterers' shops and dairies look pleasant, and ices are the only things to those who can get them. Now ladies loiter in baths; and people make presents of flowers; and wine is put into ice; and the after-dinner lounger recreates his head with applications of perfumed water out of long-necked bottles. Now the lounger, who cannot resist riding his new horse, feels his boots burn him. Now buck-skins are not the lawn of Cos. Now jockies, walking in great coats to lose flesh, curse inwardly. Now five fat people in a stage-coach, hate the sixth fat one

[1] *Eclogues* (from Virgil) II.13.
[2] Spenser, *Virgil's Gnat* 163.

who is coming in, and think he has no right to be so large. Now
clerks in offices do nothing but drink soda-water and spruce-beer, and
read the newspaper. Now the old clothesman drops his solitary cry
more deeply into the areas on the hot and forsaken side of the street;
and bakers look vicious; and cooks are aggravated: and the steam of
a tavern-kitchen catches hold of us like the breath of Tartarus. Now
delicate skins are beset with gnats: and boys make their sleeping
companion start up, with playing a burning-glass on his hand; and
blacksmiths are super-carbonated; and cobblers in their stalls almost
feel a wish to be transplanted; and butter is too easy to spread; and
the dragoons wonder whether the Romans liked their helmets; and
old ladies, with their lappets unpinned, walk along in a state of dila-
pidation; and the servant-maids are afraid they look vulgarly hot; and
the author, who has a plate of strawberries brought him, finds that
he has come to the end of his writing. . . .[3]

What Is Poetry?

❬ The critical volume by Hunt most frequently consulted and cited bore a
descriptive title when it first appeared in March 1844: *Imagination and
Fancy; or, Selections from the English Poets, Illustrative of those First
Requisites of their Art; with Markings of the Best Passages, Critical Notices
of the Writers, and an Essay in Answer to the Question "What Is Poetry?"*
The introductory essay was edited with careful notes by Albert S. Cook in
1893. The first ten pages of this essay, given below from the first edition,
contain the essence of Hunt's theories, which were gathered almost at random from other writers of his century but unified by his own emotional
attitude and taste. ❭

Poetry, strictly and artistically so called, that is to say, considered
not merely as poetic feeling, which is more or less shared by all the
world, but as the operation of that feeling, such as we see it in the
poet's book, is the utterance of a passion for truth, beauty, and power,
embodying and illustrating its conceptions by imagination and fancy,
and modulating its language on the principle of variety in unformity.
Its means are whatever the universe contains; and its ends, pleasure
and exaltation. Poetry stands between nature and convention, keeping alive among us the enjoyment of the external and the spiritual

[3] tittle-bats: sticklebacks, small fish; lawn of Cos: fine linen from the
Aegean island of Kos.

world: it has constituted the most enduring fame of nations; and, next to Love and Beauty, which are its parents, is the greatest proof to man of the pleasure to be found in all things, and of the probable riches of infinitude.

Poetry is a passion,[1] because it seeks the deepest impressions; and because it must undergo, in order to convey, them.

It is a passion for truth, because without truth the impression would be false or defective.

It is a passion for beauty, because its office is to exalt and refine by means of pleasure, and because beauty is nothing but the loveliest form of pleasure.

It is a passion for power, because power is impression triumphant, whether over the poet, as desired by himself, or over the reader, as affected by the poet.

It embodies and illustrates its impressions by imagination, or images of the objects of which it treats, and other things brought in to throw light on those objects, in order that it may enjoy and impart the feeling of their truth in its utmost conviction and affluence.

It illustrates them by fancy, which is a lighter play of imagination, or the feeling of analogy coming short of seriousness, in order that it may laugh with what it loves, and show how it can decorate it with fairy ornament.

It modulates what it utters, because in running the whole round of beauty it must needs include beauty of sound; and because, in the height of its enjoyment, it must show the perfection of its triumph, and make difficulty itself become part of its facility and joy.

And lastly, Poetry shapes this modulation into uniformity for its outline, and variety for its parts, because it thus realizes the last idea of beauty itself, which includes the charm of diversity within the flowing round of habit and ease.

Poetry is imaginative passion. The quickest and subtlest test of the possession of its essence is in expression; the variety of things to be expressed shows the amount of its resources; and the continuity of the song completes the evidence of its strength and greatness. He who has thought, feeling, expression, imagination, action, character, and continuity, all in the largest amount and highest degree, is the greatest poet.

Poetry includes whatsoever of painting can be made visible to the mind's eye, and whatsoever of music can be conveyed by sound and proportion without singing or instrumentation. But it far surpasses those divine arts in suggestiveness, range, and intellectual wealth; — the first, in expression of thought, combination of images, and the triumph over space and time; the second, in all that can be done by speech, apart from the tones and modulations of pure sound. Painting

[1] *Passio*, suffering in a good sense, — ardent subjection of one's-self to emotion. [L.H.]

and music, however, include all those portions of the gift of poetry that can be expressed and heightened by the visible and melodious. Painting, in a certain apparent manner, is things themselves; music, in a certain audible manner, is their very emotion and grace. Music and painting are proud to be related to poetry, and poetry loves and is proud of them.

Poetry begins where matter of fact or of science ceases to be merely such, and to exhibit a further truth; that is to say, the connexion it has with the world of emotion, and its power to produce imaginative pleasure. Inquiring of a gardener, for instance, what flower it is we see yonder, he answers, "a lily." This is matter of fact. The botanist pronounces it to be of the order of "Hexandria Monogynia." This is matter of science. It is the "lady" of the garden, says Spenser; and here we begin to have a poetical sense of its fairness and grace. It is

The plant and flower of *light*,

says Ben Jonson; and poetry then shows us the beauty of the flower in all its mystery and splendour.[2]

If it be asked, how we know perceptions like these to be true, the answer is, by the fact of their existence, — by the consent and delight of poetic readers. And as feeling is the earlist teacher, and perception the only final proof, of things the most demonstrable by science, so the remotest imaginations of the poets may often be found to have the closest connexion with matter of fact; perhaps might always be so, if the subtlety of our perceptions were a match for the causes of them. Consider this image of Ben Jonson's — of a lily being the flower of light. Light, undecomposed, is white; and as the lily is white, and light is white, and whiteness itself is nothing *but* light, the two things, so far, are not merely similar, but identical. A poet might add, by an analogy drawn from the connexion of light and colour, that there is a "golden dawn" issuing out of the white lily, in the rich yellow of the stamens. I have no desire to push this similarity farther than it may be worth. Enough has been stated to show that, in poetical as in other analogies, "the same feet of Nature," as Bacon says, may be seen "treading in different paths;"[3] and that the most scornful, that is to say, dullest disciple of fact, should be cautious how he betrays the shallowness of his philosophy by discerning no poetry in its depths.

But the poet is far from dealing only with these subtle and analogical truths. Truth of every kind belongs to him, provided it can bud into any kind of beauty, or is capable of being illustrated and impressed by the poetic faculty. Nay, the simplest truth is often so beautiful and impressive of itself, that one of the greatest proofs of his genius consists in his leaving it to stand alone, illustrated

[2] *The Faerie Queene* II.vi.16; Jonson, *To the Immortal Memory of Cary and Morison* 72.

[3] Cf. *Advancement of Learning* II.v.3.

by nothing but the light of its own tears or smiles, its own wonder, might, or playfulness. Hence the complete effect of many a simple passage in our old English ballads and romances, and of the passionate sincerity in general of the greatest early poets, such as Homer and Chaucer, who flourished before the existence of a "literary world," and were not perplexed by a heap of notions and opinions, or by doubts how emotion ought to be expressed. The greatest of their successors never write equally to the purpose, except when they can dismiss every thing from their minds but the like simple truth. In the beautiful poem of "Sir Eger, Sir Graham, and Sir Gray-Steel" (see it in Ellis's Specimens, or Laing's Early Metrical Tales), a knight thinks himself disgraced in the eyes of his mistress: —

> Sir Eger said, "If it be so,
> Then wot I well I must forego
> Love-liking, and manhood, all clean!"
> *The water rush'd out of his een!*

Sir Gray-Steel is killed: —

> Gray-Steel into his death thus thraws (throes?)
> He *walters* (welters, — throws himself about) *and the*
> grass up draws;
>
> ❖   ❖   ❖   ❖   ❖
>
> *A little while then lay he still*
> (*Friends that him saw, liked full ill*)
> *And bled into his armour bright.*

The abode of Chaucer's *Reve*, or Steward, in the Canterbury Tales, is painted in two lines, which nobody ever wished longer: —

> His wonning (dwelling) was full fair upon an heath,
> With greeny trees yshadowed was his place.[4]

Every one knows the words of Lear, "most *matter-of-fact*, most melancholy."

> Pray do not mock me;
> I am a very foolish fond old man
> Fourscore and upwards:
> Not an hour more, nor less; and to deal plainly
> I fear I am not in my perfect mind.[5]

It is thus, by exquisite pertinence, melody, and the implied power of writing with exuberance, if need be, that beauty and truth become identical in poetry, and that pleasure, or at the very worst, a balm in our tears, is drawn out of pain.

[4] Prologue 606–607.
[5] Cf. Milton, *Il Penseroso* 62 ("Most musical, most melancholy"); *King Lear* IV.vii.59–63.

It is a great and rare thing, and shows a lovely imagination, when the poet can write a commentary, as it were, of his own, on such sufficing passages of nature, and be thanked for the addition. There is an instance of this kind in Warner, an old Elizabethan poet, than which I know nothing sweeter in the world. He is speaking of Fair Rosamond, and of a blow given her by Queen Eleanor.

> With that she dash'd her on the lips,
>   So dyèd double red:
> Hard was the heart that gave the blow,
>   Soft were those lips that bled.[6]

There are different kinds and degrees of imagination, some of them necessary to the formation of every true poet, and all of them possessed by the greatest. Perhaps they may be enumerated as follows: — First, that which presents to the mind any object or circumstance in every-day life; as when we imagine a man holding a sword, or looking out of a window; — Second, that which presents real, but not every-day circumstances; as King Alfred tending the loaves, or Sir Philip Sidney giving up the water to the dying soldier; — Third, that which combines character and events directly imitated from real life, with imitative realities of its own invention; as the probable parts of the histories of Priam and Macbeth, or what may be called natural fiction as distinguished from supernatural; — Fourth, that which conjures up things and events not to be found in nature; as Homer's gods, and Shakspeare's witches, enchanted horses and spears, Ariosto's hippogriff,[7] &c.; — Fifth, that which, in order to illustrate or aggravate one image, introduces another; sometimes in simile, as when Homer compares Apollo descending in his wrath at noon-day to the coming of night-time: sometimes in metaphor, or simile comprised in a word, as in Milton's "motes that *people* the sunbeams;" sometimes in concentrating into a word the main history of any person or thing, past or even future, as in the "starry Galileo" of Byron, and that ghastly foregone conclusion of the epithet "murdered" applied to the yet living victim in Keats's story from Boccaccio, —

> So the two brothers and their *murder'd* man
> Rode towards fair Florence; —

sometimes in the attribution of a certain representative quality which makes one circumstance stand for others; as in Milton's grey-fly winding its "*sultry* horn," which epithet contains the heat of a summer's day;[8] — Sixth, that which reverses this process, and makes a variety of circumstances take colour from one, like nature seen with jaundiced

---

[6] William Warner, *Albion's England*, 1596, VIII.xli.53.

[7] Lodovico Ariosto (1474–1533), *Orlando Furioso* IV.iv.

[8] See *Iliad* I.47; *Il Penseroso* 8; Byron, *Childe Harold* IV.liv.8; Keats, *Isabella* xxvii.1–2; Milton, *Lycidas* 28.

or glad eyes, or under the influence of storm or sunshine; as when in Lycidas, or the Greek pastoral poets, the flowers and the flocks are made to sympathize with a man's death; or, in the Italian poet, the river flowing by the sleeping Angelica seems talking of love —

> Parea che l'erba le fiorisse intorno,
> E d'amor ragionasse quella riva! —
> > Orlando Innamorato [I.iii.69]

or in the voluptuous homage paid to the sleeping Imogen by the very light in the chamber and the reaction of her own beauty upon itself; or in the "witch element" of the tragedy of Macbeth and the May-day night of Faust;[9] — Seventh, and last, that which by a single expression, apparently of the vaguest kind, not only meets but surpasses in its effect the extremest force of the most particular description; as in that exquisite passage of Coleridge's Christabel, where the unsuspecting object of the witch's malignity is bidden to go to bed: —

> Quoth Christabel, So let it be!
> And as the lady bade, did she.
> Her gentle limbs did she undress,
> *And lay down in her loveliness;* —

a perfect verse surely, both for feeling and music. The very smoothness and gentleness of the limbs is in the series of the letter *l's.*

I am aware of nothing of the kind surpassing that most lovely inclusion of physical beauty in moral, neither can I call to mind any instances of the imagination that turns accompaniments into accessories, superior to those I have alluded to. Of the class of comparison, one of the most touching (many a tear must it have drawn from parents and lovers) is in a stanza which has been copied into the "Friar of Orders Grey," out of Beaumont and Fletcher: —

> Weep no more, lady, weep no more,
> > Thy sorrow is in vain;
> *For violets pluck'd the sweetest showers*
> *Will ne'er make grow again.*[10]

And Shakspeare and Milton abound in the very grandest; such as Antony's likening his changing fortunes to the cloud-rack; Lear's appeal to the old age of the heavens; Satan's appearance in the horizon, like a fleet "hanging in the clouds;" and the comparisons of him with the comet and the eclipse. Nor unworthy of this glorious company, for its extraordinary combination of delicacy and vastness, is that enchanting one of Shelley's in the Adonais: —

[9] Goethe, *Faust* I.3835–4222; Shelley's translation of this *Walpurgisnacht* episode appeared in the *Liberal,* No. I.

[10] As modified in Thomas Percy's *Reliques,* 1765, from a play printed in 1647 as Beaumont and Fletcher's: *The Queen of Corinth* III.ii.1–4.

> Life, like a dome of many-coloured glass,
> Stains the white radiance of eternity.[11]

I multiply these particulars in order to impress upon the reader's mind the great importance of imagination in all its phases, as a constituent part of the highest poetic faculty.

The happiest instance I remember of imaginative metaphor, is Shakspeare's moonlight "sleeping" on a bank;[12] but half his poetry may be said to be made up of it, metaphor indeed being the common coin of discourse. . . .

Poems by John Keats

❡ The *Examiner* of May 5, 1816, contained the first poem by Keats to be published. In an article titled "Young Poets," on December 1, Hunt asked his readers to note and remember three names: P. B. Shelley, J. H. Reynolds, and John Keats. He ended with the sonnet "On First Looking into Chapman's Homer." His review of Keats's first volume (dedicated to Hunt) came in three installments on June 1, July 6, and July 13, 1817. It is given here with the omission of paragraphs in which Hunt quotes at various lengths from Keats and comments briefly. ❫

This is the production of the young writer, whom we had the pleasure of announcing to the public a short time since, and several of whose Sonnets have appeared meanwhile in the *Examiner* with the signature of J. K. From these and stronger evidences in the book itself, the readers will conclude that the author and his critic are personal friends; and they are so, — made however, in the first instance, by nothing but his poetry, and at no greater distance of time than the announcement above-mentioned. We had published one of his Sonnets in our paper, without knowing more of him than any other anonymous correspondent; but at the period in question, a friend brought us one morning some copies of verses, which he said were from the pen of a youth. We had not been led, generally speaking, by a good deal of experience in these matters, to expect pleasure from introductions of the kind, so much as pain; but we had not read more than a dozen lines, when we recognised "a young poet indeed."

It is no longer a new observation, that poetry has of late years

---

[11] Cf. *Antony and Cleopatra* IV.xiv.2–11; *King Lear* II.iv.192–195; *Paradise Lost* II.637, 708–718, I.594–599; *Adonais* 462–463.

[12] *Merchant of Venice* V.i.54.

undergone a very great change, or rather, to speak properly, poetry
has undergone no change, but something which was not poetry has
made way for the return of something which is. The school which existed till lately since the restoration of Charles the 2d, was rather a
school of wit and ethics in verse, than any thing else; nor was the
verse, with the exception of Dryden's, of the best order. The authors,
it is true, are to be held in great honour. Great wit there certainly
was, excellent satire, excellent sense, pithy sayings; and Pope distilled
as much real poetry as could be got from the drawing-room world in
which the art then lived, — from the flowers and luxuries of artificial
life, — into that exquisite little toilet-bottle of essence, the *Rape of
the Lock*. But there was little imagination, of a higher order, no intense feeling of nature, no sentiment, no real music or variety. Even
the writers who gave evidences meanwhile of a truer poetical faculty,
Gray, Thomson, Akenside, and Collins himself, were content with a
great deal of second-hand workmanship, and with false styles made
up of other languages and a certain kind of inverted cant. It has been
thought that Cowper was the first poet who re-opened the true way to
nature and a natural style; but we hold this to be a mistake, arising
merely from certain negations on the part of that amiable but by no
means powerful writer. Cowper's style is for the most part as inverted
and artificial as that of the others; and we look upon him to have
been by nature not so great a poet as Pope: but Pope, from certain
infirmities on his part, was thrown into the society of the world, and
thus had to get what he could out of an artificial sphere: — Cowper,
from other and more distressing infirmities, (which by the way the
wretched superstition that undertook to heal, only burnt in upon him)
was confined to a still smaller though more natural sphere, and in truth
did not much with it, though quite as much perhaps as was to be
expected from an organization too sore almost to come in contact with
any thing.

It was the Lake Poets in our opinion (however grudgingly we say
it, on some accounts) that were the first to revive a true taste for
nature; and like most Revolutionists, especially of the cast which they
have since turned out to be, they went to an extreme, calculated
rather at first to make the readers of poetry disgusted with originality
and adhere with contempt and resentment to their magazine commonplaces. This had a bad effect also in the way of re-action; and none
of those writers have ever since been able to free themselves from
certain stubborn affectations, which having been ignorantly confounded by others with the better part of them, have been retained
by their self-love with a still less pardonable want of wisdom. The
greater part indeed of the poetry of Mr. Southey, a weak man in all
respects, is really made up of little else. Mr. Coleridge still trifles
with his poetical as he has done with his metaphysical talent. Mr.
Lamb, in our opinion, has a more real tact of humanity, a modester,

Shakspearean wisdom, than any of them; and had he written more, might have delivered the school victoriously from all it's defects. But it is Mr. Wordsworth who has advanced it the most, and who in spite of some morbidities as well as mistaken theories in other respects, has opened upon us a fund of thinking and imagination, that ranks him as the successor of the true and abundant poets of the older time. Poetry, like Plenty, should be represented with a cornucopia, but it should be a real one; not swelled out and insidiously *optimized* at the top, like Mr. Southey's stale strawberry baskets, but fine and full to the depth, like a heap from the vintage. Yet from the time of Milton till lately, scarcely a tree had been planted that could be called a poet's own. People got shoots from France, that ended in nothing but a little barren wood, from which they made flutes for young gentlemen and fan-sticks for ladies. The rich and enchanted ground of real poetry, fertile with all that English succulence could produce, bright with all that Italian sunshine could lend, and haunted with exquisite humanities, had become invisible to mortal eyes like the garden of Eden: —

"And from that time those Graces were not found."

These Graces, however, are re-appearing; and one of the greatest evidences is the little volume before us; for the work is not one of mere imitation, or a compilation of ingenious and promising things that merely announce better, and that after all might only help to keep up a bad system; but here is a young poet giving himself up to his own impressions, and revelling in real poetry for its' own sake. He has had his advantages, because others have cleared the way into those happy bowers; but it shews the strength of his natural tendency, that he has not been turned aside by the lingering enticements of a former system, and by the self-love which interests others in enforcing them. We do not, of course, mean to say, that Mr. Keats has as much talent as he will have ten years hence, or that there are no imitations in his book, or that he does not make mistakes common to inexperience; — the reverse is inevitable at his time of life. In proportion to our ideas, or impressions of the images of things, must be our acquaintance with the things themselves. But our author has all the sensitiveness of temperament requisite to receive these impressions; and wherever he has turned hitherto, he has evidently felt them deeply.

The very faults indeed of Mr. Keats arise from a passion for beauties, and a young impatience to vindicate them; and as we have mentioned these, we shall refer to them at once. They may be comprised in two; — first, a tendency to notice every thing too indiscriminately and without an eye to natural proportion and effect; and second, a sense of the proper variety of versification without a due consideration of its principles.

The former error is visible in several parts of the book, but chiefly though mixed with great beauties in the Epistles, and more between pages 28 and 47, where are collected the author's earliest pieces, some of which, we think, might have been omitted, especially the string of magistrate-interrogatories about a shell and a copy of verses. See also (p. 61) a comparison of wine poured out in heaven to the appearance of a falling star, and (p. 62) the sight of far-seen fountains in the same region to "silver streaks across a dolphin's fin." It was by thus giving way to every idea that came across him, that Marino, a man of real poetical fancy, but no judgment, corrupted the poetry of Italy;[1] a catastrophe, which however we by no means anticipate from our author, who with regard to this point is much more deficient in age than in good taste. We shall presently have to notice passages of a reverse nature, and these are by far the most numerous. But we warn him against a fault, which is the more tempting to a young writer of genius, inasmuch as it involves something so opposite to the contented common-place and vague generalities of the late school of poetry. There is a super-abundance of detail, which, though not so wanting, of course, in power of perception, is as faulty and unseasonable sometimes as common-place. It depends upon circumstances, whether we are to consider ourselves near enough, as it were, to the subject we are describing to grow microscopical upon it. A person basking in a landscape for instance, and a person riding through it, are in two very different situations for the exercise of their eyesight; and even where the license is most allowable, care must be taken not to give to small things and great, to nice detail and to general feeling, the same proportion of effect. Errors of this kind in poetry answer to a want of perspective in painting, and of a due distribution of light and shade. . . .

Mr. Keats's other fault, the one in his versification, arises from a similar cause, — that of contradicting over-zealously the fault on the opposite side. It is this which provokes him now and then into mere roughnesses and discords for their own sake, not for that of variety and contrasted harmony. We can manage, by substituting a greater feeling for a smaller, a line like the following: —

I shall roll on the grass with two-fold ease; —[2]

but by no contrivance of any sort can we prevent this from jumping out of the heroic measure into mere rhythmicality, —

How many bards gild the lapses of time![3]

We come now however to the beauties; and the reader will easily perceive that they not only outnumber the faults a hundred fold, but that they are of a nature decidedly opposed to what is false and inharmonious. Their characteristics indeed are a fine ear, a fancy and

---

[1] G. B. Marini, "il Cavalier Marino" (1569–1625).
[2] *To Charles Cowden Clark* 79.
[3] Sonnet IV, first line.

imagination at will, and an intense feeling of external beauty in it's most natural and least expressible simplicity.

We shall give some specimens of the least beauty first, and conclude with a noble extract or two that will shew the second, as well as the powers of our young poet in general. The harmony of his verses will appear throughout.

The first poem consists of a piece of luxury in a rural spot, ending with an allusion to the story of Endymion and to the origin of other lovely tales of mythology, on the ground suggested by Mr. Wordsworth in a beautiful passage of his *Excursion*. Here, and in the other largest poem, which closes the book, Mr. Keats is seen to his best advantage, and displays all that fertile power of association and imagery which constitutes the abstract poetical faculty as distinguished from every other. He wants age for a greater knowledge of humanity, but evidences of this also bud forth here and there. . . .

The best poem is certainly the last and longest, entitled *Sleep and Poetry*. It originated in sleeping in a room adorned with busts and pictures, and is a striking specimen of the restlessness of the young poetical appetite, obtaining its food by the very desire of it, and glancing for fit subjects of creation "from earth to heaven." Nor do we like it the less for an impatient, and as it may be thought by some, irreverent assault upon the late French school of criticism and monotony, which has held poetry chained long enough to render it somewhat indignant when it has got free. . . .

Amiableness Superior to Intellect

《 In this piece, which appeared as an editorial in *Leigh Hunt's London Journal* for October 29, 1834, Hunt as usual defends Hazlitt and exalts Shelley. The insistence on amiability, which continues at greater length than is represented here, especially marks the *London Journal* and Hunt's other works of this period. 》

. . . It is Sir Walter Scott, we believe, who has observed somewhere, that men of superior endowments, or other advantages, are accustomed to pay too little regard to the intercourse of their less gifted fellow-creatures, and to regret all the time that is passed in their company. He says, they accustom themselves so much to the living upon sweets and spices, that they lose a proper relish for ordinary food, and grow contemptuous of those who live upon it, to the injury of their own enjoyment. They keep their palate in a constant state of thirst and irritation, rather than of healthy satisfaction. And we recollect Mr Hazlitt making a remark to a similar effect, namely, that the being accustomed to the society of men of genius renders the conversation of others tiresome, as consisting of a parcel of things that have been heard a thousand times, and from which no stimulus is to be obtained. He lamented this, as an effect unbecoming a reflecting man and a fellow-creature (for though irritable, and sometimes resentful, his heart was large and full of humanity); and the consequence was, that nobody paid greater attention than he to common conversation, or showed greater respect towards any endeavours to interest him, however trite. Youths of his acquaintance are fond of calling to mind the footing of equality on which he treated them, even when children, gravely interchanging remarks with them, as he sat side by side, like one grown person with another, and giving them now and then (though without the pomp) a Johnsonian "Sir." The serious earnestness of his "Indeed, m'um!" with lifted eyebrows, and protruded lips, while listening to the surprising things told him by good housewives about their shopping or their preserves, is now sounding in our ears; and makes us long to see again the splenetic but kindly philosopher, who worried himself to death about the good of the nations. . . .

A total want of ideas in a companion, or of the power to receive them, is indeed to be avoided by men who require intellectual excitement; but it is a great mistake to suppose that the most discerning men demand intellect above every thing else in their most habitual associates, much less in general intercourse. Happy would they be to see intellect more universally extended, but as a means, not as an end, — as a help to the knowledge of what is amiable, and not what is merely knowing. Clever men are sometimes said even to be jealous of clever companions, especially female ones. Men of genius, it is notorious, for a very different reason, and out of their own imagination of what is excellent, and their power to adorn what they love, will be enamoured, in their youth, of women neither intelligent, nor amiable, nor handsome. They make them all three, with their fancy; and are sometimes too apt, in after-life, to resent what is nobody's fault but their own. However, their faults have their excuses, as well as those of other men; only they who know most, should excuse most. But the reader may take our word for it, from the experience of long intercourse with such men, that what they value above every other consideration, in a companion, female or male, is amiableness; that is to say, evenness of temper, and the willingness (general as well as particular) to please and be pleased, without egotism and without exaction. This is what we have ever felt to be the highest thing in themselves, and what gave us a preference for them, infinite, above others of their own class of power. We know of nothing capable of standing by the side of it, or of supplying its place, but one; and that is, a deep interest in the welfare of mankind. The possession of this will sometimes render the very want of amiableness touching, because it seems to arise from the reverse of what is unamiable and selfish, and to be exasperated, not because itself is unhappy, but because others are so. It was this, far more than his intellectual endowments (great as they were), which made us like Mr Hazlitt. Many a contest has it saved us with him, many a sharp answer, and interval of alienation; and often, perhaps, did he attribute to an apprehension of his formidable powers (for which, in our animal spirits, we did not care twopence) what was owing intirely to our love of the sweet drop at the bottom of his heart. But only imagine a man, who should feel this interest too, and be deeply amiable, and have great sufferings, bodily and mental, and know his own errors, and waive the claims of his own virtues, and manifest an unceasing considerateness for the comfort of those about him, in the very least as well as greatest things, surviving, in the pure life of his heart, all mistake, all misconception, all exasperation, and ever having a soft word in his extremity, not only for those who consoled, but for those who distressed him; and imagine how we must have loved *him!* It was Mr Shelley. His genius, transcendent as it was, would not have bound us to him; his poetry, his tragedy, his philosophy, would not have bound us; no, not even his generosity, had it been less amiable. It was his unbounded heart, and his ever kind speech. . . .

FROM *Theatrical Examiner, No.* 52

September 24, 1809

❨ Covent Garden Theater, managed by John Philip Kemble (1757–1823) and owned by Kemble together with Thomas Harris, burned in September 1808. Hunt, in the part given here of his *Examiner* review of the reopening, describes the "aristocratic" interior of the new building, of which the facade was modeled lavishly on the Parthenon. In the part omitted, Hunt describes the beginning of the O.P. (old price) riots, which continued until the sixty-first night, when lower prices were granted. The price for one person in the pit approximated an average day's pay for a lower clerk or a skilled laborer. Although always a partisan, Hunt like Southey and the diarists recorded a wide range of factual information about Regency England. Of such information this review is typical. ❩

COVENT GARDEN.

It was ardently hoped by all the lovers of the Theatre, that the Managers of Covent Garden, in shewing their taste for the fine arts, would have shewn also a liberality worthy of the taste, and thus increased the respectability and the true interest of the stage: but people, it seems, are destined to be disappointed, who expect from these men any thing but the merest feelings of tradesmen. The new theatre opened on Monday night with the increased prices of 4s. to the Pit, and 7s. to the Boxes, and if the town at least expected an increase of comfort on the occasion, it was to be disappointed even in that respect.

The *appearance,* indeed, was classical and magnificent throughout. On your entrance through the portico, you turn to the left, and pay your money at the top of a short flight of steps, adorned on each side by a bronze Grecian lamp on a tripod: immediately beyond this is the grand staircase, rising through a landing place adorned on each side with large Ionic pillars in imitation of porphyry, between each of which hangs another lamp of bronze: this brings you directly opposite Mr. Rossi's statue of SHAKSPEARE in the anti-room; it stands in an easy assured attitude, making a sling of it's cloak with it's left arm, and holding a scroll in the other; it's countenance does not much remind you of any of the faces attributed to the Great Poet, nor was it desireable that it should, for of the two commonly received likenesses, the Chandos and the Felton, the former is the head of a coxcomb, and the latter that of a dolt; but Mr. Rossi has very poorly supplied what was deficient in dignity and genius; the poet merely looks as if he good humouredly enjoyed his elevation, an expression certainly very distant from the noble simplicity of the antique, and in short, the figure altogether exhibits the usual feebleness of this artist, resulting from want of invention. This anti-room leads to the principal lobby, which disappoints one at first sight with regard to size, but it is quite large enough for the proper purposes of ingress and egress, and is very classically adorned with eight casts from the antique, among which are *Minerva, Venus,* and *Bacchus,* the *Apollo de Medicis,* and the *Farnesian Flora,* so justly celebrated for it's magnificent breadth of drapery. These entrances are certainly worthy of introducing you to a stage over which SHAKSPEARE presides.

In the audience part of the theatre, *appearances* are still as magnificent, but there is a sad abridgement of comfort. Those who had obtained seats in the *lower boxes* or *pit* might certainly feel themselves comfortable enough to look about and admire the aspect of the place. It is of a chaste and classical elegance. The boxes are of a dove-colour ground in front, the lower circle ornamented with a simple Etruscan border in gold, and the rest with the Grecian honeysuckle alternately upright and inverted. The light pillars that support them remind you of Drury-lane Theatre; they are of a gold colour, and furnished with superb chandeliers, which, however, do not shew the backs of the boxes to advantage, smeared as they are with glaring red, and abruptly patched with doors of new mahogany that look like common unfinished wood: the slips and galleries are improved in *appearance* by

being formed into a row of semicircular arcades, and the arched front
of the stage is adorned at top by a short curtain like the Greek peplum,
festooned at intervals, and ornamented in each festoon by an Apollo's
wreath: the pilasters at the side are in imitation of yellow stained
marble, but unaccountably supported upon bases of most evident
wood. The drop-scene is worthy the general classicality, and represents
a temple dedicated to SHAKSPEARE, who stands in the vista in his
usual attitude, while your eye approaches him through two rows of
statues, consisting of the various founders of the drama in various
nations, ÆSCHYLUS, MENANDER, PLAUTUS, LOPE DE VEGA, BEN JOHN-
SON, MOLIERE, &c. They seemed to be looking over the way at each
other with surprise, to find themselves on a spot so new to a set of
wits.

But the Managers, in all this display of taste, seem to have had no
eye to the improvement of the public taste, but to have obeyed a certain aristocratic impulse of their pride, and consulted little but the accommodation of the higher orders. The people felt this immediately.
It is certainly monstrous to pay seven shillings for admission to the
garrets at the top of the house, where you can neither see nor hear,
and still more monstrous, when you see a whole circle taken from the
public by way of private boxes with anti-chambers, to make room for
which the places and comforts of the lower orders have been so
circumscribed: that old nuisance, the basket, as it is called, has been
preserved to give the usual effect to the noise and interruption of the
lobbies, and thus if the accommodations are confined in some respects,
the theatre is altogether as large in others, as the avarice of the Managers and their contempt for a real taste in the drama could make it. In
no such theatre can a true taste be excited, because a true drama, which
requires nicety of expression in the voice and countenance, cannot be
felt in it: SHAKSPEARE may be played to the pit and side boxes, but
he will be little better than dumb and blind shew to the people in
the basket, who pay seven shillings to hear nothing but noise, or to
those in the upper boxes, who pay seven shillings to see nothing but
indecency. Naturally therefore the rise of the old prices entirely disgusted the public, and their disgust was increased by various attempts
on the part of the Managers and their friends to plead the excuse
of *necessity*. . . .

Theatrical Examiner, No. 338

October 4, 1818

([Hunt was in prison when Edmund Kean first appeared at the Drury Lane Theater, as Shylock, in January 1814. From the time of his release, however, despite occasional adverse reports, he explained in detail his enthusiasm for Kean's vehemence in Shakespearean roles. **])**

DRURY-LANE.

Mr. KEAN has returned from his tour to France and Italy, — a very proper relaxation for a man of his talents, — and has performed in the course of the week *Richard the Third* and *Othello*. We saw the latter on Thursday evening; and with all our experience of the stage, and with all our scepticism as to the powers of the very best actors in characters from SHAKSPEARE, we never witnessed a performance that struck us so forcibly. It brought back upon us the earnestness and implicit attention of our younger days. We have admired Mrs. SIDDONS, been infinitely amused with LEWIS, been sore with laughing at MUNDEN, been charmed with Mrs. JORDAN; but we never saw any thing that so completely held us suspended and heart-stricken, as Mr. KEAN's *Othello*. In all parts it is as complete as actor can shew it, — in the previous composure of it's dignity, in it's soldier-like repression of common impulse, in the deep agitation of it's first jealousy, in the low-voiced and faltering affectation of occasional ease, in the burst of intolerable anguish, in the consciousness that rage has hurt its dignity and ruined the future completeness of it's character, in the consequent melancholy farewell to it's past joys and greatness, in the desperate savageness of it's revenge, in it's half-exhausted reception of the real truth, and lastly, in the final resumption of a kind of moral attitude and dignity, at the moment when it uses that fine deliberate artifice, and sheathes the dagger in it's breast.

If we might venture to point out any parts the most admirable in this performance, it would be the low and agitated affectation of quiet discourse, in which he first canvasses the subject with *Iago*, the mild and tremulous farewell to "the tranquil mind, the plumed troop," &c. in which his voice occasionally uttered little tones of endearment, his head shook, and his visage quivered; and thirdly, those still more awfully mild tones in which he trembles and halts through those dreadful lines beginning —

> "Had it pleased heaven
> "To try me with affliction; had he rained
> "All kinds of sores and shames on my bare head."
>   [IV.ii.47–49]

His louder bitterness and his rage were always fine; but such passages as these, we think, were still finer. You might fancy you saw the water quivering in his eyes.

And here two things struck us very forcibly; first, how impossible it is for actor and audience to be both as they ought to be in such large theatres, since Mr. KEAN's quietest and noblest passages could certainly not have been audible in the galleries; — and second, how much an actor's talent must be modified by his own character off the stage, — an observation we may reasonably make when it leans to the favourable side; for we conjecture from anecdotes that are before the public, that Mr. KEAN's temper is hasty, and his disposition excellent and generous; and it is of passion and natural generosity that *Othello's* character is made up. For this reason we can never help being sceptical about GARRICK's excellence in characters of deep and serious interest; since, off the stage, he was little better than a quick-eyed trifler, full of phrases of gabbling jargon, and coarse-minded withal.

Of the two new performers — Mrs. WEST, who repeated *Desdemona,* and Mr. CLEARY, who changed from *Othello* to *Iago* — we have nothing to add to our former observations, except that the lady performed still better than before.

There is a new afterpiece here, which is below criticism.

Mr. KEAN's *Othello* is the masterpiece of the living stage.

Thomas De Quincey

THOMAS DE QUINCEY

CHRONOLOGY

1785   Born August 15 at Manchester, son of a merchant who died in 1792.
1799   February, withdrawn from Bath Grammar School after accidental but severe injury by a master.
1802   Ran away from Manchester Grammar School, headed for Wordsworth; wandered through North Wales and then London.
1803   Discovered by guardians; sent to Worcester College, Oxford.
1809   October, moved into Dove Cottage, Grasmere.
1813   Permanently confirmed in use of opium.
1817   February 15, married his rustic mistress, Margaret Simpson, aged 20.
1818   (July 18)–1819 (November 5)   Edited the *Westmorland Gazette*, a Tory newspaper.
1820   (December)–1821 (January)   In Edinburgh promising articles to *Blackwood's Magazine*.
1821   (September)–1825 (July)   Mostly in London; contributed "Confessions" and essays to *London Magazine*.
1822   August (?), *Confessions of an English Opium Eater* reprinted as a book (anonymous); enlarged, 1856.
1826   November, began frequent contributions to *Blackwood's*.
1830   December, settled in Edinburgh, where he wrote for several periodicals and became increasingly the eccentric recluse.
1832   March (?), *Klosterheim*, a novel.
1833–41   Autobiographic and other sketches in *Tait's Edinburgh Magazine*.
1844   March, *The Logic of Political Economy*.
1845   "Suspiria de Profundis" in *Blackwood's*.
1847   "Joan of Arc" in *Tait's*.
1849   "The English Mail-Coach" in *Blackwood's*.
1850–53   Contributed to *Hogg's Weekly Instructor*.
1853   January, began work on a collective edition, titled "Selections Grave and Gay": Volume I appeared May 21 (Volume XIV appeared January 26, 1860).
1859   Died December 8.

Confessions of an English Opium-Eater

❮ "Confessions of an English Opium-Eater: Being an Extract from the Life of a Scholar" began anonymously in the *London Magazine*, September 1821, with assurances of a basis in fact. For the second installment, in October, the editors called their readers' attention to "the deep, eloquent, and masterly paper which stands first in our present Number." The two installments were published as a separate book the next year, with an Appendix giving details of De Quincey's recent experiment in decreasing his daily dosage of opium. His artistic purpose, as he explained it in retrospect in 1845, was "to reveal something of the grandeur which belongs *potentially* to human dreams." In 1856 he revised the work for clarity and euphony, phrase by phrase, and expanded it to more than twice its original length. In this form it was published on November 13 as the fifth volume of the collective edition. In typical overflow, he added at the end an apologue, "The Daughter of Lebanon," and a further Appendix of notes. In both versions, 1821–22 and 1856, the main body of the work is divided into three parts: I. Untitled "preliminary confessions, or introductory narrative." II. The Pleasures of Opium. III. The Pains of Opium. A section originally entitled "Introduction to the Pains of Opium" — including the episode of the migrant Malay whom the author unintentionally introduced to drugs — was transferred in 1856 to "The Pleasures of Opium." At every stage, the work contained frequent digressions and sudden transitions. To suggest the extent of De Quincey's stylistic changes, one passage is given here in the text of 1821 as well as that of 1856, from which the other selections are drawn. ❯

FROM *The Pleasures of Opium*

It is very long since I first took opium; *so* long, that if it had been a trifling incident in my life, I might have forgotten its date: but cardinal events are not to be forgotten; and, from circumstances connected with it, I remember that this inauguration into the use of opium must be referred to the spring or to the autumn of 1804; during which seasons I was in London, having come thither for the first time since my entrance at Oxford. And this event arose in the following way: from an early age I had been accustomed to wash my head in cold water at least once a-day; being suddenly seized with toothache, I attributed it to some relaxation caused by a casual intermission of that practice; jumped out of bed, plunged my head into a basin of cold water, and with hair thus wetted went to sleep. The next morning, as I need hardly say, I awoke with excruciating rheumatic pains of the head and face, from which I had hardly any respite for about twenty days. On the twenty-first day I think it was, and on a Sunday, that I went out into the streets; rather to run away, if possible, from my torments, than with any distinct purpose of relief. By accident, I met a college acquaintance, who recommended opium. Opium! dread agent of unimaginable pleasure and pain! I had heard of it as I had heard of manna or of ambrosia, but no further. How unmeaning a sound was opium at that time! what solemn chords does it now strike upon my heart! what heart-quaking vibrations of sad and happy remembrances! . . .

O just, subtle, and all-conquering opium! that, to the hearts of rich and poor alike, for the wounds that will never heal, and for the pangs of grief that "tempt the spirit to rebel," bringest an assuaging balm; — eloquent opium! that with thy potent rhetoric stealest away the purposes of wrath, pleadest effectually for relenting pity, and through one night's heavenly sleep callest back to the guilty man the visions of his infancy, and hands washed pure from blood; — O just and righteous opium! that to the chancery of dreams summonest, for the triumphs of despairing innocence, false witnesses; and confoundest perjury; and dost reverse the sentences of unrighteous judges; — thou buildest upon the bosom of darkness, out of the fantastic imagery of the brain, cities and temples, beyond the art of Phidias and Praxiteles — beyond the splendours of Babylon and Hekatómpylos;[1] and, "from the anarchy of dreaming sleep," callest into sunny light the faces of long-buried beauties, and the blessed household countenances, cleansed from the "dishonours of the grave." Thou only givest these gifts to man; and thou hast the keys of Paradise, O just, subtle, and mighty opium! . . .

FROM THE *Confessions* OF 1821

Oh! just, subtle, and mighty opium! that to the hearts of poor and rich alike, for the wounds that will never heal, and for "the pangs that tempt the spirit to rebel,"[2] bringest an assuaging balm; eloquent opium! that with thy potent rhetoric stealest away the purposes of wrath; and to the guilty man, for one night givest back the hopes of his youth, and hands washed pure from blood; and to the proud man, a brief oblivion for

Wrongs unredress'd, and insults unavenged;[3]

[1] *i.e.*, the *hundred-gated* (from ἑκατον, *hekaton*, a hundred, and πυλη, *pyle*, a gate). This epithet of hundred-gated was applied to the Egyptian Thebes in contradistinction to the ἑπτάπυλος (*heptápylos*, or *seven-gated*) which designated the Grecian Thebes, within one day's journey of Athens. [De Q.]

[2] Wordsworth, *The White Doe of Rylstone*, Dedication 36.

[3] Wordsworth, *The Excursion* III.374.

that summonest to the chancery of dreams, for the triumphs of suffering innocence, false witnesses; and confoundest perjury; and dost reverse the sentences of unrighteous judges: — thou buildest upon the bosom of darkness, out of the fantastic imagery of the brain, cities and temples, beyond the art of Phidias and Praxiteles — beyond the splendour of Babylon and Hekatómpylos: and "from the anarchy of dreaming sleep,"[4] callest into sunny light the faces of long-buried beauties, and the blessed household countenances, cleansed from the "dishonours of the grave."[5] Thou only givest these gifts to man; and thou hast the keys of Paradise, oh, just, subtle, and mighty opium![6]

FROM *The Pains of Opium*

For nearly two years I believe that I read nothing and studied nothing. Analytic studies are continuous studies, and not to be pursued by fits and starts, or fragmentary efforts. All these were become insupportable to me; I shrank from them with a sense of powerless and infantine feebleness that gave me an anguish the greater from remembering the time when I grappled with them to my own hourly delight; and for this further reason, because I had devoted the labour of my whole life, had dedicated my intellect, blossoms and fruits, to the slow and elaborate toil of constructing one single work, to which I had presumed to give the title of an unfinished work of Spinosa's — viz., "*De Emendatione Humani Intellectûs.*" This was now lying locked up as by frost, like any Spanish bridge or aqueduct begun upon too great a scale for the resources of the architect; and, instead of surviving me, as a monument of wishes at least, and aspirations, and long labours, dedicated to the exaltation of human nature in that way in which God had best fitted me to promote so great an object, it was likely to stand a memorial to my children of hopes defeated, of baffled efforts, of materials uselessly accumulated, of foundations laid that were never to support a superstructure, of the grief and the ruin of the architect. In this state of imbecility, I had, for amusement, turned my attention to political economy; my understanding, which formerly had been as active and restless as a panther, could not, I suppose (so long as I lived at all), sink into utter lethargy; and political economy offers this advantage to a person in my state, that though it is eminently an organic science (no part, that is to say, but what acts on the whole, as the whole again reacts on and through each part), yet still the several parts may be detached and contemplated singly. Great as was the

[4] *Ibid.*, IV.87.
[5] Cf. 1 Corinthians 15:43.
[6] Cf. Walter Ralegh, *History of the World,* 1614: "O, eloquent, just, and mighty Death!"

prostration of my powers at this time, yet I could not forget my knowledge; and my understanding had been for too many years intimate with severe thinkers, with logic, and the great masters of knowledge, not to be aware of a great call made by political economy at this crisis for a new law and a transcendent legislator. Suddenly, in 1818, a friend in Edinburgh sent me down Mr Ricardo's book; and, recurring to my own prophetic anticipation of some coming legislator for this science, I said, before I had finished the first chapter, "Thou art the man!" Wonder and curiosity were emotions that had long been dead in me. Yet I wondered once more — wondered at myself that could once again be stimulated to the effort of reading; and much more I wondered at the book. Had this profound work been really written during the tumultuous hurry of the nineteenth century? Could it be that an Englishman, and he not in academic bowers, but oppressed by mercantile and senatorial cares, had accomplished what all the universities of Europe, and a century of thought, had failed even to advance by one hair's-breadth? Previous writers had been crushed and overlaid by the enormous weights of facts, details, and exceptions; Mr Ricardo had deduced, *a priori*, from the understanding itself, laws which first shot arrowy light into the dark chaos of materials, and had thus constructed what hitherto was but a collection of tentative discussions into a science of regular proportions, now first standing upon an eternal basis.

Thus did one simple work of a profound understanding avail to give me a pleasure and an activity which I had not known for years; it roused me even to write, or, at least, to dictate what M—— wrote for me. It seemed to me that some important truths had escaped even "the inevitable eye" of Mr Ricardo; and, as these were, for the most part, of such a nature that I could express or illustrate them briefly and elegantly by algebraic symbols, the whole would hardly have reached the bulk of a pamphlet. With M—— for my amanuensis, even at this time, incapable as I was of all general exertion, I drew up, therefore, my "Prolegomena to all Future Systems of Political Economy."

This exertion, however, was but a momentary flash, as the sequel showed. Arrangements were made at a provincial press, about eighteen miles distant, for printing it. An additional compositor was retained for some days, on this account. The work was even twice advertised; and I was, in a manner, pledged to the fulfilment of my intention. But I had a preface to write, and a dedication, which I wished to make impressive, to Mr Ricardo. I found myself quite unable to accomplish all this. The arrangements were countermanded, the compositor dismissed, and my "Prolegomena" rested peacefully by the side of its elder and more dignified brother.

In thus describing and illustrating my intellectual torpor, I use terms that apply, more or less, to every part of the years during which

I was under the Circean spells of opium. But for misery and suffering, I might, indeed, be said to have existed in a dormant state. I seldom could prevail on myself to write a letter; an answer of a few words, to any that I received, was the utmost that I could accomplish; and often *that* not until the letter had lain for weeks, or even months, on my writing-table. Without the aid of M——, my whole domestic economy, whatever became of political economy, must have gone into irretrievable confusion. I shall not afterwards allude to this part of the case; it is one, however, which the opium-eater will find, in the end, most oppressive and tormenting, from the sense of incapacity and feebleness, from the direct embarrassments incident to the neglect or procrastination of each day's appropriate labours, and from the remorse which must often exasperate the stings of these evils to a conscientious mind. The opium-eater loses none of his moral sensibilities or aspirations; he wishes and longs as earnestly as ever to realise what he believes possible, and feels to be exacted by duty; but his intellectual apprehension of what is possible infinitely outruns his power, not of execution only, but even of proposing or willing. He lies under a world's weight of incubus and nightmare; he lies in sight of all that he would fain perform, just as a man forcibly confined to his bed by the mortal languor of paralysis, who is compelled to witness injury or outrage offered to some object of his tenderest love: — he would lay down his life if he might but rise and walk; but he is powerless as an infant, and cannot so much as make an effort to move.

But from this I now pass to what is the main subject of these latter Confessions — to the history and journal of what took place in my dreams; for these were the immediate and proximate cause of shadowy terrors that settled and brooded over my whole waking life.

The first notice I had of any important change going on in this part of my physical economy, was from the re-awaking of a state of eye oftentimes incident to childhood. I know not whether my reader is aware that many children have a power of painting, as it were, upon the darkness all sorts of phantoms; in some that power is simply a mechanic affection of the eye; others have a voluntary or semi-voluntary power to dismiss or summon such phantoms; or, as a child once said to me, when I questioned him on this matter, "I can tell them to go, and they go; but sometimes they come when I don't tell them to come." He had by one-half as unlimited a command over apparitions as a Roman centurion over his soldiers. In the middle of 1817 this faculty became increasingly distressing to me: at night, when I lay awake in bed, vast processions moved along continually in mournful pomp; friezes of never-ending stories, that to my feelings were as sad and solemn as stories drawn from times before Œdipus or Priam, before Tyre, before Memphis. And, concurrently with this, a corresponding change took place in my dreams; a theatre seemed suddenly opened and lighted up within my brain, which presented nightly spectacles of more than earthly splendour. And the four following facts may be mentioned, as noticeable at this time: —

1. That, as the creative state of the eye increased, a sympathy seemed to arise between the waking and the dreaming states of the brain in one point — that whatsoever I happened to call up and to trace by a voluntary act upon the darkness was very apt to transfer itself to my dreams; and at length I feared to exercise this faculty; for, as Midas turned all things to gold that yet baffled his hopes and defrauded his human desires, so whatsoever things capable of being visually represented I did but think of in the darkness, immediately shaped themselves into phantoms for the eye; and, by a process apparently no less inevitable, when thus once traced in faint and visionary colours, like writings in sympathetic ink, they were drawn out, by the fierce chemistry of my dreams, into insufferable splendour that fretted my heart.

2. This and all other changes in my dreams were accompanied by deep-seated anxiety and funereal melancholy, such as are wholly incommunicable by words. I seemed every night to descend — not metaphorically, but literally to descend — into chasms and sunless abysses, depths below depths, from which it seemed hopeless that I could ever re-ascend. Nor did I, by waking, feel that I *had* re-ascended. Why should I dwell upon this? For indeed the state of gloom which attended these gorgeous spectacles, amounting at last to utter darkness, as of some suicidal despondency, cannot be approached by words.

3. The sense of space, and in the end the sense of time, were both powerfully affected. Buildings, landscapes, &c., were exhibited in proportions so vast as the bodily eye is not fitted to receive. Space swelled, and was amplified to an extent of unutterable and self-repeating infinity. This disturbed me very much less than the vast expansion of time. Sometimes I seemed to have lived for seventy or a hundred years in one night; nay, sometimes had feelings representative of a duration far beyond the limits of any human experience.

4. The minutest incidents of childhood, or forgotten scenes of later years, were often revived. I could not be said to recollect them; for, if I had been told of them when waking, I should not have been able to acknowledge them as parts of my past experience. But placed as they were before me, in dreams like intuitions, and clothed in all their evanescent circumstances and accompanying feelings, I *recognised* them instantaneously. . . . Of this, at least, I feel assured, that there is no such thing as ultimate *forgetting;* traces once impressed upon the memory are indestructible; a thousand accidents may and will interpose a veil between our present consciousness and the secret inscriptions on the mind. Accidents of the same sort will also rend away this veil. But alike, whether veiled or unveiled, the inscription remains

for ever; just as the stars seem to withdraw before the common light
of day, whereas, in fact, we all know that it is the light which is drawn
over them as a veil; and that they are waiting to be revealed, whenever
the obscuring daylight itself shall have withdrawn. . . .

Many years ago, when I was looking over Piranesi's "Antiquities of
Rome," Coleridge, then standing by, described to me a set of plates
from that artist, called his "Dreams," and which record the scenery of
his own visions during the delirium of a fever. Some of these (I describe only from memory of Coleridge's account) represented vast
Gothic halls; on the floor of which stood mighty engines and machinery, wheels, cables, catapults, &c., expressive of enormous power
put forth, or resistance overcome. Creeping along the sides of the
walls, you perceived a staircase; and upon this, groping his way upwards, was Piranesi himself. Follow the stairs a little farther, and you
perceive them reaching an abrupt termination, without any balustrade,
and allowing no step onwards to him who should reach the extremity,
except into the depths below. Whatever is to become of poor Piranesi,
at least you suppose that his labours must now in some way terminate.
But raise your eyes, and behold a second flight of stairs still higher,
on which again Piranesi is perceived, by this time standing on the very
brink of the abyss. Once again elevate your eye, and a still more aerial
flight of stairs is descried; and there, again, is the delirious Piranesi,
busy on his aspiring labours: and so on, until the unfinished stairs and
the hopeless Piranesi both are lost in the upper gloom of the hall. With
the same power of endless growth and self-reproduction did my architecture proceed in dreams. In the early stage of the malady, the
splendours of my dreams were indeed chiefly architectural; and I
beheld such pomp of cities and palaces as never yet was beheld by
the waking eye, unless in the clouds. . . .

To my architecture succeeded dreams of lakes and silvery expanses
of water. . . .

The waters gradually changed their character — from translucent
lakes, shining like mirrors, they became seas and oceans. And now
came a tremendous change, which, unfolding itself slowly like a
scroll, through many months, promised an abiding torment; and, in
fact, it never left me, though recurring more or less intermittingly.
Hitherto the human face had often mixed in my dreams, but not
despotically, nor with any special power of tormenting. But now that
affection, which I have called the tyranny of the human face, began to
unfold itself. Perhaps some part of my London life (the searching for
Ann amongst fluctuating crowds) might be answerable for this. Be that
as it may, now it was that upon the rocking waters of the ocean the
human face began to reveal itself; the sea appeared paved with innumerable faces, upturned to the heavens; faces, imploring, wrathful,
despairing; faces that surged upwards by thousands, by myriads, by
generations: infinite was my agitation; my mind tossed, as it seemed,

upon the billowy ocean, and weltered upon the weltering waves.

May, 1818. — The Malay has been a fearful enemy for months. Every night, through his means, I have been transported into Asiatic scenery. I know not whether others share in my feelings on this point; but I have often thought that if I were compelled to forego England, and to live in China, among Chinese manners and modes of life and scenery, I should go mad. The causes of my horror lie deep, and some of them must be common to others. Southern Asia, in general, is the seat of awful images and associations. As the cradle of the human race, if on no other ground, it would have a dim, reverential feeling connected with it. But there are other reasons. No man can pretend that the wild, barbarous, and capricious superstitions of Africa, or of savage tribes elsewhere, affect him in the way that he is affected by the ancient, monumental, cruel, and elaborate religions of Hindostan. The mere antiquity of Asiatic things, of their institutions, histories, above all, of their mythologies, &c., is so impressive, that to me the vast age of the race and name overpowers the sense of youth in the individual. A young Chinese seems to me an antediluvian man renewed. Even Englishmen, though not bred in any knowledge of such institutions, cannot but shudder at the mystic sublimity of *castes* that have flowed apart, and refused to mix, through such immemorial tracts of time; nor can any man fail to be awed by the sanctity of the Ganges, or by the very name of the Euphrates. It contributes much to these feelings, that South-eastern Asia is, and has been for thousands of years, the part of the earth most swarming with human life, the great *officina gentium*. Man is a weed in those regions. The vast empires, also, into which the enormous population of Asia has always been cast, give a further sublimity to the feelings associated with all oriental names or images. In China, over and above what it has in common with the rest of Southern Asia, I am terrified by the modes of life, by the manners, by the barrier of utter abhorrence placed between myself and *them*, by counter-sympathies deeper than I can analyse. I could sooner live with lunatics, with vermin, with crocodiles or snakes. All this, and much more than I can say, the reader must enter into, before he can comprehend the unimaginable horror which these dreams of oriental imagery and mythological tortures impressed upon me. Under the connecting feeling of tropical heat and vertical sunlights, I brought together all creatures, birds, beasts, reptiles, all trees and plants, usages and appearances, that are found in all tropical regions, and assembled them together in China or Hindostan. From kindred feelings, I soon brought Egypt and her gods under the same law. I was stared at, hooted at, grinned at, chattered at, by monkeys, by paroquets, by cockatoos. I ran into pagodas, and was fixed for centuries at the summit, or in secret rooms; I was the idol; I was the priest; I was worshipped; I was sacrificed. I fled from the wrath of Brama through all the forests of Asia; Vishnu hated me; Seeva lay in wait for me. I came suddenly upon Isis and Osiris: I had done a deed, they said, which the ibis and the crocodile trembled at. Thousands of years I lived and was buried in stone coffins, with mummies and sphinxes, in narrow chambers at the heart of eternal pyramids. I was kissed, with cancerous kisses, by crocodiles, and was laid, confounded with all unutterable abortions, amongst reeds and Nilotic mud.

Some slight abstraction I thus attempt of my oriental dreams, which filled me always with such amazement at the monstrous scenery, that horror semed absorbed for awhile in sheer astonishment. Sooner or later came a reflux of feeling that swallowed up the astonishment, and left me, not so much in terror, as in hatred and abomination of what I saw. Over every form, and threat, and punishment, and dim sightless incarceration, brooded a killing sense of eternity and infinity. Into these dreams only it was, with one or two slight exceptions, that any circumstances of physical horror entered. All before had been moral and spiritual terrors. But here the main agents were ugly birds, or snakes, or crocodiles, especially the last. The cursed crocodile became to me the object of more horror than all the rest. I was compelled to live with him; and (as was always the case in my dreams) for centuries. Sometimes I escaped, and found myself in Chinese houses. All the feet of the tables, sofas, &c., soon became instinct with life: the abominable head of the crocodile, and his leering eyes, looked out at me, multiplied into ten thousand repetitions; and I stood loathing and fascinated. So often did this hideous reptile haunt my dreams, that many times the very same dream was broken up in the very same way: I heard gentle voices speaking to me (I hear everything when I am sleeping), and instantly I awoke; it was broad noon, and my children were standing, hand in hand, at my bedside, come to show me their coloured shoes, or new frocks, or to let me see them dressed for going out. No experience was so awful to me, and at the same time so pathetic, as this abrupt translation from the darkness of the infinite to the gaudy summer air of highest noon, and from the unutterable abortions of miscreated gigantic vermin to the sight of infancy, and innocent *human* natures.

June, 1819. — I have had occasion to remark, at various periods of my life, that the deaths of those whom we love, and, indeed, the contemplation of death generally, is (*cæteris paribus*) more affecting in summer than in any other season of the year. And the reasons are these three, I think: first, that the visible heavens in summer appear far higher, more distant, and (if such a solecism may be excused) more infinite; the clouds by which chiefly the eye expounds the distance of the blue pavilion stretched over our heads are in summer more voluminous, more massed, and are accumulated in far grander and more towering piles; secondly, the light and the appearances of the declining and the setting sun are much more fitted to be types and characters of the infinite; and, thirdly (which is the main reason), the exuberant and riotous prodigality of life naturally forces the mind more powerfully upon the antagonist thought of death, and the wintry sterility of the grave. For it may be observed generally, that wherever two thoughts stand related to each other by a law of antagonism, and exist, as it were, by mutual repulsion, they are apt to suggest each other. On these accounts it is that I find it impossible to banish the thought of death when I am walking alone in the endless days of summer; and any particular death, if not actually more affecting, at least haunts my mind more obstinately and besiegingly, in that season. Perhaps this cause, and a slight incident which I omit, might have been the immediate occasions of the following dream, to which, however, a predisposition must always have existed in my mind; but, having been once roused, it never left me, and split into a thousand fantastic variations, which often suddenly re-combined; locked back into startling unity, and restored the original dream.

I thought that it was a Sunday morning in May; that it was Easter Sunday, and as yet very early in the morning. I was standing, as it seemed to me, at the door of my own cottage. Right before me lay the very scene which could really be commanded from that situation, but exalted, as was usual, and solemnised by the power of dreams. There were the same mountains, and the same lovely valley at their feet; but the mountains were raised to more than Alpine height, and there was interspace far larger between them of savannahs and forest lawns; the hedges were rich with white roses; and no living creature was to be seen, excepting that in the green churchyard there were cattle tranquilly reposing upon the verdant graves, and particularly round about the grave of a child whom I had once tenderly loved, just as I had really beheld them, a little before sunrise, in the same summer when that child died. I gazed upon the well-known scene, and I said to myself, "It yet wants much of sunrise; and it is Easter Sunday; and that is the day on which they celebrate the first-fruits of Resurrection. I will walk abroad; old griefs shall be forgotten to-day: for the air is cool and still, and the hills are high, and stretch away to heaven; and the churchyard is as verdant as the forest lawns, and the forest lawns are as quiet as the churchyard; and with the dew I can wash the fever from my forehead; and then I shall be unhappy no longer." I turned, as if to open my garden gate, and immediately I saw upon the left a scene far different; but which yet the power of dreams had reconciled into harmony. The scene was an oriental one; and there also it was Easter Sunday, and very early in the morning. And at a vast distance were visible, as a stain upon the horizon, the domes and cupolas of a great city — an image or faint abstraction, caught perhaps in childhood from some picture of Jerusalem. And not a bow-shot from me, upon a stone, shaded by Judean palms, there sat a woman; and I looked, and it was — Ann! She fixed her eyes upon me earnestly; and I said to her at length, "So, then, I have found you at

last." I waited; but she answered me not a word. Her face was the
same as when I saw it last; the same, and yet, again, how different!
Seventeen years ago, when the lamp-light of mighty London fell upon
her face, as for the last time I kissed her lips (lips, Ann, that to me
were not polluted!), her eyes were streaming with tears. The tears
were now no longer seen. Sometimes she seemed altered; yet again
sometimes *not* altered; and hardly older. Her looks were tranquil, but
with unusual solemnity of expression, and I now gazed upon her with
some awe. Suddenly her countenance grew dim; and, turning to the
mountains, I perceived vapours rolling between us; in a moment all
had vanished; thick darkness came on; and in the twinkling of an eye
I was far away from mountains, and by lamp-light in London, walking
again with Ann — just as we had walked, when both children, eighteen
years before, along the endless terraces of Oxford Street. . . .[1]

Suspiria de Profundis

❡ De Quincey regarded his *Confessions* as an "Extract" only. Several fragments contributing to a mythology of dreams, and indeed most of De
Quincey's imaginative prose, grew from his vision of one great confessional
work. "Suspiria de Profundis: Being a Sequel to the Confessions of an
English Opium-Eater" was issued, for the only time by De Quincey, in
Blackwood's Edinburgh Magazine, March–July 1845. Because he later pil-
fered extensive passages from these "Sighs from the Depths" for his *Autobiographic Sketches,* editors have usually reduced and shifted about the
original sections: Introductory Notice. Part I: The Affliction of Childhood,
The Palimpsest, Levana and Our Ladies of Sorrow, The Apparition of the
Brocken, Finale to Part I: Savannah-la-Mar. Part II [untitled and unfin-
ished]. In 1853 De Quincey ranked his *Confessions,* "but more emphatically" the *Suspiria,* as "modes of impassioned prose ranging under no
precedents that I am aware of" — and thus as superior to any other works
of his then collected. In a note at the end of "Levana and Our Ladies of
Sorrow," he warned: "The reader, who wishes at all to understand the
course of these Confessions, ought not to pass over this dream-legend.
There is no great wonder that a vision, which occupied my waking thoughts

---

[1] M— is Margaret, De Quincey's wife. As an urchin in London, 1802–
03, according to the introductory narrative, he walked nightly with "noble-
minded Ann," a prostitute about sixteen years old.

Spinoza, "On the Improvement of Human Understanding"; David Ricardo
(1772–1823), *Principles of Political Economy and Taxation,* 1817; G. B.
Piranesi (1720–78), Italian engraver and architect.

officina gentium: workshop of the nations; *caeteris paribus:* other things
being equal.

in those years, should re-appear in my dreams. It was in fact a legend
recurring in sleep, most of which I had myself silently written or sculptured
in my daylight reveries. But its importance to the present Confessions is
this — that it rehearses or prefigures their course." Except for the rest of
that note, which described a plan never realized, the "dream-legend" is
given here as it appeared in *Blackwood's* for June 1845.]❱

Levana and Our Ladies of Sorrow

Oftentimes at Oxford I saw Levana in my dreams. I knew her by
her Roman symbols. Who is Levana? Reader, that do not pretend to
have leisure for very much scholarship, you will not be angry with me
for telling you. Levana was the Roman goddess that performed for
the new-born infant the earliest office of ennobling kindness — typical,
by its mode, of that grandeur which belongs to man every where, and
of that benignity in powers invisible, which even in Pagan worlds sometimes descends to sustain it. At the very moment of birth, just as the
infant tasted for the first time the atmosphere of our troubled planet, it
was laid on the ground. *That* might bear different interpretations. But
immediately, lest so grand a creature should grovel there for more
than one instant, either the paternal hand, as proxy for the goddess
Levana, or some near kinsman, as proxy for the father, raised it upright, bade it look erect as the king of all this world, and presented
its forehead to the stars, saying, perhaps, in his heart, "Behold what
is greater than yourselves!" This symbolic act represented the function
of Levana. And that mysterious lady, who never revealed her face,
(except to me in dreams,) but always acted by delegation, had her
name from the Latin verb (as still it is the Italian verb) *levare*, to
raise aloft.

This is the explanation of Levana. And hence it has arisen that some
people have understood by Levana the tutelary power that controls the
education of the nursery. She, that would not suffer at his birth
even a prefigurative or mimic degradation for her awful ward, far less
could be supposed to suffer the real degradation attaching to the non-
development of his powers. She therefore watches over human education. Now, the word *edŭco*, with the penultimate short, was derived
(by a process often exemplified in the crystallization of languages)
from the word *edūco*, with the penultimate long. Whatsoever *educes*
or developes — *educates*. By the education of Levana, therefore, is
meant — not the poor machinery that moves by spelling-books and
grammars, but that mighty system of central forces hidden in the deep
bosom of human life, which by passion, by strife, by temptation, by the
energies of resistance, works for ever upon children — resting not day
or night, any more than the mighty wheel of day and night themselves,

whose moments, like restless spokes, are glimmering[1] for ever as they revolve.

If, then, *these* are the ministries by which Levana works, how profoundly must she reverence the agencies of grief! But you, reader! think — that children generally are not liable to grief such as mine. There are two senses in the word *generally* — the sense of Euclid where it means *universally*, (or in the whole extent of the *genus*,) and a foolish sense of this world where it means *usually*. Now I am far from saying that children universally are capable of grief like mine. But there are more than you ever heard of, who die of grief in this island of ours. I will tell you a common case. The rules of Eton require that a boy on the *foundation* should be there twelve years: he is superannuated at eighteen, consequently he must come at six. Children torn away from mothers and sisters at that age not unfrequently die. I speak of what I know. The complaint is not entered by the registrar as grief; but *that* it is. Grief of that sort, and at that age, has killed more than ever have been counted amongst its martyrs.

Therefore it is that Levana often communes with the powers that shake man's heart: therefore it is that she doats upon grief. "These ladies," said I softly to myself, on seeing the ministers with whom Levana was conversing, "these are the Sorrows; and they are three in number, as the *Graces* are three, who dress man's life with beauty; the *Parcae* are three, who weave the dark arras of man's life in their mysterious loom always with colours sad in part, sometimes angry with tragic crimson and black; the *Furies* are three, who visit with retributions called from the other side of the grave offences that walk upon this; and once even the *Muses* were but three, who fit the harp, the trumpet, or the lute, to the great burdens of man's impassioned creations. These are the Sorrows, all three of whom I know." The last words I say *now;* but in Oxford I said — "one of whom I know, and the others too surely I *shall* know." For already, in my fervent youth, I saw (dimly relieved upon the dark background of my dreams) the imperfect lineaments of the awful sisters. These sisters — by what name shall we call them?

If I say simply — "The Sorrows," there will be a chance of mistaking the term; it might be understood of individual sorrow — sepa-

---

[1] *"Glimmering."* — As I have never allowed myself to covet any man's ox nor his ass, nor any thing that is his, still less would it become a philosopher to covet other people's images, or metaphors. Here, therefore, I restore to Mr Wordsworth this fine image of the revolving wheel, and the glimmering spokes, as applied by him to the flying successions of day and night. I borrowed it for one moment in order to point my own sentence; which being done, the reader is witness that I now pay it back instantly by a note made for that sole purpose. On the same principle I often borrow their seals from young ladies — when closing my letters. Because there is sure to be some tender sentiment upon them about "memory," or "hope," or "roses," or "reunion:" and my correspondent must be a sad brute who is not touched by the eloquence of the seal, even if his taste is so bad that he remains deaf to mine. [De Q.]

rate cases of sorrow, — whereas I want a term expressing the mighty abstractions that incarnate themselves in all individual sufferings of man's heart; and I wish to have these abstractions presented as impersonations, that is, as clothed with human attributes of life, and with functions pointing to flesh. Let us call them, therefore, *Our Ladies of Sorrow*. I know them thoroughly, and have walked in all their kingdoms. Three sisters they are, of one mysterious household; and their paths are wide apart; but of their dominion there is no end. Them I saw often conversing with Levana, and sometimes about myself. Do they talk, then? Oh, no! Mighty phantoms like these disdain the infirmities of language. They may utter voices through the organs of man when they dwell in human hearts, but amongst themselves is no voice nor sound — eternal silence reigns in *their* kingdoms. *They* spoke not as they talked with Levana. *They* whispered not. *They* sang not. Though oftentimes methought they *might* have sung; for I upon earth had heard their mysteries oftentimes deciphered by harp and timbrel, by dulcimer and organ. Like God, whose servants they are, they utter their pleasure, not by sounds that perish, or by words that go astray, but by signs in heaven — by changes on earth — by pulses in secret rivers — heraldries painted on darkness — and hieroglyphics written on the tablets of the brain. *They* wheeled in mazes; *I* spelled the steps. *They* telegraphed from afar; *I* read the signals. *They* conspired together; and on the mirrors of darkness *my* eye traced the plots. *Theirs* were the symbols, — *mine* are the words.

What is it the sisters are? What is it that they do? Let me describe their form, and their presence; if form it were that still fluctuated in its outline; or presence it were that for ever advanced to the front, or for ever receded amongst shades.

The eldest of the three is named *Mater Lachrymarum*, Our Lady of Tears. She it is that night and day raves and moans, calling for vanished faces. She stood in Rama, when a voice was heard of lamentation — Rachel weeping for her children, and refusing to be comforted. She it was that stood in Bethlehem on the night when Herod's sword swept its nurseries of Innocents, and the little feet were stiffened for ever, which, heard at times as they tottered along floors overhead, woke pulses of love in household hearts that were not unmarked in heaven.

Her eyes are sweet and subtle, wild and sleepy by turns; oftentimes rising to the clouds; oftentimes challenging the heavens. She wears a diadem round her head. And I knew by childish memories that she could go abroad upon the winds, when she heard the sobbing of litanies or the thundering of organs, and when she beheld the mustering of summer clouds. This sister, the elder, it is that carries keys more than Papal at her girdle, which open every cottage and every palace. She, to my knowledge, sate all last summer by the bedside of the blind beggar, him that so often and so gladly I talked with, whose pious daughter, eight years old, with the sunny countenance, resisted the temptations of play and village mirth to travel all day long on dusty roads with her afflicted father. For this did God send her a great reward. In the spring-time of the year, and whilst yet her own spring was budding, he recalled her to himself. But her blind father mourns for ever over *her;* still he dreams at midnight that the little guiding hand is locked within his own; and still he wakens to a darkness that is *now* within a second and a deeper darkness. This *Mater Lachrymarum* also has been sitting all this winter of 1844–5 within the bedchamber of the Czar, bringing before his eyes a daughter (not less pious) that vanished to God not less suddenly, and left behind her a darkness not less profound. By the power of her keys it is that Our Lady of Tears glides a ghostly intruder into the chambers of sleepless men, sleepless women, sleepless children, from Ganges to the Nile, from Nile to Mississippi. And her, because she is the first-born of her house, and has the widest empire, let us honour with the title of "Madonna."

The second sister is called *Mater Suspiriorum*, Our Lady of Sighs. She never scales the clouds, nor walks abroad upon the winds. She wears no diadem. And her eyes, if they were ever seen, would be neither sweet nor subtle; no man could read their story; they would be found filled with perishing dreams, and with wrecks of forgotten delirium. But she raises not her eyes; her head, on which sits a dilapidated turban, droops for ever; for ever fastens on the dust. She weeps not. She groans not. But she sighs inaudibly at intervals. Her sister, Madonna, is oftentimes stormy and frantic; raging in the highest against heaven; and demanding back her darlings. But Our Lady of Sighs never clamours, never defies, dreams not of rebellious aspirations. She is humble to abjectness. Hers is the meekness that belongs to the hopeless. Murmur she may, but it is in her sleep. Whisper she may, but it is to herself in the twilight. Mutter she does at times, but it is in solitary places that are desolate as she is desolate, in ruined cities, and when the sun has gone down to his rest. This sister is the visitor of the Pariah, of the Jew, of the bondsman to the oar in Mediterranean galleys, of the English criminal in Norfolk Island, blotted out from the books of remembrance in sweet far-off England, of the baffled penitent reverting his eye for ever upon a solitary grave, which to him seems the altar overthrown of some past and bloody sacrifice, on which altar no oblations can now be availing, whether towards pardon that he might implore, or towards reparation that he might attempt. Every slave that at noonday looks up to the tropical sun with timid reproach, as he points with one hand to the earth, our general mother, but for *him* a stepmother, as he points with the other hand to the Bible, our general teacher, but against *him* sealed and sequestered;[2] — every

---

[2] This, the reader will be aware, applies chiefly to the cotton and tobacco States of North America; but not to them only: on which account I have not scrupled to figure the sun, which looks down upon slavery, as *tropical* — no matter if strictly within the tropics, or simply so near to them as to produce a similar climate. [De Q.]

woman sitting in darkness, without love to shelter her head, or hope to illumine her solitude, because the heaven-born instincts kindling in her nature germs of holy affections, which God implanted in her womanly bosom, having been stifled by social necessities, now burn sullenly to waste, like sepulchral lamps amongst the ancients; — every nun defrauded of her unreturning May-time by wicked kinsmen, whom God will judge; — every captive in every dungeon; — all that are betrayed, and all that are rejected; outcasts by traditionary law, and children of *hereditary* disgrace — all these walk with "Our Lady of Sighs." She also carries a key; but she needs it little. For her kingdom is chiefly amongst the tents of Shem, and the houseless vagrant of every clime. Yet in the very highest ranks of man she finds chapels of her own; and even in glorious England there are some that, to the world, carry their heads as proudly as the reindeer, who yet secretly have received her mark upon their foreheads.

But the third sister, who is also the youngest ——! Hush! whisper, whilst we talk of *her!* Her kingdom is not large, or else no flesh should live; but within that kingdom all power is hers. Her head, turreted like that of Cybèle, rises almost beyond the reach of sight. She droops not; and her eyes rising so high, *might* be hidden by distance. But, being what they are, they cannot be hidden; through the treble veil of crape which she wears, the fierce light of a blazing misery, that rests not for matins or for vespers — for noon of day or noon of night — for ebbing or for flowing tide — may be read from the very ground. She is the defier of God. She also is the mother of lunacies, and the suggestress of suicides. Deep lie the roots of her power; but narrow is the nation that she rules. For she can approach only those in whom a profound nature has been upheaved by central convulsions; in whom the heart trembles and the brain rocks under conspiracies of tempest from without and tempest from within. Madonna moves with uncertain steps, fast or slow, but still with tragic grace. Our Lady of Sighs creeps timidly and stealthily. But this youngest sister moves with incalculable motions, bounding, and with a tiger's leaps. She carries no key; for, though coming rarely amongst men, she storms all doors at which she is permitted to enter at all. And *her* name is *Mater Tenebrarum* — Our Lady of Darkness.

These were the *Semnai Theai,* or Sublime Goddesses[3] — these were the *Eumenides,* or Gracious Ladies, (so called by antiquity in shuddering propitiation) — of my Oxford dreams. MADONNA spoke. She spoke by her mysterious hand. Touching my head, she beckoned to Our Lady of Sighs; and *what* she spoke, translated out

[3] *"Sublime Goddesses."* — The word σεμνος is usually rendered *venerable* in dictionaries; not a very flattering epithet for females. But by weighing a number of passages in which the word is used pointedly, I am disposed to think that it comes nearest to our idea of the *sublime;* as near as a Greek word *could* come. [De Q.]

of the signs which (except in dreams) no man reads, was this: —
"Lo! here is he, whom in childhood I dedicated to my altars. This
is he that once I made my darling. Him I led astray, him I beguiled,
and from heaven I stole away his young heart to mine. Through me
did he become idolatrous; and through me it was, by languishing desires, that he worshipped the worm, and prayed to the wormy grave.
Holy was the grave to him; lovely was its darkness; saintly its corruption. Him, this young idolater, I have seasoned for thee, dear
gentle Sister of Sighs! Do thou take him now to *thy* heart, and season
him for our dreadful sister. And thou" — turning to the *Mater Tenebrarum,* she said — "wicked sister, that temptest and hatest, do thou
take him from *her.* See that thy sceptre lie heavy on his head. Suffer
not woman and her tenderness to sit near him in his darkness. Banish
the frailties of hope — wither the relentings of love — scorch the
fountains of tears: curse him as only thou canst curse. So shall he be
accomplished in the furnace — so shall he see the things that ought
not to be seen — sights that are abominable, and secrets that are unutterable. So shall he read elder truths, sad truths, grand truths, fearful truths. So shall he rise again *before* he dies. And so shall our commission be accomplished which from God we had — to plague his
heart until we had unfolded the capacities of his spirit."[4]

The English Mail-Coach

❪ In 1849, when Carlyle, Macaulay, Dickens, and Thackeray were near
the midpoint of their careers, "The English Mail-Coach, or the Glory of
Motion" appeared in *Blackwood's Magazine* for October. Two further fragments followed in December. De Quincey then described Section III,
"Dream Fugue," as "an attempt to wrestle with the utmost efforts of music
in dealing with a colossal form of impassioned horror." Although originally
written as parts of the "Suspiria de Profundis," the three sections of "The
English Mail-Coach" form De Quincey's most sustained single work. The
second volume of *Miscellanies* in his collective edition, issued November 16,
1854, included the revision which is here given in full. ❫

Section the First. — The Glory of Motion

Some twenty or more years before I matriculated at Oxford, Mr
Palmer, at that time M.P. for Bath, had accomplished two things, very

[4] De Quincey's third paragraph misrepresents the rules for scholarship
students at Eton.
Rama, Herod: see Matthew 2:16–18; Norfolk Island: penal colony near
Australia; Shem: nomad, from Genesis 9:27.

hard to do on our little planet, the Earth, however cheap they may be held by eccentric people in comets — he had invented mail-coaches, and he had married the daughter[1] of a duke. He was, therefore, just twice as great a man as Galileo, who did certainly invent (or, which is the same thing,[2] discover) the satellites of Jupiter, those very next things extant to mail-coaches in the two capital pretensions of speed and keeping time, but, on the other hand, who did *not* marry the daughter of a duke.

These mail-coaches, as organised by Mr Palmer, are entitled to a circumstantial notice from myself, having had so large a share in developing the anarchies of my subsequent dreams; an agency which they accomplished, 1st, through velocity, at that time unprecedented — for they first revealed the glory of motion; 2dly, through grand effects for the eye between lamp-light and the darkness upon solitary roads; 3dly, through animal beauty and power so often displayed in the class of horses selected for this mail service; 4thly, through the conscious presence of a central intellect, that, in the midst of vast distances[3] — of storms, of darkness, of danger — overruled all obstacles into one steady co-operation to a national result. For my own feeling, this post-office service spoke as by some mighty orchestra, where a thousand intruments, all disregarding each other, and so far in danger of discord, yet all obedient as slaves to the supreme *baton* of some great leader, terminate in a perfection of harmony like that of heart, brain, and lungs, in a healthy animal organisation. But, finally, that particular element in this whole combination which most impressed myself, and through which it is that to this hour Mr Palmer's mail-coach system tyrannises over my dreams by terror and terrific beauty, lay in the awful *political* mission which at that time it fulfilled. The mail-coach it was that distributed over the face of the land, like the opening of apocalyptic vials, the heart-shaking news of Trafalgar, of Salamanca, of Vittoria, of Waterloo. These were the harvests that, in the grandeur of their reaping, redeemed the tears and blood in which they had been sown. Neither was the meanest peasant so much below the grandeur and the sorrow of the times as to confound battles such as these, which were gradually moulding the destinies of Christendom, with the vulgar conflicts of ordinary warfare, so often no more than gladiatorial trials of national prowess. The

---

[1] Lady Madeline Gordon. [De Q. An error; she married Charles Palmer, not John Palmer (1742–1818).]

[2] *"The same thing:"* — Thus, in the calendar of the Church Festivals, the discovery of the true cross (by Helen, the mother of Constantine) is recorded (and one might think — with the express consciousness of sarcasm) as the *Invention* of the Cross. [De Q.]

[3] *"Vast distances:"* — One case was familiar to mail-coach travellers, where two mails in opposite directions, north and south, starting at the same minute from points six hundred miles apart, met almost constantly at a particular bridge which bisected the total distance. [De Q.]

victories of England in this stupendous contest rose of themselves as natural *Te Deums* to heaven; and it was felt by the thoughtful that such victories, at such a crisis of general prostration, were not more beneficial to ourselves than finally to France, our enemy, and to the nations of all western or central Europe, through whose pusillanimity it was that the French domination had prospered.

The mail-coach, as the national organ for publishing these mighty events thus diffusively influential, became itself a spiritualised and glorified object to an impassioned heart; and naturally, in the Oxford of that day, *all* hearts were impassioned, as being all (or nearly all) in *early* manhood. In most universities there is one single college; in Oxford there were five-and-twenty, all of which were peopled by young men, the *élite* of their own generation; not boys, but men; none under eighteen. In some of these many colleges, the custom permitted the student to keep what are called "short terms;" that is, the four terms of Michaelmas, Lent, Easter, and Act, were kept by a residence, in the aggregate, of ninety-one days, or thirteen weeks. Under this interrupted residence, it was possible that a student might have a reason for going down to his home four times in the year. This made eight journeys to and fro. But, as these homes lay dispersed through all the shires of the island, and most of us disdained all coaches except his majesty's mail, no city out of London could pretend to so extensive a connection with Mr Palmer's establishment as Oxford. Three mails, at the least, I remember as passing every day through Oxford, and benefiting by my personal patronage — viz., the Worcester, the Gloucester, and the Holyhead mail. Naturally, therefore, it became a point of some interest with us, whose journeys revolved every six weeks on an average, to look a little into the executive details of the system. With some of these Mr Palmer had no concern; they rested upon bye-laws enacted by posting-houses for their own benefit, and upon other bye-laws, equally stern, enacted by the inside passengers for the illustration of their own haughty exclusiveness. These last were of a nature to rouse our scorn, from which the transition was not very long to systematic mutiny. Up to this time, say 1804, or 1805 (the year of Trafalgar), it had been the fixed assumption of the four inside people (as an old tradition of all public carriages derived from the reign of Charles II.), that they, the illustrious quaternion, constituted a porcelain variety of the human race, whose dignity would have been compromised by exchanging one word of civility with the three miserable delf-ware outsides. Even to have kicked an outsider, might have been held to attaint the foot concerned in that operation; so that, perhaps, it would have required an act of parliament to restore its purity of blood. What words, then, could express the horror, and the sense of treason, in that case, which *had* happened, where all three outsides (the trinity of Pariahs) made a vain attempt to sit down at the same breakfast-table or dinner-table with the consecrated four? I myself witnessed such an attempt; and on that occasion a benevolent old gentleman endeavoured to soothe his three holy associates, by suggesting that, if the outsides were indicted for this criminal attempt at the next assizes, the court would regard it as a case of lunacy, or *delirium tremens*, rather than of treason. England owes much of her grandeur to the depth of the aristocratic element in her social composition, when pulling against her strong democracy. I am not the man to laugh at it. But sometimes, undoubtedly, it expressed itself in comic shapes. The course taken with the infatuated outsiders, in the particular attempt which I have noticed, was, that the waiter, beckoning them away from the privileged *salle-à-manger*, sang out, "This way, my good men," and then enticed these good men away to the kitchen. But that plan had not always answered. Sometimes, though rarely, cases occurred where the intruders, being stronger than usual, or more vicious than usual, resolutely refused to budge, and so far carried their point, as to have a separate table arranged for themselves in a corner of the general room. Yet, if an Indian screen could be found ample enough to plant them out from the very eyes of the high table, or *dais*, it then became possible to assume as a fiction of law — that the three delf fellows, after all, were not present. They could be ignored by the porcelain men, under the maxim, that objects not appearing, and not existing, are governed by the same logical construction.[4]

Such being, at that time, the usages of mail-coaches, what was to be done by us of young Oxford? We, the most aristocratic of people, who were addicted to the practice of looking down superciliously even upon the insides themselves as often very questionable characters — were we, by voluntarily going outside, to court indignities? If our dress and bearing sheltered us, generally, from the suspicion of being "raff" (the name at that period for "snobs"[5]) we really *were* such constructively, by the place we assumed. If we did not submit to the deep shadow of eclipse, we entered at least the skirts of its penumbra. And the analogy of theatres was valid against us, where no man can complain of the annoyances incident to the pit or gallery, having his instant remedy in paying the higher price of the boxes. But the soundness of this analogy we disputed. In the case of the theatre, it cannot be pretended that the inferior situations have any separate attractions, unless the pit may be supposed to have an advantage for the purposes of the critic or the dramatic reporter. But the critic or reporter is a rarity. For most people, the sole benefit is in the price. Now, on the contrary, the outside of the mail had its own incommunicable ad-

4 *De non apparentibus, &c.* [De Q. A maxim of Roman law.]

5 "*Snobs*," and its antithesis, "*nobs*," arose among the internal factions of shoemakers perhaps ten years later. Possibly enough, the terms may have existed much earlier; but they were then first made known, picturesquely and effectively, by a trial at some assizes which happened to fix the public attention. [De Q.]

vantages. These we could not forego. The higher price we would willingly have paid, but not the price connected with the condition of riding inside; which condition we pronounced insufferable. The air, the freedom of prospect, the proximity to the horses, the elevation of seat — these were what we required; but, above all, the certain anticipation of purchasing occasional opportunities of driving.

Such was the difficulty which pressed us; and under the coercion of this difficulty, we instituted a searching inquiry into the true quality and valuation of the different apartments about the mail. We conducted this inquiry on metaphysical principles; and it was ascertained satisfactorily, that the roof of the coach, which by some weak men had been called the attics, and by some the garrets, was in reality the drawing-room; in which drawing-room the box was the chief ottoman or sofa; whilst it appeared that the *inside,* which had been traditionally regarded as the only room tenantable by gentlemen, was, in fact, the coal-cellar in disguise.

Great wits jump. The very same idea had not long before struck the celestial intellect of China. Amongst the presents carried out by our first embassy to that country was a state-coach. It had been specially selected as a personal gift by George III.; but the exact mode of using it was an intense mystery to Pekin. The ambassador, indeed (Lord Macartney), had made some imperfect explanations upon this point; but, as his excellency communicated these in a diplomatic whisper, at the very moment of his departure, the celestial intellect was very feebly illuminated, and it became necessary to call a cabinet council on the grand state question, "Where was the emperor to sit?" The hammer-cloth happened to be unusually gorgeous; and partly on that consideration, but partly also because the box offered the most elevated seat, was nearest to the moon, and undeniably went foremost, it was resolved by acclamation that the box was the imperial throne, and for the scoundrel who drove, he might sit where he could find a perch. The horses, therefore, being harnessed, solemnly his imperial majesty ascended his new English throne under a flourish of trumpets, having the first lord of the treasury on his right hand, and the chief jester on his left. Pekin gloried in the spectacle; and in the whole flowery people, constructively present by representation, there was but one discontented person, and *that* was the coachman. This mutinous individual audaciously shouted, "Where am *I* to sit?" But the privy council, incensed by his disloyalty, unanimously opened the door, and kicked him into the inside. He had all the inside places to himself; but such is the rapacity of ambition, that he was still dissatisfied. "I say," he cried out in an extempore petition, addressed to the emperor through the window — "I say, how am I to catch hold of the reins?" — "Anyhow," was the imperial answer; "don't trouble *me,* man, in my glory. How catch the reins? Why, through the windows, through the keyholes — *any*how." Finally this contumacious coachman length-

ened the check-strings into a sort of jury-reins, communicating with
the horses; with these he drove as steadily as Pekin had any right to
expect. The emperor returned after the briefest of circuits; he descended in great pomp from his throne, with the severest resolution
never to remount it. A public thanksgiving was ordered for his
majesty's happy escape from the disease of broken neck; and the
state-coach was dedicated thenceforward as a votive offering to the
god Fo, Fo — whom the learned more accurately called Fi, Fi.

A revolution of this same Chinese character did young Oxford of
that era effect in the constitution of mail-coach society. It was a perfect French revolution; and we had good reason to say, *ça ira*. In
fact, it soon became *too* popular. The "public" — a well-known
character, particularly disagreeable, though slightly respectable, and
notorious for affecting the chief seats in synagogues[6] — had at first
loudly opposed this revolution; but when the opposition showed itself
to be ineffectual, our disagreeable friend went into it with headlong
zeal. At first it was a sort of race between us; and, as the public is
usually from thirty to fifty years old, naturally we of young Oxford,
that averaged about twenty, had the advantage. Then the public
took to bribing, giving fees to horse-keepers, &c., who hired out their
persons as warming-pans on the box-seat. *That*, you know, was shocking to all moral sensibilities. Come to bribery, said we, and there is
an end to all morality, Aristotle's, Zeno's, Cicero's, or anybody's. And,
besides, of what use was it? For *we* bribed also. And as our bribes
to those of the public were as five shillings to sixpence, here again
young Oxford had the advantage. But the contest was ruinous to the
principles of the stables connected with the mails. This whole corporation was constantly bribed, rebribed, and often sur-rebribed; a
mail-coach yard was like the hustings in a contested election; and a
horse-keeper, ostler, or helper, was held by the philosophical at that
time to be the most corrupt character in the nation.

There was an impression upon the public mind, natural enough
from the continually augmenting velocity of the mail, but quite erroneous, that an outside seat on this class of carriages was a post of
danger. On the contrary, I maintained that, if a man had become
nervous from some gipsy prediction in his childhood, allocating to a
particular moon now approaching some unknown danger, and he
should inquire earnestly, "Whither can I fly for shelter? Is a prison
the safest retreat? or a lunatic hospital? or the British Museum?" I
should have replied, "Oh, no; I'll tell you what to do. Take lodgings
for the next forty days on the box of his majesty's mail. Nobody can
touch you there. If it is by bills at ninety days after date that you are
made unhappy — if noters and protesters are the sort of wretches
whose astrological shadows darken the house of life — then note you

[6] So the scribes and Pharisees in Matthew 23:6.

what I vehemently protest — viz., that no matter though the sheriff and under-sheriff in every county should be running after you with his *posse*, touch a hair of your head he cannot whilst you keep house, and have your legal domicile on the box of the mail. It is felony to stop the mail; even the sheriff cannot do that. And an *extra* touch of the whip to the leaders (no great matter if it grazes the sheriff) at any time guarantees your safety." In fact, a bedroom in a quiet house seems a safe enough retreat, yet it is liable to its own notorious nuisances — to robbers by night, to rats, to fire. But the mail laughs at these terrors. To robbers, the answer is packed up and ready for delivery in the barrel of the guard's blunderbuss. Rats again! — there *are* none about mail-coaches, any more than snakes in Von Troil's Iceland;[7] except, indeed, now and then a parliamentary rat, who always hides his shame in what I have shown to be the "coal cellar." And as to fire, I never knew but one in a mail-coach, which was in the Exeter mail, and caused by an obstinate sailor bound to Devonport. Jack, making light of the law and the law-giver that had set their faces against his offence, insisted on taking up a forbidden seat[8] in the rear of the roof, from which he could exchange his own yarns with those of the guard. No greater offence was then known to mail-coaches; it was treason, it was *læsa majestas*, it was by tendency arson; and the ashes of Jack's pipe, falling amongst the straw of the hinder boot containing the mail-bags, raised a flame which (aided by the wind of our motion) threatened a revolution in the republic of letters. Yet even this left the sanctity of the box unviolated. In dignified re-

---

[7] *"Von Troil's Iceland:"* — The allusion is to a well-known chapter in Von Troil's work, entitled, "Concerning the Snakes of Iceland." The entire chapter consists of these six words — *"There are no snakes in Iceland."* [De Q. Actually in Niels Horrebow, *The Natural History of Iceland,* 1758.]

[8] *"Forbidden seat:"* — The very sternest code of rules was enforced upon the mails by the Post-office. Throughout England, only three outsides were allowed, of whom one was to sit on the box, and the other two immediately behind the box; none, under any pretext, to come near the guard; an indispensable caution; since else, under the guise of passenger, a robber might by any one of a thousand advantages — which sometimes are created, but always are favoured, by the animation of frank social intercourse — have disarmed the guard. Beyond the Scottish border, the regulation was so far relaxed as to allow of *four* outsides, but not relaxed at all as to the mode of placing them. One, as before, was seated on the box, and the other three on the front of the roof, with a determinate and ample separation from the little insulated chair of the guard. This relaxation was conceded by way of compensating to Scotland her disadvantages in point of population. England, by the superior density of her population, might always count upon a large fund of profits in the fractional trips of chance passengers riding for short distances of two or three stages. In Scotland, this chance counted for much less. And therefore, to make good the deficiency, Scotland was allowed a compensatory profit upon one *extra* passenger. [De Q.]

pose, the coachman and myself sat on, resting with benign composure upon our knowledge that the fire would have to burn its way through four inside passengers before it could reach ourselves. I remarked to the coachman, with a quotation from Virgil's "Æneid" really too hackneyed —

> "Jam proximus ardet
> Ucalegon."   [II.311–312]

But, recollecting that the Virgilian part of the coachman's education might have been neglected, I interpreted so far as to say, that perhaps at that moment the flames were catching hold of our worthy brother and inside passenger, Ucalegon. The coachman made no answer, which is my own way when a stranger addresses me either in Syriac or in Coptic, but by his faint sceptical smile he seemed to insinuate that he knew better; for that Ucalegon, as it happened, was not in the way-bill, and therefore could not have been booked.

No dignity is perfect which does not at some point ally itself with the mysterious. The connection of the mail with the state and the executive government — a connection obvious, but yet not strictly defined — gave to the whole mail establishment an official grandeur which did us service on the roads, and invested us with seasonable terrors. Not the less impressive were those terrors, because their legal limits were imperfectly ascertained. Look at those turnpike gates; with what deferential hurry, with what an obedient start, they fly open at our approach! Look at that long line of carts and carters ahead, audaciously usurping the very crest of the road. Ah! traitors, they do not hear us as yet; but, as soon as the dreadful blast of our horn reaches them with proclamation of our approach, see with what frenzy of trepidation they fly to their horses' heads, and deprecate our wrath by the precipitation of their crane-neck quarterings. Treason they feel to be their crime; each individual carter feels himself under the ban of confiscation and attainder; his blood is attainted through six generations; and nothing is wanting but the headsman and his axe, the block and the saw-dust, to close up the vista of his horrors. What! shall it be within benefit of clergy to delay the king's message on the high road? — to interrupt the great respirations, ebb and flood, *systole* and *diastole*, of the national intercourse? — to endanger the safety of tidings, running day and night between all nations and languages? Or can it be fancied, amongst the weakest of men, that the bodies of the criminals will be given up to their widows for Christian burial? Now the doubts which were raised as to our powers did more to wrap them in terror, by wrapping them in uncertainty, than could have been effected by the sharpest definitions of the law from the Quarter Sessions. We, on our parts (we, the collective mail, I mean), did our utmost to exalt the idea of our privileges by the insolence with which we wielded them. Whether this insolence rested upon law that gave it a sanction, or upon conscious power that haughtily dispensed with that sanction, equally it spoke from a potential station; and the agent, in each particular insolence of the moment, was viewed reverentially, as one having authority.

Sometimes after breakfast his majesty's mail would become frisky; and in its difficult wheelings amongst the intricacies of early markets, it would upset an apple-cart, a cart loaded with eggs, &c. Huge was the affliction and dismay, awful was the smash. I, as far as possible, endeavoured in such a case to represent the conscience and moral sensibilities of the mail; and, when wildernesses of eggs were lying poached under our horses' hoofs, then would I stretch forth my hands in sorrow, saying (in words too celebrated at that time, from the false echoes[9] of Marengo), "Ah! wherefore have we not time to weep over you?" which was evidently impossible, since, in fact, we had not time to laugh over them. Tied to post-office allowance, in some cases of fifty minutes for eleven miles, could the royal mail pretend to undertake the offices of sympathy and condolence? Could it be expected to provide tears for the accidents of the road? If even it seemed to trample on humanity, it did so, I felt, in discharge of its own more peremptory duties.

Upholding the morality of the mail, *à fortiori* I upheld its rights; as a matter of duty, I stretched to the uttermost its privilege of imperial precedency, and astonished weak minds by the feudal powers which I hinted to be lurking constructively in the charters of this proud establishment. Once I remember being on the box of the Holyhead mail, between Shrewsbury and Oswestry, when a tawdry thing from Birmingham, some "Tallyho" or "Highflyer," all flaunting with green and gold, came up alongside of us. What a contrast to our royal simplicity of form and colour in this plebeian wretch! The single ornament on our dark ground of chocolate colour was the mighty shield of the imperial arms, but emblazoned in proportions as modest as a signet-ring bears to a seal of office. Even this was displayed only on a single pannel, whispering, rather than proclaiming, our relations to the mighty state; whilst the beast from Birmingham, our green-and-gold friend from false, fleeting, perjured Brummagem, had as much writing and painting on its sprawling flanks as would have puzzled a decipherer from the tombs of Luxor. For some time this Birmingham machine ran along by our side — a piece of familiarity that already of itself seemed to me sufficiently jacobinical. But all at

---

[9] *"False echoes:"* — Yes, false! for the words ascribed to Napoleon, as breathed to the memory of Desaix, never were uttered at all. They stand in the same category of theatrical fictions as the cry of the foundering line-of-battle ship Vengeur, as the vaunt of General Cambronne at Waterloo, "*La Garde meurt, mais ne se rend pas,*" or as the repartees of Talleyrand. [De Q. "The guard dies, but does not surrender." Talleyrand (1754–1838), French statesman and wit, earned distrust by intrigue.]

once a movement of the horses announced a desperate intention of
leaving us behind. "Do you see *that?*" I said to the coachman. — "I
see," was his short answer. He was wide awake, yet he waited longer
than seemed prudent; for the horses of our audacious opponent had
a disagreeable air of freshness and power. But his motive was loyal;
his wish was, that the Birmingham conceit should be full-blown before
he froze it. When *that* seemed right, he unloosed, or, to speak by a
stronger word, he *sprang*, his known resources: he slipped our royal
horses like cheetahs, or hunting-leopards, after the affrighted game.
How they could retain such a reserve of fiery power after the work
they had accomplished, seemed hard to explain. But on our side,
besides the physical superiority, was a tower of moral strength, namely,
the king's name, "which they upon the adverse faction wanted."[10]
Passing them without an effort, as it seemed, we threw them into the
rear with so lengthening an interval between us, as proved in itself
the bitterest mockery of their presumption; whilst our guard blew
back a shattering blast of triumph, that was really too painfully full of
derision.

I mention this little incident for its connection with what followed.
A Welsh rustic, sitting behind me, asked if I had not felt my heart
burn within me during the progress of the race? I said, with philosophic calmness, *No;* because we were not racing with a mail, so
that no glory could be gained. In fact, it was sufficiently mortifying
that such a Birmingham thing should dare to challenge us. The
Welshman replied, that he didn't see *that;* for that a cat might look
at a king, and a Brummagem coach might lawfully race the Holyhead
mail. "*Race* us, if you like," I replied, "though even *that* has an air of
sedition, but not *beat* us. This would have been treason; and for its
own sake I am glad that the 'Tallyho' was disappointed." So dissatisfied did the Welshman seem with this opinion, that at last I was
obliged to tell him a very fine story from one of our elder dramatists
— viz., that once, in some far oriental kingdom, when the sultan of all
the land, with his princes, ladies, and chief omrahs, were flying their
falcons, a hawk suddenly flew at a majestic eagle; and in defiance of
the eagle's natural advantages, in contempt also of the eagle's traditional royalty, and before the whole assembled field of astonished
spectators from Agra and Lahore, killed the eagle on the spot. Amazement seized the sultan at the unequal contest, and burning admiration
for its unparalleled result. He commanded that the hawk should be
brought before him; he caressed the bird with enthusiasm; and he
ordered that, for the commemoration of his matchless courage, a
diadem of gold and rubies should be solemnly placed on the hawk's
head; but then that, immediately after this solemn coronation, the
bird should be led off to execution, as the most valiant indeed of

[10] Cf. *Richard III* V.iii.13.

traitors, but not the less a traitor, as having dared to rise rebelliously against his liege lord and anointed sovereign, the eagle. "Now," said I to the Welshman, "to you and me, as men of refined sensibilities, how painful it would have been that this poor Brummagem brute, the 'Tallyho,' in the impossible case of a victory over us, should have been crowned with Birmingham tinsel, with paste diamonds, and Roman pearls, and then led off to instant execution." The Welshman doubted if that could be warranted by law. And when I hinted at the 6th of Edward Longshanks, chap. 18, for regulating the precedency of coaches, as being probably the statute relied on for the capital punishment of such offences, he replied drily, that if the attempt to pass a mail really were treasonable, it was a pity that the "Tallyho" appeared to have so imperfect an acquaintance with law.

The modern modes of travelling cannot compare with the old mail-coach system in grandeur and power. They boast of more velocity, not, however, as a consciousness, but as a fact of our lifeless knowledge, resting upon *alien* evidence; as, for instance, because somebody *says* that we have gone fifty miles in the hour, though we are far from feeling it as a personal experience, or upon the evidence of a result, as that actually we find ourselves in York four hours after leaving London. Apart from such an assertion, or such a result, I myself am little aware of the pace. But, seated on the old mail-coach, we needed no evidence out of ourselves to indicate the velocity. On this system the word was, *Non magna loquimur*, as upon railways, but *vivimus.*[11] Yes, "magna *vivimus;*" we do not make verbal ostentation of our grandeurs, we realise our grandeurs in act, and in the very experience of life. The vital experience of the glad animal sensibilities made doubts impossible on the question of our speed; we heard our speed, we saw it, we felt it as a thrilling; and this speed was not the product of blind insensate agencies, that had no sympathy to give, but was incarnated in the fiery eyeballs of the noblest amongst brutes, in his dilated nostril, spasmodic muscles, and thunder-beating hoofs. The sensibility of the horse, uttering itself in the maniac light of his eye, might be the last vibration of such a movement; the glory of Salamanca might be the first. But the intervening links that connected them, that spread the earthquake of battle into the eyeball of the horse, were the heart of man and its electric thrillings — kindling in the rapture of the fiery strife, and then propagating its own tumults by contagious shouts and gestures to the heart of his servant the horse.

But now, on the new system of travelling, iron tubes and boilers have disconnected man's heart from the ministers of his locomotion. Nile nor Trafalgar has power to raise an extra bubble in a steam-kettle. The galvanic cycle is broken up for ever; man's imperial nature no longer sends itself forward through the electric sensibility of the

[11] We live, not speak, great things.

horse; the inter-agencies are gone in the mode of communication between the horse and his master, out of which grew so many aspects of sublimity under accidents of mists that hid, or sudden blazes that revealed, of mobs that agitated, or midnight solitudes that awed. Tidings, fitted to convulse all nations, must henceforwards travel by culinary process; and the trumpet that once announced from afar the laurelled mail, heart-shaking, when heard screaming on the wind, and proclaiming itself through the darkness to every village or solitary house on its route, has now given way for ever to the pot-wallopings of the boiler.

Thus have perished multiform openings for public expressions of interest, scenical yet natural, in great national tidings; for revelations of faces and groups that could not offer themselves amongst the fluctuating mobs of a railway station. The gatherings of gazers about a laurelled mail had one centre, and acknowledged one sole interest. But the crowds attending at a railway station have as little unity as running water, and own as many centres as there are separate carriages in the train.

How else, for example, than as a constant watcher for the dawn, and for the London mail that in summer months entered about daybreak amongst the lawny thickets of Marlborough forest, couldst thou, sweet Fanny of the Bath road, have become the glorified inmate of my dreams? Yet Fanny, as the loveliest young woman for face and person that perhaps in my whole life I have beheld, merited the station which even now, from a distance of forty years, she holds in my dreams; yes, though by links of natural association she brings along with her a troop of dreadful creatures, fabulous and not fabulous, that are more abominable to the heart, than Fanny and the dawn are delightful.

Miss Fanny of the Bath road, strictly speaking, lived at a mile's distance from that road; but came so continually to meet the mail, that I on my frequent transits rarely missed her, and naturally connected her image with the great thoroughfare where only I had ever seen her. Why she came so punctually, I do not exactly know; but I believe with some burden of commissions to be executed in Bath, which had gathered to her own residence as a central rendezvous for converging them. The mail-coachman who drove the Bath mail, and wore the royal livery,[12] happened to be Fanny's grandfather. A good

[12] "*Wore the royal livery:*" — The general impression was, that the royal livery belonged of right to the mail-coachmen as their professional dress. But that was an error. To the guard it *did* belong, I believe, and was obviously essential as an official warrant, and as a means of instant identification for his person, in the discharge of his important public duties. But the coachman, and especially if his place in the series did not connect him immediately with London and the General Post-office, obtained the scarlet coat only as an honorary distinction after long (or, if not long, trying and special) service. [De Q.]

man he was, that loved his beautiful granddaughter; and, loving her
wisely, was vigilant over her deportment in any case where young
Oxford might happen to be concerned. Did my vanity then suggest
that I myself, individually, could fall within the line of his terrors?
Certainly not, as regarded any physical pretensions that I could plead;
for Fanny (as a chance passenger from her own neighbourhood once
told me) counted in her train a hundred and ninety-nine professed
admirers, if not open aspirants to her favour; and probably not one
of the whole brigade but excelled myself in personal advantages.
Ulysses even, with the unfair advantage of his accursed bow, could
hardly have undertaken that amount of suitors. So the danger might
have seemed slight — only that woman is universally aristocratic; it
is amongst her nobilities of heart that she *is* so. Now, the aristocratic
distinctions in my favour might easily with Miss Fanny have compensated my physical deficiencies. Did I then make love to Fanny?
Why, yes; about as much love as one *could* make whilst the mail was
changing horses — a process which, ten years later, did not occupy
above eighty seconds; but *then* — viz., about Waterloo — it occupied
five times eighty. Now, four hundred seconds offer a field quite ample
enough for whispering into a young woman's ear a great deal of truth,
and (by way of parenthesis) some trifle of falsehood. Grandpapa did
right, therefore, to watch me. And yet, as happens too often to the
grandpapas of earth, in a contest with the admirers of granddaughters,
how vainly would he have watched me had I meditated any evil
whispers to Fanny! She, it is my belief, would have protected herself against any man's evil suggestions. But he, as the result showed,
could not have intercepted the opportunities for such suggestions.
Yet, why not? Was he not active? Was he not blooming? Blooming
he was as Fanny herself.

> "Say, all our praises why should lords ——"[13]

Stop, that's not the line.

> "Say, all our roses why should girls engross?"

The coachman showed rosy blossoms on his face deeper even than
his granddaughter's — *his* being drawn from the ale cask, Fanny's
from the fountains of the dawn. But, in spite of his blooming face,
some infirmities he had; and one particularly in which he too much re-
sembled a crocodile. This lay in a monstrous inaptitude for turning
round. The crocodile, I presume, owes that inaptitude to the absurd
length of his back; but in our grandpapa it arose rather from the absurd
breadth of his back, combined, possibly, with some growing stiffness
in his legs. Now, upon this crocodile infirmity of his I planted a
human advantage for tendering my homage to Miss Fanny. In de-

---

[13] Cf. Pope, *Moral Essays* III.249.

fiance of all his honourable vigilance, no sooner had he presented to us
his mighty Jovian back (what a field for displaying to mankind his
royal scarlet!), whilst inspecting professionally the buckles, the straps,
and the silvery turrets[14] of his harness, than I raised Miss Fanny's hand
to my lips, and, by the mixed tenderness and respectfulness of my
manner, caused her easily to understand how happy it would make me
to rank upon her list as No. 10 or 12, in which case a few casualties
amongst her lovers (and observe, they *hanged* liberally in those days)
might have promoted me speedily to the top of the tree; as, on the
other hand, with how much loyalty of submission I acquiesced by anticipation in her award, supposing that she should plant me in the
very rear-ward of her favour, as No. 199+1. Most truly I loved this
beautiful and ingenuous girl; and had it not been for the Bath mail,
timing all courtships by post-office allowance, heaven only knows what
might have come of it. People talk of being over head and ears in
love; now, the mail was the cause that I sank only over ears in love,
which, you know, still left a trifle of brain to overlook the whole conduct of the affair.

Ah, reader! when I look back upon those days, it seems to me that
all things change — all things perish. "Perish the roses and the palms
of kings:"[15] perish even the crowns and trophies of Waterloo: thunder
and lightning are not the thunder and lightning which I remember.
Roses are degenerating. The Fannies of our island — though this I
say with reluctance — are not visibly improving; and the Bath road is
notoriously superannuated. Crocodiles, you will say, are stationary.
Mr Waterton tells me that the crocodile does *not* change; that a cayman, in fact, or an alligator, is just as good for riding upon as he
was in the time of the Pharaohs. *That* may be; but the reason is, that
the crocodile does not live fast — he is a slow coach. I believe it is
generally understood among naturalists, that the crocodile is a block-
head. It is my own impression that the Pharaohs were also block-
heads. Now, as the Pharaohs and the crocodile domineered over
Egyptian society, this accounts for a singular mistake that prevailed
through innumerable generations on the Nile. The crocodile made
the ridiculous blunder of supposing man to be meant chiefly for his
own eating. Man, taking a different view of the subject, naturally
met that mistake by another: he viewed the crocodile as a thing sometimes to worship, but always to run away from. And this continued

---

14 *"Turrets:"* — As one who loves and venerates Chaucer for his unrivalled merits of tenderness, of picturesque characterisation, and of narrative skill, I noticed with great pleasure that the word *torrettes* is used by
him to designate the little devices through which the reins are made to
pass. This same word, in the same exact sense, I heard uniformly used by
many scores of illustrious mail-coachmen, to whose confidential friendship
I had the honour of being admitted in my younger days. [De Q.]

15 Cf. Wordsworth, *The Excursion* VII.980.

until Mr Waterton[16] changed the relations between the animals. The mode of escaping from the reptile he showed to be, not by running away, but by leaping on its back, booted and spurred. The two animals had misunderstood each other. The use of the crocodile has now been cleared up — viz., to be ridden; and the final cause of man is, that he may improve the health of the crocodile by riding him a fox-hunting before breakfast. And it is pretty certain that any crocodile, who has been regularly hunted through the season, and is master of the weight he carries, will take a six-barred gate now as well as ever he would have done in the infancy of the pyramids.

If, therefore, the crocodile does *not* change, all things else undeniably *do*: even the shadow of the pyramids grows less. And often the restoration in vision of Fanny and the Bath road, makes me too pathetically sensible of that truth. Out of the darkness, if I happen to call back the image of Fanny, up rises suddenly from a gulf of forty years a rose in June; or, if I think for an instant of the rose in June, up rises the heavenly face of Fanny. One after the other, like the antiphonies in the choral service, rise Fanny and the rose in June, then back again the rose in June and Fanny. Then come both together, as in a chorus — roses and Fannies, Fannies and roses, without end, thick as blossoms in paradise. Then comes a venerable crocodile, in a royal livery of scarlet and gold, with sixteen capes; and the crocodile is driving four-in-hand from the box of the Bath mail. And suddenly we upon the mail are pulled up by a mighty dial, sculptured with the hours, that mingle with the heavens and the heavenly host. Then all at once we are arrived at Marlborough forest, amongst the lovely households[17] of the roe-deer; the deer and their fawns retire into the dewy thickets; the thickets are rich with roses; once again the roses call up the sweet countenance of Fanny; and she, being the granddaughter of a crocodile, awakens a dreadful host of semi-leg-

[16] *"Mr Waterton:"* — Had the reader lived through the last generation, he would not need to be told that some thirty or thirty-five years back, Mr Waterton, a distinguished country gentleman of ancient family in Northumberland, publicly mounted and rode in top-boots a savage old crocodile, that was restive and very impertinent, but all to no purpose. The crocodile jibbed and tried to kick, but vainly. He was no more able to throw the squire, than Sinbad was to throw the old scoundrel who used his back without paying for it, until he discovered a mode (slightly immoral, perhaps, though some think not) of murdering the old fraudulent jockey, and so circuitously of unhorsing him. [De Q. Charles Waterton (1782–1865), *Wanderings in South America . . .* , London, 1825, pp. 231–232, on riding a cayman (alligator); Sinbad's Fifth Voyage, in *Arabian Nights*.]

[17] *"Households:"* — Roe-deer do not congregate in herds like the fallow or the red deer, but by separate families, parents and children; which feature of approximation to the sanctity of human hearths, added to their comparatively miniature and graceful proportions, conciliate to them an interest of peculiar tenderness, supposing even that this beautiful creature is less characteristically impressed with the grandeurs of savage and forest life. [De Q.]

endary animals — griffins, dragons, basilisks, sphinxes — till at length
the whole vision of fighting images crowds into one towering armorial
shield, a vast emblazonry of human charities and human loveliness
that have perished, but quartered heraldically with unutterable and
demoniac natures, whilst over all rises, as a surmounting crest, one
fair female hand, with the forefinger pointing, in sweet, sorrowful
admonition, upwards to heaven, where is sculptured the eternal writing
which proclaims the frailty of earth and her children.[18]

Going Down with Victory

But the grandest chapter of our experience, within the whole mail-
coach service, was on those occasions when we went down from London with the news of victory. A period of about ten years stretched
from Trafalgar to Waterloo; the second and third years of which
period (1806 and 1807) were comparatively sterile; but the other nine
(from 1805 to 1815 inclusively) furnished a long succession of victories; the least of which, in such a contest of Titans, had an inap-
preciable value of position — partly for its absolute interference with
the plans of our enemy, but still more from its keeping alive through
central Europe the sense of a deep-seated vulnerability in France.
Even to tease the coasts of our enemy, to mortify them by continual
blockades, to insult them by capturing if it were but a baubling
schooner under the eyes of their arrogant armies, repeated from time
to time a sullen proclamation of power lodged in one quarter to which
the hopes of Christendom turned in secret. How much more loudly
must this proclamation have spoken in the audacity[19] of having
bearded the *élite* of their troops, and having beaten them in pitched
battles! Five years of life it was worth paying down for the privilege
of an outside place on a mail-coach, when carrying down the first tid-

18 In 1849 this passage continued about one page further.

laesa majestas: crime against the sovereign; hinder boot: rear luggage-
space; benefit of clergy: exemption from secular trial (abolished 1827);
Oriental kingdom: in *The Royal King and the Loyal Subject,* by Thomas
Heywood (c.1570–1641), reprinted in 1815; law of Edward I: invented
by De Quincey.

19 *"Audacity:"* — Such the French accounted it; and it has struck me that
Soult would not have been so popular in London, at the period of her present Majesty's coronation, or in Manchester, on occasion of his visit to that
town, if they had been aware of the insolence with which he spoke of us in
notes written at intervals from the field of Waterloo. As though it had been
mere felony in our army to look a French one in the face, he said in more
notes than one, dated from two to four P.M. on the field of Waterloo,
"Here are the English — we have them; they are caught *en flagrant delit.*"
Yet no man should have known us better; no man had drunk deeper from
the cup of humiliation than Soult had in 1809, when ejected by us with
headlong violence from Oporto, and pursued through a long line of wrecks
to the frontier of Spain; subsequently at Albuera, in the bloodiest of recorded battles, to say nothing of Toulouse, he should have learned our
pretensions. [De Q.]

ings of any such event. And it is to be noted that, from our insular situation, and the multitude of our frigates disposable for the rapid transmission of intelligence, rarely did any unauthorised rumour steal away a prelibation from the first aroma of the regular despatches. The government news was generally the earliest news.

From eight P.M., to fifteen or twenty minutes later, imagine the mails assembled on parade in Lombard Street, where, at that time,[20] and not in St. Martin's-le-Grand, was seated the General Post-office. In what exact strength we mustered I do not remember; but, from the length of each separate *attelage,* we filled the street, though a long one, and though we were drawn up in double file. On *any* night the spectacle was beautiful. The absolute perfection of all the appointments about the carriages and the harness, their strength, their brilliant cleanliness, their beautiful simplicity — but, more than all, the royal magnificence of the horses — were what might first have fixed the attention. Every carriage, on every morning in the year, was taken down to an official inspector for examination — wheels, axles, linch-pins, pole, glasses, lamps, were all critically probed and tested. Every part of every carriage had been cleaned, every horse had been groomed, with as much rigour as if they belonged to a private gentleman; and that part of the spectacle offered itself always. But the night before us is a night of victory; and, behold! to the ordinary display, what a heart-shaking addition! — horses, men, carriages, all are dressed in laurels and flowers, oak-leaves and ribbons. The guards, as being officially his Majesty's servants, and of the coachmen such as are within the privilege of the post-office, wear the royal liveries of course; and as it is summer (for all the *land* victories were naturally won in summer), they wear, on this fine evening, these liveries exposed to view, without any covering of upper coats. Such a costume, and the elaborate arrangement of the laurels in their hats, dilate their hearts, by giving to them openly a personal connection with the great news, in which already they have the general interest of patriotism. That great national sentiment surmounts and quells all sense of ordinary distinctions. Those passengers who happen to be gentlemen are now hardly to be distinguished as such except by dress; for the usual reserve of their manner in speaking to the attendants has on this night melted away. One heart, one pride, one glory, connects every man by the transcendent bond of his national blood. The spectators, who are numerous beyond precedent, express their sympathy with these fervent feelings by continual hurrahs. Every moment are shouted aloud by the post-office servants, and summoned to draw up, the great ancestral names of cities known to history through a thousand years — Lincoln, Winchester, Portsmouth, Gloucester, Oxford, Bristol, Manchester, York, Newcastle, Edinburgh, Glasgow, Perth, Stirling, Aberdeen — expressing the grandeur of the empire by the antiquity of its towns,.

[20] *"At that time:"* — I speak of the era previous to Waterloo. [De Q.]

and the grandeur of the mail establishment by the diffusive radiation
of its separate missions. Every moment you hear the thunder of lids
locked down upon the mail-bags. That sound to each individual mail
is the signal for drawing off, which process is the finest part of the
entire spectacle. Then come the horses into play. Horses! can these
be horses that bound off with the action and gestures of leopards?
What stir! — what sea-like ferment! — what a thundering of wheels!
— what a trampling of hoofs! — what a sounding of trumpets! —
what farewell cheers — what redoubling peals of brotherly congratu-
lation, connecting the name of the particular mail — "Liverpool for
ever!" — with the name of the particular victory — "Badajoz for ever!"
or "Salamanca for ever!" The half-slumbering consciousness that, all
night long, and all the next day — perhaps for even a longer period —
many of these mails, like fire racing along a train of gunpowder, will
be kindling at every instant new successions of burning joy, has an obscure effect of multiplying the victory itself, by multiplying to the
imagination into infinity the stages of its progressive diffusion. A
fiery arrow seems to be let loose, which from that moment is destined
to travel, without intermission, westwards for three hundred miles[21] —

[21] *"Three hundred:"* — Of necessity, this scale of measurement, to an
American, if he happens to be a thoughtless man, must sound ludicrous.
Accordingly, I remember a case in which an American writer indulges himself in the luxury of a little fibbing, by ascribing to an Englishman a pompous account of the Thames, constructed entirely upon American ideas of
grandeur, and concluding in something like these terms: — "And, sir, arriving
at London, this mighty father of rivers attains a breadth of at least two fur-
longs, having, in its winding course, traversed the astonishing distance of one
hundred and seventy miles." And this the candid American thinks it fair
to contrast with the scale of the Mississippi. Now, it is hardly worth while
to answer a pure fiction gravely, else one might say that no Englishman out
of Bedlam ever thought of looking in an island for the rivers of a continent;
nor, consequently, could have thought of looking for the peculiar grandeur
of the Thames in the length of its course, or in the extent of soil which it
drains; yet, if he *had* been so absurd, the American might have recollected
that a river, not to be compared with the Thames even as to volume of water
— viz., the Tiber — has contrived to make itself heard of in this world for
twenty-five centuries to an extent not reached as yet by any river, however
corpulent, of his own land. The glory of the Thames is measured by the
destiny of the population to which it ministers, by the commerce which it
supports, by the grandeur of the empire in which, though far from the
largest, it is the most influential stream. Upon some such scale, and not by a
transfer of Columbian standards, is the course of our English mails to be
valued. The American may fancy the effect of his own valuations to our
English ears, by supposing the case of a Siberian glorifying his country in
these terms: — "These wretches, sir, in France and England, cannot march
half a mile in any direction without finding a house where food can be had
and lodging; whereas, such is the noble desolation of our magnificent country, that in many a direction for a thousand miles, I will engage that a dog
shall not find shelter from a snow-storm, nor a wren find an apology for
breakfast." [De Q.]

northwards for six hundred; and the sympathy of our Lombard Street friends at parting is exalted a hundredfold by a sort of visionary sympathy with the yet slumbering sympathies which in so vast a succession we are going to awake.

Liberated from the embarrassments of the city, and issuing into the broad uncrowded avenues of the northern suburbs, we soon begin to enter upon our natural pace of ten miles an hour. In the broad light of the summer evening, the sun, perhaps, only just at the point of setting, we are seen from every storey of every house. Heads of every age crowd to the windows — young and old understand the language of our victorious symbols — and rolling volleys of sympathising cheers run along us, behind us, and before us. The beggar, rearing himself against the wall, forgets his lameness — real or assumed — thinks not of his whining trade, but stands erect, with bold exulting smiles, as we pass him. The victory has healed him, and says, Be thou whole! Women and children, from garrets alike and cellars, through infinite London, look down or look up with loving eyes upon our gay ribbons and our martial laurels; sometimes kiss their hands; sometimes hang out, as signals of affection, pocket-handkerchiefs, aprons, dusters, anything that, by catching the summer breezes, will express an aerial jubilation. On the London side of Barnet, to which we draw near within a few minutes after nine, observe that private carriage which is approaching us. The weather being so warm, the glasses are all down; and one may read, as on the stage of a theatre, everything that goes on within. It contains three ladies — one likely to be "mamma," and two of seventeen or eighteen, who are probably her daughters. What lovely animation, what beautiful unpremeditated pantomime, explaining to us every syllable that passes, in these ingenuous girls! By the sudden start and raising of the hands, on first discovering our laurelled equipage! — by the sudden movement and appeal to the elder lady from both of them — and by the heightened colour of their animated countenances, we can almost hear them saying, "See, see! Look at their laurels! Oh, mamma! there has been a great battle in Spain; and it has been a great victory." In a moment we are on the point of passing them. We passengers — I on the box, and the two on the roof behind me — raise our hats to the ladies; the coachman makes his professional salute with the whip; the guard even, though punctilious on the matter of his dignity as an officer under the crown, touches his hat. The ladies move to us, in return, with a winning graciousness of gesture; all smile on each side in a way that nobody could misunderstand, and that nothing short of a grand national sympathy could so instantaneously prompt. Will these ladies say that we are nothing to *them?* Oh, no; they will not say *that.* They cannot deny — they do not deny — that for this night they are our sisters; gentle or simple, scholar or illiterate servant, for twelve hours to come, we on the outside have the honour to be their brothers. Those poor

women, again, who stop to gaze upon us with delight at the entrance
of Barnet, and seem, by their air of weariness, to be returning from
labour — do you mean to say that they are washerwomen and char-
women? Oh, my poor friend, you are quite mistaken. I assure you
they stand in a far higher rank; for this one night they feel themselves
by birth-right to be daughters of England, and answer to no humbler
title.

Every joy, however, even rapturous joy — such is the sad law of earth
— may carry with it grief, or fear of grief, to some. Three miles beyond
Barnet, we see approaching us another private carriage, nearly repeating
the circumstances of the former case. Here, also, the glasses are all
down — here, also, is an elderly lady seated; but the two daughters are
missing; for the single young person sitting by the lady's side, seems
to be an attendant — so I judge from her dress, and her air of
respectful reserve. The lady is in mourning; and her countenance expresses sorrow. At first she does not look up; so that I believe she is
not aware of our approach, until she hears the measured beating of
our horses' hoofs. Then she raises her eyes to settle them painfully on
our triumphal equipage. Our decorations explain the case to her at
once; but she beholds them with apparent anxiety, or even with terror. Some time before this, I, finding it difficult to hit a flying mark,
when embarrassed by the coachman's person and reins intervening,
had given to the guard a "Courier" evening paper, containing the
gazette, for the next carriage that might pass. Accordingly he tossed
it in, so folded that the huge capitals expressing some such legend as —
GLORIOUS VICTORY, might catch the eye at once. To see the paper,
however, at all, interpreted as it was by our ensigns of triumph, explained everything; and, if the guard were right in thinking the lady
to have received it with a gesture of horror, it could not be doubtful
that she had suffered some deep personal affliction in connection with
this Spanish war.

Here, now, was the case of one who, having formerly suffered,
might, erroneously perhaps, be distressing herself with anticipations
of another similar suffering. That same night, and hardly three hours
later, occurred the reverse case. A poor woman, who too probably
would find herself, in a day or two, to have suffered the heaviest of
afflictions by the battle, blindly allowed herself to express an exultation
so unmeasured in the news and its details, as gave to her the appearance which amongst Celtic Highlanders is called *fey*. This was at
some little town where we changed horses an hour or two after midnight. Some fair or wake had kept the people up out of their beds,
and had occasioned a partial illumination of the stalls and booths, presenting an unusual but very impressive effect. We saw many lights
moving about as we drew near; and perhaps the most striking scene
on the whole route was our reception at this place. The flashing of
torches and the beautiful radiance of blue lights (technically, Bengal

lights) upon the heads of our horses; the fine effect of such a showery
and ghostly illumination falling upon our flowers and glittering laurels;[22] whilst all around ourselves, that formed a centre of light, the
darkness gathered on the rear and flanks in massy blackness; these
optical splendours, together with the prodigious enthusiasm of the
people, composed a picture at once scenical and affecting, theatrical
and holy. As we staid for three or four minutes, I alighted; and immediately from a dismantled stall in the street, where no doubt she had
been presiding through the earlier part of the night, advanced eagerly
a middle-aged woman. The sight of my newspaper it was that had
drawn her attention upon myself. The victory which we were carrying
down to the provinces on *this* occasion, was the imperfect one of
Talavera — imperfect for its results, such was the virtual treachery
of the Spanish general, Cuesta, but not imperfect in its ever-memorable
heroism. I told her the main outline of the battle. The agitation of her
enthusiasm had been so conspicuous when listening, and when first
applying for information, that I could not but ask her if she had not
some relative in the Peninsular army. Oh, yes; her only son was there.
In what regiment? He was a trooper in the 23d Dragoons. My heart
sank within me as she made that answer. This sublime regiment,
which an Englishman should never mention without raising his hat
to their memory, had made the most memorable and effective charge
recorded in military annals. They leaped their horses — *over* a trench
where they could, *into* it, and with the result of death or mutilation
when they could *not*. What proportion cleared the trench is nowhere
stated. Those who *did,* closed up and went down upon the enemy
with such divinity of fervour (I use the word *divinity* by design: the
inspiration of God must have prompted this movement to those whom
even then he was calling to his presence), that two results followed. As
regarded the enemy, this 23d Dragoons, not, I believe, originally
three hundred and fifty strong, paralysed a French column, six thousand strong, then ascended the hill, and fixed the gaze of the whole
French army. As regarded themselves, the 23d were supposed at first
to have been barely not annihilated; but eventually, I believe, about
one in four survived. And this, then, was the regiment — a regiment
already for some hours glorified and hallowed to the ear of all London,
as lying stretched, by a large majority, upon one bloody aceldama —
in which the young trooper served whose mother was now talking in
a spirit of such joyous enthusiasm. Did I tell her the truth? Had I
the heart to break up her dreams? No. To-morrow, said I to myself
— to-morrow, or the next day, will publish the worst. For one night
more, wherefore should she not sleep in peace? After to-morrow, the
chances are too many that peace will forsake her pillow. This brief

[22] *"Glittering laurels:"* — I must observe, that the colour of *green* suffers
almost a spiritual change and exaltation under the effect of Bengal lights.
[De Q.]

respite, then, let her owe to *my* gift and *my* forbearance. But, if I told
her not of the bloody price that had been paid, not, therefore, was I
silent on the contributions from her son's regiment to that day's service
and glory. I showed her not the funeral banners under which the noble
regiment was sleeping. I lifted not the overshadowing laurels from
the bloody trench in which horse and rider lay mangled together.
But I told her how these dear children of England, officers and privates,
had leaped their horses over all obstacles as gaily as hunters to the
morning's chase. I told her how they rode their horses into the mists
of death (saying to myself, but not saying to *her*), and laid down their
young lives for thee, O mother England! as willingly — poured out
their noble blood as cheerfully — as ever, after a long day's sport,
when infants, they had rested their wearied heads upon their mother's
knees, or had sunk to sleep in her arms. Strange it is, yet true, that she
seemed to have no fears for her son's safety, even after this knowledge
that the 23d Dragoons had been memorably engaged; but so much
was she enraptured by the knowledge that *his* regiment, and therefore
that *he*, had rendered conspicuous service in the dreadful conflict —
a service which had actually made them, within the last twelve hours,
the foremost topic of conversation in London — so absolutely was
fear swallowed up in joy — that, in the mere simplicity of her fervent
nature, the poor woman threw her arms round my neck, as she thought
of her son, and gave to *me* the kiss which secretly was meant for *him*.[23]

Section the Second. — The Vision of Sudden Death

What is to be taken as the predominant opinion of man, reflective
and philosophic, upon SUDDEN DEATH? It is remarkable that, in different conditions of society, sudden death has been variously regarded as the consummation of an earthly career most fervently to be
desired, or, again, as that consummation which is with most horror to
be deprecated. Cæsar the Dictator, at his last dinner party (*cœna*),
on the very evening before his assassination, when the minutes of his
earthly career were numbered, being asked what death, in *his* judg-

[23] At the indecisive battle of Talavera on July 27–28, 1809, General
Cuesta acted independently of the British commander, Sir Arthur Wellesley.
   attelage: carriage with team; gazette: here a list of honors and promotions; aceldama: field of blood (see Acts 1:19).
   In the episode at Pekin, De Quincey embroiders a single sentence from
Sir George Staunton, *An Authentic Account of an Embassy . . .* , London,
1797, I, 164: "When a splendid chariot intended as a present for the Emperor was unpacked and put together, nothing could be more admired; but
it was necessary to give directions for taking off the box; for when the
mandarines found out that so elevated a seat was destined for the coachman
who was to drive the horses, they expressed the utmost astonishment that it
should be proposed to place any man in a situation *above* the Emperor."

ment, might be pronounced the most eligible, replied, "That which should be most sudden." On the other hand, the divine Litany of our English Church, when breathing forth supplications, as if in some representative character for the whole human race prostrate before God, places such a death in the very van of horrors: — "From lightning and tempest; from plague, pestilence, and famine; from battle and murder, and from SUDDEN DEATH — *Good Lord, deliver us.*" Sudden death is here made to crown the climax in a grand ascent of calamities; it is ranked among the last of curses; and yet, by the noblest of Romans, it was ranked as the first of blessings. In that difference, most readers will see little more than the essential difference between Christianity and Paganism. But this, on consideration, I doubt. The Christian Church may be right in its estimate of sudden death; and it is a natural feeling, though after all it may also be an infirm one, to wish for a quiet dismissal from life — as that which *seems* most reconcilable with meditation, with penitential retrospects, and with the humilities of farewell prayer. There does not, however, occur to me any direct scriptural warrant for this earnest petition of the English Litany, unless under a special construction of the word "sudden." It seems a petition — indulged rather and conceded to human infirmity, than exacted from human piety. It is not so much a doctrine built upon the eternities of the Christian system, as a plausible opinion built upon special varieties of physical temperament. Let that, however, be as it may, two remarks suggest themselves as prudent restraints upon a doctrine, which else *may* wander, and *has* wandered, into an uncharitable superstition. The first is this: that many people are likely to exaggerate the horror of a sudden death, from the disposition to lay a false stress upon words or acts, simply because by an accident they have become *final* words or acts. If a man dies, for instance, by some sudden death when he happens to be intoxicated, such a death is falsely regarded with peculiar horror; as though the intoxication were suddenly exalted into a blasphemy. But *that* is unphilosophic. The man was, or he was not, *habitually* a drunkard. If not, if his intoxication were a solitary accident, there can be no reason for allowing special emphasis to this act, simply because through misfortune it became his final act. Nor, on the other hand, if it were no accident, but one of his *habitual* transgressions, will it be the more habitual or the more a transgression, because some sudden calamity, surprising him, has caused this habitual transgression to be also a final one. Could the man have had any reason even dimly to foresee his own sudden death, there would have been a new feature in his act of intemperance — a feature of presumption and irreverence, as in one that, having known himself drawing near to the presence of God, should have suited his demeanour to an expectation so awful. But this is no part of the case supposed. And the only new element in the man's act is not any element of special immorality, but simply of special misfortune.

The other remark has reference to the meaning of the word *sudden*. Very possibly Cæsar and the Christian Church do not differ in the way supposed; that is, do not differ by any difference of doctrine as between Pagan and Christian views of the moral temper appropriate to death, but perhaps they are contemplating different cases. Both contemplate a violent death, a βιαθανατος — death that is βιαιος, or, in other words, death that is brought about, not by internal and spontaneous change, but by active force having its origin from without. In this meaning the two authorities agree. Thus far they are in harmony. But the difference is, that the Roman by the word "sudden" means *unlingering;* whereas the Christian Litany by "sudden death" means a death *without warning,* consequently without any available summons to religious preparation. The poor mutineer, who kneels down to gather into his heart the bullets from twelve firelocks of his pitying comrades, dies by a most sudden death in Cæsar's sense; one shock, one mighty spasm, one (possibly *not* one) groan, and all is over. But, in the sense of the Litany, the mutineer's death is far from sudden; his offence originally, his imprisonment, his trial, the interval between his sentence and its execution, having all furnished him with separate warnings of his fate — having all summoned him to meet it with solemn preparation.

Here at once, in this sharp verbal distinction, we comprehend the faithful earnestness with which a holy Christian Church pleads on behalf of her poor departing children, that God would vouchsafe to them the last great privilege and distinction possible on a death-bed — viz., the opportunity of untroubled preparation for facing this mighty trial. Sudden death, as a mere variety in the modes of dying, where death in some shape is inevitable, proposes a question of choice which, equally in the Roman and the Christian sense, will be variously answered according to each man's variety of temperament. Meantime, one aspect of sudden death there is, one modification, upon which no doubt can arise, that of all martyrdoms it is the most agitating — viz., where it surprises a man under circumstances which offer (or which seem to offer) some hurrying, flying, inappreciably minute chance of evading it. Sudden as the danger which it affronts, must be any effort by which such an evasion can be accomplished. Even *that,* even the sickening necessity for hurrying in extremity where all hurry seems destined to be vain, even that anguish is liable to a hideous exasperation in one particular case — viz., where the appeal is made not exclusively to the instinct of self-preservation, but to the conscience, on behalf of some other life besides your own, accidentally thrown upon *your* protection. To fail, to collapse in a service merely your own, might seem comparatively venial; though, in fact, it is far from venial. But to fail in a case where Providence has suddenly thrown into your hands the final interests of another — a fellow-creature shuddering between the gates of life and death; this, to a man of apprehensive conscience, would mingle the misery of an atrocious criminality with the misery of a bloody calamity. You are called upon, by the case supposed, possibly to die; but to die at the very moment when, by any even partial failure, or effeminate collapse of your energies, you will be self-denounced as a murderer. You had but the twinkling of an eye for your effort, and that effort might have been unavailing; but to have risen to the level of such an effort, would have rescued you, though not from dying, yet from dying as a traitor to your final and farewell duty.

The situation here contemplated exposes a dreadful ulcer, lurking far down in the depths of human nature. It is not that men generally are summoned to face such awful trials. But potentially, and in shadowy outline, such a trial is moving subterraneously in perhaps all men's natures. Upon the secret mirror of our dreams such a trial is darkly projected, perhaps, to every one of us. That dream, so familiar to childhood, of meeting a lion, and, through languishing prostration in hope and the energies of hope, that constant sequel of lying down before the lion, publishes the secret fraility of human nature — reveals its deep-seated falsehood to itself — records its abysmal treachery. Perhaps not one of us escapes that dream; perhaps, as by some sorrowful doom of man, that dream repeats for every one of us, through every generation, the original temptation in Eden. Every one of us, in this dream, has a bait offered to the infirm places of his own individual will; once again a snare is presented for tempting him into captivity to a luxury of ruin; once again, as in aboriginal Paradise, the man falls by his own choice; again, by infinite iteration, the ancient Earth groans to Heaven, through her secret caves, over the weakness of her child: "Nature, from her seat, sighing through all her works," again "gives signs of wo that all is lost;"[1] and again the counter sigh is repeated to the sorrowing heavens for the endless rebellion against God. It is not without probability that in the world of dreams every one of us ratifies for himself the original transgression. In dreams, perhaps under some secret conflict of the midnight sleeper, lighted up to the consciousness at the time, but darkened to the memory as soon as all is finished, each several child of our mysterious race completes for himself the treason of the aboriginal fall.

* * * * *[2]

The incident, so memorable in itself by its features of horror, and so scenical by its grouping for the eye, which furnished the text for this reverie upon *Sudden Death,* occurred to myself in the dead of night, as a solitary spectator, when seated on the box of the Manchester and Glasgow mail, in the second or third summer after Waterloo. I find it necessary to relate the circumstances, because they are

[1] *Paradise Lost* IX.782–784.
[2] The asterisks are De Quincey's.

such as could not have occurred unless under a singular combination of accidents. In those days, the oblique and lateral communications with many rural post-offices were so arranged, either through necessity or through defect of system, as to make it requisite for the main northwestern mail (*i.e.*, the *down* mail), on reaching Manchester, to halt for a number of hours; how many, I do not remember; six or seven, I think; but the result was, that, in the ordinary course, the mail recommenced its journey northwards about midnight. Wearied with the long detention at a gloomy hotel, I walked out about eleven o'clock at night for the sake of fresh air; meaning to fall in with the mail and resume my seat at the post-office. The night, however, being yet dark, as the moon had scarcely risen, and the streets being at that hour empty, so as to offer no opportunities for asking the road, I lost my way; and did not reach the post-office until it was considerably past midnight; but, to my great relief (as it was important for me to be in Westmoreland by the morning), I saw in the huge saucer eyes of the mail, blazing through the gloom, an evidence that my chance was not yet lost. Past the time it was; but, by some rare accident, the mail was not even yet ready to start. I ascended to my seat on the box, where my cloak was still lying as it had lain at the Bridgewater Arms. I had left it there in imitation of a nautical discoverer, who leaves a bit of bunting on the shore of his discovery, by way of warning off the ground the whole human race, and notifying to the Christian and the heathen worlds, with his best compliments, that he has hoisted his pocket-handkerchief once and for ever upon that virgin soil; thenceforward claiming the *jus dominii* to the top of the atmosphere above it, and also the right of driving shafts to the centre of the earth below it; so that all people found after this warning, either aloft in upper chambers of the atmosphere, or groping in subterraneous shafts, or squatting audaciously on the surface of the soil, will be treated as trespassers — kicked, that is to say, or decapitated, as circumstances may suggest, by their very faithful servant, the owner of the said pocket-handkerchief. In the present case, it is probable that my cloak might not have been respected, and the *jus gentium* might have been cruelly violated in my person — for, in the dark, people commit deeds of darkness, gas being a great ally of morality — but it so happened that, on this night, there was no other outside passenger; and thus the crime, which else was but too probable, missed fire for want of a criminal.

Having mounted the box, I took a small quantity of laudanum, having already travelled two hundred and fifty miles — viz., from a point seventy miles beyond London. In the taking of laudanum there was nothing extraordinary. But by accident it drew upon me the special attention of my assessor on the box, the coachman. And in *that* also there was nothing extraordinary. But by accident, and with great delight, it drew my own attention to the fact that this coachman was a monster in point of bulk, and that he had but one eye. In fact, he had been foretold by Virgil as

"Monstrum horrendum, informe, ingens cui lumen ademptum."[3]

He answered to the conditions in every one of the items: — 1. a monster he was; 2. dreadful; 3. shapeless; 4. huge; 5. who had lost an eye. But why should *that* delight me? Had he been one of the Calendars in the "Arabian Nights," and had paid down his eye as the price of his criminal curiosity, what right had *I* to exult in his misfortune? I did *not* exult: I delighted in no man's punishment, though it were even merited. But these personal distinctions (Nos. 1, 2, 3, 4, 5) identified in an instant an old friend of mine, whom I had known in the south for some years as the most masterly of mail-coachmen. He was the man in all Europe that could (if *any* could) have driven six-in-hand full gallop over *Al Sirat* — that dreadful bridge of Mahomet, with no side battlements, and of *extra* room not enough for a razor's edge — leading right across the bottomless gulf. Under this eminent man, whom in Greek I cognominated Cyclops *diphrélates* (Cyclops the charioteer), I, and others known to me, studied the diphrelatic art. Excuse, reader, a word too elegant to be pedantic. As a pupil, though I paid extra fees, it is to be lamented that I did not stand high in his esteem. It showed his dogged honesty (though, observe, not his discernment), that he could not see my merits. Let us excuse his absurdity in this particular, by remembering his want of an eye. Doubtless *that* made him blind to my merits. In the art of conversation, however, he admitted that I had the whip-hand of him. On this present occasion, great joy was at our meeting. But what was Cyclops doing here? Had the medical men recommended northern air, or how? I collected, from such explanations as he volunteered, that he had an interest at stake in some suit-at-law now pending at Lancaster; so that probably he had got himself transferred to this station, for the purpose of connecting with his professional pursuits an instant readiness for the calls of his lawsuit.

Meantime, what are we stopping for? Surely we have now waited long enough. Oh, this procrastinating mail, and this procrastinating post-office! Can't they take a lesson upon that subject from *me?* Some people have called *me* procrastinating. Yet you are witness, reader, that I was here kept waiting for the post-office. Will the post-office lay its hand on its heart, in its moments of sobriety, and assert that ever it waited for me? What are they about? The guard tells me that there is a large extra accumulation of foreign mails this night, owing to irregularities caused by war, by wind, by weather, in the packet service, which as yet does not benefit at all by steam. For an *extra* hour, it seems, the post-office has been engaged in threshing out the

---

[3] *Aeneid* III.658, of Polyphemus, a Cyclops.

pure wheaten correspondence of Glasgow, and winnowing it from the chaff of all baser intermediate towns. But at last all is finished. Sound your horn, guard. Manchester, good-bye; we've lost an hour by your criminal conduct at the post-office: which, however, though I do not mean to part with a serviceable ground of complaint, and one which really *is* such for the horses, to me secretly is an advantage, since it compels us to look sharply for this lost hour amongst the next eight or nine, and to recover it (if we can) at the rate of one mile extra per hour. Off we are at last, and at eleven miles an hour; and for the moment I detect no changes in the energy or in the skill of Cyclops.

From Manchester to Kendal, which virtually (though not in law) is the capital of Westmoreland, there were at this time seven stages of eleven miles each. The first five of these, counting from Manchester, terminate in Lancaster, which is therefore fifty-five miles north of Manchester, and the same distance exactly from Liverpool. The first three stages terminate in Preston (called, by way of distinction from other towns of that name, *proud* Preston), at which place it is that the separate roads from Liverpool and from Manchester to the north become confluent.[4] Within these first three stages lay the foundation, the progress, and termination of our night's adventure. During the first stage, I found out that Cyclops was mortal: he was liable to the shocking affection of sleep — a thing which previously I had never suspected. If a man indulges in the vicious habit of sleeping, all the skill in aurigation of Apollo himself, with the horses of Aurora to execute his notions, avail him nothing. "Oh, Cyclops!" I exclaimed, "thou art mortal. My friend, thou snorest." Through the first eleven miles, however, this infirmity — which I grieve to say that he shared with the whole Pagan Pantheon — betrayed itself only by brief snatches. On waking up, he made an apology for himself, which, instead of mending matters, laid open a gloomy vista of coming disasters. The summer assizes, he reminded me, were now going on at Lancaster: in consequence of which, for three nights and three days, he had not lain down in a bed. During the day, he was waiting for his own summons as a witness on the trial in which he was interested; or else, lest he should be missing at the critical moment, was drinking with the other witnesses, under the pastoral surveillance of the attorneys. During the night, or that part of it which at sea would form the middle watch, he was driving. This explanation certainly accounted for his drowsiness, but in a way which made it much more alarming; since now, after several days' resistance to this infirmity, at

---

[4] *"Confluent:"* — Suppose a capital Y (the Pythagorean letter): Lancaster is at the foot of this letter; Liverpool at the top of the *right* branch; Manchester at the top of the *left;* proud Preston at the centre, where the two branches unite. It is thirty-three miles along either of the two branches; it is twenty-two miles along the stem — viz., from Preston in the middle, to Lancaster at the root. There's a lesson in geography for the reader. [De Q.]

length he was steadily giving way. Throughout the second stage he grew more and more drowsy. In the second mile of the third stage, he surrendered himself finally and without a struggle to his perilous temptation. All his past resistance had but deepened the weight of this final oppression. Seven atmospheres of sleep rested upon him; and to consummate the case, our worthy guard, after singing "Love amongst the Roses" for perhaps thirty times, without invitation, and without applause, had in revenge moodily resigned himself to slumber — not so deep, doubtless, as the coachman's, but deep enough for mischief. And thus at last, about ten miles from Preston, it came about that I found myself left in charge of his Majesty's London and Glasgow mail, then running at the least twelve miles an hour.

What made this negligence less criminal than else it must have been thought, was the condition of the roads at night during the assizes. At that time, all the law business of populous Liverpool, and also of populous Manchester, with its vast cincture of populous rural districts, was called up by ancient usage to the tribunal of Lilliputian Lancaster. To break up this old tradition usage required, 1. a conflict with powerful established interests; 2. a large system of new arrangements; and 3. a new parliamentary statute. But as yet this change was merely in contemplation. As things were at present, twice in the year[5] so vast a body of business rolled northwards, from the southern quarter of the county, that for a fortnight at least it occupied the severe exertions of two judges in its despatch. The consequence of this was, that every horse available for such a service, along the whole line of road, was exhausted in carrying down the multitudes of people who were parties to the different suits. By sunset, therefore, it usually happened that, through utter exhaustion amongst men and horses, the road sank into profound silence. Except the exhaustion in the vast adjacent county of York from a contested election, no such silence succeeding to no such fiery uproar was ever witnessed in England.

On this occasion, the usual silence and solitude prevailed along the road. Not a hoof nor a wheel was to be heard. And to strengthen this false luxurious confidence in the noiseless roads, it happened also that the night was one of peculiar solemnity and peace. For my own part, though slightly alive to the possibilities of peril, I had so far yielded to the influence of the mighty calm as to sink into a profound reverie. The month was August, in the middle of which lay my own birthday — a festival to every thoughtful man suggesting solemn and often sigh-born[6] thoughts. The county was my own native county — upon which, in its southern section, more than upon any equal area

[5] *"Twice in the year:"* — There were at that time only two assizes even in the most populous counties — viz., the Lent Assizes, and the Summer Assizes. [De Q.]

[6] *"Sigh-born:"* — I owe the suggestion of this word to an obscure remembrance of a beautiful phrase in "Giraldus Cambrensis" — viz., *suspiriosæ cogitationes.* [De Q.]

known to man past or present, had descended the original curse of labour in its heaviest form, not mastering the bodies only of men as of slaves, or criminals in mines, but working through the fiery will. Upon no equal space of earth was, or ever had been, the same energy of human power put forth daily. At this particular season also of the assizes, that dreadful hurricane of flight and pursuit, as it might have seemed to a stranger, which swept to and from Lancaster all day long, hunting the county up and down, and regularly subsiding back into silence about sunset, could not fail (when united with this permanent distinction of Lancashire as the very metropolis and citadel of labour) to point the thoughts pathetically upon that counter vision of rest, of saintly repose from strife and sorrow, towards which, as to their secret haven, the profounder aspirations of man's heart are in solitude continually travelling. Obliquely upon our left we were nearing the sea, which also must, under the present circumstances, be repeating the general state of halcyon repose. The sea, the atmosphere, the light, bore each an orchestral part in this universal lull. Moonlight, and the first timid tremblings of the dawn, were by this time blending; and the blendings were brought into a still more exquisite state of unity by a slight silvery mist, motionless and dreamy, that covered the woods and fields, but with a veil of equable transparency. Except the feet of our own horses, which, running on a sandy margin of the road, made but little disturbance, there was no sound abroad. In the clouds, and on the earth, prevailed the same majestic peace; and in spite of all that the villain of a schoolmaster has done for the ruin of our sublimer thoughts, which are the thoughts of our infancy, we still believe in no such nonsense as a limited atmosphere. Whatever we may swear with our false feigning lips, in our faithful hearts we still believe, and must for ever believe, in fields of air traversing the total gulf between earth and the central heavens. Still, in the confidence of children that tread without fear *every* chamber in their father's house, and to whom no door is closed, we, in that Sabbatic vision which sometimes is revealed for an hour upon nights like this, ascend with easy steps from the sorrow-stricken fields of earth, upwards to the sandals of God.

Suddenly, from thoughts like these, I was awakened to a sullen sound, as of some motion on the distant road. It stole upon the air for a moment; I listened in awe; but then it died away. Once roused, however, I could not but observe with alarm the quickened motion of our horses. Ten years' experience had made my eye learned in the valuing of motion; and I saw that we were now running thirteen miles an hour. I pretend to no presence of mind. On the contrary, my fear is, that I am miserably and shamefully deficient in that quality as regards action. The palsy of doubt and distraction hangs like some guilty weight of dark unfathomed remembrances upon my energies, when the signal is flying for *action*. But, on the other hand, this accursed gift I have, as regards *thought*, that in the first step towards the possibility of a misfortune, I see its total evolution; in the radix of the series I see too certainly and too instantly its entire expansion; in the first syllable of the dreadful sentence, I read already the last. It was not that I feared for ourselves. *Us*, our bulk and impetus charmed against peril in any collision. And I had ridden through too many hundreds of perils that were frightful to approach, that were matter of laughter to look back upon, the first face of which was horror — the parting face a jest, for any anxiety to rest upon *our* interests. The mail was not built, I felt assured, nor bespoke, that could betray *me* who trusted to its protection. But any carriage that we could meet would be frail and light in comparison of ourselves. And I remarked this ominous accident of our situation. We were on the wrong side of the road. But then, it may be said, the other party, if other there was, might also be on the wrong side; and two wrongs might make a right. *That* was not likely. The same motive which had drawn *us* to the right-hand side of the road — viz., the luxury of the soft beaten sand, as contrasted with the paved centre — would prove attractive to others. The two adverse carriages would therefore, to a certainty, be travelling on the same side; and from this side, as not being ours in law, the crossing over to the other would, of course, be looked for from *us*.[7] Our lamps, still lighted, would give the impression of vigilance on our part. And every creature that met us, would rely upon *us* for quartering.[8] All this, and if the separate links of the anticipation had been a thousand times more, I saw, not discursively, or by effort, or by succession, but by one flash of horrid simultaneous intuition.

Under this steady though rapid anticipation of the evil which *might* be gathering ahead, ah! what a sullen mystery of fear, what a sigh of wo, was that which stole upon the air, as again the far-off sound of a wheel was heard! A whisper it was — a whisper from, perhaps, four miles off — secretly announcing a ruin that, being foreseen, was not the less inevitable; that, being known, was not, therefore, healed. What could be done — who was it that could do it — to check the storm-flight of these maniacal horses? Could I not seize the reins from the grasp of the slumbering coachman? You, reader, think that it would have been in *your* power to do so. And I quarrel not with your estimate of yourself. But, from the way in which the coachman's hand was viced between his upper and lower thigh, this was

[7] It is true that, according to the law of the case as established by legal precedents, all carriages were required to give way before Royal equipages, and therefore before the mail as one of them. But this only increased the danger, as being a regulation very imperfectly made known, very unequally enforced, and therefore often embarrassing the movements on both sides. [De Q.]

[8] *"Quartering:"* — This is the technical word, and, I presume, derived from the French *cartayer*, to evade a rut or any obstacle. [De Q.]

impossible. Easy, was it? See, then, that bronze equestrian statue. The cruel rider has kept the bit in his horse's mouth for two centuries. Unbridle him, for a minute, if you please, and wash his mouth with water. Easy, was it? Unhorse me, then, that imperial rider; knock me those marble feet from those marble stirrups of Charlemagne.

The sounds ahead strengthened, and were now too clearly the sounds of wheels. Who and what could it be? Was it industry in a taxed cart? Was it youthful gaiety in a gig? Was it sorrow that loitered, or joy that raced? For as yet the snatches of sound were too intermitting, from distance, to decipher the character of the motion. Whoever were the travellers, something must be done to warn them. Upon the other party rests the active responsibility, but upon *us* — and, wo is me! that *us* was reduced to my frail opium-shattered self — rests the responsibility of warning. Yet, how should this be accomplished? Might I not sound the guard's horn? Already, on the first thought, I was making my way over the roof to the guard's seat. But this, from the accident which I have mentioned, of the foreign mails' being piled upon the roof was a difficult and even dangerous attempt to one cramped by nearly three hundred miles of outside travelling. And, fortunately, before I had lost much time in the attempt, our frantic horses swept round an angle in the road, which opened upon us that final stage where the collision must be accomplished, and the catastrophe sealed. All was apparently finished. The court was sitting; the case was heard; the judge had finished; and only the verdict was yet in arrear.

Before us lay an avenue, straight as an arrow, six hundred yards, perhaps, in length; and the umbrageous trees, which rose in a regular line from either side, meeting high overhead, gave to it the character of a cathedral aisle. These trees lent a deeper solemnity to the early light; but there was still light enough to perceive, at the further end of this Gothic aisle, a frail reedy gig, in which were seated a young man, and by his side a young lady. Ah, young sir! what are you about? If it is requisite that you should whisper your communications to this young lady — though really I see nobody, at an hour and on a road so solitary, likely to overhear you — is it therefore requisite that you should carry your lips forward to hers? The little carriage is creeping on at one mile an hour; and the parties within it being thus tenderly engaged, are naturally bending down their heads. Between them and eternity, to all human calculation, there is but a minute and a-half. Oh heavens! what is it that I shall do? Speaking or acting, what help can I offer? Strange it is, and to a mere auditor of the tale might seem laughable, that I should need a suggestion from the "Iliad" to prompt the sole resource that remained. Yet so it was. Suddenly I remembered the shout of Achilles, and its effect. But could I pretend to shout like the son of Peleus, aided by Pallas? No: but then I needed not the shout that should alarm all Asia militant;

such a shout would suffice as might carry terror into the hearts of two thoughtless young people, and one gig-horse. I shouted — and the young man heard me not. A second time I shouted — and now he heard me, for now he raised his head.

Here, then, all had been done that, by me, *could* be done: more on *my* part was not possible. Mine had been the first step; the second was for the young man; the third was for God. If, said I, this stranger is a brave man, and if, indeed, he loves the young girl at his side — or, loving her not, if he feels the obligation, pressing upon every man worthy to be called a man, of doing his utmost for a woman confided to his protection — he will, at least, make some effort to save her. If *that* fails, he will not perish the more, or by a death more cruel, for having made it; and he will die as a brave man should, with his face to the danger, and with his arm about the woman that he sought in vain to save. But, if he makes no effort, shrinking, without a struggle, from his duty, he himself will not the less certainly perish for this baseness of poltroonery. He will die no less: and why not? Wherefore should we grieve that there is one craven less in the world? No; *let* him perish, without a pitying thought of ours wasted upon him; and, in that case, all our grief will be reserved for the fate of the helpless girl who now, upon the least shadow of failure in *him*, must, by the fiercest of translations — must, without time for a prayer — must, within seventy seconds, stand before the judgment-seat of God.

But craven he was not: sudden had been the call upon him, and sudden was his answer to the call. He saw, he heard, he comprehended, the ruin that was coming down: already its gloomy shadow darkened above him; and already he was measuring his strength to deal with it. Ah! what a vulgar thing does courage seem, when we see nations buying it and selling it for a shilling a-day: ah! what a sublime thing does courage seem, when some fearful summons on the great deeps of life carries a man, as if running before a hurricane, up to the giddy crest of some tumultuous crisis, from which lie two courses, and a voice says to him audibly, "One way lies hope; take the other, and mourn for ever!" How grand a triumph, if, even then, amidst the raving of all around him, and the frenzy of the danger, the man is able to confront his situation — is able to retire for a moment into solitude with God, and to seek his counsel from *him!*

For seven seconds, it might be, of his seventy, the stranger settled his countenance steadfastly upon us, as if to search and value every element in the conflict before him. For five seconds more of his seventy he sat immovably, like one that mused on some great purpose. For five more, perhaps, he sat with eyes upraised, like one that prayed in sorrow, under some extremity of doubt, for light that should guide him to the better choice. Then suddenly he rose; stood upright; and by a powerful strain upon the reins, raising his horse's fore-feet from the ground, he slewed him round on the pivot of his hind-legs, so as to plant the little equipage in a position nearly at right angles to ours. Thus far his condition was not improved; except as a first step had been taken towards the possibility of a second. If no more were done, nothing was done; for the little carriage still occupied the very centre of our path, though in an altered direction. Yet even now it may not be too late; fifteen of the seventy seconds may still be unexhausted; and one almighty bound may avail to clear the ground. Hurry, then, hurry! for the flying moments — *they* hurry. Oh, hurry, hurry, my brave young man! for the cruel hoofs of our horses — *they* also hurry! Fast are the flying moments, faster are the hoofs of our horses. But fear not for *him*, if human energy can suffice; faithful was he that drove to his terrific duty; faithful was the horse to *his* command. One blow, one impulse given with voice and hand, by the stranger, one rush from the horse, one bound as if in the act of rising to a fence, landed the docile creature's fore-feet upon the crown or arching centre of the road. The larger half of the little equipage had then cleared our over-towering shadow: *that* was evident even to my own agitated sight. But it mattered little that one wreck should float off in safety, if upon the wreck that perished were embarked the human freightage. The rear part of the carriage — was *that* certainly beyond the line of absolute ruin? What power could answer the question? Glance of eye, thought of man, wing of angel, which of these had speed enough to sweep between the question and the answer, and divide the one from the other? Light does not tread upon the steps of light more indivisibly, than did our all-conquering arrival upon the escaping efforts of the gig. *That* must the young man have felt too plainly. His back was now turned to us; not by sight could he any longer communicate with the peril; but by the dreadful rattle of our harness, too truly had his ear been instructed — that all was finished as regarded any further effort of *his*. Already in resignation he had rested from his struggle; and perhaps in his heart he was whispering, "Father, which art in heaven, do thou finish above what I on earth have attempted." Faster than ever mill-race we ran past them in our inexorable flight. Oh, raving of hurricanes that must have sounded in their young ears at the moment of our transit! Even in that moment the thunder of collision spoke aloud. Either with the swingle-bar, or with the haunch of our near leader, we had struck the off-wheel of the little gig, which stood rather obliquely, and not quite so far advanced, as to be accurately parallel with the near-wheel. The blow, from the fury of our passage, resounded terrifically. I rose in horror, to gaze upon the ruins we might have caused. From my elevated station I looked down, and looked back upon the scene, which in a moment told its own tale, and wrote all its records on my heart for ever.

Here was the map of the passion that now had finished. The horse was planted immovably, with his fore-feet upon the paved crest of the central road. He of the whole party might be supposed untouched by the passion of death. The little cany carriage — partly, perhaps, from the violent torsion of the wheels in its recent movement, partly from the thundering blow we had given to it — as if it sympathised with human horror, was all alive with tremblings and shiverings. The young man trembled not, nor shivered. He sat like a rock. But *his* was the steadiness of agitation frozen into rest by horror. As yet he dared not to look around; for he knew that, if anything remained to do, by him it could no longer be done. And as yet he knew not for certain if their safety were accomplished. But the lady ——

But the lady ——! Oh, heavens! will that spectacle ever depart from my dreams, as she rose and sank upon her seat, sank and rose, threw up her arms wildly to heaven, clutched at some visionary object in the air, fainting, praying, raving, despairing? Figure to yourself, reader, the elements of the case; suffer me to recall before your mind the circumstances of that unparalleled situation. From the silence and deep peace of this saintly summer night — from the pathetic blending of this sweet moonlight, dawnlight, dreamlight — from the manly tenderness of this flattering, whispering, murmuring love — suddenly as from the woods and fields — suddenly as from the chambers of the air opening in revelation — suddenly as from the ground yawning at her feet, leaped upon her, with the flashing of cataracts, Death the crownéd phantom, with all the equipage of his terrors, and the tiger roar of his voice.

The moments were numbered; the strife was finished; the vision was closed. In the twinkling of an eye, our flying horses had carried us to the termination of the umbrageous aisle; at right angles we wheeled into our former direction; the turn of the road carried the scene out of my eyes in an instant, and swept it into my dreams for ever.[9]

Section the Third. — Dream-Fugue

FOUNDED ON THE PRECEDING THEME OF SUDDEN DEATH

'Whence the sound
Of instruments, that made melodious chime,
Was heard, of harp and organ; and who moved
Their stops and chords, was seen; his volant touch
Instinct through all proportions, low and high,
Fled and pursued transverse the resonant fugue.'

Par. Lost, B. xi.[558–563]

[9] For Caesar on death, see Suetonius, *Life of Julius Caesar*, ch. 87.

jus dominii: law of ownership; *jus gentium:* law of nations; Calendars: three mendicants in the *Arabian Nights* who tell how each lost one eye; aurigation: chariot-driving.

The shout of Achilles, aided by Pallas Athene, terrorized the Trojans, *Iliad* IX.217ff.

Tumultuosissimamente.[1]

Passion of sudden death! that once in youth I read and interpreted by the shadows of thy averted signs![2] — rapture of panic taking the shape (which amongst tombs in churches I have seen) of woman bursting her sepulchral bonds — of woman's Ionic form bending forward from the ruins of her grave with arching foot, with eyes upraised, with clasped adoring hands — waiting, watching, trembling, praying for the trumpet's call to rise from dust for ever! Ah, vision too fearful of shuddering humanity on the brink of almighty abysses! — vision that didst start back, that didst reel away, like a shrivelling scroll from before the wrath of fire racing on the wings of the wind! Epilepsy so brief of horror, wherefore is it that thou canst not die? Passing so suddenly into darkness, wherefore is it that still thou sheddest thy sad funeral blights upon the gorgeous mosaics of dreams? Fragment of music too passionate, heard once, and heard no more, what aileth thee, that thy deep rolling chords come up at intervals through all the worlds of sleep, and after forty years, have lost no element of horror?

I.

Lo, it is summer — almighty summer! The everlasting gates of life and summer are thrown open wide; and on the ocean, tranquil and verdant as a savannah, the unknown lady from the dreadful vision and I myself are floating — she upon a fairy pinnace, and I upon an English three-decker. Both of us are wooing gales of festal happiness within the domain of our common country, within that ancient watery park, within that pathless chase of ocean, where England takes her pleasure as a huntress through winter and summer, from the rising to the setting sun. Ah, what a wilderness of floral beauty was hidden, or was suddenly revealed, upon the tropic islands through which the pinnace moved! And upon her deck what a bevy of human flowers — young women how lovely, young men how noble, that were dancing together, and slowly drifting towards *us* amidst music and incense, amidst blossoms from forests and gorgeous corymbi from vintages, amidst natural carolling and the echoes of sweet girlish laughter. Slowly the pinnace nears us, gaily she hails us, and silently she disappears beneath the shadow of our mighty bows. But then, as at some signal from heaven, the music, and the carols, and the sweet echoing of girlish laughter — all are hushed. What evil has smitten the pinnace, meeting or overtaking her? Did ruin to our friends couch within

---

[1] most tempestuously — a musical direction for reading the "fugue."
[2] *"Averted signs:"* — I read the course and changes of the lady's agony in the succession of her involuntary gestures; but it must be remembered that I read all this from the rear, never once catching the lady's full face, and even her profile imperfectly. [De Q.]

our own dreadful shadow? Was our shadow the shadow of death? I looked over the bow for an answer, and, behold! the pinnace was dismantled; the revel and the revellers were found no more; the glory of the vintage was dust; and the forests with their beauty were left without a witness upon the seas. "But where," and I turned to our crew — "where are the lovely women that danced beneath the awning of flowers and clustering corymbi? Whither have fled the noble young men that danced with *them?*" Answer there was none. But suddenly the man at the mast-head, whose countenance darkened with alarm, cried out, "Sail on the weather beam! Down she comes upon us: in seventy seconds she also will founder."

II.

I looked to the weather side, and the summer had departed. The sea was rocking, and shaken with gathering wrath. Upon its surface sat mighty mists, which grouped themselves into arches and long cathedral aisles. Down one of these, with the fiery pace of a quarrel[3] from a crossbow, ran a frigate right athwart our course. "Are they mad?" some voice exclaimed from our deck. "Do they woo their ruin?" But in a moment, as she was close upon us, some impulse of a heady current or local vortex gave a wheeling bias to her course, and off she forged without a shock. As she ran past us, high aloft amongst the shrouds stood the lady of the pinnace. The deeps opened ahead in malice to receive her, towering surges of foam ran after her, the billows were fierce to catch her. But far away she was borne into desert spaces of the sea: whilst still by sight I followed her, as she ran before the howling gale, chased by angry sea-birds and by maddening billows; still I saw her, as at the moment when she ran past us, standing amongst the shrouds, with her white draperies streaming before the wind. There she stood, with hair dishevelled, one hand clutched amongst the tackling — rising, sinking, fluttering, trembling, praying — there for leagues I saw her as she stood, raising at intervals one hand to heaven, amidst the fiery crests of the pursuing waves and the raving of the storm; until at last, upon a sound from afar of malicious laughter and mockery, all was hidden for ever in driving showers; and afterwards, but when I know not, nor how,

III.

Sweet funeral bells from some incalculable distance, wailing over the dead that die before the dawn, awakened me as I slept in a boat moored to some familiar shore. The morning twilight even then was breaking; and, by the dusky revelations which it spread, I saw a girl,

[3] arrow with four-edged head.

adorned with a garland of white roses about her head for some great
festival, running along the solitary strand in extremity of haste. Her
running was the running of panic; and often she looked back as to
some dreadful enemy in the rear. But when I leaped ashore, and
followed on her steps to warn her of a peril in front, alas! from me
she fled as from another peril, and vainly I shouted to her of quicksands that lay ahead. Faster and faster she ran; round a promontory
of rocks she wheeled out of sight; in an instant I also wheeled round
it, but only to see the treacherous sands gathering above her head.
Already her person was buried; only the fair young head and the diadem of white roses around it were still visible to the pitying heavens;
and, last of all, was visible one white marble arm. I saw by the early
twilight this fair young head, as it was sinking down to darkness —
saw this marble arm, as it rose above her head and her treacherous
grave, tossing, faltering, rising, clutching as at some false deceiving
hand stretched out from the clouds — saw this marble arm uttering
her dying hope, and then uttering her dying despair. The head, the
diadem, the arm — these all had sunk; at last over these also the cruel
quicksand had closed; and no memorial of the fair young girl remained
on earth, except my own solitary tears, and the funeral bells from
the desert seas, that, rising again more softly, sang a requiem over
the grave of the buried child, and over her blighted dawn.

I sat, and wept in secret the tears that men have ever given to the
memory of those that died before the dawn, and by the treachery
of earth, our mother. But suddenly the tears and funeral bells were
hushed by a shout as of many nations, and by a roar as from some
great king's artillery, advancing rapidly along the valleys, and heard
afar by echoes from the mountains. "Hush!" I said, as I bent my ear
earthwards to listen — "hush! — this either is the very anarchy of
strife, or else" — and then I listened more profoundly, and whispered as I raised my head — "or else, oh heavens! it is *victory* that
is final, victory that swallows up all strife."

IV.

Immediately, in trance, I was carried over land and sea to some
distant kingdom, and placed upon a triumphal car, amongst companions crowned with laurel. The darkness of gathering midnight,
brooding over all the land, hid from us the mighty crowds that were
weaving restlessly about ourselves as a centre: we heard them, but
saw them not. Tidings had arrived, within an hour, of a grandeur
that measured itself against centuries; too full of pathos they were,
too full of joy, to utter themselves by other language than by tears,
by restless anthems, and *Te Deums* reverberated from the choirs and
orchestras of earth. These tidings we that sat upon the laurelled car
had it for our privilege to publish amongst all nations. And already,

by signs audible through the darkness, by snortings and tramplings, our angry horses, that knew no fear of fleshly weariness, upbraided us with delay. Wherefore *was* it that we delayed? We waited for a secret word, that should bear witness to the hope of nations, as now accomplished for ever. At midnight the secret word arrived; which word was — Waterloo and Recovered Christendom! The dreadful word shone by its own light; before us it went; high above our leaders' heads it rode, and spread a golden light over the paths which we traversed. Every city, at the presence of the secret word, threw open its gates. The rivers were conscious as we crossed. All the forests, as we ran along their margins, shivered in homage to the secret word. And the darkness comprehended it.

Two hours after midnight we approached a mighty Minster. Its gates, which rose to the clouds, were closed. But when the dreadful word, that rode before us, reached them with its golden light, silently they moved back upon their hinges; and at a flying gallop our equipage entered the grand aisle of the cathedral. Headlong was our pace; and at every altar, in the little chapels and oratories to the right hand and left of our course, the lamps, dying or sickening, kindled anew in sympathy with the secret word that was flying past. Forty leagues we might have run in the cathedral, and as yet no strength of morning light had reached us, when before us we saw the aerial galleries of organ and choir. Every pinnacle of the fretwork, every station of advantage amongst the traceries, was crested by white-robed choristers, that sang deliverance; that wept no more tears, as once their fathers had wept; but at intervals that sang together to the generations, saying,

"Chant the deliverer's praise in every tongue,"

and receiving answers from afar,

"Such as once in heaven and earth were sung."

And of their chanting was no end; of our headlong pace was neither pause nor slackening.

Thus, as we ran like torrents — thus, as we swept with bridal rapture over the Campo Santo[4] of the cathedral graves — suddenly we

---

[4] *"Campo Santo:"* — It is probable that most of my readers will be acquainted with the history of the Campo Santo (or cemetery) at Pisa, composed of earth brought from Jerusalem from a bed of sanctity, as the highest prize which the noble piety of crusaders could ask or imagine. To readers who are unacquainted with England, or who (being English) are yet unacquainted with the cathedral cities of England, it may be right to mention that the graves within-side the cathedrals often form a flat pavement over which carriages and horses *might* run; and perhaps a boyish remembrance of one particular cathedral, across which I had seen passengers walk and burdens carried, as about two centuries back they were through the middle of St Paul's in London, may have assisted my dream. [De Q.]

became aware of a vast necropolis rising upon the far-off horizon —
a city of sepulchres, built within the saintly cathedral for the warrior
dead that rested from their feuds on earth. Of purple granite was the
necropolis; yet, in the first minute, it lay like a purple stain upon the
horizon, so mighty was the distance. In the second minute it trembled
through many changes, growing into terraces and towers of wondrous
altitude, so mighty was the pace. In the third minute already, with
our dreadful gallop, we were entering its suburbs. Vast sarcophagi
rose on every side, having towers and turrets that, upon the limits of
the central aisle, strode forward with haughty intrusion, that ran back
with mighty shadows into answering recesses. Every sarcophagus
showed many bas-reliefs — bas-reliefs of battles and of battle-fields;
battles from forgotten ages — battles from yesterday — battle-fields
that, long since, nature had healed and reconciled to herself with the
sweet oblivion of flowers — battle-fields that were yet angry and crimson with carnage. Where the terraces ran, there did *we* run; where the
towers curved, there did *we* curve. With the flight of swallows our
horses swept round every angle. Like rivers in flood, wheeling round
headlands — like hurricanes that ride into the secrets of forests —
faster than ever light unwove the mazes of darkness, our flying equipage carried earthly passions, kindled warrior instincts, amongst the
dust that lay around us — dust oftentimes of our noble fathers that
had slept in God from Créci to Trafalgar.[5] And now had we reached
the last sarcophagus, now were we abreast of the last bas-relief, already had we recovered the arrow-like flight of the illimitable central
aisle, when coming up this aisle to meet us we beheld afar off a
female child, that rode in a carriage as frail as flowers. The mists,
which went before her, hid the fawns that drew her, but could not
hide the shells and tropic flowers with which she played — but could
not hide the lovely smiles by which she uttered her trust in the mighty
cathedral, and in the cherubim that looked down upon her from the
mighty shafts of its pillars. Face to face she was meeting us; face to
face she rode, as if danger there were none. "Oh, baby!" I exclaimed,
"shalt thou be the ransom for Waterloo? Must we, that carry tidings
of great joy to every people, be messengers of ruin to thee!" In horror I rose at the thought; but then also, in horror at the thought, rose
one that was sculptured on a bas-relief — a Dying Trumpeter. Solemnly from the field of battle he rose to his feet; and, unslinging his
stony trumpet, carried it, in his dying anguish, to his stony lips —
sounding once, and yet once again; proclamation that, in *thy* ears,
oh baby! spoke from the battlements of death. Immediately deep
shadows fell between us, and aboriginal silence. The choir had ceased
to sing. The hoofs of our horses, the dreadful rattle of our harness,
the groaning of our wheels, alarmed the graves no more. By horror

[5] Crécy, battle won under Edward III, 1346.

the bas-relief had been unlocked unto life. By horror we, that were so full of life, we men and our horses, with their fiery fore-legs rising in mid air to the everlasting gallop, were frozen to a bas-relief. Then a third time the trumpet sounded; the seals were taken off all pulses; life, and the frenzy of life, tore into their channels again; again the choir burst forth in sunny grandeur, as from the muffling of storms and darkness; again the thunderings of our horses carried temptation into the graves. One cry burst from our lips, as the clouds, drawing off from the aisle, showed it empty before us — "Whither has the infant fled? — is the young child caught up to God?" Lo! afar off, in a vast recess, rose three mighty windows to the clouds; and on a level with their summits, at height insuperable to man, rose an altar of purest alabaster. On its eastern face was trembling a crimson glory. A glory was it from the reddening dawn that now streamed *through* the windows? Was it from the crimson robes of the martyrs painted *on* the windows? Was it from the bloody bas-reliefs of earth? There, suddenly, within that crimson radiance, rose the apparition of a woman's head, and then of a woman's figure. The child it was — grown up to woman's height. Clinging to the horns of the altar, voice-less she stood — sinking, rising, raving, despairing; and behind the volume of incense, that, night and day, streamed upwards from the altar, dimly was seen the fiery font, and the shadow of that dreadful being who should have baptised her with the baptism of death. But by her side was kneeling her better angel, that hid his face with wings; that wept and pleaded for *her;* that prayed when *she* could *not;* that fought with Heaven by tears for *her* deliverance; which also, as he raised his immortal countenance from his wings, I saw, by the glory in his eye, that from Heaven he had won at last.

V.

Then was completed the passion of the mighty fugue. The golden tubes of the organ, which as yet had but muttered at intervals — gleaming amongst clouds and surges of incense — threw up, as from fountains unfathomable, columns of heart-shattering music. Choir and anti-choir were filling fast with unknown voices. Thou also, Dying Trumpeter! — with thy love that was victorious, and thy anguish that was finishing — didst enter the tumult; trumpet and echo — farewell love, and farewell anguish — rang through the dreadful *sanctus.* Oh, darkness of the grave! that from the crimson altar and from the fiery font wert visited and searched by the effulgence in the angel's eye — were these indeed thy children? Pomps of life, that, from the burials of centuries, rose again to the voice of perfect joy, did ye indeed mingle with the festivals of Death? Lo! as I looked back for seventy leagues through the mighty cathedral, I saw the quick and the dead that sang together to God, together that sang to the generations of man. All the hosts of jubilation, like armies that ride in pursuit, moved with one step. Us, that, with laurelled heads, were passing from the cathedral, they overtook, and, as with a garment, they wrapped us round with thunders greater than our own. As brothers we moved together; to the dawn that advanced — to the stars that fled; rendering thanks to God in the highest — that, having hid his face through one generation behind thick clouds of War, once again was ascending — from the Campo Santo of Waterloo was ascending — in the visions of Peace; rendering thanks for thee, young girl! whom, having overshadowed with his ineffable passion of death, suddenly did God relent; suffered thy angel to turn aside his arm; and even in thee, sister unknown! shown to me for a moment only to be hidden for ever, found an occasion to glorify his goodness. A thousand times, amongst the phantoms of sleep, have I seen thee entering the gates of the golden dawn — with the secret word riding before thee — with the armies of the grave behind thee; seen thee sinking, rising, raving, despairing; a thousand times in the worlds of sleep have seen thee followed by God's angel through storms; through desert seas; through the darkness of quicksands; through dreams, and the dreadful revelations that are in dreams — only that at the last, with one sling of his victorious arm, he might snatch thee back from ruin, and might emblazon in thy deliverance the endless resurrections of his love!

FROM *Explanatory Notices,* 1854[1]

4. "The English Mail-Coach:" — This little paper, according to my original intention, formed part of the "Suspiria de Profundis," from which, for a momentary purpose, I did not scruple to detach it, and to publish it apart, as sufficiently intelligible even when dislocated from its place in a larger whole. To my surprise, however, one or two critics, not carelessly in conversation, but deliberately in print, professed their inability to apprehend the meaning of the whole, or to follow the links of the connection between its several parts. I am myself as little able to understand where the difficulty lies, or to detect any lurking obscurity, as those critics found themselves to unravel my logic. Possibly I may not be an indifferent and neutral judge in such a case. I will therefore sketch a brief abstract of the little paper according to my own original design, and then leave the reader to judge how far this design is kept in sight through the actual execution.

Thirty-seven years ago, or rather more, accident made me, in the dead of night, and of a night memorably solemn, the solitary witness to an appalling scene, which threatened instant death in a shape the

---

[1] Usually, but not by De Quincey, titled "Postscript."

most terrific to two young people, whom I had no means of assisting, except in so far as I was able to give them a most hurried warning of their danger; but even *that* not until they stood within the very shadow of the catastrophe, being divided from the most frightful of deaths by scarcely more, if more at all, than seventy seconds.

Such was the scene, such in its outline, from which the whole of this paper radiates as a natural expansion. This scene is circumstantially narrated in Section the Second, entitled, "The Vision of Sudden Death."

But a movement of horror, and of spontaneous recoil from this dreadful scene, naturally carried the whole of that scene, raised and idealised, into my dreams, and very soon into a rolling succession of dreams. The actual scene, as looked down upon from the box of the mail, was transformed into a dream, as tumultuous and changing as a musical fugue. This troubled Dream is circumstantially reported in Section the Third, entitled, "Dream-Fugue upon the Theme of Sudden Death." What I had beheld from my seat upon the mail; the scenical strife of action and passion, of anguish and fear, as I had there witnessed them moving in ghostly silence; this duel between life and death narrowing itself to a point of such exquisite evanescence as the collision neared; all these elements of the scene blended, under the law of association, with the previous and permanent features of distinction investing the mail itself: which features at that time lay — 1st, in velocity unprecedented; 2dly, in the power and beauty of the horses; 3dly, in the official connection with the government of a great nation; and, 4thly, in the function, almost a consecrated function, of publishing and diffusing through the land the great political events, and especially the great battles during a conflict of unparalleled grandeur. These honorary distinctions are all described circumstantially in the FIRST or introductory section ("The Glory of Motion"). The three first were distinctions maintained at all times; but the fourth and grandest belonged exclusively to the war with Napoleon; and this it was which most naturally introduced Waterloo into the dream. Waterloo, I understood, was the particular feature of the "Dream-Fugue" which my censors were least able to account for. Yet surely Waterloo, which, in common with every other great battle, it had been our special privilege to publish over all the land, most naturally entered the Dream under the license of our privilege. If not — if there be anything amiss — let the Dream be responsible. The Dream is a law to itself; and as well quarrel with a rainbow for showing, or for *not* showing, a secondary arch. So far as I know, every element in the shifting movements of the Dream derived itself either primarily from the incidents of the actual scene, or from secondary features associated with the mail. For example, the cathedral aisle derived itself from the mimic combination of features which grouped themselves together at the point of approaching collision — viz., an arrow-like section of the road, six hundred yards long, under the solemn lights described, with lofty trees meeting overhead in arches. The guard's horn, again — a humble instrument in itself — was yet glorified as the organ of publication for so many great national events. And the incident of the Dying Trumpeter, who rises from a marble bas-relief, and carries a marble trumpet to his marble lips for the purpose of warning the female infant, was doubtless secretly suggested by my own imperfect effort to seize the guard's horn, and to blow a warning blast. But the Dream knows best; and the Dream, I say again, is the responsible party.

Literature of Knowledge and Literature of Power

❲ In the *North British Review* for August 1848, De Quincey reviewed *The Works of Alexander Pope*, edited by William Roscoe of Liverpool. Under the title "Alexander Pope," he reprinted the review in *Leaders in Literature*, 1858, in the ninth volume of his collective works. Historians of criticism have been interested only in the several paragraphs distinguishing between the literatures of knowledge and of power. For discussion of such matters as De Quincey's general indebtedness to Wordsworth, his inconsistencies in logic, and his success in popularizing the idea of literature as a fine art, the student should go to Sigmund K. Proctor, *Thomas De Quincey's Theory of Literature*, Ann Arbor, 1943. Except for two corrections, the present text follows that of 1848. ❳

What is it that we mean by *literature?* Popularly, and amongst the thoughtless, it is held to include everything that is printed in a book. Little logic is required to disturb *that* definition; the most thoughtless person is easily made aware that in the idea of *literature* one essential element is — some relation to a general and common interest of man, so that what applies only to a local — or professional — or merely personal interest, even though presenting itself in the shape of a book, will not belong to literature. So far the definition is easily narrowed; and it is as easily expanded. For not only is much that takes a station in books not literature; but inversely, much that really *is* literature never reaches a station in books. The weekly sermons of Christendom, that vast pulpit literature which acts so extensively upon the popular mind — to warn, to uphold, to renew, to comfort, to alarm, does not attain the sanctuary of libraries in the ten thousandth part of its extent. The drama again, as, for instance, the finest of Shakspere's plays in England, and all leading Athenian plays in the noontide of the Attic stage, operated as a literature on the public mind, and were (according to the strictest letter of that term) *published* through the audiences that witnessed[1] their representation some time before they were published as things to be read; and they were published in this scenical mode of publication with much more effect than they could have had as books, during ages of costly copying or of costly printing.

Books, therefore, do not suggest an idea co-extensive and interchangeable with the idea of literature; since much literature, scenic, forensic, or didactic, (as from lectures and public orators,) may never come into books; and much that *does* come into books, may connect itself with no literary interest. But a far more important correction, applicable to the common vague idea of literature, is to be sought — not so much in a better definition of literature, as in a sharper distinction of the two functions which it fulfils. In that great social organ, which collectively we call literature, there may be distinguished two separate offices that may blend and often *do* so, but capable severally of a severe insulation, and naturally fitted for reciprocal repulsion. There is first the literature of *knowledge*, and secondly, the literature of *power*. The function of the first is — to *teach;* the function of the second is — to *move:* the first is a rudder, the second an oar or a sail. The first speaks to the *mere* discursive understanding; the second speaks ultimately it may happen to the higher understanding or reason, but always *through* affections of pleasure and sympathy. Remotely, it may travel towards an object seated in what Lord Bacon calls *dry* light;[2] but proximately it does and must operate, else it ceases to be a literature of *power*, on and through that *humid* light which clothes itself in the mists and glittering *iris* of human passions, desires, and genial emotions. Men have so little reflected on the higher functions of literature, as to find it a paradox if one should describe it as a mean or subordinate purpose of books to give information. But this is a paradox only in the sense which makes it honourable to be paradoxical. Whenever we talk in ordinary language of seeking information or gaining knowledge, we understand the words as connected with something of absolute novelty. But it is the grandeur of all truth which *can* occupy a very high place in human interests, that it is never absolutely novel to the meanest of minds: it

---

[1] Charles I., for example, when Prince of Wales, and many others in his father's court, gained their known familiarity with Shakspere — not through the original quartos, so slenderly diffused, nor through the first folio of 1623, but through the court representations of his chief dramas at Whitehall. [De Q.]

[2] After Heraclitus, in Apophthegm 268 (188) and *On Friendship*.

exists eternally by way of germ or latent principle in the lowest as in the highest, needing to be developed but never to be planted. To be capable of transplantation is the immediate criterion of a truth that ranges on a lower scale. Besides which, there is a rarer thing than truth, namely, *power* or deep sympathy with truth. What is the effect, for instance, upon society — of children? By the pity, by the tenderness, and by the peculiar modes of admiration, which connect themselves with the helplessness, with the innocence, and with the simplicity of children, not only are the primal affections strengthened and continually renewed, but the qualities which are dearest in the sight of heaven — the frailty for instance, which appeals to forbearance, the innocence which symbolizes the heavenly, and the simplicity which is most alien from the worldly, are kept up in perpetual remembrance, and their ideals are continually refreshed. A purpose of the same nature is answered by the higher literature, viz. the literature of power. What do you learn from Paradise Lost? Nothing at all. What do you learn from a cookery-book? Something new, something that you did not know before, in every paragraph. But would you therefore put the wretched cookery-book on a higher level of estimation than the divine poem? What you owe to Milton is not any knowledge, of which a million separate items are still but a million of advancing steps on the same earthly level; what you owe — is *power*, that is, exercise and expansion to your own latent capacity of sympathy with the infinite, where every pulse and each separate influx is a step upwards — a step ascending as upon a Jacob's ladder from earth to mysterious altitudes above the earth. *All* the steps of knowledge, from first to last, carry you farther on the same plane, but could never raise you one foot above your ancient level of earth: whereas, the very *first* step in power is a flight — is an ascending into another element where earth is forgotten.

Were it not that human sensibilities are ventilated and continually called out into exercise by the great phenomena of infancy, or of real life as it moves through chance and change, or of literature as it recombines these elements in the mimicries of poetry, romance, &c., it is certain that, like any animal power or muscular energy falling into disuse, all such sensibilities would gradually droop and dwindle. It is in relation to these great *moral* capacities of man that the literature of power, as contradistinguished from that of knowledge, lives and has its field of action. It is concerned with what is highest in man: for the Scriptures themselves never condescend to deal by suggestion or co-operation, with the mere discursive understanding: when speaking of man in his intellectual capacity, the Scriptures speak not of the understanding, but of *"the understanding heart,"*[3] — making the heart, *i. e.*, the great *intuitive* (or non-discursive) organ, to

[3] 1 Kings 3:9,12.

be the interchangeable formula for man in his highest state of capacity for the infinite. Tragedy, romance, fairy-tale, or epopee, all alike restore to man's mind the ideals of justice, of hope, of truth, of mercy, of retribution, which else, (left to the support of daily life in its realities,) would languish for want of sufficient illustration. What is meant for instance by *poetic justice?* — It does not mean a justice that differs by its object from the ordinary justice of human jurisprudence; for then it must be confessedly a very bad kind of justice; but it means a justice that differs from common forensic justice by the degree in which it *attains* its object, a justice that is more omnipotent over its own ends, as dealing — not with the refractory elements of earthly life — but with elements of its own creation, and with materials flexible to its own purest preconceptions. It is certain that, were it not for the literature of power, these ideals would often remain amongst us as mere arid notional forms; whereas, by the creative forces of man put forth in literature, they gain a vernal life of restoration, and germinate into vital activities. The commonest novel, by moving in alliance with human fears and hopes, with human instincts of wrong and right, sustains and quickens those affections. Calling them into action, it rescues them from torpor. And hence the pre-eminence over all authors that merely *teach,* of the meanest that *moves;* or that teaches, if at all, indirectly *by* moving. The very highest work that has ever existed in the literature of knowledge, is but a *provisional* work: a book upon trial and sufferance, and *quamdiu bene se gesserit.*[4] Let its teaching be even partially revised, let it be but expanded, nay, even let its teaching be but placed in a better order, and instantly it is superseded. Whereas the feeblest works in the literature of power, surviving at all, survive as finished and unalterable amongst men. For instance, the *Principia* of Sir Isaac Newton was a book *militant* on earth from the first. In all stages of its progress it would have to fight for its existence: 1*st,* as regards absolute truth; 2*dly,* when that combat was over, as regards its form or mode of presenting the truth. And as soon as a La Place, or anybody else, builds higher upon the foundations laid by this book, effectually he throws it out of the sunshine into decay and darkness; by weapons won from this book he superannuates and destroys this book, so that soon the name of Newton remains, as a mere *nominis umbra,*[5] but his book, as a living power, has transmigrated into other forms. Now, on the contrary, the Iliad, the Prometheus of Æschylus, — the Othello or King Lear, — the Hamlet or Macbeth, — and the Paradise Lost, are not militant but triumphant for ever as long as the languages exist in which they speak or can be taught to speak. They never *can* transmigrate into new incarnations. To reproduce *these* in new forms, or variations, even if

[4] during good behavior.
[5] shadow of a name. P. S. de Laplace's astronomical work, *Mécanique céleste,* 1799–1825, built upon Newton's *Principia,* 1687.

in some things they should be improved, would be to plagiarize. A good steam-engine is properly superseded by a better. But one lovely pastoral valley is not superseded by another, nor a statue of Praxiteles by a statue of Michael Angelo. These things are not separated by imparity, but by disparity. They are not thought of as unequal under the same standard, but as differing in *kind,* and as equal under a different standard. Human works of immortal beauty and works of nature in one respect stand on the same footing: they never absolutely repeat each other: never approach so near as not to differ; and they differ not as better and worse, or simply by more and less: they differ by undecipherable and incommunicable differences, that cannot be caught by mimicries, nor be reflected in the mirror of copies, nor become ponderable in the scales of vulgar comparison. . . .

All the literature of knowledge builds only ground-nests, that are swept away by floods, or confounded by the plough; but the literature of power builds nests in aerial altitudes of temples sacred from violation, or of forests inaccessible to fraud. *This* is a great prerogative of the *power* literature: and it is a greater which lies in the mode of its influence. The *knowledge* literature, like the fashion of this world, passeth away. An Encyclopædia is its abstract; and, in this respect, it may be taken for its speaking symbol — that, before one generation has passed, an Encyclopædia is superannuated; for it speaks through the dead memory and unimpassioned understanding, which have not the *rest* of higher faculties, but are continually enlarging and varying their phylacteries.[6] But all literature, properly so called — literature κατ' ἐξοχην,[7] for the very same reason that it is so much more durable than the literature of knowledge, is (and by the very same proportion it is) more intense and electrically searching in its impressions. The directions in which the tragedy of this planet has trained our human feelings to play, and the combinations into which the poetry of this planet has thrown our human passions of love and hatred, of admiration and contempt, exercise a power bad or good over human life, that cannot be contemplated when seen stretching through many generations, without a sentiment allied to awe.[8] And of this

[6] *rest:* repose (1858 ed.).

[7] pre-eminently.

[8] The reason why the broad distinctions between the two literatures of power and knowledge so little fix the attention, lies in the fact, that a vast proportion of books — history, biography, travels, miscellaneous essays, &c., lying in a middle zone, confound these distinctions by interblending them. All that we call "amusement" or "entertainment," is a diluted form of the power belonging to passion, and also a mixed form; and where threads of direct *instruction* intermingle in the texture with these threads of *power,* this absorption of the duality into one representative *nuance* neutralises the separate perception of either. Fused into a *tertium quid,* or neutral state, they disappear to the popular eye as the repelling forces, which in fact they are. [De Q.]

let every one be assured — that he owes to the impassioned books which he has read, many a thousand more of emotions than he can consciously trace back to them. Dim by their origination, these emotions yet arise in him, and mould him through life like the forgotten incidents of childhood.

On the Knocking at the Gate in Macbeth

⟦ This famous example of Romantic criticism is here taken from the *London Magazine* of October 1823, where it appeared for the first and only time during De Quincey's life. The passage on the "hammer murders" by John Williams, a seaman, was later expanded by De Quincey into the essay "On Murder Considered as One of the Fine Arts." In *Thomas De Quincey, Literary Critic,* University of California English Studies, No. 4 (Berkeley and Los Angeles, 1952), John E. Jordan has described the eclectic procedure in this essay of De Quincey as dreamer, logician, intuitionalist, upholder of precept and genre, amateur student of murder, and stylist. ⟧

From my boyish days I had always felt a great perplexity on one point in Macbeth: it was this: the knocking at the gate, which succeeds to the murder of Duncan, produced to my feelings an effect for which I never could account: the effect was — that it reflected back upon the murder a peculiar awfulness and a depth of solemnity: yet, however obstinately I endeavoured with my understanding to comprehend this, for many years I never could see *why* it should produce such an effect. ——

Here I pause for one moment to exhort the reader never to pay any attention to his understanding when it stands in opposition to any other faculty of his mind. The mere understanding, however useful and indispensable, is the meanest faculty in the human mind and the most to be distrusted: and yet the great majority of people trust to nothing else; which may do for ordinary life, but not for philosophic purposes. Of this, out of ten thousand instances that I might produce, I will cite one. Ask of any person whatsoever, who is not previously prepared for the demand by a knowledge of perspective, to draw in the rudest way the commonest appearance which depends upon the laws of that science — as for instance, to represent the effect of two walls standing at right angles to each other, or the appearance of the houses on each side of a street, as seen by a person looking down the street from one extremity. Now in all cases, unless the person has happened to observe in pictures how it is that artists produce these effects, he will be utterly unable to make the smallest approximation to it. Yet why? — For he has actually seen the effect every day of his life. The reason is — that he allows his understanding to overrule his eyes. His understanding, which includes no intuitive knowledge of the laws of vision, can furnish him with no reason why a line which is known and can be proved to be a horizontal line, should not *appear* a horizontal line: a line, that made any angle with the perpendicular less than a right angle, would seem to him to indicate that his houses were all tumbling down together. Accordingly he makes the line of his houses a horizontal line, and fails of course to produce the effect demanded. Here then is one instance out of many, in which not only the understanding is allowed to overrule the eyes, but where the understanding is positively allowed to obliterate the eyes as it were: for not only does the man believe the evidence of his understanding in opposition to that of his eyes, but (which is monstrous!) the idiot is not aware that his eyes ever gave such evidence. He does not know that he has seen (and therefore *quoad* his consciousness has *not* seen) that which he *has* seen every day of his life. But, to return from this digression, — my understanding could furnish no reason why the knocking at the gate in Macbeth should produce any effect direct or reflected: in fact, my understanding said positively that it could *not* produce any effect. But I knew better: I felt that it did: and I waited and clung to the problem until further knowledge should enable me to solve it. — At length, in 1812, Mr. Williams made his *début* on the stage of Ratcliffe Highway, and executed those unparalleled murders which have procured for him such a brilliant and undying reputation. On which murders, by the way, I must observe, that in one respect they have had an ill effect, by making the connoisseur in murder very fastidious in his taste, and dissatisfied with any thing that has been since done in that line. All other murders look pale by the deep crimson of his: and, as an amateur once said to me in a querulous tone, "There has been absolutely nothing *doing* since his time, or nothing that's worth speaking of." But this is wrong: for it is unreasonable to expect all men to be great artists, and born with the genius of Mr. Williams. — Now it will be remembered that in the first of these murders (that of the Marrs) the same incident (of a knocking at the door soon after the work of extermination was complete) did actually occur which the genius of Shakspeare had invented: and all good judges and the most eminent dilettanti acknowledged the felicity of Shakspeare's suggestion as soon as it was actually realized. Here then was a fresh proof that I had been right in relying on my own feeling in opposition to my understanding; and again I set myself to study the problem: at length I solved it to my own satisfaction; and my solution is this. Murder in ordinary cases, where the sympathy is wholly directed to the case of the murdered person, is an incident of coarse and vulgar horror; and for this reason — that it flings the interest exclusively upon the natural but ignoble instinct by which we cleave to life; an instinct which, as being indispensable to the primal law of self-preservation, is the same in kind (though different in degree) amongst all living creatures; this instinct therefore, because it annihilates all distinctions, and degrades the greatest of men to the level of "the poor beetle that we tread on,"[1] exhibits human nature in its most abject and humiliating attitude. Such an attitude would little suit the purposes of the poet. What then must he do? He must throw the interest on the murderer: our sympathy must be with *him;* (of course I mean a sympathy of comprehension, a sympathy by which we enter into his feelings, and are made to understand them, — not a sympathy[2] of pity or approbation:) in the murdered person all strife of thought, all flux and reflux of passion and of purpose, are crushed by one overwhelming panic: the fear of instant death smites him "with its petrific mace."[3] But in the murderer, such a murderer as a poet will condescend to, there must be raging some great storm of passion, — jealousy, ambition, vengeance, hatred, — which will create a hell within him; and into this hell we are to look. In Macbeth, for the sake of gratifying his own enormous and teeming faculty of creation, Shakspeare has introduced two murderers: and, as usual in his hands, they are remarkably discriminated: but, though in Macbeth the strife of mind is greater than in his wife, the tiger spirit not so awake, and his feelings caught chiefly by contagion from her, — yet, as both were finally involved in the guilt of murder, the murderous mind of necessity is finally to be presumed in both. This was to be expressed; and on its own account, as well as to make it a more proportionable antagonist to the unoffending nature of their victim, "the gracious Duncan," and adequately to expound "the deep damnation of his taking off," this was to be expressed with peculiar energy. We were to be made to feel that the human nature, *i. e.* the divine nature of love and mercy, spread through the hearts of all creatures, and seldom utterly withdrawn from man, — was gone, vanished, extinct; and that the fiendish nature had taken its place. And, as this effect is marvellously

---

[1] *Measure for Measure* III.i.79.

[2] It seems almost ludicrous to guard and explain my use of a word in a situation where it should naturally explain itself. But it has become necessary to do so, in consequence of the unscholarlike use of the word sympathy, at present so general, by which, instead of taking it in its proper sense, as the act of reproducing in our minds the feelings of another, whether for hatred, indignation, love, pity, or approbation, it is made a mere synonyme of the word *pity;* and hence, instead of saying, "sympathy *with* another," many writers adopt the monstrous barbarism of "sympathy *for* another." [De Q.]

[3] Cf. *Paradise Lost* X.294.

accomplished in the dialogues and soliloquies themselves, so it is finally consummated by the expedient under consideration; and it is to this that I now solicit the reader's attention. If the reader has ever witnessed a wife, daughter, or sister, in a fainting fit, he may chance to have observed that the most affecting moment in such a spectacle, is *that* in which a sigh and a stirring announce the recommencement of suspended life. Or, if the reader has ever been present in a vast metropolis on the day when some great national idol was carried in funeral pomp to his grave, and chancing to walk near to the course through which it passed, has felt powerfully, in the silence and desertion of the streets and in the stagnation of ordinary business, the deep interest which at that moment was possessing the heart of man, — if all at once he should hear the death-like stillness broken up by the sound of wheels rattling away from the scene, and making known that the transitory vision was dissolved, he will be aware that at no moment was his sense of the complete suspension and pause in ordinary human concerns so full and affecting as at that moment when the suspension ceases, and the goings-on of human life are suddenly resumed. All action in any direction is best expounded, measured, and made apprehensible, by reaction. Now apply this to the case in Macbeth. Here, as I have said, the retiring of the human heart and the entrance of the fiendish heart was to be expressed and made sensible. Another world has stepped in; and the murderers are taken out of the region of human things, human purposes, human desires. They are transfigured: Lady Macbeth is "unsexed;" Macbeth has forgot that he was born of woman; both are conformed to the image of devils; and the world of devils is suddenly revealed. But how shall this be conveyed and made palpable? In order that a new world may step in, this world must for a time disappear. The murderers, and the murder, must be insulated — cut off by an immeasurable gulph from the ordinary tide and succession of human affairs — locked up and sequestered in some deep recess: we must be made sensible that the world of ordinary life is suddenly arrested — laid asleep — tranced — racked into a dread armistice: time must be annihilated; relation to things without abolished; and all must pass self-withdrawn into a deep syncope and suspension of earthly passion. Hence it is that when the deed is done — when the work of darkness is perfect, then the world of darkness passes away like a pageantry in the clouds: the knocking at the gate is heard; and it makes known audibly that the reaction has commenced: the human has made its reflux upon the fiendish: the pulses of life are beginning to beat again: and the re-establishment of the goings-on of the world in which we live, first makes us profoundly sensible of the awful parenthesis that had suspended them.

Oh! mighty poet! — Thy works are not as those of other men, simply and merely great works of art; but are also like the phenomena of nature, like the sun and the sea, the stars and the flowers, — like frost and snow, rain and dew, hail-storm and thunder, which are to be studied with entire submission of our own faculties, and in the perfect faith that in them there can be no too much or too little, nothing useless or inert — but that, the further we press in our discoveries, the more we shall see proofs of design and self-supporting arrangement where the careless eye had seen nothing but accident!

N.B. In the above specimen of psychological criticism, I have purposely omitted to notice another use of the knocking at the gate, viz. the opposition and contrast which it produces in the porter's comments to the scenes immediately preceding; because this use is tolerably obvious to all who are accustomed to reflect on what they read. A third use also, subservient to the scenical illusion, has been lately noticed by a critic in the LONDON MAGAZINE: I fully agree with him; but it did not fall in my way to insist on this.

X. Y. Z.[4]

[4] Concentrating on *Macbeth* II.ii-iii, De Quincey quotes III.i.65, I.vii.20, I.v.42.

The last sentence of the essay may refer to an analysis of the dialogue beginning at *Macbeth* II.ii.15 in "A Third Letter to the Dramatists of the Day," by John Lacy (a pseudonym for George Darley), in the *London Magazine* for September 1823.

quoad: as far as; syncope: swoon.

Lord Byron

GEORGE GORDON, LORD BYRON

CHRONOLOGY

1788   Born January 22 in London, to "an hysterical Scotch heiress."

1789–98   Lived with his mother; attended Aberdeen Grammar School.

1798   May 21, inherited the Byron barony and the estate of Newstead Abbey, near Nottingham.

1801   April, entered Harrow School; began a series of intense friendships.

1805   (October 24)–1807 (December)   Enrolled at Trinity College, Cambridge (granted M.A., 1808). Often away at Southwell or London.

1807   Second revision of privately printed *Fugitive Pieces* published in June as *Hours of Idleness*.

1809   March, *English Bards and Scotch Reviewers*.

1809–11   Extended a grand tour into Albania, Greece, and Turkey.

1812   March 10, *Childe Harold's Pilgrimage*, Cantos I and II. In 1812–13, made three speeches in House of Lords.

1813   June, *The Giaour*. December 2, *The Bride of Abydos*.

1814   February 1 (?), *The Corsair*. August 6, *Lara*.

1815   January 2, married Annabella Milbanke. April, *Hebrew Melodies*.

1816   January 15, Lady Byron returned to her parents. April 25, Byron left England. November 18, *Childe Harold*, Canto III.

1817   Began energetic dissipation and writing in and near Venice. June 16, *Manfred*.

1818   February 28, *Beppo* (anonymous). April 28, *Childe Harold*, Canto IV.

1819   Settled on one mistress, Countess Teresa Guiccioli, aged 19. June 28, *Mazeppa*. July 15, *Don Juan*, Cantos I and II (anonymous).

1821   At Ravenna, aided Carbonari in revolutionary acts against Austrians. Wrote and published poems and poetic dramas. March, *A Letter on Bowles' Strictures on Pope*. August 8, *Don Juan*, Cantos III–V. November, joined Shelley in Pisa.

1822   October 15, "The Vision of Judgment" in the *Liberal*, No. 1.

1823   January 1, "Letter to My Grandmother's Review" in the *Liberal*, No. 2. July 24, sailed for Greece, where he joined the revolutionaries, loaned money, and organized his own troops.

1823–24   *Don Juan*, Cantos VI–XVI.

1824   Died April 19 at Missolonghi.

Letters and Journals

❲ Lord Byron's most enthusiastic supporter, G. Wilson Knight, gave and published at Nottingham, in 1953, a lecture on *Byron's Dramatic Prose.* Referring not to Byron's dramas but to his letters and journals, Mr. Knight wrote: "The language is bold, lucid and definite, with a firm diction, a fine play of antithesis, and sentences of structural weight. The native pith and sap of English speech tingles in it, but it is also, the more so for all its wealth of literary reference and allusion, a literary speech. It is colloquial on a sound basis of Augustan tradition and Augustan learning; the language of a man in whom a literary heritage has become a natural colloquialism." Whether glad or angry, Byron was consistently at his best in letters to two correspondents: his publisher, John Murray (1778–1843), and the Anglo-Irish poet, Thomas Moore (1779–1852), who became Byron's editor and biographer. The selections below are taken from the edition by Rowland E. Prothero, 1898–1901. ❳

TO LEIGH HUNT

13, Terrace, Piccadilly,
September–October 30, 1815.

MY DEAR HUNT,

Many thanks for your books, of which you already know my opinion. Their external splendour should not disturb you as inappropriate — they have still more within than without. I take leave to differ with you on Wordsworth, as freely as I once agreed with you; at that time I gave him credit for a promise, which is unfulfilled. I still think his capacity warrants all you say of *it* only, but that his performances since *Lyrical Ballads* are miserably inadequate to the ability which lurks within him: there is undoubtedly much natural talent spilt over the *Excursion;* but it is rain upon rocks — where it stands and stagnates, or rain upon sands — where it falls without fertilizing. Who can understand him? Let those who do, make him intelligible. Jacob Behmen, Swedenborg, and Joanna Southcote, are mere types of this archapostle of mystery and mysticism. But I have done, — no, I have not done, for I have two petty, and perhaps unworthy objections in small matters to make to him, which, with his pretensions to accurate observation, and fury against Pope's false translation of "the Moonlight scene in Homer", I wonder he should have fallen into; — these be they: — He says of Greece in the body of his book — that it is a land of

> "*Rivers, fertile plains,* and *sounding* shores,
> Under a cope of *variegated* sky."[1]

[1] *The Excursion* IV.719–720. See Pope's translation, *Iliad* VIII.687–698, and Wordsworth's "Essay Supplementary to the Preface," 1815.

The rivers are dry half the year, the plains are barren, and the shores *still* and *tideless* as the Mediterranean can make them; the sky is any thing but variegated, being for months and months but "darkly, deeply, beautifully blue"[2]. — The next is in his notes, where he talks of our "Monuments crowded together in the busy, etc., of a large town", as compared with the "still seclusion of a Turkish cemetery in some *remote* place". This is pure stuff; for *one* monument in our churchyards there are *ten* in the Turkish, and so crowded, that you cannot walk between them; that is, divided merely by a path or road; and as to "*remote* places", men never take the trouble in a barbarous country, to carry their dead very far; they must have lived near to where they were buried. There are no cemeteries in "remote places", except such as have the cypress and the tombstone still left, where the olive and the habitation of the living have perished. . . .

These things I was struck with, as coming peculiarly in my own way; and in both of these he is wrong; yet I should have noticed neither, but for his attack on Pope for a like blunder, and a peevish affectation about him of despising a popularity which he will never obtain. I write in great haste, and, I doubt, *not* much to the purpose; but you have it hot and hot, just as it comes, and so let it go. By-the-way, both he and you go too far against Pope's "So when the moon", etc.; it is no translation, I know; but it is not such false description as asserted. I have read it on the spot; there is a burst, and a lightness, and a glow about the night in the Troad, which makes the "planets vivid", and the "pole glowing". The moon is — at least the sky is, clearness itself; and I know no more appropriate expression for the expansion of such a heaven — o'er the scene — the plain — the sky — Ida — the Hellespont — Simois — Scamander — and the Isles — than that of a "flood of glory". I am getting horribly lengthy, and must stop: to the whole of your letter "I say ditto to Mr. Burke", as the Bristol candidate cried by way of electioneering harangue. You need not speak of morbid feelings and vexations to me; I have plenty; but I must blame partly the times, and chiefly myself: but let us forget them. *I* shall be very apt to do so when I see you next. Will you come to the theatre and see our new management? You shall cut it up to your heart's content, root and branch, afterwards, if you like; but come and see it! If not, I must come and see you.[3]

Ever yours, very truly and affectionately,

BYRON.

[2] Robert Southey, *Madoc in Wales* (1805) V.102.

[3] Hunt had sent Byron a copy of *The Feast of the Poets*, 2nd ed., 1815, wherein Wordsworth is favorably judged. In May, Byron had become a member of the Sub-Committee of Management of Drury Lane.

Joanna Southcott (1750–1814), hysterical prophetess.

TO THOMAS MOORE

Venice, January 28, 1817.

. . . I think of being in England in the spring. If there is a row, by the sceptre of King Ludd, but I'll be one; and if there is none, and only a continuance of "this meek, piping time of peace",[1] I will take a cottage a hundred yards to the south of your abode, and become your neighbour; and we will compose such canticles, and hold such dialogues, as shall be the terror of the *Times* (including the newspaper of that name), and the wonder, and honour, and praise, of the *Morning Chronicle* and posterity.

I rejoice to hear of your forthcoming in February — though I tremble for the "magnificence" which you attribute to the new *Childe Harold*. I am glad you like it; it is a fine indistinct piece of poetical desolation, and my favourite. I was half mad during the time of its composition, between metaphysics, mountains, lakes, love unextinguishable, thoughts unutterable, and the nightmare of my own delinquencies. I should, many a good day, have blown my brains out, but for the recollection that it would have given pleasure to my mother-in-law; and, even *then*, if I could have been certain to haunt her —— but I won't dwell upon these trifling family matters.

Venice is in the *estro* of her carnival, and I have been up these last two nights at the ridotto and the opera, and all that kind of thing. Now for an adventure. A few days ago a gondolier brought me a billet without a subscription, intimating a wish on the part of the writer to meet me either in gondola or at the island of San Lazaro, or at a third rendezvous, indicated in the note. "I know the country's disposition well;" — in Venice "they do let Heaven see those tricks they dare not show",[2] etc., etc.; so, for all response, I said that neither of the three places suited me; but that I would either be at home at ten at night *alone*, or be at the ridotto at midnight, where the writer might meet me masked. At ten o'clock I was at home and alone (Marianna was gone with her husband to a conversazione), when the door of my apartment opened, and in walked a well-looking and (for an Italian) *bionda* girl of about nineteen, who informed me that she was married to the brother of my *amorosa*, and wished to have some conversation with me. I made a decent reply, and we had some talk in Italian and Romaic (her mother being a Greek of Corfu), when lo! in a very few minutes in marches, to my very great astonishment, Marianna Segati, *in propriâ personâ*, and after making a most polite curtsy to her sister-in-law and to me, without a single word seizes her said sister-in-law by

---

[1] *Richard III* I.i.24.
[2] *Othello* III.iii.201–203.

the hair, and bestows upon her some sixteen slaps, which would have made your ear ache only to hear their echo. I need not describe the screaming which ensued. The luckless visitor took flight. I seized Marianna, who, after several vain efforts to get away in pursuit of the enemy, fairly went into fits in my arms; and, in spite of reasoning, eau de Cologne, vinegar, half a pint of water, and God knows what other waters beside, continued so till past midnight.

After damning my servants for letting people in without apprizing me, I found that Marianna in the morning had seen her sister-in-law's gondolier on the stairs, and, suspecting that his apparition boded her no good, had either returned of her own accord, or been followed by her maids or some other spy of her people to the conversazione, from whence she returned to perpetrate this piece of pugilism. I had seen fits before, and also some small scenery of the same genus in and out of our island: but this was not all. After about an hour, in comes — who? why, Signor Segati, her lord and husband, and finds me with his wife fainting upon the sofa, and all the apparatus of confusion, dishevelled hair, hats, handkerchiefs, salts, smelling-bottles — and the lady as pale as ashes, without sense or motion. His first question was, "What is all this?" The lady could not reply — so I did. I told him the explanation was the easiest thing in the world; but in the mean time it would be as well to recover his wife — at least, her senses. This came about in due time of suspiration and respiration.

You need not be alarmed — jealousy is not the order of the day in Venice, and daggers are out of fashion; while duels, on love matters, are unknown — at least, with the husbands. But, for all this, it was an awkward affair; and though he must have known that I made love to Marianna, yet I believe he was not, till that evening, aware of the extent to which it had gone. It is very well known that almost all the married women have a lover; but it is usual to keep up the forms, as in other nations. I did not, therefore, know what the devil to say. I could not out with the truth, out of regard to her, and I did not choose to lie for my sake; — besides, the thing told itself. I thought the best way would be to let her explain it as she chose (a woman being never at a loss — the devil always sticks by them) — only determining to protect and carry her off, in case of any ferocity on the part of the Signor. I saw that he was quite calm. She went to bed, and next day — how they settled it, I know not, but settle it they did. Well — then I had to explain to Marianna about this never-to-be-sufficiently-confounded sister-in-law; which I did by swearing innocence, eternal constancy, etc., etc. . . .[3]

[3] Ned Ludd was a legendary leader in 1812 among weavers who destroyed new machinery in protest. Byron defended the Luddites by a speech in the House of Lords.

bionda: fair; *extra:* heat, fervor; *ridotto:* masked ball.

TO JOHN MURRAY

Venice, May 30, 1817.

DEAR SIR,

I returned from Rome two days ago, and have received your letter; but no sign nor tidings of the parcel sent through Sir —— Stuart, which you mention. After an interval of months, a packet of *Tales*, etc., found me at Rome; but this is all, and may be all that ever will find me. The post seems to be the only sane conveyance; and *that only for letters.* From Florence I sent you a poem on Tasso, and from Rome the new third act of *Manfred,* and by Dr. Polidori two pictures for my sister. I left Rome, and made a rapid journey home. You will continue to direct here as usual. Mr. Hobhouse is gone to Naples: I should have run down there too for a week, but for the quantity of English whom I heard of there. I prefer hating them at a distance; unless an earthquake, or a good real eruption of Vesuvius, were insured to reconcile me to their vicinity.

I know no other situation except Hell which I should feel inclined to participate with them — as a race, always excepting several individuals. There were few of them in Rome, and I believe none whom you know, except that old Blue-*bore* Sotheby, who will give a fine account of Italy, in which he will be greatly assisted by his total ignorance of Italian, and yet this is the translator of Tasso.

The day before I left Rome I saw three robbers guillotined. The ceremony — including the *masqued* priests; the half-naked executioners; the bandaged criminals; the black Christ and his banner; the scaffold; the soldiery; the slow procession, and the quick rattle and heavy fall of the axe; the splash of the blood, and the ghastliness of the exposed heads — is altogether more impressive than the vulgar and ungentlemanly dirty "new drop", and dog-like agony of infliction upon the sufferers of the English sentence. Two of these men behaved calmly enough, but the first of the three died with great terror and reluctance, which was very horrible. He would not lie down; then his neck was too large for the aperture, and the priest was obliged to drown his exclamations by still louder exhortations. The head was off before the eye could trace the blow; but from an attempt to draw back the head, notwithstanding it was held forward by the hair, the first head was cut off close to the ears: the other two were taken off more cleanly. It is better than the oriental way, and (I should think) than the axe of our ancestors. The pain seems little; and yet the effect to the spectator, and the preparation to the criminal, are very striking and chilling. The first turned me quite hot and thirsty, and made me shake so that I could hardly hold the opera-glass (I was close, but determined to see, as one should see every thing, once, with attention);

the second and third (which shows how dreadfully soon things grow indifferent), I am ashamed to say, had no effect on me as a horror, though I would have saved them if I could.

It is some time since I heard from you — the 12*th April* I believe.[4]

Yours ever truly,

B.

TO JOHN MURRAY

September 15, 1817.

DEAR SIR,

I enclose a sheet for correction, if ever you get to another edition.[1] You will observe that the blunder in printing makes it appear as if the Château was *over* St. Gingo, instead of being on the opposite shore of the Lake, over Clarens. So, separate the paragraphs, otherwise my *to*pography will seem as inaccurate as your *ty*pography on this occasion.

The other day I wrote to convey my proposition with regard to the 4th and concluding canto. I have gone over and extended it to one hundred and fifty stanzas, which is almost as long as the two first were originally, and longer by itself than any of the smaller poems except *The Corsair*. Mr. Hobhouse has made some very valuable and accurate notes of considerable length, and you may be sure I will do for the text all that I can to finish with decency. I look upon *Childe Harold* as my best; and as I begun, I think of concluding with it. But I make no resolutions on that head, as I broke my former intention with regard to *The Corsair*. However, I fear that I shall never do better; and yet, not being thirty years of age, for some moons to come, one ought to be progressive as far as Intellect goes for many a good year. But I have had a devilish deal of wear and tear of mind and body in my time, besides having published too often and much already. God grant me some judgement! to do what may be most fitting in that and every thing else, for I doubt my own exceedingly.

I have read *Lalla Rookh,* but not with sufficient attention yet, for I ride about, and lounge, and ponder, and — two or three other things; so that my reading is very desultory, and not so attentive as it used to be. I am very glad to hear of its popularity, for Moore is a very noble fellow in all respects, and will enjoy it without any of the bad feeling which success — good or evil — sometimes engenders in the men of rhyme. Of the poem itself, I will tell you my opinion when I have mastered it: I say of the *poem,* for I don't like the *prose* at all — at all;

---

[4] John Cam Hobhouse (1786–1869), statesman, Byron's traveling companion and executor. William Sotheby (1757–1833), wealthy author and translator.

[1] of *The Prisoner of Chillon.*

and in the mean time, the "Fire worshippers" is the best, and the "Veiled Prophet" the worst, of the volume.

With regard to poetry in general, I am convinced, the more I think of it, that he and *all* of us — Scott, Southey, Wordsworth, Moore, Campbell, I, — are all in the wrong, one as much as another; that we are upon a wrong revolutionary poetical system, or systems, not worth a damn in itself, and from which none but Rogers and Crabbe are free; and that the present and next generations will finally be of this opinion. I am the more confirmed in this by having lately gone over some of our classics, particularly *Pope*, whom I tried in this way, — I took Moore's poems and my own and some others, and went over them side by side with Pope's, and I was really astonished (I ought not to have been so) and mortified at the ineffable distance in point of sense, harmony, effect, and even *Imagination*, passion, and *Invention*, between the little Queen Anne's man, and us of the Lower Empire. Depend upon it, it is all Horace then, and Claudian now, among us; and if I had to begin again, I would model myself accordingly. Crabbe's the man, but he has got a coarse and impracticable subject, and Rogers, the Grandfather of living Poetry, is retired upon half-pay, (I don't mean as a Banker), —

> Since pretty Miss Jaqueline,
> With her nose aquiline,[2]

and has done enough, unless he were to do as he did formerly.

TO JOHN MURRAY

Venice, April 6, 1819.

Dear Sir,

The Second Canto of *Don Juan* was sent, on Saturday last, by post, in 4 packets, two of 4, and two of three sheets each, containing in all two hundred and seventeen stanzas, octave measure. But I will permit no curtailments, except those mentioned about Castlereagh and the two *Bobs* in the Introduction. You sha'n't make *Canticles* of my Cantos. The poem will please, if it is lively; if it is stupid, it will fail; but I will have none of your damned cutting and slashing. If you please, you may publish *anonymously*; it will perhaps be better; but I will battle my way against them all, like a Porcupine.

[2] Byron's verses on *Jacqueline*, by Samuel Rogers (1763–1855), published with Byron's *Lara* in 1814.

Thomas Campbell (1777–1844); George Crabbe (1754–1832); Thomas Moore, *Lalla Rookh*, 1817.

Claudian: died c. 408 A.D., known as "the last great poet" of the Greco-Roman world.

So you and Mr. Foscolo, etc., want me to undertake what you call a "great work"? an Epic poem, I suppose, or some such pyramid. I'll try no such thing; I hate tasks. And then "seven or eight years!" God send us all well this day three months, let alone years. If one's years can't be better employed than in sweating poesy, a man had better be a ditcher. And works, too! — is *Childe Harold* nothing? You have so many "*divine*" poems, is it nothing to have written a *Human* one? without any of your worn-out machinery. Why, man, I could have spun the thoughts of the four cantos of that poem into twenty, had I wanted to book-make, and its passion into as many modern tragedies. Since you want *length,* you shall have enough of *Juan,* for I'll make 50 cantos.

And Foscolo, too! Why does *he* not do something more than the *Letters of Ortis,* and a tragedy, and pamphlets?[1] He has good fifteen years more at his command than I have: what has he done all that time? — proved his Genius, doubtless, but not fixed its fame, nor done his utmost.

Besides, I mean to write my best work in *Italian,* and it will take me nine years more thoroughly to master the language; and then if my fancy exist, and I exist too, I will try what I *can* do *really.* As to the Estimation of the English which you talk of, let them calculate what it is worth, before they insult me with their insolent condescension.

I have not written for their pleasure. If they are pleased, it is that they chose to be so; I have never flattered their opinions, nor their pride; nor will I. Neither will I make "Ladies books" *al dilettar le femine e la plebe.*[2] I have written from the fullness of my mind, from passion, from impulse, from many motives, but not for their "sweet voices".[3]

I know the precise worth of popular applause, for few Scribblers have had more of it; and if I chose to swerve into their paths, I could retain it, or resume it, or increase it. But I neither love ye, nor fear ye; and though I buy with ye and sell with ye, and talk with ye, I will neither eat with ye, drink with ye, nor pray with ye.[4] They made me, without my search, a species of popular Idol; they, without reason or judgement, beyond the caprice of their good pleasure, threw down the Image from its pedestal; it was not broken with the fall, and they would, it seems, again replace it — but they shall not.

You ask about my health: about the beginning of the year I was in a state of great exhaustion, attended by such debility of Stomach that nothing remained upon it; and I was obliged to reform my "way of

---

[1] Ugo Foscolo (1778–1827), Italian critic, poet, dramatist, and patriot, moved to London in 1816.

[2] for the delight of women and the populace.

[3] *Coriolanus* II.iii.119.

[4] Cf. *The Merchant of Venice* I.iii.36.

life", which was conducting me from the "yellow leaf" to the Ground,[5] with all deliberate speed. I am better in health and morals, and very much yours ever,

B[n]

P.S. — Tell Mrs. Leigh I have never had "my Sashes", and I want some tooth-powder, the red, by all or any means.

TO JOHN MURRAY

Bologna, June 7, 1819.

DEAR SIR,

Tell Mr. Hobhouse that I wrote to him a few days ago from Ferrara. It will therefore be idle in him or you to wait for any further answers or returns of proofs from Venice, as I have directed that no English letters be sent after me. The publication can be proceeded in without, and I am already sick of your remarks, to which I think not the least attention ought to be paid.

Tell Mr. Hobhouse that, since I wrote to him, I had availed myself of my Ferrara letters, and found the society much younger and better there than at Venice. I was very much pleased with the little the shortness of my stay permitted me to see of the Gonfaloniere Count Mosti, and his family and friends in general.

I have been picture-gazing this morning at the famous Domenichino and Guido, both of which are superlative. I afterwards went to the beautiful Cimetery of Bologna, beyond the walls, and found, besides the superb Burial-ground, an original of a *Custode*, who reminded me of the grave-digger in Hamlet. He has a collection of Capuchins' skulls, labelled on the forehead, and taking down one of them, said, "This was Brother Desiderio Berro, who died at forty — one of my best friends. I begged his head of his brethren after his decease, and they gave it me. I put it in lime and then boiled it. Here it is, teeth and all, in excellent preservation. He was the merriest, cleverest fellow I ever knew. Wherever he went, he brought joy; and when any one was melancholy, the sight of him was enough to make him cheerful again. He walked so actively, you might have taken him for a dancer — he joked — he laughed — oh! he was such a Frate as I never saw before, nor ever shall again!"

He told me that he had himself planted all the Cypresses in the Cimetery; that he had the greatest attachment to them and to his dead people; that since 1801 they had buried fifty three thousand persons. In showing some older monuments, there was that of a Roman girl of twenty, with a bust by Bernini. She was a Princess Barberini, dead two centuries ago: he said that, on opening her grave, they had

[5] *Macbeth* V.iii.22–23.

found her hair complete, and "as yellow as gold". Some of the epitaphs at Ferrara pleased me more than the more splendid monuments of Bologna; for instance: —

"Martini Luigi
Implora pace.

Lucrezia Picini
Implora eterna quiete."

Can any thing be more full of pathos? Those few words say all that can be said or sought: the dead had had enough of life; all they wanted was rest, and this they "*implore*". There is all the helplessness, and humble hope, and deathlike prayer, that can arise from the grave — "*implora pace*". I hope, whoever may survive me, and shall see me put in the foreigners' burying-ground at the Lido, within the fortress by the Adriatic, will see those two words, and no more, put over me. I trust they won't think of "pickling, and bringing me home to Clod or Blunderbuss Hall".[1] I am sure my bones would not rest in an English grave, or my clay mix with the earth of that country. I believe the thought would drive me mad on my deathbed, could I suppose that any of my friends would be base enough to convey my carcase back to your soil. I would not even feed your worms, if I could help it.

So, as Shakespeare says of Mowbray, the banished Duke of Norfolk, who died at Venice (see *Richard II*), that he, after fighting

"Against black pagans, Turks, and Saracens,
And toil'd with works of war, retir'd himself
To Italy; and there, at *Venice*, gave
His body to that *pleasant* country's earth,
And his pure soul unto his Captain Christ,
Under whose colours he had fought so long."[2]

Before I left Venice, I had returned to you your late, and Mr. Hobhouse's, sheets of *Juan*. Don't wait for further answers from me, but address yours to Venice, as usual. I know nothing of my own movements; I may return there in a few days, or not for some time. All this depends on circumstances. I left Mr. Hoppner very well, as well as his son and Mrs. Hoppner. My daughter Allegra was well too, and is growing pretty; her hair is growing darker, and her eyes are blue. Her temper and her ways, Mr. Hoppner says, are like mine, as well as her features: she will make, in that case, a manageable young lady.

I never hear any thing of Ada, the little Electra of my Mycenæ; the moral Clytemnestra is not very communicative of her tidings, but there will come a day of reckoning, even if I should not live to see it.

I have at least seen Romilly shivered who was one of the assassins.

[1] Sheridan, *The Rivals* V.iii.
[2] *Richard II* IV.i.95–100.

When that felon, or lunatic (take your choice he must be one and
might be both), was doing his worst to uproot my whole family tree,
branch, and blossoms; when, after taking my retainer, he went over
to them; when he was bringing desolation on my hearth and destruction on my household Gods, did he think that, in less than three years,
a natural event — a severe domestic — but an expected and common domestic calamity, — would lay his carcase in a cross road, or
stamp his name in a verdict of Lunacy? Did he (who in his drivelling
sexagenary dotage had not the courage to survive his Nurse — for
what else was a wife to him at his time of life?) — reflect or consider
what my feelings must have been, when wife, and child, and sister,
and name, and fame, and country were to be my sacrifice on his legal
altar — and this at a moment when my health was declining, my
fortune embarrassed, and my mind had been shaken by many kinds of
disappointment, while I was yet young and might have reformed what
might be wrong in my conduct, and retrieved what was perplexing
in my affairs. But the wretch is in his grave. I detested him living,
and I will not affect to pity him dead; I still loathe him — as much as
we can hate dust — but that is nothing.

What a long letter I have scribbled!

Yours truly,

B.

P.S. — Here, as in Greece, they strew flowers on the tombs. I saw
a quantity of rose-leaves, and entire roses, scattered over the graves
at Ferrara. It has the most pleasing effect you can imagine.[3]

TO JOHN MURRAY

Bologna, August 12, 1819.

DEAR SIR,

I do not know how far I may be able to reply to your letter, for I
am not very well to-day. Last night I went to the representation of
Alfieri's *Mirra*, the last two acts of which threw me into convulsions.
I do not mean by that word a lady's hysterics, but the agony of reluctant tears, and the choking shudder, which I do not often undergo
for fiction. This is but the second time for anything under reality;
the first was on seeing Kean's Sir Giles Overreach. The worst was,
that the *"dama"*, in whose box I was, went off in the same way, I
really believe more from fright than any other sympathy — at least
with the players: but she has been ill, and I have been ill, and we

[3] Sir Samuel Romilly, Lady Byron's legal adviser, had committed suicide
soon after the death of his wife.

Allegra: daughter of Claire Clairmont; Ada: Byron's legitimate daughter;
Clytemnestra: murdered her husband, Agamemnon (Electra was their
daughter).

are all languid and pathetic this morning, with great expenditure of
Sal Volatile. But to return to your letter of the 23d of July.

You are right, Gifford is right, Crabbe is right, Hobhouse is right —
you are all right, and I am all wrong; but do, pray, let me have that
pleasure. Cut me up root and branch; quarter me in the *Quarterly;*
send round my *disjecti membra poetæ,*[1] like those of the Levite's
Concubine; make me, if you will, a spectacle to men and angels; but
don't ask me to alter, for I can't: — I am obstinate and lazy — and
there's the truth.

But, nevertheless, I will answer your friend C[ohen], who objects
to the quick succession of fun and gravity, as if in that case the
gravity did not (in intention, at least) heighten the fun. His metaphor
is, that "we are never scorched and drenched at the same time".
Blessings on his experience! Ask him these questions about "scorching
and drenching". Did he never play at Cricket, or walk a mile in hot
weather? Did he never spill a dish of tea over himself in handing the
cup to his charmer, to the great shame of his nankeen breeches? Did
he never swim in the sea at Noonday with the Sun in his eyes and on
his head, which all the foam of Ocean could not cool? Did he never
draw his foot out a tub of too hot water, damning his eyes and his
valet's? * * * * * Was he ever in a Turkish bath, that marble paradise
of sherbet and Sodomy? Was he ever in a cauldron of boiling oil,
like St. John? or in the sulphureous waves of hell? (where he ought
to be for his "scorching and drenching at the same time"). Did he
never tumble into a river or lake, fishing, and sit in his wet cloathes
in the boat, or on the bank, afterwards "scorched and drenched", like
a true sportsman? "Oh for breath to utter!"[2] — but make him my
compliments; he is a clever fellow for all that — a very clever fellow.

You ask me for the plan of Donny Johnny: I *have* no plan — I *had*
no plan; but I had or have materials; though if, like Tony Lumpkin,
I am "to be snubbed so when I am in spirits",[3] the poem will be
naught, and the poet turn serious again. If it don't take, I will leave
it off where it is, with all due respect to the Public; but if continued,
it must be in my own way. You might as well make Hamlet (or Diggory) "act mad" in a strait waistcoat as trammel my buffoonery, if
I am to be a buffoon: their gestures and my thoughts would only be
pitiably absurd and ludicrously constrained. Why, Man, the Soul of
such writing is its licence; at least the *liberty* of that *licence,* if one
likes — *not* that one should abuse it: it is like trial by Jury and Peerage
and the Habeas Corpus — a very fine thing, but chiefly in the *reversion;* because no one wishes to be tried for the mere pleasure of proving his possession of the privilege.

But a truce with these reflections. You are too earnest and eager

[1] scattered poetic limbs. See Judges 19:29.
[2] *1 Henry IV* II.iv.248.
[3] *She Stoops to Conquer* II.

about a work never intended to be serious. Do you suppose that I could have any intention but to giggle and make giggle? — a playful satire, with as little poetry as could be helped, was what I meant: and as to the indecency, do, pray, read in Boswell what *Johnson*, the sullen moralist, says of *Prior* and Paulo Purgante.[4]

* * * * * *

EXTRACTS FROM A DIARY

January 6, 1821 [Ravenna].

Mist — thaw — slop — rain. No stirring out on horseback. Read Spence's *Anecdotes.* Pope a fine fellow — always thought him so. Corrected blunders in *nine* apophthegms of Bacon — all historical — and read Mitford's *Greece.* Wrote an epigram. . . .

The crow is lame of a leg — wonder how it happened — some fool trod upon his toe, I suppose. The falcon pretty brisk — the cats large and noisy — the monkeys I have not looked to since the cold weather, as they suffer by being brought up. Horses must be gay — get a ride as soon as weather serves. Deuced muggy still — an Italian winter is a sad thing, but all the other seasons are charming.

What is the reason that I have been, all my lifetime, more or less *ennuyé?* and that, if any thing, I am rather less so now than I was at twenty, as far as my recollection serves? I do not know how to answer this, but presume that it is constitutional, — as well as the waking in low spirits, which I have invariably done for many years. Temperance and exercise, which I have practised at times, and for a long time together vigorously and violently, made little or no difference. Violent passions did; — when under their immediate influence — it is odd, but — I was in agitated, but *not* in depressed, spirits.

A dose of salts has the effect of a temporary inebriation, like light champagne, upon me. But wine and spirits make me sullen and savage to ferocity — silent, however, and retiring, and not quarrelsome, if not spoken to. Swimming also raises my spirits, — but in general they are low, and get daily lower. That is *hopeless;* for I do not think I am so much *ennuyé* as I was at nineteen. The proof is, that then I must game, or drink, or be in motion of some kind, or I was miserable. At

---

[4] Matthew Prior, *Paulo Purganti and His Wife* — see *Life of Johnson,* entry of Sept. 22, 1777.

Vittorio Alfieri (1749–1803), *Mirra,* the tragedy of Myrrha, mother of Adonis. Francis Cohen (1788–1861), later Sir Francis Palgrave.

Overreach: in Philip Massinger's *A New Way to Pay Old Debts,* 1626; Lumpkin and Diggory: in Goldsmith's *She Stoops to Conquer,* 1773 (Diggery Ducklin, in Isaac Jackman's *All the World's a Stage,* 1777, imagines every situation as dramatic).

present, I can mope in quietness; and like being alone better than any
company — except the lady's whom I serve. But I feel a something,
which makes me think that, if I ever reach near to old age, like Swift,
"I shall die at top" first. Only I do not dread idiotism or madness
so much as he did. On the contrary, I think some quieter stages of
both must be preferable to much of what men think the possession
of their senses.

                                                    January 7, 1821, Sunday.

. . . The Count Pietro G[amba] took me aside to say that the
Patriots have had notice from Forli (twenty miles off) that to-night
the government and its party mean to strike a stroke — that the Cardinal here has had orders to make several arrests immediately, and that,
in consequence, the Liberals are arming, and have posted patroles in
the streets, to sound the alarm and give notice to fight for it.

He asked me "what should be done?" I answered, "Fight for it,
rather than be taken in detail;" and offered, if any of them are in
immediate apprehension of arrest, to receive them in my house (which
is defensible), and to defend them, with my servants and themselves
(we have arms and ammunition), as long as we can, — or to try to
get them away under cloud of night. On going home, I offered him
the pistols which I had about me — but he refused, but said he
would come off to me in case of accidents. . . .

                                                              January 23, 1821.

Fine day. Read — rode — fired pistols, and returned. Dined —
read. Went out at eight — made the usual visit. Heard of nothing
but war, — "the cry is still, They come."[1] The Carbonari seem to
have no plan — nothing fixed among themselves, how, when, or what
to do. In that case, they will make nothing of this project, so often
postponed, and never put in action.

Came home, and gave some necessary orders, in case of circumstances requiring a change of place. I shall act according to what
may seem proper, when I hear decidedly what the Barbarians mean
to do.[2] At present, they are building a bridge of boats over the Po,
which looks very warlike. A few days will probably show. I think
of retiring towards Ancona, nearer the northern frontier; that is to
say, if Teresa and her father are obliged to retire, which is most
likely, as all the family are Liberals. If not, I shall stay. But my
movements will depend upon the lady's wishes — for myself, it is
much the same.

I am somewhat puzzled what to do with my little daughter, and

[1] *Macbeth* V.v.2.
[2] An Austrian army was about to cross the river Po and march on the
insurgents at Naples.

my effects, which are of some quantity and value, — and neither of them do in the seat of war, where I think of going. . . . Half the city are getting their affairs in marching trim. A pretty Carnival! The blackguards might as well have waited till Lent.

January 28, 1821.
Past Midnight. One o' the clock.

I have been reading Frederick Schlegel (brother to the other of the name) till now, and I can make out nothing. He evidently shows a great power of words, but there is nothing to be taken hold of. He is like Hazlitt, in English, who *talks pimples* — a red and white corruption rising up (in little imitation of mountains upon maps), but containing nothing, and discharging nothing, except their own humours.

I dislike him the worse, (that is, Schlegel,) because he always seems upon the verge of meaning; and, lo, he goes down like sunset, or melts like a rainbow, leaving a rather rich confusion, — to which, however, the above comparisons do too much honour.

Continuing to read Mr. Frederick Schlegel. He is not such a fool as I took him for, that is to say, when he speaks of the North. But still he speaks of things *all over the world* with a kind of authority that a philosopher would disdain, and a man of common sense, feeling, and knowledge of his own ignorance, would be ashamed of. The man is evidently wanting to make an impression, like his brother, — or like George in the Vicar of Wakefield, who found out that all the good things had been said already on the right side, and therefore "dressed up some paradoxes" upon the wrong side — ingenious, but false, as he himself says — to which "the learned world said nothing, nothing at all, sir."[3] The "learned world," however, *has* said something to the brothers Schlegel. . . .

February 16, 1821.

Last night Il Conte P. G[amba]. sent a man with a bag full of bayonets, some muskets, and some hundreds of cartridges to my house, without apprizing me, though I had seen him not half an hour before. About ten days ago, when there was to be a rising here, the Liberals and my brethren C[i]. asked me to purchase some arms for a certain few of our ragamuffins. I did so immediately, and ordered ammunition, etc., and they were armed accordingly. Well — the rising is prevented by the Barbarians marching a week sooner than appointed; and an *order* is issued, and in force, by the Government, "that all persons having arms concealed, etc., etc., shall be liable to, etc., etc." — and what do my friends, the patriots, do two days afterwards?

[3] Goldsmith, *The Vicar of Wakefield* xx. Byron was probably reading Friedrich Schlegel (1772–1829), *Lectures on the History of Literature,* trans. J. Lockhart, Edinburgh, 1818.

Why, they throw back upon my hands, and into my house, these very arms (without a word of warning previously) with which I had furnished them at their own request, and at my own peril and expense.

It was lucky that Lega was at home to receive them. If any of the servants had (except Tita and F[letcher]. and Lega) they would have betrayed it immediately. In the mean time, if they are denounced or discovered, I shall be in a scrape.

At nine went out — at eleven returned. Beat the crow for stealing the falcon's victuals. Read *Tales of my Landlord*[4] — wrote a letter — and mixed a moderate beaker of water with other ingredients.

February 18, 1821.

. . . To-day I have had no communication with my Carbonari cronies; but, in the mean time, my lower apartments are full of their bayonets, fusils, cartridges, and what not. I suppose that they consider me as a depôt, to be sacrificed, in case of accidents. It is no great matter, supposing that Italy could be liberated, who or what is sacrificed. It is a grand object — the very *poetry* of politics. Only think — a free Italy!!! Why, there has been nothing like it since the days of Augustus. I reckon the times of Caesar (Julius) free; because the commotions left every body a side to take, and the parties were pretty equal at the set out. But, afterwards, it was all praetorian and legionary business — and since! — we shall see, or, at least, some will see, what card will turn up. It is best to hope, even of the hopeless. The Dutch did more than these fellows have to do, in the Seventy Years' War.

February 19, 1821.

Came home *solus* — very high wind — lightning — moonshine — solitary stragglers muffled in cloaks — women in masks — white houses — clouds hurrying over the sky, like spilt milk blown out of the pail — altogether very poetical. It is still blowing hard — the tiles flying, and the house rocking — rain splashing — lightning flashing — quite a fine Swiss Alpine evening, and the sea roaring in the distance.

Visited — conversazione. All the women frightened by the squall: they *won't* go to the masquerade because it lightens — the pious reason!

Still blowing away. A. has sent me some news to-day. The war approaches nearer and nearer. Oh those scoundrel sovereigns! Let us but see them beaten — let the Neapolitans but have the pluck of the Dutch of old, or the Spaniards of now, or of the German Protestants, the Scotch Presbyterians, the Swiss under Tell, or the Greeks under Themistocles — *all* small and solitary nations (except the

[4] by Sir Walter Scott, 1816–18.

Spaniards and German Lutherans), and there is yet a resurrection
for Italy, and a hope for the world.

February 24, 1821.

Rode, etc., as usual. The secret intelligence arrived this morning
from the frontier to the C^i. is as bad as possible. The *plan* has missed
— the Chiefs are betrayed, military, as well as civil — and the
Neapolitans not only have *not* moved, but have declared to the
P[apal] government, and to the Barbarians, that they know nothing
of the matter!!!

Thus the world goes; and thus the Italians are always lost for
lack of union among themselves. What is to be done *here*, between the
two fires, and cut off from the N^n. frontier, is not decided. My
opinion was, — better to rise than be taken in detail; but how it will
be settled now, I cannot tell. Messengers are despatched to the delegates of the other cities to learn their resolutions.

I always had an idea that it would be *bungled;* but was willing
to hope, and am so still. Whatever I can do by money, means, or
person, I will venture freely for their freedom; and have so repeated
to them (some of the Chiefs here) half an hour ago. I have two
thousand five hundred scudi, better than five hundred pounds, in the
house, which I offered to begin with.

TO THOMAS MOORE

Ravenna, April 28, 1821.

You cannot have been more disappointed than myself, nor so much
deceived. I have been so at some personal risk also, which is not yet
done away with. However, no time nor circumstances shall alter my
tone nor my feelings of indignation against tyranny triumphant. The
present business has been as much a work of treachery as of cowardice,
— though both may have done their part. If ever you and I meet
again, I will have a talk with you upon the subject. At present, for
obvious reasons, I can write but little, as all letters are opened. In
mine they shall always find *my* sentiments, but nothing that can lead
to the oppression of others.

You will please to recollect that the Neapolitans are now nowhere
more execrated than in Italy, and not blame a whole people for the
vices of a province. That would be like condemning Great Britain
because they plunder wrecks in Cornwall.

And now let us be literary; — a sad falling off, but it is always a
consolation. If "Othello's occupation be gone", let us take to the
next best; and, if we cannot contribute to make mankind more free and
wise, we may amuse ourselves and those who like it. What are you

writing? I have been scribbling at intervals, and Murray will be publishing about now.

Lady Noel has, as you say, been dangerously ill; but it may console you to learn that she is dangerously well again.

I have written a sheet or two more of Memoranda for you; and I kept a little Journal for about a month or two, till I had filled the paper-book. I then left it off, as things grew busy, and, afterwards, too gloomy to set down without a painful feeling. This I should be glad to send you, if I had an opportunity; but a volume, however small, don't go well by such posts as exist in this Inquisition of a country.

I have no news. As a very pretty woman said to me a few nights ago, with the tears in her eyes, as she sat at the harpsichord, "Alas! the Italians must now return to making operas". I fear *that* and maccaroni are their forte, and "motley their only wear". However, there are some high spirits among them still. Pray write.

                                               And believe me, etc.[1]

TO JOHN MURRAY

                                    Ravenna, September 12th 1821.

DEAR SIR,

By Tuesday's post, I forwarded, in three packets, the drama of *"Cain"*, in three acts, of which I request the acknowledgement when arrived. To the last speech of *Eve*, in the last act (i.e. where she curses Cain), add these three lines to the concluding one —

> May the Grass wither from thy foot! the Woods
> Deny thee shelter! Earth a home! the Dust
> A Grave! the Sun his light! and Heaven her God!

There's as pretty a piece of Imprecation for you, when joined to the lines already sent, as you may wish to meet with in the course of your business. But don't forget the addition of the above three lines, which are clinchers to Eve's speech.

Let me know what Gifford thinks (if the play arrives in safety); for I have a good opinion of the piece, as poetry: it is in my gay metaphysical style, and in the *Manfred* line.

You must at least commend my facility and variety, when you consider what I have done within the last fifteen months, with my head, too, full of other and of mundane matters. But no doubt you will avoid saying any good of it, for fear I should raise the price upon

[1] Quoted: *Othello* III.iii.357; *As You Like It* II.vii.34. Lady Noel: Lady Byron's mother.

you: that's right — stick to business! Let me know what your other ragamuffins are writing, for I suppose you don't like starting too many of your Vagabonds at once. You may give them the start, for any thing I care.

If this arrives in time to be added to the other two dramas, publish them *together:* if not, publish it separately, in the *same* form, to tally for the purchasers. Let me have a proof of the whole speedily. It is longer than *Manfred.*

Why don't you publish my *Pulci?* the best thing I ever wrote, with the Italian to it.[1] I wish I was alongside of you: nothing is ever done in a man's absence; every body runs counter, because they *can.* If ever I *do* return to England, (which I shan't though,) I will write a poem to which *English Bards,* etc., shall be New Milk, in comparison. Your present literary world of mountebanks stands in need of such an Avatar; but I am not yet quite bilious enough: a season or two more, and a provocation or two, will wind me up to the point, and then, have at the whole set!

I have no patience with the sort of trash you send me out by way of books; except Scott's novels, and three or four other things, I never saw such work or works. Campbell is lecturing, Moore idling, Southey twaddling, Wordsworth driveling, Coleridge muddling, Joanna Baillie piddling, Bowles quibbling, squabbling, and sniveling. Milman will *do,* if he don't cant too much, nor imitate Southey: the fellow has poesy in him; but he is envious, and unhappy, as all the envious are. Still he is among the best of the day. Barry Cornwall will do better by and bye, I dare say, if he don't get spoilt by green tea, and the praises of Pentonville and Paradise Row. The pity of these men *is,* that they never lived either in *high life,* nor in *solitude:* there is no medium for the knowledge of the *busy* or the *still* world. If admitted into high life for a season, it is merely as *spectators* — they form no part of the Mechanism thereof. Now Moore and I, the one by circumstances, and the other by birth, happened to be free of the corporation, and to have entered into its pulses and passions, *quarum partes fuimus.*[2] Both of us have learnt by this much which nothing else could have taught us.

Yours,[3]

B.

---

[1] Byron's translation from Luigi Pulci, *Il Morgante maggiore,* 1485, appeared in the *Liberal,* No. 4.

[2] which we have been part of.

[3] Postscript omitted.

TO JOHN MURRAY

Ravenna, September 24. 1821.

DEAR MURRAY,

I have been thinking over our late correspondence, and wish to propose to you the following articles for our future: —

1^{stly} That you shall write to me of yourself, of the health, wealth, and welfare of all friends; but of *me* (*quoad me*) little or nothing.

2dly That you shall send me Soda powders, tooth-powder, tooth-brushes, or any such anti-odontalgic or chemical articles, as heretofore, *ad libitum*, upon being re-imbursed for the same.

3dly That you shall *not* send me any modern, or (as they are called) *new*, publications in *English whatsoever*, save and excepting any writing, prose or verse, of (or reasonably presumed to be of) Walter Scott, Crabbe, Moore, Campbell, Rogers, Gifford, Joanna Baillie, *Irving* (the American), Hogg, Wilson (*Isle of Palms* Man), or *any* especial *single* work of fancy which is thought to be of considerable merit; *Voyages* and *travels*, provided that they are *neither in Greece, Spain, Asia Minor, Albania, nor Italy*, will be welcome: having travelled the countries mentioned, I know that what is said of them can convey nothing further which I desire to know about them. No other English works whatsoever.

4^{thly} That you send me *no periodical works* whatsoever — *no Edinburgh, Quarterly, Monthly*, nor any Review, Magazine, Newspaper, English or foreign, of any description.

5^{thly} That you send me *no* opinions whatsoever, either *good, bad,* or *indifferent*, of yourself, or your friends, or others, concerning any work, or works, of mine, past, present, or to come.

6^{thly} That all negotiations in matters of business between you and me pass through the medium of the Honble Douglas Kinnaird, my friend and trustee, or Mr. Hobhouse, as *Alter Ego*, and tantamount to myself during my absence, or presence.

Some of these propositions may at first seem strange, but they are founded. The quantity of trash I have received as books is incalculable, and neither amused nor instructed. Reviews and Magazines are at the best but ephemeral and superficial reading: *who thinks* of the *grand article* of *last year* in any *given review?* in the next place, if they regard *myself*, they tend to increase *Egotism;* if favourable, I do not deny that the praise *elates*, and if unfavourable, that the abuse *irritates* — the latter may conduct me to inflict a species of Satire, which would neither do good to you nor to your friends: *they* may smile *now*, and so may *you;* but if I took you all in hand, it would not be difficult to cut you up like gourds. I did as much by as powerful people at nineteen years old, and I know little as yet, in three and thirty, which should prevent me from making all your ribs Gridirons for your hearts, if such were my propensity. But it is *not.* Therefore let me hear none of your provocations. If any thing occurs so very *gross* as to require my notice, I shall hear it from my personal friends. For the rest, I merely request to be left in ignorance.

The same applies to opinions, *good, bad,* or *indifferent,* of persons in conversation or correspondence: these do not *interrupt,* but they *soil* the *current* of my *Mind.* I am sensitive enough, but *not* till I am *touched;* and *here* I am beyond the touch of the short arms of literary England, except the few feelers of the Polypus that crawl over the Channel in the way of Extract.

All these precautions *in* England would be useless: the libeller or the flatterer would there reach me in spite of all; but in Italy we know little of literary England, and think less, except what reaches us through some garbled and brief extract in some miserable Gazette. For *two years* (excepting two or three articles cut out and sent to *you,* by the post) I never read a newspaper which was not forced upon me by some accident, and know, upon the whole, as little of England as you all do of Italy, and God knows *that* is little enough, with all your travels, etc., etc., etc. The English travellers *know Italy* as *you* know Guernsey: how much is *that?*

If any thing occurs so violently gross or personal as to require notice, Mr. D^s Kinnaird will let me *know;* but of *praise* I desire to hear *nothing.*

You will say, "to what tends all this?" I will answer THAT; — to keep my mind *free and unbiassed* by all paltry and personal irritabilities of praise or censure; — to let my Genius take its natural direction, while my feelings are like the dead, who know nothing and feel nothing of all or aught that is said or done in their regard.

If you can observe these conditions, you will spare yourself and others some pain: let me not be worked upon to rise up; for if I do, it will not. be for a little: if you can *not* observe these conditions, we shall cease to be correspondents, but *not friends;* for I shall always be

Yours ever and truly,[1]

BYRON.

TO THE GENERAL GOVERNMENT OF GREECE

Cephalonia, November 30, 1823.

The affair of the Loan, the expectations so long and vainly indulged of the arrival of the Greek fleet, and the danger to which Messolonghi is still exposed, have detained me here, and will detain me till some of them are removed. But when the money shall be advanced for the

[1] Postscript omitted.

fleet, I will start for the Morea; not knowing, however, of what use my presence can be in the present state of things. We have heard some rumours of new dissensions, nay, of the existence of a civil war. With all my heart I pray that these reports may be false or exaggerated, for I can imagine no calamity more serious than this; and I must frankly confess that unless union and order are established, all hopes of a Loan will be vain; and all the assistance which the Greeks could expect from abroad — and assistance neither trifling nor worthless — will be suspended or destroyed; and, what is worse, the great powers of Europe, of whom no one was an enemy to Greece, but seemed to favour her establishment of an independent power, will be persuaded that the Greeks are unable to govern themselves, and will, perhaps, themselves undertake to settle your disorders in such a way as to blast the brightest hopes of yourselves and of your friends.

Allow me to add, once for all, — I desire the well-being of Greece, and nothing else; I will do all I can to secure it; but I cannot consent, I never will consent, that the English public, or English individuals, should be deceived as to the real state of Greek affairs. The rest, Gentlemen, depends on you. You have fought gloriously; — act honourably towards your fellow-citizens and the world, and it will then no more be said, as has been repeated for two thousand years with the Roman historians, that Philopœmen was the last of the Grecians.[1] Let not calumny itself (and it is difficult, I own, to guard against it in so arduous a struggle) compare the patriot Greek, when resting from his labours, to the Turkish pacha, whom his victories have exterminated.

I pray you to accept these my sentiments as a sincere proof of my attachment to your real interests, and to believe that I am and always shall be

Yours, etc.

TO THE HON. DOUGLAS KINNAIRD

Messalonghi, March 30th 1824.

. . . The Greek Cause up to this present writing hath cost me of mine own monies about thirty thousand Spanish dollars *advanced,* without counting my own contingent expences of every kind. It is true, however, that every thing would have been at a stand-still in Messalonghi if I had not done so. Part of this money, more particularly the 4000 £ advanced, and guaranteed by the G[k] Deputies is, or ought to be, repaid. To this you will look, but I shall still spend it in the

---

[1] So Plutarch, in *Parallel Lives.*

Cause, for I have some hundred men under my command, regularly paid and pretty men enough.

I have written to you repeatedly, imploring you to sell out of the Funds while they are high, and to take four per cent. — or any per cent. — on landed security for the monies.

I have also been, and am, anxious to hear how you have succeeded with Rochdale, the Kirkby Arrears, the new publications, the settling of lawsuits, etc., etc., etc., and always concluding by a request for all possible credits to the extent of my resources, for I must do the thing handsomely.

I have been very unwell, but am supposed to be better, and almost every body else has been ill too — Parry and all, tho' he is a sort of hardworking Hercules. We have had strange weather and strange incidents — natural, moral, physical, martial and political, all which you will hear of perhaps, truly or falsely, from other quarters — I can't gossip just now. I am called to a Congress at Salona with P. Mavrocordato to meet Ulysses and the Eastern Chiefs on State affairs, and on the opening Campaign. What the result is likely to be I cannot say. The General Gov^t have assured me the direction of this province, or to join them in the Morea. I am willing to do anything that may be useful.

We were to have besieged Lepanto, but the Suliotes did not like the service "against Stone walls", and have had a row besides with some foreigners, in which blood was spilt on both sides, so that that scheme was postponed. Capt Parry is doing all that circumstances will permit in his department, and indeed in many others, for he does *all* that is done here, without any aid except the Committee's and mine, for the G^k local Gov^t have not a *sou*, *they* say, and are in debt besides. I have two hundred and twenty five regulars and irregulars in my pay — and had five hundred of the latter, but when they quarrelled amongst themselves, and tried to heighten their pretensions besides, I boomed them off; and by dint of so doing, and turning restive when fair means would not do, the rest are reduced to very good order, and the *regulars* have all along behaved very well, upon the whole — as well as any other troops anywhere. Six Guns belong to this auxiliary Corps of Artillery, which, by the way, is the only *regularly paid* corps in Greece. The Gov^t only give them rations — and those reluctantly: they have mutinied twice on account of bad bread, and really with cause, for it was quite unmasticable; but we have gotten a new Commissary, and a Baker, instead of the Bricklayer who furnished the former loaves, apparently, — and with not very good bricks neither. Yesterday there was a Court Martial on a man for stealing; the German Officers wanted to flog, but I positively prohibited anything of the kind: the culprit was dismissed the service — publicly, and conducted through the town to the Police Office to have him punished according to the Civil law. Same day, one amicable officer challenged two others; I had the parties put under arrest until the affair was accommodated: if there is any more challenging, I will call them all out and wafer one half of them.

Matters, however, go on very tolerably, and we expect them to mend still further now that the Greeks have got their loan, and may be organized. Believe me,

Ever yours and truly,

N[1] B[n1]

[1] On the death of his mother-in-law in 1822, Byron had taken the name Noel, and could spend in the Greek cause income from the Noel (Kirkby) estates as well as from the Rochdale (Byron) estate.

Percy Bysshe Shelley

PERCY BYSSHE SHELLEY

CHRONOLOGY

1792   Born August 4 at father's country estate in Sussex.

1804–10   At Eton. Conducted "terrific" scientific experiments; wrote tales of horror and poems.

1810   October 10, entered University College, Oxford. Read Godwin's *Political Justice.*

1811   March 25, expelled, with T. J. Hogg, for issuing *The Necessity of Atheism.* August 29, in Edinburgh, married Harriet Westbrook.

1812   With Harriet in Ireland and Wales. February 24, *An Address to the Irish People.* July, printed *A Letter to Lord Ellenborough.*

1813   May (?), *Queen Mab.* Became a vegetarian.

1814   Spring, *A Refutation of Deism.* July 27–29, eloped to France with Godwin's daughter Mary.

1816   February, *Alastor.* May–August, with Mary and her half-sister, Claire Clairmont, near Byron in Switzerland. December 30, married Mary after suicide of Harriet. Mary began *Frankenstein* (published 1817).

1817   March, settled at Marlow, near London. March 2 (?), *A Proposal for Putting Reform to the Vote* ("By the Hermit of Marlow"). November, wrote *An Address to the People on the Death of the Princess Charlotte* (published 1843).

1818   January, *The Revolt of Islam* (revised from *Laon and Cythna,* 1817). February, removed to Italy.

1819   May (?), *Rosalind and Helen.* Worked on major poems and *A Philosophical View of Reform* (published 1920).

1820   January 26, settled in Pisa. March, *The Cenci.* September, *Prometheus Unbound.*

1821   February–March, wrote *A Defence of Poetry* (published 1840). February 16, completed *Epipsychidion.* June 8, completed *Adonais.*

1822   March (?), *Hellas.* Worked on *The Triumph of Life.* In his boat the *Don Juan,* drowned at sea July 8.

A Philosophical View of Reform

¶ Shelley worked on *A Philosophical View of Reform,* the longest of his political essays, concurrently with *Prometheus Unbound* and *The Cenci* late in 1819 and probably until May 1820, when he asked if Leigh Hunt knew of a publisher for it in London. The surviving manuscript, unfinished, begins with an outline of the projected work: "1st. Sentiment of the Necessity of change. 2nd. Practicability and Utility of such a change. 3rd. State of Parties as regards it. 4th. Probable Mode — Desirable Mode." Of the three chapters written, Chapter I, "Introduction," traces the history of European despotism from the dissolution of the Roman Empire to the French Revolution and into contemporary England, with judicious (if inaccurate) paragraphs on the Americas, India, and the Turkish Near East. Chapter II, corresponding to the first topic in Shelley's outline, ascribes current conditions to inequalities of property and of access to justice, the national debt, sinecures, religious tithes, and a standing army. It includes a sharp attack on the proposal by Malthus that marriages be delayed for the poor. The three chapters were first published one hundred years after they were written. The passages below follow the transcription by Walter E. Peck for the *Complete Works,* Volume VII, 1930. ▶

from CHAPTER III

Probable Means

The great principle of Reform consists in every individual of mature age and perfect understanding giving his consent to the institution and the continued existence of the social system, which is instituted for his advantage and for the advantage of others in his situation. As in a great nation this is practically impossible, masses of individuals consent to qualify other individuals, whom they delegate to superintend their concerns. These delegates have constitutional authority to exercise the functions of sovereignty; they unite in the highest degree the legislative and executive functions. A government that is founded on any other basis is a government of fraud or force and ought on the first convenient occasion to be overthrown. The broad principle of political reform is the natural equality of men, not with relation to their property but to their rights. That equality in possessions which Jesus Christ so passionately taught is a moral rather than a political truth and is such as social institutions cannot without mischief inflexibly secure. Morals and politics can only be considered as portions of the same science, with relation to a system of such absolute perfection as Christ and Plato and Rousseau and other reasoners have asserted, and as Godwin has, with irresistible eloquence, systematised and developed. Equality in possessions must be the last result of the utmost refinements of civilization; it is one of the conditions of that system of society, towards which with whatever hope of ultimate success, it is our duty to tend. We may and ought to advert to it as to the elementary principle, as to the goal, unattainable, perhaps, by us, but which, as it were, we revive in our posterity to pursue. We derive tranquillity and courage and grandeur of soul from contemplating an object which is, because we will it, and may be, because we hope and desire it, and must be if succeeding generations of the enlightened sincerely and earnestly seek it. . . .

If Reform shall be begun by the existing government, let us be contented with a limited *beginning*, with any whatsoever opening; let the rotten boroughs be disfranchised and their rights transferred to the unrepresented cities and districts of the Nation; it is no matter how slow, gradual and cautious be the change; we shall demand more and more with firmness and moderation, never anticipating but never deferring the moment of successful opposition, so that the people may become habituated [to] exercising the functions of sovereignty, in proportion as they acquire the possession of it. If reform could begin from within the Houses of Parliament, as constituted at present, it appears to me that what is called moderate reform, that is a suffrage whose qualification should be the possession of a certain small property, and triennial parliaments, would be principles — a system in which for the sake of obtaining without bloodshed or confusion ulterior improvements of a more important character, all reformers ought to acquiesce. Not that such are first principles, or that they would produce a system of perfect social institutions or one approaching to [such]. But nothing is more idle than to reject a limited benefit because we cannot without great sacrifices obtain an unlimited one. We might thus reject a Representative Republic, if it were obtainable, on the plea that the imagination of man can conceive of something more absolutely perfect. Towards whatsoever we regard as perfect, undoubtedly it is no less our duty than it is our nature to press forward; this is the generous enthusiasm which accomplishes not indeed the consummation after which it aspires, but one which approaches it in a degree far nearer than if the whole powers had not been developed by a delusion. — It is in politics rather than in religion that faith is meritorious. —

. . . The true patriot will endeavor to enlighten and to unite the nation and animate it with enthusiasm and confidence. For this purpose he will be indefatigable in promulgating political truth. He will endeavor to rally round one standard the divided friends of liberty, and make them forget the subordinate objects with regard to which they differ by appealing to that respecting which they are all agreed. He will promote such open confederations among men of

principle and spirit as may tend to make their intentions and their
efforts converge to a common centre. He will discourage all secret
associations, which have a tendency, by making national will develop
itself in a partial and premature manner, to cause tumult and confusion. He will urge the necessity of exciting the people frequently
to exercise their right of assembling, in such limited numbers as that
all present may be actual parties to the proceedings of the day. Lastly,
if circumstances had collected a more considerable number as at
Manchester on the memorable 16th of August, if the tyrants command
their troops to fire upon them or cut them down unless they disperse,
he will exhort them peaceably to risque the danger, and to expect
without resistance the onset of the cavalry, and wait with folded arms
the event of the fire of the artillery and receive with unshrinking
bosoms the bayonets of the charging battalions. Men are every day
persuaded to incur greater perils for a less manifest advantage. And
this, not because active resistance is not justifiable when all other
means shall have failed, but because in this instance temperance and
courage would produce greater advantages than the most decisive
victory. . . .

The public opinion in England ought first to [be] excited to action,
and the durability of those forms within which the oppressors in-
trench themselves brought perpetually to the test of its operation.
No law or institution can last if this opinion be distinctly pronounced
against it. For this purpose government ought to be defied, in cases of
questionable result, to prosecute for political libel. All questions relating to the jurisdiction of magistrates and courts of law respecting
which any doubt could be raised ought to be agitated with indefatigable pertinacity. Some two or three of the popular leaders have
shown the best spirit in this respect; they only want system and co-
operation. The taxgatherer ought to be compelled in every practicable
instance to distrain, whilst the right to impose taxes, as was the case
in the beginning of the resistance to the tyranny of Charles the 1st,
is formally contested by an overwhelming multitude of defendants
before the courts of common law. Confound the subtlety of lawyers
with the subtlety of the law. All of the nation would thus be excited
to develop itself, and to declare whether it acquiesced in the existing
forms of government. — The manner in which all questions of this
nature might be decided would develop the occasions, and afford a
prognostic as to the success, of more decisive measures. Simultaneously with this active and vigilant system of opposition, means ought
to be taken of solemnly conveying the sense of large bodies and
various denominations of the people in a manner the most explicit to
the existing depositaries of power. Petitions, couched in the actual
language of the petitioners, and emanating from distinct assemblies,
ought to load the tables of the House of Commons. The poets, philosophers and artists ought to remonstrate, and the memorials entitled
their petitions might shew the diversity [of] convictions they enter-

tain of the inevitable connection between national prosperity and freedom, and the cultivation of the imagination and the cultivation of scientific truth, and the profound development of moral and metaphysical enquiry. Suppose these memorials to be severally written by Godwin, Hazlitt, Bentham and Hunt, they would be worthy of the age and of the cause; these, radiant and irresistible like the meridian sun would strike all but the eagles who dared to gaze upon its beams, with blindness and confusion. These appeals of solemn and emphatic argument from those who have already a predestined existence among posterity, would appal the enemies of mankind by their echoes from every corner of the world in which the majestic literature of England is cultivated; it would be like a voice from beyond the dead of those who will live in the memories of men, when they must be forgotten; it would be Eternity warning Time. . . .

A Defence of Poetry

❪ Soon after receiving *Ollier's Literary Miscellany*, in January 1821, Shelley determined to answer Peacock's essay there, "The Four Ages of Poetry." About March 14, Mary Shelley began to copy out Part I of the answer, which was ready by March 20 to send to the Olliers; but the *Miscellany* had ceased with the first number. In 1822 a copy of the *Defence* was edited for publication in the *Liberal*, but the death of that periodical again frustrated the attempt. The projected Parts II and III were never written. Shelley's *Defence* resembles, and in several passages paraphrases, *An Apology for Poetry* by Sir Philip Sidney. From Sidney's sober Aristotelian arguments, however, Shelley rises to the idealism of Plato's *Ion* and *Phaedrus*. He rises also to a metaphorical radiance of his own. In the midst of an excellent discussion of the *Defence*, in *Oxford Lectures on Poetry*, 1905, A. C. Bradley repeated Tennyson's remark about one of Shelley's poems: "He seems to go up into the air and burst." Yet Bradley aptly summarized Shelley's argument: "Love talking musically is Poetry." In 1840 Mary published the *Defence*, with the allusions to Peacock's essay removed, in a collection of Shelley's *Essays, Letters from Abroad, Translations, and Fragments*. The text of Ingpen and Peck, based on an incomplete manuscript, is here amended from a transcription by Mary Shelley (printed in *Shelley's Prose in the Bodleian Library*, edited by A. H. Koszul, Oxford, 1910) and from Mary's corrected edition of the *Essays* in 1852. ❫

PART I

According to one mode of regarding those two classes of mental action, which are called reason and imagination, the former may be considered as mind contemplating the relations borne by one thought to another, however produced; and the latter, as mind acting upon those thoughts so as to colour them with its own light, and composing from them as from elements, other thoughts, each containing within itself the principle of its own integrity. The one is the τὸ ποιεῖν, or the principle of synthesis, and has for its objects those forms which are common to universal nature and existence itself; the other is the τὸ λογίζειν, or principle of analysis, and its action regards the relations of things, simply as relations; considering thoughts, not in their integral unity, but as the algebraical representations which conduct to certain general results. Reason is the enumeration of quantities already known; imagination is the perception of the value of those quantities, both separately and as a whole. Reason respects the differences, and Imagination the similitudes of things. Reason is to Imagination as the instrument to the agent, as the body to the spirit, as the shadow to the substance.

Poetry, in a general sense, may be defined to be "the expression of the Imagination": and poetry is connate with the origin of man. Man is an instrument over which a series of external and internal impressions are driven, like the alternations of an ever-changing wind over an Æolian lyre, which move it by their motion to ever-changing melody. But there is a principle within the human being, and perhaps within all sentient beings, which acts otherwise than in the lyre, and produces not melody alone, but harmony, by an internal adjustment of the sounds or motions thus excited to the impressions which excite them. It is as if the lyre could accommodate its chords to the motions of that which strikes them, in a determined proportion of sound; even as the musician can accommodate his voice to the sound of the lyre. A child at play by itself will express its delight by its voice and motions; and every inflexion of tone and gesture will bear exact relation to a corresponding antitype in the pleasurable impressions which awakened it; it will be the reflected image of that impression; and as the lyre trembles and sounds after the wind has died away, so the child seeks, by prolonging in its voice and motions the duration of the effect, to prolong also a consciousness of the cause. In relation to the objects which delight a child, these expressions are what poetry is to higher objects. The savage (for the savage is to ages what the child is to years) expresses the emotions produced in him by surrounding objects in a similar manner; and language and gesture, together with plastic or pictorial imitation, become the image of the combined effect of those objects, and of his apprehension of them. Man in society, with all his passions and his pleasures, next becomes the object of the passions and pleasures of man; an additional class of emotions produces an augmented treasure of expressions; and language, gesture, and the imitative arts, become at once the representation and the medium, the pencil and the picture, the chisel and the statue, the chord and the harmony. The social sympathies, or those laws from which, as from its elements, society results, begin to develop themselves from the moment that two human beings coexist; the future is contained within the present as the plant within the seed; and equality, diversity, unity, contrast, mutual dependence, become the principles alone capable of affording the motives according to which the will of a social being is determined to action, inasmuch as he is social; and constitute pleasure in sensation, virtue in sentiment, beauty in art, truth in reasoning, and love in the intercourse of kind. Hence men, even in the infancy of society, observe a certain order in their words and actions, distinct from that of the objects and the impressions represented by them, all expression being subject to the laws of that from which it proceeds. But let us dismiss those more general considerations which might involve an inquiry into the principles of society itself, and restrict our view to the manner in which the imagination is expressed upon its forms.

In the youth of the world, men dance and sing and imitate natural objects, observing in these actions, as in all others, a certain rhythm or order. And, although all men observe a similar, they observe not the same order, in the motions of the dance, in the melody of the song, in the combinations of language, in the series of their imitations of natural objects. For there is a certain order or rhythm belonging to each of these classes of mimetic representation, from which the hearer and the spectator receive an intenser and purer pleasure than from any other: the sense of an approximation to this order has been called taste by modern writers. Every man in the infancy of art, observes an order which approximates more or less closely to that from which this highest delight results: but the diversity is not sufficiently marked, as that its gradations should be sensible, except in those instances where the predominance of this faculty of approximation to the beautiful (for so we may be permitted to name the relation between this highest pleasure and its cause) is very great. Those in whom it exists in excess are poets, in the most universal sense of the word; and the pleasure resulting from the manner in which they express the influence of society or nature upon their own minds, communicates itself to others, and gathers a sort of reduplication from that community. Their language is vitally metaphorical; that is, it marks the before un- apprehended relations of things and perpetuates their apprehension, until the words which represent them, become, through time, signs for portions or classes of thoughts, instead of pictures of integral thoughts; and then if no new poets should arise to create afresh the associations which have been thus disorganised, language will be dead to all the nobler purposes of human intercourse. These similitudes or relations are finely said by Lord Bacon to be "the same footsteps of nature im- pressed upon the various subjects of the world"[1] — and he considers the faculty which perceives them as the storehouse of axioms com-

---

[1] De Augment. Scient., cap. I, lib. iii. [P.B.S.]

mon to all knowledge. In the infancy of society every author is necessarily a poet, because language itself is poetry; and to be a poet is to apprehend the true and the beautiful, in a word, the good which exists in the relation, subsisting, first between existence and perception, and secondly between perception and expression. Every original language near to its source is in itself the chaos of a cyclic poem: the copiousness of lexicography and the distinctions of grammar are the works of a later age, and are merely the catalogue and the form of the creations of Poetry.

But Poets, or those who imagine and express this indestructible order, are not only the authors of language and of music, of the dance, and architecture, and statuary, and painting; they are the institutors of laws, and the founders of civil society, and the inventors of the arts of life, and the teachers who draw into a certain propinquity with the beautiful and the true, that partial apprehension of the agencies of the invisible world which is called religion. Hence all original religions are allegorical or susceptible of allegory, and, like Janus, have a double face of false and true. Poets, according to the circumstances of age and nation in which they appeared, were called, in the earlier epochs of the world, legislators or prophets: a poet essentially comprises and unites both these characters. For he not only beholds intensely the present as it is, and discovers those laws according to which present things ought to be ordered, but he beholds the future in the present, and his thoughts are the germs of the flower and the fruit of latest time. Not that I assert poets to be prophets in the gross sense of the word, or that they can foretell the form as surely as they foreknow the spirit of events: such is the pretence of superstition, which would make poetry an attribute of prophecy, rather than prophecy an attribute of poetry. A Poet participates in the eternal, the infinite, and the one; as far as relates to his conceptions, time and place and number are not. The grammatical forms which express the moods of time, and the difference of persons, and the distinction of place, are convertible with respect to the highest poetry without injuring it as poetry; and the choruses of Æschylus, and the book of Job, and Dante's Paradise, would afford, more than any other writings, examples of this fact, if the limits of this paper did not forbid citation. The creations of sculpture, painting, and music, are illustrations still more decisive.

Language, colour, form, and religious and civil habits of action, are all the instruments and materials of poetry; they may be called poetry by that figure of speech which considers the effect as a synonyme of the cause. But poetry in a more restricted sense expresses those arrangements of language, and especially metrical language, which are created by that imperial faculty, whose throne is curtained within the invisible nature of man. And this springs from the nature itself of language, which is a more direct representation of the actions and passions of our internal being, and is susceptible of more various and delicate combinations, than colour, form, or motion, and is more plastic and obedient to the control of that faculty of which it is the creation. For language is arbitrarily produced by the Imagination, and has relation to thoughts alone; but all other materials, instruments, and conditions of art, have relations among each other, which limit and interpose between conception and expression. The former is as a mirror which reflects, the latter as a cloud which enfeebles, the light of which both are mediums of communication. Hence the fame of sculptors, painters, and musicians, although the intrinsic powers of the great masters of these arts may yield in no degree to that of those who have employed language as the hieroglyphic of their thoughts, has never equalled that of poets in the restricted sense of the term; as two performers of equal skill will produce unequal effects from a guitar and a harp. The fame of legislators and founders of religion, so long as their institutions last, alone seems to exceed that of poets in the restricted sense; but it can scarcely be a question, whether, if we deduct the celebrity which their flattery of the gross opinions of the vulgar usually conciliates, together with that which belonged to them in their higher character of poets, any excess will remain.

We have thus circumscribed the word Poetry within the limits of that art which is the most familiar and the most perfect expression of the faculty itself. It is necessary, however, to make the circle still narrower, and to determine the distinction between measured and unmeasured language; for the popular division into prose and verse is inadmissible in accurate philosophy.

Sounds as well as thoughts have relation both between each other and towards that which they represent, and a perception of the order of those relations has always been found connected with a perception of the order of the relations of thoughts. Hence the language of poets has ever affected a certain uniform and harmonious recurrence of sound, without which it were not poetry, and which is scarcely less indispensable to the communication of its action, than the words themselves, without reference to that peculiar order. Hence the vanity of translation; it were as wise to cast a violet into a crucible that you might discover the formal principle of its colour and odour, as seek to transfuse from one language into another the creations of a poet. The plant must spring again from its seed, or it will bear no flower — and this is the burthen of the curse of Babel.

An observation of the regular mode of the recurrence of this harmony in the language of poetical minds, together with its relation to music, produced metre, or a certain system of traditional forms of harmony and language. Yet it is by no means essential that a poet should accommodate his language to this traditional form, so that the harmony, which is its spirit, be observed. The practice is indeed convenient and popular, and to be preferred, especially in such composition as includes much form and action: but every great poet must inevitably innovate upon the example of his predecessors in the exact structure of his peculiar versification. The distinction between poets and prose writers is a vulgar error. The distinction between philosophers and poets has been anticipated. Plato was essentially a poet — the truth and splendour of his imagery, and the melody of his language, are the most intense that it is possible to conceive. He rejected the measure of the epic, dramatic, and lyrical forms, because he sought to kindle a harmony in thoughts divested of shape and action, and he forbore to invent any regular plan of rhythm which should include under determinate forms, the varied pauses of his style. Cicero sought to imitate the cadence of his periods, but with little success. Lord Bacon was a poet.[2] His language has a sweet and majestic rhythm, which satisfies the sense, no less than the almost superhuman wisdom of his philosphy satisfies the intellect; it is a strain which distends, and then bursts the circumference of the hearer's mind, and pours itself forth together with it into the universal element with which it has perpetual sympathy. All the authors of revolutions in opinion are not only necessarily poets as they are inventors, nor even as their words unveil the permanent analogy of things by images which participate in the life of truth; but as their periods are harmonious and rhythmical, and contain in themselves the elements of verse; being the echo of the eternal music. Nor are those supreme poets, who have employed traditional forms of rhythm on account of the form and action of their subjects, less capable of perceiving and teaching the truth of things, than those who have omitted that form. Shakspeare, Dante, and Milton (to confine ourselves to modern writers) are philosophers of the very loftiest power.

A poem is the very image of life expressed in its eternal truth. There is this difference between a story and a poem, that a story is a catalogue of detached facts, which have no other bond of connexion than time, place, circumstance, cause, and effect; the other is the creation of actions according to the unchangeable forms of human nature, as existing in the mind of the creator, which is itself the image of all other minds. The one is partial, and applies only to a definite period of time, and a certain combination of events which can never again recur; the other is universal, and contains within itself the germ of a relation to whatever motives or actions have place in the possible varieties of human nature. Time, which destroys the beauty and the use of the story of particular facts, stript of the poetry which should invest them, augments that of Poetry, and for ever develops new and wonderful applications of the eternal truth which it contains. Hence epitomes have been called the moths of just history;[3] they eat out the poetry of it. The story of particular facts is as a mirror which obscures

[2] See the *Filum Labyrinthi*, and the *Essay on Death* particularly. [P.B.S.]
[3] Bacon, *Advancement of Learning* II.ii.4.

and distorts that which should be beautiful: Poetry is a mirror which
makes beautiful that which is distorted.

The parts of a composition may be poetical, without the composition as a whole being a poem. A single sentence may be considered
as a whole, though it may be found in a series of unassimilated portions; a single word even may be a spark of inextinguishable thought.
And thus all the great historians, Herodotus, Plutarch, Livy, were poets;
and although the plan of these writers, especially that of Livy,
restrained them from developing this faculty in its highest degree,
they make copious and ample amends for their subjection, by filling all
the interstices of their subjects with living images.

Having determined what is poetry, and who are poets, let us proceed to estimate its effects upon society.

Poetry is ever accompanied with pleasure: all spirits upon which
it falls open themselves to receive the wisdom which is mingled with
its delight. In the infancy of the world, neither poets themselves nor
their auditors are fully aware of the excellence of poetry: for it acts
in a divine and unapprehended manner, beyond and above consciousness; and it is reserved for future generations to contemplate and
measure the mighty cause and effect in all the strength and splendour
of their union. Even in modern times, no living poet ever arrived at
the fulness of his fame; the jury which sits in judgment upon a poet,
belonging as he does to all time, must be composed of his peers: it
must be impanneled by Time from the selectest of the wise of many
generations. A Poet is a nightingale, who sits in darkness and sings
to cheer its own solitude with sweet sounds; his auditors are as men
entranced by the melody of an unseen musician, who feel that they
are moved and softened, yet know not whence or why. The poems of
Homer and his contemporaries were the delight of infant Greece;
they were the elements of that social system which is the column upon
which all succeeding civilization has reposed. Homer embodied the
ideal perfection of his age in human character; nor can we doubt that
those who read his verses were awakened to an ambition of becoming
like to Achilles, Hector, and Ulysses: the truth and beauty of friendship, patriotism, and persevering devotion to an object, were unveiled
to their depths in these immortal creations: the sentiments of the
auditors must have been refined and enlarged by a sympathy with
such great and lovely impersonations, until from admiring they imitated, and from imitation they identified themselves with the objects
of their admiration. Nor let it be objected, that these characters are
remote from moral perfection, and that they are by no means to be
considered as edifying patterns for general imitation. Every epoch,
under names more or less specious, has deified its peculiar errors;
Revenge is the naked Idol of the worship of a semi-barbarous age; and
Self-deceit is the veiled Image of unknown evil, before which luxury
and satiety lie prostrate. But a poet considers the vices of his con-

temporaries as the temporary dress in which his creations must be
arrayed, and which cover without concealing the eternal proportions
of their beauty. An epic or dramatic personage is understood to wear
them around his soul, as he may the antient armour or the modern
uniform around his body; whilst it is easy to conceive a dress more
graceful than either. The beauty of the internal nature cannot be so far
concealed by its accidental vesture, but that the spirit of its form shall
communicate itself to the very disguise, and indicate the shape it hides
from the manner in which it is worn. A majestic form and graceful
motions will express themselves through the most barbarous and
tasteless costume. Few poets of the highest class have chosen to exhibit the beauty of their conceptions in its naked truth and splendour;
and it is doubtful whether the alloy of costume, habit, &c., be not
necessary to temper this planetary music for mortal ears.

The whole objection, however, of the immorality of poetry rests
upon a misconception of the manner in which poetry acts to produce
the moral improvement of man. Ethical science arranges the elements
which poetry has created, and propounds schemes and proposes examples of civil and domestic life: nor is it for want of admirable doctrines that men hate, and despise, and censure, and deceive, and sub-
jugate one another. But Poetry acts in another and diviner manner.
It awakens and enlarges the mind itself by rendering it the receptacle
of a thousand unapprehended combinations of thought. Poetry lifts
the veil from the hidden beauty of the world, and makes familiar
objects be as if they were not familiar; it reproduces all that it represents, and the impersonations clothed in its Elysian light stand thenceforward in the minds of those who have once contemplated them, as
memorials of that gentle and exalted content which extends itself over
all thoughts and actions with which it coexists. The great secret of
morals is Love; or a going out of our own nature, and an identification
of ourselves with the beautiful which exists in thought, action, or person, not our own. A man, to be greatly good, must imagine intensely
and comprehensively; he must put himself in the place of another and
of many others; the pains and pleasures of his species must become
his own. The great instrument of moral good is the imagination; and
poetry administers to the effect by acting upon the cause. Poetry enlarges the circumference of the imagination by replenishing it with
thoughts of ever new delight, which have the power of attracting and
assimilating to their own nature all other thoughts, and which form
new intervals and interstices whose void for ever craves fresh food.
Poetry strengthens the faculty which is the organ of the moral nature of
man, in the same manner as exercise strengthens a limb. A Poet therefore would do ill to embody his own conceptions of right and wrong,
which are usually those of his place and time, in his poetical creations,
which participate in neither. By this assumption of the inferior office
of interpreting the effect, in which perhaps after all he might acquit

himself but imperfectly, he would resign a glory in the participation of the cause. There was little danger that Homer, or any of the eternal Poets, should have so far misunderstood themselves as to have abdicated this throne of their widest dominion. Those in whom the poetical faculty, though great, is less intense, as Euripides, Lucan, Tasso, Spenser, have frequently affected a moral aim, and the effect of their poetry is diminished in exact proportion to the degree in which they compel us to advert to this purpose.

Homer and the cyclic poets were followed at a certain interval by the dramatic and lyrical Poets of Athens, who flourished contemporaneously with all that is most perfect in the kindred expressions of the poetical faculty; architecture, painting, music, the dance, sculpture, philosophy, and we may add, the forms of civil life. For although the scheme of Athenian society was deformed by many imperfections which the poetry existing in Chivalry and Christianity has erased from the habits and institutions of modern Europe; yet never at any other period has so much energy, beauty and virtue, been developed; never was blind strength and stubborn form so disciplined and rendered subject to the will of man, or that will less repugnant to the dictates of the beautiful and the true, as during the century which preceded the death of Socrates. Of no other epoch in the history of our species have we records and fragments stamped so visibly with the image of the divinity in man. But it is Poetry alone, in form, in action, or in language, which has rendered this epoch memorable above all others, and the storehouse of examples to everlasting time. For written poetry existed at that epoch simultaneously with the other arts, and it is an idle enquiry to demand which gave and which received the light, which all, as from a common focus, have scattered over the darkest periods of succeeding age. We know no more of cause and effect than a constant conjunction of events: Poetry is ever found to coexist with whatever other arts contribute to the happiness and perfection of man. I appeal to what has already been established to distinguish between the cause and the effect.

It was at the period here adverted to, that the Drama had its birth; and however a succeeding writer may have equalled or surpassed those few great specimens of the Athenian drama which have been preserved to us, it is indisputable that the art itself never was understood or practised according to the true philosophy of it, as at Athens. For the Athenians employed language, action, music, painting, the dance, and religious institutions, to produce a common effect in the representation of the loftiest idealisms of passion and of power; each division in the art was made perfect in its kind by artists of the most consummate skill, and was disciplined into a beautiful proportion and unity one towards another. On the modern stage a few only of the elements capable of expressing the image of the poet's conception are employed at once. We have tragedy without music and dancing; and

music and dancing without the high impersonations of which they
are the fit accompaniment, and both without religion and solemnity.
Religious institution has indeed been usually banished from the stage.
Our system of divesting the actor's face of a mask, on which the many
expressions appropriated to his dramatic character might be moulded
into one permanent and unchanging expression, is favourable only to
a partial and inharmonious effect; it is fit for nothing but a monologue,
where all the attention may be directed to some great master of ideal
mimicry. The modern practice of blending comedy with tragedy,
though liable to great abuse in point of practice, is undoubtedly an
extension of the dramatic circle; but the comedy should be as in King
Lear, universal, ideal, and sublime. It is perhaps the intervention of
this principle which determines the balance in favour of King Lear
against the Œdipus Tyrannus or the Agamemnon, or, if you will, the
trilogies with which they are connected; unless the intense power of
the choral poetry, especially that of the latter, should be considered as
restoring the equilibrium. King Lear, if it can sustain this comparison,
may be judged to be the most perfect specimen of the dramatic art
existing in the world; in spite of the narrow conditions to which the
poet was subjected by the ignorance of the philosophy of the drama
which has prevailed in modern Europe. Calderon, in his religious
Autos, has attempted to fulfil some of the high conditions of dramatic
representation neglected by Shakspeare; such as the establishing a
relation between the drama and religion, and the accommodating
them to music and dancing; but he omits the observation[4] of conditions still more important, and more is lost than gained by a substitution of the rigidly-defined and ever-repeated idealisms of a distorted
superstition for the living impersonations of the truth of human
passion.[5]

But we digress. — The Author of the Four Ages of Poetry has
prudently omitted to dispute on the effect of the Drama upon life
and manners. For, if I know the Knight by the device of his shield,
I have only to inscribe Philoctetes or Agamemnon or Othello upon
mine to put to flight the giant sophisms which have enchanted him,
as the mirror of intolerable light though on the arm of one of the
weakest of the Paladines could blind and scatter whole armies of
necromancers and pagans.[6] The connexion of scenic exhibitions with
the improvement or corruption of the manners of men, has been universally recognized: in other words, the presence or absence of poetry
in its most perfect and universal form, has been found to be connected with good and evil in conduct and habit. The corruption which

[4] observance.

[5] Calderon (1600–81) wrote over seventy *Autos sacramentales*. Shelley
translated scenes from his *El Mágico prodigioso*.

[6] In legends of Charlemagne and his twelve paladins or knightly
champions.

has been imputed to the drama as an effect, begins, when the poetry employed in its constitution ends: I appeal to the history of manners whether the gradations of the growth of the one and the decline of the other have not corresponded with an exactness equal to any other example of moral cause and effect.

The drama at Athens, or wheresoever else it may have approached to its perfection, ever coexisted with the moral and intellectual greatness of the age. The tragedies of the Athenian poets are as mirrors in which the spectator beholds himself, under a thin disguise of circumstance, stript of all but that ideal perfection and energy which every one feels to be the internal type of all that he loves, admires, and would become. The imagination is enlarged by a sympathy with pains and passions so mighty, that they distend in their conception the capacity of that by which they are conceived; the good affections are strengthened by pity, indignation, terror and sorrow; and an exalted calm is prolonged from the satiety of this high exercise of them into the tumult of familiar life: even crime is disarmed of half its horror and all its contagion by being represented as the fatal consequence of the unfathomable agencies of nature; error is thus divested of its wilfulness; men can no longer cherish it as the creation of their choice. In the drama of the highest order there is little food for censure or hatred; it teaches rather self-knowledge and self-respect. Neither the eye nor the mind can see itself, unless reflected upon that which it resembles. The drama, so long as it continues to express poetry, is a prismatic and many-sided mirror, which collects the brightest rays of human nature and divides and reproduces them from the simplicity of these elementary forms, and touches them with majesty and beauty, and multiplies all that it reflects, and endows it with the power of propagating its like wherever it may fall.

But in periods of the decay of social life, the drama sympathises with that decay. Tragedy becomes a cold imitation of the form of the great masterpieces of antiquity, divested of all harmonious accompaniment of the kindred arts; and often the very form misunderstood, or a weak attempt to teach certain doctrines, which the writer considers as moral truths; and which are usually no more than specious flatteries of some gross vice or weakness, with which the author, in common with his auditors, are infected. Hence what has been called the classical and domestic drama. Addison's "Cato" is a specimen of the one; and would it were not superfluous to cite examples of the other! To such purposes poetry cannot be made subservient. Poetry is a sword of lightning, ever unsheathed, which consumes the scabbard that would contain it. And thus we observe that all dramatic writings of this nature are unimaginative in a singular degree; they affect sentiment and passion, which, divested of imagination, are other names for caprice and appetite. The period in our own history of the grossest degradation of the drama is the reign of Charles II., when all forms in which poetry had been accustomed to be expressed became hymns to the triumph of kingly power over liberty and virtue. Milton stood alone illuminating an age unworthy of him. At such periods the calculating principle pervades all the forms of dramatic exhibition, and poetry ceases to be expressed upon them. Comedy loses its ideal universality: wit succeeds to humour; we laugh from self complacency and triumph, instead of pleasure; malignity, sarcasm, and contempt, succeed to sympathetic merriment; we hardly laugh, but we smile. Obscenity, which is ever blasphemy against the divine beauty in life, becomes, from the very veil which it assumes, more active if less disgusting: it is a monster for which the corruption of society for ever brings forth new food, which it devours in secret.

The drama being that form under which a greater number of modes of expression of poetry are susceptible of being combined than any other, the connexion of poetry and social good is more observable in the drama than in whatever other form. And it is indisputable that the highest perfection of human society has ever corresponded with the highest dramatic excellence; and that the corruption or the extinction of the drama in a nation where it has once flourished, is a mark of a corruption of manners, and an extinction of the energies which sustain the soul of social life. But, as Machiavelli says of political institutions, that life may be preserved and renewed, if men should arise capable of bringing back the drama to its principles. And this is true with respect to poetry in its most extended sense: all language, institution and form, require not only to be produced but to be sustained: the office and character of a poet participates in the divine nature as regards providence, no less than as regards creation.

Civil war, the spoils of Asia, and the fatal predominance first of the Macedonian, and then of the Roman arms, were so many symbols of the extinction or suspension of the creative faculty in Greece. The bucolic writers,[7] who found patronage under the lettered tyrants of Sicily and Egypt, were the latest representatives of its most glorious reign. Their poetry is intensely melodious; like the odour of the tuberose, it overcomes and sickens the spirit with excess of sweetness; whilst the poetry of the preceding age was as a meadow-gale of June, which mingles the fragrance of all the flowers of the field, and adds a quickening and harmonising spirit of its own which endows the sense with a power of sustaining its extreme delight. The bucolic and erotic delicacy in written poetry is correlative with that softness in statuary, music, and the kindred arts, and even in manners and institutions, which distinguished the epoch to which we now refer. Nor is it the poetical faculty itself, or any misapplication of it, to which this want of harmony is to be imputed. An equal sensibility to the influence of the senses and the affections is to be found in the writings of

[7] Theocritus, Bion, Moschus.

Homer and Sophocles: the former, especially, has clothed sensual and
pathetic images with irresistible attractions. Their superiority over
these succeeding writers consists in the presence of those thoughts
which belong to the inner faculties of our nature, not in the absence
of those which are connected with the external: their incomparable
perfection consists in an harmony of the union of all. It is not what
the erotic writers have, but what they have not, in which their imperfection consists. It is not inasmuch as they were Poets, but inasmuch as they were not Poets, that they can be considered with any
plausibility as connected with the corruption of their age. Had that
corruption availed so as to extinguish in them the sensibility to
pleasure, passion, and natural scenery, which is imputed to them as
an imperfection, the last triumph of evil would have been achieved.
For the end of social corruption is to destroy all sensibility to pleasure;
and, therefore, it is corruption. It begins at the imagination and the
intellect as at the core, and distributes itself thence as a paralysing
venom, through the affections into the very appetites, until all become
a torpid mass in which sense hardly survives. At the approach of such
a period, Poetry ever addresses itself to those faculties which are the
last to be destroyed, and its voice is heard, like the footsteps of Astræa,
departing from the world. Poetry ever communicates all the pleasure
which men are capable of receiving: it is ever still the light of life;
the source of whatever of beautiful or generous or true can have place
in an evil time. It will readily be confessed that those among the
luxurious citizens of Syracuse and Alexandria, who were delighted
with the poems of Theocritus, were less cold, cruel, and sensual than
the remnant of their tribe. But corruption must have utterly destroyed
the fabric of human society before poetry can ever cease. The sacred
links of that chain have never been entirely disjoined, which descending through the minds of many men is attached to those great minds,
whence as from a magnet the invisible effluence is sent forth, which
at once connects, animates, and sustains the life of all. It is the faculty
which contains within itself the seeds at once of its own and of social
renovation. And let us not circumscribe the effects of the bucolic
and erotic poetry within the limits of the sensibility of those to whom
it was addressed. They may have perceived the beauty of those immortal compositions, simply as fragments and isolated portions: those
who are more finely organised, or born in a happier age, may recognise
them as episodes to that great poem, which all poets, like the co-
operating thoughts of one great mind, have built up since the beginning of the world.

The same revolution within a narrower sphere had place in antient
Rome; but the actions and forms of its social life never seem to have
been perfectly saturated with the poetical element. The Romans appear to have considered the Greeks as the selectest treasuries of the
selectest forms of manners and of nature, and to have abstained from

creating in measured language, sculpture, music, or architecture, any thing which might bear a particular relation to their own condition, whilst it might bear a general one to the universal constitution of the world. But we judge from partial evidence, and we judge perhaps partially. Ennius, Varro, Pacuvius, and Accius, all great poets, have been lost. Lucretius is in the highest, and Virgil in a very high sense, a creator. The chosen delicacy of the expressions of the latter, are as a mist of light which conceal from us the intense and exceeding truth of his conceptions of nature. Livy is instinct with poetry. Yet Horace, Catullus, Ovid, and generally the other great writers of the Virgilian age, saw man and nature in the mirror of Greece. The institutions also, and the religion of Rome, were less poetical than those of Greece, as the shadow is less vivid than the substance. Hence poetry in Rome, seemed to follow, rather than accompany, the perfection of political and domestic society. The true poetry of Rome lived in its institutions; for whatever of beautiful, true, and majestic, they contained, could have sprung only from the faculty which creates the order in which they consist. The life of Camillus, the death of Regulus; the expectation of the Senators, in their godlike state, of the victorious Gauls; the refusal of the Republic to make peace with Hannibal, after the battle of Cannæ, were not the consequences of a refined calculation of the probable personal advantage to result from such a rhythm and order in the shews of life, to those who were at once the poets and the actors of these immortal dramas. The imagination beholding the beauty of this order, created it out of itself according to its own idea; the consequence was empire, and the reward ever-living fame. These things are not the less poetry, *quia carent vate sacro*.[8] They are the episodes of that cyclic poem written by Time upon the memories of men. The Past, like an inspired rhapsodist, fills the theatre of everlasting generations with their harmony.

At length the antient system of religion and manners had fulfilled the circle of its revolutions. And the world would have fallen into utter anarchy and darkness, but that there were found poets among the authors of the Christian and Chivalric systems of manners and religion, who created forms of opinion and action never before conceived; which, copied into the imaginations of men, became as generals to the bewildered armies of their thoughts. It is foreign to the present purpose to touch upon the evil produced by these systems: except that we protest, on the ground of the principles already established, that no portion of it can be imputed to the poetry they contain.

It is probable that the astonishing poetry of Moses, Job, David, Solomon, and Isaiah, had produced a great effect upon the mind of Jesus and his disciples. The scattered fragments preserved to us by the biographers of this extraordinary person, are all instinct with the

---

[8] "because they lack a sacred poet" — cf. Horace, *Odes*, IV.ix.28.

most vivid poetry. But his doctrines seem to have been quickly distorted. At a certain period after the prevalence of doctrines founded upon those promulgated by him, the three forms into which Plato had distributed the faculties of mind underwent a sort of apotheosis, and became the object of the worship of Europe. Here it is to be confessed that "Light seems to thicken," and

> "The crow makes wing to the rooky wood,
> Good things of day begin to droop and drowse,
> And night's black agents to their preys do rouse."[9]

But mark how beautiful an order has sprung from the dust and blood of this fierce chaos! how the World, as from a resurrection, balancing itself on the golden wings of knowledge and of hope, has reassumed its yet unwearied flight into the Heaven of time. Listen to the music, unheard by outward ears, which is as a ceaseless and invisible wind, nourishing its everlasting course with strength and swiftness.

The poetry in the doctrines of Jesus Christ, and the mythology and institutions of the Celtic conquerors of the Roman empire, outlived the darkness and the convulsions connected with their growth and victory, and blended themselves into a new fabric of manners and opinion. It is an error to impute the ignorance of the dark ages to the Christian doctrines or the predominance of the Celtic nations. Whatever of evil their agencies may have contained sprang from the extinction of the poetical principle, connected with the progress of despotism and superstition. Men, from causes too intricate to be here discussed, had become insensible and selfish: their own will had become feeble, and yet they were its slaves, and thence the slaves of the will of others: lust, fear, avarice, cruelty, and fraud, characterised a race amongst whom no one was to be found capable of *creating* in form, language, or institution. The moral anomalies of such a state of society are not justly to be charged upon any class of events immediately connected with them, and those events are most entitled to our approbation which could dissolve it most expeditiously. It is unfortunate for those who cannot distinguish words from thoughts, that many of these anomalies have been incorporated into our popular religion.

It was not until the eleventh century that the effects of the poetry of the Christian and Chivalric systems began to manifest themselves. The principle of equality had been discovered and applied by Plato in his Republic, as the theoretical rule of the mode in which the materials of pleasure and of power produced by the common skill and labour of human beings ought to be distributed among them. The limitations of this rule were asserted by him to be determined only by the sensibility of each, or the utility to result to all. Plato, following

9 Cf. *Macbeth* III.ii.50–53.

the doctrines of Timæus and Pythagoras, taught also a moral and intellectual system of doctrine, comprehending at once the past, the present, and the future condition of man. Jesus Christ divulged the sacred and eternal truths contained in these views to mankind, and Christianity, in its abstract purity, became the exoteric expression of the esoteric doctrines of the poetry and wisdom of antiquity. The incorporation of the Celtic nations with the exhausted population of the south, impressed upon it the figure of the poetry existing in their mythology and institutions. The result was a sum of the action and reaction of all the causes included in it; for it may be assumed as a maxim that no nation or religion can supersede any other without incorporating into itself a portion of that which it supersedes. The abolition of personal and domestic slavery, and the emancipation of women from a great part of the degrading restraints of antiquity, were among the consequences of these events.

The abolition of personal slavery is the basis of the highest political hope that it can enter into the mind of man to conceive. The freedom of women produced the poetry of sexual love. Love became a religion, the idols of whose worship were ever present. It was as if the statues of Apollo and the Muses had been endowed with life and motion, and had walked forth among their worshippers; so that earth became peopled by the inhabitants of a diviner world. The familiar appearance and proceedings of life became wonderful and heavenly; and a paradise was created as out of the wrecks of Eden. And as this creation itself is poetry, so its creators were poets; and language was the instrument of their art: "Galeotto fù il libro, e chi lo scrisse."[10] The Provençal Trouveurs, or inventors, preceded Petrarch, whose verses are as spells, which unseal the inmost enchanted fountains of the delight which is in the grief of love. It is impossible to feel them without becoming a portion of that beauty which we contemplate: it were superfluous to explain how the gentleness and the elevation of mind connected with these sacred emotions can render men more amiable, and generous and wise, and lift them out of the dull vapours of the little world of self. Dante understood the secret things of love even more than Petrarch. His *Vita Nuova* is an inexhaustible fountain of purity of sentiment and language: it is the idealised history of that period, and those intervals of his life which were dedicated to love. His apotheosis of Beatrice in Paradise, and the gradations of his own love and her loveliness, by which as by steps he feigns himself to have ascended to the throne of the Supreme Cause, is the most glorious imagination of modern poetry. The acutest critics have justly reversed the judgment of the vulgar, and the order of the great acts of the "Divine Drama," in the measure of the admiration which they accord to the Hell, Purgatory, and Paradise. The latter is a perpetual hymn

[10] "Galeotto was the book, and he who wrote it." — Dante, *Inferno* V.137.

of everlasting Love. Love, which found a worthy poet in Plato alone of all the antients, has been celebrated by a chorus of the greatest writers of the renovated world; and the music has penetrated the caverns of society, and its echoes still drown the dissonance of arms and superstition. At successive intervals, Ariosto, Tasso, Shakspeare, Spenser, Calderon, Rousseau, and the great writers of our own age, have celebrated the dominion of love, planting as it were trophies in the human mind of that sublimest victory over sensuality and force. The true relation borne to each other by the sexes into which human kind is distributed, has become less misunderstood; and if the error which confounded diversity with inequality of the powers of the two sexes has become partially recognised in the opinions and institutions of modern Europe, we owe this great benefit to the worship of which Chivalry was the law, and poets the prophets.

The poetry of Dante may be considered as the bridge thrown over the stream of time, which unites the modern and antient World. The distorted notions of invisible things which Dante and his rival Milton have idealised, are merely the mask and the mantle in which these great poets walk through eternity enveloped and disguised. It is a difficult question to determine how far they were conscious of the distinction which must have subsisted in their minds between their own creeds and that of the people. Dante at least appears to wish to mark the full extent of it by placing Riphæus, whom Virgil calls *justissimus unus*,[11] in Paradise, and observing a most heretical caprice in his distribution of rewards and punishments. And Milton's poem contains within itself a philosophical refutation of that system, of which, by a strange and natural antithesis, it has been a chief popular support. Nothing can exceed the energy and magnificence of the character of Satan as expressed in "Paradise Lost." It is a mistake to suppose that he could ever have been intended for the popular personification of evil. Implacable hate, patient cunning, and a sleepless refinement of device to inflict the extremest anguish on an enemy, these things are evil; and, although venial in a slave, are not to be forgiven in a tyrant; although redeemed by much that ennobles his defeat in one subdued, are marked by all that dishonours his conquest in the victor. Milton's Devil as a moral being is as far superior to his God, as One who perseveres in some purpose which he has conceived to be excellent in spite of adversity and torture, is to One who in the cold security of undoubted triumph inflicts the most horrible revenge upon his enemy, not from any mistaken notion of inducing him to repent of a perseverance in enmity, but with the alleged design of exasperating him to deserve new torments. Milton has so far violated the popular creed (if this shall be judged to be a violation) as to have alleged no superiority of moral virtue to his God over his Devil. And this bold neglect of a direct moral purpose is the most

11 "the most just" — *Aeneid* II.426. See *Paradiso* XX.67–126.

decisive proof of the supremacy of Milton's genius. He mingled as it were the elements of human nature as colours upon a single pallet, and arranged them in the composition of his great picture according to the laws of epic truth; that is, according to the laws of that principle by which a series of actions of the external universe and of intelligent and ethical beings is calculated to excite the sympathy of succeeding generations of mankind. The Divina Commedia and Paradise Lost have conferred upon modern mythology a systematic form; and when change and time shall have added one more superstition to the mass of those which have arisen and decayed upon the earth, commentators will be learnedly employed in elucidating the religion of ancestral Europe, only not utterly forgotten because it will have been stamped with the eternity of genius.

Homer was the first and Dante the second epic poet: that is, the second poet, the series of whose creations bore a defined and intelligible relation to the knowledge and sentiment and religion and political conditions of the age in which he lived, and of the ages which followed it: developing itself in correspondence with their development. For Lucretius had limed the wings of his swift spirit in the dregs of the sensible world; and Virgil, with a modesty that ill became his genius, had affected the fame of an imitator, even whilst he created anew all that he copied; and none among the flock of mock-birds, though their notes were sweet, Apollonius Rhodius, Quintus Calaber Smyrnæus, Nonnus, Lucan, Statius, or Claudian, have sought even to fulfil a single condition of epic truth. Milton was the third epic poet. For if the title of epic in its highest sense be refused to the Æneid, still less can it be conceded to the Orlando Furioso, the Gerusalemme Liberata, the Lusiad, or the Fairy Queen.[12]

Dante and Milton were both deeply penetrated with the antient religion of the civilised world; and its spirit exists in their poetry probably in the same proportion as its forms survived in the unreformed worship of modern Europe. The one preceded and the other followed the Reformation at almost equal intervals. Dante was the first religious reformer, and Luther surpassed him rather in the rudeness and acrimony, than in the boldness of his censures of papal usurpation. Dante was the first awakener of entranced Europe; he created a language, in itself music and persuasion, out of a chaos of inharmonious barbarisms. He was the congregator of those great spirits who presided over the resurrection of learning; the Lucifer of that starry flock which in the thirteenth century shone forth from republican Italy, as from a heaven, into the darkness of the benighted world. His very words are instinct with spirit; each is as a spark, a burning atom of inextinguishable thought; and many yet lie covered in the ashes of their birth, and pregnant with a lightning which has yet found no conductor. All high poetry is infinite; it is as the first acorn, which con-

[12] Poems by Ariosto, Tasso, Camoëns, and Spenser.

tained all oaks potentially. Veil after veil may be undrawn, and the inmost naked beauty of the meaning never exposed. A great poem is a fountain for ever overflowing with the waters of wisdom and delight; and after one person and one age has exhausted all its divine effluence which their peculiar relations enable them to share, another and yet another succeeds, and new relations are ever developed, the source of an unforeseen and an unconceived delight.

The age immediately succeeding to that of Dante, Petrarch, and Boccaccio, was characterized by a revival of painting, sculpture, music, and architecture. Chaucer caught the sacred inspiration, and the superstructure of English literature is based upon the materials of Italian invention.

But let us not be betrayed from a defence into a critical history of Poetry and its influence on Society. Be it enough to have pointed out the effects of poets, in the large and true sense of the word, upon their own and all succeeding times, and to revert to the partial instances cited as illustrations of an opinion the reverse of that attempted to be established by the Author of the Four Ages of Poetry.

But poets have been challenged to resign the civic crown to reasoners and mechanists on another plea. It is admitted that the exercise of the imagination is most delightful, but it is alleged, that that of reason is more useful. Let us examine as the grounds of this distinction, what is here meant by utility. Pleasure or good, in a general sense, is that which the consciousness of a sensitive and intelligent being seeks, and in which, when found, it acquiesces. There are two modes or degrees of pleasure, one durable, universal and permanent; the other transitory and particular. Utility may either express the means of producing the former or the latter. In the former sense, whatever strengthens and purifies the affections, enlarges the imagination, and adds spirit to sense, is useful. But the meaning in which the Author of the Four Ages of Poetry seems to have employed the word utility is the narrower one of banishing the importunity of the wants of our animal nature, the surrounding men with security of life, the dispersing the grosser delusions of superstition, and the conciliating such a degree of mutual forbearance among men as may consist with the motives of personal advantage.

Undoubtedly the promoters of utility, in this limited sense, have their appointed office in society. They follow the footsteps of poets, and copy the sketches of their creations into the book of common life. They make space, and give time. Their exertions are of the highest value, so long as they confine their administration of the concerns of the inferior powers of our nature within the limits due to the superior ones. But whilst the sceptic destroys gross superstitions, let him spare to deface, as some of the French writers have defaced, the eternal truths charactered upon the imaginations of men. Whilst the mechanist abridges, and the political economist combines, labour, let them beware that their speculations, for want of correspondence with those first principles which belong to the imagination, do not tend, as they have in modern England, to exasperate at once the extremes of luxury and want. They have exemplified the saying, "To him that hath, more shall be given; and from him that hath not, the little that he hath shall be taken away."[13] The rich have become richer, and the poor have become poorer; and the vessel of the state is driven between the Scylla and Charybdis of anarchy and despotism. Such are the effects which must ever flow from an unmitigated exercise of the calculating faculty.

It is difficult to define pleasure in its highest sense; the definition involving a number of apparent paradoxes. For, from an inexplicable defect of harmony in the constitution of human nature, the pain of the inferior is frequently connected with the pleasures of the superior portions of our being. Sorrow, terror, anguish, despair itself, are often the chosen expressions of an approximation to the highest good. Our sympathy in tragic fiction depends on this principle; tragedy delights by affording a shadow of that pleasure which exists in pain. This is the source also of the melancholy which is inseparable from the sweetest melody. The pleasure that is in sorrow is sweeter than the pleasure of pleasure itself. And hence the saying, "It is better to go to the house of mourning, than to the house of mirth."[14] Not that this highest species of pleasure is necessarily linked with pain. The delight of love and friendship, the ecstacy of the admiration of nature, the joy of the perception and still more of the creation of poetry, is often wholly unalloyed.

The production and assurance of pleasure in this highest sense is true utility. Those who produce and preserve this pleasure are Poets or poetical philosophers.

The exertions of Locke, Hume, Gibbon, Voltaire, Rousseau,[15] and their disciples, in favour of oppressed and deluded humanity, are entitled to the gratitude of mankind. Yet it is easy to calculate the degree of moral and intellectual improvement which the world would have exhibited, had they never lived. A little more nonsense would have been talked for a century or two; and perhaps a few more men, women, and children, burnt as heretics. We might not at this moment have been congratulating each other on the abolition of the Inquisition in Spain.[16] But it exceeds all imagination to conceive what would have been the moral condition of the world if neither Dante, Petrarch, Boccaccio, Chaucer, Shakspeare, Calderon, Lord Bacon, nor Milton, had ever existed; if Raphael and Michael Angelo had never been born; if the Hebrew poetry had never been translated; if a revival of the

[13] Cf. Mark 4:25.
[14] Cf. Ecclesiastes 7:2.
[15] I follow the classification adopted by the Author of the Four Ages of Poetry; but he [Rousseau] was essentially a Poet. The others, even Voltaire, were mere reasoners. [P.B.S.]
[16] In March 1820.

study of Greek literature had never taken place; if no monuments of antient sculpture had been handed down to us; and if the poetry of the religion of the antient world had been extinguished together with its belief. The human mind could never, except by the intervention of these excitements, have been awakened to the invention of the grosser sciences, and that application of analytical reasoning to the aberrations of society, which it is now attempted to exalt over the direct expression of the inventive and creative faculty itself.

We have more moral, political, and historical wisdom, than we know how to reduce into practice; we have more scientific and economical knowledge than can be accommodated to the just distribution of the produce which it multiplies. The poetry in these systems of thought, is concealed by the accumulation of facts and calculating processes. There is no want of knowledge respecting what is wisest and best in morals, government, and political economy, or at least what is wiser and better than what men now practise and endure. But we let *"I dare not* wait upon *I would,* like the poor cat i' the adage."[17] We want the creative faculty to imagine that which we know; we want the generous impulse to act that which we imagine; we want the poetry of life: our calculations have outrun conception; we have eaten more than we can digest. The cultivation of those sciences which have enlarged the limits of the empire of man over the external world, has, for want of the poetical faculty, proportionally circumscribed those of the internal world; and man, having enslaved the elements, remains himself a slave. To what but a cultivation of the mechanical arts in a degree disproportioned to the presence of the creative faculty, which is the basis of all knowledge, is to be attributed the abuse of all invention for abridging and combining labour, to the exasperation of the inequality of mankind? From what other cause has it arisen that these inventions which should have lightened, have added a weight to the curse imposed on Adam? Thus Poetry, and the principle of Self, of which Money is the visible incarnation, are the God and Mammon of the world.

The functions of the poetical faculty are twofold; by one it creates new materials for knowledge, and power and pleasure; by the other it engenders in the mind a desire to reproduce and arrange them according to a certain rhythm and order which may be called the beautiful and the good. The cultivation of poetry is never more to be desired than at periods when, from an excess of the selfish and calculating principle, the accumulation of the materials of external life exceed the quantity of the power of assimilating them to the internal laws of human nature. The body has then become too unwieldy for that which animates it.

Poetry is indeed something divine. It is at once the centre and circumference of knowledge; it is that which comprehends all science,

[17] *Macbeth* I.vii.44–45.

and that to which all science must be referred. It is at the same time the root and blossom of all other systems of thought; it is that from which all spring, and that which adorns all; and that which, if blighted, denies the fruit and the seed, and withholds from the barren world the nourishment and the succession of the scions of the tree of life. It is the perfect and consummate surface and bloom of things; it is as the odour and the colour of the rose to the texture of the elements which compose it, as the form and the splendour of unfaded beauty to the secrets of anatomy and corruption. What were Virtue, Love, Patriotism, Friendship — what were the scenery of this beautiful Universe which we inhabit; what were our consolations on this side of the grave, and what were our aspirations beyond it, if poetry did not ascend to bring light and fire from those eternal regions where the owl-winged faculty of calculation dare not ever soar? Poetry is not like reasoning, a power to be exerted according to the determination of the will. A man cannot say, "I will compose poetry." The greatest poet even cannot say it: for the mind in creation is as a fading coal, which some invisible influence, like an inconstant wind, awakens to transitory brightness: this power arises from within, like the colour of a flower which fades and changes as it is developed, and the conscious portions of our natures are unprophetic either of its approach or its departure. Could this influence be durable in its original purity and force, it is impossible to predict the greatness of the results; but when composition begins, inspiration is already on the decline, and the most glorious poetry that has ever been communicated to the world is probably a feeble shadow of the original conception of the Poet. I appeal to the great poets of the present day, whether it be not an error to assert that the finest passages of poetry are produced by labour and study. The toil and the delay recommended by critics, can be justly interpreted to mean no more than a careful observation of the inspired moments, and an artificial connexion of the spaces between their suggestions by the intertexture of conventional expressions; a necessity only imposed by the limitedness of the poetical faculty itself: for Milton conceived the Paradise Lost as a whole before he executed it in portions. We have his own authority also for the muse having "dictated" to him the "unpremeditated song."[18] And let this be an answer to those who would allege the fifty-six various readings of the first line of the Orlando Furioso. Compositions so produced are to poetry what mosaic is to painting. This instinct and intuition of the poetical faculty is still more observable in the plastic and pictorial arts: a great statue or picture grows under the power of the artist as a child in the mother's womb; and the very mind which directs the hands in formation, is incapable of accounting to itself for the origin, the gradations, or the media of the process.

Poetry is the record of the best and happiest moments of the hap-

[18] Cf. *Paradise Lost* IX.21–26.

piest and best minds. We are aware of evanescent visitations of thought and feeling, sometimes associated with place or person, sometimes regarding our own mind alone, and always arising unforeseen and departing unbidden, but elevating and delightful beyond all expression: so that even in the desire and the regret they leave, there cannot but be pleasure, participating as it does in the nature of its object. It is as it were the interpenetration of a diviner nature through our own; but its footsteps are like those of a wind over a sea, which the coming calm erases, and whose traces remain only, as on the wrinkled sand which paves it. These and corresponding conditions of being are experienced principally by those of the most delicate sensibility and the most enlarged imagination; and the state of mind produced by them is at war with every base desire. The enthusiasm of virtue, love, patriotism, and friendship, is essentially linked with these emotions; and whilst they last, self appears as what it is, an atom to a Universe. Poets are not only subject to these experiences as spirits of the most refined organisation, but they can colour all that they combine with the evanescent hues of this ethereal world; a word, or a trait in the representation of a scene or a passion, will touch the enchanted chord, and reanimate, in those who have ever experienced these emotions, the sleeping, the cold, the buried image of the past. Poetry thus makes immortal all that is best and most beautiful in the world; it arrests the vanishing apparitions which haunt the interlunations of life, and veiling them, or in language or in form, sends them forth among mankind, bearing sweet news of kindred joy to those with whom their sisters abide — abide, because there is no portal of expression from the caverns of the spirit which they inhabit into the universe of things. Poetry redeems from decay the visitations of the divinity in Man.

Poetry turns all things to loveliness; it exalts the beauty of that which is most beautiful, and it adds beauty to that which is most deformed; it marries exultation and horror, grief and pleasure, eternity and change; it subdues to union under its light yoke, all irreconcilable things. It transmutes all that it touches, and every form moving within the radiance of its presence is changed by wondrous sympathy to an incarnation of the spirit which it breathes: its secret alchemy turns to potable gold the poisonous waters which flow from death through life; it strips the veil of familiarity from the world, and lays bare the naked and sleeping beauty, which is the spirit of its forms.

All things exist as they are perceived; at least in relation to the percipient. "The mind is its own place, and of itself can make a Heaven of Hell, a Hell of Heaven,"[19] But poetry defeats the curse which binds us to be subjected to the accident of surrounding impressions. And whether it spreads its own figured curtain, or with-

[19] *Paradise Lost* I.254–255.

draws life's dark veil from before the scene of things, it equally creates for us a being within our being. It makes us the inhabitants of a world to which the familiar world is a chaos. It reproduces the common Universe of which we are portions and percipients, and it purges from our inward sight the film of familiarity which obscures from us the wonder of our being. It compels us to feel that which we perceive, and to imagine that which we know. It creates anew the universe, after it has been annihilated in our minds by the recurrence of impressions blunted by reiteration. It justifies that bold and true word of Tasso: *Non merita nome di creatore, se non Iddio ed il Poeta.*[20]

A poet, as he is the author to others of the highest wisdom, pleasure, virtue and glory, so he ought personally to be the happiest, the best, the wisest, and the most illustrious of men. As to his glory, let Time be challenged to declare whether the fame of any other institutor of human life be comparable to that of a poet. That he is the wisest, the happiest, and the best, inasmuch as he is a poet, is equally incontrovertible: the greatest Poets have been men of the most spotless virtue, of the most consummate prudence, and, if we would look into the interior of their lives, the most fortunate of men: and the exceptions, as they regard those who possessed the imaginative faculty in a high yet inferior degree, will be found on consideration to confirm[21] rather than destroy the rule. Let us for a moment stoop to the arbitration of popular breath, and usurping and uniting in our own persons the incompatible characters of accuser, witness, judge and executioner, let us without trial, testimony, or form, determine that certain motives of those who are "there sitting where we dare not soar," are reprehensible.[22] Let us assume that Homer was a drunkard, that Virgil was a flatterer, that Horace was a coward, that Tasso was a madman, that Lord Bacon was a peculator, that Raphael was a libertine, that Spenser was a poet laureate. It is inconsistent with this division of our subject to cite living poets, but Posterity has done ample justice to the great names now referred to. Their errors have been weighed and found to have been dust in the balance; if their sins were as scarlet, they are now white as snow: they have been washed in the blood of the mediator and redeemer, Time. Observe in what a ludicrous chaos the imputations of real or fictitious crime have been confused in the contemporary calumnies against poetry and poets; consider how little is, as it appears — or appears, as it is; look to your own motives, and judge not, lest ye be judged.[23]

Poetry, as has been said, in this respect differs from logic, that it is not subject to the controul of the active powers of the mind, and

[20] "None merits the name of creator except the Deity and the poet."
[21] confirm: confine *in 1840 edition and afterward.*
[22] Cf. *Paradise Lost* IV. 829.
[23] Shelley paraphrases Daniel 5:27; Isaiah 1:18, 40:15; Revelations 7:14; Hebrews 9:15, 12:24; Matthew 7:1.

that its birth and recurrence has no necessary connexion with consciousness or will. It is presumptuous to determine that these are the necessary conditions of all mental causation, when mental effects are experienced insusceptible of being referred to them. The frequent recurrence of the poetical power, it is obvious to suppose, may produce in the mind an habit of order and harmony correlative with its own nature and with its effects upon other minds. But in the intervals of inspiration, and they may be frequent without being durable, a Poet becomes a man, and is abandoned to the sudden reflux of the influences under which others habitually live. But as he is more delicately organized than other men, and sensible to pain and pleasure, both his own and that of others, in a degree unknown to them, he will avoid the one and pursue the other with an ardour proportioned to this difference. And he renders himself obnoxious to calumny, when he neglects to observe the circumstances under which these objects of universal pursuit and flight have disguised themselves in one another's garments.

But there is nothing necessarily evil in this error, and thus cruelty, envy, revenge, avarice, and the passions purely evil, have never formed any portion of the popular imputations on the lives of poets.

I have thought it most favourable to the cause of truth to set down these remarks according to the order in which they were suggested to my mind, by a consideration of the subject itself, instead of following that of the treatise that excited me to make them public. Thus although devoid of the formality of a polemical reply; if the view they contain be just, they will be found to involve a refutation of the doctrines of the Four Ages of Poetry, so far at least as regards the first division of the subject. I can readily conjecture what should have moved the gall of the learned and intelligent author of that paper; I confess myself, like him, unwilling to be stunned by the Theseids of the hoarse Codri of the day. Bavius and Mævius undoubtedly are, as they ever were, insufferable persons.[24] But it belongs to a philosophical critic to distinguish rather than confound.

The first part of these remarks has related to Poetry in its elements and principles; and it has been shewn, as well as the narrow limits assigned them would permit, that what is called poetry, in a restricted sense, has a common source with all other forms of order and of beauty, according to which the materials of human life are susceptible of being arranged, and which is Poetry in an universal sense.

The second part will have for its object an application of these principles to the present state of the cultivation of Poetry, and a defence of the attempt to idealize the modern forms of manners and opinions, and compel them into a subordination to the imaginative and creative faculty. For the literature of England, an energetic devel-

[24] Codrus, Bavius, Mævius: poetasters satirized in Juvenal, *Satires* I.1–2; Virgil, *Eclogues* III.90–91; Horace, *Epodes* X.

opment of which has ever preceded or accompanied a great and free development of the national will, has arisen as it were from a new birth. In spite of the low-thoughted envy which would undervalue contemporary merit, our own will be a memorable age in intellectual achievements, and we live among such philosophers and poets as surpass beyond comparison any who have appeared since the last national struggle for civil and religious liberty. The most unfailing herald, companion, and follower of the awakening of a great people to work a beneficial change in opinion or institution, is Poetry. At such periods there is an accumulation of the power of communicating and receiving intense and impassioned conceptions respecting man and nature. The persons in whom this power resides, may often as far as regards many portions of their nature, have little apparent correspondence with that spirit of good of which they are the ministers. But even whilst they deny and abjure, they are yet compelled to serve, the Power which is seated on the throne of their own soul. It is impossible to read the compositions of the most celebrated writers of the present day without being startled with the electric life which burns within their words. They measure the circumference and sound the depths of human nature with a comprehensive and all-penetrating spirit, and they are themselves perhaps the most sincerely astonished at its manifestations; for it is less their spirit than the spirit of the age. Poets are the hierophants of an unapprehended inspiration; the mirrors of the gigantic shadows which futurity casts upon the present; the words which express what they understand not; the trumpets which sing to battle, and feel not what they inspire; the influence which is moved not, but moves. Poets are the unacknowledged legislators of the world.

John Keats

JOHN KEATS

CHRONOLOGY

1795   Born October 31 at the Swan and Hoop Livery Stables, London, to the head ostler and the daughter of the owner.

1803–11   Attended Clarke's school at Enfield.

1809   Became a passionate reader of poetry, with Charles Cowden Clarke (son of the schoolmaster) as guide.

1810   July, the four Keats children, as orphans, placed by their grandmother under a trust fund, with Richard Abbey, a tea-merchant, as principal guardian.

1811   Summer, apprenticed to a surgeon in nearby Edmonton.

1815   Came under the influence of Leigh Hunt, who published several of Keats's early poems in *Examiner*. October 1, began medical course at Guy's Hospital, London.

1816   July 25, certified to practice as apothecary, physician, and surgeon.

1817   March 3, *Poems*. Frequently with Haydon, Hunt, the Shelleys, and (probably) Hazlitt; met Lamb and Wordsworth. December 21 (and January 4, 1818), three theatrical critiques in the *Champion*, for J. H. Reynolds.

1818   February, attended lectures by Hazlitt. April 27 (?), *Endymion: A Poetic Romance*. June–August, walked and climbed in Lake District, Scotland, and Ireland. By December, fell in love with Fanny Brawne, aged 18.

1819   Wrote his great odes and narrative poems. Began revising "Hyperion" into "The Fall of Hyperion: A Vision."

1820   About July 1, *Lamia, Isabella, The Eve of St. Agnes, and Other Poems*. Doomed by tuberculosis, sailed September 18 for Italy.

1821   Died February 23 in Rome.

Letters

◖ In *The Use of Poetry and the Use of Criticism*, T. S. Eliot called the letters of John Keats "the most important ever written by an English poet." They are, he said, "what letters ought to be." Thoughts arose too rapidly for Keats to notice spelling, punctuation, or grammar. Most of the letters, despite their headlong informality, deserve formal designations, such as Letter on Negative Capability, On Essential Beauty, On Palpable Design, Chamber of Maiden Thought, Breakfast of Robins, Egotistical Sublime, Pouncing Rhymes, Vale of Soul-Making. Treasured by their first recipients and by later collectors, the letters have had the good fortune of a definitive edition by Hyder Rollins. ◗

TO BENJAMIN ROBERT HAYDON

[10–11 May 1817]
Margate Saturday Eve

My dear Haydon,

> Let Fame, which all hunt after in their Lives,
> Live register'd upon our brazen tombs,
> And so grace us in the disgrace of death:
> When spite of cormorant devouring time
> The endeavour of this pre⟨a⟩sent breath may buy
> That Honor which shall bate his Scythe's keen edge
> And make us heirs of all eternity.[1]

To think that I have no right to couple myself with you in this speech would be death to me so I have e'en written it — and I pray God that our brazen Tombs be nigh neighbors. It cannot be long first the endeavor of this present breath will soon be over — and yet it is as well to breathe freely during our sojourn — it is as well if you have not been teased with that Money affair — that bill-pestilence. However I must think that difficulties nerve the Spirit of a Man — they make our Prime Objects a Refuge as well as a Passion. The Trumpet of Fame is as a tower of Strength the ambitious bloweth it and is safe — I suppose by your telling me not to give way to fore-

[1] *Love's Labor's Lost* I.i.1–7. Both the texts of the letters and these notes are based on Rollins, largely by way of Douglas Bush's volume of selections from Keats in the Riverside series. Canceled words and letters are here enclosed in shaped brackets(⟨⟩); editorial insertions are enclosed in square brackets ([]).

bodings George has mentioned to you what I have lately said in my
Letters to him — truth is I have been in such a state of Mind as to
read over my Lines and hate them. I am "one that gathers Samphire
dreadful trade"[2] the Cliff of Poesy Towers above me — yet when, Tom
who meets with some of Pope's Homer in Plutarch's Lives reads some
of those to me they seem like Mice[3] to mine. I read and write about
eight hours a day. There is an old saying well begun is half done" —
't is a bad one. I would use instead — Not begun at all 'till half done"
so according to that I have not begun my Poem and consequently
(a priori) can say nothing about it. Thank God! I do begin arduously
where I leave off, nothwithstanding occasional depressions: and I hope
for the support of a High Power while I clime this little eminence and
especially in my Years of more momentous Labor. I remember your
saying that you had notions of a good Genius presiding over you —
I have of late had the same thought. for things which [I] do half at
Random are afterwards confirmed by my judgment in a dozen features
of Propriety — Is it too daring to Fancy Shakspeare this Presider?
When in the Isle of W⟨h⟩ight I met with a Shakspeare in the Passage
of the House at which I lodged — it comes nearer to my idea of him
than any I have seen — I was but there a Week yet the old Woman
made me take it with me though I went off in a hurry — Do you not
think this is ominous of good? I am glad you say every Man of great
Views is at times tormented as I am —
    Sunday Aft. This Morning I received a letter from George by which
it appears that Money Troubles are to follow us up for some time to
come perhaps for always — these vexations are a great hindrance to
one — they are not like Envy and detraction stimulants to further
exertion as being immediately relative and reflected on at the same
time with the prime object — but rather like a nettle leaf or two in
your bed. So now I revoke my Promise of finishing my Poem by the
Autumn which I should have done had I gone on as I have done —
but I cannot write while my spirit is fe⟨a⟩vered in a contrary direction
and I am now sure of having plenty of it this Summer — At this moment I am in no enviable Situation — I feel that I am not in a Mood
to write any to day; and it appears that the lo⟨o⟩ss of it is the beginning of all sorts of irregularities. I am extremely glad that a time
must come when every thing will leave not a wrack behind.[4] You tell
me never to despair — I wish it was as easy for me to observe the
saying — truth is I have a horrid Morbidity of Temperament which
has shown itself at intervals — it is I have no doubt the greatest
Enemy and stumbling block I have to fear — I may even say that it
is likely to be the cause of my disappointment. How ever every ill
has its share of good — this very bane would at any time enable me

---

[2] *King Lear* IV.vi.15.
[3] *Ibid.*, IV.vi.18.
[4] *The Tempest* IV.i.155–156.

to look with an obstinate eye on the Devil Himself — ay to be as proud of being the lowest of the human race as Alfred could be in being of the highest. I feel confident I should have been a rebel Angel had the opportunity been mine. I am very sure that you do love me as your own Brother — I have seen it in your continual anxiety for me — and I assure you that your wellfare and fame is and will be a chief pleasure to me all my Life. I know no one but you who can be fully sensible of the turmoil and anxiety, the sacrifice of all what is called comfort the readiness to Measure time by what is done and to die in 6 hours could plans be brought to conclusions. — the looking upon the Sun the Moon the Stars, the Earth and its contents as materials to form greater things — that is to say ethereal things — but here I am talking like a Madman greater things that [*for* than] our Creator himself made!! I wrote to Hunt yesterday — scar[c]ely know what I said in it — I could not talk about Poetry in the way I should have liked for I was not in humor with either his or mine. His self delusions are very lamentable they have inticed him into a Situation which I should be less eager after than that of a galley Slave — what you observe thereon is very true must be in time. Perhaps it is a self delusion to say so — but I think I could not be be dece[i]ved in the Manner that Hunt is — may I die tomorrow if I am to be. There is no greater Sin after the 7 deadly than to flatter oneself into an idea of being a great Poet — or one of those beings who are privileged to wear out their Lives in the pursuit of Honor — how comfortable a feel it is that such a Crime must bring its heavy Penalty? That if one be a Self-deluder accounts will be balanced? I am glad you are hard at Work — 't will now soon be done — I long to see Wordsworth's as well as to have mine in:[5] but I would rather not show my face in Town till the end of the Year — if that will be time enough — if not I shall be disappointed if you do not write for me even when you think best — I never quite despair and I read Shakspeare — indeed I shall I think never read any other Book much — Now this might lead me into a long Confab but I desist. I am very near Agreeing with Hazlit that Shakspeare is enough for us — By the by what a tremendous Southean Article his last was — I wish he had left out "grey hairs"[6]

    ❋   ❋   ❋   ❋   ❋   ❋

So now in the Name of Shakespeare Raphael and all our Saints I commend you to the care of heaven!

Your everlasting friend
John Keats —

[5] *I.e.*, his head painted into Haydon's *Christ's Entry into Jerusalem;* see p. 595.

[6] Hazlitt reviewed Southey's *Letter to William Smith* in the *Examiner,* May 4, 11, and 18.

TO BENJAMIN BAILEY

[8 October 1817]
Hamps[t]ead Octr Wednesday

My dear Bailey,

. . . I am quite disgusted with literary Men and will never know
another except Wordsworth — no not even Byron — Here is an in-
stance of the friendships of such — Haydon and Hunt have known
each other many years — now they live pour ainsi dire[1] jealous
Neighbours. Haydon says to me Keats dont show your Lines to Hunt
on any account or he will have done half for you — so it appears
Hunt wishes it to be thought. When he met Reynolds in the Theatre
John told him that I was getting on to the completion of 4000 Lines.
Ah! says Hunt, had it not been for me they would have been 7000!
If he will say this to Reynolds what would he to other People?
Haydon received a Letter a little while back on this subject from some
Lady — which contains a caution to me through him on this subject
— Now is not all this a most paultry thing to think about? You may
see the whole of the case by the following extract from a Letter I
wrote to George in the spring "As to what you say about my being a
Poet, I can retu[r]n no answer but by saying that the high Idea I
have of poetical fame makes me think I see it towering to high above
me. At any rate I have no right to talk until Endymion is finished —
it will be a test, a trial of my Powers of Imagination and chiefly of
my invention which is a rare thing indeed — by which I must make
4000 Lines of one bare circumstance and fill them with Poetry; and
when I consider that this is a great task, and that when done it will
take me but a dozen paces towards the Temple of Fame — it makes
me say — God forbid that I should be without such a task! I have
heard Hunt say and may be asked — why endeavour after a long
Poem? To which I should answer — Do not the Lovers of Poetry like
to have a little Region to wander in where they may pick and choose,
and in which the images are so numerous that many are forgotten and
found new in a second Reading: which may be food for a Week's
stroll in the Summer? Do not they like this better than what they
can read through before Mrs Williams comes down stairs? a Morning
work at most. Besides a long Poem is a test of Invention which I
take to be the Polar Star of Poetry, as Fancy is the Sails, and Imagination the Rudder. Did our great Poets ever write short Pieces? I
mean in the shape of Tales — This same invention seems indeed of

[1] so to say.

late Years to have been forgotten as a Poetical excellence. But enough
of this, I put on no Laurels till I shall have finished Endymion, and
I hope Apollo is not angered at my having made a Mockery at him
at Hunt's" You see Bailey how independant my writing has been —
Hunts dissuasion was of no avail — I refused to visit Shelley, that I
might have my own unfetterd scope — and after all I shall have the
Reputation of Hunt's elevé — His corrections and amputations will
by the knowing ones be trased in the Poem — This is to be sure the
vexation of a day — nor would I say so many Words about it to any
but those whom I know to have my wellfare and Reputation at
Heart . . .

> your sincere friend & brother
> John Keats

TO BENJAMIN BAILEY

[22 November 1817]

My dear Bailey,
    I will get over the first part of this (*un*said) Letter as soon as pos-
sible for it relates to the affair of poor Crips — To a Man of your
nature, such a Letter as Haydon's must have been extremely cutting —
What occasions the greater part of the World's Quarrels? simply this,
two Minds meet and do not understand each other time enough to
p[r]aevent any shock or surprise at the conduct of either party — As
soon as I had known Haydon three days I had got enough of his
character not to have been surp[r]ised at such a Letter as he has hurt
you with. Nor when I knew it was it a principle with me to drop his
acquaintance although with you it would have been an imperious
feeling. I wish you knew all that I think about Genius and the Heart
— and yet I think you are thoroughly acquainted with my innermost
breast in that respect or you could not have known me even thus long
and still hold me worthy to be your dear friend. In passing however
I must say of one thing that has pressed upon me lately and encreased
my Humility and capability of submission and that is this truth — Men
of Genius are great as certain ethereal Chemicals operating on the
Mass of neutral intellect — by [*for* but] they have not any individuality, any determined Character. I would call the top and head of those
who have a proper self Men of Power —
    But I am running my head into a Subject which I am certain I
could not do justice to under five years s[t]udy and 3 vols octavo —
and moreover long to be talking about the Imagination — so my dear
Bailey do not think of this unpleasant affair if possible — do not —
I defy any ha[r]m to come of it — I defy — I'll shall write to Crips

this Week and reque[s]t him to tell me all his goings on from time
to time by Letter whererever I may be — it will all go on well —
so dont because you have suddenly discover'd a Coldness in Haydon
suffer yourself to be teased. Do not my dear fellow. O I wish I was as
certain of the end of all your troubles as that of your momentary
start about the authenticity of the Imagination. I am certain of
nothing but of the holiness of the Heart's affections and the truth of
Imagination — What the imagination seizes as Beauty must be truth
— whether it existed before or not — for I have the same Idea of all
our Passions as of Love they are all in their sublime, creative of
essential Beauty — In a Word, you may know my favorite Speculation by my first Book and the little song I sent in my last[1] — which
is a representation from the fancy of the probable mode of operating
in these Matters — The Imagination may be compared to Adam's
dream[2] — he awoke and found it truth. I am the more zealous in this
affair, because I have never yet been able to perceive how any
thing can be known for truth by consequitive reasoning — and yet it
must be — Can it be that even the greatest Philosopher ever ⟨when⟩
arrived at his goal without putting aside numerous objections — However it may be, O for a Life of Sensations rather than of Thoughts!
It is 'a Vision in the form of Youth' a Shadow of reality to come —
and this consideration has further conv[i]nced me for it has come as
auxiliary to another favorite Speculation of mine, that we shall enjoy
ourselves here after by having what we called happiness on Earth
repeated in a finer tone and so repeated — And yet such a fate can
only befall those who delight in sensation rather than hunger as you
do after Truth — Adam's dream will do here and seems to be a conviction that Imagination and its empyreal reflection is the same as
human Life and its spiritual repetition. But as I was saying — the
simple imaginative Mind may have its rewards in the repeti[ti]on of
its own silent Working coming continually on the spirit with a fine
suddenness — to compare great things with small — have you never
by being surprised with an old Melody — in a delicious place — by
a delicious voice, fe[l]t over again your very speculations and surmises
at the time it first operated on your soul — do you not remember
forming to yourself the singer's face more beautiful that [for than]
it was possible and yet with the elevation of the Moment you did not
think so — even then you were mounted on the Wings of Imagination so high — that the Prototype must be here after — that delicious
face you will see — What a time! I am continually running away from
the subject — sure this cannot be exactly the case with a complex
Mind — one that is imaginative and at the same time careful of its
fruits — who would exist partly on sensation partly on thought — to

[1] *Endymion* I; "Ode to Sorrow."
[2] *Paradise Lost* VIII.460–490.

whom it is necessary that years should bring the philosophic Mind[3]
— such an one I consider your's and therefore it is necessary to your
eternal Happiness that you not only ⟨have⟩ drink this old Wine of
Heaven which I shall call the redigestion of our most ethereal Musings
on Earth; but also increase in knowledge and know all things. I am
glad to hear you are in a fair Way for Easter — you will soon get
through your unpleasant reading and then! — but the world is full
of troubles and I have not much reason to think myself pesterd with
many — I think Jane or Marianne has a better opinion of me than I
deserve — for really and truly I do not think my Brothers illness connected with mine — you know more of the real Cause than they do —
nor have I any chance of being rack'd as you have been — you perhaps
at one time thought there was such a thing as Worldly Happiness to
be arrived at, at certain periods of time marked out — you have of
necessity from your disposition been thus led away — I scarcely remember counting upon any Happiness — I look not for it if it be not
in the present hour — nothing startles me beyond the Moment. The
setting sun will always set me to rights — of if a Sparrow come before
my Window I take part in its existince and pick about the Gravel.
The first thing that strikes me on hea[r]ing a Misfortune having be-
falled another is this. 'Well it cannot be helped. — he will have the
pleasure of trying the resourses of his spirit, and I beg now my dear
Bailey that hereafter should you observe any thing cold in me not
to but [*for* put] it to the account of heartlessness but abstraction —
for I assure you I sometimes feel not the influence of a Passion or Affection during a whole week — and so long this sometimes continues
I begin to suspect myself and the genui[ne]ness of my feelings at
other times — thinking them a few barren Tragedy-tears — My
Brother Tom is much improved — he is going to Devonshire —
whither I shall follow him — at present I am just arrived at Dorking
to change the Scene — change the Air and give me a spur to wind
up my Poem, of which there are wanting 500 Lines. I should have
been here a day sooner but the Reynoldses persuaded me to spop [*for*
stop] in Town to meet your friend Christie — There were Rice and
Martin — we talked about Ghosts — I will have some talk with Taylor
and let you know — when please God I come down a[t] Christmas —
I will find that Examiner if possible. My best regards to Gleig. My
Brothers to you and Mrs Bentley['s]

Your affectionate friend
John Keats —

I want to say much more to you — a few hints will set me going
Direct Burford Bridge near dorking

---

[3] Wordsworth, *Intimations of Immortality* 190.

TO GEORGE AND THOMAS KEATS

[21, 27 (?) December 1817]
Hampstead Sunday

My dear Brothers

I must crave your pardon for not having written ere this. ***
I saw Kean return to the public in Richard III, & finely he did it,
& at the request of Reynolds I went to criticise his Luke in Riches
— the critique is in todays champion, which I send you with the
Examiner in which you will find very proper lamentation on the obso-
letion of christmas Gambols & pastimes: but it was mixed up with so
much egotism of that drivelling nature that pleasure is entirely lost.
Hone the publisher's trial, you must find very amusing; & as Englishmen very ⟨amusing⟩ encouraging — his *Not Guilty* is a thing, which not
to have been, would have dulled still more Liberty's Emblazoning —
Lord Ellenborough has been paid in his own coin — Wooler & Hone
have done us an essential service[1] — I have had two very pleasant
evenings with Dilke yesterday & today; & am at this moment just come
from him & feel in the humour to go on with this, began in the morning, & from which he came to fetch me. I spent Friday evening with
Wells & went the next morning to see *Death on the Pale horse*. It
is a wonderful picture, when West's[2] age is considered; But there
is nothing to be intense upon; no women one feels mad to kiss; no
face swelling into reality. the excellence of every Art is its intensity,
capable of making all disagreeables evaporate, from their being in
close relationship with Beauty & Truth — Examine King Lear & you
will find this examplified throughout; but in this picture we have
unpleasantness without any momentous depth of speculation excited,
in which to bury its repulsiveness — The picture is larger than Christ
rejected — I dined with Haydon the sunday after you left, & had a
very pleasant day, I dined too (for I have been out too much lately)
with Horace Smith & met his two Brothers with Hill & Kingston & one
Du Bois, they only served to convince me, how superior humour is to
wit in respect to enjoyment — These men say things which make one
start, without making one feel, they are all alike; their manners are
alike; they all know fashionables; they have a mannerism in their very
eating & drinking, in their mere handling a Decanter — They talked
of Kean & his low company — Would I were with that company
instead of yours said I to myself! I know such like acquaintance will

---

[1] As judge in trials for libel, Ellenborough had dealt harshly with John
and Leigh Hunt; William Hone (tried under Ellenborough) and Thomas
Wooler won acquittals.
[2] Benjamin West (1738–1820).

never do for me & yet I am going to Reynolds, on wednesday —
Brown & Dilke walked with me & back from the Christmas pantomime.
I had not a dispute but a disquisition with Dilke, on various subjects;
several things dovetailed in my mind, & at once it struck me, what
quality went to form a Man of Achievement especially in Literature
& which Shakespeare posessed so enormously — I mean *Negative
Capability*, that is when man is capable of being in uncertainties,
Mysteries, doubts, without any irritable reaching after fact & reason —
Coleridge, for instance, would let go by a fine isolated verisimilitude
caught from the Penetralium of mystery, from being incapable of remaining content with half knowledge. This pursued through Volumes
would perhaps take us no further than this, that with a great poet the
sense of Beauty overcomes every other consideration, or rather obliter-
ates all consideration.

Shelley's poem is out, & there are words about its being objected too,
as much as Queen Mab was. Poor Shelley I think he has his Quota of
good qualities, in sooth la!! Write soon to your most sincere friend &
affectionate Brother.

John

TO BENJAMIN BAILEY

Friday Jany 23rd [1818]

My dear Bailey,

Twelve days have pass'd since your last reached me — what has
gone through the myriads of human Minds since the 12th we talk of
the immense number of Books, the Volumes ranged thousands by
thousands — but perhaps more goes through the human intelligence
in 12 days than ever was written. How has that unfortunate Family
lived through the twelve? One saying of your's I shall never forget —
you may not recollect it — it being perhaps said when you were looking on the surface and seeming of Humanity alone, without a thought
of the past or the future — or the deeps of good and evil — you were
at the moment estranged from speculation and I think you have arguments ready for the Man who would utter it to you — this is a formidable preface for a simple thing — merely you said; *"Why should
Woman suffer?"* Aye. Why should she? 'By heavens I'd coin my very
Soul and drop my Blood for Drachmas"![1]. These things are, and he who
feels how incompetent the most skyey Knight errantry its [*for is*] to
heal this bruised fairness is like a sensitive leaf on the hot hand of
thought. Your tearing, my dear friend, a spiritless and gloomy Letter

---

[1] *Julius Caesar* IV.iii.72–73.

up ⟨and⟩ to rewrite to me is what I shall never forget — it was to me a real thing. Things have happen'd lately of great Perplexity — You must have heard of them — Reynolds and Haydon retorting and re-crimminating — and parting for ever — the same thing has happened between Haydon and Hunt — It is unfortunate — Men should bear with each other — there lives not the Man who may not be cut up, aye hashed to pieces on his weakest side. The best of Men have but a por-tion of good in them — a kind of spiritual yeast in their frames which creates the ferment of existence — by which a Man is propell'd to act and strive and buffet with Circumstance. The sure way Bailey, is first to know a Man's faults, and then be passive, if after that he insensibly draws you towards him then you have no Power to break the link. Before I felt interested in either Reynolds or Haydon — I was well read in their faults yet knowing them I have been cementing gradually with both — I have an affection for them both for reasons almost op-posite — and to both must I of necessity cling — supported always by the hope that when a little time — a few years shall have tried me more fully in their esteem I may be able to bring them together — the time must come because they have both hearts — and they will recol-lect the best parts of each other when this gust is overblown.

*   *   *   *   *

. . . My Brother Tom is getting stronger but his Spitting of blood continues — I sat down to read King Lear yesterday, and felt the greatness of the thing up to the writing of a Sonnet preparatory thereto — in my next you shall have it. There were some miserable reports of Rice's health — I went and lo! Master Jemmy had been to the play the night before and was out at the time — he always comes on his Legs like a Cat — I have seen a good deal of Wordsworth. Hazlitt is lectu[r]ing on Poetry at the Surr[e]y institution — I shall be there next Tuesday.

Your most affectionate Friend
John Keats —

TO JOHN HAMILTON REYNOLDS

[3 February 1818]
Hampstead Tuesday.

My dear Reynolds,

I thank you for your dish of Filberts — Would I could get a basket of them by way of des[s]ert every day for the sum of two pence — Would we were a sort of ethereal Pigs, & turn'd loose to feed upon spiritual Mast & Acorns — which would be merely being a squirrel

& feed[ing] upon filberts. for what is a squirrel but an airy pig, or a filbert but a sort of archangelical acorn. About the nuts being worth cracking, all I can say is that where there are a throng of delightful Images ready drawn simplicity is the only thing. the first is the best on account of the first line, and the "arrow — foil'd of its antler'd food" — and moreover (and this is the only ⟨only⟩ word or two I find fault with, the more because I have had so much reason to shun it as a quicksand) the last has "tender and true" — We must cut this, and not be rattle-snaked into any more of the like — It may be said that we ought to read our Contemporaries. that Wordsworth &c should have their due from us. but for the sake of a few fine imaginative or domestic passages, are we to be bullied into a certain Philosophy engendered in the whims of an Egotist — Every man has his speculations, but every man does not brood and peacock over them till he makes a false coinage and deceives himself — Many a man can travel to the very bourne of Heaven, and yet want confidence to put down his halfseeing. Sancho[1] will invent a Journey heavenward as well as any body. We hate poetry that has a palpable design upon us — and if we do not agree, seems to put its hand in its breeches pocket. Poetry should be great & un-obtrusive, a thing which enters into one's soul, and does not startle it or amaze it with itself but with its subject. — How beautiful are the retired flowers! how would they lose their beauty were they to throng into the highway crying out, "admire me I am a violet! dote upon me I am a primrose! Modern poets differ from the Elizabethans in this. Each of the moderns like an Elector of Hanover governs his petty state, & knows how many straws are swept daily from the Causeways in all his dominions & has a continual itching that all the Housewives should have their coppers well scoured: the antients were ⟨Emperors of large⟩ Emperors of vast Provinces, they had only heard of the remote ones and scarcely cared to visit them. — I will cut all this — I will have no more of Wordsworth or Hunt in particular — Why should we be of the tribe of Manasseh, when we can wander with Esau? why should we kick against the Pricks, when we can walk on Roses? Why should we be owls, when we can be Eagles? Why be teased with "nice Eyed wag-tails",[2] when we have in sight "the Cherub Contemplation"?[3] — Why with Wordsworths "Matthew with a bough of wilding in his hand"[4] when we can have Jacques "under an oak &c."?[5] — The secret of the Bough of Wilding will run through your head faster than I can write it — Old Matthew spoke to him some years ago on some nothing, & be-cause he happens in an Evening Walk to imagine the figure of the old man — he must stamp it down in black & white, and it is henceforth

[1] Don Quixote's squire.
[2] Leigh Hunt, *The Nymphs* ii.170.
[3] *Il Penseroso* 54.
[4] Wordsworth, *The Two April Mornings* 57–60.
[5] *As You Like It* II.i.31.

sacred — I don't mean to deny Wordsworth's grandeur & Hunt's merit, but I mean to say we need not be teazed with grandeur & merit — when we can have them uncontaminated & unobtrusive. Let us have the old Poets, & robin Hood Your letter and its sonnets gave me more pleasure than will the 4th Book of Childe Harold & the whole of any body's life & opinions. In return for your dish of filberts, I have gathered a few Catkins, I hope they'll look pretty.

[Here follow *Robin Hood* and *Lines on the Mermaid Tavern.*]

*   *   *   *   *   *

Yr sincere friend and Coscribbler
John Keats.

TO JOHN HAMILTON REYNOLDS

[19 February 1818]

My dear Reynolds,
    I have an idea that a Man might pass a very pleasant life in this manner — let him on any certain day read a certain Page of full Poesy or distilled Prose and let him wander with it, and muse upon it, and reflect from it, and bring home to it, and prophesy upon it, and dream upon it — untill it becomes stale — but when will it do so? Never — When Man has arrived at a certain ripeness in intellect any one grand and spiritual passage serves him as a starting post towards all "the two-and-thirty Pallaces" How happy is such a "voyage of conception,' what delicious diligent Indolence! A doze upon a Sofa does not hinder it, and a nap upon Clover engenders ethereal finger-pointings — the prattle of a child gives it wings, and the converse of middle age a strength to beat them — a strain of musick conducts to 'an odd angle of the Isle'[1] and when the leaves whisper it puts a 'girdle round the earth.'[2] Nor will this sparing touch of noble Books be any irreverance to their Writers — for perhaps the honors paid by Man to Man are trifles in comparison to the Benefit done by great Works to the 'Spirit and pulse of good'[3] by their mere passive existence. Memory should not be called knowledge — Many have original minds who do not think it — they are led away by Custom — Now it appears to me that almost any Man may like the Spider spin from his own inwards his own airy Citadel — the points of leaves and twigs on which the Spider begins her work are few and she fills the Air with a beautiful circuiting: man should be content with as few points to tip with the fine Webb

[1] *The Tempest* I.ii.223.
[2] *A Midsummer Night's Dream* II.i.175.
[3] Wordsworth, *The Old Cumberland Beggar* 77.

of his Soul and weave a tapestry empyrean — full of Symbols for his
spiritual eye, of softness for his spiritual touch, of space for his wandering of distinctness for his Luxury — But the Minds of Mortals are so
different and bent on such diverse Journeys that it may at first appear
impossible for any common taste and fellowship to exist ⟨bettween⟩
between two or three under these suppositions — It is however quite
the contrary — Minds would leave each other in contrary directions,
traverse each other in Numberless points, and all [*for* at] last greet
each other at the Journeys end — An old Man and a child would talk
together and the old Man be led on his Path, and the child left thinking — Man should not dispute or assert but whisper results to his
neighbour, and thus by every germ of Spirit sucking the Sap from
mould ethereal every human might become great, and Humanity instead of being a wide heath of Furse[4] and Briars with here and there a
remote Oak or Pine, would become a grand democracy of Forest Trees.
It has been an old Comparison for our urging on — the Bee hive —
however it seems to me that we should rather be the flower than the
Bee — for it is a false notion that more is gained by receiving than
giving — no the receiver and the giver are equal in their benefits —
The f[l]ower I doubt not receives a fair guerdon from the Bee — its
leaves blush deeper in the next spring — and who shall say between
Man and Woman which is the most delighted? Now it is more noble
to sit like Jove that [*for* than] to fly like Mercury — let us not therefore go hurrying about and collecting honey-bee like, buzzing here
and there impatiently from a knowledge of what is to be arrived at:
but let us open our leaves like a flower and be passive and receptive —
budding patiently under the eye of Apollo and taking hints from every
noble insect that favors us with a visit — sap will be given us for Meat
and dew for drink — I was led into these thoughts, my dear Reynolds,
by the beauty of the morning operating on a sense of Idleness — I have
not read any Books — the Morning said I was right — I had no Idea
but of the Morning and the Thrush said I was right — seeming to
say —

[Here follows *What the Thrush Said.*]

Now I am sensible all this is a mere sophistication, however it may
neighbour to any truths, to excuse my own indolence — so I will not
deceive myself that Man should be equal with jove — but think himself very well off as a sort of scullion-Mercury or even a humble Bee —
It is not [*for* no] matter whether I am right or wrong either one way
or another, if there is sufficient to lift a little time from your Shoulders.

Your affectionate friend
John Keats —

[4] *The Tempest* I.i.68–69.

TO JOHN TAYLOR

Hampstead 27 Feby [1818] . . .

My dear Taylor,

Your alteration strikes me as being a great improvement — the page looks much better. And now I will attend to the Punctuations you speak of — the comma should be at *soberly,* and in the other passage the comma should follow *quiet,.* I am extremely indebted to you for this attention and also for your after admonitions — It is a sorry thing for me that any one should have to overcome Prejudices in reading my Verses — that affects me more than any hyper-criticism on any particular Passage. In *Endymion* I have most likely but moved into the Go-cart from the leading strings. In Poetry I have a few Axioms, and you will see how far I am from their Centre. 1st I think Poetry should surprise by a fine excess and not by Singularity — it should strike the Reader as a wording of his own highest thoughts, and appear almost a Remembrance — 2nd Its touches of Beauty should never be half way ther[e]by making the reader breathless instead of content: the rise, the progress, the setting of imagery should like the Sun come natural natural too him — shine over him and set soberly although in magnificence leaving him in the Luxury of twilight — but it is easier to think what Poetry should be than to write it — and this leads me on to another axiom. That if Poetry comes not as naturally as the Leaves to a tree it had better not come at all. However it may be with me I cannot help looking into new countries with 'O for a Muse of fire to ascend!'[1] — If Endymion serves me as a Pioneer perhaps I ought to be content. I have great reason to be content, for thank God I can read and perhaps understand Shakspeare to his depths, and I have I am sure many friends, who, if I fail, will attribute any change in my Life and Temper to Humbleness rather than to Pride — to a cowering under the Wings of great Poets rather than to a Bitterness that I am not appreciated. I am anxious to get Endymion printed that I may forget it and proceed. I have coppied the 3rd Book and have begun the 4th. On running my Eye over the Proofs — I saw one Mistake I will notice it presently and also any others if there be any — There should be no comma in 'the raft branch down sweeping from a tall Ash top' — I have besides made one or two alteration[s] and also altered the 13 Line Page 32 to make sense of it as you will see. I will take care the Printer shall not trip up my Heels — There should be no dash after

1 *Henry V*, Prologue 1.

Dryope in this Line 'Dryope's lone lulling of her Child. Remember me
to Percy Street.[2]

Your sincere and oblig[d] friend
John Keats —

P. S. You shall have a sho[r]t *Preface* in good time —

TO BENJAMIN BAILEY

[13 March 1818]
Teignmouth Friday

My dear Bailey,

❖   ❖   ❖   ❖   ❖   ❖

. . . I think it well for the honor of Brittain that Julius Caesar did
not first land in this County — A Devonshirer standing on his native
hills is not a distinct object — he does not show against the light —
a wolf or two would dispossess him. I like, I love England, I like
its strong Men — Give me a "long brown plain"[1] for my Morning [*for*
Money?] so I may meet with some of Edmond Iron side's des[c]endants
— Give me a barren mould so I may meet with some shadowing of
Alfred in the shape of a Gipsey, a Huntsman or as [*for* a] Shepherd.
Scenery is fine — but human nature is finer — The Sward is richer for
the tread of a real, nervous, english foot — the eagles nest is finer for
the Mountaineer has look'd into it — Are these facts or prejudices?
Whatever they are, for them I shall never be able to relish entirely any
devonshire scenery — Homer is very fine, Achilles is fine, Diomed is
fine, Shakspeare is fine, Hamlet is fine, Lear is fine, but dwindled
englishmen are not fine — Where too the Women are so passable,
and have such english names, such as Ophelia, Cordelia & — that they
should have such Paramours or rather Imparamours — As for them I
cannot, in thought help wishing as did the cruel Emperour,[2] that they
had but one head and I might cut it off to deliver them from any
horrible Courtesy they may do their undeserving Countrymen — I
wonder I meet with no born Monsters — O Devonshire, last night I
thought the Moon had dwindled in heaven — I have never had your
Sermon from Wordsworth but M[rs] Dilke lent it me — You know my
ideas about Religion — I do not think myself more in the right than
other people and that nothing in this world is proveable. I wish I

---

[2] *I.e.,* to friends there.
For Taylor and Hessey, his publishers, Keats corrects *Endymion*
I.149,247,335,495. The "13 Line" is unidentified.
[1] *The Tempest* I.i.68–69.
[2] Caligula (12–41 A.D.) of Rome.

could enter into all your feelings on the subject merely for one short
10 Minutes and give you a Page or two to your liking. I am sometimes so very sceptical as to think Poetry itself a mere Jack a lanthern
to amuse whoever may chance to be struck with its brilliance — As
Tradesmen say every thing is worth what it will fetch, so probably
every mental pursuit takes its reality and worth from the ardour of the
pursuer — being in itself a nothing — Ethereal thing[s] may at least
be thus real, divided under three heads — Things real — things semireal — and no things — Things real — such as existences of Sun Moon
& Stars and passages of Shakspeare — Things semireal such as Love,
the Clouds &c which require a greeting of the Spirit to make them
wholly exist — and Nothings which are made Great and dignified by
an ardent pursuit — Which by the by stamps the burgundy mark on
the bottles of our Minds, insomuch as they are able to *"consec[r]ate
whate'er they look upon"*[3] . . .

        . . . It is an old maxim of mine and of course must be well known
that eve[r]y point of thought is the centre of an intellectual world —
the two uppermost thoughts in a Man's mind are the two poles of
his World he revolves on them and every thing is southward or north-
ward to him through their means — We take but three steps from
feathers to iron. Now my dear fellow I must once for all tell you I
have not one Idea of the truth of any of my speculations — I shall
never be a Reasoner because I care not to be in the right, when retired
from bickering and in a proper philosophical temper — . . .

                                                    Your affectionate friend
                                                    John Keats —

TO JOHN HAMILTON REYNOLDS

                                                    Teignmouth May 3ᵈ [1818]

My dear Reynolds.
        What I complain of is that I have been in so an uneasy a state of
Mind as not to be fit to write to an invalid. I cannot write to any
length under a dis-guised feeling. I should have loaded you with an
addition of gloom, which I am sure you do not want. I am now thank
God in a humour to give you a good groats worth — for Tom, after a
Night without a Wink of sleep, and overburdened with fever, has got
up after a refreshing day sleep and is better than he has been for a
long time; and you I trust have been again round the Common without

[3] Shelley, *Hymn to Intellectual Beauty* 13–14.

any effect but refreshment. — As to the Matter I hope I can say with Sir Andrew "I have matter enough in my head"[1] in your favor And now, in the second place, for I reckon that I have finished my Imprimis, I am glad you blow up the weather — all through your letter there is a leaning towards a climate-curse. and you know what a delicate satisfaction there is in having a vexation anathematized: one would think there has been growing up for these last four thousand years, a grandchild Scion of the old forbidden tree, and that some modern Eve had just violated it; and that there was come with double charge, "Notus and Afer black with thunderous clouds, from Sierra-leona" —[2] I shall breathe worsted stockings sooner than I thought for. Tom wants to be in Town — we will have some such days upon the heath like that of last summer and why not with the same book: or what say you to a black Letter Chaucer printed in 1596: aye I've got one huzza! I shall have it bounden gothique a nice sombre binding — it will go a little way to unmodernize. And also I see no reason, because I have been away this last month, why I should not have a peep at your Spencerian — notwithstanding you speak of your office, in my thought a little too early, for I do not see why a Mind like yours is not capable of harbouring and digesting the whole Mystery of Law as easily as Parson Hugh does Pepins[3] — which did not hinder him from his poetic Canary — Were I study physic or rather Medicine again, — I feel it would not make the least difference in my Poetry; when the Mind is in its infancy a Bias ⟨in⟩ is in reality a Bias, but when we have acquired more strength, a Bias becomes no Bias. Every department of knowledge we see excellent and calculated towards a great whole. I am so convinced of this, that I am glad at not having given away my medical Books, which I shall again look over to keep alive the little I know thitherwards; and moreover intend through you and Rice to become a sort of Pip-civilian. An extensive knowledge is needful to thinking people — it takes away the heat and fever; and helps, by widening speculation, to ease the Burden of the Mystery:[4] a thing I begin to understand a little, and which weighed upon you in the most gloomy and true sentence in your Letter. The difference of high Sensations with and without knowledge appears to me this — in the latter case we are falling continually ten thousand fathoms deep and being blown up again without wings and with all [the] horror of a ⟨Case⟩ bare shoulderd Creature — in the former case, our shoulders are fledge⟨d⟩, and we go thro' the same ⟨Fir⟩ air and space without fear.[5] This is running one's rigs on the score of abstracted benefit — when we come to human Life and the affections it is impossible [to know] how

---

[1] Slender, in *Merry Wives of Windsor* I.i.127.
[2] *Paradise Lost* X.702–703.
[3] *Merry Wives of Windsor* I.ii.13.
[4] Wordsworth, *Tintern Abbey* 38.
[5] Cf. *Paradise Lost* II.933f., III.627.

a parallel of breast and head can be drawn — (you will forgive me
for thus privately ⟨heading⟩ treading out [of] my depth, and take it
for treading as schoolboys ⟨head⟩ tread the water⟨s⟩) — it is impossible to know how far knowlege will console ⟨as⟩ us for the death of
a friend and the ill "that flesh is heir to⟨o⟩"[6] — With respect to the affections and Poetry you must know by a sympathy my thoughts that
way; and I dare say these few lines will be but a ratification: I wrote
them on May-day — and intend to finish the ode all in good time. —

[Here follows *Fragment of an Ode to Maia.*]

You may be anxious to know for fact to what sentence in your
Letter I allude. You say "I fear there is little chance of any thing else
in this life". You seem by that to have been going through with a more
painful and acute ⟨test⟩ zest the same labyrinth that I have — I have
come to the same conclusion thus far. My Branchings out therefrom
have been numerous: one of them is the consideration of Wordsworth's
genius and as a help, in the manner of gold being the meridian Line
of worldly wealth, — how he differs from Milton. — And here I have
nothing but surmises, from an uncertainty whether Miltons apparently
less anxiety for Humanity proceeds from his seeing further or no than
Wordsworth: And whether Wordsworth has in truth epic passion⟨s⟩,
and martyrs himself to the human heart, the main region of his song[7]
— In regard to his genius alone — we find what he says true as far as
we have experienced and we can judge no further but by larger experience — for axioms in philosophy are not axioms until they are
proved upon our pulses: We read fine — things but never feel them
to the full until we have gone the same steps as the Author. — I know
this is not plain; you will know exactly my meaning when I say, that
now I shall relish Hamlet more than I ever have done — Or, better —
You are sensible no Man can set down Venery as a bestial or joyless
thing until he is sick of it and therefore all philosophizing on it would
be mere wording. Until we are sick, we understand not; — in fine, as
Byron says, "Knowledge is Sorrow";[8] and I go on to say that "Sorrow
is Wisdom" — and further for aught we can know for certainty! "Wisdom is folly" — So you see how I have run away from Wordsworth,
and Milton, and shall still run away from what was in my head, to
observe, that some kind of letters are good squares others handsome
ovals, and others some orbicular, others spheroid — and why should
there not be another species with two rough edges like a Rat-trap?
I hope you will find all my long letters of that species, and all will be
well; for by merely touching the spring delicately and etherially, the
rough edged will fly immediately into a proper compactness; and thus

---

[6] *Hamlet* III.i.63.
[7] Cf. line 41 in the passage from *The Recluse* quoted by Wordsworth in
the Preface to *The Excursion.*
[8] *Manfred* I.i.10.

you may make a good wholesome loaf, with your own le[a]ven in it, of my fragments — If you cannot find this said Rat-trap sufficiently tractable — alas for me, it being an impossibility in grain for my ink to stain otherwise: If I scribble long letters I must play my vagaries. I must be too heavy, or too light, for whole pages — I must be quaint and free of Tropes and figures — I must play my draughts as I please, and for my advantage and your erudition, crown a white with a black, or a black with a white, and move into black or white, far and near as I please — I must go from Hazlitt to Patmore, and make Wordsworth and Coleman play at leap-frog — or keep one of them down a whole half holiday at fly the garter — "From Gray to Gay, from Little to Shakespeare"[9] — Also, as a long cause requires two or more sittings of the Court, so a long letter will require two or more sittings of the Breech wherefore I shall resume after dinner. —

Have you not seen a Gull, an orc, a Sea Mew,[10] or any thing to bring this Line to a proper length, and also fill up this clear part; that like the Gull I may *dip* — I hope, not out of sight — and also, like a Gull, I hope to be lucky in a good sized fish — This crossing a letter is not without its association[11] — for chequer work leads us naturally to a Milkmaid, a Milkmaid to Hogarth Hogarth to Shakespeare Shakespear to Hazlitt — Hazlitt to Shakespeare and thus by merely pulling an apron string we set a pretty peal of Chimes at work — Let them chime on while, with your patience, — I will return to Wordsworth — whether or no he has an extended vision or a circumscribed grandeur — whether he is an eagle in his nest, or on the wing — And to be more explicit and to show you how tall I stand by the giant, I will put down a simile of human life as far as I now perceive it; that is, to the point to which I say we both have arrived at —' Well — I compare human life to a large Mansion of Many Apartments, two of which I can only describe, the doors of the rest being as yet shut upon me — The first we step into we call the infant or thoughtless Chamber, in which we remain as long as we do not think — We remain there a long while, and notwithstanding the doors of the second Chamber remain wide open, showing a bright appearance, we care not to hasten to it; but are at length imperceptibly impelled by the awakening of the thinking principle — within us — we no sooner get into the second Chamber, which I shall call the Chamber of Maiden-Thought, than we become intoxicated with the light and the atmosphere, we see nothing but

[9] Cf. Pope, *Essay on Man* IV.380, "From grave to gay, from lively to severe." "Thomas Little" was a pseudonym used by Thomas Moore. P. G. Patmore (1786–1855); George Colman (1762–1836).

[10] Cf. *Paradise Lost* XI.835.

[11] To save paper and postage, the original of this letter was "crossed," like a net, with vertical writing over the face of the horizontal writing. As the original is lost, Keats's corrections in this letter cannot be distinguished from those made in the transcription by his friend Woodhouse.

pleasant wonders, and think of delaying there for ever in delight: However among the effects this breathing is father of is that tremendous
one of sharpening one's vision into the ⟨head⟩ heart and nature of Man
— of convincing ones nerves that the World is full of Misery and Heart-
break, Pain, Sickness and oppression — whereby This Chamber of
Maiden Thought becomes gradually darken'd and at the same time on
all sides of it many doors are set open — but all dark — all leading to
dark passages — We see not the ballance of good and evil. We are in a
Mist — *We* are now in that state — We feel the "burden of the Mystery," To this Point was Wordsworth come, as far as I can conceive
when he wrote 'Tintern Abbey' and it seems to me that his Genius is
explorative of those dark Passages. Now if we live, and go on thinking, we too shall explore them. he is a Genius and superior [to] us, in
so far as he can, more than we, make discoveries, and shed a light
in them — Here I must think Wordsworth is deeper than Milton —
though I think it has depended more upon the general and gregarious
advance of intellect, than individual greatness of Mind — From the
Paradise Lost and the other Works of Milton, I hope it is not too
presuming, even between ourselves to say, his Philosophy, human and
divine, may be tolerably understood by one not much advanced in
years, In his time englishmen were just emancipated from a great
superstition — and Men had got hold of certain points and resting
places in reasoning which were too newly born to be doubted, and
too much ⟨oppressed⟩ opposed by the Mass of Europe not to be thought
etherial and authentically divine — who could gainsay his ideas on
virtue, vice, and Chastity in Comus, just at the time of the dismissal
of Cod-pieces and a hundred other disgraces? who would not rest
satisfied with his hintings at good and evil in the Paradise Lost, when
just free from the inquisition and burrning in Smithfield? The Reformation produced such immediate and great⟨s⟩ benefits, that Protestantism
was considered under the immediate eye of heaven, and its own remaining Dogmas and superstitions, then, as it were, regenerated, constituted those resting places and seeming sure points of Reasoning —
from that I have mentioned, Milton, whatever he may have thought in
the sequel, appears to have been content with these by his writings —
He did not think into the human heart, as Wordsworth has done —
Yet Milton as a Philosop[h]er, had sure as great powers as Wordsworth — What is then to be inferr'd? O many things — It proves
there is really a grand march of intellect —, It proves that a mighty
providence subdues the mightiest Minds to the service of the time
being, whether it be in human Knowledge or Religion — I have
often pitied a Tutor who has to hear "Nomᵉ: Musa" — so often
dinn'd into his ears — I hope you may not have the same pain in
this scribbling — I may have read these things before, but I never
had even a thus dim perception of them; and moreover I like to
say my lesson to one who will endure my tediousness for my own

sake — After all there is certainly something real in the World — Moore's present to Hazlitt is real — I like that Moore, and am glad ⟨that⟩ I saw him at the Theatre just before I left Town. Tom has spit a leetle blood this afternoon, and that is rather a damper — but I know — the truth is there is something real in the World Your third Chamber of Life shall be a lucky and a gentle one — stored with the wine of love — and the Bread of Friendship. When you see George if he should not have recēd a letter from me tell him he will find one at home most likely — tell Bailey I hope soon to see him — Remember me to all The leaves have been out here, for mony a day — I have written to George for the first stanzas of my Isabel — I shall have them soon and will copy the whole out for you.

> Your affectionate friend
> John Keats.

TO JAMES AUGUSTUS HESSEY

[8 October 1818]

My dear Hessey.

You are very good in sending me the letter from the Chronicle — and I am very bad in not acknowledging such a kindness sooner. — pray forgive me. — It has so chanced that I have had that paper every day — I have seen today's. I cannot but feel indebted to those Gentlemen who have taken my part — As for the rest, I begin to get a little acquainted with my own strength and weakness. — Praise or blame has but a momentary effect on the man whose love of beauty in the abstract makes him a severe critic on his own Works. My own domestic criticism has given me pain without comparison beyond what Blackwood or the ⟨Edinburgh⟩ Quarterly could possibly inflict. and also when I feel I am right, no external praise can give me such a glow as my own solitary reperception & ratification of what is fine. J. S.[1] is perfectly right in regard to the slip-shod Endymion. That it is so is no fault of mine. — No! — though it may sound a little paradoxical. It is as good as I had power to make it — by myself — Had I been nervous about its being a perfect piece, & with that view asked advice, & trembled over every page, it would not have been written; for it is not in my nature to fumble — I will write independantly. — I have written independently *without Judgment.* — I may write independently & *with judgment* hereafter. — The Genius of Poetry must work out its own salvation in a man: It cannot be matured by law & precept, but by sensation & watchfulness in itself — That which is creative

[1] Probably John Scott, in the *Morning Chronicle*, October 3.

must create itself — In Endymion, I leaped headlong into the Sea, and thereby have become better acquainted with the Soundings, the quicksands, & the rocks, than if I had ⟨stayed⟩ stayed upon the green shore, and piped a silly pipe, and took tea & comfortable advice. — I was never afraid of failure; for I would sooner fail than not be among the greatest — But I am nigh getting into a rant. So, with remembrances to Taylor and Woodhouse &c I am

Yrs very sincerely
John Keats.

TO RICHARD WOODHOUSE

[27th October 1818]

My dear Woodhouse,

Your Letter gave me a great satisfaction; more on account of its friendliness, than any relish of that matter in it which is accounted so acceptable in the 'genus irritabile'.[1] The best answer I can give you is in a clerklike manner to make some observations on two principle points, which seem to point like indices into the midst of the whole pro and con, about genius, and views and atchievements and ambition and cœtera. 1st As to the poetical Character itself, (I mean that sort of which, if I am any thing, I am a Member; that sort distinguished from the wordsworthian or egotistical sublime; which is a thing per se and stands alone[2]) it is not itself — it has no self — it is every thing and nothing — it has no character — it enjoys light and shade; it lives in gusto, be it foul or fair, high or low, rich or poor, mean or elevated — It has as much delight in conceiving an Iago as an Imogen. What shocks the virtuous philosop[h]er, delights the camelion Poet. It does no harm from its relish of the dark side of things any more than from its taste for the bright one; because they both end in speculation. A Poet is the most unpoetical of any thing in existence; because he has no Identity — he is continually in for — and filling some other Body — The Sun, the Moon, the Sea and Men and Women who are creatures of impulse are poetical and have about them an unchangeable attribute — the poet has none; no identity — he is certainly the most unpoetical of all God's Creatures. If then he has no self, and if I am a Poet, where is the Wonder that I should say I would ⟨right⟩ write no more? Might I not at the very instant [have] been cogitating on the Characters of saturn and Ops? It is a wretched thing to confess; but is a very fact that not one word I ever utter can be taken for granted as an opinion growing out of my identical nature — how can it, when I have no nature? When I am in a room with People if I ever am

---

1 "The irritable tribe [of poets]." Horace, *Epistles* II.ii.102.
2 Cf. Shakespeare, *Troilus and Cressida* I.ii.15f.

free from speculating on creations of my own brain, then not myself
goes home to myself:[3] but the identity of every one in the room begins
to [*for* so?] to press upon me that, I am in a very little time an[ni]hi-
lated — not only among Men; it would be the same in a Nursery of
children: I know not whether I make myself wholly understood: I
hope enough so to let you see that no dependence is to be placed on
what I said that day.

In the second place I will speak of my views, and of the life I
purpose to myself — I am ambitious of doing the world some good:
if I should be spared that may be the work of maturer years — in
the interval I will assay to reach to as high a summit in Poetry as
the nerve bestowed upon me will suffer. The faint conceptions I have
of Poems to come brings the blood frequently into my forehead —
All I hope is that I may not lose all interest in human affairs — that
the solitary indifference I feel for applause even from the finest Spirits,
will not blunt any acuteness of vision I may have. I do not think it
will — I feel assured I should write from the mere yearning and fondness I have for the Beautiful even if my night's labours should be
burnt every morning and no eye ever shine upon them. But even now
I am perhaps not speaking from myself; but from some character in
whose soul I now live. I am sure however that this next sentence is
from myself. I feel your anxiety, good opinion and friendliness in the
highest degree, and am

Your's most sincerely
John Keats

TO GEORGE AND GEORGIANA KEATS

[14 February–3 May 1819]
sunday Morn Feby 14[th]

My dear Brother &   Sister —

. . . I went out twice at Chichester to old Dowager card parties —
I see very little now, and very few Persons — being almost tired of
Men and things — Brown and Dilke are very kind and considerate
towards me — The Miss Reynoldses have been stoppi[n]g next door
lately — but all very dull — Miss Brawne and I have every now and
then a chat and a tiff — Brown and Dilke are walking round their
Garden hands in Pockets making observations. The Literary world I
know nothing about — There is a Poem from Rogers dead born — and
another Satire is expected from Byron call'd Don Giovanni —

❉   ❉   ❉   ❉   ❉   ❉

Friday [March] *19th* . . . I have this moment received a note from
Haslam in which he expects the death of his Father who has been for

[3] Cf. *ibid.,* III.iii.105,107.

some time in a state of insensibility — his mother bears up he says very well — I shall go to twon [*for* town] tommorrow to see him. This is the world — thus we cannot expect to give way many hours to pleasure — Circumstances are like Clouds continually gathering and bursting — While we are laughing the seed of some trouble is put into ⟨he⟩ the wide arable land of events — while we are laughing it sprouts is [*for* it] grows and suddenly bears a poison fruit which we must pluck — Even so we have leisure to reason on the misfortunes of our friends; our own touch us too nearly for words. Very few men have ever arrived at a complete disinterestedness of Mind: very few have been influenced by a pure desire of the benefit of others — in the greater part of the Benefactors ⟨of⟩ & to Humanity some meretricious motive has sullied their greatness — some melodramatic scenery has fa[s]cinated them — From the manner in which I feel Haslam's misfortune I perceive how far I am from any humble standard of disinterestedness — Yet this feeling ought to be carried to its highest pitch, as there is no fear of its ever injuring society — which it would do I fear pushed to an extremity — For in wild nature the Hawk would loose his Breakfast of Robins and the Robin his of Worms The Lion must starve as well as the swallow — The greater part of Men make their way with the same instinctiveness, the same unwandering eye from their purposes, the same animal eagerness as the Hawk — The Hawk wants a Mate, so does the Man — look at them both they set about it and procure on[e] in the same manner — They want both a nest and they both set about one in the same manner — they get their food in the same manner — The noble animal Man for his amusement smokes his pipe — the Hawk balances about the Clouds — that is the only difference of their leisures. This it is that makes the Amusement of Life — to a speculative Mind. I go among the Feilds and catch a glimpse of a stoat or a fieldmouse peeping out of the withered grass — the creature hath a purpose and its eyes are bright with it — I go amongst the buildings of a city and I see a Man hurrying along — to what? The Creature has a purpose and his eyes are bright with it. But then as Wordsworth says, "we have all one human heart"[1] — there is an ellectric fire in human nature tending to purify — so that among these human creature[s] there is continu[a]lly some birth of new heroism — The pity is that we must wonder at it: as we should at finding a pearl in rubbish — I have no doubt that thousands of people never heard of have had hearts comp[l]etely disinterested: I can remember but two — Socrates and Jesus — their Histories evince it — What I heard a little time ago, Taylor observe with respect to Socrates, may be said of Jesus — That he was so great a⟨s⟩ man that though he transmitted no writing of his own to posterity, we have his Mind and his sayings and his greatness handed to us by others. It is to be lamented that the history of the latter was written and revised by Men interested

---

[1] *The Old Cumberland Beggar* 153.

in the pious frauds of Religion. Yet through all this I see his splendour. Even here though I myself am pursueing the same instinctive course as the veriest human animal you can think of — I am however young writing at random — straining at particles of light in the midst of a great darkness — without knowing the bearing of any one assertion of any one opinion. Yet may I not in this be free from sin? May there not be superior beings amused with any graceful, though instinctive attitude my mind m[a]y fall into, as I am entertained with the alertness of a Stoat or the anxiety of a Deer? Though a quarrel in the streets is a thing to be hated, the energies displayed in it are fine; the commonest Man shows a grace in his quarrel — By a superior being our reasoning[s] may take the same tone — though erroneous they may be fine — This is the very thing in which consists poetry; and if so it is not so fine a thing as philosophy — For the same reason that an eagle is not so fine a thing as a truth — Give me this credit — Do you not think I strive — to know myself? Give me this credit — and you will not think that on my own accou[n]t I repeat Milton's lines

"How charming is divine Philosophy
Not harsh and crabbed as dull fools suppose
But musical as is Apollo's lute" — 2

No — no[t?] for myself — feeling grateful as I do to have got into a state of mind to relish them properly — Nothing ever becomes real till it is experienced — Even a Proverb is no proverb to you till your Life has illustrated it — I am ever affraid that your anxiety for me will lead you to fear for the violence of my temperament continually smothered down: for that reason I did not intend to have sent you the following sonnet — but look over the two last pages and ask yourselves whether I have not that in me which will well bear the buffets of the world. It will be the best comment on my sonnet; it will show you that it was written with no Agony but that of ignorance; with no thirst of any thing but knowledge when pushed to the point though the first steps to it were throug[h] my human passions — they went away, and I wrote with my Mind — and perhaps I must confess a little bit of my heart —

[Here follows *Why Did I Laugh Tonight?*]

I went to ⟨bead⟩ bed, and enjoyed an uninterrupted sleep — Sane I went to bed and sane I ⟨aose⟩ arose.

❊   ❊   ❊   ❊   ❊   ❊

[15 April]. . . . Last Sunday I took a Walk towards highgate and in the lane that winds by the side of Lord Mansfield's park I met

2 *Comus* 475–477.

Mr Green our Demonstrator at Guy's in conversation with Coleridge
— I joined them, after enquiring by a look whether it would be agreeable — I walked with him a[t] his alderman-after dinner pace for
near two miles I suppose In those two Miles he broached a thousand
things — let me see if I can give you a list — Nightingales, Poetry —
on Poetical sensation — Metaphysics — Different genera and species
of Dreams — Nightmare — a dream accompanied ⟨with⟩ by a sense of
touch — single and double touch — A dream related — First and second consciousness — the difference explained between will and Voli-
tion — so m[an]y metaphysicians from a want of smoking the second
consciousness — Monsters — the Kraken — Mermaids — southey believes in them — southeys belief too much diluted — A Ghost story —
Good morning — I heard his voice as he came towards me — I heard
it as he moved away — I had heard it all the interval — if it may be
called so. He was civil enough to ask me to call on him at Highgate
Good night!

*   *   *   *   *   *

[21 April]. . . . I have been reading lately two very different books
Robertson's America and Voltaire's Siecle De Louis XIV It is like
walking arm and arm between Pizzaro and the great-little Monarch.
In How lementabl[e] a case do we see the great body of the people
in both instances: in the first, where Men might seem to inherit quiet of
Mind from unsophisticated senses; from uncontamination of civilisa-
tion; and especially from their being as it were estranged from the
mutual helps of Society and its mutual injuries — and thereby more
immediately under the Protection of Providence — even there they
had mortal pains to bear as bad; or even worse than Ba[i]liffs, Debts
and Poverties of civilised Life — The whole appears to resolve into
this — that Man is originally 'a poor forked creature'[3] subject to the
same mischances as the beasts of the forest, destined to hardships and
disquietude of some kind or other. If he improves by degrees his
bodily accom[m]odations and comforts — at each stage, at each accent
[for ascent] there are waiting for him a fresh set of annoyances — he
is mortal and there is still a heaven with its Stars abov[e] his head.
The most interesting question that can come before us is, How far by
the persevering endeavours of a seldom appearing Socrates Mankind
may be made happy — I can imagine such happiness carried to an
extreme — but what must it end in? — Death — and who could in
such a case bear with death — the whole troubles of life which are
now frittered away in a series of years, would the[n] be accumulated
for the last days of a being who instead of hailing its approach, would
leave this world as Eve left Paradise — But in truth I do not at all
believe in this sort of perfectibility — the nature of the world will not
admit of it — the inhabitants of the world will correspond to itself —

[3] *King Lear* III.iv.112–113.

Let the fish philosophise the ice away from the Rivers in winter time
and they shall be at continual play in the tepid delight of summer.
Look at the Poles and at the sands of Africa, Whirlpools and vol-
canoes — Let men exterminate them and I will say that they may
arrive at earthly Happiness — The point at which Man may arrive is
as far as the paral[l]el state in inanimate nature and no further — For
instance suppose a rose to have sensation, it blooms on a beautiful
morning it enjoys itself — but there comes a cold wind, a hot sun — it
can not escape it, it cannot destroy its annoyances — they are as native
to the world as itself: no more can man be happy in spite, the
world[l]y elements will prey upon his nature — The common cogno-
men of this world among the misguided and superstitious is 'a vale of
tears' from which we are to be redeemed by a certain arbit[r]ary
interposition of God and taken to Heaven — What a little circumscribe[d] straightened notion! Call the world if you Please "The vale
of Soul-making" Then you will find out the use of the world (I am
speaking now in the highest terms for human nature admitting it to
be immortal which I will here take for granted for the purpose of
showing a thought which has struck me concerning it) I say 'Soul
making' Soul as distinguished from an Intelligence — There may be
intelligences or sparks of the divinity in millions — but they are not
Souls ⟨the⟩ till they acquire identities, till each one is personally itself.
I[n]telligences are atoms of perception — they know and they see and
they are pure, in short they are God — How then are Souls to be
made? How then are these sparks which are God to have identity
given them — so as ever to possess a bliss peculiar to each ones individual existence? How, but by the medium of a world like this?
This point I sincerely wish to consider because I think it a grander
system of salvation than the chryst⟨e⟩ain religion — or rather it is a system of Spirit-creation — This is effected by three grand materials
acting the one upon the other for a series of years. These three Materials are the *Intelligence* — the *human heart* (as distinguished from
intelligence or Mind) and the *World* or *Elemental space* suited for the
proper action of *Mind and Heart* on each other for the purpose of
forming the Soul or *Intelligence destined to possess the sense of Identity*. I can scarcely express what I but dimly perceive — and yet I think
I perceive it — that you may judge the more clearly I will put it in
the most homely form possible — I will call the *world* a School instituted for the purpose of teaching little children to read — I will call
the *human heart* the *horn Book* used in that School — and I will call
the *Child able to read, the Soul* made from that *school* and its *hornbook*. Do you not see how necessary a World of Pains and troubles
is to school an Intelligence and make it a soul? A Place where the
heart must feel and suffer in a thousand diverse ways! Not merely is
the Heart a Hornbook, It is the Minds Bible, it is the Minds experience,
it is the teat from which the Mind or intelligence sucks its identity —

As various as the Lives of Men are — so various become their souls, and thus does God make individual beings, Souls, Identical Souls of the sparks of his own essence — This appears to me a faint sketch of a system of Salvation which does not affront our reason and humanity — I am convinced that many difficulties which christians labour under would vanish before it — there is one wh[i]ch even now Strikes me — the Salvation of Children — In them the Spark or intelligence returns to God without any identity — it having had no time to learn of, and be altered by, the heart — or seat of the human Passions — It is pretty generally suspected that the chr[i]stian scheme has been coppied from the ancient persian and greek Philosophers. Why may they not have made this simple thing even more simple for common apprehension by introducing Mediators and Personages in the same manner as in the he[a]then mythology abstractions are personified — Seriously I think it probable that this System of Soul-making — may have been the Parent of all the more palpable and personal Schemes of Redemption, among the Zoroastrians the Christians and the Hindoos. For as one part of the human species must have their carved Jupiter; so another part must have the palpable and named Mediatior and saviour, their Christ their Oromanes and their Vishnu — If what I have said should not be plain enough, as I fear it may not be, I will but [*for* put] you in the place where I began in this series of thoughts — I mean, I began by seeing how man was formed by circumstances — and what are circumstances? — but touchstones of his heart — ? and what are touchstones? — but proovings of his hearrt? and what are proovings of his heart but fortifiers or alterers of his nature? and what is his altered nature but his soul? — and what was his soul before it came into the world and had These provings and alterations and perfection-ings? — An intelligence⟨s⟩ without Identity — and how is this Iden-tity to be made? Through the medium of the Heart? And how is the heart to become this Medium but in a world of Circumstances?

*   *   *   *   *   *

I have been endeavouring to discover a better sonnet stanza than we have. The legitimate does not suit the language over-well from the pouncing rhymes — the other kind appears too elegai⟨a⟩c — and the couplet at the end of it has seldom a pleasing effect — I do not pre-tend to have succeeded — it will explain itself —

> If by dull rhymes our english must be chaind
> And, like Andromeda, the Sonnet sweet,
> Fetterd in spite of pained Loveliness;
> Let us find out, if we must be constrain'd,
> Sandals more interwoven & complete
> To fit the naked foot of Poesy;
> Let us inspect the Lyre & weigh the stress
> Of every chord & see what may be gained

By ear industrious & attention meet,
Misers of sound & syllable no less,
Than Midas of his coinage, let us be
Jealous of dead leaves in the bay wreath Crown;
So if we may not let the Muse be free,
She will be bound with Garlands of her own.

Here endeth the other Sonnet — this is the 3ᵈ of May & every thing is
in delightful forwardness; the violets are not withered, before the
peeping of the first rose; You must let me know every thing, how
parcels go & come, what papers you have, & what Newspapers you
want, & other things — God bless you my dear Brother & Sister

Your ever Affectionate Brother,
John Keats —

TO BENJAMIN BAILEY

[14 August 1819]

❖   ❖   ❖   ❖   ❖   ❖

We removed to Winchester for the convenience of a Library and
find it an exceeding pleasant Town, enriched with a beautiful
Cathedrall and surrounded by a fresh-looking country. We are in
tolerably good and cheap Lodgings. Within these two Months I have
written 1500 Lines, most of which besides many more of prior composition you will probably see by next Winter. I have written two
Tales, one from Boccac[c]io call'd the Pot of Basil; and another call'd
Sᵗ Agnes' Eve on a popular superstition; and a third call'd Lamia —
(half finished — I have also been writing parts of my Hyperion and
completed 4 Acts of a Tragedy. It was the opinion of most of my
friends that I should never be able to write a scene — I will endeavour
to wipe away the prejudice — I sincerely hope you will be pleased
when my Labours since we last saw each other shall reach you — One
of my Ambitions is to make as great a revolution in modern dramatic
writing as Kean has done in acting — another to upset the drawling
of the blue stocking literary world — if in the course of a few years
I do these two things I ought to die content — and my friends should
drink a dozen of Claret on my Tomb — I am convinced more and
more every day that (excepting the human friend Philosopher) a fine
writer is the most genuine Being in the World. Shakspeare and the
paradise Lost every day become greater wonders to me — I look upon
fine Phrases like a Lover — I was glad to see, by a Passage in one of
Brown's Letters sometime ago from the north that you were in such
good Spirits — Since that you have been married and in congra[tu]-
lating you I wish you every continuance of them — Present my

Respects to Mrs Bailey. This sounds oddly to me, and I dare say I do
it awkwardly enough: but I suppose by this time it is nothing new to
you — Brown's remembrances to you — As far as I know we shall
remain at Winchester for a goodish while —

Ever your sincere friend
John Keats.

TO JOHN HAMILTON REYNOLDS

[24 August 1819]
Winchest^r Augt 25th

My dear Reynolds,
      By this Post I write to Rice who will tell you why we have left
Shanklin; and how we like this Place — I have indeed scar[c]ely any
thing else to say, leading so monotonous a life except I was to give you
a history of sensations, and day-night mares. You would not find me
at all unhappy in it; as all my thoughts and feelings which are of the
selfish nature, home speculations every day continue to make me more
Iron — I am convinced more and more day by day that fine writing
is next to fine doing the top thing in the world; the Paradise Lost
becomes a greater wonder — The more I know what my diligence
may in time probably effect; the more does my heart distend with
Pride and Obstinacy[1] — I feel it in my power to become a popular
writer — I feel it in my strength to refuse the poisonous suffrage of a
public — My own being which I know to be becomes of more consequence to me than the crowds of Shadows in the Shape of Man
and women that inhabit a kingdom. The Soul is a world of itself and
has enough to do in its own home — Those whom I know already and
who have grown as it were a part of myself I could not do without:
but for the rest of Mankind they are as much a dream to me as Miltons
Hierarchies. I think if I had a free and healthy and lasting organisation
of heart and Lungs — as strong as an ox⟨e⟩'s — so as to be able [to
bear] unhurt the shock of extreme thought and sensation without
weariness, I could pass my Life very nearly alone though it should
last eighty years. But I feel my Body too weak to support me to the
height; I am obliged continually to check myself and strive to be
nothing. It would be vain for me to endeavour after a more reasonable
manner of writing to you: I have nothing to speak of but myself —
and what can I say but what I feel? If you should have any reason to
regret this state of excitement in me, I will turn the tide of your feelings in the right channel by mentioning that it is the only state for the
best sort of Poetry — that is all I care for, all I live for. Forgive me for

---

[1] Cf. *Paradise Lost* I.571–572.

not filling up the whole sheet; Letters become so irksome to me that
the next time I leave London I shall petition them all to be spar'd me.
To give me credit for constancy and at the same time wa[i]ve letter
writing will be the highest indulgence I can think of.

Ever your affectionate friend
John Keats

TO FANNY BRAWNE

[March (?), 1820]

My dearest Fanny, I slept well last night and am no worse this
morning for it. Day by day if I am not deceived I get a more un-
restrain'd use of my Chest. The nearer a racer gets to the Goal the
more his anxiety becomes so I lingering upon the borders of health
feel my impatience increase. Perhaps on your account I have imagined
my illness more serious than it is: how horrid was the chance of slipping into the ground instead of into your arms — the difference is
amazing Love. Death must come at last; Man must die, as Shallow
says[1]; but before that is my fate I feign [*for* fain] would try what
more pleasures than you have given so sweet a creature as you can
give. Let me have another op[p]ortunity of years before me and I will
not die without being remember'd. Take care of yourself dear that
we may both be well in the Summer. I do not at all fatigue myself
with writing, having merely to put a line or two here and there, a
Task which would worry a stout state of the body and mind, but
which just suits me as I can do no more.

Your affectionate
J. K —

TO PERCY BYSSHE SHELLEY

Hampstead August 16th [1820]

My dear Shelley,

I am very much gratified that you, in a foreign country, and with
a mind almost over occupied, should write to me in the strain of the
Letter beside me. If I do not take advantage of your invitation it will
be prevented by a circumstance I have very much at heart to prophesy
— There is no doubt that an english winter would put an end to me,
and do so in a lingering hateful manner, therefore I must either

[1] *2 Henry IV* III.ii.42.

voyage or journey to Italy as a soldier marches up to a battery. My nerves at present are the worst part of me, yet they feel soothed when I think that come what extreme may, I shall not be destined to remain in one spot long enough to take a hatred of any four particular bed-posts. I am glad you take any pleasure in my poor Poem; — which I would willingly take the trouble to unwrite, if possible, did I care so much as I have done about Reputation. I received a copy of the Cenci, as from yourself from Hunt. There is only one part of it I am judge of; the Poetry, and dramatic effect, which by many spirits now a days is considered the mammon. A modern work it is said must have a purpose, which may be the God — *an artist* must serve Mammon — he must have "self concentration" selfishness perhaps. You I am sure will forgive me for sincerely remarking that you might curb your magnanimity and be more of an artist, and 'load every rift' of your subject with ore.[1] The thought of such discipline must fall like cold chains upon you, who perhaps never sat with your wings furl'd for six Months together. And is not this extraordina[r]y talk for the writer of Endymion? whose mind was like a pack of scattered cards — I am pick'd up and sorted to a pip. My Imagination is a Monastry and I am its Monk — you must explain my metap^cs [*for* metaphysics] to your-self. I am in expectation of Prometheus every day. Could I have my own wish for its interest effectèd you would have it still in manuscript — or be but now putting an end to the second act. I remember you advising me not to publish my first-blights, on Hampstead heath — I am returning advice upon your hands. Most of the Poems in the volume I send you have been written above two years, and would never have been publish'd but from a hope of gain; so you see I am inclined enough to take your advice now. I must exp[r]ess once more my deep sense of your kindness, adding my sincere thanks and respects for Mrs Shelley. In the hope of soon seeing you I remain

> most sincerely yours,
> John Keats —

TO CHARLES BROWN

Rome. 30 November 1820

My dear Brown,

'Tis the most difficult thing in the world ⟨for⟩ to me to write a letter. My stomach continues so bad, that I feel it worse on opening any book, — yet I am much better than I was in Quarantine. Then I am afraid to encounter the proing and conning of any thing interesting

---

[1] *The Faerie Queene* II.vii.28.5.

to me in England. I have an habitual feeling of my real life having past, and that I am leading a posthumous existence. God knows how it would have been — but it appears to me — however, I will not speak of that subject. I must have been at Bedhampton nearly at the time you were writing to me from Chichester — how unfortunate — and to pass on the river too! There was my star predominant! I cannot answer any thing in your letter, which followed me from Naples to Rome, because I am afraid to look it over again. I am so weak (in mind) that I cannot bear the sight of any hand writing of a friend I love so much as I do you. Yet I ride the little horse, — and, at my worst, even in Quarantine, summoned up more puns, in a sort of desperation, in one week than in any year of my life. There is one thought enough to kill me — I have been well, healthy, alert &c, walking with her — and now — the knowledge of contrast, feeling for light and shade, all that information (primitive sense) necessary for a poem are great enemies to the recovery of the stomach. There, you rogue, I put you to the torture, — but you must bring your philosophy to bear — as I do mine, really — or how should I be able to live? Dr Clarke is very attentive to me; he says, there is very little the matter with my lungs, but my stomach, he says, is very bad. I am well disappointed in hearing good news from George, — for it runs in my head we shall all die young. I have not written to * * * * *[1] yet, which he must think very neglectful; being anxious to send him a good account of my health, I have delayed it from week to week. If I recover, I will do all in my power to correct the mistakes made during sickness; and if I should not, all my faults will be forgiven. I shall write to * * * tomorrow, or next day. I will write to * * * * * in the middle of next week. Severn is very well, though he leads so dull a life with me. Remember me to all friends, and tell * * * * I should not have left London without taking leave of him, but from being so low in body and mind. Write to George as soon as you receive this, and tell him how I am, as far as you can guess; and also a note to my sister — who walks about my imagination like a ghost — she is so like Tom. I can scarcely bid you good bye even in a letter. I always made an awkward bow.

> God bless you!
> John Keats

[1] Rollins suggested that the four friends whose names Brown deleted were Haslam, Dilke, Woodhouse, and Reynolds.

Critical and Imaginative

CRITICAL AND IMAGINATIVE

CHRONOLOGY

1790   Thomas Bewick (1753–1828), wood-engravings to *A General History of Quadrupeds.*

1791   William Gilpin (1724–1804), *Remarks on Forest Scenery and Other Woodland Views.*

1792   March 24, Benjamin West, historical painter from Pennsylvania, succeeded Sir Joshua Reynolds as president of the Royal Academy.

1798–1800   Melodramas by Kotzebue (1761–1819) were more popular on the London stage than German tragedies by Lessing (1729–81) or Schiller (1759–1805).

1800–01   Recent oratorios by Haydn, *The Creation* and *The Seasons,* performed in London, where the composer had worked since 1794.

1801–03   Lord Elgin brought to London sculpture from the frieze of the Parthenon.

1802   October 10, *Edinburgh Review* commenced; soon became the Whig quarterly, with Francis Jeffrey as sole editor from May 1803. In France, F. R. Chateaubriand (1768–1848), *Le Génie du christianisme* and *René.*

1802–03   Walter Scott (1771–1832), *Minstrelsy of the Scottish Border.*

1805   Richard Payne Knight (1750–1824), *An Analytical Inquiry into the Principles of Taste.*

1806   British Institution founded to promote living British artists and to exhibit old masters.

1807   J. M. W. Turner (1775–1851), *Sun Rising through Vapour* exhibited at the Royal Academy.

1808   In Germany, J. W. von Goethe (1749–1832), *Faust,* Part I. (Part II, 1833.)

1808–14   In Spain, Francisco Goya (1746–1828) etched *Los Desastres de la guerra.*

1808–09   In Vienna, A. W. Schlegel delivered influential Romantic lectures, published in 1809–11 as *Vorlesungen über dramatische Kunst und Literatur.*

1809   February, *Quarterly Review* commenced by Tories; edited by William Gifford (1756–1826). May–September, London exhibition of paintings by William Blake. September 18, Covent Garden Theater reopened after fire of September 19, 1808. R. P. Knight, *Ancient Sculpture,* depreciated the Elgin Marbles.

1811   November, Jane Austen, *Sense and Sensibility.*

1812   October 12, Drury Lane Theater reopened after fire of February 24, 1809.

1813   Madame de Staël (1766–1817), *De l'Allemagne,* written 1808–11, but suppressed in France; propagated admiration of German literature and thought. London Philharmonic Society founded; promoted works of Beethoven (1770–1827).

1814   *New Monthly Magazine* founded; edited 1821–30 by Thomas Campbell (1777–1844).

1816   June, Elgin Marbles, praised by Haydon and other artists, were acquired for the British Museum.

1817   October, Blackwood's *Edinburgh Magazine* reorganized as a Tory monthly edited by J. G. Lockhart (1794–1854) with John Wilson (1785–1854, "Christopher North"), James Hogg (1770–1835, "the Ettrick Shepherd"), and from 1819 William Maginn (1793–1842).

1818   October, T. L. Peacock, *Nightmare Abbey.* Scott, *Rob Roy.*

1819–20   Washington Irving (1783–1859), *The Sketch-Book,* by "Geoffrey Crayon."

1820   January, *London Magazine* commenced, with John Scott as editor. March 11, Sir Thomas Lawrence (1769–1830), Court portraitist, elected president of the Royal Academy.

1821   February, John Scott killed in a duel by Lockhart's second, J. Christie.

1823–24   Thomas Carlyle (1795–1881), "Schiller's Life and Writings," published serially in *London Magazine.*

1824   John Constable (1776–1837), Richard Bonington (1801–28), and other English landscape painters exhibited at Paris Salon. May 10, National Gallery opened (Parliament had purchased house and collection of J. J. Angerstein).

1826   Karl Maria von Weber (1786–1826), *Oberon,* opera, commissioned for Covent Garden Theater.

1830   February, in Paris, performance of *Hernani,* by Victor Hugo (1802–85), caused riots between classicists and Romantics.

Archibald Alison

Essays on the Nature and Principles of Taste

❨ As a member of the Scottish school of associational psychology, taste, sympathy, and common sense, Alison (1757–1839) represents both the intellectual pettiness against which the Romantics rebelled and at the same time the movement from objective observation of general nature toward subjective reporting of personal impressions. In emphasizing the effects of a sublime or beautiful object on the observer, the school of taste made no distinction between natural objects and works of art. From 1790 until its revision in 1811 (the source of the selections below), "Alison on Taste" was the standard work. After 1811 Francis Jeffrey's review of it in the *Edinburgh Review* became the accepted statement of Alison's theories. ❩

FROM *Introduction*

TASTE is, in general, considered as that Faculty of the human Mind, by which we perceive and enjoy whatever is BEAUTIFUL or SUBLIME in the works of Nature or Art.

The perception of these qualities is attended with an Emotion of Pleasure, very distinguishable from every other pleasure of our Nature, and which is accordingly distinguished by the name of the EMOTION of TASTE. The distinction of the objects of Taste into the Sublime and the Beautiful, has produced a similar division of this Emotion, into the EMOTION of SUBLIMITY, and the EMOTION of BEAUTY.

The Qualities that produce these Emotions, are to be found in almost every class of the objects of human knowledge, and the Emotions themselves afford one of the most extensive sources of human delight. They occur to us, amid every variety of EXTERNAL Scenery, and among many diversities of disposition and affection in the MIND of Man. The most pleasing Arts of human invention are altogether directed to their pursuit: and even the necessary Arts are exalted into dignity, by the Genius that can unite Beauty with Use. From the earliest period of Society, to its last stage of improvement, they afford an innocent and elegant amusement to private life, at the same time that they increase the Splendour of National Character; and in the progress of Nations, as well as of Individuals, while they attract attention from the pleasures they bestow, they serve to exalt the human Mind, from corporeal to intellectual pursuits. . . .

Of the Relative Beauty of Forms[1]

BESIDES those qualities of which Forms in themselves are expressive
to us, and which constitute what I have called their NATURAL Beauty,
there are other qualities of which they are the Signs, from their being
the subjects of Art, or produced by Wisdom or Design, for some end.
Whatever is the effect of Art, naturally leads us to the consideration of
that Art which is its cause, and of that end or purpose for which it
was produced. When we discover skill or wisdom in the one, or use-
fulness or propriety in the other, we are conscious of a very pleasing
Emotion; and the Forms which we have found by experience to be
associated with such qualities, become naturally and necessarily expressive of them, and affect us with the Emotions which properly
belong to the qualities they signify. There is therefore an additional
source of Beauty in Forms, from the Expression of such qualities;
which, for the sake of perspicuity, I shall beg leave to call their
RELATIVE Beauty.

Every work of Design may be considered in one or other of the
following lights: Either in relation to the Art or Design which produced it, — to the nature of its construction, for the purpose or end
intended, — or to the nature of the end which it is thus destined to
serve; and its Beauty accordingly depends, either upon the excellence
or wisdom of this Design, upon the Fitness or propriety of this construction, or upon the Utility of this end. The considerations of Design, of Fitness, and of Utility, therefore, may be considered as the
three great sources of the Relative Beauty of Forms. . . .

Of the Accidental Beauty of Forms[2]

BESIDE the Expressions that have now been enumerated, and which
constitute the two great and permanent sources of the Beauty of
Forms, there are others of a casual or accidental kind, which have a
very observable effect in producing the same Emotion in our minds,
and which constitute what may be called the ACCIDENTAL Beauty of
Forms. Such associations, instead of being common to all mankind,
are peculiar to the individual. They take their rise from education,
from peculiar habits of thought, from situation, from profession; and
the Beauty they produce is felt only by those whom similar causes
have led to the formation of similar associations. There are few men
who have not associations of this kind, with particular Forms, from

[1] Essay II, *Of the Sublimity and Beauty of the Material World,* Chapter
IV, Introduction to Section II.
[2] Essay II, Chapter IV, Section III.

their being familiar to them from their infancy, and thus connected
with the gay and pleasing imagery of that period of life; from their
connection with scenes to which they look back with pleasure; or
people whose memories they love: and such Forms, from this accidental connection, are never seen, without being in some measure the
Signs of all those affecting and endearing recollections. When such
associations are of a more general kind, and are common to many
individuals, they sometimes acquire a superiority over the more permanent principles of Beauty, and determine even for a time the Taste
of nations. The admiration which is paid to the Forms of Architecture,
of Furniture, of Ornament, which we derive from Antiquity, though
undoubtedly very justly due to these Forms themselves, originates, in
the greater part of mankind, from the associations which they connect
with these Forms. These associations, however, are merely accidental;
and were these Forms much inferior in point of Beauty, the admiration
which Modern Europe bestows on them, would not be less enthusiastic than it is now. There are even cases where, in a few years, the
Taste of a nation, in such respects, undergoes an absolute change,
from associations of a different kind becoming general or fashionable;
and where the beautiful Form is always found to correspond to the
prevailing association. They who are learned in the History of Dress,
will recollect many instances of this kind. In every other species of
ornament it is also observable. A single instance will be sufficient.

In the succession of Fashions which have taken place in the article
of ornamental Furniture, within these few years, every one must have
observed how much their Beauty has been determined by accidental
associations of this kind, and how little the real and permanent Beauty
of such Forms has been regarded. Some years ago, every article of
this kind was made in what was called the Chinese Taste, and however fantastic and uncouth the Forms in reality were, they were yet
universally admired, because they brought to mind those images of
Eastern magnificence and splendour, of which we have heard so much,
and which we are always willing to believe, because they are distant.
To this succeeded the Gothic Taste. Every thing was now made in
imitation, not indeed of Gothic furniture, but in imitation of the Forms
and ornament of Gothic Halls and Cathedrals. This slight association,
however, was sufficient to give Beauty to such Forms, because it led
to ideas of Gothic manners and adventure, which had become fashionable in the world from many beautiful Compositions both in Prose
and Verse. The Taste which now reigns is that of the Antique. Every
thing we now use, is made in imitation of those models which have
been lately discovered in Italy; and they serve in the same manner to
occupy our imagination, by leading to those recollections of Grecian
or Roman Taste, which have so much the possession of our minds,
from the studies and amusements of our youth.

I shall only further observe upon this subject, that all such instances of the effect of accidental Expression, in bestowing a temporary Beauty upon Forms, conclude immediately against the doctrine of their absolute or independent Beauty; and that they afford a very strong presumption, if not a direct proof, that their permanent Beauty arises also from the Expressions they permanently convey to us.

From the illustrations that I have offered in this long chapter, on the Beauty of FORMS, we seem to have sufficient reason for concluding in general, that no Forms, or species of Forms, are in themselves originally beautiful; but that their Beauty in all cases arises from their being expressive to us of some pleasing or affecting Qualities.

If the views also that I have presented on the subject are just, we may perhaps still farther conclude, that the principal sources of the Beauty of Forms are, 1st, The Expressions we connect with peculiar Forms, either from the Form itself, or the nature of the subject thus Formed. 2dly, The qualities of Design, and Fitness, and Utility, which they indicate: And, 3dly, The accidental Associations which we happen to connect with them. . . .

(()

William Blake

The Marriage of Heaven and Hell

❨ *The Marriage of Heaven and Hell,* begun about 1790, was etched about 1793 in the hidden process of "illuminated printing" practiced by William Blake (1757–1827). In the first book-length critical study of Blake, in 1868, A. C. Swinburne declared the work "full of that passionate wisdom and bright rapid strength proper to the step and speech of gods." It satirizes the *Heaven and Hell* of Emanuel Swedenborg. In *Fearful Symmetry: A Study of William Blake,* Princeton, 1947, Northrop Frye has said that the *Marriage,* "with its blistering ridicule of the wisdom that dwells with prudence, with its rowdy guffaws at the doctrines of a torturing hell and a boring heaven which are taught by cowards to dupes, is perhaps the epilogue to the golden age of English satire." Blake's "contraries," whose interaction can make life dynamic, are basic to the Proverbs of Hell. Martin K. Nurmi, in *Blake's Marriage of Heaven and Hell: A Critical Study,* Kent, Ohio, 1957, has described the contraries as "opposed yet positive and complementary forces which, when allowed to interact without external restraint, impart to life a motion and a tension that make it creative." Few copies of the work have survived; the text here is taken from published facsimiles. ❩

Proverbs of Hell

In seed time learn, in harvest teach, in winter enjoy.
Drive your cart and your plow over the bones of the dead.
The road of excess leads to the palace of wisdom.
Prudence is a rich ugly old maid courted by Incapacity.
He who desires but acts not, breeds pestilence.
The cut worm forgives the plow.
Dip him in the river who loves water.
A fool sees not the same tree that a wise man sees.
He whose face gives no light, shall never become a star.
Eternity is in love with the productions of time.
The busy bee has no time for sorrow.
The hours of folly are measur'd by the clock, but of wisdom no clock
    can measure.
All wholsom food is caught without a net or a trap.
Bring out number weight & measure in a year of dearth.
No bird soars too high, if he soars with his own wings.
A dead body revenges not injuries.
The most sublime act is to set another before you.
If the fool would persist in his folly he would become wise.
Folly is the cloke of knavery.
Shame is Prides cloke.
Prisons are built with stones of Law, Brothels with bricks of Religion.
The pride of the peacock is the glory of God.
The lust of the goat is the bounty of God.
The wrath of the lion is the wisdom of God.
The nakedness of woman is the work of God.
Excess of sorrow laughs. Excess of joy weeps.
The roaring of lions, the howling of wolves, the raging of the stormy
    sea, and the destructive sword, are portions of eternity too great for
    the eye of man.
The fox condemns the trap, not himself.
Joys impregnate. Sorrows bring forth.
Let man wear the fell of the lion, woman the fleece of the sheep.
The bird a nest, the spider a web, man friendship.
The selfish smiling fool, & the sullen frowning fool, shall be both
    thought wise, that they may be a rod.
What is now proved was once only imagin'd.
The rat, the mouse, the fox, the rabbet watch the roots; the lion, the
    tyger, the horse, the elephant watch the fruits.
The cistern contains: the fountain overflows.
One thought fills immensity.
Always be ready to speak your mind, and a base man will avoid you.

Every thing possible to be believ'd is an image of truth.

The eagle never lost so much time, as when he submitted to learn of the crow.

The fox provides for himself, but God provides for the lion.

Think in the morning. Act in the noon. Eat in the evening. Sleep in the night.

He who has sufferd you to impose on him knows you.

As the plow follows words, so God rewards prayers.

The tygers of wrath are wiser than the horses of instruction.

Expect poison from the standing water.

You never know what is enough unless you know what is more than enough.

Listen to the fools reproach! it is a kingly title!

The eyes of fire, the nostrils of air, the mouth of water, the beard of earth.

The weak in courage is strong in cunning.

The apple tree never asks the beech how he shall grow, nor the lion the horse how he shall take his prey.

The thankful rec[ei]ver bears a plentiful harvest.

If others had not been foolish, we should be so.

The soul of sweet delight can never be defil'd.

When thou seest an Eagle, thou seest a portion of Genius: lift up thy head!

As the catterpiller chooses the fairest leaves to lay her eggs on, so the priest lays his curse on the fairest joys.

To create a little flower is the labour of ages.

Damn braces: Bless relaxes.

The best wine is the oldest, the best water the newest.

Prayers plow not! Praises reap not!

Joys laugh not! Sorrows weep not!

The head Sublime, the heart Pathos, the genitals Beauty, the hands & feet Proportion.

As the air to a bird or the sea to a fish, so is contempt to the contemptible.

The crow wish'd every thing was black, the owl, that every thing was white.

Exuberance is Beauty.

If the lion was advised by the fox, he would be cunning.

Improv[em]ent makes strait roads, but the crooked roads without Improvement are roads of Genius.

Sooner murder an infant in its cradle than nurse unacted desires.

Where man is not, nature is barren.

Truth can never be told so as to be understood, and not be believ'd.
Enough! or Too much.

Annotations to Reynolds' Discourses

❡ About 1808, in the margins of his three-volume set of *The Works of Sir Joshua Reynolds*, edited by Edmund Malone, Second Edition, 1798 (now in the British Museum), Blake made extensive remarks on Reynolds' "Discourses," or presidential addresses delivered to the Royal Academy between 1769 and 1790. The following selections from his annotations are taken, without indication of the omissions, from *The Complete Writings of William Blake*, edited by Geoffrey Keynes, London and New York, 1957. ❞

The Arts & Sciences are the Destruction of Tyrannies or Bad Governments. Why should A Good Government endeavour to Depress what is its Chief & only Support?

The Foundation of Empire is Art & Science. Remove them or Degrade them, & the Empire is No More. Empire follows Art & Not Vice Versa as Englishmen suppose.

Invention depends Altogether upon Execution or Organization; as that is right or wrong so is the Invention perfect or imperfect.

Whoever is set to Undermine the Execution of Art is set to Destroy Art. Michael Angelo's Art depends on Michael Angelo's Execution Altogether.

To Generalize is to be an Idiot. To Particularize is the Alone Distinction of Merit. General Knowledges are those Knowledges that Idiots possess.

Minute Discrimination is Not Accidental. All Sublimity is founded on Minute Discrimination.

I do not believe that Rafael taught Mich. Angelo, or that Mich. Angelo taught Rafael, any more than I believe that the Rose teaches the Lilly how to grow, or the Apple tree teaches the Pear tree how to bear Fruit. I do not believe the tales of Anecdote writers when they militate against Individual Character.

Knowledge of Ideal Beauty is Not to be Acquired. It is Born with us. Innate Ideas are in Every Man, Born with him; they are truly Himself. The Man who says that we have No Innate Ideas must be a Fool & Knave, Having No Con-Science or Innate Science.

Obscurity is Neither the Source of the Sublime nor of any Thing Else.

God forbid that Truth should be Confined to Mathematical Demonstration!

He who does not Know Truth at Sight is unworthy of Her Notice.

Burke's Treatise on the Sublime & Beautiful is founded on the Opinions of Newton & Locke; on this Treatise Reynolds has grounded many of his assertions in all his Discourses. I read Burke's Treatise when very Young; at the same time I read Locke on Human Understanding & Bacon's Advancement of Learning; on Every one of these Books I wrote my Opinions, & on looking them over find that my Notes on Reynolds in this Book are exactly Similar. I felt the Same Contempt & Abhorrence then that I do now. They mock Inspiration & Vision. Inspiration & Vision was then, & now is, & I hope will always Remain, my Element, my Eternal Dwelling place; how can I then hear it Contemned without returning Scorn for Scorn?

A Descriptive Catalogue
of Pictures, Poetical and Historical Inventions

❨ A *Descriptive Catalogue*, 1809, describes sixteen of the pictures in the exhibit that Blake opened in May of that year. Mr. B., as he calls himself in the *Catalogue*, announced that the exhibit would close on September 29. Harsh reviews in the *Examiner*, by Leigh Hunt's brother Robert, were almost the only public notice the exhibition received. The fourth picture is Blake's interpretation of the poem by Thomas Gray which most affected the Romantics, "The Bard: A Pindaric Ode." The text here follows the copy of the *Catalogue* in the Huntington Library. ❩

NUMBER IV

The Bard, from Gray.

> On a rock, whose haughty brow
> Frown'd o'er old Conway's foaming flood,
> Robed in the sable garb of woe,
> With haggard eyes the Poet stood,
> Loose his beard, and hoary hair
> Stream'd like a meteor to the troubled air.
>
> Weave the warp, and weave the woof,
> The winding sheet of Edward's race.[1]

Weaving the winding sheet of Edward's race by means of sounds

[1] Blake quotes from Gray's ode lines 15–20, 49–50, 47–48, and 12.

of spiritual music and its accompanying expressions of articulate speech is a bold, and daring, and most masterly conception, that the public have embraced and approved with avidity. Poetry consists in these conceptions; and shall Painting be confined to the sordid drudgery of fac-simile representations of merely mortal and perishing substances, and not be as poetry and music are, elevated into its own proper sphere of invention and visionary conception? No, it shall not be so! Painting, as well as poetry and music, exists and exults in immortal thoughts. If Mr. B.'s Canterbury Pilgrims had been done by any other power than that of the poetic visionary, it would have been as dull as his adversary's.

The Spirits of the murdered bards assist in weaving the deadly woof.

> With me in dreadful harmony they join,
> And weave, with bloody hands, the tissue of thy line.

The connoisseurs and artists who have made objections to Mr. B.'s mode of representing spirits with real bodies, would do well to consider that the Venus, the Minerva, the Jupiter, the Apollo, which they admire in Greek statues, are all of them representations of spiritual existences of God's immortal, to the mortal perishing organ of sight; and yet they are embodied and organized in solid marble. Mr. B. requires the same latitude and all is well. The Prophets describe what they saw in Vision as real and existing men whom they saw with their imaginative and immortal organs; the Apostles the same; the clearer the organ the more distinct the object. A Spirit and a Vision are not, as the modern philosophy supposes, a cloudy vapour or a nothing: they are organized and minutely articulated beyond all that the mortal and perishing nature can produce. He who does not imagine in stronger and better lineaments, and in stronger and better light than his perishing mortal eye can see does not imagine at all. The painter of this work asserts that all his imaginations appear to him infinitely more perfect and more minutely organized than any thing seen by his mortal eye. Spirits are organized men: Moderns wish to draw figures without lines, and with great and heavy shadows; are not shadows more unmeaning than lines, and more heavy? O who can doubt this!

King Edward and his Queen Elenor are prostrated, with their horses, at the foot of a rock on which the Bard stands; prostrated by the terrors of his harp on the margin of the river Conway, whose waves bear up a corse of a slaughtered bard at the foot of the rock. The armies of Edward are seen winding among the mountains.

> "He wound with toilsome march his long array."

Mortimer and Gloucester lie spell bound behind their king.

The execution of this picture is also in Water Colours, or Fresco.

Dorothy Wordsworth

Journals

⟨[Without publishing a word, Dorothy Wordsworth (1771–1855) kept invaluable journals of residences, walks, and extended tours (in Germany, 1798; Scotland, 1803 and 1822; five Continental countries, 1820; and the Isle of Man, 1828), nearly always in the company of her brother William. Although both Wordsworth and Coleridge sometimes referred to Dorothy's journals in composing poems, the details and language recorded there may have come just as frequently from the poets' conversation. With or without their aid, she was extremely sensitive to her surroundings, to people, and to language. The complete journals were published in two volumes by Ernest de Selincourt in 1941. The entries below are taken from the text of the Dove Cottage (Grasmere) journal as revised by Helen Darbishire in 1958.]⟩

[*1801, November*] *24th, Tuesday.* A rainy morning. We all were well except that my head ached a little, and I took my Breakfast in bed. I read a little of Chaucer, prepared the goose for dinner, and then we all walked out. I was obliged to return for my fur tippet and Spenser,[1] it was so cold. We had intended going to Easedale, but we shaped our course to Mr. Gell's cottage. It was very windy, and we heard the wind everywhere about us as we went along the lane, but the walls sheltered us. John Green's house looked pretty under Silver How. As we were going along we were stopped at once, at the distance perhaps of 50 yards from our favorite Birch tree. It was yielding to the gusty wind with all its tender twigs, the sun shone upon it, and it glanced in the wind like a flying sunshiny shower. It was a tree in shape, with stem and branches, but it was like a Spirit of water. The sun went in, and it resumed its purplish appearance, the twigs still yielding to the wind, but not so visibly to us. The other Birch trees that were near it looked bright and chearful, but it was a creature by its own self among them. We could not get into Mr. Gell's grounds — the old tree fallen from its undue exaltation above the Gate. A shower came on when we were at Benson's. We went through the wood — it became fair. There was a rainbow which spanned the lake from the island-house to the foot of Bainriggs. The village looked populous and beautiful. Catkins are coming out; palm trees budding; the alder, with its plumb-coloured buds. We came home over the stepping-stones.

[1] a jacket (from the 2nd Earl Spencer, 1758–1834).

The Lake was foamy with white waves. I saw a solitary butter-flower in the wood. I found it not easy to get over the stepping stones. Reached home at dinner time. Sent Peggy Ashburner some goose. She sent me some honey, with a thousand thanks. "Alas! the gratitude of men has", etc.[2] I went in to set her right about this, and sate a while with her. She talked about Thomas's having sold his land. "Ay," says she, "I said many a time he's not come fra London to buy our Land, however." Then she told me with what pains and industry they had made up their taxes, interest, etc. etc., how they all got up at 5 o'clock in the morning to spin and Thomas carded, and that they had paid off a hundred pound of the interest. She said she used to take such pleasure in the cattle and sheep. "O how pleased I used to be when they fetched them down, and when I had been a bit poorly I would gang out upon a hill and look ower t' fields and see them, and it used to do me so much good you cannot think." Molly said to me when I came in, "Poor Body! she's very ill, but one does not know how long she may last. Many a fair face may gang before her." We sate by the fire without work for some time, then Mary read a poem of Daniel upon Learning. After tea Wm. read Spenser, now and then a little aloud to us. We were making his waistcoat. We had a note from Mrs. C[oleridge]., with bad news from poor C. — very ill. William walked to John's Grove. I went to meet him. Moonlight, but it rained. I met him before I had got as far as John Baty's — he had been surprized and terrified by a sudden rushing of winds, which seemed to bring earth sky and lake together, as if the whole were going to enclose him in; he was glad he was in a high Road.

In speaking of our walk on Sunday evening, the 22nd November, I forgot to notice one most impressive sight. It was the moon and the moonlight seen through hurrying driving clouds immediately behind the Stone-Man upon the top of the hill on the Forest Side. Every tooth and every edge of Rock was visible, and the Man stood like a Giant watching from the Roof of a lofty castle. The hill seemed perpendicular from the darkness below it. It was a sight that I could call to mind at any time, it was so distinct.

November 28, Saturday. — A very fine sunny morning. Soldiers still going by. I should have mentioned that yesterday when we went with Wm. to Mr. Luff's we met a soldier and his wife, he with a child in his arms, she carrying a bundle and his gun — we gave them some halfpence, it was such a pretty sight. William having slept ill lay in bed till after one o'clock. Mary and I walked up to Mr. Simpson's between 20 minutes before 2 and 20 minutes before 3 to desire them not to come. We drank tea and supped at Mr. Olliff's — a keen frost with sparkling stars when we came home at ½ past 11.

[*1802, April*] *15, Thursday.* It was a threatening, misty morning,

---

[2] Wordsworth, *Simon Lee* 75–76.

but mild. We set off after dinner from Eusemere. Mrs. Clarkson went a short way with us, but turned back. The wind was furious, and we thought we must have returned. We first rested in the large Boathouse, then under a furze bush opposite Mr. Clarkson's. Saw the plough going in the field. The wind seized our breath. The Lake was rough. There was a Boat by itself floating in the middle of the Bay below Water Millock. We rested again in the Water Millock Lane. The hawthorns are black and green, the birches here and there greenish, but there is yet more of purple to be seen on the twigs. We got over into a field to avoid some cows — people working. A few primroses by the roadside — woodsorrel flower, the anemone, scentless violets, strawberries, and that starry, yellow flower which Mrs. C. calls pile wort. When we were in the woods beyond Gowbarrow park we saw a few daffodils close to the water-side. We fancied that the lake had floated the seeds ashore, and that the little colony had so sprung up. But as we went along there were more and yet more; and at last, under the boughs of the trees, we saw that there was a long belt of them along the shore, about the breadth of a country turnpike road. I never saw daffodils so beautiful. They grew among the mossy stones about and about them; some rested their heads upon these stones as on a pillow for weariness; and the rest tossed and reeled and danced, and seemed as if they verily laughed with the wind, that blew upon them over the lake; they looked so gay, ever glancing, ever changing. This wind blew directly over the lake to them. There was here and there a little knot, and a few stragglers a few yards higher up; but they were so few as not to disturb the simplicity, unity, and life of that one busy highway. We rested again and again. The bays were stormy, and we heard the waves at different distances, and in the middle of the water, like the sea. Rain came on — we were wet when we reached Luff's, but we called in. Luckily all was chearless and gloomy, so we faced the storm — we *must* have been wet if we had waited — put on dry clothes at Dobson's. I was very kindly treated by a young woman, the Landlady looked sour, but it is her way. She gave us a goodish supper, excellent ham and potatoes. We paid 7/- when we came away. William was sitting by a bright fire when I came downstairs. He soon made his way to the library, piled up in a corner of the window. He brought out a volume of Enfield's *Speaker,* another miscellany, and an odd volume of Congreve's plays. We had a glass of warm rum and water. We enjoyed ourselves, and wished for Mary. It rained and blew, when we went to bed. N.B. Deer in Gowbarrow park like skeletons.

April 16th, Friday (Good Friday). When I undrew my curtains in the morning, I was much affected by the beauty of the prospect, and the change. The sun shone, the wind had passed away, the hills looked chearful, the river was very bright as it flowed into the lake. The Church rises up behind a little knot of Rocks, the steeple not so

high as an ordinary three-story house. Trees in a row in the garden
under the wall. After Wm. had shaved we set forward; the valley is
at first broken by little rocky wooden knolls that make retiring places,
fairy valleys in the vale; the river winds along under these hills, travelling, not in a bustle but not slowly, to the lake. We saw a fisherman
in the flat meadow on the other side of the water. He came towards
us, and threw his line over the two-arched Bridge. It is a Bridge of a
heavy construction, almost bending inwards in the middle, but it is
grey, and there is a look of ancientry in the architecture of it that
pleased me. As we go on the vale opens out more into one vale, with
somewhat of a cradle bed. Cottages, with groups of trees, on the side
of the hills. We passed a pair of twin Children, 2 years old. Sate on
the next bridge which we crossed — a single arch. We rested again
upon the Turf, and looked at the same bridge. We observed arches in
the water, occasioned by the large stones sending it down in two
streams. A Sheep came plunging through the river, stumbled up the
bank, and passed close to us, it had been frightened by an insignificant
little Dog on the other side. Its fleece dropped a glittering shower
under its belly. Primroses by the road-side, pile wort that shone like
stars of gold in the Sun, violets, strawberries, retired and half-buried
among the grass. When we came to the foot of Brothers Water, I left
William sitting on the bridge, and went along the path on the right
side of the Lake through the wood. I was delighted with what I saw.
The water under the boughs of the bare old trees, the simplicity of the
mountains, and the exquisite beauty of the path. There was one grey
cottage. I repeated *The Glow-worm*,[3] as I walked along. I hung over
the gate, and thought I could have stayed for ever. When I returned,
I found William writing a poem descriptive of the sights and sounds
we saw and heard.[4] . . .

[*1802, entry of July 27 continued:*] On Thursday morning, 29th,
we arrived in London. Wm. left me at the Inn. I went to bed, etc. etc.
After various troubles and disasters, we left London on Saturday
morning at $\frac{1}{2}$-past 5 or 6, the 31st of July. (I have forgot which.)
We mounted the Dover Coach at Charing Cross. It was a beautiful
morning. The City, St. Paul's, with the river and a multitude of little
Boats, made a most beautiful sight as we crossed Westminster Bridge.
The houses were not overhung by their cloud of smoke, and they were
spread out endlessly, yet the sun shone so brightly, with such a fierce
light, that there was even something like the purity of one of nature's
own grand spectacles.

We rode on chearfully, now with the Paris Diligence before us,
now behind. We walked up the steep hills, beautiful prospects everywhere, till we even reached Dover. At first the rich, populous, wide-

[3] "Among all lovely things my Love had been."
[4] "The Cock is crowing" (published as *Written in March* . . .).

spreading, woody country about London, then the River Thames, ships sailing, chalk cliffs, trees, little villages. Afterwards Canterbury, situated on a plain, rich and woody, but the City and Cathedral disappointed me. Hop grounds on each side of the road some miles from Canterbury, then we came to a common, the race ground, an elevated plain, villages among trees in the bed of a valley at our right, and, rising above this valley, green hills scattered over with wood, neat gentlemen's houses. One white house, almost hid with green trees, which we longed for, and the parson's house, as neat a place as could be, which would just have suited Coleridge. No doubt we might have found one for Tom Hutchinson and Sara, and a good farm too. We halted at a halfway house — fruit carts under the shade of trees, seats for guests, a tempting place to the weary traveller. Still, as we went along, the country was beautiful, hilly, with cottages lurking under the hills, and their little plots of hop ground like vineyards. It was a bad hop year. A woman on the top of the coach said to me, "It is a sad thing for the poor people, for the hop-gathering is the women's harvest; there is employment about the hops both for women and children".

* * * * *

On Monday, 4th October 1802, my Brother William was married to Mary Hutchinson. I slept a good deal of the night, and rose fresh and well in the morning. At a little after 8 o'clock I saw them go down the avenue towards the church. William had parted from me upstairs. I gave him the wedding ring — with how deep a blessing! I took it from my forefinger where I had worn it the whole of the night before — he slipped it again onto my finger and blessed me fervently. When they were absent my dear little Sara prepared the breakfast. I kept myself as quiet as I could, but when I saw the two men running up the walk, coming to tell us it was over, I could stand it no longer, and threw myself on the bed, where I lay in stillness, neither hearing or seeing anything till Sara came upstairs to me, and said, "They are coming". This forced me from the bed where I lay, and I moved, I knew not how, straight forward, faster than my strength could carry me, till I met my beloved William, and fell upon his bosom. He and John Hutchinson led me to the house, and there I stayed to welcome my dear Mary. As soon as we had breakfasted, we departed. It rained when we set off. Poor Mary was much agitated, when she parted from her Brothers and Sisters, and her home. Nothing particular occurred till we reached Kirby. We had sunshine and showers, pleasant talk, love and chearfulness. . . .[5]

[5] Samuel Daniel's "Musophilus," 1599, is a poetic dialogue on learning; William Enfield, *The Speaker*, 1774, a popular anthology; William Congreve (1670–1729), dramatist.

Jane Austen

Letter to the Regent's Librarian

❆ Jane Austen (1775–1817) prudently kept a copy of this letter to the Rev. James S. Clarke, which was first published by members of the Austen-Leigh family in *A Memoir of Jane Austen,* 1870, and freshly transcribed in *Jane Austen: Her Life and Letters,* 1913. Her collected *Letters,* in an edition revised by R. W. Chapman in 1952, illustrate in detail the manners of Miss Austen's social class, her gay malice, and her "zest for the small concerns" of friends as well as of created characters. ❂

Dec. 11 [1815]

Dear Sir

My "Emma" is now so near publication that I feel it right to assure you of my not having forgotten your kind recommendation of an early copy for Carlton House, and that I have Mr. Murray's promise of its being sent to His Royal Highness, under cover to you, three days previous to the work being really out.[1] I must make use of this opportunity to thank you, dear Sir, for the very high praise you bestow on my other novels. I am too vain to wish to convince you that you have praised them beyond their merits. My greatest anxiety at present is that this fourth work should not disgrace what was good in the others. But on this point I will do myself the justice to declare that, whatever may be my wishes for its success, I am very strongly haunted with the idea that to those readers who have preferred "Pride and Prejudice" it will appear inferior in wit, and to those who have preferred "Mansfield Park" very inferior in good sense. Such as it is, however, I hope you will do me the favour of accepting a copy. Mr. Murray will have directions for sending one. I am quite honoured by your thinking me capable of drawing such a clergyman as you gave the sketch of in your note of Nov. 16th. But I assure you I am *not*. The comic part of the character I might be equal to, but not the good, the enthusiastic, the literary. Such a man's conversation must at times be on subjects of science and philosophy, of which I know nothing; or at least be occasionally abundant in quotations and allusions which a woman who, like me, knows only her own mother tongue, and has read very little in that, would be totally without the power of giving. A classical education, or at any rate a very extensive acquaintance with English literature, ancient and modern, appears to

[1] John Murray (1778–1843), publisher of *Emma,* of Byron, and of the *Quarterly Review.*

me quite indispensable for the person who would do any justice to your clergyman; and I think I may boast myself to be, with all possible vanity, the most unlearned and uninformed female who ever dared to be an authoress.

Believe me, dear Sir,
Your obliged and faithful hum^{bl} Ser^t.
Jane Austen

❲❳

Thomas Love Peacock

The Four Ages of Poetry

❲ *The Four Ages of Poetry* appeared anonymously in *Ollier's Literary Miscellany*, No. 1, November 1820. Its author, Thomas Love Peacock (1785–1866), a friend and later biographer of Shelley, scattered among his imaginatively original novels various lyrics expressing the "pensive passion of the moment" (the phrase is Oliver Elton's). Macaulay was soon to argue, without irony, that civilization and enlightenment require the eclipse of poetry. Peacock's similar thesis contains not only satirical paradox, but also irony turned against himself and his friends. Because the deliberately flat opening prepares for the sting of the close, and because the structure of Peacock's essay helps to explain the structure of Shelley's answering *Defence*, the entire essay is given here, from the copy of *Ollier's Miscellany* at Harvard University, with a few corrections from the manuscript in the British Museum. ❳

Qui inter hæc nutriuntur non magis sapere possunt, quam bene olere qui in culinâ habitant.   PETRONIUS.[1]

Poetry, like the world, may be said to have four ages, but in a different order: the first age of poetry being the age of iron; the second, of gold; the third, of silver; and the fourth, of brass.

The first, or iron age of poetry, is that in which rude bards celebrate in rough numbers the exploits of ruder chiefs, in days when every man is a warrior, and when the great practical maxim of every form of society, "to keep what we have and to catch what we can," is not yet disguised under names of justice and forms of law, but is the naked motto of the naked sword, which is the only judge and jury in every

---

[1] "Nourished on this stuff, how can they have acquired taste? — whoever lives in a kitchen will have a strong smell." — *Satyricon* 2.

question of *meum* and *tuum*. In these days, the only three trades flourishing (besides that of priest which flourishes always) are those of king, thief, and beggar: the beggar being for the most part a king deject, and the thief a king expectant. The first question asked of a stranger is, whether he is a beggar or a thief:[2] the stranger, in reply, usually assumes the first, and awaits a convenient opportunity to prove his claim to the second appellation.

The natural desire of every man to engross to himself as much power and property as he can acquire by any of the means which might makes right, is accompanied by the no less natural desire of making known to as many people as possible the extent to which he has been a winner in this universal game. The successful warrior becomes a chief; the successful chief becomes a king: his next want is an organ to disseminate the fame of his achievements and the extent of his possessions; and this organ he finds in a bard, who is always ready to celebrate the strength of his arm, being first duly inspired by that of his liquor. This is the origin of poetry, which, like all other trades, takes its rise in the demand for the commodity, and flourishes in proportion to the extent of the market.

Poetry is thus in its origin panegyrical. The first rude songs of all nations appear to be a sort of brief historical notices, in a strain of tumid hyperbole, of the exploits and possessions of a few pre-eminent individuals. They tell us how many battles such an one has fought, how many helmets he has cleft, how many breastplates he has pierced, how many widows he has made, how much land he has appropriated, how many houses he has demolished for other people, what a large one he has built for himself, how much gold he has stowed away in it, and how liberally and plentifully he pays, feeds, and intoxicates the divine and immortal bards, the sons of Jupiter, but for whose everlasting songs the names of heroes would perish.

This is the first stage of poetry before the invention of written letters. The numerical modulation is at once useful as a help to memory, and pleasant to the ears of uncultured men, who are easily caught by sound: and from the exceeding flexibility of the yet unformed language, the poet does no violence to his ideas in subjecting them to the fetters of number. The savage indeed lisps in numbers, and all rude and uncivilized people express themselves in the manner which we call poetical.

The scenery by which he is surrounded, and the superstitions which are the creed of his age, form the poet's mind. Rocks, mountains, seas, unsubdued forests, unnavigable rivers, surround him with forms of power and mystery, which ignorance and fear have peopled with spirits, under multifarious names of gods, goddesses, nymphs, genii, and dæmons. Of all these personages marvellous tales are in existence:

---

[2] See the Odyssey, passim: and Thucydides, I.5. [Peacock's note.]

the nymphs are not indifferent to handsome young men, and the gentlemen-genii are much troubled and very troublesome with a propensity to be rude to pretty maidens: the bard therefore finds no difficulty in tracing the genealogy of his chief to any of the deities in his neighbourhood with whom the said chief may be most desirous of claiming relationship.

In this pursuit, as in all others, some of course will attain a very marked pre-eminence; and these will be held in high honor, like Demodocus in the Odyssey, and will be consequently inflated with boundless vanity, like Thamyris in the Iliad. Poets are as yet the only historians and chroniclers of their time, and the sole depositories of all the knowledge of their age; and though this knowledge is rather a crude congeries of traditional phantasies than a collection of useful truths, yet, such as it is, they have it to themselves. They are observing and thinking, while others are robbing and fighting: and though their object be nothing more than to secure a share of the spoil, yet they accomplish this end by intellectual, not by physical, power: their success excites emulation to the attainment of intellectual eminence: thus they sharpen their own wits and awaken those of others, at the same time that they gratify vanity and amuse curiosity. A skilful display of the little knowledge they have gains them credit for the possession of much more which they have not. Their familiarity with the secret history of gods and genii obtains for them, without much difficulty, the reputation of inspiration; thus they are not only historians but theologians, moralists, and legislators: delivering their oracles *ex cathedrâ,* and being indeed often themselves (as Orpheus and Amphion) regarded as portions and emanations of divinity: building cities with a song, and leading brutes with a symphony; which are only metaphors for the faculty of leading multitudes by the nose.

The golden age of poetry finds its materials in the age of iron. This age begins when poetry begins to be retrospective; when something like a more extended system of civil polity is established; when personal strength and courage avail less to the aggrandising of their possessor and to the making and marring of kings and kingdoms, and are checked by organised bodies, social institutions, and hereditary successions. Men also live more in the light of truth and within the interchange of observation; and thus perceive that the agency of gods and genii is not so frequent among themselves as, to judge from the songs and legends of the past time, it was among their ancestors. From these two circumstances, really diminished personal power, and apparently diminished familiarity with gods and genii, they very easily and naturally deduce two conclusions: 1st, That men are degenerated, and 2nd, That they are less in favour with the gods. The people of the petty states and colonies, which have now acquired stability and form, which owed their origin and first prosperity to the talents and courage of a single chief, magnify their founder through the mists of distance and tradition, and perceive him achieving wonders with a god or goddess always at his elbow. They find his name and his exploits thus magnified and accompanied in their traditionary songs, which are their only memorials. All that is said of him is in this character. There is nothing to contradict it. The man and his exploits and his tutelary deities are mixed and blended in one invariable association. The marvellous too is very much like a snow-ball: it grows as it rolls downward, till the little nucleus of truth which began its descent from the summit is hidden in the accumulation of superinduced hyperbole.

When tradition, thus adorned and exaggerated, has surrounded the founders of families and states with so much adventitious power and magnificence, there is no praise which a living poet can, without fear of being kicked for clumsy flattery, address to a living chief, that will not still leave the impression that the latter is not so great a man as his ancestors. The man must in this case be praised through his ancestors. Their greatness must be established, and he must be shown to be their worthy descendant. All the people of a state are interested in the founder of their state. All states that have harmonized into a common form of society, are interested in their respective founders. All men are interested in their ancestors. All men love to look back into the days that are past. In these circumstances traditional national poetry is reconstructed and brought like chaos into order and form. The interest is more universal: understanding is enlarged: passion still has scope and play: character is still various and strong: nature is still unsubdued and existing in all her beauty and magnificence, and men are not yet excluded from her observation by the magnitude of cities or the daily confinement of civic life: poetry is more an art: it requires greater skill in numbers, greater command of language, more extensive and various knowledge, and greater comprehensiveness of mind. It still exists without rivals in any other department of literature; and even the arts, painting and sculpture certainly, and music probably, are comparatively rude and imperfect. The whole field of intellect is its own. It has no rivals in history, nor in philosophy, nor in science. It is cultivated by the greatest intellects of the age, and listened to by all the rest. This is the age of Homer, the golden age of poetry. Poetry has now attained its perfection: it has attained the point which it cannot pass: genius therefore seeks new forms for the treatment of the same subjects: hence the lyric poetry of Pindar and Alcæus, and the tragic poetry of Æschylus and Sophocles. The favor of kings, the honour of the Olympic crown, the applause of present multitudes, all that can feed vanity and stimulate rivalry, await the successful cultivator of this art, till its forms become exhausted, and new rivals arise around it in new fields of literature, which gradually acquire more influence as, with the progress of reason and civilization, facts become more interesting than fiction: indeed the maturity of poetry may be considered the infancy of history. The transition from Homer to Herodotus is scarcely more remarkable than that from Herodotus to Thucydides: in the gradual dereliction of fabulous incident and ornamented language, Herodotus is as much a poet in relation to Thucydides as Homer is in relation to Herodotus. The history of Herodotus is half a poem: it was written while the whole field of literature yet belonged to the Muses, and the nine books of which it was composed were therefore of right, as well as courtesy, superinscribed with their nine names.

Speculations, too, and disputes, on the nature of man and of mind; on moral duties and on good and evil; on the animate and inanimate components of the visible world; begin to share attention with the eggs of Leda and the horns of Io, and to draw off from poetry a portion of its once undivided audience.

Then comes the silver age, or the poetry of civilized life. This poetry is of two kinds, imitative and original. The imitative consists in recasting, and giving an exquisite polish to, the poetry of the age of gold: of this Virgil is the most obvious and striking example. The original is chiefly comic, didactic, or satiric: as in Menander, Aristophanes, Horace, and Juvenal. The poetry of this age is characterised by an exquisite and fastidious selection of words, and a laboured and somewhat monotonous harmony of expression: but its monotony consists in this, that experience having exhausted all the varieties of modulation, the civilized poetry selects the most beautiful, and prefers the repetition of these to ranging through the variety of all. But the best expression being that into which the idea naturally falls, it requires the utmost labour and care so to reconcile the inflexibility of civilized language and the laboured polish of versification with the idea intended to be expressed, that sense may not appear to be sacrificed to sound. Hence numerous efforts and rare success.

This state of poetry is however a step towards its extinction. Feeling and passion are best painted in, and roused by, ornamental and figurative language; but the reason and the understanding are best addressed in the simplest and most unvarnished phrase. Pure reason and dispassionate truth would be perfectly ridiculous in verse, as we may judge by versifying one of Euclid's demonstrations. This will be found true of all dispassionate reasoning whatever, and of all reasoning that requires comprehensive views and enlarged combinations. It is only the more tangible points of morality, those which command assent at once, those which have a mirror in every mind, and in which the severity of reason is warmed and rendered palatable by being mixed up with feeling and imagination, that are applicable even to what is called moral poetry: and as the sciences of morals and of mind advance towards perfection, as they become more enlarged and comprehensive in their views, as reason gains the ascendancy in them over imagination and feeling, poetry can no longer accompany them in their progress, but drops into the back ground, and leaves them to advance alone.

Thus the empire of thought is withdrawn from poetry, as the empire of facts had been before. In respect of the latter, the poet of the age of iron celebrates the achievements of his contemporaries; the poet of the age of gold celebrates the heroes of the age of iron; the poet of the age of silver re-casts the poems of the age of gold: we may here see how very slight a ray of historical truth is sufficient to dissipate all the illusions of poetry. We know no more of the men than of the gods of the Iliad; no more of Achilles than we do of Thetis; no more of Hector and Andromache than we do of Vulcan and Venus: these belong altogether to poetry; history has no share in them: but Virgil knew better than to write an epic about Cæsar; he left him to Livy; and travelled out of the confines of truth and history into the old regions of poetry and fiction.

Good sense and elegant learning, conveyed in polished and some-what monotonous verse, are the perfection of the original and imitative poetry of civilized life. Its range is limited, and when exhausted, nothing remains but the *crambe repetita* of common-place, which at length becomes thoroughly wearisome, even to the most indefatigable readers of the newest new nothings.

It is now evident that poetry must either cease to be cultivated, or strike into a new path. The poets of the age of gold have been imitated and repeated till no new imitation will attract notice: the limited range of ethical and didactic poetry is exhausted: the associa-tions of daily life in an advanced state of society are of very dry, methodical, unpoetical matters-of-fact: but there is always a multitude of listless idlers, yawning for amusement, and gaping for novelty: and the poet makes it his glory to be foremost among their purveyors.

Then comes the age of brass, which, by rejecting the polish and the learning of the age of silver, and taking a retrograde stride to the barbarisms and crude traditions of the age of iron, professes to return to nature and revive the age of gold. This is the second childhood of poetry. For the comprehensive energy of the Homeric Muse, which, by giving at once the grand outline of things, presented to the mind a vivid picture in one or two verses, inimitable alike in simplicity and magnificence, is substituted a verbose and minutely-detailed description of thoughts, passions, actions, persons, and things, in that loose ram-bling style of verse, which any one may write, *stans pede in uno*,[3] at the rate of two hundred lines in an hour. To this age may be referred all the poets who flourished in the decline of the Roman Empire. The best specimen of it, though not the most generally known, is the Dionysiaca of Nonnus, which contains many passages of exceeding beauty in the midst of masses of amplification and repetition.

[3] standing on one foot.

The iron age of classical poetry may be called the bardic; the golden, the Homeric; the silver, the Virgilian; and the brass, the Nonnic.

Modern poetry has also its four ages: but "it wears its rue with a difference."[4]

To the age of brass in the ancient world succeeded the dark ages, in which the light of the Gospel began to spread over Europe, and in which, by a mysterious and inscrutable dispensation, the darkness thickened with the progress of the light. The tribes that overran the Roman Empire brought back the days of barbarism, but with this difference, that there were many books in the world, many places in which they were preserved, and occasionally some one by whom they were read, who indeed (if he escaped being burned *pour l'amour de Dieu*),[5] generally lived an object of mysterious fear, with the reputation of magician, alchymist, and astrologer. The emerging of the nations of Europe from this superinduced barbarism, and their settling into new forms of polity, was accompanied, as the first ages of Greece had been, with a wild spirit of adventure, which, co-operating with new manners and new superstitions, raised up a fresh crop of chimæras, not less fruitful, though far less beautiful, than those of Greece. The semi-deification of women by the maxims of the age of chivalry, combining with these new fables, produced the romance of the middle ages. The founders of the new line of heroes took the place of the demi-gods of Grecian poetry. Charlemagne and his Paladins, Arthur and his knights of the round table, the heroes of the iron age of chivalrous poetry, were seen through the same magnifying mist of distance, and their exploits were celebrated with even more extravagant hyperbole. These legends, combined with the exaggerated love that pervades the songs of the troubadours, the reputation of magic that attached to learned men, the infant wonders of natural philosophy, the crazy fanaticism of the crusades, the power and privileges of the great feudal chiefs, and the holy mysteries of monks and nuns, formed a state of society in which no two laymen could meet without fighting, and in which the three staple ingredients of lover, prize-fighter, and fanatic, that composed the basis of the character of every true man, were mixed up and diversified, in different individuals and classes, with so many distinctive excellencies, and under such an infinite motley variety of costume, as gave the range of a most extensive and picturesque field to the two great constituents of poetry, love and battle.

From these ingredients of the iron age of modern poetry, dispersed in the rhymes of minstrels and the songs of the troubadours, arose the golden age, in which the scattered materials were harmonized and blended about the time of the revival of learning; but with this

[4] Cf. *Hamlet* IV.v.183.
[5] for the love of God.

peculiar difference, that Greek and Roman literature pervaded all the poetry of the golden age of modern poetry, and hence resulted a heterogeneous compound of all ages and nations in one picture; an infinite licence, which gave to the poet the free range of the whole field of imagination and memory. This was carried very far by Ariosto, but farthest of all by Shakspeare and his contemporaries, who used time and locality merely because they could not do without them, because every action must have its when and where: but they made no scruple of deposing a Roman Emperor by an Italian Count, and sending him off in the disguise of a French pilgrim to be shot with a blunderbuss by an English archer. This makes the old English drama very picturesque, at any rate, in the variety of costume, and very diversified in action and character; though it is a picture of nothing that ever was seen on earth except a Venetian carnival.

The greatest of English poets, Milton, may be said to stand alone between the ages of gold and silver, combining the excellencies of both; for with all the energy, and power, and freshness of the first, he united all the studied and elaborate magnificence of the second.

The silver age succeeded; beginning with Dryden, coming to perfection with Pope, and ending with Goldsmith, Collins, and Gray.

Cowper divested verse of its exquisite polish; he thought in metre, but paid more attention to his thoughts than his verse. It would be difficult to draw the boundary of prose and blank verse between his letters and his poetry.

The silver age was the reign of authority; but authority now began to be shaken, not only in poetry but in the whole sphere of its dominion. The contemporaries of Gray and Cowper were deep and elaborate thinkers. The subtle scepticism of Hume, the solemn irony of Gibbon, the daring paradoxes of Rousseau, and the biting ridicule of Voltaire, directed the energies of four extraordinary minds to shake every portion of the reign of authority. Enquiry was roused, the activity of intellect was excited, and poetry came in for its share of the general result. The changes had been rung on lovely maid and sylvan shade, summer heat and green retreat, waving trees and sighing breeze, gentle swains and amorous pains, by versifiers who took them on trust, as meaning something very soft and tender, without much caring what: but with this general activity of intellect came a necessity for even poets to appear to know something of what they professed to talk of. Thomson and Cowper looked at the trees and hills which so many ingenious gentlemen had rhymed about so long without looking at them at all, and the effect of the operation on poetry was like the discovery of a new world. Painting shared the influence, and the principles of picturesque beauty were explored by adventurous essayists with indefatigable pertinacity. The success which attended these experiments, and the pleasure which resulted from them, had the usual effect of all new enthusiasms, that of turning the heads of a few unfortunate persons, the patriarchs of the age of brass, who, mistaking the prominent novelty for the all-important totality, seem to have ratiocinated much in the following manner: "Poetical genius is the finest of all things, and we feel that we have more of it than any one ever had. The way to bring it to perfection is to cultivate poetical impressions exclusively. Poetical impressions can be received only among natural scenes: for all that is artificial is anti-poetical. Society is artificial, therefore we will live out of society. The mountains are natural, therefore we will live in the mountains. There we shall be shining models of purity and virtue, passing the whole day in the innocent and amiable occupation of going up and down hill, receiving poetical impressions, and communicating them in immortal verse to admiring generations." To some such perversion of intellect we owe that egregious confraternity of rhymesters, known by the name of the Lake Poets; who certainly did receive and communicate to the world some of the most extraordinary poetical impressions that ever were heard of, and ripened into models of public virtue, too splendid to need illustration. They wrote verses on a new principle; saw rocks and rivers in a new light; and remaining studiously ignorant of history, society, and human nature, cultivated the phantasy only at the expence of the memory and the reason; and contrived, though they had retreated from the world for the express purpose of seeing nature as she was, to see her only as she was not, converting the land they lived in into a sort of fairy-land, which they peopled with mysticisms and chimæras. This gave what is called a new tone to poetry, and conjured up a herd of desperate imitators, who have brought the age of brass prematurely to its dotage.

The descriptive poetry of the present day has been called by its cultivators a return to nature. Nothing is more impertinent than this pretension. Poetry cannot travel out of the regions of its birth, the uncultivated lands of semi-civilized men. Mr. Wordsworth, the great leader of the returners to nature, cannot describe a scene under his own eyes without putting into it the shadow of a Danish boy or the living ghost of Lucy Gray, or some similar phantastical parturition of the moods of his own mind.

In the origin and perfection of poetry, all the associations of life were composed of poetical materials. With us it is decidedly the reverse. We know too that there are no Dryads in Hyde-park nor Naiads in the Regent's-canal. But barbaric manners and supernatural interventions are essential to poetry. Either in the scene, or in the time, or in both, it must be remote from our ordinary perceptions. While the historian and the philosopher are advancing in, and accelerating, the progress of knowledge, the poet is wallowing in the rubbish of departed ignorance, and raking up the ashes of dead savages to find gewgaws and rattles for the grown babies of the age. Mr. Scott digs up the poachers and cattle-stealers of the ancient border. Lord Byron cruizes for thieves and pirates on the shores of the Morea and among the Greek islands. Mr. Southey wades through ponderous volumes of travels and old chronicles, from which he carefully selects all that is false, useless, and absurd, as being essentially poetical; and when he has a common-place book full of monstrosities, strings them into an epic. Mr. Wordsworth picks up village legends from old women and sextons; and Mr. Coleridge, to the valuable information acquired from similar sources, superadds the dreams of crazy theologians and the mysticisms of German metaphysics, and favours the world with visions in verse, in which the quadruple elements of sexton, old woman, Jeremy Taylor, and Emanuel Kant, are harmonized into a delicious poetical compound. Mr. Moore presents us with a Persian, and Mr. Campbell with a Pennsylvanian tale, both formed on the same principle as Mr. Southey's epics, by extracting from a perfunctory and desultory perusal of a collection of voyages and travels, all that useful investigation would not seek for and that common sense would reject.[6]

These disjointed relics of tradition and fragments of second-hand observation, being woven into a tissue of verse, constructed on what Mr. Coleridge calls a new principle (that is, no principle at all), compose a modern-antique compound of frippery and barbarism, in which the puling sentimentality of the present time is grafted on the misrepresented ruggedness of the past into a heterogeneous congeries of unamalgamating manners, sufficient to impose on the common readers of poetry, over whose understandings the poet of this class possesses that commanding advantage, which, in all circumstances and conditions of life, a man who knows something, however little, always possesses over one who knows nothing.

A poet in our times is a semi-barbarian in a civilized community. He lives in the days that are past. His ideas, thoughts, feelings, associations, are all with barbarous manners, obsolete customs, and exploded superstitions. The march of his intellect is like that of a crab, backward. The brighter the light diffused around him by the progress of reason, the thicker is the darkness of antiquated barbarism, in which he buries himself like a mole, to throw up the barren hillocks of his Cimmerian labours. The philosophic mental tranquillity which looks round with an equal eye on all external things, collects a store of ideas, discriminates their relative value, assigns to all their proper place, and from the materials of useful knowledge thus collected, appreciated, and arranged, forms new combinations that impress the stamp of their power and utility on the real business of life, is diametrically the reverse of that frame of mind which poetry inspires, or from which poetry can emanate. The highest inspirations of poetry are resolvable into three ingredients: the rant of unregulated passion,

[6] Thomas Moore, *Lalla Rookh,* 1817; Thomas Campbell, *Gertrude of Wyoming,* 1809.

the whine of exaggerated feeling, and the cant of factitious sentiment: and can therefore serve only to ripen a splendid lunatic like Alexander, a puling driveller like Werter, or a morbid dreamer like Wordsworth. It can never make a philosopher, nor a statesman, nor in any class of life an useful or rational man. It cannot claim the slightest share in any one of the comforts and utilities of life of which we have witnessed so many and so rapid advances. But though not useful, it may be said it is highly ornamental, and deserves to be cultivated for the pleasure it yields. Even if this be granted, it does not follow that a writer of poetry in the present state of society is not a waster of his own time, and a robber of that of others. Poetry is not one of those arts which, like painting, require repetition and multiplication, in order to be diffused among society. There are more good poems already existing than are sufficient to employ that portion of life which any mere reader and recipient of poetical impressions should devote to them, and these having been produced in poetical times, are far superior in all the characteristics of poetry to the artificial reconstructions of a few morbid ascetics in unpoetical times. To read the promiscuous rubbish of the present time to the exclusion of the select treasures of the past, is to substitute the worse for the better variety of the same mode of enjoyment.

But in whatever degree poetry is cultivated, it must necessarily be to the neglect of some branch of useful study: and it is a lamentable spectacle to see minds, capable of better things, running to seed in the specious indolence of these empty aimless mockeries of intellectual exertion. Poetry was the mental rattle that awakened the attention of intellect in the infancy of civil society: but for the maturity of mind to make a serious business of the playthings of its childhood, is as absurd as for a full-grown man to rub his gums with coral, and cry to be charmed to sleep by the jingle of silver bells.

As to that small portion of our contemporary poetry, which is neither descriptive, nor narrative, nor dramatic, and which, for want of a better name, may be called ethical, the most distinguished portion of it, consisting merely of querulous, egotistical rhapsodies, to express the writer's high dissatisfaction with the world and every thing in it, serves only to confirm what has been said of the semi-barbarous character of poets, who from singing dithyrambics and "Io Triumphe," while society was savage, grow rabid, and out of their element, as it becomes polished and enlightened.

Now when we consider that it is not to the thinking and studious, and scientific and philosophical part of the community, not to those whose minds are bent on the pursuit and promotion of permanently useful ends and aims, that poets must address their minstrelsy, but to that much larger portion of the reading public, whose minds are not awakened to the desire of valuable knowledge, and who are indifferent to any thing beyond being charmed, moved, excited, affected,

and exalted: charmed by harmony, moved by sentiment, excited by
passion, affected by pathos, and exalted by sublimity: harmony, which
is language on the rack of Procrustes; sentiment, which is canting
egotism in the mask of refined feeling; passion, which is the commotion
of a weak and selfish mind; pathos, which is the whining of an unmanly spirit; and sublimity, which is the inflation of an empty head:
when we consider that the great and permanent interests of human
society become more and more the main spring of intellectual pursuit;
that in proportion as they become so, the subordinacy of the ornamental to the useful will be more and more seen and acknowledged;
and that therefore the progress of useful art and science, and of moral
and political knowledge, will continue more and more to withdraw
attention from frivolous and unconducive, to solid and conducive
studies: that therefore the poetical audience will not only continually
diminish in the proportion of its number to that of the rest of the
reading public, but will also sink lower and lower in the comparison
of intellectual acquirement: when we consider that the poet must
still please his audience, and must therefore continue to sink to their
level, while the rest of the community is rising above it: we may easily
conceive that the day is not distant, when the degraded state of every
species of poetry will be as generally recognized as that of dramatic
poetry has long been: and this not from any decrease either of intellectual power, or intellectual acquisition, but because intellectual
power and intellectual acquisition have turned themselves into other
and better channels, and have abandoned the cultivation and the fate
of poetry to the degenerate fry of modern rhymesters, and their olympic judges, the magazine critics, who continue to debate and promulgate oracles about poetry, as if it were still what it was in the Homeric
age, the all-in-all of intellectual progression, and as if there were no
such things in existence as mathematicians, astronomers, chemists,
moralists, metaphysicians, historians, politicians, and political econo-
mists, who have built into the upper air of intelligence a pyramid, from
the summit of which they see the modern Parnassus far beneath them,
and, knowing how small a place it occupies in the comprehensiveness
of their prospect, smile at the little ambition and the circumscribed
perceptions with which the drivellers and mountebanks upon it are
contending for the poetical palm and the critical chair.[7]

[7] Demodocus: blind bard in *Odyssey* VIII; Thamyris: musician blinded
for challenging the Muses to a trial of skill (*Iliad* II. 594); Leda: visited
by Zeus in the form of a swan, she hatched Helen of Troy; *Dionysiaca:* a
Greek epic, 5th century A.D.; Werter: in Goethe's *Sorrows of Werther,*
the despairing hero takes his own life.
    crambe repetita: warmed-over cabbage.

Francis Jeffrey

Thalaba, the Destroyer; a Metrical Romance, by Robert Southey

❡ Francis, later Lord, Jeffrey (1773–1850), was the chief reviewer and after May 1803 sole editor of the *Edinburgh Review*. As John Clive observes in *Scotch Reviewers* (London 1957), Jeffrey reviewed works of poetry, fiction, drama, aesthetic theory, history, biography, philosophy, jurisprudence, religion, geography, and other subjects. All reviews of the time were anonymous. Most, as Leigh Hunt explains in his *Autobiography*, were politically biased. Aesthetically, Jeffrey belonged to the school of common sense. He accepted the associationist doctrines of Archibald Alison's *Essays on the Nature and Principles of Taste*. But it was partly from his position as a Whig, and partly from the editorial practice of making "one or two examples of great delinquents in every number," that Jeffrey chastised Wordsworth and other "Lake Poets." He began the chastisement promptly, with Southey's *Thalaba* as his excuse, in Article VIII of the first number of the *Edinburgh*, October 1802. His attack actually centers on Wordsworth's Preface to *Lyrical Ballads* rather than on *Thalaba*. Jeffrey collected the most important of his contributions in four volumes in 1844, but the selections here are taken directly from the *Edinburgh*. ❫

Poetry has this much, at least, in common with religion, that its standards were fixed long ago, by certain inspired writers, whose authority it is no longer lawful to call in question; and that many profess to be entirely devoted to it, who have no *good works* to produce in support of their pretensions. The catholic poetical church, too, has worked but few miracles since the first ages of its establishment; and has been more prolific, for a long time, of doctors than of saints: It has had its corruptions, and reformation also, and has given birth to an infinite variety of heresies and errors, the followers of which have hated and persecuted each other as cordially as other bigots.

The author who is now before us belongs to a *sect* of poets, that has established itself in this country within these ten or twelve years, and is looked upon, we believe, as one of its chief champions and apostles. The peculiar doctrines of this sect, it would not, perhaps, be very easy to explain; but, that they are *dissenters* from the established systems in poetry and criticism is admitted, and proved, indeed, by the whole tenor of their compositions. Though they lay claim, we believe, to a creed and a revelation of their own, there can be little

doubt, that their doctrines are of *German* origin, and have been derived from some of the great modern reformers in that country. Some
of their leading principles, indeed, are probably of an earlier date, and
seem to have been borrowed from the great apostle of Geneva.[1] As
Mr. Southey is the first author, of this persuasion, that has yet
been brought before us for judgment, we cannot discharge our inquisi-
torial office conscientiously, without premising a few words upon the
nature and tendency of the tenets he has helped to promulgate.

The disciples of this school boast much of its originality, and seem
to value themselves very highly, for having broken loose from the
bondage of ancient authority, and re-asserted the independence of
genius. Originality, however, we are persuaded, is rarer than mere
alteration; and a man may change a good master for a bad one, without finding himself at all nearer to independence. That our new poets
have abandoned the old models, may certainly be admitted; but we
have not been able to discover that they have yet created any models
of their own; and are very much inclined to call in question the worthiness of those to which they have transferred their admiration. The
productions of this school, we conceive, are so far from being entitled
to the praise of originality, that they cannot be better characterised
than by an enumeration of the sources from which their materials have
been derived. The greatest part of them, we apprehend, will be found
to be composed of the following elements: 1. The antisocial principles,
and distempered sensibility of Rousseau — his discontent with the
present constitution of society — his paradoxical morality, and his perpetual hankerings after some unattainable state of voluptuous virtue and
perfection. 2. The simplicity and energy (*horresco referens*)[2] of Kotzebue and Schiller. 3. The homeliness and harshness of some of Cowper's
language and versification, interchanged occasionally with the *innocence* of Ambrose Philips, or the quaintness of Quarles and Dr. Donne.
From the diligent study of these few originals, we have no doubt that
an entire art of poetry may be collected, by the assistance of which
the very *gentlest* of our readers may soon be qualified to compose a
poem as correctly versified as Thalaba, and to deal out sentiment and
description with all the sweetness of Lambe, and all the magnificence
of Coleridge.

The authors of whom we are now speaking have, among them, unquestionably, a very considerable portion of poetical talent, and have,
consequently, been enabled to seduce many into an admiration of the
false taste (as it appears to us) in which most of these productions
are composed. They constitute, at present, the most formidable conspiracy that has lately been formed against sound judgment in matters poetical; and are entitled to a larger share of our censorial notice,
than could be spared for an individual delinquent. We shall hope for
the indulgence of our readers, therefore, in taking this opportunity

[1] J.–J. Rousseau, "the father of Romanticism," born at Geneva in 1712.
[2] "I shudder at the recollection."

to inquire a little more particularly into their merits, and to make a few remarks upon those peculiarities which seem to be regarded by their admirers as the surest proofs of their excellence.

Their most distinguishing symbol is undoubtedly an affectation of great simplicity and familiarity of language. They disdain to make use of the common poetical phraseology, or to ennoble their diction by a selection of fine or dignified expressions. There would be too much *art* in this, for that great love of nature with which they are all of them inspired; and their sentiments, they are determined, shall be indebted, for their effect, to nothing but their intrinsic tenderness or elevation. There is something very noble and conscientious, we will confess, in this plan of composition; but the misfortune is, that there are passages in all poems that can neither be pathetic nor sublime; and that, on these occasions, a neglect of the establishments of language is very apt to produce absolute meanness and insipidity. The language of passion, indeed, can scarcely be deficient in elevation; and when an author is wanting in that particular, he may commonly be presumed to have failed in the truth, as well as in the dignity of his expression. The case, however, is extremely different with the subordinate parts of composition; with the narrative and description, that are necessary to preserve its connection; and the explanation, that must frequently prepare us for the great scenes and splendid passages. In these, all the requisite ideas may be conveyed, with sufficient clearness, by the meanest and most negligent expressions; and if magnificence or beauty is ever to be observed in them, it must have been introduced from some other motive than that of adapting the style to the subject. It is in such passages, accordingly, that we are most frequently offended with low and inelegant expressions; and that the language, which was intended to be simple and natural, is found oftenest to degenerate into mere slovenliness and vulgarity. It is in vain, too, to expect that the meanness of those parts may be redeemed by the excellence of others. A poet who aims at all at sublimity or pathos, is like an actor in a high tragic character, and must sustain his dignity throughout, or become altogether ridiculous. We are apt enough to laugh at the mock-majesty of those whom we know to be but common mortals in private; and cannot permit Hamlet to make use of a single provincial intonation, although it should only be in his conversation with the grave-diggers.

The followers of simplicity are, therefore, at all times in danger of occasional degradation; but the simplicity of this new school seems intended to ensure it. *Their* simplicity does not consist, by any means, in the rejection of glaring or superfluous ornament, — in the substitution of elegance to splendour, — or in that refinement of art which seeks concealment in its own perfection. It consists, on the contrary, in a very great degree, in the positive and *bonâ fide* rejection of art altogether, and in the bold use of those rude and negligent expressions, which would be banished by a little discrimination. One of their own authors, indeed, has very ingeniously set forth, (in a kind of manifesto, that preceded one of their most flagrant acts of hostility,) that it was their capital object "to adapt to the uses of poetry the ordinary language of conversation among the middling and lower orders of the people." What advantages are to be gained by the success of this project, we confess ourselves unable to conjecture. The language of the higher and more cultivated orders may fairly be presumed to be better than that of their inferiors; at any rate, it has all those associations in its favour, by means of which a style can ever appear beautiful or exalted, and is adapted to the purposes of poetry, by having been long consecrated to its use. The language of the vulgar, on the other hand, has all the opposite associations to contend with; and must seem unfit for poetry, (if there were no other reason,) merely because it has scarcely ever been employed in it. A great genius may indeed overcome these disadvantages; but we scarcely conceive that he should court them. We may excuse a certain homeliness of language in the productions of a ploughman or a milkwoman; but we cannot bring ourselves to admire it in an author, who has had occasion to indite odes to his college-bell, and inscribe hymns to the Penates.

But the mischief of this new system is not confined to the depravation of language only; it extends to the sentiments and emotions, and leads to the debasement of all those feelings which poetry is designed to communicate. It is absurd to suppose, that an author should make use of the language of the vulgar, to express the sentiments of the refined. His professed object, in employing that language, is to bring his compositions nearer to the true standard of nature; and his intention to copy the sentiments of the lower orders, is implied in his resolution to make use of their style. Now, the different classes of society have each of them a distinct character, as well as a separate idiom; and the names of the various passions to which they are subject respectively have a signification that varies essentially, according to the condition of the persons to whom they are applied. The love or grief, or indignation of an enlightened and refined character, is not only expressed in a different language, but is in itself a different emotion from the love, or grief, or anger of a clown, a tradesman or a market-wench. The things themselves are radically and obviously distinct; and the representation of them is calculated to convey a very different train of sympathies and sensations to the mind. The question, therefore, comes simply to be — Which of them is the most proper object for poetical imitation? It is needless for us to answer a question, which the practice of all the world has long ago decided irrevocably. The poor and vulgar may interest us, in poetry, by their *situation;* but never, we apprehend, by any sentiments that are peculiar to their condition, and still less by any language that is characteristic of it. The truth is, that it is impossible to copy their diction or their sentiments correctly, in a serious composition; and this, not merely

because poverty makes men ridiculous, but because just taste and refined sentiment are rarely to be met with among the uncultivated part
of mankind; and a language fitted for their expression, can still more
rarely form any part of their "ordinary conversation."

The low-bred heroes, and interesting rustics of poetry, have no sort
of affinity to the real vulgar of this world; they are imaginary beings,
whose characters and language are in contrast with their situation; and
please those who can be pleased with them, by the marvellous, and not
by the nature of such a combination. In serious poetry, a man of the
middling or lower order *must necessarily* lay aside a great deal of his
ordinary language; he must avoid errors in grammar and orthography;
and steer clear of the cant of particular professions, and of every impropriety that is, ludicrous or disgusting; nay, he must speak in good
verse, and observe all the graces in prosody and collocation. After all
this, it may not be very easy to say how we are to find him out to be
a low man, or what marks can remain of the ordinary language of conversation in the inferior orders of society. If there be any phrases that
are not used in good society, they will appear as blemishes in the
composition, no less palpably than errors in syntax or quantity; and if
there be no such phrases, the style cannot be characteristic of that
condition of life, the language of which it professes to have adopted.
All approximation to that language, in the same manner, implies a
deviation from that purity and precision, which no one, we believe,
ever violated spontaneously.

It has been argued, indeed, (for men will argue in support of what
they do not venture to practise,) that, as the middling and lower
orders of society constitute by far the greater part of mankind, so their
feelings and expressions should interest more extensively, and may be
taken, more fairly than any other, for the standards of what is natural
and true. To this it seems obvious to answer, that the arts that aim at
exciting admiration and delight, do not take their models from what is
ordinary, but from what is excellent; and that our interest in the representation of any event does not depend upon our familiarity with the
original, but on its intrinsic importance, and the celebrity of the parties
it concerns. The sculptor employs his art in delineating the graces of
Antinous or Apollo, and not in the representation of those ordinary
forms that belong to the crowd of his admirers. When a chieftain
perishes in battle, his followers mourn more for him than for thousands
of their equals that may have fallen around him.

After all, it must be admitted, that there is a class of persons, (we
are afraid they cannot be called readers,) to whom the representation
of vulgar manners, in vulgar language, will afford much entertainment. We are afraid, however, that the ingenious writers who supply
the hawkers and ballad-singers have very nearly monopolized that department, and are probably better qualified to hit the taste of their
customers than Mr. Southey, or any of his brethren, can yet pretend

to be. To fit them for the higher task of original composition, it would not be amiss if they were to undertake a translation of Pope or Milton into the vulgar tongue, for the benefit of those children of nature.

There is another disagreeable effect of this affected simplicity, which, though of less importance than those which have been already noticed, it may yet be worth while to mention: This is, the extreme difficulty of supporting the same low tone of expression throughout, and the inequality that is consequently introduced into the texture of the composition. To an author of reading and education, it is a style that must always be assumed and unnatural, and one from which he will be perpetually tempted to deviate. He will rise, therefore, every now and then, above the level to which he has professedly degraded himself, and make amends for that transgression by a fresh effort of descension. His composition, in short, will be like that of a person who is attempting to speak in an obsolete or provincial dialect; he will betray himself by expressions of occasional purity and elegance, and exert himself to efface that impression, by passages of unnatural meanness or absurdity.

In making these strictures on the perverted taste for simplicity, that seems to distinguish our modern school of poetry, we have no particular allusion to Mr. Southey, or the production now before us: On the contrary, he appears to us to be less addicted to this fault than most of his fraternity; and if we were in want of examples to illustrate the preceding observations, we should certainly look for them in the effusions of that poet who commemorates, with so much effect, the chattering of Harry Gill's teeth, tells the tale of the one-eyed huntsman, "who had a cheek like a cherry," and beautifully warns his studious friend of the risk he ran of "growing double.". . .[3]

The Excursion, by William Wordsworth

❨ Jeffrey's review of *The Excursion, being a portion of the Recluse, a Poem,* appeared as the first article in the *Edinburgh Review* for November 1814. ❩

This will never do. It bears no doubt the stamp of the author's heart and fancy; but unfortunately not half so visibly as that of his peculiar system. His former poems were intended to recommend that

[3] Wordsworth, *Goody Blake and Harry Gill; Simon Lee* 7–8; *The Tables Turned* 2.
    Philips (1675?–1749), nicknamed "Namby-Pamby"; Lambe: Charles Lamb; Antinoüs: a handsome favorite of the Roman emperor Hadrian.

system, and to bespeak favour for it by their individual merit; — but this, we suspect, must be recommended by the system — and can only expect to succeed where it has been previously established. It is longer, weaker, and tamer, than any of Mr. Wordsworth's other productions; with less boldness and originality, and less even of that extreme simplicity and lowliness of tone which wavered so prettily, in the Lyrical Ballads, between silliness and pathos. We have imitations of Cowper, and even of Milton here, engrafted on the natural drawl of the Lakers — and all diluted into harmony by that profuse and irrepressible wordiness which deluges all the blank verse of this school of poetry, and lubricates and weakens the whole structure of their style.

Though it fairly fills four hundred and twenty good quarto pages, without note, vignette, or any sort of extraneous assistance, it is stated in the title — with something of an imprudent candour — to be but "a portion" of a larger work; and in the preface, where an attempt is rather unsuccessfully made to explain the whole design, it is still more rashly disclosed, that it is but "a part of the second part of a *long* and laborious work" — which is to consist of three parts.

What Mr. Wordsworth's ideas of length are, we have no means of accurately judging; but we cannot help suspecting that they are liberal, to a degree that will alarm the weakness of most modern readers. As far as we can gather from the preface, the entire poem — or one of them, for we really are not sure whether there is to be one or two — is of a biographical nature; and is to contain the history of the author's mind, and of the origin and progress of his poetical powers, up to the period when they were sufficiently matured to qualify him for the great work on which he has been so long employed. Now, the quarto before us contains an account of one of his youthful rambles in the vales of Cumberland, and occupies precisely the period of three days; so that, by the use of a very powerful *calculus*, some estimate may be formed of the probable extent of the entire biography.

This small specimen, however, and the statements with which it is prefaced, have been sufficient to set our minds at rest in one particular. The case of Mr. Wordsworth, we perceive, is now manifestly hopeless; and we give him up as altogether incurable, and beyond the power of criticism. We cannot indeed altogether omit taking precautions now and then against the spreading of the malady; — but for himself, though we shall watch the progress of his symptoms as a matter of professional curiosity and instruction, we really think it right not to harass him any longer with nauseous remedies, — but rather to throw in cordials and lenitives, and wait in patience for the natural termination of the disorder. In order to justify this desertion of our patient, however, it is proper to state why we despair of the success of a more active practice.

A man who has been for twenty years at work on such matter as is now before us, and who comes complacently forward with a whole quarto of it after all the admonitions he has received, cannot reasonably be expected to "change his hand, or check his pride," upon the suggestion of far weightier monitors than we can pretend to be. Inveterate habit must now have given a kind of sanctity to the errors of early taste; and the very powers of which we lament the perversion, have probably become incapable of any other application. The very quantity, too, that he has written, and is at this moment working up for publication upon the old pattern, makes it almost hopeless to look for any change of it. All this is so much capital already sunk in the concern; which must be sacrificed if it be abandoned: and no man likes to give up for lost the time and talent and labour which he has embodied in any permanent production. We were not previously aware of these obstacles to Mr. Wordsworth's conversion; and, considering the peculiarities of his former writings merely as the result of certain wanton and capricious experiments on public taste and indulgence, conceived it to be our duty to discourage their repetition by all the means in our power. We now see clearly, however, how the case stands; — and, making up our minds, though with the most sincere pain and reluctance, to consider him as finally lost to the good cause of poetry, shall endeavour to be thankful for the occasional gleams of tenderness and beauty which the natural force of his imagination and affections must still shed over all his productions, — and to which we shall ever turn with delight, in spite of the affectation and mysticism and prolixity, with which they are so abundantly contrasted.

Long habits of seclusion, and an excessive ambition of originality, can alone account for the disproportion which seems to exist between this author's taste and his genius; or for the devotion with which he has sacrificed so many precious gifts at the shrine of those paltry idols which he has set up for himself among his lakes and his mountains. Solitary musings, amidst such scenes, might no doubt be expected to nurse up the mind to the majesty of poetical conception, — (though it is remarkable, that all the greater poets lived, or had lived, in the full current of society;) — But the collision of equal minds, — the admonition of prevailing impressions — seems necessary to reduce its redundancies, and repress that tendency to extravagance or puerility, into which the self-indulgence and self-admiration of genius is so apt to be betrayed, when it is allowed to wanton, without awe or restraint, in the triumph and delight of its own intoxication. That its flights should be graceful and glorious in the eyes of men, it seems almost to be necessary that they should be made in the consciousness that men's eyes are to behold them, — and that the inward transport and vigour by which they are inspired, should be tempered by an occasional reference to what will be thought of them by those ultimate dispensers of glory. An habitual and general knowledge of the few settled and permanent maxims, which form the canon of general taste in all large and polished societies — a certain tact, which informs us at once that many things, which we still love and are moved by in secret, must necessarily be despised as childish or derided as absurd, in all such societies — though it will not stand in the place of genius, seems necessary to the success of its exertions; and though it will never enable any one to produce the higher beauties of art, can alone secure the talent which does produce them, from errors that must render it useless. Those who have most of the talent, however, commonly acquire this knowledge with the greatest facility; — and if Mr. Wordsworth, instead of confining himself almost entirely to the society of the dalesmen and cottagers, and little children, who form the subjects of his book, had condescended to mingle a little more with the people that were to read and judge of it, we cannot help thinking, that its texture would have been considerably improved: At least it appears to us to be absolutely impossible, that any one who had lived or mixed familiarly with men of literature and ordinary judgment in poetry, (of course we exclude the coadjutors and disciples of his own school,) could ever have fallen into such gross faults, or so long mistaken them for beauties. His first essays[1] we looked upon in a good degree as poetical paradoxes, — maintained experimentally, in order to display talent, and court notoriety; — and so maintained, with no more serious belief in their truth, than is usually generated by an ingenious and animated defence of other paradoxes. But when we find, that he has been for twenty years exclusively employed upon articles of this very fabric, and that he has still enough of raw material on hand to keep him so employed for twenty years to come, we cannot refuse him the justice of believing that he is a sincere convert to his own system, and must ascribe the peculiarities of his composition, not to any transient affectation, or accidental caprice of imagination, but to a settled perversity of taste or understanding, which has been fostered, if not altogether created, by the circumstances to which we have already alluded.

The volume before us, if we were to describe it very shortly, we should characterize as a tissue of moral and devotional ravings, in which innumerable changes are rung upon a few very simple and familiar ideas: — but with such an accompaniment of long words, long sentences, and unwieldy phrases — and such a hubbub of strained raptures and fantastical sublimities, that it is often extremely difficult for the most skilful and attentive student to obtain a glimpse of the author's meaning — and altogether impossible for an ordinary reader to conjecture what he is about. Moral and religious enthusiasm, though undoubtedly poetical emotions, are at the same time but dangerous inspirers of poetry; nothing being so apt to run into interminable dulness or mellifluous extravagance, without giving the unfortunate author the slightest intimation of his danger. His laudable zeal for the efficacy of his preachments, he very naturally mistakes for the ardour of poetical inspiration; — and, while dealing out the high words and glowing phrases which are so readily supplied by themes of this description, can scarcely avoid believing that he is eminently original

[1] poems in *Lyrical Ballads,* 1798.

and impressive: — All sorts of commonplace notions and expressions
are sanctified in his eyes, by the sublime ends for which they are
employed; and the mystical verbiage of the methodist pulpit is repeated, till the speaker entertains no doubt that he is the elected organ
of divine truth and persuasion. But if such be the common hazards
of seeking inspiration from those potent fountains, it may easily be
conceived what chance Mr. Wordsworth had of escaping their enchantment, with his natural propensities to wordiness, and his unlucky habit
of debasing pathos with vulgarity. The fact accordingly is, that in this
production he is more obscure than a Pindaric poet of the seventeenth
century:[2] and more verbose "than even himself of yore;" while the
wilfulness with which he persists in choosing his examples of intellectual dignity and tenderness exclusively from the lowest ranks of society,
will be sufficiently apparent, from the circumstance of his having
thought fit to make his chief prolocutor in this poetical dialogue, and
chief advocate of Providence and Virtue, *an old Scotch Pedlar* —
retired indeed from business — but still rambling about in his former
haunts, and gossiping among his old customers, without his pack on
his shoulders. The other persons of the drama are, a retired military
chaplain, who has grown half an atheist and half a misanthrope — the
wife of an unprosperous weaver — a servant girl with her infant — a
parish pauper, and one or two other personages of equal rank and
dignity.

The character of the work is decidedly didactic; and more than nine
tenths of it are occupied with a species of dialogue, or rather a series
of long sermons or harangues which pass between the pedlar, the
author, the old chaplain, and a worthy vicar, who entertains the whole
party at dinner on the last day of their excursion. The incidents which
occur in the course of it are as few and trifling as can be imagined; —
and those which the different speakers narrate in the course of their
discourses, are introduced rather to illustrate their arguments or opinions, than for any interest they are supposed to possess of their own.
— The doctrine which the work is intended to enforce, we are by no
means certain that we have discovered. In so far as we can collect,
however, it seems to be neither more nor less than the old familiar
one, that a firm belief in the providence of a wise and beneficent
Being must be our great stay and support under all afflictions and perplexities upon earth — and that there are indications of his power and
goodness in all the aspects of the visible universe, whether living or
inanimate — every part of which should therefore be regarded with
love and reverence, as exponents of those great attributes. We can
testify, at least, that these salutary and important truths are incul-
cated at far greater length, and with more repetitions, than in any
ten volumes of sermons that we ever perused. It is also maintained,
with equal conciseness and originality, that there is frequently much

[2] Abraham Cowley, for example.

good sense, as well as much enjoyment, in the humbler conditions of life; and that in spite of great vices and abuses, there is a reasonable allowance both of happiness and goodness in society at large. If there be any deeper or more recondite doctrines in Mr. Wordsworth's book, we must confess that they have escaped us; — and, convinced as we are of the truth and soundness of those to which we have alluded, we cannot help thinking that they might have been better enforced with less parade and prolixity. His effusions on what may be called the physiognomy of external nature, or its moral and theological expression, are eminently fantastic, obscure, and affected. — It is quite time, however, that we should give the reader a more particular account of this singular performance.

It opens with a picture of the author toiling across a bare common in a hot summer day, and reaching at last a ruined hut surrounded with tall trees, where he meets by appointment with a hale old man, with an iron-pointed staff lying beside him. Then follows a retrospective account of their first acquaintance — formed, it seems, when the author was at a village school; and his aged friend occupied "one room, — the fifth part of a house," in the neighbourhood. After this, we have the history of this reverend person at no small length. He was born, we are happy to find, in Scotland — among the hills of Athol; and his mother, after his father's death, married the parish schoolmaster — so that he was taught his letters betimes: But then, as it is here set forth with much solemnity,

> "From his sixth year, the boy, of whom I speak,
> In summer tended cattle on the hills."

And again, a few pages after, that there may be no risk of mistake as to a point of such essential importance —

> "From early childhood, even, as hath been said,
> From his *sixth year,* he had been sent abroad,
> *In summer,* to tend herds: Such was his task!"

In the course of this occupation, it is next recorded, that he acquired such a taste for rural scenery and open air, that when he was sent to teach a school in a neighbouring village, he found it "a misery to him," and determined to embrace the more romantic occupation of a Pedlar — or, as Mr. Wordsworth more musically expresses it,

> "A vagrant merchant bent beneath his load;"

— and in the course of his peregrinations had acquired a very large acquaintance, which, after he had given up dealing, he frequently took a summer ramble to visit.

The author, on coming up to this interesting personage, finds him sitting with his eyes half shut; — and, not being quite sure whether he

is asleep or awake, stands "some minutes space" in silence beside him.
"At length," says he, with his own delightful simplicity —

> "At length I hailed him — *seeing that his hat*
> *Was moist* with water-drops, as if the brim
> Had newly scooped a running stream! —
> —————— ' 'Tis,' said I, 'a burning day;
> My lips are parched with thirst; — but you, I guess,
> Have somewhere found relief.' "

Upon this, the benevolent old man points him out a well in a corner,
to which the author repairs; and after minutely describing its situation,
beyond a broken wall, and between two alders, that "grew in a cold
damp nook," he thus faithfully chronicles the process of his return.

> "My thirst I slaked — and from the cheerless spot
> Withdrawing, straightway to the shade returned,
> Where sate the old man on the cottage bench."[3]

The Pedlar then gives an account of the last inhabitants of the
deserted cottage beside them. These were, a good industrious weaver,
and his wife and children. They were very happy for a while; till
sickness and want of work came upon them; and then the father
enlisted as a soldier, and the wife pined in the lonely cottage — growing every year more careless and desponding, as her anxiety and fears
for her absent husband, of whom no tidings ever reached her, accumulated. Her children died, and left her cheerless and alone; and at last
she died also; and the cottage fell to decay. We must say, that there
is very considerable pathos in the telling of this simple story; and that
they who can get over the repugnance excited by the triteness of its
incidents, and the lowness of its objects, will not fail to be struck with
the author's knowledge of the human heart, and the power he possesses
of stirring up its deepest and gentlest sympathies. His prolixity, indeed, it is not so easy to get over. This little story fills about twenty-
five quarto pages; and abounds, of course, with mawkish sentiment,
and details of preposterous minuteness. . . .

[For 22 pages, Jeffrey gives long quotations from the poem to demon-
strate its "rapturous mysticism" and its "tamer and more creeping
prolixity."]

These examples, we perceive, are not very well chosen — but we
have not leisure to improve the selection; and, such as they are, they
may serve to give the reader a notion of the sort of merit which we
meant to illustrate by their citation. — When we look back to them,
indeed, and to the other passages which we have now extracted, we
feel half inclined to rescind the severe sentence which we passed on
the work at the beginning: — But when we look into the work itself,
we perceive that it cannot be rescinded. Nobody can be more disposed

[3] Quoted from the version of 1814: I.118–119, 197–199, 314, 324, 443ff.,
461, 463–465.

to do justice to the great powers of Mr. Wordsworth than we are; and, from the first time that he came before us, down to the present moment, we have uniformly testified in their favour, and assigned indeed our high sense of their value as the chief ground of the bitterness with which we resented their perversion. That perversion, however, is now far more visible than their original dignity; and while we collect the fragments, it is impossible not to lament the ruins from which we are condemned to pick them. If any one should doubt of the existence of such a perversion, or be disposed to dispute about the instances we have hastily brought forward, we would just beg leave to refer him to the general plan and the characters of the poem now before us. — Why should Mr. Wordsworth have made his hero a superannuated Pedlar? What but the most wretched and provoking perversity of taste and judgment, could induce any one to place his chosen advocate of wisdom and virtue in so absurd and fantastic a condition? Did Mr. Wordsworth really imagine, that his favourite doctrines were likely to gain any thing in point of effect or authority by being put into the mouth of a person accustomed to higgle about tape, or brass sleeve-buttons? Or is it not plain that, independent of the ridicule and disgust which such a personification must give to many of his readers, its adoption exposes his work throughout to the charge of revolting incongruity, and utter disregard of probability or nature? For, after he has thus wilfully debased his moral teacher by a low occupation, is there one word that he puts into his mouth, or one sentiment of which he makes him the organ, that has the most remote reference to that occupation? Is there any thing in his learned, abstracted, and logical harangues, that savours of the calling that is ascribed to him? Are any of their materials such as a pedlar could possibly have dealt in? Are the manners, the diction, the sentiments, in any, the very smallest degree, accommodated to a person in that condition? or are they not eminently and conspicuously such as could not by possibility belong to it? A man who went about selling flannel and pocket-handkerchiefs in this diction, would soon frighten away all his customers; and would infallibly pass either for a madman, or for some learned and affected gentleman, who, in a frolic, had taken up a character which he was peculiarly ill qualified for supporting.

The absurdity in this case, we think, is palpable and glaring; but it is exactly of the same nature with that which infects the whole substance of the work — a puerile ambition of singularity engrafted on an unlucky predilection for truisms; and an affected passion for simplicity and humble life, most awkwardly combined with a taste for mystical refinements, and all the gorgeousness of obscure phraseology. His taste for simplicity is evinced, by sprinkling up and down his interminable declamations, a few descriptions of baby-houses, and of old hats with wet brims; and his amiable partiality for humble life, by assuring us, that a wordy rhetorician, who talks about Thebes, and allegorizes all the heathen mythology, was once a pedlar — and making him break in upon his magnificent orations with two or three awkward notices of something that he had seen when selling winter raiment about the country — or of the changes in the state of society, which had almost annihilated his former calling.

(I)

Benjamin Robert Haydon

Autobiography

❡ Other diarists, particularly the artist Joseph Farington (1747–1821) and the cosmopolitan lawyer Henry Crabb Robinson (1775–1867), are extremely useful to students in search of fact concerning the English Romantics. But the historical painter Haydon (1786–1846), with an equally large circle of acquaintance, had fuller powers of observation, of expression in prose, and of self-revelation. From his original journals, he began about 1839 to prepare an autobiography for publication, but it remained uncompleted when he committed suicide on June 22, 1846. The account below, of a dinner in December 1817, is typical, except that it conveys little of Haydon's naive vanity and passionate egoism. It comes from the end of Chapter XVII, as given in the second of two editions of the autobiography and journals issued by Haydon's executor, Tom Taylor, in 1853. The manuscript used by Taylor for the "Autobiography" has since disappeared, but W. B. Pope began in 1960 to publish the complete journals, under the title of *Diary*, directly from Haydon's manuscripts. ❱

In December Wordsworth was in town, and as Keats wished to know him I made up a party to dinner of Charles Lamb, Wordsworth, Keats and Monkhouse, his friend, and a very pleasant party we had.

I wrote to Lamb, and told him the address was "22, Lisson Grove, North, at Rossi's, half way up, right hand corner." I received his characteristic reply.

"My dear Haydon,

"I will come with pleasure to 22. Lisson Grove, North, at Rossi's, half way up, right hand side, if I can find it.

"Yours,
"C. LAMB.

"20. Russel Court,
Covent Garden East,
half way up, next the corner,
left hand side."

On December 28th the immortal dinner came off in my painting-room, with Jerusalem towering up behind us as a background.[1] Wordsworth was in fine cue, and we had a glorious set-to, — on Homer, Shakespeare, Milton and Virgil. Lamb got exceedingly merry and exquisitely witty; and his fun in the midst of Wordsworth's solemn intonations of oratory was like the sarcasm and wit of the fool in the intervals of Lear's passion. He made a speech and voted me absent, and made them drink my health. "Now," said Lamb, "you old lake poet, you rascally poet, why do you call Voltaire dull?" We all defended Wordsworth, and affirmed there was a state of mind when Voltaire would be dull. "Well," said Lamb, "here's Voltaire — the Messiah of the French nation, and a very proper one too."

He then, in a strain of humour beyond description, abused me for putting Newton's head into my picture, — "a fellow," said he, "who believed nothing unless it was as clear as the three sides of a triangle." And then he and Keats agreed he had destroyed all the poetry of the rainbow by reducing it to the prismatic colours. It was impossible to resist him, and we all drank "Newton's health, and confusion to mathematics." It was delightful to see the good-humour of Wordsworth in giving in to all our frolics without affectation and laughing as heartily as the best of us.

By this time other friends joined, amongst them poor Ritchie who was going to penetrate by Fezzan to Timbuctoo. I introduced him to all as "a gentleman going to Africa." Lamb seemed to take no notice; but all of a sudden he roared out, "Which is the gentleman we are going to lose?" We then drank the victim's health, in which Ritchie joined.

In the morning of this delightful day, a gentleman, a perfect stranger, had called on me. He said he knew my friends, had an enthusiasm for Wordsworth and begged I would procure him the happiness of an introduction. He told me he was a comptroller of stamps, and often had correspondence with the poet. I thought it a liberty; but still, as he seemed a gentleman, I told him he might come.

When we retired to tea we found the comptroller. In introducing him to Wordsworth I forgot to say who he was.[2] After a little time the comptroller looked down, looked up and said to Wordsworth, "Don't you think, sir, Milton was a great genius?" Keats looked at me, Wordsworth looked at the comptroller. Lamb who was dozing by the fire turned round and said, "Pray, sir, did you say Milton was a great genius?" "No, sir; I asked Mr. Wordsworth if he were not." "Oh,"

[1] Haydon's large painting, *Christ's Entry into Jerusalem,* into which he had recently worked striking portraits of Keats, Wordsworth, and Hazlitt.

[2] In his original notes Haydon wrote: "The moment he was introduced he let Wordsworth know *who* he officially was." — *Diary,* ed. W. B. Pope, Cambridge, Mass., 1960, II, 174. Wordsworth, as distributor of stamps for Westmorland, was subordinate to the comptroller.

said Lamb, "then you are a silly fellow." "Charles! my dear Charles!"
said Wordsworth; but Lamb, perfectly innocent of the confusion he
had created, was off again by the fire.

After an awful pause the comptroller said, "Don't you think Newton a great genius?" I could not stand it any longer. Keats put his
head into my books. Ritchie squeezed in a laugh. Wordsworth seemed
asking himself, "Who is this?" Lamb got up, and taking a candle, said,
"Sir, will you allow me to look at your phrenological development?"
He then turned his back on the poor man, and at every question of
the comptroller he chaunted —

> "Diddle diddle dumpling, my son John
> Went to bed with his breeches on."

The man in office, finding Wordsworth did not know who he was, said
in a spasmodic and half-chuckling anticipation of assured victory, "I
have had the honour of some correspondence with you, Mr. Wordsworth." "With me, sir?" said Wordsworth, "not that I remember."
"Don't you, sir? I am a comptroller of stamps." There was a dead
silence; — the comptroller evidently thinking that was enough. While
we were waiting for Wordsworth's reply, Lamb sung out

> "Hey diddle diddle,
> The cat and the fiddle."

"My dear Charles!" said Wordsworth, —

> "Diddle diddle dumpling, my son John,"

chaunted Lamb, and then rising, exclaimed, "Do let me have another
look at that gentleman's organs." Keats and I hurried Lamb into the
painting-room, shut the door and gave way to inextinguishable laughter. Monkhouse followed and tried to get Lamb away. We went
back but the comptroller was irreconcilable. We soothed and smiled
and asked him to supper. He stayed though his dignity was sorely
affected. However, being a good-natured man, we parted all in good-
humour, and no ill effects followed.

All the while, until Monkhouse succeeded, we could hear Lamb
struggling in the painting-room and calling at intervals, "Who is that
fellow? Allow me to see his organs once more."

It was indeed an immortal evening. Wordsworth's fine intonation as
he quoted Milton and Virgil, Keats' eager inspired look, Lamb's quaint
sparkle of lambent humour, so speeded the stream of conversation, that
in my life I never passed a more delightful time. All our fun was
within bounds. Not a word passed that an apostle might not have
listened to. It was a night worthy of the Elizabethan age, and my
solemn Jerusalem flashing up by the flame of the fire, with Christ
hanging over us like a vision, all made up a picture which will long
glow upon —

> "that inward eye
> Which is the bliss of solitude."[3]

Keats made Ritchie promise he would carry his Endymion to the great desert of Sahara and fling it in the midst.

Poor Ritchie went to Africa, and died, as Lamb foresaw, in 1819. Keats died in 1821, at Rome. C. Lamb is gone, joking to the last. Monkhouse is dead, and Wordsworth and I are the only two now living (1841) of that glorious party.

❮❯

John Gibson Lockhart (?)

Cockney School of Poetry

❮ Lockhart (1794–1854), favorably remembered as the son-in-law and biographer of Scott, sharply attacked Leigh Hunt in the first three articles of his series on the Cockney School in *Blackwood's Edinburgh Magazine*. Keats, his victim in the fourth article, of August 1818, qualified as a Cockney by birth in London and as a dangerous radical by association with Hunt and Hazlitt. Lockhart may have received aid from John Wilson in writing the review. Shelley and others who befriended Keats held J. W. Croker's attack in the *Quarterly Review* responsible for dispiriting the author of *Endymion*, but the *Blackwood's* review is more personal and more slashing. ❯

No. IV

——————————— OF KEATS,
THE MUSES' SON OF PROMISE, AND WHAT FEATS
HE YET MAY DO, &C.
CORNELIUS WEBB.[1]

Of all the manias of this mad age, the most incurable, as well as the most common, seems to be no other than the *Metromanie*. The just celebrity of Robert Burns and Miss Baillie has had the melancholy effect of turning the heads of we know not how many farm-servants

---

[3] Wordsworth, "I wandered lonely as a cloud" 21–22.
[1] Webb (c.1790–c.1848) belonged to the edge of Keats's circle; further lines from his poem were quoted in No. I (October 1817) and No. II (November).

and unmarried ladies; our very footmen compose tragedies, and there is scarcely a superannuated governess in the island that does not leave a roll of lyrics behind her in her band-box. To witness the disease of any human understanding, however feeble, is distressing; but the spectacle of an able mind reduced to a state of insanity is of course ten times more afflicting. It is with such sorrow as this that we have contemplated the case of Mr John Keats. This young man appears to have received from nature talents of an excellent, perhaps even of a superior order — talents which, devoted to the purposes of any useful profession, must have rendered him a respectable, if not an eminent citizen. His friends, we understand, destined him to the career of medicine, and he was bound apprentice some years ago to a worthy apothecary in town. But all has been undone by a sudden attack of the malady to which we have alluded. Whether Mr John had been sent home with a diuretic or composing draught to some patient far gone in the poetical mania, we have not heard. This much is certain, that he has caught the infection, and that thoroughly. For some time we were in hopes, that he might get off with a violent fit or two; but of late the symptoms are terrible. The phrenzy of the "Poems" was bad enough in its way; but it did not alarm us half so seriously as the calm, settled, imperturbable drivelling idiocy of "Endymion." We hope, however, that in so young a person, and with a constitution originally so good, even now the disease is not utterly incurable. Time, firm treatment, and rational restraint, do much for many apparently hopeless invalids; and if Mr Keats should happen, at some interval of reason, to cast his eye upon our pages, he may perhaps be convinced of the existence of his malady, which, in such cases, is often all that is necessary to put the patient in a fair way of being cured.

The readers of the Examiner newspaper were informed, some time ago, by a solemn paragraph, in Mr Hunt's best style, of the appearance of two new stars of glorious magnitude and splendour in the poetical horizon of the land of Cockaigne. One of these turned out, by and by, to be no other than Mr John Keats. This precocious adulation confirmed the wavering apprentice in his desire to quit the gallipots, and at the same time excited in his too susceptible mind a fatal admiration for the character and talents of the most worthless and affected of all the versifiers of our time. One of his first productions was the following sonnet, "written on the day when Mr Leigh Hunt left prison." It will be recollected, that the cause of Hunt's confinement was a series of libels against his sovereign, and that its fruit was the odious and incestuous "Story of Rimini."

> "What though, for shewing truth to flattered state,
>   Kind Hunt was shut in prison, yet has he,
>   In his immortal spirit been as free
> As the sky-searching lark, and as elate.

> Minion of grandeur! think you he did wait?
> Think you he nought but prison walls did see,
> Till, so unwilling, thou unturn'dst the key?
> Ah, no! far happier, nobler was his fate!
> *In Spenser's halls!* he strayed, and bowers fair,
> Culling enchanted flowers; and he flew
> *With daring Milton!* through the fields of air;
> To regions of his own his genius true
> Took happy flights. Who shall his fame impair
> When thou art dead, and all thy wretched crew?

The absurdity of the thought in this sonnet is, however, if possible, surpassed in another, *"addressed to Haydon"* the painter, that clever, but most affected artist, who as little resembles Raphael in genius as he does in person, notwithstanding the foppery of having his hair curled over his shoulders in the old Italian fashion. In this exquisite piece it will be observed, that Mr Keats classes together WORDSWORTH, HUNT, and HAYDON, as the three greatest spirits of the age, and that he alludes to himself, and some others of the rising brood of Cockneys, as likely to attain hereafter an equally honourable elevation. Wordsworth and Hunt! what a juxta-position! The purest, the loftiest, and, we do not fear to say it, the most classical of living English poets, joined together in the same compliment with the meanest, the filthiest, and the most vulgar of Cockney poetasters. . . .

From his prototype Hunt, John Keats has acquired a sort of vague idea, that the Greeks were a most tasteful people, and that no mythology can be so finely adapted for the purposes of poetry as theirs. It is amusing to see what a hand the two Cockneys make of this mythology; the one confesses that he never read the Greek Tragedians, and the other knows Homer only from Chapman; and both of them write about Apollo, Pan, Nymphs, Muses, and Mysteries, as might be expected from persons of their education. We shall not, however, enlarge at present upon this subject, as we mean to dedicate an entire paper to the classical attainments and attempts of the Cockney poets. As for Mr Keats' "Endymion," it has just as much to do with Greece as it has with "old Tartary the fierce;" no man, whose mind has ever been imbued with the smallest knowledge or feeling of classical poetry or classical history, could have stooped to profane and vulgarise every association in the manner which has been adopted by this "son of promise." Before giving any extracts, we must inform our readers, that this romance is meant to be written in English heroic rhyme. To those who have read any of Hunt's poems, this hint might indeed be needless. Mr Keats has adopted the loose, nerveless versification, and Cockney rhymes of the poet of Rimini; but in fairness to that gentleman, we must add, that the defects of the system are tenfold more conspicuous in his disciple's work than in his own. Mr Hunt is a small poet, but he is a clever man. Mr Keats is a still smaller poet, and he is only a boy of pretty abilities, which he has done every thing in his power to spoil. . . .

We had almost forgot to mention, that Keats belongs to the Cockney School of Politics, as well as the Cockney School of Poetry.

It is fit that he who holds Rimini to be the first poem, should believe the Examiner to be the first politician of the day. We admire consistency, even in folly. Hear how their bantling has already learned to lisp sedition.

[Here follows *Endymion* III.1–22, beginning "There are who lord it o'er their fellow-men."]

And now, good-morrow to "the Muses' son of Promise;" as for "the feats he yet may do," as we do not pretend to say, like himself, "Muse of my native land am I inspired," we shall adhere to the safe old rule of *pauca verba*. We venture to make one small prophecy, that his bookseller will not a second time venture £50 upon any thing he can write. It is a better and a wiser thing to be a starved apothecary than a starved poet; so back to the shop Mr John, back to "plasters, pills, and ointment boxes," &c. But, for Heaven's sake, young Sangrado, be a little more sparing of extenuatives and soporifics in your practice than you have been in your poetry.   Z.[2]

[2] "Z" is the usual signature of attacks in *Blackwood's* on Hunt and other Cockneys.

Joanna Baillie (1762–1851), sprightly Scottish poetess; Sangrado: a medical quack in Le Sage's *Gil Blas*.